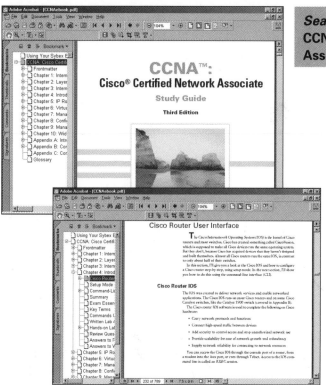

Search through the entire CCNA: Cisco Certified Network Associate Study Guide!

- Access the entire *CCNA: Cisco Certified Network Associate Study Guide*, complete with figures and tables, in electronic format.

- Search the *CCNA: Cisco Certified Network Associate Study Guide* chapters to find information on any topic in seconds.

- Use Adobe Acrobat Reader (included on the CD-ROM) to view the electronic book.

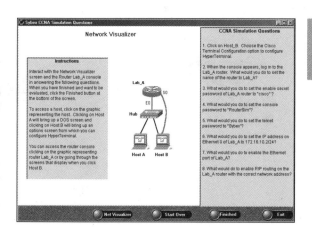

Use the Router Fundamentals Simulator *to gain valuable hands-on experience with a Cisco-equipped lab!*

- Practice on your own or use in conjunction with the 14 labs detailed in Appendix A.

- Sharpen your skills by logging onto a Cisco router, setting passwords, configuring router interfaces, setting router hostnames, and more.

SYBEX

CCNA: Cisco Certified Network Associate Study Guide

Exam 640-607

OBJECTIVE	CHAPTER
Bridging/Switching	**2, 6**
Name and describe two switching methods.	2
Distinguish between cut-through and store-and-forward LAN switching.	2
Describe the operation of the Spanning Tree Protocol and its benefits.	2
Describe the benefits of virtual LANs.	6
OSI Reference Model and Layered Communications	**1, 3, 8**
Describe data link and network addresses and identify key differences between them.	1
Define and describe the function of the MAC address.	1
List the key internetworking functions for the OSI Network layer.	1
Identify at least three reasons why the industry uses a layered model.	1
Describe the two parts of network addressing; then identify the parts in specific protocol address examples.	3, 8
Define and explain the five conversion steps of data encapsulation.	1
Describe connection-oriented network service and connectionless network service, and identify their key differences.	1
Identify the parts in specific protocol address examples.	1, 3, 8
Describe the advantages of LAN segmentation.	1
Describe LAN segmentation using bridges.	1
Describe LAN segmentation using routers.	1
Describe LAN segmentation using switches.	1
Describe the benefits of network segmentation with bridges.	1
Describe the benefits of network segmentation with routers.	1
Describe the benefits of network segmentation with switches.	1
Network Protocols	**3, 4, 5, 7, 8**
Describe the different classes of IP addresses (and subnetting).	3
Identify the functions of the TCP/IP network-layer protocol.	3
Identify the functions performed by ICMP.	3
Configure IP addresses.	3, 4, 5
Verify IP addresses.	3, 4, 7
List the required IPX address and encapsulation type.	8

SYBEX

Exam objectives are subject to change at any time without prior notice and at Cisco's sole discretion. Please visit the Cisco website (www.cisco.com) and click the Training/Certifications link for the most current listing of exam objectives.

SYBEX®

CCNA:
Cisco Certified Network Associate
Study Guide

Third Edition

CCNA™:
Cisco® Certified Network Associate
Study Guide

Third Edition

Todd Lammle

San Francisco • London

Associate Publisher: Neil Edde
Acquisitions and Developmental Editor: Maureen Adams
Editor: Pete Gaughan
Production Editor: Elizabeth Campbell
Technical Editors: Rod Jackson, Errol Robichaux
Book Designer: Bill Gibson
Graphic Illustrator: Tony Jonick
Electronic Publishing Specialist: Interactive Composition Corporation
Proofreaders: Yariv Rabinovitch, Nancy Riddiough, Sarah Tannehill
Indexer: Ted Laux
CD Coordinator: Dan Mummert
CD Technician: Kevin Ly
Cover Designer: Archer Design
Cover Photographer: Tony Stone

SYBEX

To Our Valued Readers:

Since its inception, the Cisco Certified Network Associate program has established itself as the premier internetworking certification. Sybex is proud to have helped hundreds of thousands of CCNA candidates prepare for their exams in recent years, and we are excited about the opportunity to continue to provide individuals with the knowledge and skills they'll need to succeed in the highly competitive IT industry.

With the recent revision of the CCNA exam, Cisco raised the bar considerably, adding simulation questions to verify the skills associated with hands-on router configuration. Sybex welcomes this new testing feature as we strongly advocate a comprehensive and practical instructional approach to certification exam preparation. It has always been Sybex's mission to teach exam candidates how new technologies work in the real world, not to simply feed them answers to test questions. Sybex was founded on the premise of providing technical skills to IT professionals, and we have continued to build on that foundation. Over the years, we have made significant improvements to our study guides based on feedback from readers, suggestions from instructors, and comments from industry leaders.

Cisco's new CCNA exam is indeed challenging. The author, renowned Cisco authority Todd Lammle, and Sybex's editors and technical reviewers have worked hard to ensure that this *CCNA: Cisco Certified Network Associate Study Guide* is comprehensive, in-depth, and pedagogically sound. We're confident that this book, along with the collection of cutting-edge software study tools included on the CD, will meet and exceed the demanding standards of the certification marketplace and help you, the CCNA exam candidate, succeed in your endeavors.

Good luck in pursuit of your CCNA certification!

Neil Edde
Associate Publisher—Certification
Sybex, Inc.

Acknowledgments

Elizabeth Campbell, Pete Gaughan, and Maureen Adams were instrumental in helping me get this book out in time, without stressing out too much, and working together as a well-oiled machine. Thank you.

I'd also like to thank Rod Jackson and Errol Robichaux, who scrutinized every word, figure, and line of code in the book for technical accuracy. (Of course, any mistakes remaining in the text are my responsibility, not theirs.) Additional thanks go out to Interactive Composition Corporation who carefully set every single page in the book; Yariv Rabinovitch, Nancy Riddiough, Sarah Tannehill, who all did marvelous jobs proofreading; Tony Jonick, who created all the great illustrations; and Ted Laux, who crafted the index. The book would not exist without all of you.

Contents at a Glance

Contents

Chapter   2   Layer-2 Switching   75

Introduction

Welcome to the exciting world of Cisco certification! You have picked up this book because you want something better; namely, a better job with more satisfaction. Rest assured that you have made a good decision. Cisco certification can help you get your first networking job, or more money and a promotion if you are already in the field.

Cisco certification can also improve your understanding of the internetworking of more than just Cisco products: You will develop a complete understanding of networking and how different network topologies work together to form a network. This is beneficial to every networking job and is the reason Cisco certification is in such high demand, even at companies with few Cisco devices.

Cisco is the king of routing and switching, the Microsoft of the internetworking world. The Cisco certifications reach beyond the popular certifications, such as the MCSE and CNE, to provide you with an indispensable factor in understanding today's network—insight into the Cisco world of internetworking. By deciding that you want to become Cisco certified, you are saying that you want to be the best—the best at routing and the best at switching. This book will lead you in that direction.

How to Use This Book

If you want a solid foundation for the serious effort of preparing for the Cisco Certified Network Associate (CCNA) exam, then look no further. I have spent hundreds of hours putting together this book with the sole intention of helping you to pass the CCNA exam and learn how to configure Cisco routers and switches.

This book is loaded with lots of valuable information, and you will get the most out of your studying time if you understand how I put this book together.

To best benefit from this book, I recommend the following study method:

1. Take the assessment test immediately following this introduction. (The answers are at the end of the test.) It's OK if you don't know any of the answers; that is why you bought this book! Carefully read over the explanations for any question you get wrong and note which chapters the material comes from. This information should help you plan your study strategy.

2. Study each chapter carefully, making sure that you fully understand the information and the test objectives listed at the beginning of each chapter. Pay extra-close attention to any chapter where you missed questions in the assessment test.

3. Complete each written lab at the end of each chapter. Do *not* skip this written exercise, as it directly relates to the CCNA exam and what you must glean from the chapter you just read. Do not just skim this lab! Make sure you understand completely the reason for each answer.

4. Complete all hands-on labs in the chapter, referring to the text of the chapter so that you understand the reason for each step you take. If you do not have Cisco equipment available, be sure to study the examples carefully, or use the Router Fundamentals Simulator found on the CD of this book. Also, check www.routersim.com for router simulator software that provides drag-and-drop networking configurations. This will help you gain hands-on experience configuring Cisco routers.

5. If you do not have Cisco equipment or the RouterSim Cisco simulator product, then go through all the core hands-on labs (contained in Appendix A) using the Router Fundamentals Simulator product found on the CD of this book. This will help you gain hands-on experience configuring Cisco routers. (The Router Fundamentals Simulator will not run the hands-on labs that are printed at the end of each chapter. Within the software product, only use the simulator's labs.)

6. Answer all of the review questions related to that chapter. (The answers appear at the end of the chapter.) Note the questions that confuse you and study those sections of the book again. Do not just skim these questions! Make sure you understand completely the reason for each answer.

7. Try your hand at the practice exams that are included on the companion CD. The questions in these exams appear only on the CD. This will give you a complete overview of what you can expect to see on the real CCNA exam. Check out www.lammleprep.com for more Cisco exam prep questions.

8. Also on the companion CD is a software simulation program that will help you prepare for the new simulation questions on the CCNA 607 exam. The router simulator on the CD or at www.routersim.com is the best form of study, but be sure and practice with the software simulation program as well.

9. Test yourself using all the flashcards on the CD. There are brand new and updated flashcard programs on the CD to help you prepare completely for the CCNA exam. These are a great study tool!

The electronic flashcards can be used on your Windows computer, Pocket PC, or on your Palm device.

10. Make sure you read the "Key Terms" and "Commands Used in This Chapter" lists at the end of the chapters. Appendix B lists all the commands used in the book, including an explanation for each command.

To learn every bit of the material covered in this book, you'll have to apply yourself regularly, and with discipline. Try to set aside the same time period every day to study, and select a comfortable and quiet place to do so. If you work hard, you will be surprised at how quickly you learn this material.

If you follow the steps listed above, and really study and practice the review questions, CD exams, electronic flashcards, and written and hands-on labs, it would be hard to fail the CCNA exam.

What's on the CD?

We worked hard to provide some really great tools to help you with your certification process. All of the following tools should be loaded on your workstation when studying for the test.

Router Fundamentals Simulator

The companion CD contains the Router Fundamentals Simulator, a "mini" version of Sybex's best-selling CCNA Virtual Lab e-trainer. The Virtual Lab is a stand-alone product that allows readers to gain hands-on experience without buying expensive Cisco gear. This practical experience is a must-have for anyone hoping to pass the CCNA exam. Its smaller counterpart, the Router Fundamentals Simulator bundled with this book's CD, covers the absolute essentials for the exam, represented by the 14 hands-on labs contained in Appendix A. (The Router Fundamental Simulator requires Real-Player, which is also included on the CD.) You can find more router simulator software available for purchase at www.routersim.com.

The EdgeTest Test Preparation Software

The test preparation software, provided by EdgeTek Learning Systems, prepares you to pass the CCNA exam. In this test engine, you will find all the review and assessment questions from the book, plus five additional bonus exams that appear exclusively on the CD. You can take the assessment test, test yourself by chapter or by topic, take the practice exams, or take a randomly generated exam comprising all the questions.

In addition to multiple-choice and drag-and-drop questions, Cisco has included some questions on the CCNA exam that simulate working on routers and switches in a network environment. In response, we have included a simulation question program on our test engine. We designed our program to help further your hands-on networking skills and better prepare you for when you are faced with a simulation question at the testing center.

Please visit the Cisco training and certification website (http://www.cisco .com/public/training_cert.shtml) for the latest exam information.

Electronic Flashcards for PC, Pocket PC, and Palm Devices

To prepare for the exam, you can read this book, study the review questions at the end of each chapter, and work through the practice exams included in the book and on the companion CD. But wait, there's more! You can also test yourself with the flashcards included on the CD. If you can get through these difficult questions and understand the answers, you'll know you're ready for the CCNA exam.

The flashcards include over 300 questions specifically written to hit you hard and make sure you are ready for the exam. Between the review questions, practice exams, and flashcards, you'll be more than prepared for the exam.

CCNA Study Guide in PDF

Sybex offers the *CCNA Study Guide* in PDF format on the CD so you can read the book on your PC or laptop. This will be helpful to readers who travel and don't want to carry a book, as well as to readers who prefer to read from their computer. (Acrobat Reader 5 is also included on the CD.)

Bonus Chapter: Configuring the Catalyst 1900 Switch

The CCNA exam is mostly theory on layer-2 switching; however, this easy-to-read Acrobat file will add to your overall Cisco knowledge and help further your CCNA studies.

Cisco—A Brief History

Many readers may already be familiar with Cisco and what they do. However, those of you who are new to the field, just coming in fresh from your MCSE, and those of you who maybe have 10 or more years in the field but wish to brush up on the new technology may appreciate a little background on Cisco.

In the early 1980s, Len and Sandy Bosack, a married couple who worked in different computer departments at Stanford University, were having trouble getting their individual systems to communicate (like many married people). So in their living room they created a gateway server that made it easier for their disparate computers in two different departments to communicate using the IP protocol. In 1984, they founded cisco Systems (notice the small *c*) with a small commercial gateway server product that changed networking forever. Some people think the name was intended to be San Francisco Systems but the paper got ripped on the way to the incorporation lawyers—who knows? In 1992, the company name was changed to Cisco Systems, Inc.

The first product the company marketed was called the Advanced Gateway Server (AGS). Then came the Mid-Range Gateway Server (MGS), the Compact Gateway Server (CGS), the Integrated Gateway Server (IGS), and the AGS+. Cisco calls these "the old alphabet soup products."

In 1993, Cisco came out with the amazing 4000 router and then created the even more amazing 7000, 2000, and 3000 series routers. These are still around and evolving (almost daily, it seems).

Cisco has since become an unrivaled worldwide leader in networking for the Internet. Its networking solutions can easily connect users who work from diverse devices on disparate networks. Cisco products make it simple for people to access and transfer information without regard to differences in time, place, or platform.

In the big picture, Cisco provides end-to-end networking solutions that customers can use to build an efficient, unified information infrastructure of their own or to connect to someone else's. This is an important piece in the Internet/networking–industry puzzle because a common architecture that delivers consistent network services to all users is now a functional imperative. Because Cisco Systems offers such a broad range of networking and

Internet services and capabilities, users who need to regularly access their local network or the Internet can do so unhindered, making Cisco's wares indispensable.

Cisco answers this need with a wide range of hardware products that form information networks using the Cisco Internetwork Operating System (IOS) software. This software provides network services, paving the way for networked technical support and professional services to maintain and optimize all network operations.

Along with the Cisco IOS, one of the services Cisco created to help support the vast amount of hardware it has engineered is the Cisco Certified Internetwork Expert (CCIE) program, which was designed specifically to equip people to effectively manage the vast quantity of installed Cisco networks. The business plan is simple: If you want to sell more Cisco equipment and have more Cisco networks installed, ensure that the networks you install run properly.

Clearly, having a fabulous product line isn't all it takes to guarantee the huge success that Cisco enjoys—lots of companies with great products are now defunct. If you have complicated products designed to solve complicated problems, you need knowledgeable people who are fully capable of installing, managing, and troubleshooting them. That part isn't easy, so Cisco began the CCIE program to equip people to support these complicated networks. This program, known colloquially as the Doctorate of Networking, has also been very successful, primarily due to its extreme difficulty. Cisco continuously monitors the program, changing it as it sees fit, to make sure that it remains pertinent and accurately reflects the demands of today's internetworking business environments.

Building upon the highly successful CCIE program, Cisco Career Certifications permit you to become certified at various levels of technical proficiency, spanning the disciplines of network design and support. So, whether you're beginning a career, changing careers, securing your present position, or seeking to refine and promote your position, this is the book for you!

Cisco's Network Support Certifications

Initially, to secure the coveted CCIE, you took only one test and then you were faced with the (extremely difficult) lab, an all-or-nothing approach that made it tough to succeed. In response, Cisco created a series of new certifications to help you get the coveted CCIE, as well as aid prospective employers in measuring skill levels. With these new certifications, which added a better approach to preparing for that almighty lab, Cisco opened doors that few were allowed through before. So, what are these stepping-stone certifications and how do they help you get your CCIE?

Cisco Certified Network Associate (CCNA)

The CCNA certification was the first in the new line of Cisco certifications, and was the precursor to all current Cisco certifications. With the new certification programs, Cisco has created a type of stepping-stone approach to CCIE certification. Now, you can become a Cisco Certified Network Associate for the meager cost of this book, plus $120 for the test. And you don't have to stop there—you can choose to continue with your studies and achieve a higher certification, called the Cisco Certified Network Professional (CCNP). Someone with a CCNP has all the skills and knowledge he or she needs to attempt the CCIE lab. However, because no textbook can take the place of practical experience, we'll discuss what else you need to be ready for the CCIE lab shortly.

Why Become a CCNA?

Cisco, not unlike Microsoft or Novell, has created the certification process to give administrators a set of skills and to equip prospective employers with a way to measure skills or match certain criteria. Becoming a CCNA can be the initial step of a successful journey toward a new, highly rewarding, and sustainable career.

The CCNA program was created to provide a solid introduction not only to the Cisco Internetwork Operating System (IOS) and Cisco hardware, but also to internetworking in general, making it helpful to you in areas that are not exclusively Cisco's. At this point in the certification process, it's not unrealistic to imagine that future network managers—even those without Cisco equipment—could easily require Cisco certifications for their job applicants.

If you make it through the CCNA and are still interested in Cisco and internetworking, you're headed down a path to certain success.

What Skills Do You Need to Become a CCNA?

To meet the CCNA certification skill level, you must be able to understand or do the following:

- Install, configure, and operate simple-routed LAN, routed WAN, and switched LAN and LANE networks.

- Understand and be able to configure IP, IGRP, IPX, serial, AppleTalk, Frame Relay, IP RIP, VLANs, IPX RIP, Ethernet, and access lists.

- Install and/or configure a network.

- Optimize WAN through Internet-access solutions that reduce bandwidth and WAN costs, using features such as filtering with access lists, bandwidth on demand (BOD), and dial-on-demand routing (DDR).

- Provide remote access by integrating dial-up connectivity with traditional, remote LAN-to-LAN access, as well as supporting the higher levels of performance required for new applications such as Internet commerce, multimedia, etc.

How Do You Become a CCNA?

The first step to becoming a CCNA is to pass one little test and—poof!— you're a CCNA. (Don't you wish it were that easy?) True, it's just one test, but you still have to possess enough knowledge to understand (and read between the lines—trust me) what the test writers are saying.

I can't stress this enough—it's critical that you have some hands-on experience with Cisco routers. If you can get a hold of some 2500 routers, you're set. But if you can't, we've worked hard to provide hundreds of configuration examples throughout this book to help network administrators (or people who want to become network administrators) learn what they need to know to pass the CCNA exam.

One way to get the hands-on router experience you'll need in the real world is to attend one of the seminars offered by GlobalNet Training Solutions, Inc., which is owned and run by myself. The seminars are 5 days and 11 days long and will teach you everything you need to become a CCNA (or even a CCNP). Each student gets hands-on experience by configuring at least two routers and a switch. See www.globalnettraining.com for more information.

For hands-on training with Todd Lammle, please see www.globalnettraining. com.

Cisco Certified Network Professional (CCNP)

So you're thinking, "Great, what do I do after passing the CCNA exam?" Well, if you want to become a CCIE in Routing and Switching (the most popular certification), understand that there's more than one path to that much-coveted CCIE certification. The first way is to continue studying and become a Cisco Certified Network Professional (CCNP), which means four more tests, in addition to the CCNA certification.

The CCNP program will prepare you to understand and comprehensively tackle the internetworking issues of today and beyond—and it is not limited to the Cisco world. You will undergo an immense metamorphosis, vastly increasing your knowledge and skills through the process of obtaining these certifications.

While you don't need to be a CCNP or even a CCNA to take the CCIE lab, it's extremely helpful if you already have these certifications.

What Skills Do You Need to Become a CCNP?

Cisco demands a certain level of proficiency for its CCNP certification. In addition to mastering the skills required for the CCNA, you should be able to do the following:

- Install, configure, operate, and troubleshoot complex routed LAN, routed WAN, and switched LAN networks, along with dial-access services.

- Understand complex networks, such as IP, IGRP, IPX, async routing, AppleTalk, extended access lists, IP RIP, route redistribution, IPX RIP, route summarization, OSPF, VLSM, BGP, serial, IGRP, Frame Relay, ISDN, ISL, X.25, DDR, PSTN, PPP, VLANs, Ethernet, ATM LAN emulation, access lists, 802.10, FDDI, and transparent and translational bridging.

- Install and/or configure a network to increase bandwidth, quicker network response times, and improve reliability and quality of service.

- Maximize performance through campus LANs, routed WANs, and remote access.

- Improve network security.

- Create a global intranet.

- Provide access security to campus switches and routers.

- Provide increased switching and routing bandwidth—end-to-end resiliency services.

- Provide custom queuing and routed priority services.

How Do You Become a CCNP?

After becoming a CCNA, the four exams you must take to get your CCNP are as follows:

Exam 640-503: Routing This exam continues to build on the fundamentals learned in the CCNA course. It focuses on large multiprotocol internetworks and how to manage them with access lists, queuing, tunneling, route distribution, route maps, BGP, EIGRP, OSPF, and route summarization. The *CCNP: Routing Study Guide* (Sybex) covers all the objectives you need to understand to pass the Routing exam.

Exam 640-504: Switching   This exam tests your knowledge of the 1900 and 5000 series of Catalyst switches. The *CCNP: Switching Study Guide* (Sybex) covers all the objectives you need to understand to pass the Switching exam.

Exam 640-506: Support   This tests you on the Cisco troubleshooting skills needed for Ethernet and Token Ring LANs, IP, IPX, and AppleTalk networks, as well as ISDN, PPP, and Frame Relay networks. The *CCNP: Support Study Guide* (Sybex) covers all the objectives you need to understand to pass the Support exam.

Exam 640-505: Remote Access   This exam tests your knowledge of installing, configuring, monitoring, and troubleshooting Cisco ISDN and dial-up access products. You must understand PPP, ISDN, Frame Relay, and authentication. The *CCNP: Remote Access Study Guide* (Sybex) covers all the exam objectives.

www.routersim.com has a complete Cisco router simulator for all CCNP exams.

If you hate tests, you can take fewer of them by signing up for the CCNA exam and the Support exam and then taking just one more long exam called the Foundation R/S exam (640-509). Doing this also gives you your CCNP—but beware; it's a really long test that fuses all the material Routing, Switching, and Remote Access exams into one exam. Good luck! However, by taking this exam, you get three tests for the price of two, which saves you $100 (if you pass). Some people think it's easier to take the Foundation R/S exam because you can leverage the areas that you would score higher in against the areas in which you wouldn't.

Remember that test objectives and tests can change at any time without notice. Always check the Cisco website for the most up-to-date information (www.cisco.com).

Cisco Certified Internetwork Expert (CCIE)

You've become a CCNP, and now you fix your sights on getting your Cisco Certified Internetwork Expert (CCIE) in Routing and Switching—what do you do next? Cisco recommends that before you take the lab, you take the Cisco Internetwork Design (CID) exam (640-025) and the Cisco-authorized course called Installing and Maintaining Cisco Routers (IMCR). By the way, no Prometric test for IMCR exists at the time of this writing, and Cisco recommends a *minimum* of two years of on-the-job experience before taking the CCIE lab. After jumping those hurdles, you then have to pass the CCIE-R/S Exam Qualification (350-001) before taking the actual lab.

How Do You Become a CCIE?

To become a CCIE, Cisco recommends you do the following:

1. Attend all the recommended courses at an authorized Cisco training center and pony up around $15,000–$20,000, depending on your corporate discount.

2. Pass the Drake/Prometric exam ($200 per exam—so hopefully, you'll pass it the first time).

3. Pass the one-day, hands-on lab at Cisco. This costs $1,000 per lab, and many people fail two or more times. (Some never make it through!) Also, there are a limited number of places to take the lab: San Jose, California; Research Triangle Park, North Carolina; Sydney, Australia; Halifax, Nova Scotia; Tokyo, Japan; and Brussels, Belgium. This means that you might just need to add travel costs to that $1,000. Cisco has added new sites lately for the CCIE lab; it is best to check the Cisco website for the most current information.

Cisco has changed the CCIE lab from a two-day to a one-day lab. Please see www.cisco.com for the latest information.

What Skills Do You Need to Become a CCIE?

The CCIE Routing and Switching exam includes the advanced technical skills that are required to maintain optimum network performance and reliability, as well as advanced skills in supporting diverse networks that use disparate technologies. CCIEs just don't have problems getting jobs; these experts are basically inundated with offers to work for six-figure salaries.

But that's because it isn't easy to attain the level of capability that is mandatory for Cisco's CCIE. For example, a CCIE can easily do the following:

- Install, configure, operate, and troubleshoot complex routed LAN, routed WAN, switched LAN, and ATM LANE networks, and dial-access services.

- Diagnose and resolve network faults.

- Use packet/frame analysis and Cisco debugging tools.

- Document and report the problem-solving processes used.

- Understand general LAN/WAN characteristics, including data encapsulation and layering; windowing and flow control, and their relation to delay; error detection and recovery; link-state, distance vector, and switching algorithms; management, monitoring, and fault isolation.

- Understand a variety of corporate technologies—including major services provided by Desktop, WAN, and Internet groups—as well as the functions; addressing structures; and routing, switching, and bridging implications of each of their protocols.

- Understand Cisco-specific technologies, including router/switch platforms, architectures, and applications; communication servers; protocol translation and applications; configuration commands and system/network impact; and LAN/WAN interfaces, capabilities, and applications.

- Design, configure, install, and verify voice-over-IP and voice-over-ATM networks.

Sybex's CCIE: Cisco Certified Internetwork Expert Study Guide (2001) will help you prepare for and pass the CCIE exam.

Cisco's Network Design Certifications

In addition to the network support certifications, Cisco has created another certification track for network designers. The two certifications within this track are the Cisco Certified Design Associate and Cisco Certified Design

Professional certifications. If you're reaching for the CCIE stars, we highly recommend the CCNP and CCDP certifications before attempting the lab (or attempting to advance your career).

This certification will give you the knowledge you need to design routed LAN, routed WAN, and switched LAN and ATM LANE networks.

Cisco Certified Design Associate (CCDA)

To become a CCDA, you must pass the Designing Cisco Networks (DCN) exam (640-441). To pass this test, you must understand how to do the following:

- Design simple routed LAN, routed WAN, and switched LAN and ATM LANE networks.

- Use Network-layer addressing.

- Filter with access lists.

- Use and propagate VLAN.

- Size networks.

The Sybex *CCDA: Cisco Certified Design Associate Study Guide* (1999) is the most cost-effective way to study for and pass your CCDA exam.

Cisco Certified Design Professional (CCDP)

If you're already a CCNP and want to get your CCDP, you can simply take the CID 640-025 test. If you're not yet a CCNP, however, you must take the CCDA, CCNA, Routing, Switching, Remote Access, and CID exams. CCDP certification skills include the following:

- Designing complex routed LAN, routed WAN, and switched LAN and ATM LANE networks

- Building upon the base level of the CCDA technical knowledge

CCDPs must also demonstrate proficiency in the following:

- Network-layer addressing in a hierarchical environment

- Traffic management with access lists

- Hierarchical network design

- VLAN use and propagation

- Performance considerations: required hardware and software; switching engines; memory, cost, and minimization

What Does This Book Cover?

This book covers everything you need to know in order to become CCNA certified. However, taking the time to study and practice with routers or a router simulator is the real key to success.

The information you will learn in this book, and need to know for the CCNA exam, is listed in the following bullet points:

- Chapter 1 introduces you to internetworking. You will learn the basics of the Open Systems Interconnection model the way Cisco wants you to learn it. Ethernet networking and standards are discussed in detail in this chapter as well. There are written labs and plenty of review questions to help you. Do not skip the labs in this chapter!

- Chapter 2 gives you a background on layer-2 switching and how switches perform address learning and make forwarding and filtering decisions. Network loops and how to avoid them with the Spanning Tree Protocol (STP) will be discussed, as well as the different LAN switch types used by Cisco switches. Go through the written lab and review questions.

- Chapter 3 provides you with the background necessary for success on the exam as well as in the real world by discussing TCP/IP. This in-depth chapter covers the very beginnings of the Internet Protocol stack and then goes all the way to IP addressing and subnetting. If you read this chapter carefully, you will be able to subnet a network in your head! Plenty of help is found in this chapter if you do not skip the written lab and review questions.

- Chapter 4 introduces you to the Cisco Internetwork Operating System (IOS) and command-line interface (CLI). In this chapter you will learn how to turn on a router and configure the basics of the IOS, including setting passwords, banners, and more. IP configuration will be discussed and a hands-on lab will help you gain a firm grasp of the concepts taught in the chapter. Before you go through the hands-on lab, be sure and complete the written lab and review questions.

- Chapter 5 teaches you about IP routing. This is a fun chapter, because you will begin to build your network, add IP addresses, and route data between routers. You will also learn about static, default, and dynamic routing. Written and hands-on labs will help you understand IP routing to the fullest.

- Chapter 6 covers virtual LANs and how you can use them in your internetwork. This chapter also covers the nitty-gritty of VLANs and the different concepts and protocols used with VLANs. A written lab and review questions will reinforce the VLAN material.

- Chapter 7 provides you with the management skills needed to run a Cisco ISO network. Backing up and restoring the IOS, as well as router configuration, is covered, as are the troubleshooting tools necessary to keep a network up and running. Before performing the hands-on labs in this chapter, complete the written lab and review questions.

- Chapter 8 introduces you to the wonderful world of Novell IPX. Since IPX is still around, Cisco thinks it is important to understand IPX routing. Actually, after IP routing, IPX is a breeze. Both written and hands-on labs, along with review questions, will give you the understanding of IPX you need to pass the CCNA exam.

- Chapter 9 covers access lists, which are created on routers to filter the network. Both IP and IPX access lists are covered in detail. Written and hands-on labs, along with review questions, will help you study for the access-list portion of the CCNA exam.

- Chapter 10 concentrates on Cisco wide area network (WAN) protocols. This chapter covers HDLC, PPP, Frame Relay, and ISDN in depth. You must be proficient in all these protocols to be successful on the CCNA exam. Do not skip the written lab, review questions, or hands-on labs found in this chapter.

- Appendix A contains the hands-on labs for the Router Fundamentals Simulator on the CD of this book.

- Appendix B lists all the Cisco IOS commands used in this book. It is a great reference if you need to look up what a certain command does and is used for.

- The Glossary is a handy resource for Cisco terms. This is a great tool for understanding some of the more obscure terms used in this book.

Where Do You Take the Exams?

You may take the exams at any of the more than 800 Sylvan Prometric Authorized Testing Centers around the world (www.2test.com), or call 800-204-EXAM (3926). You can also register and take the exams at a VUE authorized center as well (www.vue.com) or call (877) 404-EXAM (3926).

To register for a Cisco Certified Network Professional exam:

1. Determine the number of the exam you want to take. (The CCNA exam number is 640-607.)

2. Register with the nearest Sylvan Prometric Registration Center or VUE testing center. At this point, you will be asked to pay in advance for the exam. At the time of this writing, the exams are $100 each and must be taken within one year of payment. You can schedule exams up to six weeks in advance or as late as the same day you want to take it—but if you fail a Cisco exam, you must wait 72 hours before you will be allowed to retake the exam. If something comes up and you need to cancel or reschedule your exam appointment, contact Sylvan Prometric or VUE at least 24 hours in advance.

3. When you schedule the exam, you'll get instructions regarding all appointment and cancellation procedures, the ID requirements, and information about the testing-center location.

Tips for Taking Your CCNA Exam

The CCNA test contains about 50 questions to be completed in about 90 minutes. This can change per exam. You must get a score of about 82% to 85% to pass this exam, but again, each exam can be different.

Many questions on the exam have answer choices that at first glance look identical—especially the syntax questions! Remember to read through the choices carefully, because close doesn't cut it. If you get commands in the wrong order or forget one measly character, you'll get the question wrong.

So, to practice, do the hands-on exercises at the end of the chapters over and over again until they feel natural to you.

Also, never forget that the right answer is the Cisco answer. In many cases, more than one appropriate answer is presented, but the *correct* answer is the one that Cisco recommends.

The CCNA 640-607 exam includes the following test formats:

- Multiple-choice single answer
- Multiple-choice multiple answer
- Drag-and-drop
- Fill-in-the-blank
- Router simulations

In addition to multiple choice and fill-in response questions, Cisco Career Certifications exams may include performance simulation exam items.

As practice in Cisco router command sequences, both router simulator and question simulation software has been included on this book's CD. However, RouterSim.com has created a perfect companion for the Sybex CCNA 3rd Edition study guide, called the Cisco 607 CCNA Simulator, that matches perfectly to the new Cisco CCNA 607 exam. Use the software included in this book, and for extra study material, check out the software at www.routersim.com that accepts partial responses just as an actual Cisco router will.

The software on the CD and at RouterSim.com provides step-by-step instruction on how to configure both Cisco routers and switches. However, router simulations in Cisco proctored exams will not show the steps to follow in completing a router interface configuration. They do allow partial command responses. For example, show config or sho config or sh conf would be acceptable. Router #show ip protocol or router # show ip prot would be acceptable. The exam commands must include the correct spacing, spelling, and punctuation marks (such as #@!?).

Here are some general tips for exam success:

- Arrive early at the exam center, so you can relax and review your study materials.
- Read the questions *carefully*. Don't jump to conclusions. Make sure you're clear about *exactly* what each question asks.

- When answering multiple-choice questions that you're not sure about, use the process of elimination to get rid of the obviously incorrect answers first. Doing this greatly improves your odds if you need to make an educated guess.

- You can no longer move forward and backward through the Cisco exams, so double-check your answer before clicking Next since you can't change your mind.

After you complete an exam, you'll get immediate, online notification of your pass or fail status, a printed Examination Score Report that indicates your pass or fail status, and your exam results by section. (The test administrator will give you the printed score report.) Test scores are automatically forwarded to Cisco within five working days after you take the test, so you don't need to send your score to them. If you pass the exam, you'll receive confirmation from Cisco, typically within two to four weeks.

How to Contact the Author

You can reach Todd Lammle through GlobalNet Training Solutions, Inc. (www.globalnettraining.com), his training and systems integration company in Dallas, Texas—or through his software company (www.routersim .com) in Denver, Colorado, which creates both Cisco and Microsoft software simulation programs.

Assessment Test

1. What protocol does PPP use to identify the Network layer protocol?

   A. NCP

   B. ISDN

   C. HDLC

   D. LCP

2. You work in a large application-development company providing MIS services. This company has four 10Mbps shared hubs providing network services to an NT server. To meet the business requirements, you must provide many different types of hosts to allow the application developers to test the different applications they create. These hosts must be able to share data between each host and also send data to and from an enterprise server. The hosts run at 10Mbps and the server at 100Mbps. Some applications only need 3Mbps of bandwidth to run at any given time. What network recommendation would you give this company if money were an issue?

   A. Replace the 10Mbps hubs with 100Mbps hubs.

   B. Install a router and connect all the hubs into separate collision domains and one large broadcast domain.

   C. Install a layer-2 switch and run a 10Mbps connection to the hosts and a 100Mbps connection to the server.

   D. Uses bridges to break up the collision domains and create one large broadcast domain.

3. How does a host in a Novell network receive a logical address?

   A. DHCP Server.

   B. DNS Server.

   C. It uses the MAC address of the NIC and the network ID assigned to a router and/or server.

   D. A Novell server dynamically assigns all logical addresses to hosts for routing purposes.

4. What does the command routerA(config)#**line cons 0** allow you to perform next?

 A. Set the Telnet password.

 B. Shut down the router.

 C. Set your console password.

 D. Disable console connections.

5. What ISDN command will bring up the second BRI at 50 percent load?

 A. load balance 50

 B. load share 50

 C. dialer load-threshold 125

 D. dialer idle-timeout 125

6. What PPP protocol provides dynamic addressing, authentication, and multilink?

 A. NCP

 B. HDLC

 C. LCP

 D. X.25

7. What command will display the line, protocol, DLCI, and LMI information of an interface?

 A. sh pvc

 B. show interface

 C. show frame-rely pvc

 D. sho runn

8. What type of access list uses the numbers 1–99?

   A. IP standard

   B. IPX standard

   C. IP extended

   D. IPX extended

   E. IPX SAP filter

9. What does the `passive` command provide to dynamic routing protocols?

   A. Stops an interface from sending or receiving periodic dynamic updates

   B. Stops an interface from sending periodic dynamic updates but still receives updates

   C. Stops the router from receiving any dynamic updates

   D. Stops the router from sending any dynamic updates

10. Which protocol does Ping use?

   A. TCP

   B. ARP

   C. ICMP

   D. BootP

11. Which command will show the IPX RIP and SAP information sent and received on a router?

   A. `show ipx traffic`

   B. `show ipx server`

   C. `show ipx interface`

   D. `show ipx rip sap`

12. Which of the following commands will set your Telnet password on a Cisco router?

  A. `line telnet 0 4`

  B. `line aux 0 4`

  C. `line vty 0 4`

  D. `line con 0`

13. Which router command allows you to view the entire contents of all access-lists?

  A. `show all access-lists`

  B. `show access-lists`

  C. `show ip interface`

  D. `show interface`

14. What does a VLAN provide?

  A. The fastest port to all servers

  B. Multiple collision domains on one switch port

  C. Breaking up broadcast domains in a layer-2 switches internetwork

  D. Multiple broadcast domains within a single collision domain

15. If you wanted to delete the configuration stored in NVRAM, what would you type?

  A. `erase startup`

  B. `erase nvram`

  C. `delete nvram`

  D. `erase running`

16. What Cisco command is used to allow the 802.2 IPX frame type on an Ethernet interface?

A. Novell-Ether

B. SAP

C. SNAP

D. 802.2

17. Which class of IP address has the most host addresses available by default?

A. A

B. B

C. C

D. A and B

18. How often are BPDU sent from a layer-2 device?

A. Never

B. Every two seconds

C. Every 10 minutes

D. Every 30 seconds

19. Which of the following is true regarding VLANs? (Choose all that apply.)

A. Two VLANs are configured by default on all Cisco switches.

B. VLANs only work if you have a complete Cisco switched internetwork. No off-brand switches are allowed.

C. You should not have more than 10 switches in the same VTP domain.

D. VTP is used to send VLAN information to switches in a configured VTP domain.

20. What LAN switch mode keeps CRC errors to a minimum but still has a fixed latency rate?

A. STP

B. Store and forward

C. Cut-through

D. FragmentFree

21. How many broadcast domains are created when you segment a network with a 12-port switch?

A. One

B. Two

C. Five

D. 12

22. What PDU is at the Transport layer?

A. User data

B. Session

C. Segment

D. Frame

23. What protocols are used to configure trunking on a switch? (Choose all that apply.)

A. Virtual Trunk Protocol

B. VLAN

C. 802.1q

D. ISL

24. What is a stub network?

A. A network with more than one exit point

B. A network with more than one exit and entry point

C. A network with only one entry and no exit point

D. A network that has only one entry and exit

25. Where is a hub specified in the OSI model?

A. Session layer

B. Physical layer

C. Data Link layer

D. Application layer

26. If you wanted to configure ports on a Cisco switch, what are the different ways available to configure VLAN memberships? (Choose all that apply.)

A. Via a DHCP server

B. Statically

C. Dynamically

D. Via a VTP database

27. What does the command `show controllers s 0` provide?

A. The type of serial port connection (e.g., Ethernet or Token Ring)

B. The type of connection (e.g., DTE or DCE)

C. The configuration of the interface including the IP address and clock rate

D. The controlling processor of that interface

28. What is a pre-10.3 IOS command that copies the contents of NVRAM to DRAM?

   A. config t

   B. config net

   C. config mem

   D. wr mem

29. What is the main reason the OSI model was created?

   A. To create a layered model larger than the DoD model

   B. So application developers can change only one layer's protocols at a time

   C. So different networks could communicate

   D. So Cisco could use the model

30. Which layer of the OSI model creates a virtual circuit between hosts before transmitting data?

   A. Application

   B. Session

   C. Transport

   D. Network

   E. Data Link

31. Which protocol does DHCP use at the Transport layer?

   A. IP

   B. TCP

   C. UDP

   D. ARP

32. How do you copy a router IOS to a TFTP host?

    A. `copy run starting`

    B. `copy start running`

    C. `copy running tftp`

    D. `copy flash tftp`

33. If your router is facilitating a CSU/DSU, which of the following commands do you need to use to provide the router with a 64000bps serial link?

    A. `RouterA(config)#`**`bandwidth 64`**

    B. `RouterA(config-if)#`**`bandwidth 64000`**

    C. `RouterA(config)#`**`clockrate 64000`**

    D. `RouterA(config-if)`**`clock rate 64`**

    E. `RouterA(config-if)`**`clock rate 64000`**

34. Which command is used to determine if an IP access-list is enabled on a particular interface?

    A. `show access-lists`

    B. `show interface`

    C. `show ip interface`

    D. `show interface access-lists`

35. Which of the following commands will set your Telnet password on a Cisco router?

    A. `Line telnet 0 4`

    B. `Line aux 0 4`

    C. `Line vty 0 4`

    D. `Line con 0`

36. What command do you use to set the enable secret password on a Cisco router?

   A. RouterA(config)#`enable password todd`

   B. RouterA(config)#`enable secret todd`

   C. RouterA(config)#`enable secret password todd`

   D. RouterA(config-if)#`enable secret todd`

37. Which protocol is used to find an Ethernet address from a known IP address?

   A. IP

   B. ARP

   C. RARP

   D. BootP

38. Which command is used to upgrade an IOS on a Cisco router?

   A. `copy tftp run`

   B. `copy tftp start`

   C. `config net`

   D. `copy tftp flash`

39. If you want to copy a configuration from the router's DRAM to NVRAM, which command do you use?

   A. `copy run start`

   B. `copy start run`

   C. `config net`

   D. `config mem`

   E. `copy flash nvram`

40. If an interface is administratively down, what is the problem?

    A. The interface is bad.

    B. The interface is not connected to another device.

    C. There is no problem.

    D. The interface is looped.

41. What is used in a reliable session to make sure all data was received properly?

    A. Route selection

    B. Acknowledgements

    C. System authentication

    D. Holddowns

42. How many collision domains are created when you segment a network with a 12-port switch?

    A. 1

    B. 2

    C. 5

    D. 12

43. What is the administrative distance of static routes by default?

    A. 0

    B. 1

    C. 10

    D. 100

44. What was the first solution for counting to infinity?

    A. Holddowns

    B. Triggered updates

    C. Setting a maximum hop count

    D. Reverse poison

45. Which protocol is used to send a Destination Network Unknown message back to originating hosts?

   A. TCP

   B. ARP

   C. ICMP

   D. BootP

46. What is the maximum distance of 100BaseT?

   A. 100 meters

   B. 260 meters

   C. 400 meters

   D. 1000 feet

47. At which layer do packets occur?

   A. Session

   B. Transport

   C. Network

   D. Data Link

48. Which of the following is not one of the advantages of using static routes over dynamic routing?

   A. Fast convergence

   B. No CPU usage

   C. No bandwidth usage

   D. Security

49. How do you copy a configuration stored on a TFTP host to DRAM?

   A. `copy run start`

   B. `copy start run`

   C. `copy tftp flash`

   D. `copy tftp running`

50. What keystrokes will return a Telnet session back to an originating routers console?

   A. Ctrl+Z

   B. Ctrl+C

   C. Ctrl+Shift+6, then X

   D. Ctrl+Break

51. What type of access list uses the numbers 100–199?

   A. IP standard

   B. IPX standard

   C. IP extended

   D. IPX extended

   E. IPX SAP filter

52. What Cisco command will configure IPX on an Ethernet network running 802.3?

   A. SAP

   B. Novell-ether

   C. 802.3

   D. SNAP

53. Which of the following routing protocols uses bandwidth and delay of the line when making routing decisions?

   A. RIP

   B. Static

   C. IGRP

   D. OSPF

54. What type of access list uses the numbers 1000–1099?

    A. IP standard

    B. IPX standard

    C. IP extended

    D. IPX extended

    E. IPX SAP filter

55. What is a pre-10.3 IOS command that lets you copy a configuration from a TFTP host to DRAM?

    A. config t

    B. config net

    C. config mem

    D. wr mem

56. Which of the following commands is a way of turning on RIP routing?

    A. RouterA#**routing rip**

    B. Router(config)#**routing rip**

    C. RouterA#**router rip**

    D. Router(config)#**router rip**

    E. router(config-router)#**router rip**

57. What type of access list uses the numbers 800–899?

    A. IP standard

    B. IPX standard

    C. IP extended

    D. IPX extended

    E. IPX SAP filter

58. What two commands will show you all your configured PVCs?

  A. sh pvc

  B. show interface

  C. show frame-rely pvc

  D. sho runn

59. If you connect a Cisco router and a 3Com router through a T-1, why won't they work by default?

  A. Cisco and 3Com are not compatible.

  B. 3Com was purchased by Cisco and scrapped.

  C. The serial encapsulations are not compatible by default.

  D. The Ethernet frame types are not compatible by default.

60. You have a large Ethernet network in your office. Which of the following is true regarding this network?

  A. You can use a FastEthernet full-duplex connection using 10Base2.

  B. You can use full duplex when connecting a point-to-point connection between two nodes.

  C. You can use store and forward with a full-duplex connection.

  D. You can use cut-through with half duplex.

61. You have large files that you need to transfer from your home to your remote corporate office. You need to do this periodically and quickly. What technology would be best suited for your situation?

  A. Frame Relay

  B. Ethernet

  C. ISDN

  D. Token Ring

  E. ATM

62. What command is used to see the NetWare servers running on your network?

   A. show servers

   B. show ipx servers

   C. show novell

   D. show all servers

63. What protocol is used at layer-2 to help stop network loops?

   A. BPDU

   B. STP

   C. VLANs

   D. Switches

64. What Cisco command is used to set the IPX Ethernet frame type to Ethernet_II?

   A. SNAP

   B. ARPA

   C. Ethernet_II

   D. SAP

65. What is not a characteristic of a network segment on a switch?

   A. The segment has its own collision domain.

   B. The segment can translate from one media to a different media.

   C. All devices in the segment are part of the same broadcast domain.

   D. One device per segment can concurrently send frames to the switch.

66. BECN is used for what?

   A. PPP authentication

   B. ISDN BRI load balancing

   C. Frame Relay congestion control

   D. HDLC protocol identification of the Network layer

67. What is the bit length and expression form of a MAC address?

    A. 24 bits, hex

    B. 48 bits, hex

    C. 24 bits, binary

    D. 48 bits, binary

68. Which of the following is the valid host range for the IP address 192.168.168.188 255.255.255.192?

    A. 192.168.168.129–190

    B. 192.168.168.129–191

    C. 192.168.168.128–190

    D. 192.168.168.128–192

69. What type of access list uses the numbers 900–999?

    A. IP standard

    B. IPX standard

    C. IP extended

    D. IPX extended

    E. PX SAP filter

70. In a network with dozens of switches, how many root bridges would you have?

    A. One

    B. Two

    C. Five

    D. 12

Answers to Assessment Test

1. **A.** Network Control Protocol identifies the Network layer protocol used in the packet. See Chapter 10 for more information.

2. **C.** The best answer is to use a layer-2 switch and provide collision domains to each device. This will provide the most bang for the buck in terms of network equipment. See Chapter 2 for more information.

3. **C.** The IPX logical address of a host is typically a combination of the host's MAC address of the NIC and the network ID of the LAN. See Chapter 8 for more information.

4. **C.** The command `line console 0` places you at a prompt where you can then set your console user-mode password. See Chapter 4 for more information.

5. **C.** The `dialer load-threshold 125` command tells the router to bring up the second BRI at 50 percent load. See Chapter 10 for more information.

6. **C.** Link Control Protocol in the PPP stack provides dynamic addressing, authentication, and multilink. See Chapter 10 for more information.

7. **B.** The `show interface` command shows the line, protocol, DLCI, and LMI information of an interface. See Chapter 10 for more information.

8. **A.** IP standard access lists use the numbers 1–99. See Chapter 9 for more information.

9. **B.** The `passive` command, short for `passive-interface`, stops regular updates from being sent out an interface. However, the interface can still receive updates. See Chapter 5 for more information.

10. **C.** ICMP is the protocol at the Network layer that is used to send echo requests and replies. See Chapter 3 for more information.

11. **A.** The `show ipx traffic` command shows the RIP and SAP information being sent and received on a router. The `show ipx interface` command shows the IPX RIP and SAP information being sent and received on a specific interface. See Chapter 8 for more information.

12. C.   The command `line vty 0 4` places you in a prompt that will allow you to set or change your Telnet password. See Chapter 4 for more information.

13. B.   To see the contents of all access-lists, use the `show access-lists` command.

14. C.   VLAN's break up broadcast domains at layer-2. See Chapter 6 for more information.

15. A.   The command `erase-startup-config` deletes the configuration stored in NVRAM. See Chapter 4 for more information.

16. B.   The Cisco encapsulation of SAP will set the Ethernet encapsulation to 802.2. See Chapter 8 for more information.

17. A.   Class A addressing provides 24 bits for hosts addressing. See Chapter 3 for more information.

18. B.   Every two seconds, BPDUs are sent out from all active bridge ports by default. See Chapter 2 for more information.

19. D.   Switches do not propagate VLAN information by default; you must configure the VTP domain. Virtual Trunk Protocol (VTP) is used to propagate VLAN information across a trunked link. See Chapter 6 for more information.

20. D.   FragmentFree LAN switching checks into the data portion of the frame to make sure no fragmentation has occurred. See Chapter 2 for more information.

21. A.   By default, switches break up collision domains but are one large broadcast domain. See Chapter 2 for more information.

22. C.   Segmentation happens at the Transport layer. See Chapter 1 for more information.

23. C, D.   VTP is not right because it has nothing to do with trunking, except that it sends VLAN information across a trunked link. 802.1q and ISL are used to configure trunking on a port. See Chapter 6 for more information.

24. D.   Stub networks have only one connection to an internetwork. Default routes can only be set on a stub network, or network loops may occur. See Chapter 5 for more information.

25. B. Hubs regenerate electrical signals, which are specified at the Physical layer. See Chapter 1 for more information.

26. B, C. You can configure VLAN memberships on a port either statically or dynamically. See Chapter 6 for more information.

27. B. The command `show controllers s 0` tells you what type of serial connection you have. If it is a DCE, you need to provide the clock rate. See Chapter 4 for more information.

28. C. The old command `config mem` was used to copy the configuration stored in NVRAM to RAM and append the file in DRAM, not replace it. The new command is `copy start run`. See Chapter 7 for more information.

29. C. The primary reason the OSI model was created was so that different networks could interoperate. See Chapter 1 for more information.

30. C. The Transport layer creates virtual circuits between hosts before transmitting any data. See Chapter 1 for more information.

31. C. User Datagram Protocol is a connection network service at the Transport layer, and DHCP uses this connectionless service. See Chapter 3 for more information.

32. D. The command used to copy a configuration from a router to a TFTP host is `copy flash tftp`. See Chapter 7 for more information.

33. E. The clock rate command is two words, and the speed of the line is in bps. See Chapter 4 for more information.

34. C. The `show ip interface` command will show you if any outbound or inbound interfaces have an access-lists set. See Chapter 9 for more information.

35. C. The command `line vty 0 4` places you in a prompt that will allow you to set or change your Telnet password. See Chapter 4 for more information.

36. B. The command `enable secret todd` sets the enable secret password to todd. See Chapter 4 for more information.

37. B. If a device knows the IP address of where it wants to send a packet, but doesn't know the hardware address, it will send an ARP broadcast looking for the hardware or, in this case, Ethernet address. See Chapter 3 for more information.

38. D. The `copy tftp flash` command places a new file in flash memory, which is the default location for the Cisco IOS in Cisco routers. See Chapter 7 for more information.

39. A. The command to copy `running-config`, which is the file in DRAM, to NVRAM is `copy running-config startup-config`. See Chapter 7 for more information.

40. C. If an interface is administratively shut down, it just means the administrator needs to perform a `no shutdown` on the interface. See Chapter 4 for more information.

41. B. A reliable session, typically meaning the Transport layer, uses acknowledgments to make sure all data was received properly.

42. D. Layer-2 switching creates individual collision domains. See Chapter 2 for more information.

43. B. Static routes have an administrative distance of one by default. See Chapter 5 for more information.

44. C. Before a maximum hop count was used in distance-vector networks, the only way to solve network loops was to reboot all the routers in the network. See Chapter 5 for more information.

45. C. ICMP is the protocol at the Network layer that is used to send messages back to an originating router. See Chapter 3 for more information.

46. A. Fast Ethernet, using twisted-pair, can run up to 100 meters. See Chapter 1 for more information.

47. C. PDUs at the Network layer are called packets. See Chapter 1 for more information.

48. A. Static routes do not converge and must be updated by hand. See Chapter 5 for more information.

49. D. The `copy tftp running-config` command copies the running-config file to DRAM. See Chapter 7 for more information.

50. C. The keystrokes Cntrl+Shift+6, then X, will return a Telnet session back to the originating console. See Chapter 7 for more information.

51. C. IP extended access lists use the numbers 100–199. See Chapter 9 for more information.

52. B. The Cisco command Novell-ether is the encapsulation for 802.3. However, this is the default on Ethernet links if no encapsulation is specified. See Chapter 8 for more information.

53. C. IGRP, as well as EIGRP. Use bandwidth and delay of the line, by default, when making routing decisions. See Chapter 5 for more information.

54. E. IPX SAP filters use the access list numbers 1000–1099. See Chapter 9 for more information.

55. B. The old command to copy a file from a TFTP host to DRAM is `config net`. See Chapter 7 for more information.

56. D. The global command `router rip` will turn RIP routing on in the router. You then need to tell the RIP routing protocol which network to advertise. See Chapter 5 for more information.

57. B. IPX standard access lists use the numbers 800–899. See Chapter 9 for more information.

58. C, D. The commands `show running-config` and `show frame pvc` will show you the configured PVC for each interface or subinterface. See Chapter 10 for more information.

59. C. Each vendor uses HDLC by default on the serial links. They are both proprietary. To communicate between vendors, you must use something like PPP or Frame Relay. See Chapter 10 for more information.

60. B. Full-duplex Ethernet creates a point-to-point connection between the transmitter circuitry of the transmitting station and the receiving circuitry of the receiving station. See Chapter 1 for more information.

61. C. Even though newer technologies are probably a better choice at this point for home–to–corporate office connections, Cisco's answer to this question is ISDN because of the period connection that is needed. See Chapter 10 for more information.

62. B. The `show ipx servers` command shows from which NetWare servers the routers have received SAP packets. See Chapter 8 for more information.

63. B. To stop network loops from occurring with redundant links, layer-2 devices implement the Spanning-Tree Protocol. See Chapter 2 for more information.

64. C. The keyword for Ethernet_II is ARPA. See Chapter 8 for more information.

65. B. Switches cannot translate from one media to another on the same segment. See Chapter 2 for more information.

66. C. Backward-Explicit Congestion Notification is used to tell the transmitting device to slow down because the Frame Relay switch is congested. See Chapter 10 for more information.

67. B. MAC address are 48 bits long, 6 bytes, and written in hex. See Chapter 1 for more information.

68. A. $256 - 192 = 64$. $64 + 64 = 128$. $128 + 64 = 192$. The subnet is 128, the broadcast address is 191, and the valid host range is the numbers in between, or 129–190. See Chapter 3 for more information.

69. D. IPX extended access lists use the numbers 900–999. See Chapter 9 for more information.

70. A. You should only have one root bridge per network. See Chapter 2 for more information.

Chapter

1

Internetworking

THE CCNA EXAM TOPICS COVERED IN THIS CHAPTER INCLUDE THE FOLLOWING:

✓ **OSI Reference Model & Layered Communications**

- Describe data link and network addresses and identify key differences between them.

- Define and describe the function of the MAC address.

- List the key internetworking functions for the OSI Network layer.

- Identify at least three reasons why the industry uses a layered model.

- Define and explain the five conversion steps of data encapsulation.

- Describe connection-oriented network service and connectionless network service, and identify their key differences.

- Identify the parts in specific protocol address examples.

- Describe the advantages of LAN segmentation.

- Describe LAN segmentation using bridges.

- Describe LAN segmentation using routers.

- Describe LAN segmentation using switches.

- Describe the benefits of network segmentation with bridges.

- Describe the benefits of network segmentation with routers.

- Describe the benefits of network segmentation with switches.

✓ **LAN Design**

- Describe full- and half-duplex Ethernet operation.
- Describe network congestion problem in Ethernet networks.
- Describe the features and benefits of Fast Ethernet.
- Describe the guidelines and distance limitations of Fast Ethernet.

✓ **Routing**

- Define flow control and describe the three basic methods used in networking.

Welcome to the exciting world of internetworking. This first chapter will really help you understand the basics of internetworking by focusing on how to connect networks together using Cisco routers and switches. First, you need to know exactly what an internetwork is: You create an internetwork when you take two or more LANs or WANs and connect them via a router, and configure a logical network addressing scheme with a protocol like IP.

I'll begin by exploring four things in this chapter:

- Internetworking basics

- Network segmentation

- How bridges, switches, and routers are used to physically segment a network

- How routers are employed to create an internetwork

I'm also going to dissect the Open Systems Interconnection (OSI) model and describe each part to you in detail, because you really need a good grasp of it to have a solid foundation on which to build your networking knowledge. The OSI model has seven hierarchical layers that were developed to enable different networks to communicate reliably between disparate systems. Since this book is centering upon all things CCNA, it's crucial for you to understand the OSI model as Cisco sees it, so that's how I will be presenting the seven layers of the OSI model to you.

Since there's a bunch of different types of devices specified at the different layers of the OSI model, it's also very important to understand the many types of cables and connectors used for connecting all those devices to a network. We'll go over cabling Cisco devices, discussing that along with Ethernet LANs, WAN technologies, and even how to connect a router or switch with a console connection.

Cisco makes a smorgasbord of router, hub, and switch products, so it follows that by understanding all that's available from Cisco, you can make a much more solid, informed decision about exactly which product(s) will most strategically meet your networking needs. I'll help you with that by going over Cisco's product line of hubs, routers, and switches in a special section toward the end of this chapter.

I'll end this chapter by discussing the Cisco three-layer hierarchical model. This was developed by Cisco to help you design, implement, and troubleshoot internetworks.

After you finish reading this chapter, you will encounter 25 review questions and three written labs, which will serve to lock the information from this chapter into your memory. Do not skip this part of the chapter! In addition, don't forget to go through the bonus exams as well as the flash cards on the CD.

Internetworking Basics

Before we explore internetworking models and the specifications of the OSI reference model, you've got to understand the big picture and learn the answer to the key question: "Why is it so important to learn Cisco internetworking?"

Networks and networking have grown exponentially over the last 15 years—understandably so. They've had to evolve at light speed just to keep up with huge increases in basic mission-critical user needs like sharing data and printers, as well as more advanced demands like video conferencing. Unless everyone who needs to share network resources is located in the same office area (an increasingly uncommon situation), the challenge is to connect the relevant and sometimes many networks together so all users can share the networks' wealth.

It's also likely that at some point, you'll have to break up one large network into a number of smaller ones because user response has dwindled to a trickle as the network grew and grew and created LAN traffic congestion. Breaking up a larger network into a number of smaller ones is called *network segmentation*, and it's accomplished using *routers*, *switches*, and *bridges*.

The possible causes of LAN traffic congestion are:

- Too many hosts in a broadcast domain

- Broadcast storms

- Multicasting

- Low bandwidth

Routers are used to connect networks together and route packets of data from one network to another. Cisco became the de facto standard of routers because of their high-quality router products, great selection, and fantastic service. Routers, by default, break up a *broadcast domain*, which is the set of all devices on a network segment that hear all broadcasts sent on that segment. Breaking up a broadcast domain is important because when a host or server sends a network broadcast, every device on the network must read and process that broadcast—unless you've got a router. When the router's interface receives this broadcast, it can respond by basically saying "Thanks, but no thanks," and discard the broadcast without forwarding it on to other networks. Even though routers are known for breaking up broadcast domains by default, it's important to remember that they also break up collision domains as well.

Conversely, switches aren't used to create internetworks, they're employed to add functionality to an internetwork LAN. The main purpose of a switch is to make a LAN work better—to optimize its performance—providing more bandwidth for the LAN's users. And switches don't forward packets to other networks like routers do. Instead, they only "switch" frames from one port to another within the switched network. (Theoretically, you don't know what frames and packets are yet, but don't worry: I'll tell you all about them later in this chapter, I promise!)

By default, switches break up *collision domains*. This is an Ethernet term used to describe a network scenario in which one particular device sends a packet on a network segment, forcing every other device on that same segment to pay attention to it. At the same time, a different device tries to transmit, leading to a collision, after which both devices must retransmit, one at a time. Not very efficient! This situation is typically found in a hub environment where each host segment connects to a hub that represents only one collision domain and only one broadcast domain. By contrast, each and every port on a switch represents its own collision domain.

Switches create separate collision domains, but a single broadcast domain. Routers provide a separate broadcast domain.

The term *bridging* was introduced before routers and hubs were implemented, so it's pretty common to hear people referring to bridges as "switches." That's because bridges and switches basically do the same thing—break up collision domains on a LAN. But there are differences. Switches provide this function, but they do it with greatly enhanced management ability and features. Plus, most of the time, bridges only had two or four ports. You could get your hands on a bridge with up to 16 ports, but that's nothing compared to the hundreds available on some switches!

You would use a bridge in a network to reduce collisions within broadcast domains and to increase the number of collision domains in your network, which provides more bandwidth for users.

Figure 1.1 shows how a network would look with all these internetwork devices in place. Remember that the router will break up broadcast domains for every LAN interface, but it also breaks up collision domains as well.

FIGURE 1.1 Internetworking devices

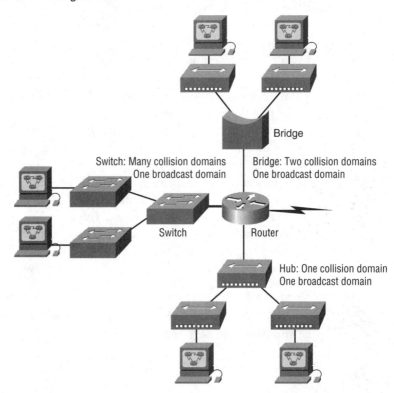

In Figure 1.1, did you notice that the router is found at center stage, and that it connects each physical network together? We have to use this layout because of the older technologies involved—bridges and hubs. Once we have only switches in our network, things change a lot! The LAN switches would then be placed at the center of the network world and the routers would be found connecting only logical networks together. If I've implemented this kind of setup, I've created virtual LANs (VLANs), which I'll go over thoroughly with you in Chapter 6.

Back to Figure 1.1: On the top network, a bridge was used to connect the hubs to a router. The bridge breaks up collision domains, but all the hosts connected to both hubs are still crammed into the same broadcast domain. Also, the bridge only created two collision domains, so each device connected to a hub is in the same collision domain as every other device connected to that same hub. This is lame, but it's still better than having one collision domain for all hosts!

Although bridges are used to segment networks, they will not isolate broadcast or multicast packets.

Notice something else: the three hubs at the bottom that are connected also connect to the router, creating one humongous collision domain and one humongous broadcast domain. This makes the bridged network look much better indeed!

The best network connected to the router is the LAN switch network on the left because, as you'll remember, each port on that switch breaks up collision domains. But it could definitely be improved because all devices are still in the same broadcast domain. Remember, this can be a bad thing, because all devices must listen to all broadcasts transmitted, and if your broadcast domains are too large, the users have less bandwidth and network response time will suffer.

The best network is a network that is correctly configured to meet the business requirements of each individual business. LAN switches with routers, correctly placed in the network, are the best network design. This book will help you understand the basics of routers and switches so you can make informed decisions on a case-by-case basis.

So now that you've gotten an introduction to internetworking, and the various devices that live in an internetwork, it's time to head into internetworking models.

Should I just replace all my hubs with switches?

Well, if you can, sure—why not? Switches really add a lot of functionality to a network that hubs just don't have. However, most of us don't have an unlimited budget. Hubs still can create a nice network—that is, if you design and implement the network correctly, of course.

Let's say that you have 40 users plugged into four hubs, 10 users each. At this point, the hubs are all connected together so that you have one large collision domain and one large broadcast domain. If you can afford to buy just one switch and plug each hub into a switch port, as well as the servers into the switch, then you now have four collision domains and one broadcast domain. Not great, but for the price of one switch, your network is much better.

Internetworking Models

When networks first came into being, computers could typically communicate only with computers from the same manufacturer. For example, companies ran either a complete DECnet solution or an IBM solution—not both together. In the late 1970s, the *Open Systems Interconnection (OSI) reference model* was created by the International Organization for Standardization (ISO) to break this barrier.

The OSI model was meant to help vendors create interoperable network devices so that different vendor networks could work with each other. Like world peace, it'll probably never happen completely, but it's still a great goal.

The OSI model is the primary architectural model for networks. It describes how data and network information are communicated from an application on one computer, through the network media, to an application on another computer. The OSI reference model breaks this approach into layers.

The Layered Approach

A *reference model* is a conceptual blueprint of how communications should take place. It addresses all the processes required for effective communication and divides these processes into logical groupings called *layers*. When a communication system is designed in this manner, it's known as *layered architecture*.

Think of it like this: You and some friends want to start a company. One of the first things you'd do is sit down and think through what tasks must be done, who will do them, what order they will be done in, and how they relate to each other. Ultimately, you might group these tasks into departments. Let's say you decide to have an order-taking department, an inventory department, and a shipping department. Each of your departments has its own unique tasks, keeping its staff members busy and requiring them to focus on only their own duties.

In this scenario, departments are a metaphor for the layers in a communication system. For things to run smoothly, the staff of each department will have to trust and rely heavily on the others to do their jobs and competently handle their unique responsibilities. In your planning sessions, you would probably take notes, recording the entire process to facilitate later discussions about standards of operation that will serve as your business blueprint, or reference model.

Once your business is launched, your department heads, armed with the part of the blueprint relating to their department, will need to develop practical methods to implement their assigned tasks. These practical methods, or protocols, will need to be compiled into a standard operating procedures manual and followed closely. Each of the various procedures in your manual will have been included for different reasons and have varying degrees of importance and implementation. If you form a partnership or acquire another company, it will be imperative for its business protocols—its business blueprint—to match yours (or at least be compatible with it).

Similarly, software developers can use a reference model to understand computer communication processes and see what types of functions need to be accomplished on any one layer. If they are developing a protocol for a certain layer, all they need to concern themselves with is the specific layer's functions, not those of any other layer. Another layer and protocol will handle the other functions. The technical term for this idea is *binding*. The communication processes that are related to each other are bound, or grouped together, at a particular layer.

Advantages of Reference Models

The OSI model is hierarchical, and the same benefits and advantages can apply to any layered model. The primary purpose of all models, and especially the OSI model, is to allow different vendors' networks to interoperate.

Advantages of using the OSI layered model include, but are not limited to, the following:

- Allows multiple-vendor development through standardization of network components

- Allows various types of network hardware and software to communicate

- Prevents changes in one layer from affecting other layers, so it does not hamper development

The OSI Reference Model

The OSI reference model was created in the late 1970s to help facilitate data transfer between network nodes. One of the greatest functions of the OSI specifications is to assist in data transfer between disparate hosts, meaning, they enable us to transfer data between a Unix host and a PC or a Mac.

The OSI isn't a physical model, though. Rather, it's a set of guidelines that application developers can use to create and implement applications that run on a network. It also provides a framework for creating and implementing networking standards, devices, and internetworking schemes.

The main reason the International Organization for Standardization (ISO) released the OSI model was so different vendor networks could work with each other.

The OSI has seven different layers, divided into two groups. The top three layers define how the applications within the end stations will communicate with each other and with users. The bottom four layers define how data is transmitted end-to-end. Figure 1.2 shows the three upper layers and their functions, and Figure 1.3 shows the four lower layers and their functions.

When you study Figure 1.2, you can see that the user interfaces with the computer at the Application layer, and also that the upper layers are responsible for applications communicating between hosts. Remember that none of the upper layers know anything about networking or network addresses. That's the responsibility of the four bottom layers.

In Figure 1.3 you can see that it's the four bottom layers that define how data is transferred through a physical wire or through switches and routers. These bottom layers also determine how to rebuild a data stream from a transmitting host to a destination host's application.

FIGURE 1.2   The upper layers

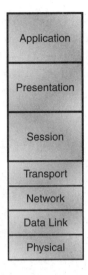

• Provides a user interface

• Presents data
• Handles processing such as encryption

• Keeps different applications'
  data separate

FIGURE 1.3   The lower layers

• Provides reliable or unreliable delivery
• Performs error correction before retransmit

• Provides logical addressing,
  which routers use for path determination

• Combines packets into bytes and bytes into frames
• Provides access to media using MAC address
• Performs error detection not correction

• Moves bits between devices
• Specifies voltage, wire speed,
  and pin-out of cables

Network devices that operate at all seven layers of the OSI model include:

- Network management stations
- Web servers
- Gateways
- Network hosts

The OSI Layers

Basically, the International Organization for Standardization (ISO) is pretty much the Emily Post of the network protocol world. Just like Ms. Post, who wrote the book setting the standards—or protocols—for human social interaction, the ISO developed the OSI reference model as the precedent and guide for an open network protocol set. Defining the etiquette of communication models, it remains today the most popular means of comparison for protocol suites.

The OSI reference model has seven layers:

- Application layer

- Presentation layer

- Session layer

- Transport layer

- Network layer

- Data Link layer

- Physical layer

Figure 1.4 shows the functions defined at each layer of the OSI model. With this in hand, we can now move on to explore each layer's function in detail.

FIGURE 1.4   Layer functions

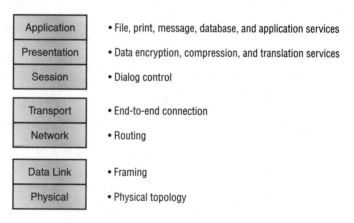

The Application Layer

The *Application layer* of the OSI model marks the spot where users actually communicate to the computer. This layer is responsible for identifying and establishing the availability of the intended communication partner, and determining if sufficient resources for the intended communication exist.

These tasks are important because, although computer applications sometimes require only desktop resources, they may (and often do) unite communicating components from more than one network application. Some examples of this include executing file transfers and e-mail, as well as enabling remote access, network management activities, client/server processes, and information location. Many network applications provide services for communication over enterprise networks, but for present and future internet-working, the need is fast developing to reach beyond the limits of current physical networking. Today, transactions and information exchanges between organizations are broadening to require internetworking applications like the following:

World Wide Web (WWW) Connects countless servers (the number seems to grow with each passing day) presenting diverse formats. Most are multimedia and include some or all of the following: graphics, text, video, and increasingly, even sound. (And as pressure to keep up the pace mounts, websites are only getting slicker and snappier. Keep in mind, the snazzier the site, the more resources it requires. You'll see why I mention this later.) Netscape Navigator and Internet Explorer simplify both accessing and viewing websites.

E-mail gateways Versatile and can use Simple Mail Transfer Protocol (SMTP) or the X.400 standard to deliver messages between different e-mail applications.

Electronic data interchange (EDI) A composite of specialized standards and processes that facilitates the flow of tasks such as accounting, shipping/receiving, and order and inventory tracking between businesses.

Special interest bulletin boards Include the many Internet chat rooms where people can "meet" (connect) and communicate with each other either by posting messages or by typing a live conversation. They can also share public-domain software.

Internet navigation utilities Include applications like Gopher and WAIS, as well as search engines like Yahoo!, Excite, and AltaVista, which help users locate the resources and information they need on the Internet.

Financial transaction services   Target the financial community. They gather and sell information pertaining to investments, market trading, commodities, currency exchange rates, and credit data to their subscribers.

The Presentation Layer

The *Presentation layer* gets its name from its purpose: It presents data to the Application layer and is responsible for data translation and code formatting.

This layer is essentially a translator and provides coding and conversion functions. A successful data-transfer technique is to adapt the data into a standard format before transmission. Computers are configured to receive this generically formatted data and then convert the data back into its native format for actual reading (for example, EBCDIC to ASCII). By providing translation services, the Presentation layer ensures that data transferred from the Application layer of one system can be read by the Application layer of another one.

The OSI has protocol standards that define how standard data should be formatted. Tasks like data compression, decompression, encryption, and decryption are associated with this layer. Some Presentation layer standards are involved in multimedia operations too. The following serve to direct graphic and visual image presentation:

PICT   This is picture format used by Macintosh or PowerPC programs for transferring QuickDraw graphics.

TIFF   The Tagged Image File Format is a standard graphics format for high-resolution, bitmapped images.

JPEG   The Joint Photographic Experts Group brings these photo standards to us.

Other standards guide movies and sound:

MIDI   The Musical Instrument Digital Interface is used for digitized music.

MPEG   The Moving Picture Experts Group's standard for the compression and coding of motion video for CDs is increasingly popular. It provides digital storage and bit rates up to 1.5Mbps.

QuickTime   This is for use with Macintosh or PowerPC programs; it manages audio and video applications.

RTF   Rich Text Format is a file format that lets you exchange text files between different word processors, even in different operating systems.

The Session Layer

The *Session layer* is responsible for setting up, managing, and then tearing down sessions between Presentation layer entities. This layer also provides dialogue control between devices, or nodes. It coordinates communication between systems, and serves to organize their communication by offering three different modes: *simplex*, *half duplex*, and *full duplex*. To sum up, the Session layer basically keeps different applications' data separate from other applications' data.

The following are some examples of Session layer protocols and interfaces (according to Cisco):

Network File System (NFS)   Developed by Sun Microsystems and used with TCP/IP and Unix workstations to allow transparent access to remote resources.

Structured Query Language (SQL)   Developed by IBM to provide users with a simpler way to define their information requirements on both local and remote systems.

Remote Procedure Call (RPC)   A broad client/server redirection tool used for disparate service environments. Its procedures are created on clients and performed on servers.

X Window   Widely used by intelligent terminals for communicating with remote Unix computers, allowing them to operate as though they were locally attached monitors.

AppleTalk Session Protocol (ASP)   Another client/server mechanism, which both establishes and maintains sessions between AppleTalk client and server machines.

Digital Network Architecture Session Control Protocol (DNA SCP)   A DECnet Session layer protocol.

The Transport Layer

The *Transport layer* segments and reassembles data into a data stream. Services located in the Transport layer both segment and reassemble data from upper-layer applications and unite it onto the same data stream. They provide end-to-end data transport services and can establish a logical connection between the sending host and destination host on an internetwork.

Some of you are probably familiar with TCP and UDP already. (But if you're not, no worries—I'll tell you all about them in Chapter 3.) If so, you know that both work at the Transport layer, and that TCP is a reliable service and UDP is not. This means that application developers have more options because they have a choice between the two protocols when working with TCP/IP protocols.

The Transport layer is responsible for providing mechanisms for multiplexing upper-layer applications, establishing sessions, and tearing down virtual circuits. It also hides details of any network-dependent information from the higher layers by providing transparent data transfer.

The term "reliable networking" can be used at the Transport layer.

Flow Control

Data integrity is ensured at the Transport layer by maintaining *flow control* and by allowing users to request reliable data transport between systems. Flow control prevents a sending host on one side of the connection from overflowing the buffers in the receiving host—an event that can result in lost data. Reliable data transport employs a connection-oriented communications session between systems, and the protocols involved ensure that the following will be achieved:

- The segments delivered are acknowledged back to the sender upon their reception.

- Any segments not acknowledged are retransmitted.

- Segments are sequenced back into their proper order upon arrival at their destination.

- A manageable data flow is maintained in order to avoid congestion, overloading, and data loss.

Connection-Oriented Communication

In reliable transport operation, one device first establishes a connection-oriented session with its peer system. This is called a *call setup*, or a *three-way handshake* (Cisco's term). Data is then transferred, and when finished, a call termination takes place to tear down the virtual circuit.

Figure 1.5 depicts a typical reliable session taking place between sending and receiving systems. By looking at it, you can see that both hosts' application programs begin by notifying their individual operating systems that a connection is about to be initiated. The two operating systems communicate by sending messages over the network confirming that the transfer is approved and that both sides are ready for it to take place. Once all this required synchronization takes place, a connection is fully established and the data transfer begins.

FIGURE 1.5 Establishing a connection-oriented session

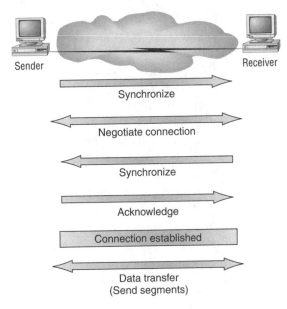

Sender

Receiver

Synchronize

Negotiate connection

Synchronize

Acknowledge

Connection established

Data transfer
(Send segments)

While the information is being transferred between hosts, the two machines periodically check in with each other, communicating through their protocol software to ensure that all is going well and that the data is being received properly.

Let me sum up the steps in the connection-oriented session—the three-way handshake—pictured in Figure 1.5:

- The first "connection agreement" segment is a request for synchronization.

- The second and third segments acknowledge the request and establish connection parameters—the rules—between hosts.

- The final segment is also an acknowledgment. It notifies the destination host that the connection agreement has been accepted and that the actual connection has been established. Data transfer can now begin.

Sounds pretty simple, but things don't always flow so smoothly. Sometimes during a transfer, congestion can occur because a high-speed computer is generating data traffic a lot faster than the network can handle transferring. A bunch of computers simultaneously sending datagrams through a single gateway or destination can also botch things up nicely. In the latter case, a gateway or destination can become congested even though no single source caused the problem. In either case, the problem is basically akin to a freeway bottleneck—too much traffic for too small a capacity. It's not usually one car that's the problem; there are simply too many cars on that freeway.

Okay, so what happens when a machine receives a flood of datagrams too quickly for it to process? It stores them in a memory section called a *buffer*. But this buffering action can only solve the problem if the datagrams are part of a small burst. If not, and the datagram deluge continues, a device's memory will eventually be exhausted, its flood capacity will be exceeded, and it will react by discarding any additional datagrams that arrive.

No huge worries here, though. Because of the transport function, network flood control systems actually work quite well. Instead of dumping resources and allowing data to be lost, the transport can issue a "not ready" indicator to the sender, or source, of the flood (as shown in Figure 1.6). This mechanism works kind of like a stop light, signaling the sending device to stop transmitting segment traffic to its overwhelmed peer. After the peer receiver processes the segments already in its memory reservoir—its buffer—it sends out a "ready" transport indicator. When the machine waiting to transmit the rest of its datagrams receives this "go" indictor, it then resumes its transmission.

In fundamental, reliable, connection-oriented data transfer, datagrams are delivered to the receiving host in exactly the same sequence they're transmitted—and the transmission fails if this order is breached! If any data segments are lost, duplicated, or damaged along the way, a failure will transmit. This problem is solved by having the receiving host acknowledge that it has received each and every data segment.

 Connectionless transfer is covered in Chapter 3.

FIGURE 1.6 Transmitting segments with flow control

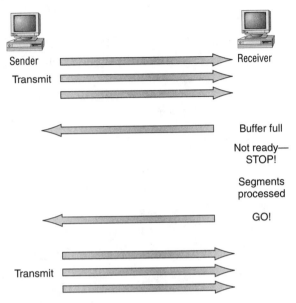

Windowing

Ideally, data throughput happens quickly and efficiently. And as you can imagine, it would be slow if the transmitting machine had to wait for an acknowledgment after sending each segment. But because there's time available *after* the sender transmits the data segment and *before* it finishes processing acknowledgments from the receiving machine, the sender uses the break as an opportunity to transmit more data. The quantity of data segments (measured in bytes) the transmitting machine is allowed to send without receiving an acknowledgment for them is called a *window*.

Windows are used to control the amount in outstanding, unacknowledged data segments.

So the size of the window controls how much information is transferred from one end to the other. While some protocols quantify information by observing the number of packets, TCP/IP measures it by counting the number of bytes.

As you can see in Figure 1.7, there are two window sizes—one set to 1, and one set to 3. When you've configured a window size of 1, the sending machine waits for an acknowledgment for each data segment it transmits before transmitting another. If you've configured a window size of 3, it's allowed to transmit three data segments before an acknowledgment is received. In our simplified example, both the sending and receiving machines are workstations. Reality is rarely that simple, and most often acknowledgments and packets will commingle as they travel over the network and pass through routers. Routing definitely complicates things, but no worries, you'll learn about applied routing in Chapter 5.

FIGURE 1.7 Windowing

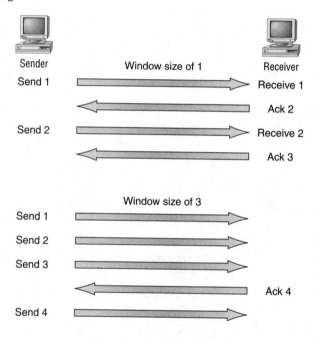

 If a TCP session is set up with a window size of 2 bytes, and during the transfer stage of the session the window size changes from 2 bytes to 3 bytes, the sending host must then transmit 3 bytes before waiting for an acknowledgment instead of the 2 bytes originally set up in the virtual circuit.

Acknowledgments

Reliable data delivery ensures the integrity of a stream of data sent from one machine to the other through a fully functional data link. It guarantees that the data won't be duplicated or lost. This is achieved through something called *positive acknowledgment with retransmission*—a technique that requires a receiving machine to communicate with the transmitting source by sending an acknowledgment message back to the sender when it receives data. The sender documents each segment it sends and waits for this acknowledgment before sending the next segment. When it sends a segment, the transmitting machine starts a timer and retransmits if it expires before an acknowledgment is returned from the receiving end.

In Figure 1.8, the sending machine transmits segments 1, 2, and 3. The receiving node acknowledges it has received them by requesting segment 4. When it receives the acknowledgment, the sender then transmits segments 4, 5, and 6. If segment 5 doesn't make it to the destination, the receiving node acknowledges that event with a request for the segment to be resent. The sending machine will then resend the lost segment and wait for an acknowledgment, which it must receive in order to move on to the transmission of segment 7.

FIGURE 1.8   Transport layer reliable delivery

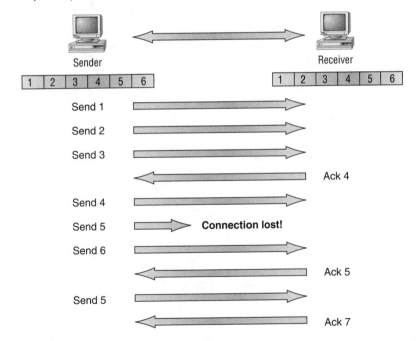

The Network Layer

The *Network layer* (also called layer 3) manages devices addressing, tracks the location of devices on the network, and determines the best way to move data, which means that the Network layer must transport traffic between devices that aren't locally attached. Routers (layer-3 devices) are specified at the Network layer and provide the routing services within an internetwork.

It happens like this: First, when a packet is received on a router interface, the destination IP address is checked. If the packet isn't destined for that particular router, it will look up the destination network address in the routing table. Once the router chooses an exit interface, the packet will be sent to that interface to be framed and sent out on the local network. If the router can't find an entry for the packet's destination network in the routing table, the router drops the packet.

Two types of packets are used at the Network layer: data and route updates.

Data packets   Used to transport user data through the internetwork. Protocols used to support data traffic are called *routed protocols*; examples of routed protocols are IP and IPX. You'll learn about IP addressing in Chapter 3 and IPX addressing in Chapter 8.

Route update packets   Used to update neighboring routers about the networks connected to all routers within the internetwork. Protocols that send route update packets are called routing protocols; examples of some common ones are RIP, EIGRP, and OSPF. Route update packets are used to help build and maintain routing tables on each router.

In Figure 1.9, I've given you an example of a routing table.

FIGURE 1.9   Routing table used in a router

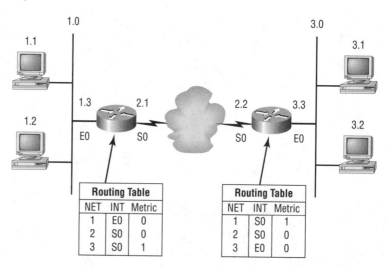

The routing table used in a router includes the following information:

Network addresses These are protocol-specific network addresses. A router must maintain a routing table for individual routing protocols because each routing protocol keeps track of a network with a different addressing scheme. Think of it as a street sign in each of the different languages spoken by the residents that live on a particular street. So, if there were American, Spanish, and French folks on a street named "Cat," the sign would read: Cat/Gato/Chat.

Interface The exit interface a packet will take when destined for a specific network.

Metric The distance to the remote network. Different routing protocols use different ways of computing this distance. I'm going to cover routing protocols in Chapter 5, but for now, know that some routing protocols use something called a *hop count* (the number of routers a packet passes through en route to a remote network), while others use bandwidth, delay of the line, or even tick count (1/18 of a second).

And as I mentioned earlier, routers break up broadcast domains, which means that by default, broadcasts aren't forwarded through a router. Do you remember why this is a good thing? Routers also break up collision domains, but you can also do that using layer-2 (Data Link layer) switches. Because each interface in a router represents a separate network, it must be assigned unique network identification numbers, and each host on the network connected to that router must use the same network number.

Here are some points about routers you should really commit to memory:

- Routers, by default, will not forward any broadcast or multicast packets.

- Routers use the logical address in a Network layer header to determine the next hop router to forward the packet to.

- Routers can use access lists, created by an administrator, to control security on the types of packets that are allowed to enter or exit an interface.

- Routers can provide layer-2 bridging functions if needed and can simultaneously route through the same interface.

- Layer-3 devices (routers in this case) provide connections between virtual LANs (VLANs).

- Routers can provide quality of service (QoS) for specific types of network traffic.

Switching and VLANs and are covered in Chapters 2 and 6, respectively.

The Data Link Layer

The *Data Link layer* provides the physical transmission of the data and handles error notification, network topology, and flow control. This means the Data Link layer will ensure that messages are delivered to the proper device on a LAN using hardware addresses, and translates messages from the Network layer into bits for the Physical layer to transmit.

The Data Link layer formats the message into pieces, each called a *data frame*, and adds a customized header containing the hardware destination and source address. This added information forms a sort of capsule that surrounds the original message in much the same way that engines, navigational devices, and other tools were attached to the lunar modules of the Apollo project. These various pieces of equipment were useful only during certain stages of space flight and were stripped off the module and discarded when their designated stage was complete. Data traveling through networks is similar.

Figure 1.10 shows the Data Link layer with the Ethernet and IEEE specifications. When you check it out, notice that the IEEE 802.2 standard is used in conjunction with and adds functionality to the other IEEE standards.

FIGURE 1.10 Data Link layer

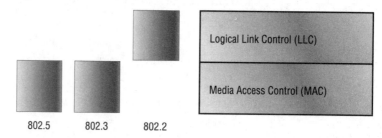

802.5   802.3   802.2

It's important for you to understand that routers, which work at the Network layer, don't care at all about where a particular host is located. They're only concerned about where networks are located, and the best way to reach them—including remote ones. Routers are totally obsessive when it comes to networks. And for once, this is a good thing! It's the Data Link layer that's responsible for the actual unique identification of each device that resides on a local network.

For a host to send packets to individual hosts and between routers, the Data Link layer uses hardware addressing. Each time a packet is sent between routers, it is framed with control information at the Data Link layer, but that information is stripped off at the receiving router and only the original packet is left completely intact. This framing of the packet continues for each hop until the packet is finally delivered to the correct receiving host. It's really important to understand that the packet itself is never altered along the route; it is only encapsulated with the type of control information required for it to be properly passed on to the different media types.

The IEEE Ethernet Data Link layer has two sublayers:

Media Access Control (MAC) 802.3 This defines how packets are placed on the media. Contention media access is "first come/first served" access where everyone shares the same bandwidth—hence the name. Physical addressing is defined here, as well as logical topologies. What's a logical topology? It's the signal path through a physical topology. Line discipline, error notification (not correction), ordered delivery of frames, and optional flow control can also be used at this sublayer.

Logical Link Control (LLC) 802.2 This sublayer is responsible for identifying Network layer protocols and then encapsulating them. An LLC header tells the Data Link layer what to do with a packet once a frame is received. It works like this: A host will receive a frame and look in the LLC header to find out the packet is destined for, say, the IP protocol at the Network layer. The LLC can also provide flow control and sequencing of control bits.

Switches and Bridges at the Data Link Layer

The switches and bridges I talked about near the beginning of the chapter both work at the Data Link layer and filter the network using hardware (MAC) addresses. Layer-2 switching is considered hardware-based bridging because it uses specialized hardware called an *application-specific integrated circuit (ASIC)*. ASICs can run up to gigabit speeds with very low latency rates.

Latency is the time measured from when a frame enters a port to the time it exits a port.

Bridges and switches read each frame as it passes through the network. The layer-2 device then puts the source hardware address in a filter table and keeps track of which port the frame was received on. This information (logged in the bridge's or switch's filter table) is what helps the machine determine the location of the specific sending device.

The real estate business is all about location, location, location, and it's the same way for both layer-2 and -3 devices. Though both need to be able to negotiate the network, it's crucial to remember that they're concerned with very different parts of it. Routers, or layer-3 machines, need to locate specific networks, whereas layer-2 machines (switches and bridges) need to locate specific devices. So, networks are to routers as individual devices are to switches and bridges. And routing tables that "map" the internetwork are for routers, as filter tables that "map" individual devices are for switches and bridges.

After a filter table is built on the layer-2 device, it will only forward frames to the segment where the destination hardware address is located. If the destination device is on the same segment as the frame, the layer-2 device will block the frame from going to any other segments. If the destination is on a different segment, the frame can only be transmitted to that segment. This is called *transparent bridging*.

When a switch interface receives a frame with a destination hardware address that isn't found in the device's filter table, it will forward the frame to all connected segments. If the unknown device that sent the "mystery frame" replies to this forwarding action, the switch updates its filter table regarding that device's location. But in the event the destination address of the transmitting frame is a broadcast address, the switch will forward all broadcasts to every connected segment by default.

All devices that the broadcast is forwarded to are considered to be in the same broadcast domain. This can be a problem; layer-2 devices propagate layer-2 broadcast storms that choke performance, and the only way to stop a broadcast storm from propagating through an internetwork is with a layer-3 device—a router.

The biggest benefit of using switches instead of hubs in your internetwork is that each switch port is actually its own collision domain. (Conversely, a hub creates one large collision domain.) But even armed with a switch, you still can't break up broadcast domains. Neither switches nor bridges will do that. They'll simply forward all broadcasts instead.

Another benefit of LAN switching over hub-centered implementations is that each device on every segment plugged into a switch can transmit simultaneously—another benefit of each segment being its own collision domain. As you might have guessed, hubs only allow one device per network to communicate at a time.

Each network segment connected to the switch must be the same type of device. What this means to you and me is, you can connect an Ethernet hub into a switch port and then connect multiple Ethernet hosts into the hub, but you can't mix Token Ring hosts in with the Ethernet gang on the same segment. Mixing hosts in this manner is called *media translation*, and Cisco says you've just got to have a router around if you need to provide this service.

The Physical Layer

Finally arriving at the bottom, we find that the *Physical layer* does two things: It sends bits and receives bits. Bits come only in values of 1 or 0—a Morse code with numerical values. The Physical layer communicates directly with the various types of actual communication media. Different kinds of media represent these bit values in different ways. Some use audio tones, while others employ *state transitions*—changes in voltage from high to low and low to high. Specific protocols are needed for each type of media to describe the proper bit patterns to be used, how data is encoded into media signals, and the various qualities of the physical media's attachment interface.

The Physical layer specifies the electrical, mechanical, procedural, and functional requirements for activating, maintaining, and deactivating a physical link between end systems. This layer is also where you identify the interface between the data terminal equipment (DTE) and the data communication equipment (DCE). The DCE is usually located at the service provider, while the DTE is the attached device. The services available to the DTE are most often accessed via a modem or channel service unit/data service unit (CSU/DSU).

The Physical layer's connectors and different physical topologies are defined by the OSI as standards, allowing disparate systems to communicate. The CCNA exam is only interested in the Ethernet standards.

Hubs at the Physical Layer

A *hub* is really a multiple-port repeater. A repeater receives a digital signal and reamplifies or regenerates that signal, and then forwards the digital signal out all active ports without looking at any data. An active hub does the same thing. Any digital signal received from a segment on a hub port is regenerated or reamplified and transmitted out all ports on the hub. This means all devices plugged into a hub are in the same collision domain as well as in the same broadcast domain.

Hubs, like repeaters, don't actually examine any of the traffic as it enters and is then transmitted out to the other parts of the physical media. Every device connected to the hub, or hubs, must listen if a device transmits. A physical star network—where the hub is a central device and cables extend in all directions out from it—is the type of topology a hub creates. Visually, the design really does resemble a star, whereas Ethernet networks run a logical bus topology, meaning that the signal has to run from end to end of the network.

Ethernet Networking

*E*thernet is a contention media access method that allows all hosts on a network to share the same bandwidth of a link. Ethernet is popular because it's readily scalable, meaning it's comparatively easy to integrate new technologies, like FastEthernet and Gigabit Ethernet, into an existing network infrastructure. It's also relatively simple to implement in the first place, and with it, troubleshooting is reasonably straightforward. Ethernet uses both Data Link and Physical layer specifications, and this section of the chapter will give you both the Data Link and Physical layer information you need to effectively implement, troubleshoot, and maintain an Ethernet network.

Ethernet networking uses *Carrier Sense Multiple Access with Collision Detect (CSMA/CD)*, a protocol that helps devices share the bandwidth evenly without having two devices transmit at the same time on the network medium. CSMA/CD was created to overcome the problem of those collisions that occur when packets are transmitted simultaneously from different nodes. And trust me, good collision management is crucial because when a node transmits in a CSMA/CD network, all the other nodes on the network receive and examine that transmission. Only bridges and routers can effectively prevent a transmission from propagating throughout the entire network!

So, how does the CSMA/CD protocol work? Like this: When a host wants to transmit over the network, it first checks for the presence of a digital signal on the wire. If all is clear (no other host is transmitting), the host will then proceed with its transmission. But it doesn't stop there. The transmitting host constantly monitors the wire to make sure no other hosts begin transmitting. If the host detects another signal on the wire, it sends out an extended jam signal that causes all nodes on the segment to stop sending data (think, busy signal). The nodes respond to that jam signal by waiting a while before attempting to transmit again. Backoff algorithms determine when the colliding stations can retransmit. If collisions keep occurring after 15 tries, the nodes attempting to transmit will then time out. Pretty clean!

The effects of having a CSMA/CD network sustaining heavy collisions include:

- Delay

- Low throughput

- Congestion

Backoff on an 802.3 network is the retransmission delay that's enforced when a collision occurs.

Half- and Full-Duplex Ethernet

Half-duplex Ethernet is defined in the original 802.3 Ethernet and uses only one wire pair with a digital signal running in both directions on the wire. It also uses the CSMA/CD protocol to help prevent collisions and to permit retransmitting if a collision does occur. If a hub is attached to a switch, it must operate in half-duplex mode because the end stations must be able to detect collisions. Half-duplex Ethernet—typically 10BaseT—is only about 30 to 40 percent efficient as Cisco sees it, because a large 10BaseT network will usually only give you 3- to 4Mbps—at most.

But full-duplex Ethernet uses two pairs of wires, instead of one wire pair like half duplex. And full duplex uses a point-to-point connection between the transmitter of the transmitting device and the receiver of the receiving device. There are no collisions to worry about because now it's like a freeway with multiple lanes instead of the single-lane road provided by half duplex. Full-duplex Ethernet is supposed to offer 100 percent efficiency in both directions, e.g., you can get 20Mbps with a 10Mbps Ethernet running full duplex, or 200Mbps for FastEthernet—woohoo! But this rate is something known as an aggregate rate, which translates, "You're supposed to get" 100 percent efficiency. No guarantees in networking as in life.

Full-duplex Ethernet can be used in three situations:

- With a connection from a switch to a host
- With a connection from a switch to a switch
- With a connection from a host to a host using a crossover cable

Full-duplex Ethernet requires a point-to-point connection when only two nodes are present.

Now, if it's capable of all that speed, why wouldn't it deliver? Well, when a full-duplex Ethernet port is powered on, it first connects to the remote end, and then negotiates with the other end of the FastEthernet link. This is called an *auto-detect mechanism*. This mechanism first decides on the exchange capability, which means it checks to see if it can run at 10 or 100Mbps. It then checks to see if it can run full duplex, and if it can't, it will run half duplex.

Remember that half-duplex Ethernet shares a collision domain and provides a lower effective throughput than full-duplex Ethernet, which typically has a private collision domain and a higher effective throughput.

Ethernet at the Data Link Layer

Ethernet at the Data Link layer is responsible for Ethernet addressing, commonly referred to as hardware addressing or MAC addressing. Ethernet is also responsible for framing packets received from the Network layer and preparing them for transmission on the local network through the Ethernet contention media access method. There are four different types of Ethernet frames available:

- Ethernet_II
- IEEE 802.3
- IEEE 802.2
- SNAP

And I promise to go over all four of the available Ethernet frames in the upcoming sections.

Ethernet Addressing

Here's where we get into how Ethernet addressing works. It uses the *Media Access Control (MAC) address* burned into each and every Ethernet Network Interface Card (NIC). The MAC, or hardware address, is a 48-bit (6 byte) address written in a hexadecimal format.

Figure 1.11 shows the 48-bit MAC addresses and how the bits are divided.

FIGURE 1.11 Ethernet addressing using MAC addresses

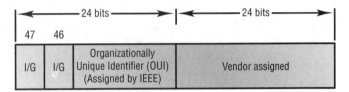

The *organizationally unique identifier (OUI)* is assigned by the IEEE to an organization. It's composed of 24 bits, or 3 bytes. The organization, in turn, assigns a globally administered address (24 bits, or 3 bytes) that is unique (supposedly, again, no guarantees) to each and every adapter they manufacture. Look closely at the figure… Notice bit 46? Bit 46 must be 0 if it's a globally assigned bit from the manufacturer, and it has to be a 1 if it's locally assigned by the network administrator.

Ethernet Frames

The Data Link layer is responsible for combining bits into bytes and bytes into frames. Frames are used at the Data Link layer to encapsulate packets handed down from the Network layer for transmission on a type of media access. There are three types of media access methods: contention (Ethernet), token passing (Token Ring and FDDI), and polling (IBM Mainframes and 100VG-AnyLAN). The CCNA exam covers primarily Ethernet (contention) media access—so shall we.

The function of Ethernet stations is to pass data frames between each other using a group of bits known as a MAC frame format. This provides error detection from a cyclic redundancy check (CRC). But remember—this is error detection, not error correction. The 802.3 frames and Ethernet frame are shown in Figure 1.12.

FIGURE 1.12 802.3 and Ethernet frame formats

Ethernet_II

Preamble 8 bytes	DA 6 bytes	SA 6 bytes	Type 2 bytes	Data	FCS 4 bytes

802.3_Ethernet

Preamble 8 bytes	DA 6 bytes	SA 6 bytes	Length 2 bytes	Data	FCS

Encapsulating a frame within a different type of frame is called *tunneling*.

The following points detail the different fields in the 802.3 and Ethernet frame types.

Preamble An alternating 1,0 pattern provides a 5MHz clock at the start of each packet, which allows the receiving devices to lock the incoming bit stream. The preamble uses either an SFD or synch field to indicate to the receiving station that the data portion of the message will follow.

Start Frame Delimiter (SFD)/Synch SFD is 1,0,1,0,1,0, etc., and the synch field is all 1s. The preamble and SFD/synch field are 64 bits long.

Destination Address (DA) This transmits a 48-bit value using the least significant bit (LSB) first. The DA is used by receiving stations to determine if an incoming packet is addressed to a particular node. The destination address can be an individual address, or a broadcast or multicast MAC address. Remember that a broadcast is all 1s (or Fs in hex) and is sent to all devices, but a multicast is only sent to a similar subset of nodes on a network.

Hex is short for hexadecimal, which is a numbering system that uses the first six letters of the alphabet (A through F) to extend beyond the available 10 digits in the decimal system. Hexadecimal has a total of 16 digits.

Source Address (SA)   The SA is a 48-bit MAC address used to identify the transmitting device, and it uses the LSB first. Broadcast and multicast address formats are illegal within the SA field.

Length or Type field   802.3 uses a Length field, but the Ethernet frame uses a Type field to identify the Network layer protocol. 802.3 cannot identify the upper-layer protocol and must be used with a proprietary LAN—IPX, for example.

Data   This is a packet sent down to the Data Link layer from the Network layer. The size can vary from 46 to 1500 bytes.

Frame Check Sequence (FCS)   FCS is a field at the end of the frame that's used to store the cyclic redundancy check (CRC).

Let's pause here for a minute and take a look at some frames caught on our trusty Etherpeek network analyzer. You can see that the frame below has only three fields: a Destination, Source, and Type field. This is an Ethernet_II frame. Notice the type field is IP, or 08-00 in hexadecimal.

```
Destination:    00:60:f5:00:1f:27
Source:         00:60:f5:00:1f:2c
Protocol Type: 08-00 IP
```

The next frame has the same fields, so it must be an Ethernet_II frame too. I included this one so you could see that the frame can carry more than just IP—it can also carry IPX, or 81-37h. Did you notice that this frame was a broadcast? You can tell because the destination hardware address is all 1s in binary, or all Fs in hexadecimal.

```
Destination:    ff:ff:ff:ff:ff:ff Ethernet Broadcast
Source:         02:07:01:22:de:a4
Protocol Type: 81-37 NetWare
```

Now, pay special attention to the length field in the next frame. This must be an 802.3 frame. The problem with this frame is this: How do you know which protocol this packet is going to be handed to at the Network layer? It doesn't specify in the frame, so it must be IPX. Why? Because when Novell created the 802.3 frame type (before the IEEE did and called it 802.3 Raw), Novell was pretty much the only LAN server out there. So, Novell was assuming that if you're running a LAN, it must be IPX, and so, they didn't include any Network layer protocol field information in the 802.3 frame.

```
Flags:          0x80 802.3
Status:         0x00
Packet Length:  64
Timestamp:      12:45:45.192000 06/26/1998
Destination:    ff:ff:ff:ff:ff:ff Ethernet Broadcast
Source:         08:00:11:07:57:28
Length:         34
```

802.2 and SNAP

Since the 802.3 Ethernet frame cannot by itself identify the upper-layer (Network) protocol, it obviously needs some help. The IEEE defined the 802.2 LLC specifications to provide this function and more. Figure 1.13 shows the IEEE 802.3 with LLC (802.2) and the Subnetwork Access Protocol (SNAP) frame types.

FIGURE 1.13 802.2 and SNAP

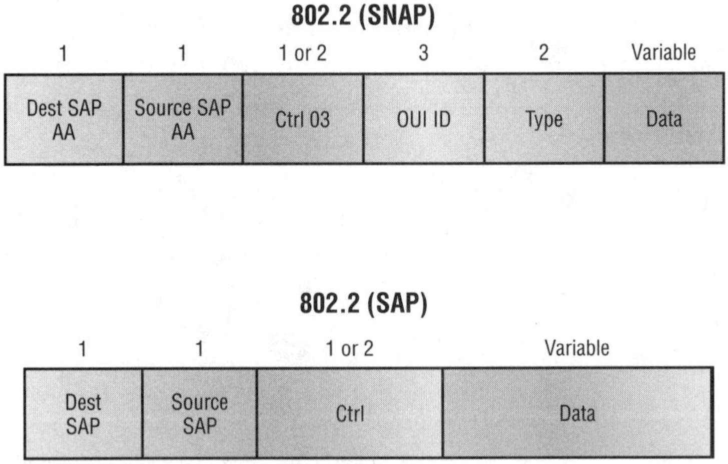

802.2 (SNAP)

1	1	1 or 2	3	2	Variable
Dest SAP AA	Source SAP AA	Ctrl 03	OUI ID	Type	Data

802.2 (SAP)

1	1	1 or 2	Variable
Dest SAP	Source SAP	Ctrl	Data

Figure 1.13 shows how the LLC header information is added to the data portion of the frame. Now, let's take a look at an 802.2 frame and SNAP captured from our analyzer.

802.2 Frame

The following is an 802.2 frame captured with a protocol analyzer. You can see that the first frame has a Length field, so it's probably an 802.3, right? Maybe. Look again... it also has a DSAP and an SSAP, so it's not an 802.3. It has to be an 802.2 frame. (Remember—an 802.2 frame is an 802.3 frame with the LLC information in the data field of the header so we know what the upper-layer protocol is.)

```
Flags:          0x80 802.3
Status:         0x02 Truncated
Packet Length:64
Slice Length: 51
Timestamp:      12:42:00.592000 03/26/1998
Destination:    ff:ff:ff:ff:ff:ff Ethernet Broadcast
Source:         00:80:c7:a8:f0:3d
LLC Length:     37
Dest. SAP:      0xe0 NetWare
Source SAP:     0xe0 NetWare Individual LLC
   SublayerManagement Function
Command:        0x03 Unnumbered Information
```

SNAP Frame

The SNAP frame has its own protocol field to identify the upper-layer protocol. This is really a way to allow an Ethernet_II Ether-Type field to be used in an 802.3 frame. Even though the following network trace shows a protocol field, it is really an Ethernet_II type (Ether-Type) field.

```
Flags:          0x80 802.3
Status:         0x00
Packet Length:78
Timestamp:      09:32:48.264000 01/04/2000
802.3 Header
Destination:    09:00:07:FF:FF:FF AT Ph 2 Broadcast
Source:         00:00:86:10:C1:6F
LLC Length:     60
```

```
802.2 Logical Link Control (LLC) Header
Dest. SAP:      0xAA SNAP
Source SAP:     0xAA SNAP
Command:        0x03 Unnumbered Information
Protocol:       0x080007809B AppleTalk
```

You can identify a SNAP frame because the DSAP and SSAP fields are always AA, and the Command field is always 3. This frame type was created because not all protocols worked well with the 802.3 Ethernet frame, which didn't have an Ether-Type field. To allow the proprietary protocols created by application developers to be used in the LLC frame, the IEEE defined the SNAP format. Up until last year or so, the SNAP frame was on its way out of the corporate market. However, the new 802.11 wireless LAN specification uses an Ethernet SNAP field to identify the Network layer protocol. Cisco also still uses a SNAP frame with their proprietary protocol Cisco Discovery Protocol (CDP)—something I'm going to talk about in Chapter 7.

Ethernet at the Physical Layer

Ethernet was first implemented by a group called DIX (Digital, Intel, and Xerox). They created and implemented the first Ethernet LAN specification, which the IEEE used to create the IEEE 802.3 Committee. This was a 10Mbps network that ran on coax, twisted-pair, and fiber physical media.

The IEEE extended the 802.3 Committee to two new committees known as 802.3U (FastEthernet) and 802.3Z (Gigabit Ethernet). These are both specified on twisted-pair and fiber physical media.

Figure 1.14 shows the IEEE 802.3 and original Ethernet Physical layer specifications.

FIGURE 1.14 Ethernet Physical layer specifications

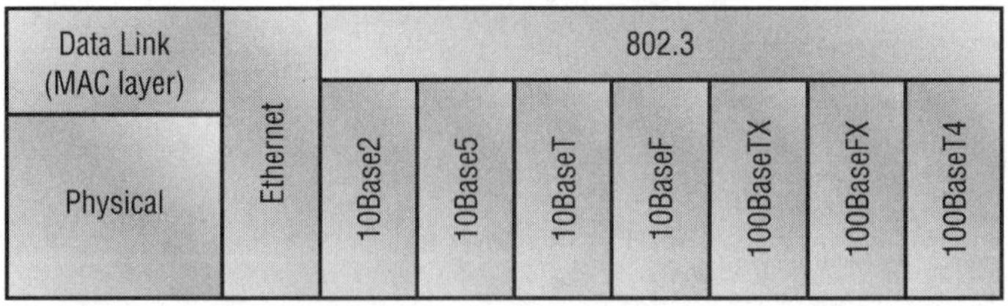

When designing your LAN, it's really important to understand the different types of Ethernet media available to you. Sure, it would certainly be great to run Gigabit Ethernet to each desktop and 10Gbps between switches, and although this might happen one day, justifying the cost of that network today really is pretty unreasonable. But if you mix and match the different types of Ethernet media methods available today, you can come up with a cost-effective network solution that works great.

The EIA/TIA (Electronic Industries Association and the newer Telecommunications Industry Association) is the standards body that creates the Physical layer specifications for Ethernet. The EIA/TIA specifies that Ethernet uses a *registered jack (RJ) connector* with a 4 5 wiring sequence on *unshielded twisted-pair (UTP)* cabling (RJ-45).

Here are the original IEEE 802.3 standards:

10Base2   10Mbps, baseband technology, up to 185 meters in length. Known as *thinnet* and can support up to 30 workstations on a single segment. Uses a physical and logical bus with AUI connectors. The 10 means 10Mbps, Base means baseband technology, and the 2 means almost 200 meters.

10Base2 Ethernet cards use BNC (British Naval Connectors) and T-Connectors to connect to a network.

10Base5   10Mbps, baseband technology, up to 500 meters in length. Known as *thicknet*. Uses a physical and logical bus with AUI connectors. Up to 2500 meters with repeaters and 1024 users for all segments.

10BaseT   10Mbps using Category 3 unshielded twisted-pair (UTP) wiring. Unlike the 10Base2 and 10Base5 networks, each device must connect into a hub or switch, and you can only have one host per segment or wire. Uses an RJ-45 connector with a physical star topology and a logical bus.

The "Base" in the preceding network standards means "baseband," which is a signaling method for communication on the network

Each of the 802.3 standards defines an Attachment Unit Interface (AUI), which allows a one-bit-at-a-time transfer to the Physical layer from the Data Link media access method. This allows the MAC to remain constant but means the Physical layer can support any existing and new technologies. The original AUI interface was a 15-pin connector, which allowed a transceiver (transmitter/receiver) that provided a 15-pin–to–twisted-pair conversion.

Typically, the AUI has a built-in transceiver, and the connections are now usually just RJ-45 connections.

The thing is, the AUI interface cannot support 100Mbps Ethernet because of the high frequencies involved. So 100BaseT needed a new interface, and the 802.3U specifications created one called the Media Independent Interface (MII), which provides 100Mbps throughput. The MII uses a *nibble*, defined as four bits. Gigabit Ethernet uses a Gigabit Media Independent Interface (GMII) and is eight bits at a time.

802.3U (FastEthernet) is compatible with 802.3 Ethernet because they share the same physical characteristics. FastEthernet and Ethernet use the same maximum transmission unit (MTU), same Media Access Control (MAC) mechanisms, and preserve the frame format that is used by 10BaseT Ethernet. Basically, FastEthernet is just based on an extension to the IEEE 802.3 specification, except it offers a speed increase of 10 times that of 10BaseT.

Here are the expanded IEEE Ethernet 802.3 standards:

100BaseTX   EIA/TIA Category 5, 6, or 7 UTP two-pair wiring. One user per segment; up to 100 meters long. It uses an RJ-45 MII connector with a physical star topology and a logical bus.

100BaseFX   Uses fiber cabling 62.5/125-micron multimode fiber. Point-to-point topology; up to 412 meters long. It uses an ST or SC connector, which are duplex media-interface connectors.

1000BaseCX   Copper shielded twisted-pair that can only run up to 25 meters.

1000BaseT   Category 5, four-pair UTP wiring up to 100 meters long.

1000BaseSX   MMF using 62.5 and 50-micron core; uses a 780-nano-meter laser and can go up to 260 meters.

1000BaseLX   Single-mode fiber that uses a 9-micron core, 1300-nano-meter laser and can go from 3km up to 10km.

100VG-AnyLAN is a twisted-pair technology that was the first 100Mbps LAN. But since it was incompatible with Ethernet signaling techniques (it used a demand priority access method), it wasn't very popular, and is now essentially dead.

Ethernet Cabling

Ethernet cabling is an important discussion, especially if you are planning on taking the Cisco CCNA exam. The types of Ethernet cables available are *straight-through cable*, *crossover cable*, and *rolled cable*.

If you are studying for your CCNA exam, you better know your Ethernet cabling types!

Straight-Through Cable

This type of Ethernet cable is used to connect:

- Host to switch or hub

- Router to switch or hub

Four wires are used in straight-through cable to connect Ethernet devices. It is relatively simple to create this type; Figure 1.15 shows the four wires used in a straight-through Ethernet cable.

FIGURE 1.15   Straight-through Ethernet cable

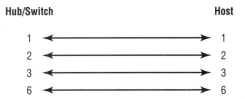

Notice that only pins 1, 2, 3 and 6 are used. Just connect 1 to 1, 2 to 2, 3 to 3 and 6 to 6, and you'll be up and networking in no time.

Crossover Cable

This type of Ethernet cable can be used to connect:

- Switch to switch

- Hub to hub

- Host to host

The same four wires are used in this cable as in the straight-through cable, but we just connect different pins together. Figure 1.16 shows how the four wires are used in a crossover Ethernet cable.

FIGURE 1.16 Crossover Ethernet cable

Notice that instead of connecting 1 to 1, etc., here we connect pins 1 to 3 and 2 to 6 on each side of the cable.

Rolled Cable

Although this type isn't used to connect any Ethernet connections together, you can use a rolled Ethernet cable to connect a host to a router console serial communication (com) port.

If you have a Cisco router or switch, you would use this cable to connect your PC running HyperTerminal to the Cisco hardware. Eight wires are used in this cable to connect serial devices. Figure 1.17 shows the eight wires used in a rolled cable.

FIGURE 1.17 Rolled Ethernet cable

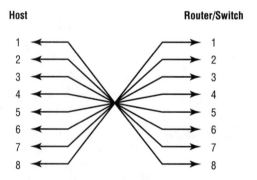

These are probably the easiest cables to make, because you just cut the end off on one side of a straight-through cable and reverse the end.

Once you have the correct cable connected from your PC to the Cisco router or switch, you can start HyperTerminal to create a console connection and configure the device. Set the configuration as follows:

1. Open HyperTerminal and enter a name for the connection. It is irrelevant what you name it, but I always just use "Cisco." Then click OK.

2. Choose the communications port—either COM1 or COM2, whichever is open on your PC.

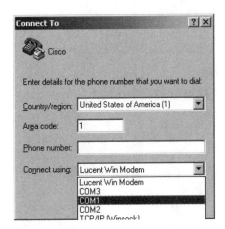

3. Now set the port settings. The default values (2400bps and no flow control) will not work; you must set the port settings as shown in Figure 1.18.

FIGURE 1.18 Port settings for a rolled cable connection

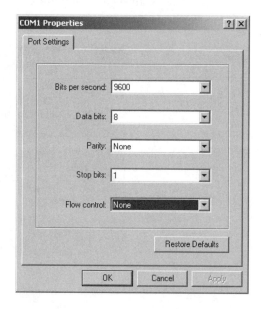

Notice the bit rate is now set to 9600 and the flow control is set to none. At this point, you can click OK and press the Enter key, and you should be connected to your Cisco device console port.

Data Encapsulation

When a host transmits data across a network to another device, the data goes through *encapsulation*: it is wrapped with protocol information at each layer of the OSI model. Each layer communicates only with its peer layer on the receiving device.

To communicate and exchange information, each layer uses *Protocol Data Units (PDUs)*. These hold the control information attached to the data at each layer of the model. They are usually attached to the header of the data field but can also be in the trailer, or end, of it.

Each PDU is attached to the data by encapsulating it at each layer of the OSI model, and each has a specific name depending on the information provided in each header. This PDU information is only read by the peer layer on the receiving device. After it's read, it's stripped off, and the data is then handed to the next layer up.

Figure 1.19 shows the PDUs and how they attach control information to each layer. This figure demonstrates how the upper-layer user data is converted for transmission on the network. The data stream is then handed down to the Transport layer, which sets up a virtual circuit to the receiving device by sending over a synch packet. The data stream is then broken up into smaller pieces, and a Transport layer header (a PDU) is created and attached to the header of the data field; now the piece of data is called a segment. Each segment is sequenced so the data stream can be put back together on the receiving side exactly as it was transmitted.

FIGURE 1.19 Data encapsulation

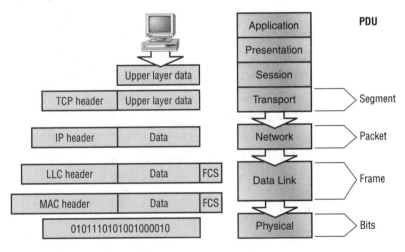

Each segment is then handed to the Network layer for network addressing and routing through the internetwork. Logical addressing (for example, IP) is used to get each segment to the correct network. The Network layer protocol adds a control header to the segment handed down from the Transport layer, and what we have now is called a *packet* or *datagram*. Remember that the Transport and Network layers work together to rebuild a data stream on a receiving host, but it's not part of their work to place their PDUs on a local network segment—which is the only way to get the information to a router or host.

It's the Data Link layer that's responsible for taking packets from the Network layer and placing them on the network medium (cable or wireless). The Data Link layer encapsulates each packet in a *frame*, and the frame's header carries the hardware address of the source and destination hosts. If the destination device is on a remote network, then the frame is sent to a router to be routed through an internetwork. Once it gets to the destination network, a new frame is used to get the packet to the destination host.

To put this frame on the network, it must first be put into a digital signal. Since a frame is really a logical group of 1s and 0s, the Physical layer is responsible for encapsulating these digits into a digital signal, which is read by devices on the same local network. The receiving devices will synchronize on the digital signal and extract the ones and zeros from the digital signal. At this point the devices build the frames, run a cyclic redundancy check (CRC), and then check their answer against the answer in the frame's FCS field. If it matches, the packet is pulled from the frame, and the frame is discarded. This process is called *de-encapsulation*. The packet is handed to the Network layer, where the address is checked. If the address matches, the segment is pulled from the packet, and the packet is discarded. The segment is processed at the Transport layer, which rebuilds the data stream and acknowledges to the transmitting station that it received each piece. It then happily hands the data stream to the upper-layer application.

At a transmitting device, the data encapsulation method works like this:

1. User information is converted to data for transmission on the network.

2. Data is converted to segments and a reliable connection is set up between the transmitting and receiving hosts.

3. Segments are converted to packets or datagrams, and a logical address is placed in the header so each packet can be routed through an internetwork.

4. Packets or datagrams are converted to frames for transmission on the local network. Hardware (Ethernet) addresses are used to uniquely identify hosts on a local network segment.

5. Frames are converted to bits, and a digital encoding and clocking scheme is used.

Cabling the Wide Area Network

There's a couple of things (well, okay, more than a couple, but we'll start with these) that you need to know in order to connect your *wide area network (WAN)*. You've got to understand the WAN Physical layer implementation provided by Cisco, and you must be familiar with the various types of WAN serial connectors. So mostly, that's what I'm going to talk about in this section, but I'm also going to discuss the cabling requirements for ISDN BRI connections.

Cisco serial connections support almost any type of WAN service. The typical WAN connections are dedicated leased lines using High-Level Data Link Control (HDLC), Point-to-Point Protocol (PPP), Integrated Services Digital Network (ISDN), and Frame Relay. Typical speeds run at anywhere from 2400bps to 1.544Mbps (T-1).

All of these WAN types are discussed in detail in Chapter 10.

HDLC, PPP, and Frame Relay can use the same Physical layer specifications, but ISDN has different pinouts and specifications at the Physical layer.

Serial Transmission

WAN serial connectors use *serial transmission*, which happens one bit at a time, over a single channel. *Parallel transmission* can pass at least 8 bits at a time, but all WANs use serial transmission.

Cisco routers use a proprietary 60-pin serial connector that you must buy from Cisco or a provider of Cisco equipment. The type of connector you have on the other end of the cable depends on your service provider or end-device requirements. The different ends available are EIA/TIA-232, EIA/TIA-449, V.35 (used to connect to a CSU/DSU), X.21 (used in X.25), and EIA-530.

Serial links are described in frequency or cycles-per-second (hertz). The amount of data that can be carried within these frequencies is called *bandwidth*. Bandwidth is the amount of data in bits-per-second that the serial channel can carry.

Data Terminal Equipment and Data Communication Equipment

Router interfaces are, by default, *data terminal equipment (DTE)*, and they connect into *data communication equipment (DCE)*, for example, a *channel service unit/data service unit (CSU/DSU)*. The CSU/DSU then plugs into a demarcation location (demarc) and is the service provider's last responsibility. Most of the time, the demarc is a jack that has an RJ-45 female connector located close to your equipment. You may have heard of demarcs if you've ever had the glorious experience of reporting a problem to your service provider—they'll always tell you it tests fine up to the demarc, and that the problem must be the CPE, or customer premise equipment. In other words, your responsibility, not theirs.

The idea behind a WAN is to be able to connect two DTE networks together through a DCE network. The DCE network includes the CSU/DSU, through the provider's wiring and switches, all the way to the CSU/DSU at the other end. The network's DCE device provides clocking to the DTE-connected interface (the router's serial interface).

Terms such as EIA/TIA-232, V.35, X.21, and HSSI (High-Speed Serial Interface), describe the physical layer between the DTE (router) and DCE device (CSU/DSU).

Fixed and Modular Interfaces

Some of the routers Cisco sells have fixed interfaces, while others are modular. The fixed routers, such as the 2500 series, have set interfaces that can't be changed. The 2501 router has two serial connections and one 10BaseT AUI interface. If you need to add a third serial interface, then you need to buy a new router—ouch! However, the 1600, 1700, 2600, 3600, and higher routers have modular interfaces that allow you to buy what you need now and add almost any type of interface you may need later. The 1600 and 1700 are limited and have both fixed and modular ports, but the 2600 and up provide many serials, FastEthernet, and even voice-module availability—now we're talking!

Integrated Services Digital Network (ISDN) Connections

Integrated Services Digital Network (ISDN) Basic Rate Interface (BRI) is two B (Bearer) channels of 64k each and one D (Data) channel of 16k for signaling and clocking.

ISDN BRI routers come with either a U interface or something known as an S/T interface. The difference between the two is that the U interface is already a two-wire ISDN convention that can plug right into the ISDN local loop. Conversely, the S/T interface is a four-wire interface and needs a Network Termination type 1 (NT 1) to convert from a four-wire to the two-wire ISDN specification.

The U interface has a built-in NT 1 device. If your service provider uses an NT 1 device, then you need to buy a router that has an S/T interface. Most Cisco router BRI interfaces are marked with a U or an S/T. When in doubt, ask Cisco or the salesperson you bought it from.

Primary Rate Interface (PRI) provides T-1 speeds (1.544Mbps) in the U.S. and E-1 speeds (2.048) in Europe, but I'm not going to tell you all about it in this book because it's not relevant for the CCNA course. See the book *CCNP: Routing Study Guide* (Sybex, 2001) for more information on PRI.

The ISDN BRI interface uses an RJ-45, Category 5, straight-through cable. It is important to avoid plugging a console cable or other LAN cable into a BRI interface on a router, because it will probably ruin the interface. Cisco says it will ruin it, but I have students do it every week and haven't lost one yet. (I probably shouldn't have said that—now I probably will lose one next week.)

Selecting Cisco Products

To select the correct Cisco products for your network, start by gathering information about where devices need to operate in the internetworking hierarchy, then consider issues like ease of installation, port-capacity requirements, and other features.

If you have remote offices or other WAN needs, you need to first find out what type of service is available. It won't do you any good to design a large Frame Relay network only to discover that Frame Relay is only supported in half the locations where you need to implement. After you research things and find out about the different options available through your service provider, you're then equipped and ready to choose the Cisco product that best meets your needs.

You usually have a few options: dial-up asynchronous connections, leased lines up to 1.544Mbps, Frame Relay, and ISDN are the most popular WAN technologies. But xDSL is the fast becoming the new front-runner and looks to lead as the fastest, most reliable, cheapest WAN technology. Obviously it's really important to consider your level of usage before buying and implementing a technology. Think about it... if your users at a remote branch are connected to the corporate office more than three to four hours a day, then you need either Frame Relay or a leased line. If they connect infrequently, then you might get away with ISDN or even dial-up connectivity.

In the next sections I'm going to discuss the different types of Cisco hubs, routers, and switches you can use to build a hierarchical network.

Cisco Hubs

It is hard for me to imagine that anyone would actually call Cisco and ask to buy a hub, but I guess somebody must be doing this, or they wouldn't be selling any. And it's true, Cisco really does have a pretty impressive list of hubs. It's so extensive that it can (and does) trigger some real confusion and an amazing variety of selection issues.

So before you buy any hub, you need to know—not think you know, but really-actually-certainly know—which users can use a shared 10Mbps or shared 100Mbps network. The lower-end model of hubs Cisco offers supports only 10Mbps, while the middle-of-the-road style offers both 10- and 100Mbps auto-sensing ports. The higher-end flavors offer network-management port and console connections. But seriously, if you're planning to pony up enough to buy a high-end hub, what not just go for a shiny-new switch instead? Figure 1.20 shows the various hub products that Cisco offers, and any of these hubs can be stacked together to give you more port density.

These are the selection issues you need to have answers for:

- Business requirements for 10- or 100Mbps

- Port density

- Management

- Ease of operation

FIGURE 1.20 Cisco hub products

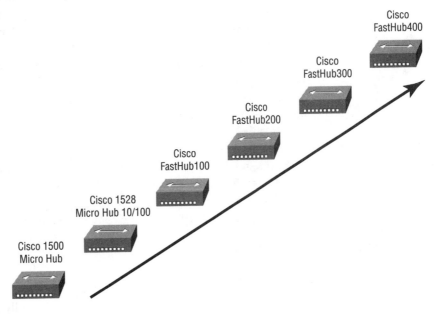

Cisco Routers

When someone says "Cisco" to you, what do you think of first? Hubs? I don't think so. You think "routers," of course. (If you thought of restaurant supplies, e.g. "Sysco," stop here and start this book over immediately!) Cisco makes the very kewlest routers in the world—everyone knows this. That's why I wrote this book, and that's why you're reading it… Period!

And it seems like Cisco comes out with a new router nearly once a month—have you noticed that? If not, you will. It truly is a challenge to keep up with Cisco's every latest and greatest. Not that Cisco would mind a bit if you decided to make buying each new rave a hobby. But your accountants would! Since these great products can also be pretty spendy, it's a good idea to always have your key criterion in mind when selecting from their ever growing list of router products: "What feature sets do I really need to meet my actual business requirements?" That way, you won't get carried away (or fired when the boss with the budget gets the bill). For example, do you need IP, Frame Relay, and VPN support? How about IPX, AppleTalk, and DECnet? Cisco has it all—and more.

You have some further considerations too: What will your fabulous network design require regarding port density and interface speeds? As you may have guessed, when you get into the higher-end models, you'll find more ports and faster speeds. For example, the new 12000 series model is Cisco's first Gigabit Switch Router (GSR), and its functions, features, and capabilities are beyond dazzling!

It's weird, but you can tell how much a product is going to cost by looking at its model number. A stripped-down 12000 series GSR with no cards or power supplies starts at about $12,000, but know that the price can end up at well over $100,000 for a loaded system.

You also need to think about WAN support when buying a router. You can get anything you want in a Cisco router, but you must first be familiar with the service provided for your area.

Figure 1.21 shows some of the router products Cisco sells.

FIGURE 1.21 Cisco router products

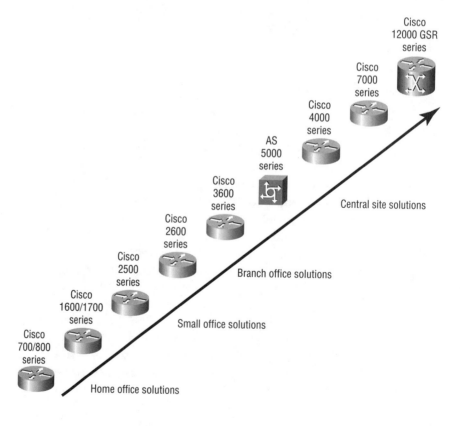

The Cisco 800 series router has mostly replaced the Cisco 700 series because the 700 series doesn't run the Cisco IOS. In fact, I personally hope Cisco will soon stop selling the 700 series routers altogether because they're difficult to configure and maintain.

The main things for you to consider when choosing Cisco routers are highlighted here:

- Scale of routing features needed

- Port density and variety requirements

- Capacity and performance

- Common user interface

Cisco Switches

It seems like switch prices are dropping almost daily. I recently received an e-mail from Cisco announcing that the Catalyst 2900 series switches have dropped in price 30 percent. About four years ago, a 12-port, 10/100 switch card for the Catalyst 5000 series switch was about $15,000. Now you can buy a complete Catalyst 5000 with a 10/100 card and supervisor module for about $7500 or thereabouts. My point is, with switch prices becoming reasonable, it's now much easier to justify installing switches in your network. Why buy hubs when you can use switches? I think every closet should have at least one switch.

And never failing us, Cisco again has a huge assortment of switches to meet absolutely every business need you can dream of. But as when buying a router, you must consider whether you need 10/100 or 1000Mbps for each desktop, and if you need to connect between switches. ATM (asynchronous transfer mode) is another factor, but, with Gigabit Ethernet out, and 10Gbps links just around the corner, who needs ATM? The next criterion to consider is again port density. Lower-end models start at 12 ports, and the higher-end jobs can provide hundreds of switched ports per switch. That's quite a range! Figure 1.22 shows the Cisco-switch product line.

And here's that list of switch-buying considerations:

- Business requirements for 10, 100, or even 1000Mbps

- Need for trunking and interswitch links

- Workgroup segmentation (VLANs)

- Port density needs

- Different user interfaces

FIGURE 1.22 Cisco Catalyst switch products

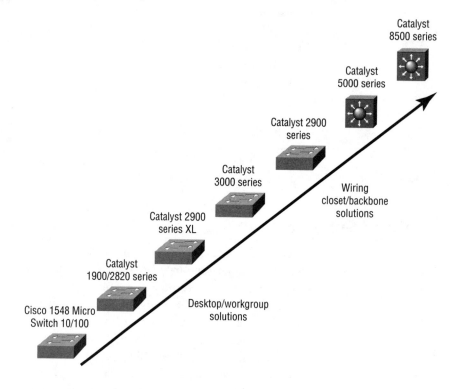

Catalyst
8500 series

Catalyst
5000 series

Catalyst 2900
series

Catalyst
3000 series

Wiring
closet/backbone
solutions

Catalyst 2900
series XL

Catalyst
1900/2820 series

Desktop/workgroup
solutions

Cisco 1548 Micro
Switch 10/100

The Cisco Three-Layer Hierarchical Model

Most of us were exposed to hierarchy early in life. Anyone with older siblings learned what it was like to be at the bottom of the hierarchy! Regardless of where you first discovered hierarchy, today most of us experience it in many aspects of our lives. It is *hierarchy* that helps us understand where things belong, how things fit together, and what functions go where. It brings order and understandability to otherwise complex models. If you want a pay raise, for instance, hierarchy dictates that you ask your boss, not your subordinate. That is the person whose role it is to grant (or deny) your request.

Hierarchy has many of the same benefits in network design that it does in other areas of life. When used properly, it makes networks more predictable.

It helps us define which areas should perform certain functions. Likewise, you can use tools such as access lists at certain levels in hierarchical networks and avoid them at others.

Let's face it, large networks can be extremely complicated, with multiple protocols, detailed configurations, and diverse technologies. Hierarchy helps us summarize a complex collection of details into an understandable model. Then, as specific configurations are needed, the model dictates the appropriate manner to apply them.

The Cisco hierarchical model can help you design, implement, and maintain a scalable, reliable, cost-effective hierarchical internetwork. Cisco defines three layers of hierarchy, as shown in Figure 1.23, each with specific functions.

FIGURE 1.23   The Cisco hierarchical model

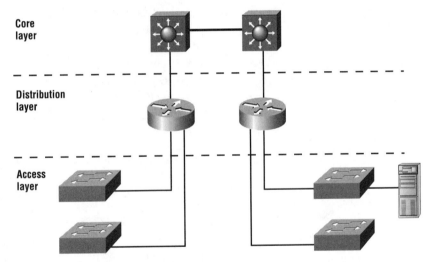

The following are the three layers:

- The core layer
- The distribution layer
- The access layer

Each layer has specific responsibilities. Remember, however, that the three layers are logical and are not necessarily physical devices. Consider the OSI model, another logical hierarchy. The seven layers describe functions but not necessarily protocols, right? Sometimes a protocol maps to more than one layer of the OSI model, and sometimes multiple protocols communicate within a single layer. In the same way, when we build physical implementations of hierarchical networks, we may have many devices in a single layer, or we might have a single device performing functions at two layers. The definition of the layers is logical, not physical.

Now, let's take a closer look at each of the layers.

The Core Layer

The *core layer* is literally the core of the network. At the top of the hierarchy, the core layer is responsible for transporting large amounts of traffic both reliably and quickly. The only purpose of the network's core layer is to switch traffic as fast as possible. The traffic transported across the core is common to a majority of users. However, remember that user data is processed at the distribution layer, which forwards the requests to the core if needed.

If there is a failure in the core, *every single user* can be affected. Therefore, fault tolerance at this layer is an issue. The core is likely to see large volumes of traffic, so speed and latency are driving concerns here. Given the function of the core, we can now consider some design specifics. Let's start with some things we don't want to do.

- Don't do anything to slow down traffic. This includes using access lists, routing between virtual local area networks (VLANs), and packet filtering.

- Don't support workgroup access here.

- Avoid expanding the core when the internetwork grows (i.e., adding routers). If performance becomes an issue in the core, give preference to upgrades over expansion.

Now, there are a few things that we want to do as we design the core. They include the following:

- Design the core for high reliability. Consider data-link technologies that facilitate both speed and redundancy, such as FDDI, Fast Ethernet (with redundant links), or even ATM.

- Design with speed in mind. The core should have very little latency.

- Select routing protocols with lower convergence times. Fast and redundant data-link connectivity is no help if your routing tables are shot!

The Distribution Layer

The *distribution layer* is sometimes referred to as the *workgroup layer* and is the communication point between the access layer and the core. The primary functions of the distribution layer are to provide routing, filtering, and WAN access and to determine how packets can access the core, if needed. The distribution layer must determine the fastest way that network service requests are handled—for example, how a file request is forwarded to a server. After the distribution layer determines the best path, it forwards the request to the core layer. The core layer then quickly transports the request to the correct service.

The distribution layer is the place to implement policies for the network. Here you can exercise considerable flexibility in defining network operation. There are several actions that generally should be done at the distribution layer. They include the following:

- Implementation of tools such as access lists, of packet filtering, and of queuing

- Implementation of security and network policies, including address translation and firewalls

- Redistribution between routing protocols, including static routing

- Routing between VLANs and other workgroup support functions

- Definitions of broadcast and multicast domains

Things to avoid at the distribution layer are limited to those functions that exclusively belong to one of the other layers.

The Access Layer

The *access layer* controls user and workgroup access to internetwork resources. The access layer is sometimes referred to as the *desktop layer*. The network resources most users need will be available locally. The distribution layer handles any traffic for remote services. The following are some of the functions to be included at the access layer:

- Continued (from distribution layer) access control and policies

- Creation of separate collision domains (segmentation)

- Workgroup connectivity into the distribution layer

Technologies such as DDR and Ethernet switching are frequently seen in the access layer. Static routing (instead of dynamic routing protocols) is seen here as well.

As already noted, three separate levels does not imply three separate routers. There could be fewer, or there could be more. Remember, this is a *layered* approach.

Summary

Phew! I know that seemed like the chapter that wouldn't end, but it did—and you made it! You're now armed with a ton of fundamental information; you're ready to build upon it, and well on your way to certification.

This chapter began with a discussion of the OSI model—the seven-layer model used to help application developers design applications that can run on any type of system or network. Each layer has its special jobs and select responsibilities within the model to ensure that solid, effective communications do, in fact, occur. I provided you with complete details of each layer and discussed how Cisco views the specifications of the OSI model.

In addition, each layer in the OSI model specifies different types of devices. I described the different types of devices, cables, and connectors used at each layer. Remember that hubs are Physical layer devices and repeat the digital signal to all segments except the one it was received from. Switches segment the network using hardware addresses and break up collision domains. Routers break up broadcast domains and use logical addressing to send packets through an internetwork.

Cisco makes a large range of router, hub, and switch products. I discussed the different products Cisco creates and sells so that you can make more informed decisions when building and buying for your internetwork.

Lastly, this chapter covered the Cisco three-layer hierarchical model. I described in detail the three layers and how each is used to help design and implement a Cisco internetwork.

Exam Essentials

Remember the possible causes of LAN traffic congestion.   Too many hosts in a broadcast domain, broadcast storms, multicasting, and low bandwidth are all possible causes of LAN traffic congestion.

Understand the difference between a collision domain and a broadcast domain.   A collision domain is an Ethernet term used to describe a network scenario in which one particular device sends a packet on a network segment, forcing every other device on that same segment to pay attention to it. A broadcast domain is where a set of all devices on a network segment hear all broadcasts sent on that segment.

Understand the difference between a hub, a bridge, a switch, and a router.   Hubs create one collision domain and one broadcast domain. Bridges break up collision domains but create one large broadcast domain. They use hardware addresses to filter the network. Switches are really just multiple port bridges with more intelligence. They break up collision domains but create one large broadcast domain by default. Switches use hardware addresses to filter the network. Routers break up broadcast domains and use logical addressing to filter the network.

Remember the Presentation layer protocols.   PICT, TIFF, JPEG, MIDI, MPEG, QuickTime, and RTF are examples of Presentation layer protocols.

Remember the difference between connection-oriented and connectionless network services.   Connection-oriented uses acknowledgments and flow control to create a reliable session. More overhead is used than in a connectionless network service. Connectionless services are used to send data with no acknowledgments or flow control. This is considered unreliable.

Remember the OSI layer.   You must remember the seven layers of the OSI model and what function each layer provides. The Application, Presentation, and Session layers are upper layers and are responsible for communicating from a user interface to an application. The Transport layer provides segmentation, sequencing, and virtual circuits. The Network layer provides logical network addressing and routing through an internetwork. The Data Link layer provides framing and placing of data on the network medium. The Physical layer is responsible for taking ones and zeros and encoding them into a digital signal for transmission on the network segment.

Remember the types of Ethernet cabling and when you would use them. The three types of cables that can be created from an Ethernet cable are: straight-through (to connect a PC or a router's Ethernet interface to a hub or switch), crossover (to connect hub to hub, hub to switch, switch to switch, or PC to PC), and rolled (for a console connection from a PC to a router or switch).

Understand how to connect a console cable from a PC to a router and start HyperTerminal. Take a rolled cable and connect it from the COM port of the host to the console port of a router. Start HyperTerminal and set the BPS to 9600 and flow control to None.

Remember the three layers in the Cisco three-layer model. The three layers in the Cisco hierarchical model are the core, distribution, and access layers.

Key Terms

Before you take the exam, be certain you are familiar with the following terms:

access layer	buffer
Application layer	call setup
application-specific integrated circuit (ASIC)	Carrier Sense Multiple Access with Collision Detect (CSMA/CD)
auto-detect mechanism	channel service unit/data service unit (CSU/DSU)
Basic Rate Interface (BRI)	collision domains
binding	core layer
bridges	crossover cable
broadcast domain	data communication equipment (DCE)

data frame	packet
Data Link layer	Physical layer
data terminal equipment (DTE)	positive acknowledgment with retransmission
datagram	Presentation layer
de-encapsulation	Protocol Data Units (PDUs)
distribution layer	reference model
encapsulation	registered jack (RJ) connector
Ethernet	rolled cable
flow control	routed protocols
frame	routers
full duplex	Session layer
half duplex	simplex
hierarchy	state transitions
hop count	straight-through cable
hub	switches
Integrated Services Digital Network (ISDN)	thicknet
layered architecture	thinnet
layers	three-way handshake
Media Access Control (MAC) address	transparent bridging
media translation	Transport layer
Network layer	tunneling
network segmentation	unshielded twisted-pair (UTP)
nibble	wide area network (WAN)
Open Systems Interconnection (OSI) reference model	window
organizationally unique identifier (OUI)	

Written Labs

In this section, you'll complete the following labs to make sure you've got the information and concepts contained within them fully dialed in:

- Lab 1.1: OSI Questions
- Lab 1.2: Defining the OSI Layers and Devices
- Lab 1.3: Identifying Collision and Broadcast Domains

Written Lab 1.1: OSI Questions

Answer the following questions about the OSI model:

1. Which layer chooses and determines the availability of communicating partners, along with the resources necessary to make the connection; coordinates partnering applications; and forms a consensus on procedures for controlling data integrity and error recovery?

2. Which layer is responsible for converting data packets from the Data Link layer into electrical signals?

3. At which layer is routing implemented, enabling connections and path selection between two end systems?

4. Which layer defines how data is formatted, presented, encoded, and converted for use on the network?

5. Which layer is responsible for creating, managing, and terminating sessions between applications?

6. Which layer ensures the trustworthy transmission of data across a physical link and is primarily concerned with physical addressing, line discipline, network topology, error notification, ordered delivery of frames, and flow control?

7. Which layer is used for reliable communication between end nodes over the network and provides mechanisms for establishing, maintaining, and terminating virtual circuits; transport-fault detection and recovery; and controlling the flow of information?

8. Which layer provides logical addressing that routers will use for path determination?

9. Which layer specifies voltage, wire speed, and pinout cables and moves bits between devices?

10. Which layer combines bits into bytes and bytes into frames, uses MAC addressing, and provides error detection?

11. Which layer is responsible for keeping the data from different applications separate on the network?

12. Which layer is represented by frames?

13. Which layer is represented by segments?

14. Which layer is represented by packets?

15. Which layer is represented by bits?

16. Put the following in order of encapsulation:

   - Packets

   - Frames

   - Bits

   - Segments

17. Which layer segments and reassembles data into a data stream?

18. Which layer provides the physical transmission of the data and handles error notification, network topology, and flow control?

19. Which manages device addressing, tracks the location of devices on the network, and determines the best way to move data?

20. What is the bit length and expression form of a MAC address?

Written Lab 1.2: Defining the OSI Layers and Devices

Fill in the blanks with the appropriate layer of the OSI or hub, switch, or router device.

Description	Device or OSI Layer
This device sends and receives information about the Network layer.	
This layer creates a virtual circuit before transmitting between two end stations.	

Description	Device or OSI Layer
This layer uses service access points.	
This device uses hardware addresses to filter a network.	
Ethernet is defined at these layers.	
This layer supports flow control and sequencing.	
This device can measure the distance to a remote network.	
Logical addressing is used at this layer.	
Hardware addresses are defined at this layer.	
This device creates one big collision domain and one large broadcast domain.	
This device creates many smaller collision domains, but the network is still one large broadcast domain.	
This device breaks up collision domains and broadcast domains.	

Written Lab 1.3: Identifying Collision and Broadcast Domains

In Figure 1.24, identify the number of collision domains and broadcast domains in each specified device. Each device is represented by a letter:

1. Hub

2. Bridge

3. Switch

4. Router

FIGURE 1.24 Identifying the number of collision and broadcast domains

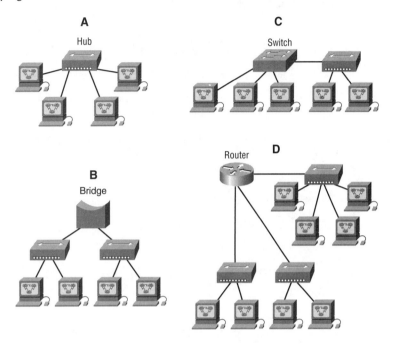

(The answers to the Written Labs can be found following the answers to the Review Questions for this chapter.)

Review Questions

1. Which is true when a broadcast is sent out in an Ethernet 802.3 LAN?

   A. The broadcast is sent only to the default gateway.

   B. The broadcast is sent only to the destination hardware address in the broadcast.

   C. The broadcast is sent to all devices in the collision domain.

   D. The broadcast is sent to all devices in the broadcast domain.

2. PDUs at the Network layer of the OSI are called what?

   A. Transport

   B. Frames

   C. Packets

   D. Segments

3. Which two statements about a reliable connection-oriented data transfer are true?

   A. Receiving hosts acknowledge receipt of data.

   B. When buffers are full, packets are discarded and are not retransmitted.

   C. Windowing is used to provide flow control and unacknowledged data segments.

   D. If the transmitting host's timer expires before receipt of an acknowledgment, the transmitting host drops the virtual circuit.

4. PDUs at the Data Link layer are named what?

   A. Transport

   B. Frames

   C. Packets

   D. Segments

5. Segmentation of a data stream happens at which layer of the OSI model?

A. Physical

B. Data Link

C. Network

D. Transport

6. What term is used if you are using the processes of placing frames from one network system into the frame of another network system?

A. Framing

B. Encapsulating

C. Tunneling

D. Frame Relay

7. What does the Data Link layer use to find hosts on a local network?

A. Logical network addresses

B. Port numbers

C. Hardware addresses

D. Default gateways

8. What were the key reasons the ISO released the OSI model? (Choose two.)

A. To allow companies to charge more for their equipment

B. To help vendors create interoperable network devices

C. To help vendors create and sell specialized software and hardware

D. So the IBM mainframe would be replaced with the PC

E. So the industry could create a standard for how host computers work

F. So that different vendor networks could work with each other

9. Which statement about Ethernet networks is true?

    A. Full duplex can run over 10Base2.

    B. Full duplex requires a point-to-point connection when only two nodes are present.

    C. Full-duplex Ethernet can be used to connect multiple hosts to a single switch interface.

    D. Half duplex uses the cut-through LAN switch method.

10. What is used at the Transport layer to stop a receiving host's buffer from overflowing?

    A. Segmentation

    B. Packets

    C. Acknowledgments

    D. Flow control

    E. PDUs

11. Which layer of the OSI provides translation of data?

    A. Application

    B. Presentation

    C. Session

    D. Transport

    E. Data Link

12. When data is encapsulated, which is the correct order?

    A. Data, frame, packet, segment, bit

    B. Segment, data, packet, frame, bit

    C. Data, segment, packet, frame, bit

    D. Data, segment, frame, packet, bit

13. Which of the following is not an advantage of a layered model?

    A. Allows multiple-vendor development through standardization of network components

    B. Allows various types of network hardware and software to communicate

    C. Allows changes to occur in all layers without having to change just one layer

    D. Prevents changes in one layer from affecting other layers, so it does not hamper development

14. What are two purposes for segmentation with a bridge?

    A. Add more broadcast domains.

    B. Create more collision domains.

    C. Add more bandwidth for users.

    D. Allow more broadcasts for users.

15. What does the term "Base" indicate in 100Base-TX?

    A. The maximum distance

    B. The type of wiring used

    C. A LAN switch method using half duplex

    D. A signaling method for communication on the network

16. What is the maximum distance of 100BaseT?

    A. 100 feet

    B. 1000 feet

    C. 100 meters

    D. 1000 meters

17. Which of the following would describe a Transport layer connection that would ensure reliable delivery?

    A. Routing

    B. Acknowledgments

    C. Switching

    D. System authentication

18. What are two reasons to segment a network with a bridge?

    A. Increase the amount of collision on a segment.

    B. Decrease the amount of broadcast on a segment.

    C. Reduce collisions within a broadcast domain.

    D. Increase the number of collision domains.

19. Which of the following types of connections can use full duplex? Select all that apply.

    A. Hub to hub

    B. Switch to switch

    C. Host to host

    D. Switch to hub

    E. Switch to host

20. Which of the following describes the Physical layer connection between a DTE (router) and a DCE (CSU/DSU) device?

    A. IP, IPX, AFP

    B. TCP, UDP

    C. EIA/TIA 232, V.35, X.21, HSSI

    D. FTP, TFPT, SMTP

21. Which of the following would be used to connect a router to an Ethernet switch?

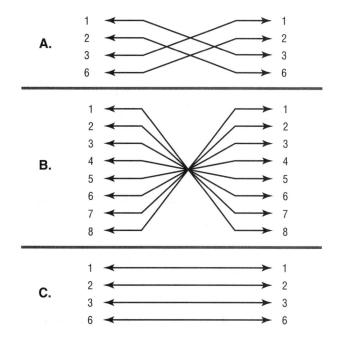

A. A

B. B

C. C

D. None of the figures

22. Which of the following are Presentation layer protocols? Select all that apply.

A. TFTP

B. IP

C. RTF

D. QuickTime

E. MIDI

23. Which of the following are considered some reasons for LAN congestion? Select all that apply.

  A. Bill Gates

  B. Low bandwidth

  C. Too many users in a broadcast domain

  D. Broadcast storms

  E. Routers

  F. Multicasting

  G. Any Cisco competitor

24. Which of the following are reasons for breaking up a network into two segments with a router? (Choose two.)

  A. To create fewer broadcast domains

  B. To create more broadcast domains

  C. To create one large broadcast domain

  D. To stop one segment's broadcasts from being sent to the second segment

25. How do you connect to a router using HyperTerminal?

  A. Connect the Ethernet port of your host to the Ethernet interface of the router using a rolled cable.

  B. Connect the COM port of your host to the Ethernet port of your router using a straight-through cable.

  C. Connect the Ethernet port of your host to the console port of the router using a rolled cable.

  D. Connect the COM port of your host to the console port of the router using a crossover cable.

  E. Connect the COM port of your host to the console port of the router using a rolled cable.

Answers to Review Questions

1. D. A broadcast sent on an Ethernet 802.3 LAN will go to all devices in the Ethernet broadcast domain.

2. C. Protocol Data Units are used to define data at each layer of the OSI model. PDUs at the Network layer are called packets.

3. A, C. When a virtual circuit is created, windowing is used for flow control and acknowledgment of data.

4. B. Data is encapsulated with a media access method at the Data Link layer, and the Protocol Data Unit (PDU) is called a frame.

5. D. The Transport layer receives large data streams from the upper layers and breaks these up into smaller pieces called segments.

6. C. If you place a frame inside another frame, this is called tunneling.

7. C. MAC addresses, also called hardware addresses, are used to uniquely identify hosts on a local network.

8. B, F. The ISO wanted all vendors equipment to be able to work together, which is the main reason for the OSI model. The second and last options are saying the same thing.

9. B. The best answer for this question is the second option. Full duplex cannot run over 10Base2; you cannot connect multiple nodes to a single switch port and run full duplex; and cut-through has nothing to do with half- or even full-duplex Ethernet.

10. D. Flow control stops a device from overflowing its buffers. Even though flow control can be used at many layers, the Transport layer's reliable connection provides the best flow control available in the model.

11. B. The only layer of the OSI model that can actually change data is the Presentation layer.

12. C. The encapsulation method is: data, segment, packet, frame, bit.

13. C. The largest advantage of a layered model is that it can allow application developers to change the aspects of a program in just one layer of the layer model's specifications.

14. B, C. Bridges break up collision domains, which allow more bandwidth for users.

15. D. *Baseband* signaling is a technique that uses the entire bandwidth of a wire when transmitting. Broadband wiring uses many signals at the same time on a wire. These are both considered an Ethernet signaling type.

16. C. 10BaseT and 100BaseT have a distance limitation of 100 meters.

17. B. A reliable Transport layer connection uses acknowledgments to make sure all data is transmitted and received reliably.

18. C, D. Bridges increase the number of collision domains in a network, which provides more bandwidth per user, which means less collision on a LAN.

19. B, C, E. Hubs cannot run full-duplex Ethernet. Full duplex must be used on a point-to-point connection between two devices capable of running full duplex. Switches and hosts can run full duplex between each other, no problem.

20. C. The EIA/TIA 232, V.35, X.21, and HSSI are examples of Physical layer specifications.

21. C. A straight-through Ethernet cable is used to connect a host or router to an Ethernet switch.

22. C, D, E. The Presentation layer defines many protocols; RTF, Quick-Time, and MIDI are correct answers. IP is a Network layer protocol; TFTP is an Application layer protocol.

23. B, C, D, F. Although, Bill Gates is a good answer for me, and Cisco probably would like the last option, the answers are: not enough bandwidth, broadcast storms, too many users, and multicasting.

24. B, D. Routers, by default, break up broadcast domains, which means that broadcasts sent on one network would not be forwarded to another network by the router.

25. E. From a COM port of a PC or other host, connect a rolled cable to the console port of the router, start HyperTerminal, set the BPS to 9600 and flow control to None, then press Enter to connect.

Answers to Written Labs

Answers to Written Lab 1.1

1. The Application layer is responsible for finding the network resources broadcast from a server and adding flow control and error control (if the application developer chooses).

2. The Physical layer takes frames from the Data Link layer and encodes the ones and zeros into a digital signal from transmission on the network medium.

3. The Network layer provides routing through an internetwork and logical addressing.

4. The Presentation layer makes sure that data is in a readable format for the Application layer.

5. The Session layer sets up, maintains, and terminates sessions between applications.

6. PDUs at the Data Link layer are called frames. As soon as you see "frame" in a question, you know the answer.

7. The Transport layer uses virtual circuits to create a reliable connection between two hosts.

8. The Network layer provides logical addressing, typically IP addressing and routing.

9. The Physical layer is responsible for the electrical and mechanical connections between devices.

10. The Data Link layer is responsible for the framing of data packets.

11. The Session layer creates sessions between different hosts' applications.

12. The Data Link layer frames packets received from the network layer.

13. The Transport layer segments user data.

14. The Network layer creates packets out of segments handed down from the Transport layer.

15. The Physical layer is responsible for transporting ones and zeros in a digital signal.

16. Segments, packets, frames, bits

17. Transport

18. Data Link

19. Network

20. 48 bits (6 bytes) expressed as a hexadecimal number

Answer to Written Lab 1.2

Description	Device or OSI Layer
This device sends and receives information about the Network layer.	Router
This layer can create a virtual circuit before transmitting between two end stations.	Transport
This layer uses service access points.	Data Link (LLC sublayer)
This device uses hardware addresses to filter a network.	Bridge or switch
Ethernet is defined at these layers.	Data Link and Physical
This layer supports flow control and sequencing.	Transport
This device can measure the distance to a remote network.	Router
Logical addressing is used at this layer.	Network
Hardware addresses are defined at this layer.	Data Link (MAC sublayer)
This device creates one big collision domain and one large broadcast domain.	Hub
This device creates many smaller collision domains but the network is still one large broadcast domain.	Switch or bridge
This device breaks up collision domains and broadcast domains.	Router

Answers to Written Lab 1.3

1. Hub: One collision domain, one broadcast domain

2. Bridge: Two collision domains, one broadcast domain

3. Switch: Four collision domains, one broadcast domain

4. Router: Three collision domains, three broadcast domains

Layer-2 Switching

THE CCNA EXAM TOPICS COVERED IN THIS CHAPTER INCLUDE THE FOLLOWING:

✓ **Bridging/Switching**

- Name and describe two switching methods.
- Distinguish between cut-through and store-and-forward LAN switching.
- Describe the operation of the Spanning Tree Protocol and its benefits.

When Cisco discusses switching, they're talking about layer-2 switching unless they say otherwise. Layer-2 switching is the process of using the hardware address of devices on a LAN to segment a network. Since you've got the basic ideas down, I'm now going to focus on the particulars of layer-2 switching and nail down how it works.

Okay, you know that switching breaks up large collision domains into smaller ones, and that a collision domain is a network segment with two or more devices sharing the same bandwidth. A hub network is a typical example of this type of technology. But since each port on a switch is actually its own collision domain, you can make a much better Ethernet LAN network just by replacing your hubs with switches!

Switches truly have changed the way networks are designed and implemented. If a pure switched design is properly implemented, it absolutely will result in a clean, cost-effective, and resilient internetwork. In this chapter, we'll survey and compare network design before and after switching technologies were introduced.

Routing protocols (such as RIP, which you'll learn about in Chapter 5) have processes for stopping network loops from occurring at the Network layer. However, if you have redundant physical links between your switches, routing protocols won't do a thing to stop loops from occurring at the Data Link layer. That's exactly the reason Spanning Tree Protocol was developed—to put a stop to loops in a layer-2 switched internetwork. The essentials of this vital protocol, as well as how it works within a switched network, are also important subjects this chapter will cover thoroughly.

When frames traverse a switched fabric (or switched internetwork), the LAN switch type determines how a frame is forwarded to an exit port on a switch. There are three different types of LAN switch methods, and each one handles frames differently as they are forwarded through a switch. This chapter will close with a discussion on the three methods used by Cisco switches.

Before Layer-2 Switching

Let's go back in time a bit and take a look at the condition of networks before switches and how switches have helped segment the corporate LAN. Before LAN switching, the typical network design looked like the network in Figure 2.1.

FIGURE 2.1   Before switching

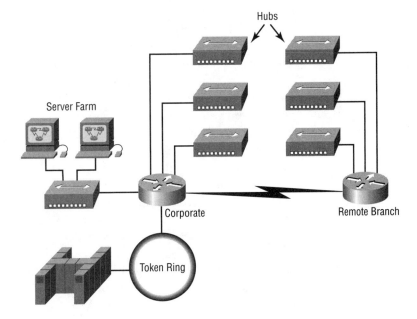

The design in Figure 2.1 was called a collapsed backbone because all hosts would need to go to the corporate backbone to reach any network services—both LAN and mainframe.

Going back even further, before networks like the one shown in Figure 2.1 had physical segmentation devices like routers and hubs, there was the mainframe network. This network included the mainframe (IBM, Honeywell, Sperry, DEC, etc.), controllers, and dumb terminals that connected into the controller. Any remote sites were connected to the mainframe with bridges.

And then the PC began its rise to stardom, and the mainframe was connected to the Ethernet or to a Token Ring LAN where the servers were installed. These servers were usually O/S 2 or LAN Manager because this was "pre-NT." Each floor of a building ran either coax or twisted-pair wiring to the corporate backbone, and was then connected to a router. PCs ran an emulating software program that allowed them to connect to the mainframe services, giving those PCs the ability to access services from the mainframe and LAN simultaneously. Eventually the PC became robust enough to allow application developers to port applications more effectively than they could ever before—an advance that markedly reduced networking prices and enabled businesses to grow at a much faster rate.

When Novell became more popular in the late 1980s and early 1990s, O/S 2 and LAN Manager servers were by and large replaced with NetWare services. This made the Ethernet network even more popular, because that's what Novell 3.x servers used to communicate with client/server software.

So that's the story about how the network in Figure 2.1 came into being. There was only one problem the corporate backbone grew and grew, and as it grew, network services became slower. A big reason for this was that, at the same time this huge burst in growth was taking place, LAN services needed even faster service, and the network was becoming totally saturated. Everyone was dumping the Macs and dumb terminals used for the mainframe service in favor of those slick new PCs so they could more easily connect to the corporate backbone and network services.

All this was taking place before the Internet's momentous popularity (Al Gore was still inventing it?), so everyone in the company needed to access the corporate network's services. Why? Because without the Internet, all network services were internal—exclusive to the company network. This created a screaming need to segment that one humongous and plodding corporate network, connected with sluggish old routers. At first, Cisco just created faster routers (no doubt about that), but more segmentation was needed, especially on the Ethernet LANs. The invention of FastEthernet was a very good and helpful thing too, but it didn't address that network segmentation need at all.

But devices called bridges did, and they were first used in the network to break up collision domains. Bridges were sorely limited by the amount of ports and other network services they could provide, and that's when layer-2 switches came to the rescue. These switches saved the day by breaking up collision domains on each and every port, and switches could provide hundreds of them! This early, switched LAN looked like the network pictured in Figure 2.2.

FIGURE 2.2   The first switched LAN

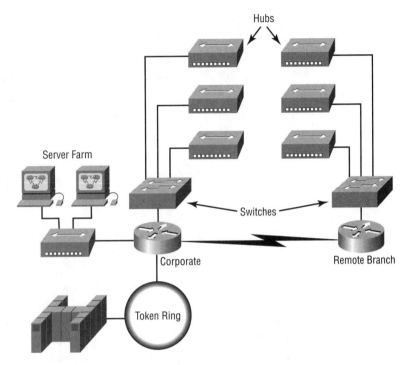

Each hub was placed into a switch port, an innovation that vastly improved the network. Now, instead of each building being crammed into the same collision domain, each hub became its own separate collision domain. But there was a catch—switch ports were still very new, and so, unbelievably expensive. Because of that, simply adding a switch into each floor of the building just wasn't going to happen—at least, not yet. Thanks to whomever you choose to thank for these things, the price has dropped dramatically, so now, having every one of your users plugged into a switch port is both good and feasible.

So there it is—if you're going to create a network design and implement it, including switching services is a must. A typical contemporary network design would look something like Figure 2.3, a complete switched network design and implementation.

"But I still see a router in there," you say! Yes, it's not a mirage—there *is* a router in there. But its job has changed. Instead of performing physical segmentation, it now creates and handles logical segmentation. Those logical segments are called VLANs, and I promise I'll explain them thoroughly—both in the duration of this chapter and in Chapter 6, where they'll be given a starring role.

FIGURE 2.3 The typical switched network design

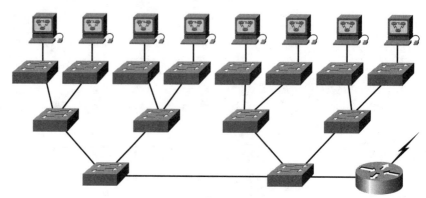

Switching Services

Layer-2 switching is hardware based, which means it uses the MAC address from the host's NIC cards to filter the network. Unlike bridges that use software to create and manage a filter table, switches use application-specific integrated circuits (ASICs) to build and maintain their filter tables. But it's still okay to think of a layer-2 switch as a multiport bridge because their basic reason for being is the same: to break up collision domains.

Layer-2 switches and bridges are faster than routers because they don't take up time looking at the Network layer header information. Instead, they look at the frame's hardware addresses before deciding to either forward the frame or drop it.

Layer-2 switching provides the following:

- Hardware-based bridging (MAC)
- Wire speed
- Low latency
- Low cost

What makes layer-2 switching so efficient is that no modification to the data packet takes place. The device only reads the frame encapsulating the packet, which makes the switching process considerably faster and less error-prone than routing processes are.

And if you use layer-2 switching for both workgroup connectivity and network segmentation (breaking up collision domains), you can create a flatter network design with more network segments than you can with traditional 10BaseT shared networks.

Plus, layer-2 switching increases bandwidth for each user because, again, each connection (interface) into the switch is its own collision domain. This feature makes it possible for you to connect multiple devices to each interface.

Limitations of Layer-2 Switching

Since we commonly stick layer-2 switching into the same category as bridged networks, we also tend to think it has the same hang-ups and issues that bridged networks do. Keep in mind that bridges are good and helpful things if we design the network correctly, keeping their features as well as their limitations in mind. And to design well with bridges, the two most important considerations are:

- We absolutely must break up the collision domains correctly.

- The right way to create a functional bridged network is to make sure that its users spend 80 percent of their time on the local segment.

Bridged networks break up collision domains, but remember, that network is still one large broadcast domain. Both layer-2 switches and bridges don't break up broadcast domains by default—something that not only limits your network's size and growth potential, but can also reduce its overall performance.

Broadcasts and multicasts, along with the slow convergence time of spanning trees, can give you some major grief as your network grows. These are the big reasons why layer-2 switches and bridges cannot completely replace routers (layer-3 devices) in the internetwork.

Bridging vs. LAN Switching

It's true—layer-2 switches really are pretty much just bridges that give us a bunch more ports, but there are some important differences you should always keep in mind:

- Bridges are software based, while switches are hardware based because they use ASIC chips to help make filtering decisions.

- Bridges can only have one spanning-tree instance per bridge, while switches can have many. (I'm going to tell you all about spanning trees in a bit.)

- Switches have a higher number of ports than most bridges.

- Both bridges and switches forward layer-2 broadcasts.

- Both bridges and switches make forwarding decisions based on layer-2 addresses.

Three Switch Functions at Layer 2

There are three distinct functions of layer-2 switching (you need to remember these!): *address learning*, forward/filter decisions, and loop avoidance.

Address learning   Layer-2 switches and bridges remember the source hardware address of each frame received on an interface, and they enter this information into a MAC database called a forward/filter table.

Forward/filter decisions   When a frame is received on an interface, the switch looks at the destination hardware address and finds the exit interface in the MAC database. The frame is only forwarded out the specified destination port.

Loop avoidance   If multiple connections between switches are created for redundancy purposes, network loops can occur. Spanning Tree Protocol (STP) is used to stop network loops while still permitting redundancy.

Address learning, forward/filtering decisions, and loop avoidance are discussed in detail in the next sections.

Address Learning

When a switch is first powered on, the MAC forward/filter table is empty, as shown in Figure 2.4.

FIGURE 2.4   Empty forward/filter table on a switch

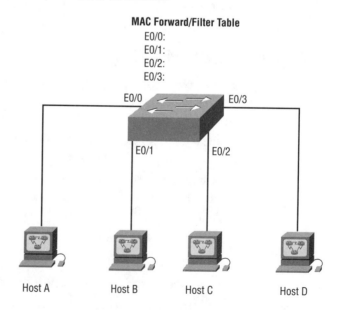

MAC Forward/Filter Table
E0/0:
E0/1:
E0/2:
E0/3:

When a device transmits and an interface receives a frame, the switch places the frame's source address in the MAC forward/filter table, allowing it to remember which interface the sending device is located on. The switch then has no choice but to flood the network with this frame because it has no idea where the destination device is actually located.

If a device answers this broadcast and sends a frame back, then the switch will take the source address from that frame and place that MAC address in its database as well, associating this address with the interface that received the frame. Since the switch now has both of the relevant MAC addresses in its filtering table, the two devices can now make a point-to-point connection. The switch doesn't need to broadcast as it did the first time, because now the frames can and will be forwarded only between the two devices. This is exactly the thing that makes layer-2 switches better than hubs. In a hub network, all frames are forwarded out all ports every time—no matter what! Figure 2.5 shows the processes involved in building a MAC database.

FIGURE 2.5   How switches learn hosts' locations

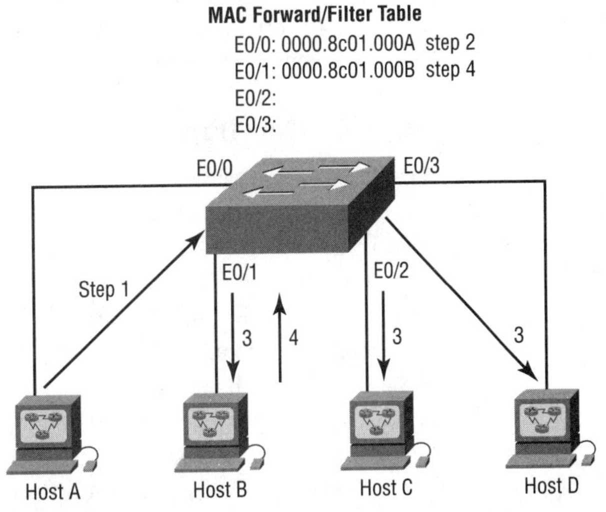

In this figure, you can see four hosts attached to a switch. When the switch is powered on, it has nothing in its MAC address forward/filter table, just like in Figure 2.4. But when the hosts start communicating, the switch places the source hardware address of each frame in the table along with which port the frame's address corresponds.

Let me give you an example of how a forward/filter table is populated:

1. Host A sends a frame to Host B. Host A's MAC address is 0000.8c01.000A; Host B's MAC address is 0000.8c01.000B.

2. The switch receives the frame on the E0/0 interface and places the source address in the MAC address table.

3. Since the destination address is not in the MAC database, the frame is forwarded out all interfaces.

4. Host B receives the frame and responds to Host A. The switch receives this frame on interface E0/1 and places the source hardware address in the MAC database.

5. Host A and Host B can now make a point-to-point connection and only the two devices will receive the frames. Hosts C and D will not see the frames, nor are their MAC addresses found in the database because they haven't yet sent a frame to the switch.

If Host A and Host B don't communicate to the switch again within a certain amount of time, the switch will flush their entries from the database to keep it as current as possible.

Forward/Filter Decisions

When a frame arrives at a switch interface, the destination hardware address is compared to the forward/filter MAC database. If the destination hardware address is known and listed in the database, the frame is only sent out the correct exit interface. The switch doesn't transmit the frame out any interface except for the destination interface. This preserves bandwidth on the other network segments and is called *frame filtering*.

If the destination hardware address is not listed in the MAC database, then the frame is broadcast out all active interfaces except the interface the frame was received on. If a device answers the broadcast, the MAC database is updated with the device's location (interface).

If a host or server sends a broadcast on the LAN, the switch will broadcast the frame out all active ports by default. Remember, the switch only creates smaller collision domains, but it's still one large broadcast domain by default.

Loop Avoidance

Redundant links between switches are a good idea because they help prevent complete network failures in the event one link stops working.

Sounds great, but even though redundant links can be extremely helpful, they often cause more problems than they solve. This is because frames can be broadcast down all redundant links simultaneously, creating network loops as well as other evils. Here's a list of some of the ugliest problems:

- If no loop avoidance schemes are put in place, the switches will flood broadcasts endlessly throughout the internetwork. This is sometimes referred to as a *broadcast storm*. (But most of the time it's referred to in ways we're not permitted to repeat in print!) Figure 2.6 illustrates how a broadcast can be propagated throughout the network. Observe how a frame is continually being broadcast through the internetwork's Physical network media.

FIGURE 2.6 Broadcast storm

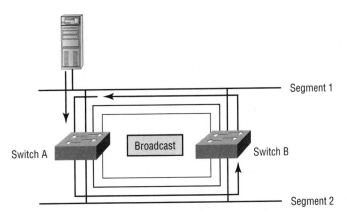

- A device can receive multiple copies of the same frame, since that frame can arrive from different segments at the same time. Figure 2.7 demonstrates how a whole bunch of frames can arrive from multiple segments simultaneously. The server in the figure sends a unicast (which is a directed broadcast) frame to Router C. Since it's a type of broadcast, Switch A forwards the frame, and Switch B provides the same service—it forwards the broadcast. This is bad because it means that Router C receives that unicast frame twice, causing additional overhead on the network.

FIGURE 2.7   Multiple frame copies

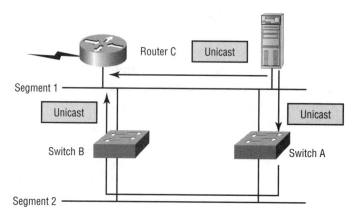

- You may have thought of this one: The MAC address filter table will be totally confused about the device's location because the switch can receive the frame from more than one link. And what's more, the bewildered switch could get so caught up in constantly updating the MAC filter table with source hardware address locations that it will fail to forward a frame! This is called thrashing the MAC table.

- One of the nastiest things that can happen is multiple loops generating throughout an internetwork. This means that loops can occur within other loops, and if a broadcast storm were to also occur, the network wouldn't be able to perform frame switching—period!

All of these problems spell "hosed" or "pretty much hosed" and are decidedly evil situations that must be avoided, or at least fixed somehow. That's where Spanning Tree Protocol comes into the game. It was developed to solve each and every one of the problems I just told you about.

Spanning Tree Protocol (STP)

Back before it was purchased and renamed Compaq, a company called Digital Equipment Corporation (DEC) created the original version of *Spanning Tree Protocol (STP)*. The IEEE later created its own version of STP called 802.1D. All Cisco switches run the IEEE 802.1D version of STP, which isn't compatible with the DEC version.

STP's main task is to stop network loops from occurring on your layer-2 network (bridges or switches). It vigilantly monitors the network to find all links, making sure that no loops occur by shutting down any redundant ones. STP uses the spanning-tree algorithm (STA) to first create a topology database, then search out and destroy redundant links. With STP running, frames will only be forwarded on the premium, STP-picked links.

Spanning-Tree Terms

Before I get into describing the details of how STP works in the network, you need to understand some basic ideas and terms and how they relate within the layer-2 switched network:

STP   Spanning Tree Protocol (STP) is a bridge protocol that uses the STA to find redundant links dynamically and create a spanning-tree topology database. Bridges exchange BPDU messages with other bridges to detect loops, and then remove them by shutting down selected bridge interfaces.

Root bridge   The *root bridge* is the bridge with the best bridge ID. With STP, the key is for all the switches in the network to elect a root bridge that becomes the focal point in the network. All other decisions in the network—like which port is to be blocked and which port is to be put in forwarding mode—are made from the perspective of this root bridge.

BPDU   All the switches exchange information to use in the selection of the root switch, as well as for subsequent configuration of the network. Each switch compares the parameters in the *Bridge Protocol Data Unit (BPDU)* that they send to one neighbor with the one that they receive from another neighbor.

Bridge ID   This is how STP keeps track of all the switches in the network. The bridge ID is determined by a combination of the bridge priority (32,768 by default on all Cisco switches) and the base MAC address. The lowest bridge ID becomes the root bridge in the network.

Nonroot bridge   All bridges that are not the root bridge. These exchange BPDUs with all bridges and update the STP topology database on all switches, preventing loops and providing a measure of defense against link failures.

Root port   Always the link directly connected to the root bridge, or the shortest path to the root bridge. If more than one link connects to the root bridge, then a port cost is determined by checking the bandwidth of each link. The lowest cost port becomes the root port.

Designated port   Either a root port or a port that has been determined as having the best (lower) cost—a *designated port* will be marked as a forwarding port.

Port cost   Determined when multiple links are used between two switches and none are root ports. The cost of a link is determined by the bandwidth of a link.

Nondesignated port   Port with a higher cost than the designated port that will be put in blocking mode—a *nondesignated port* is not a forwarding port.

Forwarding port   Port that forwards frames.

Blocked port   Port that will not forward frames, in order to prevent loops. However, a blocked port will always listen to frames.

Spanning-Tree Operations

As I've said before, STP's job is to find all links in the network and shut down any redundant ones, thereby preventing network loops from occurring. STP does this by first electing a root bridge that will preside over network topology decisions. Those decisions include determining which "roads" are the best ones for frames to travel on normally, and which ones should be reserved as backup routes if one of the primary "roads" fail.

Things tend to go a lot more smoothly when you don't have more than one person making a navigational decision, and so, there can only be one root bridge in any given network. I'll discuss the root bridge election process more completely in the next section.

Selecting the Root Bridge

The bridge ID is used to elect the root bridge in the network as well as to determine the root port. This ID is 8 bytes long, and includes both the priority and the MAC address of the device. The default priority on all devices running the IEEE STP version is 32,768.

To determine the root bridge, the priorities of the bridge and the MAC address are combined. If two switches or bridges happen to have the same priority value, then the MAC address becomes the tie breaker for figuring out which one has the lowest (best) ID. It's like this: If two switches—I'll name them A and B—both use the default priority of 32,768, then the MAC address will be used instead. If switch A's MAC address is 0000.0c00.1111.1111 and switch B's MAC address is 0000.0c00.2222.2222, then switch A would become the root bridge. Just remember that the lower value is the better one when it comes to electing a root bridge.

BPDUs are sent every 2 seconds, by default, out all active ports on a bridge/switch, and the bridge with the lowest (best) bridge ID is elected the root bridge. You can change the bridge's ID so that it will become a root bridge automatically. Being able to do that is important in a large switched network—it ensures that the best paths are chosen.

Changing STP parameters is beyond the scope of this book, but it's covered in *CCNP: Switching Study Guide* (Sybex, 2000).

Selecting the Designated Port

If more than one link is connected to the root port, then port cost becomes the factor used to determine which port will be the root port. So, to determine the port or ports that will be used to communicate with the root bridge, you must first figure out the path's cost. The STP cost is an accumulated total path cost based on the available bandwidth of each of the links. Table 2.1 shows the typical costs associated with various Ethernet networks.

TABLE 2.1   Typical Costs of Different Ethernet Networks

Speed	New IEEE Cost	Original IEEE Cost
10Gbps	2	1
1Gbps	4	1
100Mbps	19	10
10Mbps	100	100

The IEEE 802.1D specification has recently been revised to handle the new higher-speed links. The Cisco 1900 switches use the original IEEE 802.1D specifications.

Spanning-Tree Port States

The ports on a bridge or switch running STP can transition through five different modes:

Blocking   A blocked port won't forward frames; it just listens to BPDUs. All ports are in blocking state by default when the switch is powered up.

Listening   The port listens to BPDUs to make sure no loops occur on the network before passing data frames.

Learning   The switch port listens to BPDUs and learns all the paths in the switched network. It also learns MAC addresses and builds a filter table but does not forward frames.

Forwarding   The port sends and receives all data on the bridged port.

Disabled   A port in the disabled state does not participate in the frame forwarding or STP. A port in the disabled state is virtually nonoperational.

Switch ports are most often in either the blocking or forwarding state. A forwarding port is one that has been determined to have the lowest (best) cost to the root bridge. But when and if the network experiences a topology change (because of a failed link or because someone adds in a new switch), you'll find the ports on a switch in listening and learning state.

As I mentioned, blocking ports is a strategy for preventing network loops. Once a switch determines the best path to the root bridge, then all other ports will be in blocking mode. Blocked ports can still receive BPDUs; they just don't send out any frames.

If a switch determines that a blocked port should now be the designated port, it will go into listening mode and check all BPDUs it receives to make sure that it won't create a loop once the port goes to forwarding mode.

Convergence

Convergence occurs when bridges and switches have transitioned to either the forwarding or blocking modes. No data is forwarded during this time. Before data can be forwarded again, all devices must be updated. Convergence is important to make sure all devices have the same database, but it does cost you some time: it usually takes 50 seconds to go from blocking to forwarding mode, and it's not recommended that you change the default STP timers. (But you can adjust those timers if necessary.) Forward delay means the time it takes to transition a port from listening to learning mode or vice versa.

Spanning-Tree Example

So now comes D-Day—well, maybe not quite; you're not taking the test yet! But it is time to begin using and not just reading about this stuff. It's important to see how a spanning tree works in an internetwork, because it will really help you understand it better. So in the section coming up, I'll give you a chance to observe what you've learned as it takes place in a live network.

Check it out: In Figure 2.8, you can assume that all five switches have the same priority of 32,768. But now study the MAC address of each switch. By looking at the priority and MAC addresses of each device, you should be able to determine the root bridge.

FIGURE 2.8 Spanning tree example

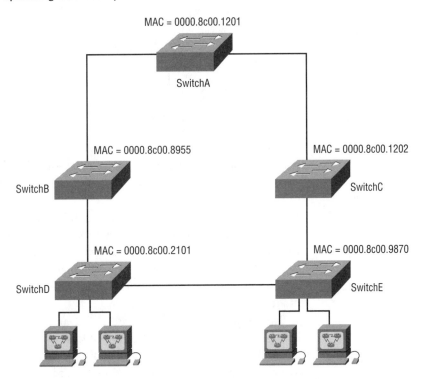

Once you've established which switch has got to be the root bridge, look at the figure again and try to figure out which is the root port on each of the switches. (Hint: Root ports are always designated ports, which means they will always be in forwarding mode.) Okay, next try and establish which of the ports will be in blocking mode.

Figure 2.9 has the answers for each of the port states for each switch.

FIGURE 2.9 Spanning tree example answers

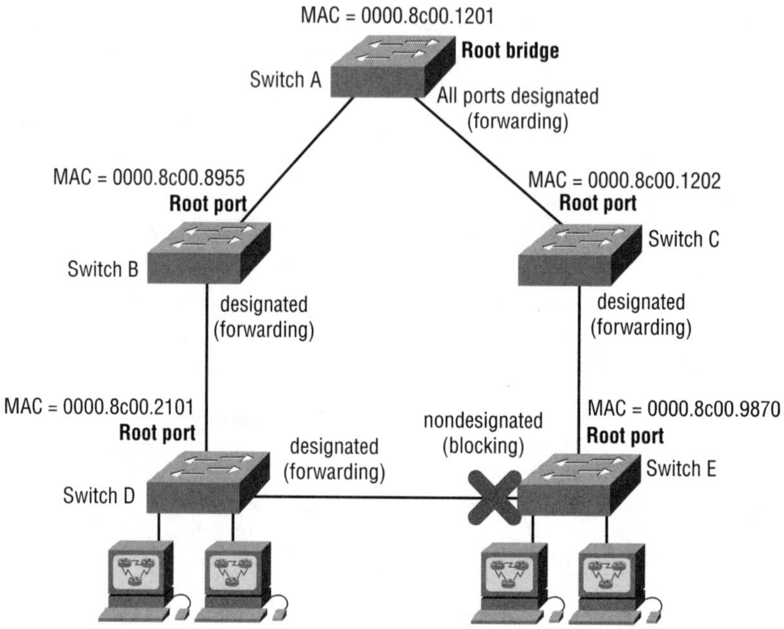

MAC = 0000.8c00.1201

Root bridge

Switch A

All ports designated
(forwarding)

MAC = 0000.8c00.8955
Root port

Switch B

MAC = 0000.8c00.1202
Root port

Switch C

designated
(forwarding)

designated
(forwarding)

MAC = 0000.8c00.2101
Root port

Switch D

designated
(forwarding)

nondesignated
(blocking)

MAC = 0000.8c00.9870
Root port

Switch E

Since Switch A has the lowest MAC address and all five switches use the default priority, Switch A gets to be the root bridge. And remember this: A root bridge always has every port in forwarding mode (designated ports).

To determine the root ports on Switch B and Switch C, just follow the connection to the root bridge. Each direct connection to the root bridge will be a root port, so it will become designated. On Switches D and E, the ports connected to Switches B and C are Switches D and E's closest ports to the root bridge (lowest cost), so those ports are root ports and in forwarding mode (designated).

Take another look at the Figure 2.9. Can you tell which of the ports between Switch D and E must be shut down so a network loop doesn't occur? Let's work it out: Since the connection from Switches D and E to Switches B and C are root ports, those can't be shut down. Next, the bridge ID is used to determine designated and nondesignated ports; so, because Switch D has the lowest (best) bridge ID, Switch E's port to Switch D will become nondesignated (blocking), and Switch D's connection to Switch E will be designated (forwarding).

> ⊕ **Real World Scenario**
>
> **When should I worry about spanning tree?**
>
> If you have fewer than six switches in your internetwork, then depending on the number of users in your network, you typically would just let STP do its job and not worry about it.
>
> However, if you have dozens of switches and hundreds of users in your network, then it is time to consider how STP is running. If you do not set the root switch in this larger switched network, your STP may never converge between switches, which could bring your network down.
>
> Setting the timers and root switch are covered in the Sybex *CCNP: Switching Study Guide.*

LAN Switch Types

LAN switch types decide how a frame is handled when it's received on a switch port. Latency—the time it takes for a frame to be sent out an exit port once the switch receives the frame—depends on the chosen switching mode. There are three switching modes:

Cut-through   When in this mode, the switch waits for the destination hardware address to be received before it looks up the destination address in the MAC filter table.

FragmentFree (modified cut-through)   This is the default mode for the Catalyst 1900 switch, and it's sometimes referred to as modified cut-through. In FragmentFree mode, the switch checks the first 64 bytes of a frame before forwarding it for fragmentation, thus guarding against possible collisions.

Store-and-forward   Herein, the complete data frame is received on the switch's buffer, a CRC is run, and then the switch looks up the destination address in the MAC filter table.

Figure 2.10 delimits the different points where the switching mode takes place in the frame.

FIGURE 2.10 Different switching modes within a frame

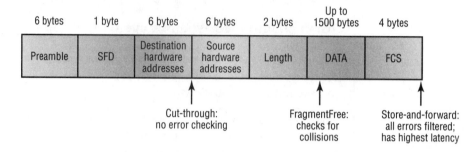

Let's now discuss these three switching modes in more detail.

Cut-Through (Real Time)

With the *cut-through* switching method, the LAN switch copies only the destination address (the first six bytes following the preamble) onto its onboard buffers. That done, it then looks up the hardware destination address in the MAC switching table, determines the outgoing interface, and proceeds to forward the frame toward its destination.

A cut-through switch really helps to reduce latency because it begins to forward the frame as soon as it reads the destination address and determines the outgoing interface. And after it determines the destination port, the following frames are immediately forwarded out through it.

With some switches, you get an extra super-cool feature: the flexibility to perform cut-through switching on a per-port basis until a user-defined error threshold is reached. At the point that threshold is attained, the ports automatically change over to store-and-forward mode so they will stop forwarding the errors. And, when the error rate on the port falls back below the threshold, the port automatically changes back to cut-through mode.

FragmentFree (Modified Cut-Through)

FragmentFree is a modified form of cut-through switching, in which the switch waits for the collision window (64 bytes) to pass before forwarding. This is because if a packet has an error, it almost always occurs within the first 64 bytes. It means each frame will be checked into the data field to make sure no fragmentation has occurred.

FragmentFree mode provides better error checking than the cut-through mode with practically no increase in latency. It's the default switching method for the 1900 switches.

Store-and-Forward

Store-and-forward switching is Cisco's primary LAN switching method. When in *store-and-forward*, the LAN switch copies the entire frame onto its onboard buffers and then computes the cyclic redundancy check (CRC). Because it copies the entire frame, latency through the switch varies with frame length.

The frame is discarded if it contains a CRC error, if it's too short (less than 64 bytes including the CRC), or if it's too long (more than 1518 bytes including the CRC). If the frame doesn't contain any errors, the LAN switch looks up the destination hardware address in its forwarding or switching table to find the correct outgoing interface. When it does, out goes the frame toward its destination. This is the mode used by the Catalyst 5000 series switches, and you can't modify it.

Summary

Y ou can think of this as the layer-2 switching background chapter because the information I presented was designed to give you everything you need before continuing with the rest of this book. Specifically, we covered the following information:

- Layer-2 switching and how switches differ from bridges

- Address learning and how the MAC address filter table is built

- Forward/filtering decisions that layer-2 switches make and how they make them

- Loop avoidance and the problems caused when loop avoidance schemes are not used in the network

- Spanning Tree Protocol and how it prevents loops

- LAN switch types used on Cisco routers and how they differ

I've got to say this... if any of the subjects in this list here aren't clear to you yet, look into the appropriate section again. These concepts are both fundamental and progressive, and if you're a little confused at this point, you'll probably just get frustrated if you move on to Chapter 3 and beyond. It will only take a few minutes, and it's worth going over again to make the rest of the course clearer and easier to understand!

Exam Essentials

Remember the three switch functions.   Address learning, forward/filter decision, and loop avoidance are the functions of a switch.

Understand the main purpose of the spanning tree in a switched LAN. The main purpose of STP is to prevent switching loops in a network with redundant switched paths.

Remember the three LAN switch methods.   The three LAN switch methods are cut-through, FragmentFree (also known as modified cut-through) and store-and-forward.

Understand how the cut-through LAN switch method works.   When in this mode, the switch waits only for the destination hardware address to be received before it looks up the address in the MAC filter table.

Understand how the FragmentFree LAN switch method works.   The FragmentFree LAN switch method checks the first 64 bytes of a frame before forwarding it for fragmentation.

Understand how the store-and-forward LAN switch method works. Store-and-forward first receives the complete data frame on the switch's buffer; a CRC is run, and then the switch looks up the destination address in the MAC filter table.

Key Terms

Before taking the exam, be sure you're familiar with the following terms:

address learning	frame filtering
Bridge Protocol Data Unit (BPDU)	nondesignated port
broadcast storm	root bridge
cut-through	Spanning Tree Protocol (STP)
designated port	store-and-forward
FragmentFree	

Written Lab 2

Write in the answers to the following questions:

1. Which LAN switch method has the highest latency?

2. Which LAN switch method only reads the hardware destination address before forwarding the frame?

3. What are the three switch functions at layer 2?

4. Which LAN switch type reads into the data field of the frame before forwarding the frame?

5. What is used at layer 2 to prevent switching loops?

6. Which LAN switch method receives the complete frame before beginning to forward it?

7. Which two LAN switch methods have a constant latency?

8. What LAN switch method is also known as "modified cut-through"?

9. What is used to prevent switching loops in a network with redundant switched paths?

10. Which LAN switch method runs a CRC on every frame the switch receives?

(The answers to Written Lab 2 can be found following the answers to the Review Questions for this chapter.)

Review Questions

1. Which LAN switch method runs a CRC on every frame?

   A. Cut-through

   B. Store-and-forward

   C. FragmentCheck

   D. FragmentFree

2. Which LAN switch type checks only the hardware address before forwarding a frame?

   A. Cut-through

   B. Store-and-forward

   C. FragmentCheck

   D. FragmentFree

3. What is the result of segmenting a network with a bridge? (Choose all that apply.)

   A. It increases the number of collision domains.

   B. It decreases the number of collision domains.

   C. It increases the number of broadcast domains.

   D. It decreases the number of broadcast domains.

   E. It makes smaller collision domains.

   F. It makes larger collision domains.

4. Layer-2 switching provides which of the following?

   A. Hardware-based bridging (MAC)

   B. Wire speed

   C. High latency

   D. High cost

5. If your network is currently congested and you are using only hubs in your network, what would be the best solution to decrease congestion on your network?

   A. Cascade your hubs.

   B. Replace your hubs with switches.

   C. Replace your hubs with routers.

   D. Add faster hubs.

6. Which LAN switch method is also known as a modified version of cut-through?

   A. Cut-throughout

   B. FragmentFree

   C. Store-and-forward

   D. Store-and-release

7. Which of the following are true regarding store-and-forward? (Select all that apply.)

   A. The latency time varies with frame size.

   B. The latency time is constant.

   C. The frame is transmitted only after the complete frame is received.

   D. The frame is transmitted as soon as the header of the frame is read.

8. What are the three distinct functions of layer-2 switching that increase available bandwidth on the network?

   A. Address learning

   B. Routing

   C. Forwarding and filtering

   D. Creating network loops

   E. Loop avoidance

   F. IP addressing

9. You are working on a network design and determine that a new testing application requires multiple hosts that must be capable of sharing data between each host and server running 10Mbps. Other departments use applications that require less than 3Mbps to the server. What should you recommend?

    A. Replace the 10Mbps Ethernet hub with a 100Mbs Ethernet hub.

    B. Install a router between departments.

    C. Use a switch with a 100Mbps uplink to the server and 10Mbps to the hosts.

    D. Use a bridge to break up collision domains.

10. What technology is a used by Catalyst switches to resolve topology loops and ensure that data flows properly through a single network path?

    A. RIP

    B. STP

    C. IGRP

    D. Store-and-forward

    E. Cut-through

11. Which of the following statements is true?

    A. A switch creates a single collision domain and a single broadcast domain. A router creates a single collision domain.

    B. A switch creates separate collision domains but one broadcast domain. A router provides a separate broadcast domain.

    C. A switch creates a single collision domain and separate broadcast domains. A router provides a separate broadcast domain as well.

    D. A switch creates separate collision domains and separate broadcast domains. A router provides separate collision domains.

12. What are the two primary operating modes for frame switching? (Choose two.)

   A. Full duplex

   B. Half duplex

   C. Cut-through

   D. FragmentFree

   E. Store-and-forward

13. What does a switch do when a frame is received on an interface and the destination hardware address is unknown or not in the filter table?

   A. Forwards the switch to the first available link

   B. Drops the frame

   C. Floods the network with the frame looking for the device

   D. Sends back a message to the originating station asking for a name resolution

14. Which LAN switch type waits for the collision window to pass before looking up the destination hardware address in the MAC filter table and forwarding the frame?

   A. Cut-through

   B. Store-and-forward

   C. FragmentCheck

   D. FragmentFree

15. What statement about switching methods are true?

   A. Store-and-forward has the lowest latency.

   B. Cut-through latency time varies by packet size.

   C. The modified version holds the packet in memory until 50% of the packet reaches the switch.

   D. The modified version holds the packet in memory until the data portion of the packet reaches the switch.

16. Which layer-2 device enables high-speed data exchange?

    A. Repeater

    B. Hub

    C. Switch

    D. Router

17. What purpose in a switched LAN does STP perform?

    A. Prevent routing loops in a network with redundant paths.

    B. Prevent switching loops in a network with redundant switched paths.

    C. Allow VLAN information be passed in a trunked link.

    D. Create multiple broadcast domains in a layer-2 switched network.

18. Which of the following is a characteristic of having a network segment on a switch?

    A. The segment is many collision domains.

    B. The segment can translate from one media to a different media.

    C. All devices on a segment are part of a different broadcast domain.

    D. One device per segment can concurrently send frames to the switch.

19. What could happen on a network if no loop avoidance schemes are put in place? (Choose two options.)

    A. Faster convergence times

    B. Broadcast storms

    C. Multiple frame copies

    D. IP routing will cause flapping on a serial link

20. Which of the following is true in regard to bridges?

A. Bridges do not isolate broadcast domains.

B. Bridges broadcast packets into the same domain they were received from.

C. Bridges use IP addresses to filter the network.

D. Bridges can translate from one media to a different media.

21. When a LAN switch has just been powered on, what happens to the first frame as it passes through the switch?

A. The appropriate MAC address of the frame and the switch port information are copied to the NVRAM. The frame is forwarded out the appropriate destination port.

B. The appropriate MAC address of the frame and the switch port information are copied to the CAM table. The frame is then forwarded out all LAN switch ports.

C. The appropriate MAC address of the frame and the switch port information are copied to NVRAM. The frame is forwarded out all LAN switch ports, except from the port on which the frame was received.

D. The source MAC address of the frame and switch port information are copied to the CAM table. The frame is then forwarded out all LAN switch ports excluding the port on which the frame was received.

22. The MAC address table in a LAN switch is used to:

A. Map the source MAC address to the source switch port.

B. Map the source MAC address to the destination switch port.

C. Map the destination MAC address to the source switch port.

D. Map the destination MAC address to the destination switch port.

23. If a switch determines that the destination of a frame is the same port from which the frame was received, the switch will:

A. Forward the frame back out the port from which it was received.

B. Drop the frame.

C. Flood the frame out all ports except the one on which it was received.

D. Flood the frame out all ports including the one on which it was received.

24. Bridged and switched networks commonly utilize redundant pathways to ensure a fault-tolerant network. If the redundancy is not properly managed, loops in the topology may cause which of the following problems? Select all that apply.

A. Conflicting MAC address entries in the MAC address table of bridges or switches

B. Unrecoverable application errors

C. Broadcast storms

D. None of the above

25. Which of the following is a true statement concerning the operation of Spanning Tree Protocol (STP)? Select all that apply.

A. It is enabled by default on Cisco Catalyst switches.

B. It is enabled by default on Cisco routers.

C. The IEEE Spanning Tree Protocol and DEC Spanning Tree Protocol are compatible and are able to exchange spanning-tree topology information.

D. The DEC Spanning Tree Protocol and IBM Spanning Tree Protocol are compatible and are able to exchange spanning-tree topology information.

Answers to Review Questions

1. **B.** Store-and-forward LAN switching checks every frame for CRC errors. It has the highest latency of any LAN switch type.

2. **A.** The cut-through method does no error checking and has the lowest latency of the three LAN switch types. Cut-through only checks the hardware destination address before forwarding the frame.

3. **A, E.** Bridges break up collision domains, which would increase the number of collision domains in a network and also make smaller collision domains.

4. **A, B.** Layer-2 switching uses ASICs to provide frame filtering and is considered hardware based. Layer-2 switching also provides wire-speed frame transfers, with low latency.

5. **B.** Layer-2 switches break up collision domains and will decrease congestion on your network.

6. **B.** The modified version of cut-through is called FragmentFree.

7. **A, C.** Store-and-forward latency (delay) will always vary because the complete frame must be received before the frame is transmitted back out the switch.

8. **A, C, E.** Layer-2 features that increase available bandwidth include address learning, forwarding and filtering of the network, and loop avoidance.

9. **C.** By adding a switch, you can effectively segment the network and provide 100Mbps to the server and 10MBps to the hosts.

10. **B.** Spanning Tree Protocol (STP) will make sure that no network loops occur at layer 2.

11. **B.** Switches break up collision domains, and routers break up broadcast domains.

12. **C, E.** There are three methods of LAN switching: cut-through, FragmentFree, and store-and-forward. Cut-through and store-and-forward are the two main methods, according to Cisco.

13. C.   Switches forward all frames that have an unknown destination address. If a device answers the frame, the switch will update the MAC address table to reflect the location of the device.

14. D.   FragmentFree looks at the first 64 bytes of a frame to make sure a collision has not occurred. It is sometimes referred to as modified cut-through.

15. D.   The last option is the best answer because the FragmentFree LAN switch method reads into the data field of every frame.

16. C.   Layer-2 switches are used to enable high-speed data exchange on a LAN.

17. B.   Spanning Tree Protocol (STP) stops loops at layer 2, and in this question, the best answer is to stop loops in a switched network because switches work at layer 2. Routing protocols (RIP, IGRP, etc.) are used to stop loops at layer 3 (routing).

18. D.   Only one device on a network segment connected to a switch can send frames to the switch. A switch cannot translate from one media type to another on the same segment.

19. B, C.   Broadcast storms and multiple frame copies are typically found in a network that has multiple links to remote locations without some type of loop-avoidance scheme.

20. A.   A bridge breaks up collision domains, but it creates one large broadcast domain by default.

21. D.   When a LAN switch is first brought online, it does not contain entries in its CAM table (stored in RAM). As the frame passes through the switch, the switch copies the frame's MAC address information, mapping the MAC address to the port on which the frame was received. Since the destination port is not known, the switch forwards the frame out every port excluding the port on which the frame was received.

22. A.   The MAC address table records a frame's source MAC address and the port on which the frame was received. This identifies the physical location of the end-device on the network. When the switch receives a frame destined for a MAC address found in its MAC address table, the switch forwards the frame to that switch port only.

23. B. If the switch port is connected to a hub, it is likely that from time to time the switch will see a frame where the destination MAC address is associated with the same port on which it was received. The switch assumes the frame has reached its intended destination and drops the frame, not wanting to create multiple copies of the same frame.

24. A, B, C. A looped topology can create a multitude of errors, including broadcast storms, unrecoverable application errors, and corruption of the MAC address table in bridges or switches.

25. A. STP is responsible for creating a loop-free topology in which only one active path exists between any two points within a broadcast domain. The protocol is enabled by default on Catalyst switches; however, it is not enabled by default on Cisco routers unless bridging has been configured. The IEEE, DEC, and IBM implementations are unique in design and are not compatible with one another.

Answers to Written Lab 2

1. Store-and-forward
2. Cut-through
3. Address learning, filter/forward, loop avoidance
4. FragmentFree
5. Spanning Tree Protocol (STP)
6. Store-and-forward
7. Cut-through, FragmentFree
8. FragmentFree
9. Spanning Tree Protocol (STP)
10. Store-and-forward

Internet Protocols

THE CCNA EXAM TOPICS COVERED IN THIS CHAPTER INCLUDE THE FOLLOWING:

✓ **OSI Reference Model & Layered Communications**

- Describe the two parts of network addressing; then identify the parts in specific protocol address examples.
- Identify the parts in specific protocol address examples.

✓ **Network Protocols**

- Describe the different classes of IP addresses (and subnetting).
- Identify the functions of the TCP/IP network-layer protocol.
- Identify the functions performed by ICMP.
- Configure IP addresses.
- Verify IP addresses.

he *Transmission Control Protocol/Internet Protocol (TCP/IP)* suite was created by the Department of Defense (DoD) to ensure and preserve data integrity, as well as maintain communications in the event of catastrophic war. If designed and implemented correctly, a TCP/IP network can be a dependable and resilient one. In this chapter, I'll cover the protocols of TCP/IP, and throughout this book, you'll learn how to create a marvelous TCP/IP network—using Cisco routers, of course.

We'll begin by taking a look at the DoD's version of TCP/IP and then compare this version and its protocols with the OSI reference model discussed in Chapter 1. Once you understand the protocols used at the various levels of the DoD model, you'll learn about IP addressing and subnetting IP network addresses.

IP addressing and subnetting isn't difficult; there is just a lot of material to understand. I'm going to present it in a very detailed manner because that will allow you to read each section over and over again until you feel you've mastered that section of IP addressing.

Your assignment, if you choose to accept it—and you'd better, if you want your Cisco certification—is to subnet IP addresses in your head. I can take you to the promised land—just follow me!

TCP/IP and the DoD Model

The DoD model is basically a condensed version of the OSI model—it's composed of four, instead of seven, layers:

- Process/Application layer

- Host-to-Host layer

- Internet layer

- Network Access layer

Figure 3.1 shows a comparison of the DoD model and the OSI reference model. As you can see, the two are similar in concept, but each has a different number of layers with different names.

FIGURE 3.1 The DoD and OSI models

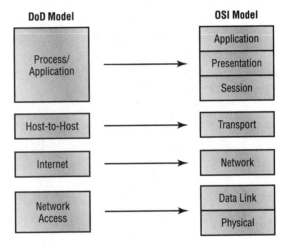

When talking about the different protocols in the IP stack, the layers of the OSI and DoD models are interchangeable. In other words, the Internet layer and the Network layer describe the same thing, as do the Host-to-Host layer and the Transport layer.

A vast array of protocols combine at the DoD model's *Process/Application layer* to integrate the various activities and duties spanning the focus of the OSI's corresponding top three layers (Application, Presentation, and Session). We'll be looking closely at those protocols in the next part of this chapter. The Process/Application layer defines protocols for node-to-node application communication and also controls user-interface specifications.

The *Host-to-Host layer* parallels the functions of the OSI's Transport layer, defining protocols for setting up the level of transmission service for applications. It tackles issues like creating reliable end-to-end communication and ensuring the error-free delivery of data. It handles packet sequencing and maintains data integrity.

The *Internet layer* corresponds to the OSI's Network layer, designating the protocols relating to the logical transmission of packets over the entire network. It takes care of the addressing of hosts by giving them an IP (Internet Protocol) address, and it handles the routing of packets among multiple networks. It also controls the communication flow between two hosts.

At the bottom of the DoD model, the *Network Access layer* monitors the data exchange between the host and the network. The equivalent of the Data Link and Physical layers of the OSI model, the Network Access layer oversees hardware addressing and defines protocols for the physical transmission of data.

While the DoD and OSI models are alike in design and concept and have similar functions in similar places, *how* those functions occur is different. Figure 3.2 shows the TCP/IP protocol suite and how its protocols relate to the DoD model layers.

FIGURE 3.2 The TCP/IP protocol suite

DoD Model

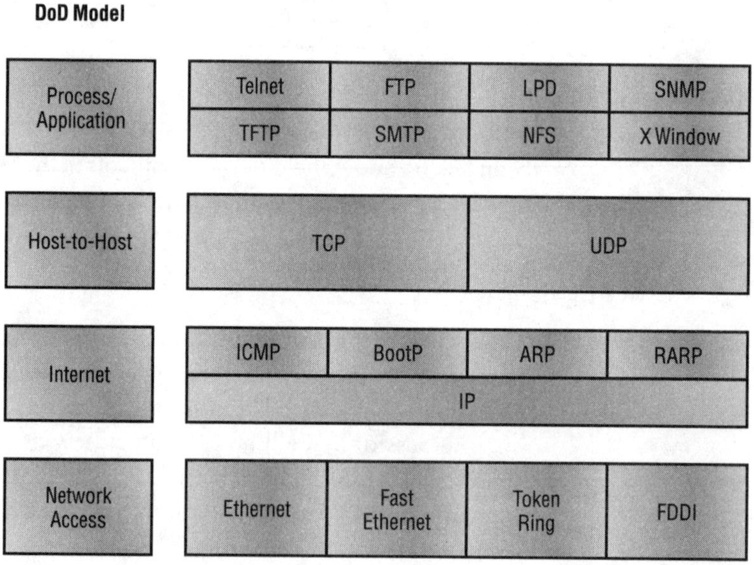

The Process/Application Layer Protocols

In this section, I'll describe the different applications and services typically used in IP networks. The different protocols and applications covered in this section include the following:

DHCP	LPD	SNMP	X Window
DNS	NFS	Telnet	
FTP	SMTP	TFTP	

Telnet

Telnet is the chameleon of protocols—its specialty is terminal emulation. It allows a user on a remote client machine, called the Telnet client, to access the resources of another machine, the Telnet server. Telnet achieves this by pulling a fast one on the Telnet server and making the client machine appear as though it were a terminal directly attached to the local network. This projection is actually a software image—a virtual terminal that can interact with the chosen remote host.

These emulated terminals are of the text-mode type and can execute refined procedures like displaying menus that give users the opportunity to choose options from them and access the applications on the duped server. Users begin a Telnet session by running the Telnet client software and then logging into the Telnet server.

The name *Telnet* comes from "telephone network," which is how most Telnet sessions used to occur.

File Transfer Protocol (FTP)

File Transfer Protocol (FTP) is the protocol that actually lets us transfer files; it can facilitate this between any two machines using it. But FTP isn't just a protocol; it's also a program. Operating as a protocol, FTP is used by applications. As a program, it's employed by users to perform file tasks by hand. FTP also allows for access to both directories and files and can accomplish certain types of directory operations, like relocating into different ones. FTP teams up with Telnet to transparently log you into the FTP server and then provides for the transfer of files.

Accessing a host through FTP is only the first step, though. Users must then be subjected to an authentication login that's probably secured with passwords and usernames implemented by system administrators to restrict access. But you can get around this somewhat by adopting the username "anonymous"—though what you'll gain access to will be limited.

Even when employed by users manually as a program, FTP's functions are limited to listing and manipulating directories, typing file contents, and copying files between hosts. It can't execute remote files as programs.

Trivial File Transfer Protocol (TFTP)

Trivial File Transfer Protocol (TFTP) is the stripped-down, stock version of FTP, but it's the protocol of choice if you know exactly what you want and where to find it. It doesn't give you the abundance of functions that FTP does, though. TFTP has no directory-browsing abilities; it can do nothing but send and receive files. This compact little protocol also skimps in the data department, sending much smaller blocks of data than FTP, and there's no authentication as with FTP, so it's insecure. Few sites support it because of the inherent security risks.

 Real World Scenario

When are FTP and TFTP used?

If you need to give someone a large file or you need to get a large file from someone, FTP is a nice choice. Smaller files (less than 5MB) can just be sent via e-mail if you have the bandwidth of DSL or a cable modem. However, most ISPs don't allow files of 5MB to be e-mailed, so FTP is an option you should consider if you are in need of sending and receiving large files (who isn't these days?). To do this, you will need to set up a FTP server on the Internet so that the files can be shared.

TFTP is completely different than FTP, not just because it is connectionless but also because you cannot just put a TFTP server on the Internet and list files for people to share. When you install a TFTP client, you choose the default directory. When you use TFTP, the file is either taken from this directory and put somewhere else or downloaded into this directory. You cannot list files with TFTP nor tell TFTP where to put the file. Later in this book, you'll use TFTP to both back up and download a new Internetwork Operating System (IOS) to and from your Cisco router.

Network File System (NFS)

Network File System (NFS) is a jewel of a protocol specializing in file sharing. It allows two different types of file systems to interoperate. It works like this: Suppose the NFS server software is running on an NT server, and the NFS client software is running on a Unix host. NFS allows for a portion of the RAM on the NT server to transparently store Unix files, which can, in turn, be used by Unix users. Even though the NT file system and Unix file system are unlike—they have different case sensitivity, filename lengths, security, and so on—both Unix users and NT users can access that same file with their normal file systems, in their normal way.

Simple Mail Transfer Protocol (SMTP)

Simple Mail Transfer Protocol (SMTP), answering our ubiquitous call to e-mail, uses a spooled, or queued, method of mail delivery. Once a message has been sent to a destination, the message is spooled to a device—usually a disk. The server software at the destination posts a vigil, regularly checking this queue for messages. When it detects them, it proceeds to deliver them to their destination. SMTP is used to send mail; POP3 is used to receive mail.

Line Printer Daemon (LPD)

The Line Printer Daemon (LPD) protocol is designed for printer sharing. The LPD, along with the LPR (Line Printer) program, allows print jobs to be spooled and sent to the network's printers using TCP/IP.

X Window

Designed for client-server operations, *X Window* defines a protocol for writing client/server applications based on a graphical user interface (GUI). The idea is to allow a program, called a client, to run on one computer and have it display a program called a window server on another computer.

Simple Network Management Protocol (SNMP)

Simple Network Management Protocol (SNMP) collects and manipulates this valuable network information. It gathers data by polling the devices on the network from a management station at fixed or random intervals, requiring them to disclose certain information. When all is well, SNMP receives something called a *baseline*—a report delimiting the operational traits of a healthy network. This protocol can also stand as a watchdog over the network, quickly notifying managers of any sudden turn of events. These network watchdogs are called *agents*, and when aberrations occur, agents send an alert called a *trap* to the management station.

Domain Name Service (DNS)

Domain Name Service (DNS) resolves host names, specifically Internet names, like www.routersim.com. You don't have to use DNS; you can just type in the *IP address* of any device you want to communicate with. An IP address identifies hosts on a network and the Internet as well. However, DNS was designed to make our lives easier. Think about this: What would happen if you wanted to move your web page to a different service provider? The IP address would change and no one would know what the new one was. DNS allows you to use a domain name to specify an IP address. You can change the IP address as often as you want, and no one will know the difference.

DNS is used to resolve a *fully qualified domain name (FQDN)*—for example, www.lammle.com or todd.lammle.com. An FQDN is a hierarchy that can logically locate a system based on its domain identifier.

If you want to resolve the name "todd," you either must type in the FQDN of todd.lammle.com or have a device like a PC or router add the suffix for you. For example, on a Cisco router, you can use the command ip domain-name lammle.com to append each request with the lammle.com domain. If you don't do that, you'll have to type in the FQDN to get DNS to resolve the name.

An important thing to remember about DNS is that if you can ping a device with an IP address but cannot use its FQDN, then you might have some type of DNS configuration failure.

Dynamic Host Configuration Protocol (DHCP)

Dynamic Host Configuration Protocol (DHCP) gives IP addresses to hosts. It allows easier administration and works well in small-to-even-very-large network environments. All types of hardware can be used as a DHCP server, including a Cisco router.

DHCP differs from BootP in that BootP gives an IP address to a host, but the host's hardware address must be entered manually in a BootP table. You can think of DHCP as a dynamic BootP. But remember that BootP is also used to send an operating system that a host can boot from. DHCP can't do that.

But there is a lot of information a DHCP server can provide to a host when the host is requesting an IP address from the DHCP server. Here's a list of the information a DHCP server can provide:

- IP address
- Subnet mask
- Domain name
- Default gateway (routers)
- DNS
- WINS information

A DHCP server can give us even more information than this, but the items in that list are the most common.

The Host-to-Host Layer Protocols

The main purpose of the Host-to-Host layer is to shield the upper-layer applications from the complexities of the network. This layer says to the upper layer, "Just give me your data stream, with any instructions, and I'll begin the process of getting your information ready to send."

The following sections describe the two protocols at this layer:

- Transmission Control Protocol (TCP)

- User Datagram Protocol (UDP)

Transmission Control Protocol (TCP)

Transmission Control Protocol (TCP) takes large blocks of information from an application and breaks them into segments. It numbers and sequences each segment so that the destination's TCP protocol can put the segments back into the order the application intended. After these segments are sent, TCP (on the transmitting host) waits for an acknowledgment of the receiving end's TCP virtual circuit session, retransmitting those that aren't acknowledged.

Before a transmitting host starts to send segments down the model, the sender's TCP protocol contacts the destination's TCP protocol to establish a connection. What is created is known as a *virtual circuit*. This type of communication is called *connection-oriented*. During this initial handshake, the two TCP layers also agree on the amount of information that's going to be sent before the recipient's TCP sends back an acknowledgment. With everything agreed upon in advance, the path is paved for reliable communication to take place.

TCP is a full-duplex, connection-oriented, reliable, and accurate protocol, but establishing all these terms and conditions, in addition to error checking, is no small task. TCP is very complicated and, not surprisingly, costly in terms of network overhead. And since today's networks are much more reliable than those of yore, this added reliability is often unnecessary.

TCP Segment Format

Since the upper layers just send a data stream to the protocols in the Transport layers, I'll demonstrate how TCP segments a data stream and prepares it for the Internet layer. The Internet layer then routes the segments as packets through an internetwork. The packets are handed to the receiving host's Host-to-Host layer protocol, which rebuilds the data stream to hand to the upper-layer applications or protocols.

Figure 3.3 shows the TCP segment format. The figure shows the different fields within the TCP header.

FIGURE 3.3   TCP segment format

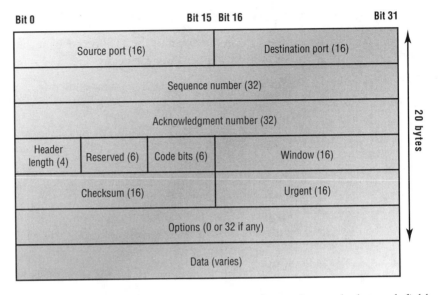

The TCP header is 20 bytes long. You need to understand what each field in the TCP segment is. The TCP segment contains the following fields:

Source port   The port number of the host sending the data. (Port numbers will be explained a little later in this section.)

Destination port   The port number of the application requested on the destination host.

Sequence number   Puts the data back in the correct order or retransmits missing or damaged data, a process called *sequencing*.

Acknowledgment number   Defines which TCP octet is expected next.

HLEN   Stands for header length, which defines the number of 32-bit words in the header.

Reserved   Always set to zero.

Code bits   Control functions used to set up and terminate a session.

Window   The window size the sender is willing to accept, in octets.

Checksum   The cyclic redundancy check (CRC), because TCP doesn't trust the lower layers and checks everything. The CRC checks the header and data fields.

Urgent pointer   Indicates the end of urgent data.

Option   Sets the maximum TCP segment size to either 0 or 32 bits, if any.

Data   Handed down to the TCP protocol at the Transport layer, which includes the upper-layer headers.

Let's take a look at a TCP segment copied from a network analyzer:

```
TCP - Transport Control Protocol
 Source Port:        5973
 Destination Port:   23
 Sequence Number:    1456389907
 Ack Number:         1242056456
 Offset:             5
 Reserved:           %000000
 Code:               %011000
       Ack is valid
       Push Request
 Window:             61320
 Checksum:           0x61a6
 Urgent Pointer:     0
 No TCP Options
 TCP Data Area:
 vL.5.+.5.+.5.+.5  76 4c 19 35 11 2b 19 35 11 2b 19 35 11
   2b 19 35 +. 11 2b 19
 Frame Check Sequence: 0x0d00000f
```

Did you notice that everything I talked about above is in the segment? As you can see from the number of fields in the header, TCP creates a lot of overhead. Application developers may opt for efficiency over reliability to save overhead, and so, User Datagram Protocol was also defined at the Transport layer as an alternative.

User Datagram Protocol (UDP)

If you were to compare *User Datagram Protocol (UDP)* with TCP, the former is basically the scaled-down economy model that's sometimes referred to as a thin protocol. Like a thin person on a park bench, a thin protocol doesn't take up a lot of room—or in this case, much bandwidth on a network.

UDP doesn't offer all the bells and whistles of TCP either, but it does do a fabulous job of transporting information that doesn't require reliable delivery—and it does so using far fewer network resources. (Please note that UDP is covered thoroughly in Request for Comments 768.)

The Requests for Comments (RFCs) form a series of notes, started in 1969, about the Internet (originally the ARPAnet). The notes discuss many aspects of computer communication, focusing on networking protocols, procedures, programs, and concepts but also including meeting notes, opinion, and sometimes humor.

There are some situations where it would definitely be wise for developers to opt for UDP rather than TCP. Remember the watchdog SNMP up there at the Process/Application layer? SNMP monitors the network, sending intermittent messages and a fairly steady flow of status updates and alerts, especially when running on a large network. The cost in overhead to establish, maintain, and close a TCP connection for each one of those little messages would reduce what would be an otherwise healthy, efficient network to a dammed-up bog in no time!

Another circumstance calling for UDP over TCP is when reliability is already handled at the Process/Application layer. Network File System (NFS) handles its own reliability issues, making the use of TCP both impractical and redundant. But ultimately, it's up to the application developer who decides whether to use UDP or TCP, not the user who wants to transfer data faster.

UDP does *not* sequence the segments and does not care in which order the segments arrive at the destination. But after that, UDP sends the segments off and forgets about them. It doesn't follow through, check up on them, or even allow for an acknowledgment of safe arrival—complete abandonment. Because of this, it's referred to as an unreliable protocol. This does not mean that UDP is ineffective, only that it doesn't handle issues of reliability.

Further, UDP doesn't create a virtual circuit, nor does it contact the destination before delivering information to it. Because of this, it's also considered a *connectionless* protocol. Since UDP assumes that the application will use its own reliability method, it doesn't use any. This gives an application developer a choice when running the Internet Protocol stack: TCP for reliability or UDP for faster transfers.

UDP Segment Format

Figure 3.4 clearly illustrates UDP's markedly low overhead as compared to TCP's hungry usage. Look at the figure carefully—can you see the fact that

UDP doesn't use windowing or provide for acknowledgments represented within it?

FIGURE 3.4 UDP segment

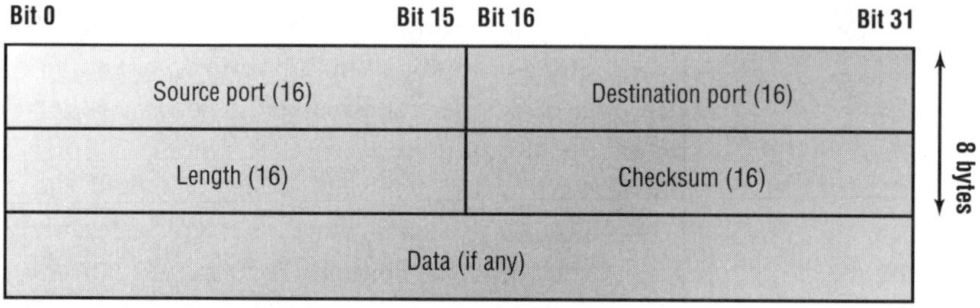

It's important for you to understand what each field in the UDP segment is. The UDP segment contains the following fields:

Source port Port number of the host sending the data.

Destination port Port number of the application requested on the destination host.

Length of the segment Length of UDP header and UDP data.

CRC Checksum of both the UDP header and UDP data fields.

Data Upper-layer data.

UDP, like TCP, doesn't trust the lower layers and runs its own CRC. Remember that the Frame Check Sequence (FCS) is the field that houses the CRC, which is why you can see the FCS information.

The following shows a UDP segment caught on a network analyzer:

```
UDP - User Datagram Protocol
 Source Port:      1085
 Destination Port: 5136
 Length:           41
 Checksum:         0x7a3c
 UDP Data Area:
 ..Z............  00 01 5a 96 00 01 00 00 00 00 00 11 00
   00 00
 ...C..2...._C._C  2e 03 00 43 02 1e 32 0a 00 0a 00 80 43
   00 80
 Frame Check Sequence: 0x00000000
```

Notice that low overhead! Try to find the sequence number, ack number, and window size in the UDP segment. You can't (I hope) because they just aren't there!

Key Concepts of Host-to-Host Protocols

Since we've seen both a connection-oriented (TCP) and connectionless (UDP) protocol in action, it would be good to summarize the two here. The following list highlights some of the key concepts that you should keep in mind regarding these two protocols. Memorize Table 3.1.

TABLE 3.1 Key Features of TCP and UDP

TCP	UDP
Sequenced	Unsequenced
Reliable	Unreliable
Connection-oriented	Connectionless
Virtual circuit	Low overhead
Three-way handshake	No acknowledgment
Windowing flow control	No windowing or flow control

A telephone analogy could really help you understand how TCP works. Most of us know that before you speak to someone on a phone, you must first establish a connection with that other person—wherever they are. This is like a virtual circuit with the TCP protocol. If you were giving someone important information during your conversation, you might say, "You know?" or ask, "Did you get that?" Saying something like this is a lot like a TCP acknowledgment—it's designed to get you verification. From time to time (especially on cell phones), people also ask, "Are you still there?" They end their conversations with a "Goodbye" of some kind, putting closure on the phone call. TCP also performs these types of functions.

Alternately, using UDP is like sending a postcard. To do that, you don't need to contact the other party first. You simply write your message, address the postcard, and mail it. This is analogous to UDP's connectionless orientation. Since the message on the postcard is probably not a matter of life or death, you don't need an acknowledgment of its receipt. Similarly, UDP does not involve acknowledgments.

Port Numbers

TCP and UDP must use *port numbers* to communicate with the upper layers, because they're what keeps track of different conversations crossing the network simultaneously. Originating-source port numbers are dynamically assigned by the source host and will equal some number starting at 1024. 1023 and below are defined in RFC 1700, which discusses what are called well-known port numbers.

Virtual circuits that don't use an application with a well-known port number are assigned port numbers randomly from a specific range instead. These port numbers identify the source and destination host in the TCP segment.

Figure 3.5 illustrates how both TCP and UDP use port numbers.

FIGURE 3.5 Port numbers for TCP and UDP

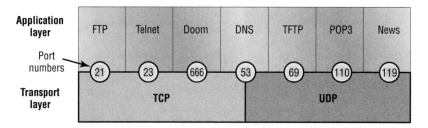

The different port numbers that can be used are explained next:

- Numbers below 1024 are considered well-known port numbers and are defined in RFC 1700.

- Numbers 1024 and above are used by the upper layers to set up sessions with other hosts, and by TCP to use as source and destination addresses in the TCP segment.

TCP Session: Source Port

The following listing shows a TCP session captured with Etherpeek analyzer software. Notice that the source host makes up the source port and, in this case, is 5973. The destination port is 23, which is used to tell the receiving host the purpose of the intended connection (Telnet).

```
TCP - Transport Control Protocol
    Source Port:      5973
```

```
Destination Port: 23
Sequence Number:   1456389907
Ack Number:        1242056456
Offset:            5
Reserved:          %000000
Code:              %011000
      Ack is valid
      Push Request
Window:            61320
Checksum:          0x61a6
Urgent Pointer:    0
No TCP Options
TCP Data Area:
vL.5.+.5.+.5.+.5  76 4c 19 35 11 2b 19 35 11 2b 19 35 11
  2b 19 35 +. 11 2b 19
Frame Check Sequence: 0x0d00000f
```

We can see by looking at this session that the source host makes up the source port. But why does the source makes up a port number? To differentiate between sessions with different hosts, silly! How else would a server know where information is coming from if it didn't have a different number from a sending host? TCP and the upper layers don't use hardware and logical addresses to understand the sending host's address like the Data Link and Network layer protocols do. Instead, they use port numbers. And it's easy to imagine the receiving host getting thoroughly confused if all the hosts used the same port number to get to FTP!

TCP Session: Destination Port

Now, you'll usually look at an analyzer and see that only the source port is above 1024 and the destination port is a well-known port, as shown in the following Etherpeek trace:

```
TCP - Transport Control Protocol
  Source Port:       1144
  Destination Port:  80 World Wide Web HTTP
  Sequence Number:   9356570
  Ack Number:        0
  Offset:            7
  Reserved:          %000000
  Code:              %000010
```

```
        Synch Sequence
Window:              8192
Checksum:            0x57E7
Urgent Pointer:      0
TCP Options:
 Option Type: 2 Maximum Segment Size
   Length:    4
   MSS:       536
 Option Type: 1 No Operation
 Option Type: 1 No Operation
 Option Type: 4
   Length:    2
   Opt Value:
 No More HTTP Data
Frame Check Sequence: 0x43697363
```

And sure enough, the source port is over 1024, but the destination port is 80, or HTTP service. The server, or receiving host, will change the destination port if it needs to.

In the preceding trace, a "syn" packet is sent to the destination device. The syn sequence is what's telling the remote destination device that it wants to create a session.

TCP Session: Syn Packet Acknowledgment

The next trace shows an acknowledgment to the syn packet. Notice the "Ack is valid," which means the source port was accepted and the device agreed to create a virtual circuit with the originating host:

```
TCP - Transport Control Protocol
  Source Port:      80 World Wide Web HTTP
  Destination Port: 1144
  Sequence Number:  2873580788
  Ack Number:       9356571
  Offset:           6
  Reserved:         %000000
  Code:             %010010
      Ack is valid
      Synch Sequence
Window:              8576
Checksum:            0x5F85
```

```
        Urgent Pointer:   0
        TCP Options:
         Option Type: 2 Maximum Segment Size
            Length:   4
            MSS:      1460
         No More HTTP Data
       Frame Check Sequence: 0x6E203132
```

And here again, you can see that the response from the server shows the source is 80 and the destination is the 1144 sent from the originating host—all's well.

The Internet Layer Protocols

In the DoD model, there are two main reasons for the Internet layer's existence: routing, and providing a single network interface to the upper layers.

None of the other upper- or lower-layer protocols have any functions relating to routing—that complex and important task belongs entirely to the Internet layer. The Internet layer's second duty is to provide a single network interface to the upper-layer protocols. Without this layer, application programmers would need to write "hooks" into every one of their applications for each different Network Access protocol. This would not only be a pain in the neck, but it would lead to different versions of each application—one for Ethernet, another one for Token Ring, and so on. To prevent this, IP provides one single network interface for the upper-layer protocols. That accomplished, it's then the job of IP and the various Network Access protocols to get along and work together.

All network roads don't lead to Rome—they lead to IP. And all the other protocols at this layer, as well as all those at the upper layers, use it. Never forget that. All paths through the DoD model go through IP. The following sections describe the protocols at the Internet layer:

- Internet Protocol (IP)

- Internet Control Message Protocol (ICMP)

- Address Resolution Protocol (ARP)

- Reverse Address Resolution Protocol (RARP)

Internet Protocol (IP)

Internet Protocol (IP) essentially is the Internet layer. The other protocols found here merely exist to support it. IP holds the big picture and could be said to "see all," in that it's aware of all the interconnected networks. It can do this because all the machines on the network have a software, or logical, address called an IP address, which I'll cover more thoroughly later in this chapter.

IP looks at each packet's address. Then, using a routing table, it decides where a packet is to be sent next, choosing the best path. The protocols of the Network Access layer at the bottom of the DoD model don't possess IP's enlightened scope of the entire network; they deal only with physical links (local networks).

Identifying devices on networks requires answering these two questions: Which network is it on? And what is its ID on that network? The first answer is the *software address*, or *logical address* (the correct street). The second answer is the hardware address (the correct mailbox). All hosts on a network have a logical ID called an IP address. This is the software, or logical, address and contains valuable encoded information greatly simplifying the complex task of routing. (Please note that IP is discussed in RFC 791.)

IP receives segments from the Host-to-Host layer and fragments them into datagrams (packets). IP then reassembles datagrams back into segments on the receiving side. Each datagram is assigned the IP address of the sender and of the recipient. Each router (layer-3 device) that receives a datagram makes routing decisions based on the packet's destination IP address.

Figure 3.6 shows an IP header. This will give you an idea of what the IP protocol has to go through every time user data is sent from the upper layers and is to be sent to a remote network.

FIGURE 3.6 IP header

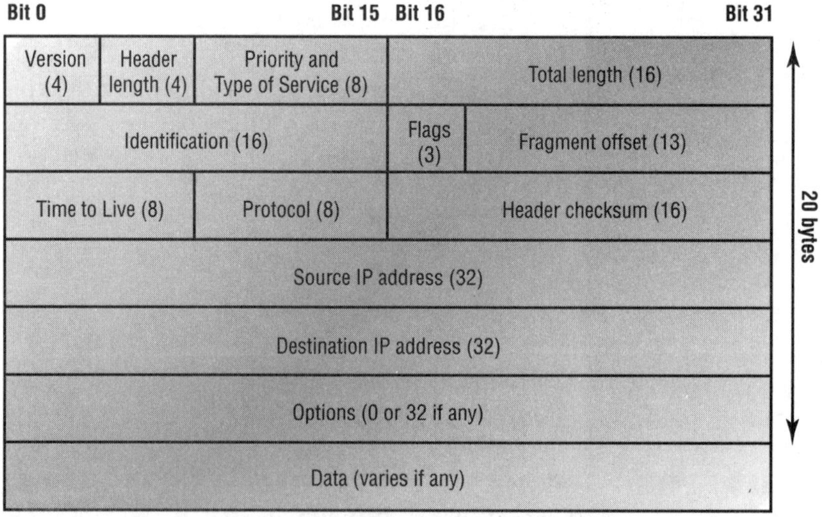

The following fields make up the IP header:

Version   IP version number.

HLEN   Header length in 32-bit words.

Priority or ToS   Type of Service tells how the datagram should be handled. The first three bits are the priority bits.

Total length   Length of the packet including header and data.

Identification   Unique IP-packet value.

Flags   Specifies whether fragmentation should occur.

Frag offset   Provides fragmentation and reassembly if the packet is too large to put in a frame. It also allows different maximum transmission units (MTUs) on the Internet.

TTL   The time to live is set into a packet when it is originally generated. If it doesn't get to where it wants to go before the TTL expires, boom— it's gone. This stops IP packets from continuously circling the network looking for a home.

Protocol   Port of upper-layer protocol (TCP is port 6 or UDP is port 17 [hex]).

Header checksum   Cyclic redundancy check (CRC) on header only.

Source IP address   32-bit IP address of sending station.

Destination IP address   32-bit IP address of the station this packet is destined for.

IP option   Used for network testing, debugging, security, and more.

Data   Upper-layer data.

Here's a snapshot of an IP packet caught on a network analyzer. Notice that all the information discussed above appears here:

```
IP Header - Internet Protocol Datagram
  Version:            4
  Header Length:      5
  Precedence:         0
  Type of Service:    %000
  Unused:             %00
```

```
Total Length:         187
Identifier:           22486
Fragmentation Flags:  %010 Do Not Fragment
Fragment Offset:      0
Time To Live:         60
IP Type:              0x06 TCP
Header Checksum:      0xd031
Source IP Address:    10.7.1.30
Dest. IP Address:     10.7.1.10
No Internet Datagram Options
```

Can you distinguish the logical, or IP, addresses in this header?

The Type field—it's typically a Protocol field, but this analyzer sees it as a Type field—is important. If the header didn't carry the protocol information for the next layer, IP wouldn't know what to do with the data carried in the packet. The example above tells IP to hand the segment to TCP.

Figure 3.7 demonstrates how the Network layer sees the protocols at the Transport layer when it needs to hand a packet to the upper-layer protocols.

FIGURE 3.7 The Protocol field in an IP header

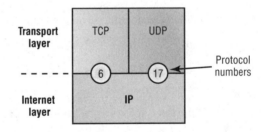

In this example, the Protocol field tells IP to send the data to either TCP port 6 or UDP port 17 (both hex addresses). However, it will only be UDP or TCP if the data is part of a data stream headed for an upper-layer service or application. It could just as easily be destined for ICMP (Internet Control Message Protocol), ARP (Address Resolution Protocol), or some other type of Network layer protocol.

Table 3.2 is a list of some other popular protocols that can be specified in the Protocol field.

TABLE 3.2 Possible Protocols Found in the Protocol Field of an IP Header

Protocol	Protocol Number
ICMP	1
IGRP	9
IPv6	41
GRE	47
IPX in IP	111
Layer-2 tunnel	115

Internet Control Message Protocol (ICMP)

Internet Control Message Protocol (ICMP) works at the Network layer and is used by IP for many different services. ICMP is a management protocol and messaging service provider for IP. Its messages are carried as IP datagrams. RFC 1256 is an annex to ICMP, which affords hosts' extended capability in discovering routes to gateways.

Periodically, router advertisements are announced over the network, reporting IP addresses for the router's network interfaces. Hosts listen for these network infomercials to acquire route information. A router solicitation is a request for immediate advertisements and may be sent by a host when it starts up.

RFC 1700 references ICMP and describes how ICMP must be implemented by all TCP/IP hosts.

The following are some common events and messages that ICMP relates to:

Destination Unreachable   If a router can't send an IP datagram any further, it uses ICMP to send a message back to the sender, advising it of the situation. For example, if a router receives a packet destined for a network that the router doesn't know about, it will send an ICMP Destination Unreachable message back to the sending station.

Buffer Full   If a router's memory buffer for receiving incoming datagrams is full, it will use ICMP to send out this message.

Hops   Each IP datagram is allotted a certain number of routers, called hops, that it may go through. If it reaches its limit of hops before arriving at its destination, the last router to receive that datagram deletes it. The executioner router then uses ICMP to send an obituary message, informing the sending machine of the demise of its datagram.

Ping   Ping (Packet Internet Groper) uses ICMP echo messages to check the physical connectivity of machines on an internetwork.

Traceroute   Using ICMP timeouts, Traceroute is used to discover the path a packet takes as it traverses an internetwork.

Both Ping and Traceroute (also just called Trace; Microsoft Windows uses tracert) allow you to verify address configurations in your internetwork.

The following data is from a network analyzer catching an ICMP echo request. Take a look at it—notice anything unusual? Do you catch the fact that even though ICMP works at the Internet layer, it still uses IP to do the Ping request? The Type field in the IP header is 0x01, which specifies the ICMP protocol.

```
Flags:          0x00
Status:         0x00
Packet Length: 78
Timestamp:      14:04:25.967000 05/06/2002
Ethernet Header
 Destination: 00:a0:24:6e:0f:a8
 Source:        00:80:c7:a8:f0:3d
 Ether-Type:  08-00 IP
IP Header - Internet Protocol Datagram
 Version:               4
 Header Length:         5
 Precedence:            0
 Type of Service:     %000
 Unused:              %00
```

```
Total Length:          60
Identifier:            56325
Fragmentation Flags:   %000
Fragment Offset:       0
Time To Live:          32
IP Type:               0x01 ICMP
Header Checksum:       0x2df0
Source IP Address:     100.100.100.2
Dest. IP Address:      100.100.100.1
No Internet Datagram Options
ICMP - Internet Control Messages Protocol
ICMP Type:             8 Echo Request
Code:                  0
Checksum:              0x395c
Identifier:            0x0300
Sequence Number: 4352
ICMP Data Area:
abcdefghijklmnop  61 62 63 64 65 66 67 68 69 6a 6b 6c 6d
qrstuvwabcdefghi  71 72 73 74 75 76 77 61 62 63 64 65 66
Frame Check Sequence: 0x00000000
```

The Ping program just uses the alphabet in the data portion of the packet as a payload, up to 100 bytes by default.

If you remember reading about the Data Link layer and the different frame types in Chapter 1, you should be able to look at the preceding trace and tell what type of Ethernet frame this is. The only fields are destination hardware address, source hardware address, and Ether-Type. The only frame that uses an Ether-Type field exclusively is an Ethernet_II frame. (SNAP uses an Ether-Type field also, but only within an 802.2 LLC field, which isn't present in the frame.)

Address Resolution Protocol (ARP)

Address Resolution Protocol (ARP) finds the hardware address of a host from a known IP address. Here's how it works: When IP has a datagram to send, it must inform a Network Access protocol, such as Ethernet or Token Ring, of the destination's hardware address on the local network. (It has already been informed by upper-layer protocols of the destination's IP address.) If IP doesn't find the destination host's hardware address in the ARP cache, it uses ARP to find this information.

As IP's detective, ARP interrogates the local network by sending out a broadcast asking the machine with the specified IP address to reply with its hardware address. In other words, ARP translates the software (IP) address into a hardware address—for example, the destination machine's Ethernet board address—and from it, deduces its whereabouts. Figure 3.8 shows how an ARP looks to a local network.

FIGURE 3.8 Local ARP broadcast

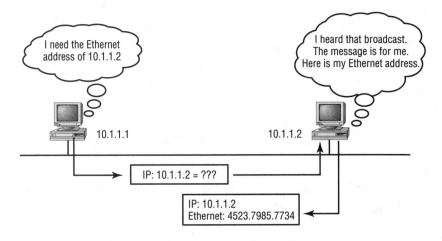

 ARP resolves IP addresses to Ethernet addresses.

The following trace shows an ARP broadcast. Notice that the destination hardware address is unknown, and is all Fs in hex (all 1s in binary), and a hardware address broadcast.

```
Flags:          0x00
Status:         0x00
Packet Length:  64
Timestamp:      09:17:29.574000 01/04/2002
```

```
Ethernet Header
 Destination:    FF:FF:FF:FF:FF:FF Ethernet Broadcast
 Source:         00:A0:24:48:60:A5
 Protocol Type: 0x0806 IP ARP
ARP - Address Resolution Protocol
 Hardware:                    1 Ethernet (10Mb)
 Protocol:                    0x0800 IP
 Hardware Address Length: 6
 Protocol Address Length: 4
 Operation:                   1 ARP Request
 Sender Hardware Address: 00:A0:24:48:60:A5
 Sender Internet Address: 172.16.10.3
 Target Hardware Address: 00:00:00:00:00:00 (ignored)
 Target Internet Address: 172.16.10.10
Extra bytes (Padding):
 ............... 0A 0A 0A 0A 0A 0A 0A 0A 0A 0A 0A 0A 0A
 0A 0A 0A 0A 0A
 Frame Check Sequence: 0x00000000
```

Reverse Address Resolution Protocol (RARP)

When an IP machine happens to be a diskless machine, it has no way of initially knowing its IP address, but it does know its MAC address. *Reverse Address Resolution Protocol (RARP)* discovers the identity of the IP address for diskless machines by sending out a packet that includes its MAC address and a request for the IP address assigned to that MAC address. A designated machine, called a *RARP server,* responds with the answer, and the identity crisis is over. RARP uses the information it does know about the machine's MAC address to learn its IP address and complete the machine's ID portrait.

RARP resolves Ethernet addresses to IP addresses.

Figure 3.9 shows a diskless workstation asking for its IP address with a RARP broadcast.

FIGURE 3.9 RARP broadcast example

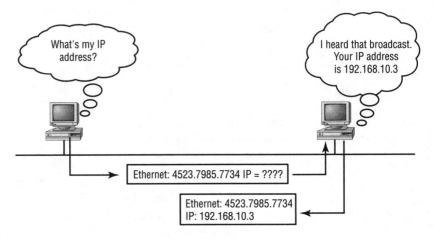

IP Addressing

One of the most important topics in any discussion of TCP/IP is IP addressing. An *IP address* is a numeric identifier assigned to each machine on an IP network. It designates the specific location of a device on the network.

An IP address is a software address, not a hardware address—the latter is hard-coded on a network interface card (NIC) and used for finding hosts on a local network. IP addressing was designed to allow a host on one network to communicate with a host on a different network, regardless of the type of LANs the hosts are participating in.

Before we get into the more complicated aspects of IP addressing, you need to understand some of the basics. First, I'm going to explain some of the fundamentals of IP addressing and its terminology. Later on, you'll learn about the hierarchical IP addressing scheme and then, subnetting.

To understand IP addressing and subnetting, it's important to have already mastered binary-to-decimal conversion and the powers of 2 (exponents). If you need to review these topics, see the upcoming sidebars that cover these subjects.

IP Terminology

Throughout this chapter you'll learn several important terms vital to your understanding of the Internet Protocol. Here are a few to get you started:

Bit   A *bit* is one digit; either a 1 or a 0.

Byte   A *byte* is 7 or 8 bits, depending on whether parity is used. For the rest of this chapter, always assume a byte is 8 bits.

Octet   Always 8 bits. Base-8 addressing scheme.

Network address   The designation used in routing to send packets to a remote network—for example, 10.0.0.0, 172.16.0.0, and 192.168.10.0.

Broadcast address   The address used by applications and hosts to send information to all nodes on a network is called the *broadcast address*. Examples include 255.255.255.255, which is all networks, all nodes; 172.16.255.255, which is all subnets and hosts on network 172.16.0.0; and 10.255.255.255, which broadcasts to all subnets and hosts on network 10.0.0.0.

The Hierarchical IP Addressing Scheme

An IP address consists of 32 bits of information. These bits are divided into four sections, referred to as *octets* or bytes, each containing 1 byte (8 bits). You can depict an IP address using one of three methods:

- Dotted-decimal, as in 172.16.30.56

- Binary, as in 10101100.00010000.00011110.00111000

- Hexadecimal, as in AC 10 1E 38

All these examples represent the same IP address. Although hexadecimal isn't used as often as dotted-decimal or binary when IP addressing is discussed, you still might find an IP address stored in hexadecimal in some programs. The Windows Registry is a good example of a program that stores a machine's IP address in hex.

The 32-bit IP address is a structured or hierarchical address, as opposed to a flat or nonhierarchical, address. Although either type of addressing scheme could have been used, *hierarchical addressing* was chosen for a good reason. The advantage of this scheme is that it can handle a large number of addresses, namely 4.3 billion (a 32-bit address space with two possible values for each position—either 0 or 1—gives you 2^{32}, or 4,294,967,296). The disadvantage of the flat addressing scheme, and the reason it's not used for IP addressing, relates to routing. If every address were unique, all routers on the Internet would need to store the address of each and every machine on the Internet. This would make efficient routing impossible, even if only a fraction of the possible addresses were used.

The solution to this dilemma is to use a two- or three-level, hierarchical addressing scheme that is structured by network and host, or network, subnet, and host.

This two- or three-level scheme is comparable to a telephone number. The first section, the area code, designates a very large area. The second section, the prefix, narrows the scope to a local calling area. The final segment, the customer number, zooms in on the specific connection. IP addresses use the same type of layered structure. Rather than all 32 bits being treated as a unique identifier, as in flat addressing, a part of the address is designated as the network address, and the other part is designated as either the subnet and host, or just the node address.

Network Addressing

The *network address* uniquely identifies each network. Every machine on the same network shares that network address as part of its IP address. In the IP address 172.16.30.56, for example, 172.16 is the network address.

The *node address* is assigned to, and uniquely identifies, each machine on a network. This part of the address must be unique because it identifies a particular machine—an individual—as opposed to a network, which is a group. This number can also be referred to as a *host address*. In the sample IP address 172.16.30.56, the 30.56 is the node address.

The designers of the Internet decided to create classes of networks based on network size. For the small number of networks possessing a very large number of nodes, they created the rank *Class A network*. At the other extreme is the *Class C network*, which is reserved for the numerous networks with a small number of nodes. The class distinction for networks between very large and very small is predictably called the *Class B network*.

Subdividing an IP address into a network and node address is determined by the class designation of one's network. Figure 3.10 summarizes the three classes of networks—a subject I'll explain in much greater detail throughout this chapter.

FIGURE 3.10 Summary of the three classes of networks

	8 bits	8 bits	8 bits	8 bits
Class A:	Network	Host	Host	Host
Class B:	Network	Network	Host	Host
Class C:	Network	Network	Network	Host
Class D:	Multicast			
Class E:	Research			

To ensure efficient routing, Internet designers defined a mandate for the leading-bits section of the address for each different network class. For example, since a router knows that a Class A network address always starts with a 0, the router might be able to speed a packet on its way after reading only the first bit of its address. This is where the address schemes define the difference between a Class A, Class B, and Class C address.

Network Address Range: Class A

The designers of the IP address scheme said that the first bit of the first byte in a Class A network address must always be off, or 0. This means a Class A address must be between 0 and 127.

Consider the following network address:

0xxxxxxx

If we turn the other 7 bits all off and then turn them all on, we'll find your Class A range of network addresses:

00000000 = 0
01111111 = 127

So, a Class A network is defined in the first octet between 0 and 127, and it can't be less or more. (I'll talk about illegal addresses in a minute.)

If you are having any difficulty with the binary-to-decimal conversions, please read the "Binary-to-Decimal Conversion Review" sidebar.

Binary-to-Decimal Conversion Review

Prior to learning about IP addressing, you must have a fundamental understanding of binary-to-decimal conversions. Here is how it works: Binary numbers use 8 bits to define a decimal number. These bits are weighted from right to left in an increment that doubles in value.

Here's an example of 8 bits and the value assigned to each bit:

```
128  64  32  16  8  4  2  1
```

Here's an example of binary-to-decimal conversion:

```
128  64  32  16  8  4  2  1  Binary value
  0   0   1   0  0  1  1  0  Byte in binary
```

Add the value of the bits that are turned on:

```
    32
     4
     2
 =  38
```

Any time you find a bit turned on (a one), you add the values of each bit position. Let's practice on a few more:

```
01010101 = 85
64
   16
       4
          1
            = 85
```

Try a few on your own:

```
00001111 = 15
10001100 = 140
11001100 = 204
```

You'll need to memorize the binary-to-decimal conversions in the following list, because you'll really find yourself using this information a lot when you practice subnetting later in this chapter:

```
00000000 = 0
10000000 = 128
11000000 = 192
11100000 = 224
11110000 = 240
11111000 = 248
11111100 = 252
11111110 = 254
11111111 = 255
```

Network Address Range: Class B

In a Class B network, the RFCs state that the first bit of the first byte must always be turned on, but the second bit must always be turned off. If you turn the other six bits all off and then all on, you will find the range for a Class B network:

10000000 = 128
10111111 = 191

As you can see, this means that a Class B network is defined when the first byte is configured from 128 to 191.

Network Address Range: Class C

For Class C networks, the RFCs define the first two bits of the first octet always turned on, but the third bit can never be on. Following the same process as the previous classes, convert from binary to decimal to find the range. Here's the range for a Class C network:

11000000 = 192
11011111 = 223

So, if you see an IP address that starts at 192 and goes to 223, you'll know it is a Class C IP address.

Network Address Ranges: Classes D and E

The addresses between 224 and 255 are reserved for Class D and E networks. Class D is used for multicast addresses (224–239) and Class E (240–255) for scientific purposes, but I'm not going into these types of addresses in this book (and you don't need to know them for the exam).

Network Addresses: Special Purpose

Some IP addresses are reserved for special purposes, so network administrators can't ever assign these addresses to nodes. Table 3.3 lists the members of this exclusive little club and why they're included in it.

TABLE 3.3   Reserved IP Addresses

Address	Function
Network address of all 0s	Interpreted to mean "this network or segment."
Network address of all 1s	Interpreted to mean "all networks."
Network 127.0.0.1	Reserved for loopback tests. Designates the local node and allows that node to send a test packet to itself without generating network traffic.
Node address of all 0s	Interpreted to mean "this node."
Node address of all 1s	Interpreted to mean "all nodes" on the specified network; for example, 128.2.255.255 means "all nodes" on network 128.2 (Class B address).
Entire IP address set to all 0s	Used by Cisco routers to designate the default route.
Entire IP address set to all 1s (same as 255.255.255.255)	Broadcast to all nodes on the current network; sometimes called an "all 1s broadcast."

Class A Addresses

In a Class A network address, the first byte is assigned to the network address, and the three remaining bytes are used for the node addresses. The Class A format is

`network.node.node.node`

For example, in the IP address 49.22.102.70, the 49 is the network address, and 22.102.70 is the node address. Every machine on this particular network would have the distinctive network address of 49.

Class A network addresses are one byte long, with the first bit of that byte reserved and the seven remaining bits available for manipulation. As a result, the maximum number of Class A networks that can be created is 128. Why? Because each of the seven bit positions can either be a 0 or a 1, thus 2^7 or 128.

To complicate matters further, the network address of all 0s (0000 0000) is reserved to designate the default route (see Table 3.3 in the previous section). Additionally, the address 127, which is reserved for diagnostics, can't be used either, which means that you can really only use the numbers 1 to 126 to designate Class A network addresses. This means the actual number of usable Class A network addresses is 128 minus 2, or 126.

Each Class A address has three bytes (24-bit positions) for the node address of a machine. This means there are 2^{24}—or 16,777,216—unique combinations and, therefore, precisely that many possible unique node addresses for each Class A network. Because addresses with the two patterns of all 0s and all 1s are reserved, the actual maximum usable number of nodes for a Class A network is 2^{24} minus 2, which equals 16,777,214. Either way, that's a huge amount of hosts on a network segment!

Class A Valid Host IDs

Here's an example of how to figure out the valid host IDs in a Class A network address:

- All host bits off is the network address: 10.0.0.0.
- All host bits on is the broadcast address: 10.255.255.255.

The valid hosts are the number in between the network address and the broadcast address: 10.0.0.1 through 10.255.255.254. Notice that 0s and 255s can be valid host IDs. All you need to remember when trying to find valid host addresses is that the host bits can't all be turned off or all be on at the same time.

Class B Addresses

In a Class B network address, the first two bytes are assigned to the network address, and the remaining two bytes are used for node addresses. The format is:

`network.network.node.node`

For example, in the IP address 172.16.30.56, the network address is 172.16, and the node address is 30.56.

With a network address being two bytes (eight bits each), there would be 2^{16} unique combinations. But the Internet designers decided that all Class B network addresses should start with the binary digit 1, then 0. This leaves 14 bit positions to manipulate, therefore 16,384 (that is, 2^{14}) unique Class B network addresses.

A Class B address uses two bytes for node addresses. This is 2^{16} minus the two reserved patterns (all 0s and all 1s), for a total of 65,534 possible node addresses for each Class B network.

Class B Valid Host IDs

Here's an example of how to find the valid hosts in a Class B network:

- All host bits turned off is the network address: 172.16.0.0.

- All host bits turned on is the broadcast address: 172.16.255.255.

The valid hosts would be the numbers in between the network address and the broadcast address: 172.16.0.1 through 172.16.255.254.

Class C Addresses

The first three bytes of a Class C network address are dedicated to the network portion of the address, with only one measly byte remaining for the node address. The format is

`network.network.network.node`

Using the example IP address 192.168.100.102, the network address is 192.168.100, and the node address is 102.

In a Class C network address, the first three bit positions are always the binary 110. The calculation is such: 3 bytes, or 24 bits, minus 3 reserved positions, leaves 21 positions. Hence, there are 2^{21}, or 2,097,152, possible Class C networks.

Each unique Class C network has one byte to use for node addresses. This leads to 2^8 or 256, minus the two reserved patterns of all 0s and all 1s, for a total of 254 node addresses for each Class C network.

Class C Valid Host IDs

Here's an example of how to find a valid host ID in a Class C network:

- All host bits turned off is the network ID: 192.168.100.0.

- All host bits turned on is the broadcast address: 192.168.100.255.

The valid hosts would be the numbers in between the network address and the broadcast address: 192.168.100.1 through 192.168.100.254.

Subnetting

Okay, you've just learned how to define and find the valid host ranges used in a Class A, Class B, and Class C network address by turning the host bits all off and then all on. This is very good, but here's the catch: You were only defining one network. What happens if you wanted to take one network address and create six networks from it? You would have to do something called *subnetting*, because that's what allows you to take one larger network and break it into a bunch of smaller networks.

There are loads of reasons in favor of subnetting. Some of the benefits include:

Reduced network traffic   We all appreciate less traffic of any kind. Networks are no different. Without trusty routers, packet traffic could grind the entire network down to a near standstill. With routers, most traffic will stay on the local network; only packets destined for other networks will pass through the router. Routers create broadcast domains. The smaller broadcast domains you create, the less network traffic on that network segment.

Optimized network performance   This is a result of reduced network traffic.

Simplified management   It's easier to identify and isolate network problems in a group of smaller connected networks than within one gigantic network.

Facilitated spanning of large geographical distances   Because WAN links are considerably slower and more expensive than LAN links, a single large network that spans long distances can create problems in every arena listed above. Connecting multiple smaller networks makes the system more efficient.

To create subnetworks, you take bits from the host portion of the IP address and reserve them to define the subnet address. This means fewer bits for hosts, so the more subnets, the fewer bits available for defining hosts.

In this section you will learn how to create subnets, starting with Class C addresses. But before you actually implement subnetting, you need to determine your current requirements as well as plan for future conditions. Follow these steps:

1. Determine the number of required network IDs:

   • One for each subnet

   • One for each wide area network connection

2. Determine the number of required host IDs per subnet:

   • One for each TCP/IP host

   • One for each router interface

3. Based on the above requirement, create the following:

   • One subnet mask for your entire network

   • A unique subnet ID for each physical segment

   • A range of host IDs for each subnet

Understanding the Powers of 2

Powers of 2 are important to understand and memorize for use with IP subnetting. To review powers of 2, remember that when you see a number with another number to its upper right (called an exponent), this means you should multiply the number by itself as many times as the upper number specifies. For example, 2^3 is $2 \times 2 \times 2$, which equals 8. Here's the list of powers of 2 you should commit to memory:

$2^1 = 2$

$2^2 = 4$

$2^3 = 8$

$2^4 = 16$

$2^5 = 32$

$2^6 = 64$

$2^7 = 128$

$2^8 = 256$

Subnet Masks

For the subnet address scheme to work, every machine on the network must know which part of the host address will be used as the subnet address. This is accomplished by assigning a *subnet mask* to each machine. A subnet mask is a 32-bit value that allows the recipient of IP packets to distinguish the network ID portion of the IP address from the host ID portion of the IP address.

The network administrator creates a 32-bit subnet mask composed of 1s and 0s. The 1s in the subnet mask represent the positions that refer to the network or subnet addresses.

Not all networks need subnets, meaning they use the default subnet mask. This is basically the same as saying that a network doesn't have a subnet address. Table 3.4 shows the default subnet masks for Classes A, B, and C. These cannot change. In other words, you can't make a Class B subnet mask read 255.0.0.0. If you try, the host will read that address as invalid and usually won't even let you type it in. For a Class A network, you can't change the first byte in a subnet mask; it must read 255.0.0.0 at a minimum. Similarly, you cannot assign 255.255.255.255, as this is all 1s—a broadcast address. A Class B address must start with 255.255.0.0, and a Class C has to start with 255.255.255.0.

TABLE 3.4   Default Subnet Mask

Class	Format	Default Subnet Mask
A	*network.node.node.node*	255.0.0.0
B	*network.network.node.node*	255.255.0.0
C	*network.network.network.node*	255.255.255.0

Subnetting Class C Addresses

There are many different ways to subnet a network. The right way is the way that works best for you. First I'll show you how to use the binary method, and then we'll look at an easier way to do the same thing.

In a Class C address, only 8 bits are available for defining the hosts. Remember that subnet bits start at the left and go to the right, without skipping bits. This means that the only Class C subnet masks can be:

```
Binary       Decimal  Shorthand
-------------------------------------------------------------
10000000 = 128        /25   (Not valid on the Cisco exams!)
11000000 = 192        /26
11100000 = 224        /27
11110000 = 240        /28
11111000 = 248        /29
11111100 = 252        /30
11111110 = 254        /31   (Not valid)
```

Now, the RFCs say that you can't have only one bit for subnetting, since that would mean that the subnet bit would always be either off or on, which is illegal. So, the first subnet mask you can legally use is 192, and the last one is 252 because you need at least two bits for defining hosts.

In production, you can use one bit for assigning subnets. This is called *subnet-zero*. But know that Cisco doesn't consider subnet-zero valid on any of their certification exams!

Okay, what the heck does the /25, /26, etc., mean? This just means how many bits are used in the subnet mask. Since all of these masks are Class C addresses, the mask at a minimum must be 255.255.255.0, which is 24 bits (8 bits in each octet), or /24. The "slash" address convention is just an easy way to identify the mask without having to write out the whole mask; you can write the combination of address 192.168.10.0 and subnet mask 255.255.255.0 as 192.168.10.0/24. (No, you cannot configure a Cisco router using this format).

Another example is 255.255.255.192, or /26. Remember that each octet has a maximum of 8 bits. The first three octets have all bits in use, so that is 24 bits ($8 \times 3 = 24$), plus two bits in the fourth octet for a total of 26 bits, or /26.

The Binary Method: Subnetting a Class C Address

In this section, I'm going to teach you how to subnet a Class C address using the binary method. I'll start by using the first subnet mask available with a Class C address, which borrows two bits from subnetting. For this example, I'll be using 255.255.255.192.

```
192 = 11000000
```

The 1s represent the subnet bits, and the 0s represent the host bits available in each subnet. 192 provides two bits for subnetting and six bits for defining the hosts in each subnet.

What are the subnets? Since the subnet bits can't be both off or on at the same time, the only two valid subnets are these two:

01000000 = 64 (all host bits off)

10000000 = 128 (all host bits off)

The valid hosts would be defined as the numbers between the subnets, minus the all-host-bits-off and all-host-bits-on numbers.

To find the hosts, first find your subnet by turning all the host bits off, then turn all the host bits on to find your broadcast address for the subnet. The valid hosts must be between those two numbers. Table 3.5 shows the 64 subnet, valid host range, and broadcast address.

TABLE 3.5 Subnet 64

Subnet	Host	Meaning
01	000000 = 64	The network (do this first)
01	000001 = 65	The first valid host
01	111110 = 126	The last valid host
01	111111 = 127	The broadcast address (do this second)

Table 3.6 shows the 128 subnet, valid host range, and broadcast address.

TABLE 3.6 Subnet 128

Subnet	Host	Meaning
10	000000 = 128	The subnet address
10	000001 = 129	The first valid host

TABLE 3.6 Subnet 128 *(continued)*

Subnet	Host	Meaning
10	111110 = 190	The last valid host
10	111111 = 191	The broadcast address

That wasn't all that hard, was it? Hopefully, you understood what I was trying to show you. The example I presented only used two subnet bits, so what if you had to subnet using 9, 10, or even 20 subnet bits? Try that with the binary method and see how long it takes you. Since the Cisco CCNA exam gives you just over a minute for each question, it's really important to know how much time you'll spend on a subnetting question. That's why committing as much as possible to memory as I suggested earlier in the chapter is vital. Using the binary method can take you way too long and you could fail the exam even if you know the material!

This is why I'm going to teach you an alternate method of subnetting that makes it easier to subnet larger numbers in no time.

The Fast Way: Subnetting a Class C Address

When you've chosen a possible subnet mask for your network and need to determine the number of subnets, valid hosts, and broadcast address that the mask provides, all you need to do is answer five simple questions:

- How many subnets does the chosen subnet mask produce?

- How many valid hosts per subnet are available?

- What are the valid subnets?

- What's the broadcast address of each subnet?

- What are the valid hosts in each subnet?

At this point it's important that you both understand and have memorized your powers of 2. Please refer to the sidebar earlier in this chapter if you need some help. Here's how you get the answers to those five big questions:

- *How many subnets?* $2^x - 2$ = number of subnets. x is the number of masked bits, or the 1s. For example, in 11000000, the number of ones gives us $2^2 - 2$ subnets. In this example, there are 2 subnets.

- *How many hosts per subnet?* $2^x - 2$ = number of hosts per subnet. x is the number of unmasked bits, or the 0s. For example, in 11000000, the number of zeros gives us $2^6 - 2$ hosts. In this example, there are 62 hosts per subnet.

- *What are the valid subnets?* 256 – subnet mask = block size, or base number. For example, 256 – 192 = 64. 64 is the first subnet. The next subnet would be the base number itself, or 64 + 64 = 128, (the second subnet). You keep adding the base number to itself until you reach the value of the subnet mask, which is not a valid subnet because all subnet bits would be turned on (1s).

- *What's the broadcast address for each subnet?* The broadcast address is all host bits turned on, which is the number immediately preceding the next subnet.

- *What are the valid hosts?* Valid hosts are the numbers between the subnets, minus all 0s and all 1s.

I know this can truly seem confusing. But it really isn't as hard as it seems to be at first—just hang in there! Why not try a few and see for yourself?

Subnetting Practice Examples: Class C Addresses

Here's your opportunity to practice subnetting Class C addresses using the method I just described. We're going to start with the first Class C subnet mask and work through every subnet that we can using a Class C address. When we're done, I'll show you how easy this is with Class A and B networks too!

Practice Example #1C: 255.255.255.192 (/26)

Let's use the Class C subnet mask from the preceding example, 255.255.255.192, to see how much simpler this method is than writing out the binary numbers. We're going to subnet the network address 192.168.10.0 and subnet mask 255.255.255.192.

192.168.10.0 = Network address

255.255.255.192 = Subnet mask

Now, let's answer the big five:

- *How many subnets?* Since 192 is two bits on (**11000000**), the answer would be $2^2 - 2 = 2$. (The minus 2 is the subnet bits all on or all off, which are not valid by default.)

- *How many hosts per subnet?* We have 6 host bits off (11000000), so the equation would be $2^6 - 2 = 62$ hosts.

- *What are the valid subnets?* $256 - 192 = 64$, which is the first subnet and our base number or variable. Keep adding the variable to itself until you reach the subnet mask. $64 + 64 = 128$. $128 + 64 = 192$, which is invalid because it is the subnet mask (all subnet bits turned on). Our two valid subnets are, then, 64 and 128.

- *What's the broadcast address for each subnet?* The number right before the next subnet is all host bits turned on and equals the broadcast address.

- *What are the valid hosts?* These are the numbers between the subnets. The easiest way to find the hosts is to write out the subnet address and the broadcast address. This way the valid hosts are obvious. The following table shows the 64 and 128 subnets, the valid host ranges of each, and the broadcast address of both subnets.

	64	128
The subnets (do this first)	64	128
Our first host (perform host addressing last)	65	129
Our last host	126	190
The broadcast address (do this second)	127	191

See? We really did come up with the same answers as when we did it the binary way, and this way is so much easier because you never have to do any binary-to-decimal conversions! About now, you might be thinking that it's not easier than the first method I showed you. And I'll admit, for the first subnet with only two subnet bits—you're right, it isn't that much easier. But remember, we're going after the gold: being able to subnet in your head. And to do that, you need one thing: practice!

Practice Example #2C: 255.255.255.224 (/27)

This time, we'll subnet the network address 192.168.10.0 and subnet mask 255.255.255.224.

192.168.10.0 = Network address

255.255.255.224 = Subnet mask

- *How many subnets?* 224 is 11100000, so our equation would be $2^3 - 2 = 6$.

- *How many hosts?* $2^5 - 2 = 30$.

- *What are the valid subnets?* $256 - 224 = 32$. $32 + 32 = 64$. $64 + 32 = 96$. $96 + 32 = 128$. $128 + 32 = 160$. $160 + 32 = 192$. $192 + 32 = 224$, which is invalid because it is our subnet mask (all subnet bits on). Our subnets are 32, 64, 96, 128, 160, and 192.

- *What's the broadcast address for each subnet (always the number right before the next subnet)?*

- *What are the valid hosts (the numbers between the subnet number and the broadcast address)?*

To answer questions 4 and 5, first just write out the subnets, then write out the broadcast addresses—the number right before the next subnet. Lastly, fill in the host addresses. The following table gives you all the subnets for the 255.255.255.224 Class C subnet mask.

The subnet address	32	64	96	128	160	192
The first valid host	33	65	97	129	161	193
The last valid host	62	94	126	158	190	222
The broadcast address	63	95	127	159	191	223

Practice Example #3C: 255.255.255.240 (/28)

Let's practice on another one:

192.168.10.0 = Network address

255.255.255.240 = Subnet mask

- *Subnets?* 240 is 11110000 in binary. $2^4 - 2 = 14$.

- *Hosts?* Four host bits, or $2^4 - 2 = 14$.

- *Valid subnets?* $256 - 240 = 16$. $16 + 16 = 32$. $32 + 16 = 48$. $48 + 16 = 64$. $64 + 16 = 80$. $80 + 16 = 96$. $96 + 16 = 112$. $112 + 16 = 128$. $128 + 16 = 144$. $144 + 16 = 160$. $160 + 16 = 176$. $176 + 16 = 192$. $192 + 16 = 208$. $208 + 16 = 224$. $224 + 16 = 240$, which is our subnet mask and therefore invalid. So, our valid subnets are 16, 32, 48, 64, 80, 96, 112, 128, 144, 160, 176, 192, 208, and 224.

- *Broadcast address for each subnet?*

- *Valid hosts?*

To answer questions 4 and 5, check out the following table. It gives you the subnets, valid hosts, and broadcast addresses for each subnet. First, find the broadcast address of each subnet (it's always the number right before the next valid subnet), then just fill in the host addresses.

Subnet	16	32	48	64	80	96	112	128	144	160	176	192	208	224
First host	17	33	49	65	81	97	113	129	145	161	177	193	209	225
Last host	30	46	62	78	94	110	126	142	158	174	190	206	222	238
Broadcast	31	47	63	79	95	111	127	143	159	175	191	207	223	239

Practice Example #4C: 255.255.255.248 (/29)

Let's keep practicing:

192.168.10.0 = Network address

255.255.255.248 = Subnet mask

- *Subnets?* 248 in binary = 11111000. $2^5 - 2 = 30$.

- *Hosts?* $2^3 - 2 = 6$.

- *Valid subnets?* $256 - 248 = 8$, 16, 24, 32, 40, 48, 56, 64, 72, 80, 88, 96, 104, 112, 120, 128, 136, 144, 152, 160, 168, 176, 184, 192, 200, 208, 216, 224, 232, and 240.

- *Broadcast address for each subnet?*

- *Valid hosts?*

Okay, take a look at the following table… it shows some of the subnets (first three and last three only), valid hosts, and broadcast addresses for the Class C 255.255.255.248 mask.

Subnet	8	16	24	...	224	232	240
First host	9	17	25	...	225	233	241
Last host	14	22	30	...	230	238	246
Broadcast	15	23	31	...	231	239	247

Practice Example #5C: 255.255.255.252 (/30)

Just a couple more:

192.168.10.0 = Network address

255.255.255.252 = Subnet mask

- *Subnets?* 62.

- *Hosts?* 2.

- *Valid subnets?* 4, 8, 12, etc., all the way to 248.

- *Broadcast address for each subnet?* (always the number right before the next subnet)

- *Valid hosts?* (the numbers between the subnet number and the broadcast address)

The following table shows you the subnet, valid host, and broadcast address of the first three and last three subnets in the 255.255.255.252 Class C subnet.

Subnet	4	8	12	...	240	244	248
First host	5	9	13	...	241	245	249
Last host	6	10	14	...	242	246	250
Broadcast	7	11	15	...	243	247	251

 Real World Scenario

Should we really use this mask that provides only two hosts?

Yes, this is a very helpful mask in wide area network (WAN) networks. Think about this as if you had dozens of WAN links connecting to your corporate office. If you use the 255.255.255.0 mask, then each network would have 254 hosts, but you only use two addresses! That is a waste of 252 hosts per subnet. If you use the 255.255.255.252 mask, then each subnet has only two hosts and you don't waste precious addresses.

Practice Example #6C: 255.255.255.128 (/25)

I know I told you that using only one subnet bit was considered illegal in the original RFCs and that you ought not to do that. But aren't most rules meant to be broken? This mask can be used when you need two subnets, each with 126 hosts. But our trusty big five questions won't work with this one—it's special—so I'll just explain it to you. First, use the global configuration command `ip subnet-zero` to tell your router to break the rules and use a 1-bit subnet mask (this is a default command on all routers running the 12.*x* Cisco IOS).

Since 128 is 1000000 in binary, there is only one bit for subnetting. Since this bit can be either off or on, the two available subnets are 0 and 128. You can determine the subnet value by looking at the decimal value of the fourth octet. If the valid of the fourth octet is below 128, then the host is in the 0 subnet. If the fourth octet value is above 128, then the host is in the 128 subnet.

The following table shows you the two subnets, valid host ranges, and broadcast addresses for the Class C 255.255.255.128 mask.

Subnet	0	128
First host	1	129
Last host	126	254
Broadcast	127	255

So, if you have an IP address of 192.168.10.5 using the 255.255.255.128 subnet mask, you know it's in the range of the 0 subnet and bit number 128 must be off. If you have an IP address of 192.168.10.189, then 128 must be on, and the host is considered to be in the 128 subnet. You'll see this again in a minute.

Okay, this is a point of much confusion. Cisco says it is okay to use this mask in production, but then considers this invalid or illegal on the Cisco exams. Cisco is saying, "do as we say, not as we do." Remember for the exam that one subnet bit is considered wrong and will be considered invalid.

Subnetting in Your Head: Class C Addresses

I'm not lying—I promise! It really is possible to subnet in your head. Even if you don't you believe me, I'll show you how. And it's not all that hard either—take the following example:

192.168.10.33 = Node address

255.255.255.224 = Subnet mask

First, determine the subnet and broadcast address of the above IP address. You can do this by answering question 3 of the big five questions. 256 − 224 = 32. 32 + 32 = 64. Woohooo! The address falls between the two subnets and must be part of the 192.168.10.32 subnet. The next subnet is 64, so the broadcast address is 63. (Remember that the broadcast address of a subnet is always the number right before the next subnet.) The valid host range is 33–62. This is too easy! No, it's not?

Okay, then let's try another one. We'll subnet another Class C address:

192.168.10.33 = Node address

255.255.255.240 = Subnet mask

What subnet and broadcast address is the above IP address a member of? 256 – 240 = 16. 16 + 16 = 32. 32 + 16 = 48. And bingo—the host address is between the 32 and 48 subnets. The subnet is 192.168.10.32, and the broadcast address is 47. The valid host range is 33–46.

Okay, we need to do more, just to make sure you have this down!

You have a node address of 192.168.10.174 with a mask of 255.255.255.240. What is the valid host range?

The mask is 240, so we'd do a 256 – 240 = 16. This our block size. Just keep adding 16 until we pass the host address of 174: 16, 32, 48, 64, 80, 96, 112, 128, 144, 160, 176. Whew... we made it. The host address of 174 is between 160 and 176, so the subnet is 160. The broadcast address is 175, so the valid host range is 161–174. That was a tough one.

One more—just for fun. This is the easiest one of all Class C subnetting:

192.168.10.17 = Node address

255.255.255.252 = Subnet mask

What subnet and broadcast address is the above IP address a member of? 256 – 252 = 4, 8, 12, 16, 20 . You've got it! The host address is between the 16 and 20 subnets. The subnet is 192.168.10.16, and the broadcast address is 19. The valid host range is 17–18.

Now that you're all over Class C subnetting, Let's move on to Class B subnetting!

Subnetting Class B Addresses

Before we dive into this, let's look at all the possible Class B subnet masks first. Notice that we have a lot more possible subnets than we do with a Class C network address:

255.255.128.0	(/17)	255.255.255.0	(/24)
255.255.192.0	(/18)	255.255.255.128	(/25)
255.255.224.0	(/19)	255.255.255.192	(/26)

```
255.255.240.0   (/20)        255.255.255.224   (/27)
255.255.248.0   (/21)        255.255.255.240   (/28)
255.255.252.0   (/22)        255.255.255.248   (/29)
255.255.254.0   (/23)        255.255.255.252   (/30)
```

We know the Class B network address has 16 bits available for host addressing. This means we can use up to 14 bits for subnetting because we have to leave at least two bits for host addressing.

By the way, do you notice anything interesting about that list of subnet values—a pattern maybe? Ah ha! That's exactly why I had you memorize the binary-to-decimal numbers at the beginning of this section. Since subnet mask bits start on the left, move to the right, and can't skip bits, the numbers are always the same. Memorize this pattern.

The process of subnetting a Class B network is pretty much the same as it is for a Class C, except that you just have more host bits. Use the same subnet numbers you used with Class C, but add a zero to the network portion and a 255 to the broadcast section in the fourth octet. The following table shows you a host range of two subnets used in a Class B subnet:

16.0   32.0

16.255   32.255

Just add the valid hosts between the numbers, and you're set!

Subnetting Practice Examples: Class B Addresses

This section will give you an opportunity to practice subnetting Class B addresses.

Practice Example #1B: 255.255.192.0 (/18)

172.16.0.0 = Network address

255.255.192.0 = Subnet mask

- *Subnets?* $2^2 - 2 = 2$.

- *Hosts?* $2^{14} - 2 = 16,382$. (6 bits in the third octet, and 8 in the fourth.)

- *Valid subnets?* $256 - 192 = 64$. $64 + 64 = 128$.

- *Broadcast address for each subnet?*

- *Valid hosts?*

The following table shows the two subnets available, the valid host range, and the broadcast address of each:

Subnet	64.0	128.0
First host	64.1	128.1
Last host	127.254	191.254
Broadcast	127.255	191.255

Notice that we just added the fourth octet's lowest and highest values and came up with the answers. Again, it's pretty much the same as it is for a Class C subnet—we just added 0 and 255 in the fourth octet.

Practice Example #2B: 255.255.240.0 (/20)

172.16.0.0 = Network address

255.255.240.0 = Subnet address

- *Subnets?* $2^4 - 2 = 14$.

- *Hosts?* $2^{12} - 2 = 4094$.

- *Valid subnets?* $256 - 240 = 16, 32, 48$, etc., up to 224. Notice these are the same numbers as a Class C 240 mask.

- *Broadcast address for each subnet?*

- *Valid hosts?*

The following table shows the first three subnets, valid hosts, and broadcast addresses in a Class B 255.255.240.0 mask:

Subnet	16.0	32.0	48.0	...
First host	16.1	32.1	48.1	...
Last host	31.254	47.254	63.254	...
Broadcast	31.255	47.255	63.255	...

Practice Example #3B: 255.255.254.0 (/23)

- *Subnets?* $2^7 - 2 = 126$.

- *Hosts?* $2^9 - 2 = 510$.

- *Valid subnets?* $256 - 254 = 2, 4, 6, 8$, etc., up to 252.

- *Broadcast address for each subnet?*

- *Valid hosts?*

The following table shows the first four subnets, valid hosts, and broadcast addresses in a Class B 255.255.254.0 mask.

Subnet	2.0	4.0	6.0	8.0	...
First host	2.1	4.1	6.1	8.1	...
Last host	3.254	5.254	7.254	9.254	...
Broadcast	3.255	5.255	7.255	9.255	...

Practice Example #4B: 255.255.255.0 (/24)

Contrary to popular belief, 255.255.255.0 used with a Class B network address is not called "a Class B network with a Class C subnet mask." It's amazing how many people see this mask used in a Class B network and think it's a Class C subnet mask. This is a "Class B subnet mask with 8 bits of subnetting"—it's considerably different from a Class C mask. Subnetting this address is fairly simple:

- *Subnets?* $2^8 - 2 = 254$.

- *Hosts?* $2^8 - 2 = 254$.

- *Valid subnets?* $256 - 255 = 1, 2, 3$, etc. all the way to 254.

- *Broadcast address for each subnet?*

- *Valid hosts?*

The next table shows the first three subnets and the last one, valid hosts, and broadcast addresses in a Class B 255.255.255.0 mask:

Subnet	1.0	2.0	3.0	...	254.0
First host	1.1	2.1	3.1	...	254.1
Last host	1.254	2.254	3.254	...	254.254
Broadcast	1.255	2.255	3.255	...	254.255

Practice Example #5B: 255.255.255.128 (/25)

Oh no! This one's got to be illegal, right? What type of mask is it? (Don't you wish it were illegal?) Well, it's a drag, but it's not. It is one of the hardest subnet masks you can play with though. And worse, it actually is a really good subnet to use in production because it creates over 500 subnets with 126 hosts for each subnet—a nice mixture. So, don't skip over it!

- *Subnets?* $2^9 - 2 = 510$.

- *Hosts?* $2^7 - 2 = 126$.

- *Valid subnets?* Okay, now for the tricky part. $256 - 255 = 1, 2, 3$, etc., for the third octet. But you can't forget the one subnet bit used in the fourth octet. Remember when I showed you how to figure one subnet bit with a Class C mask? You figure this the same way. (Now you know why I showed you the 1-bit subnet mask in the Class C section— to make this part easier.) You actually get two subnets for each fourth octet value, hence the 510 subnets. For example, if the third octet is showing subnet 3, the two subnets would actually be 3.0 and 3.128.

- *Broadcast address for each subnet?*

- *Valid hosts?*

The following table shows how you can create subnets, valid hosts, and broadcast addresses using the Class B 255.255.255.128 subnet mask. (The first seven subnets are shown, and then the last subnet).

Subnet	0.128	1.0	1.128	2.0	2.128	3.0	3.128	...	255.0
First host	0.129	1.1	1.129	2.1	2.129	3.1	3.129	...	255.1
Last host	0.254	1.126	1.254	2.126	2.254	3.126	3.254	...	255.126
Broadcast	0.255	1.127	1.255	2.127	2.255	3.127	3.255	...	255.127

Practice Example #6B: 255.255.255.192 (/26)

This one gets just a little tricky. Both the 0 subnet as well as the 192 subnet could be valid in the fourth octet. It just depends on what that third octet is doing.

- *Subnets?* $2^{10} - 2 = 1022$.

- *Hosts?* $2^6 - 2 = 62$.

- *Valid subnets?* $256 - 192 = 64$ and 128. And as long as all the subnet bits on the third are not all off, then subnet 0 in the fourth octet is valid. Also, as long as all the subnet bits in the third octet are not all on, 192 is valid in the fourth octet as a subnet.

- *Broadcast address for each subnet?*
- *Valid hosts?*

The following table shows the first seven subnet ranges, valid hosts, and broadcast addresses.

Subnet	0.64	0.128	0.192	1.0	1.64	1.128	1.192	...
First host	0.65	0.129	0.193	1.1	1.65	1.129	1.193	...
Last host	0.126	0.190	0.254	1.62	1.126	1.190	1.254	...
Broadcast	0.127	0.191	0.255	1.63	1.127	1.191	1.255	...

Notice that for each subnet value in the third octet, you get subnets 0, 64, 128, and 192 in the fourth octet. This is true for every subnet in the third octet except 0 and 255. I just demonstrated the 0-subnet value in the third octet. But notice that for the 1 subnet in the third octet, the fourth octet has four subnets: 0, 64, 128, and 192.

Practice Example #7B: 255.255.255.224 (/27)

This is done the same way as the preceding subnet mask, except that we just have more subnets and fewer hosts per subnet available.

- *Subnets?* $2^{11} - 2 = 2046$.
- *Hosts?* $2^5 - 2 = 30$.
- *Valid subnets?* $256 - 224 = 32, 64, 96, 128, 160, 192$. However, as demonstrated above, both the 0 and 224 subnets can be used as long as the third octet does not show a value of 0 or 255. Here's an example of having no subnet bits in the third octet.
- *Broadcast address for each subnet?*
- *Valid hosts?*

The following table shows the first seven subnets.

Subnet	0.32	0.64	0.96	0.128	0.160	0.192	0.224
First host	0.33	0.65	0.97	0.129	0.161	0.193	0.225
Last host	0.62	0.94	0.126	0.158	0.190	0.222	0.254
Broadcast	0.63	0.95	0.127	0.159	0.191	0.223	0.255

Let's take a look at a situation where a subnet bit is turned on in the third octet. The following table shows the full range of subnets available in the fourth octet:

Subnet	1.0	1.32	1.64	1.96	1.128	1.160	1.192	1.224
First host	1.1	1.33	1.65	1.97	1.129	1.161	1.193	1.225
Last host	1.30	1.62	1.94	1.126	1.158	1.190	1.222	1.254
Broadcast	1.31	1.63	1.95	1.127	1.159	1.191	1.223	1.255

This next table shows the last seven subnets.

Subnet	255.0	255.32	255.64	255.96	255.128	255.160	255.192
First host	255.1	255.33	255.65	255.97	255.129	255.161	255.193
Last host	255.62	255.62	255.94	255.126	255.158	255.190	255.222
Broadcast	255.63	255.63	255.95	255.127	255.159	255.191	255.223

Subnetting in Your Head: Class B Addresses

Are you nuts? Subnet Class B addresses in our heads? If you think easier equals crazy, then, yes, I'm a few sails short, but it's actually easier than writing it out—I'm not kidding! Let me show you how:

Question: What subnet and broadcast address is the IP address 172.16.10.33 255.255.255.224 a member of?

Answer: 256 – 224 = 32. 32 + 32 = 64. Bingo: 33 is between 32 and 64. However, remember that the third octet is considered part of the subnet, so the answer would be the 10.32 subnet. The broadcast is 10.63, since 10.64 is the next subnet.

Question: What subnet and broadcast address is the IP address 172.16.90.66 255.255.255.192 a member of?

Answer: 256 – 192 = 64. 64 + 64 = 128. The subnet is 172.16.90.64. The broadcast must be 172.16.90.127, since 90.128 is the next subnet.

Question: What subnet and broadcast address is the IP address 172.16.50.97 255.255.255.224 a member of?

Answer: 256 – 224 = 32, 64, 96, 128. The subnet is 172.16.50.96, and the broadcast must be 172.16.50.127 since 50.128 is the next subnet.

Question: What subnet and broadcast address is the IP address 172.16.10.10 255.255.255.192 a member of?

Answer: 256 − 192 = 64. This address must be in the 172.16.10.0 subnet, and the broadcast must be 172.16.10.63.

Question: What subnet and broadcast address is the IP address 172.16.10.10 255.255.255.252 a member of?

Answer: 256 − 252 = 4. The subnet is 172.16.10.8, with a broadcast of 172.16.10.11.

Subnetting Class A Addresses

Class A subnetting is not performed any differently from Classes B and C, but there are 24 bits to play with instead of the 16 in a Class B address and the eight bits in a Class C address.

Let's start by listing all the Class A subnets:

255.128.0.0	(/9)	255.255.240.0	(/20)
255.192.0.0	(/10)	255.255.248.0	(/21)
255.224.0.0	(/11)	255.255.252.0	(/22)
255.240.0.0	(/12)	255.255.254.0	(/23)
255.248.0.0	(/13)	255.255.255.0	(/24)
255.252.0.0	(/14)	255.255.255.128	(/25)
255.254.0.0	(/15)	255.255.255.192	(/26)
255.255.0.0	(/16)	255.255.255.224	(/27)
255.255.128.0	(/17)	255.255.255.240	(/28)
255.255.192.0	(/18)	255.255.255.248	(/29)
255.255.224.0	(/19)	255.255.255.252	(/30)

That's it. You must leave at least two bits for defining hosts. And I hope you can see the pattern by now. Remember, we're going to do this the same way as a Class B or C subnet. It's just that, again, we simply have more host bits.

Subnetting Practice Examples: Class A Addresses

When you look at an IP address and a subnet mask, you must be able to distinguish the bits used for subnets from the bits used for determining hosts. This is imperative. If you're still struggling with this concept, please reread the preceding "IP Addressing" section. It shows you how to determine the difference between the subnet and host bits, and should help clear things up.

Practice Example #1A: 255.255.0.0 (/16)

Class A addresses use a default mask of 255.0.0.0, which leaves 22 bits for subnetting since you must leave two bits for host addressing. The 255.255.0.0 mask with a Class A address is using eight subnet bits.

- *Subnets?* $2^8 - 2 = 254$.
- *Hosts?* $2^{16} - 2 = 65,534$.
- *Valid subnets?* $256 - 255 = 1$, 2, 3, etc. (all in the second octet). The subnets would be 10.1.0.0, 10.2.0.0, 10.3.0.0, etc., up to 10.254.0.0.
- *Broadcast address for each subnet?*
- *Valid hosts?*

The following table shows the first and last subnet, valid host range, and broadcast addresses:

Subnet	10.0.16.0	...	10.254.0.0
First host	10.1.0.1	...	10.254.0.1
Last host	10.1.255.254	...	10.254.255.254
Broadcast	10.1.255.255	...	10.254.255.255

Practice Example #2A: 255.255.240.0 (/20)

255.255.240.0 gives us 12 bits of subnetting and leaves us 12 bits for host addressing.

- *Subnets?* $2^{12} - 2 = 4094$.
- *Hosts?* $2^{12} - 2 = 4094$.
- *Valid subnets?* $256 - 240 = 16$. And since the second octet is 255, or all subnet bits on, we can start the third octet with 0 as long as a subnet bit is turned on in the second octet. So, the first valid subnets are 10.0.16.0, 10.0.32.0, and 10.0.48.0, all the way to 10.0.224.0. The next set of subnets would be 10.1.0.0, 10.1.16.0, 10.1.32.0, 10.1.48.0, all the way to 10.1.240.0. Notice that we can use 240 in the third octet as long as the subnet bits in the second octet are not all on (1s). In other words, 10.255.240.0 is invalid because all subnet bits are turned on. The last valid subnet would have to be 10.255.224.0.

- *Broadcast address for each subnet?*

- *Valid hosts?*

The following table shows some examples of the host ranges—the first, second, and last subnets:

Subnet	10.1.0.0	10.1.16.0	...	10.255.224.0
First host	10.1.0.1	10.1.16.1	...	10.255.224.1
Last host	10.1.15.254	10.1.31.254	...	10.255.239.254
Broadcast	10.1.15.255	10.1.31.255	...	10.255.239.255

Practice Example #3A: 255.255.255.192 (/26)

Let's do one more example using the second, third, and fourth octets for subnetting.

- *Subnets?* $2^{18} - 2 = 262,142$.

- *Hosts?* $2^6 - 2 = 62$.

- *Valid subnets?* Okay, now we need to add subnet numbers from the second, third, and fourth octets. In the second and third, they can range from 0 to 255, as long as all subnet bits in the second, third, and fourth octets are not all on at the same time. For the fourth octet, it will be $256 - 192 = 64$. And 0 will be valid as long as at least one other subnet bit is turned on in the second or third octet. Also, 192 will be valid as long as all the bits in the second and third octets are not turned on.

- *Broadcast address for each subnet?*

- *Valid hosts?*

The following table shows the first few subnets and their valid hosts and broadcast addresses in the Class A 255.255.255.192 mask:

Subnet	10.0.0.64	10.0.0.128	10.0.0.192	10.1.0.0
First host	10.0.0.65	10.0.0.129	10.0.0.193	10.1.0.1
Last host	10.0.0.126	10.0.0.190	10.0.0.254	10.1.0.62
Broadcast	10.0.0.127	10.0.0.191	10.0.0.255	10.1.0.64

The following table shows the last three subnets and their valid hosts and broadcast addresses:

Subnet	10.255.255.0	10.255.255.64	10.255.255.128
First host	10.255.255.1	10.255.255.65	10.255.255.129
Last host	10.255.255.62	10.255.255.126	10.255.255.190
Broadcast	10.255.255.63	10.255.255.127	10.255.255.191

Summary

Wow... I'm truly impressed—especially if you made it this far and understood everything the first time through! We really covered a lot of ground in this chapter, and it is the largest chapter in the book. You learned about the Internet Protocol stack, as well as IP addressing and subnetting—all in one huge bite! (Or byte.)

But it's truly priceless information—not only for the CCNA exam, of course, but also in any networking job or production environment you would ever find yourself working in—from designing and building to troubleshooting. And even if you did get it all the first time around, it really wouldn't hurt you to read this chapter more than once and to practice subnetting as much as possible. It's just that critical. You could even ask a friend to write out valid IP addresses for which you would have to reply with the subnet, broadcast address, and valid host range. Make sure it's a good friend though!

And I promise I won't throw any more gruesome chapters at you! That's your reward for getting through this one. There's still lot's of ground to cover, but it will be given to you in smaller, more manageable servings from now on. Think about it like this, since you've already come this far, there's no reason to stop now and waste all those brainwaves and new neurons. So don't stop—go through the written and review questions at the end of this chapter and make sure you understand each answer's explanation. The best is yet to come!

Exam Essentials

Remember the Process/Application layer protocols. Telnet, which is a terminal emulation program and allows you to log into a remote host and run programs. File Transfer Protocol (FTP) is a connection-oriented service that allows you to transfer files. Trivial FTP (TFTP) is a connectionless file transfer program. Simple Mail Transfer Protocol (SMTP) is a send mail program.

Remember the Host-to-Host layer protocols.   Transmission Control Protocol (TCP) is a connection-oriented protocol that provides reliable network service by using acknowledgments and flow control. User Datagram Protocol (UDP) is a connectionless protocol that provides low overhead and is considered unreliable.

Remember the Internet layer protocols.   Internet Protocol (IP) is a connectionless protocol that provides network address and routing through an internetwork. Address Resolution Protocol (ARP) finds a hardware address from a known IP address. Reverse ARP (RARP) finds an IP address from a known hardware address. Internet Control Message Protocol (ICMP) provides diagnostics and unreachable messages.

Remember the Class A range.   The IP range for a Class A network is 1–126. This provides 8 bits of network addressing and 24 bits of host addressing by default.

Remember the Class B range.   The IP range for a Class B network is 128–191. Class B addressing provides 16 bits of network addressing and 16 bits of host addressing by default.

Remember the Class C range.   The IP range for a Class C network is 192–223. Class C addressing provides 24 bits of network addressing and 8 bits of host addressing by default.

Understand the difference between a subnet address and a broadcast address.   A subnet address is calculated by turning all host bits off. A broadcast address is calculated by turning all host bits on.

Be able to calculate Class C and Class B subnets and find their valid hosts.   Make sure you can understand, by looking at the first octet, which class of address the IP address is a member of. Once you do that, you need to find your host bits and determine which bits are used for subnetting and which bits are used for host addressing. Then turn the host bits all off to get the subnet address, and turn the bits all on to get the broadcast address. The valid host addresses are always the numbers between the subnet address and the broadcast address.

Key Terms

Before taking the exam, be sure you're familiar with the following terms:

Address Resolution Protocol (ARP)	network address
bit	Network File System (NFS)
Bootstrap Protocol (BootP)	node address
broadcast address	octets
byte	port numbers
Class A network	RARP server
Class B network	Reverse Address Resolution Protocol (RARP)
Class C network	sequencing
connectionless	Simple Mail Transfer Protocol (SMTP)
connection-oriented	Simple Network Management Protocol (SNMP)
Domain Name Service (DNS)	software address
Dynamic Host Configuration Protocol (DHCP)	subnet mask
File Transfer Protocol (FTP)	subnetting
fully qualified domain name (FQDN)	Telnet
hierarchical addressing	Transmission Control Protocol (TCP)
host address	Transmission Control Protocol/Internet Protocol (TCP/IP)
Internet Control Message Protocol (ICMP)	Trivial File Transfer Protocol (TFTP)
Internet Protocol (IP)	User Datagram Protocol (UDP)
IP address	virtual circuit
logical address	X Window

Written Lab 3

Write the subnet, broadcast address, and valid host range for each of the following:

1. 172.16.10.5 255.255.255.128

2. 172.16.10.33 255.255.255.224

3. 172.16.10.65 255.255.255.192

4. 172.16.10.17 255.255.255.252

5. 172.16.10.33 255.255.255.240

6. 192.168.100.25 255.255.255.252

7. 192.168.100.17, with 4 bits of subnetting

8. 192.168.100.66, with 3 bits of subnetting

9. 192.168.100.17 255.255.255.248

10. 10.10.10.5 255.255.255.252

(The answers to Written Lab 3 can be found following the answers to the Review Questions for this chapter.)

Review Questions

1. What is the decimal and hexadecimal equivalent of this binary number 10101010?

   A. Decimal 100
      Hexadecimal 3ef2

   B. Decimal 150
      Hexadecimal AB

   C. Decimal 170
      Hexadecimal AA

   D. Decimal 180
      Hexadecimal FF

2. What valid host range is the IP address 172.16.10.22 255.255.255.240 a part of?

   A. 172.16.10.20 through 172.16.10.22

   B. 172.16.10.1 through 172.16.10.255

   C. 172.16.10.16 through 172.16.10.23

   D. 172.16.10.17 through 172.16.10.31

   E. 172.16.10.17 through 172.16.10.30

3. What range of addresses can be used in the first octet of a Class B network address?

   A. 1–126

   B. 1–127

   C. 128–190

   D. 128–191

   E. 129–192

   F. 192–220

4. Which of the following is true? (Choose all that apply.)

    A. IP is connectionless and provides routing.

    B. ARP is used to find an IP address of a host.

    C. UDP is connectionless.

    D. TCP is connection oriented.

    E. TCP uses windowing as a flow control method.

    F. ICMP is used to manage data to routers.

    G. ARP is used to find a hardware address from a known IP address.

5. Assuming a default mask, which two pieces of information can be derived from the IP address 172.16.25.11?

    A. It is a Class C address.

    B. It is a Class B address.

    C. The network address is 172.

    D. The network address is 172.16.25.

    E. The host portion is 25.11.

6. What protocol is used to find the hardware address of a local device?

    A. RARP

    B. ARP

    C. IP

    D. ICMP

    E. BootP

7. What are the two most common elements of a request/reply pair with ICMP messages when using the Ping program?

    A. Echo reply

    B. Echo request

    C. Destination unreachable

    D. Source quench

8. Which class of IP address provides a maximum of only 254 host addresses per network ID?

   A. Class A

   B. Class B

   C. Class C

   D. Class D

   E. Class E

9. What is the broadcast address of the subnet address 172.16.8.159 255.255.255.192?

   A. 172.16.255.255

   B. 172.16.8.127

   C. 172.16.8.191

   D. 172.16.8.255

10. What is the broadcast address of the subnet address 172.16.99.99 255.255.192.0?

   A. 172.16.99.255

   B. 172.16.127.255

   C. 172.16.255.255

   D. 172.16.64.127

11. If you wanted to have 12 subnets with a Class C network ID, which subnet mask would you use?

   A. 255.255.255.252

   B. 255.255.255.248

   C. 255.255.255.240

   D. 255.255.255.255

12. Which two protocol tools use ICMP?

    A. Telnet

    B. Ping

    C. ARP

    D. Traceroute

13. Which of the following is a true statement?

    A. MAC address broadcasts are all zeros.

    B. MAC addresses are defined at the Physical layer.

    C. MAC address are used by bridges and switches to make forwarding/ filtering decisions.

    D. IP addresses allow a flat address scheme, whereas MAC addresses are hierarchal.

14. What is the protocol and what is the second part of the network address 172.16.0.1 255.255.0.0?

    A. IPX, MAC address

    B. IP, private Class C directed broadcast

    C. Private IP address, node number

    D. Private IP address, directed broadcast

15. What is the result of using a hierarchical addressing scheme?

    A. Increased number of addresses

    B. Decreased amount of routers needed

    C. Increased memory usage on routers

    D. No routing tables needed on routers

16. If you need to have a Class B network address subnetted into exactly 510 subnets, what subnet mask would you assign?

    A. 255.255.255.252

    B. 255.255.255.128

    C. 255.255.0.0

    D. 255.255.255.192

17. Which of the following is a correct ping to a host?

    A. Router>**ping 172.16.0.0**

    B. Router#**ping 172.16.25.255**

    C. Router>**ping 172.16.10.2**

    D. Router#**ping 172.16.2.256**

18. If you have a 12-bit subnet mask, which of the following is a valid host range for the IP address 172.16.10.33?

    A. 1–63

    B. 33–46

    C. 33–47

    D. 1–254

19. If you are using a Class C network ID with two subnets and need 31 hosts per network, which of the following masks should you use?

    A. 255.255.255.0

    B. 255.255.255.192

    C. 255.255.255.224

    D. 255.255.255.248

20. Which of the following are true? (Choose two.)

    A. TCP is connection-oriented but doesn't use flow control.

    B. IP is not necessary on all hosts that use TCP.

    C. ICMP must be implemented by all TCP/IP hosts.

    D. ARP is used to find a hardware address from a known IP address.

21. Which of the following are the Internet Protocol (IP) protocols used at the Application layer of the OSI model? (Choose three.)

    A. IP

    B. TCP

    C. Telnet

    D. FTP

    E. TFTP

    F. Ping

22. How many subnets and hosts can you get from the network 192.168.254.0/26?

    A. 4 networks with 64 hosts

    B. 2 networks with 62 hosts

    C. 254 networks with 254 hosts

    D. 1 network with 254 hosts

23. You have the network 172.16.10.0/24. How many subnets and hosts are available?

    A. 1 subnet with 10 hosts

    B. 1 subnet with 254 hosts

    C. 192 subnets with 10 hosts

    D. 254 subnets with 254 hosts

24. What mask would you assign to the network ID of 172.16.0.0 if you needed more than 300 hosts with each subnet but fewer than 500?

    A. 255.255.255.0

    B. 255.255.254.0

    C. 255.255.252.0

    D. 255.255.0.0

25. You are the network administrator for RouterSim.com, and a user cannot reach the corporate server from their remote office. The IP address of the host is 192.168.254.10/24, the default gateway of the host is 192.168.254.1, and the server is 192.168.10.10/24. You have the user type the following from a DOS prompt: `ping 192.168.254.1`; this is unsuccessful. You then have the user type: `ping 127.0.0.1`; this is also unsuccessful. What could the problem be?

A. The router is down.

B. The server is down.

C. TCP/IP is not initialized on the host.

D. The Ethernet cable is unplugged from the host.

Answers to Review Questions

1. C. To take a binary number and put it into decimal, you just have to add the values of each bit that is a one. The values of 10101010 are 128, 32, 8, and 2. $128 + 32 = 160 + 8 = 168 + 2 = 170$. The Decimal answer is 170. Hexadecimal is a base 16 number system. The base of hexadecimal is 0, 1, 2, 3, 4, 5, 6, 7, 8, 9, 0A, 0B, 0C, 0D, 0E, 0F, 10. Sixteen digits total, from which to create all the numbers you'll ever need. So, if 1010 in binary is 10, then the hexadecimal equivalent is A. Since we have 1010 and 1010, the answer to this question is AA.

2. E. First start by using the 256 mask, which in this case is $256 - 240 = 16$. The first subnet is 16; the second subnet is 32. This host must be in the 16 subnet; the broadcast address is 31, and the valid host range is 17–30.

3. D. A Class B network is defined in the first octet with the numbers 128–191.

4. A, C, D, E, G. UDP is connectionless, TCP is connection-oriented and uses windowing, and ARP is used to find a hardware address from a known IP address.

5. B, E. 172.16.25.11 is a Class B address, and the host portion is 25.11.

6. B. Address Resolution Protocol (ARP) is used to find the hardware address from a known IP address.

7. A, B. The Ping program uses ICMP echo request and echo replies to check a host on an internetwork.

8. C. A Class C network address only has 8 bits for defining hosts. $2^8 - 2 = 254$.

9. C. The two subnets provided by this Class B mask are 64 and 128. The broadcast address for the 128 subnet is 191.

10. B. First start with 256 mask or, in this case, $256 - 192 = 64$. 64 is the first subnet; 128 is the second subnet. This host is in the 64–subnet range, the broadcast address is 127.255, and the valid host range is 64.1–127.254.

11. C. Take a look at the answers and see which subnet mask will give you what you need for subnetting. 252 gives you 62 subnets, 248 gives you 30 subnets, 240 gives you 14 subnets, and 255 is invalid. Only the third option (240) gives you what you need.

12. B, D. ICMP is used by both Ping and Traceroute.

13. C. MAC addresses are a flat address scheme and used by bridges/switches to make forwarding/filtering decisions. Routers use IP addresses, which is a hierarchical address scheme, to make routing decisions.

14. C. 172.16–31.0.0 is a private IP address that cannot be routed through the Internet. 172.16.0.1 is a host address, not a broadcast address. The network broadcast address for this address would be 172.16.255.255.

15. A. The designers created a hierarchical addressing scheme when they created the IP address so that more addresses would be available to each network.

16. B. If you use the mask 255.255.255.0, that only gives you eight subnet bits, or 254 subnets. You are going to have to use one subnet bit from the fourth octet, or 255.255.255.128. This is 9 subnet bits ($2^9 - 2 = 510$).

17. C. The only valid host address listed is 172.16.10.2.

18. B. The question is nothing short of stupid (I didn't think of it!). What Cisco wants you to do is to add "12 bits" to a default mask. Since this is a Class B address, the default mask is 255.255. Adding 12 bits would make the mask 255.255.255.240. The host is located in the 10.32 subnet with the next subnet being 10.48. The valid host range is then 33–46 because 47 is the broadcast address.

19. B. The Class C mask of 255.255.255.192 provides two subnets (four if you are using subnet-zero), each with 62 hosts. 255.255.255.224 only provides 30 hosts per subnet.

20. C, D. ICMP must be implemented by all TCP/IP hosts, and ARP is used to find a hardware address from a known IP address.

21. C, D, E. Telnet, File Transfer Protocol (FTP), and Trivial FTP are all Application layer protocols. IP is a Network layer protocol, as well as Ping. Transmission Control Protocol (TCP) is a Transport layer protocol.

22. B. I bet you struggled with this one, although it isn't difficult. But the answers will make you think. First, the 254-host answers are not even close, so you have a 50/50 chance between the four-network and two-network options. The part you probably thought about the most is whether Cisco is using subnet-zero. This would provide four networks instead of two. Makes sense. However, Cisco does not consider subnet-zero valid on any of their exams. In addition, you cannot get 64 hosts with this mask, only 62 hosts per subnet, regardless of whether you are using subnet-zero or not, which makes the four-network answer completely wrong.

23. D. Easy question, easy answer. The third octet is used for all subnets, and the fourth octet is used only for hosts. 8 bits for subnetting, 8 bits for hosts.

24. B. This one takes some thought. 255.255.255.0 would give you 254 hosts each with 254 subnets. Doesn't work for this question. 255.255.254.0 would provide 126 subnets, each with 510 hosts; the second option looks good. 255.255.252.0 is 62 subnets, each with 1022 hosts. So 255.255.254.0 is the only correct answer.

25. C. 127.0.0.1 is called the *loopback address* and is used for diagnostics on a host. If you cannot ping this address, then you have a problem with the IP stack on the host.

Answers to Written Lab 3

1. 172.16.10.5 255.255.255.128: Subnet is 172.16.10.0, broadcast is 172.16.10.127, and valid host range is 172.16.10.1 through 126.

   You need to ask yourself, "Is the subnet bit in the fourth octet on or off?" If the host address has a value of less than 128 in the fourth octet, then the subnet bit must be off. If the value of the fourth octet is higher than 128, then the subnet bit must be on. In this case, the host address is 10.5, and the bit in the fourth octet must be off. The subnet must be 172.16.10.0.

2. 172.16.10.33 255.255.255.224: Subnet is 172.16.10.32, broadcast is 172.16.10.63, and valid host range is 172.16.10.33 through 10.62.

   256 – 224 = 32. 32 + 32 = 64—bingo. The subnet is 10.32, and the next subnet is 10.64, so the broadcast address must be 10.63.

3. 172.16.10.65 255.255.255.192: Subnet is 172.16.10.64, broadcast is 172.16.10.127, and valid host range is 172.16.10.65 through 172.16.10.126.

   256 – 192 = 64. 64 + 64 = 128, so the network address must be 172.16.10.64, with a broadcast of 172.16.10.127.

4. 172.16.10.17 255.255.255.252: Subnet is 172.16.10.16, broadcast is 172.16.10.19, and valid hosts are 172.16.10.17 and 18.

   256 – 252 = 4. 4 + 4 = 8, plus 4 = 12, plus 4 = 16, plus 4 = 20—bingo. The subnet is 172.16.10.16, and the broadcast must be 10.19.

5. 172.16.10.33 255.255.255.240: Subnet is 172.16.10.32, broadcast is 172.16.10.47, and valid host range is 172.16.10.33 through 46.

   256 – 240 = 16. 16 + 16 = 32, plus 16 = 48. Subnet is 172.16.10.32; broadcast is 172.16.10.47.

6. 192.168.100.25 255.255.255.252: Subnet is 192.168.100.24, broadcast is 192.168.100.27, and valid hosts are 192.168.100.25 and 26.

   256 – 252 = 4. 4 + 4 = 8, plus 4 = 12, plus 4 = 16, plus 4 = 20, plus 4 = 24, plus 4 = 28. Subnet is 100.24; broadcast is 100.27.

7. 192.168.100.17, with 4 bits of subnetting: Subnet is 192.168.100.16, broadcast is 192.168.100.31, and valid host range is 192.168.100.17 through 30.

   $256 - 240 = 16$. $16 + 16 = 32$. Subnet is, then, 100.16, with a broadcast of 100.31 because 32 is the next subnet.

8. 192.168.100.66, with 3 bits of subnetting: Subnet is 192.168.100.64, broadcast is 192.168.100.95, and valid host range is 192.168.100.65 through 94.

   $256 - 224 = 32$. $32 + 32 = 64$, plus 32 = 96. Subnet is 100.64, and broadcast is 100.95.

9. 192.168.100.17 255.255.255.248: Subnet is 192.168.100.16, broadcast is 192.168.100.23, and valid host range is 192.168.100.17 through 22.

   $256 - 248 = 8$. $8 + 8 = 16$, plus 8 = 24. Subnet is 16, and broadcast is 23.

10. 10.10.10.5 255.255.255.252: Subnet is 10.10.10.4, broadcast is 10.10.10.7, and valid hosts are 10.10.10.5 and 6.

    $256 - 252 = 4$. $4 + 4 = 8$.

Introduction to the Cisco IOS

THE CCNA EXAM TOPICS COVERED IN THIS CHAPTER INCLUDE THE FOLLOWING:

✓ **Network Protocols**

- Configure IP addresses.
- Verify IP addresses.

✓ **Cisco Basics, IOS & Network Basics**

- Examine router elements.
- Manage configuration files from the privilege EXEC mode.
- Control router passwords, identification, and banner.
- Identify the main Cisco IOS software commands for router startup.
- Log in to a router in both user and privilege modes.
- Check an initial configuration using the setup command.
- Use the context-sensitive help facility.
- Use the command history and editing features.
- List the commands to load Cisco IOS software from: Flash memory, a TFTP server, or ROM.
- Prepare to backup, upgrade, and load a backup Cisco IOS software image.
- List problems that each routing type encounters when dealing with topology changes, and describe techniques to reduce the number of these problems.
- Prepare the initial configuration of your router and enable IP.

t's time to introduce you to the Cisco Internetwork Operating System (IOS). The IOS is what runs Cisco routers and also some Cisco switches, and it's what allows you to configure the devices as well.

In this chapter, you'll learn how to configure a Cisco IOS router using both the initial setup mode and the Cisco IOS command-line interface (CLI). Through the IOS interface, you can configure passwords, banners, and more. You'll also learn the basics of router configurations in this chapter. All these subjects are covered in this chapter:

- Understanding and configuring the Cisco Internetwork Operating System (IOS)

- Connecting to a router

- Bringing up a router

- Logging into a router

- Understanding the router prompts

- Understanding the CLI prompts

- Performing editing and help features

- Gathering basic routing information

- Setting router passwords

- Setting router banners

- Performing interface configurations

- Setting router hostnames

- Setting interface descriptions

- Viewing and saving router configurations

- Verifying routing configurations

And just as it was with the preceding chapters, the important fundamentals that you'll be taught in this chapter are the critical building blocks that you need to grasp going on to the other chapters in this book.

Cisco Router User Interface

The *Cisco Internetwork Operating System (IOS)* is the kernel of Cisco routers and most switches. Cisco has created something called CiscoFusion, which is supposed to make all Cisco devices run the same operating system. But they don't, because Cisco has acquired devices that they haven't designed and built themselves. Almost all Cisco routers run the same IOS, in contrast to only about half of their switches.

In this section, I'll give you a look at the Cisco IOS and how to configure a Cisco router step-by-step, using setup mode. In the next section, I'll show you how to do this using the command-line interface (CLI).

Cisco Router IOS

The IOS was created to deliver network services and enable networked applications. The Cisco IOS runs on most Cisco routers and on some Cisco Catalyst switches, like the Catalyst 1900 switch.

The Cisco router IOS software is used to complete the following on Cisco hardware:

- Carry network protocols and functions

- Connect high-speed traffic between devices

- Add security to control access and stop unauthorized network use

- Provide scalability for ease of network growth and redundancy

- Supply network reliability for connecting to network resources

You can access the Cisco IOS through the console port of a router, from a modem into the Aux port, or even through Telnet. Access to the IOS command line is called an *EXEC session*.

Connecting to a Cisco Router

You can connect to a Cisco router to configure the router, verify the configuration, and check statistics. There are different ways to do this, but most often, the first place you would connect to is the console port. The *console port* is usually an RJ-45 connection located at the back of the router; by default, there's no password set.

See Chapter 1 for an explanation on how to configure a PC to connect to a router console port.

But you can also connect to a Cisco router through an *auxiliary port*, which is really the same thing as a console port so you can use it as one. However, this auxiliary port also allows you to configure modem commands so a modem can be connected to the router. This is a cool feature that allows you to dial up a remote router and attach to the auxiliary port if the router is down and you need to configure it.

The third way to connect to a Cisco router is through the program *Telnet*. Telnet is a terminal emulation program that acts as though it's a dumb-terminal. You can then use Telnet to connect to any active interface on a router like an Ethernet or serial port.

Figure 4.1 shows an illustration of a 2501 Cisco router. Pay special attention to all the different kinds of interfaces and connections.

FIGURE 4.1 A Cisco 2501 router

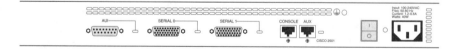

The 2501 router has two serial interfaces for WAN connection and one Attachment Unit Interface (AUI) connection for a 10Mbps Ethernet network connection. This router also has one console and one auxiliary connection via RJ-45 connectors.

Bringing Up a Router

So let's get started! When you first bring up a Cisco router, it will run a power-on self-test (POST), and if that passes, it will then look for and load the Cisco IOS from Flash memory, if a file is present. (Flash memory is an electronically erasable programmable read-only memory [EEPROM].) The IOS then proceeds to load and then look for a valid configuration—the startup-config—that's stored by default in nonvolatile RAM (NVRAM).

The following messages appear when a router is first booted or reloaded:

```
System Bootstrap, Version 12.1(3r)T2, RELEASE SOFTWARE (fc1)
Copyright (c) 2000 by cisco Systems, Inc.
C2600 platform with 32768 Kbytes of main memory
```

The first part, shown above, is the information about the bootstrap program, which first runs the POST and then tells the router how to load, which by default is to find the IOS in Flash memory.

The next part, shown below, shows the IOS is being decompressed into RAM. This does not happen the same way for all routers, but for the 2600 router in this example, the IOS is loaded into RAM. The 2500 series router runs the IOS from Flash memory and does not load the IOS into RAM.

```
program load complete, entry point: 0x80008000, size:
   0x43b7fc
Self decompressing the image :
#########################################################
#########################################################
#########################################################
#########################################################
#########################################################
#########################################################
#########################################################
#########################################################
################################### [OK]
```

After the IOS is decompressed into RAM, the IOS is then loaded and starts running the router, as shown below. Notice the IOS version is stated as version 12.1(8).

```
Cisco Internetwork Operating System Software
IOS (tm) C2600 Software (C2600-I-M), Version 12.1(8),
   RELEASE SOFTWARE (fc1)
Copyright (c) 1986-2001 by cisco Systems, Inc.
Compiled Tue 17-Apr-01 04:55 by kellythw
Image text-base: 0x80008088, data-base: 0x8080853C
```

Once the IOS is loaded, the information learned from the POST will be displayed, as shown next:

```
cisco 2621 (MPC860) processor (revision 0x101) with
  26624K/6144K bytes of memory.
Processor board ID JAD050697JB (146699779)
M860 processor: part number 0, mask 49
Bridging software.
X.25 software, Version 3.0.0.
2 FastEthernet/IEEE 802.3 interface(s)
1 Serial network interface(s)
32K bytes of non-volatile configuration memory.
8192K bytes of processor board System flash (Read/Write)
```

Once the IOS is loaded and is up and running, then a valid configuration will be loaded from NVRAM.

If there is no configuration in NVRAM, then the router will go into *setup mode*—a step-by-step process to help you configure the router. You can also enter setup mode at any time from the command line by typing the command **setup** from something called privileged mode, which I'll cover in a minute. Setup mode only covers some very global commands, but it can be really helpful if you don't know how to configure certain protocols, like bridging or DECnet.

Setup Mode

Okay, you actually have two options when using setup mode: *Basic Management* and *Extended Setup*. Basic Management only gives you enough configurations to allow connectivity to the router, but Extended Setup gives you the power to configure some global parameters as well as interface configuration parameters:

```
        --- System Configuration Dialog ---
Would you like to enter the initial configuration dialog?
  [yes/no]: y


At any point you may enter a question mark '?' for help.
Use ctrl-c to abort configuration dialog at any prompt.
Default settings are in square brackets '[]'.
```

Notice the two lines above that state you can use Ctrl+C to abort configuration dialog at any prompt and that the default settings are in square brackets: [].

Basic Management setup configures only enough connectivity for management of the system. But since you can do so much more with Extended Setup, this mode will ask you to configure each interface on the system.

```
Would you like to enter basic management setup?[yes/no]:n

First, would you like to see the current interface
    summary? [yes]:return
Any interface listed with OK? value "NO" does not have a
    valid configuration

Interface        IP-Address     OK? Method Status Protocol
FastEthernet0/0  unassigned     NO  unset  up     up
FastEthernet0/1  unassigned     NO  unset  up     up

Configuring global parameters:
  Enter host name [Router]: Todd

  The enable secret is a password used to protect access
  to privileged EXEC and configuration modes. This
  password, after entered, becomes encrypted in the
  configuration. Enter enable secret: todd

  The enable password is used when you do not specify an
  enable secret password, with some older software
  versions, and some boot images.
  Enter enable password: todd
% Please choose a password that is different from the
    enable secret
  Enter enable password: todd1
```

There's something I want you to observe here, so let's pause for a moment. Did you notice that setup mode asks you to configure two enable passwords? Passwords are covered later in this chapter, but you should understand that you really only use the enable secret password. The enable password is for pre-10.3 IOS routers (really old routers). Even so, you must configure the password when in setup mode, and it has to be different. It will never be used if the enable secret is configured, though.

The enable secret is encrypted, and the enable password is not.

The next password is for setting up Telnet sessions to the router. The reason setup mode has you configure a Telnet (VTY) password is because you can't telnet into a router by default if a password for the VTY lines hasn't been set.

```
The virtual terminal password is used to protect
access to the router over a network interface.
Enter virtual terminal password: todd
Configure SNMP Network Management? [yes]:[Enter] or n
 Community string [public]:[Enter]
Configure DECnet? [no]:[Enter]
Configure AppleTalk? [no]:[Enter]
Configure IP? [yes]:[Enter]
 Configure IGRP routing? [yes]:n
 Configure RIP routing? [no]:[Enter]
Configure bridging? [no]:[Enter]
Configure IPX? [no]:[Enter]
```

The preceding commands can help you configure a protocol if you're not sure which commands you need to configure, but if you use the command-line interface (CLI) instead of setup mode, you'll have a lot more flexibility. I'll show you the CLI soon in the next section.

If you have an Async modem card installed in your router, you can have setup mode configure the modems for you:

```
Async lines accept incoming modems calls. If you will
have users dialing in via modems, configure these lines.
 Configure Async lines? [yes]:n
```

If your router has an ISDN BRI interface, you'll be prompted for the ISDN switch type to be configured. Take a look at the router output:

```
BRI interface needs isdn switch-type to be configured
Valid switch types are:
[0] none.........Only if you don't want to configure BRI
[1] basic-1tr6....1TR6 switch type for Germany
```

```
[2] basic-5ess....AT&T 5ESS switch type for the US/Canada
[3] basic-dms100..Northern DMS-100 switch type for
                              US/Canada
[4] basic-net3....NET3 switch type for UK and Europe
[5] basic-ni......National ISDN switch type
[6] basic-ts013...TS013 switch type for Australia
[7] ntt...........NTT switch type for Japan
[8] vn3...........VN3 and VN4 switch types for France
Choose ISDN BRI Switch Type [2]:2
```

The next section of the Extended Setup is configuring the interfaces. We only have two Fast Ethernet interfaces on this router: FastEthernet 0/0 and FastEthernet 0/1. I'll go over various types of router interfaces later in this chapter.

```
Configuring interface parameters:

Do you want to configure FastEthernet0/0 interface?
  [yes]:[Enter]
 Use the 100 Base-TX (RJ-45) connector? [yes]:[Enter]
 Operate in full-duplex mode? [no]: y and [Enter]
 Configure IP on this interface? [yes]:[Enter]
   IP address for this interface: 1.1.1.1
   Subnet mask for this interface [255.0.0.0]: 255.255.0.0
   Class A network is 1.0.0.0, 16 subnet bits; mask is /16

Do you want to configure FastEthernet0/1 interface?
  [yes]:[Enter]
 Use the 100 Base-TX (RJ-45) connector? [yes]:[Enter]
 Operate in full-duplex mode? [no]:y and [Enter]
 Configure IP on this interface? [yes]:[Enter]
   IP address for this interface: 2.2.2.2
   Subnet mask for this interface [255.0.0.0]: 255.255.0.0
   Class A network is 2.0.0.0, 16 subnet bits; mask is /16
```

This configuration is very basic, I know, but it will allow you to get a router up and running quickly. Notice the mask is displayed as /16, which means 16 out of 32 bits are being used.

NOTE See Chapter 3 if you need to review IP subnetting.

The Extended Setup will now show the running configuration created:

```
The following configuration command script was created:

hostname Todd
enable secret 5 $1$BOwu$5FOm/EDdtRkQ4vy4a8qwC/
enable password todd1
line vty 0 4
password todd
snmp-server community public
!
no decnet routing
no appletalk routing
ip routing
no bridge 1
no ipx routing
!
interface FastEthernet0/0
media-type 100BaseX
full-duplex
ip address 1.1.1.1 255.255.0.0
no mop enabled
!
interface FastEthernet0/1
media-type 100BaseX
full-duplex
ip address 2.2.2.2 255.255.0.0
no mop enabled
dialer-list 1 protocol ip permit
dialer-list 1 protocol ipx permit
!
end

[0] Go to the IOS command prompt without saving this
    config.
```

```
[1] Return back to the setup without saving this config.
[2] Save this configuration to nvram and exit.

Enter your selection [2]:0
```

The most interesting part of the Extended Setup is the options you get at the end. You can go to CLI mode and discard the running-config (0); you can go back to setup to do it all over again (1); or you can save this configuration to NVRAM, which is known as startup-config (2). This file would then be loaded every time the router is rebooted.

I'm going to choose 0 to go to the IOS—we're not going to save the file we just created. Doing this will take us to the CLI.

You can exit setup mode at anytime by pressing Ctrl+C.

Command-Line Interface

Because it's so much more flexible, the *command-line interface (CLI)* is really the best way to configure a router. I sometimes refer to the CLI as "Cash Line Interface" because if you can create advanced configurations on Cisco routers and switches using the CLI, then you'll get the cash!

To use the CLI, just say No to entering the initial configuration dialog. After you do that, the router will respond with messages that tell you all about the status of each and every one of the router's interfaces.

```
Would you like to enter the initial configuration dialog?
  [yes]:n
Would you like to terminate autoinstall? [yes]:[Enter]

Press RETURN to get started!

00:00:42: %LINK-3-UPDOWN: Interface Ethernet0, changed
  state to up
00:00:42: %LINK-3-UPDOWN: Interface Serial0, changed
  state to down
00:00:42: %LINK-3-UPDOWN: Interface Serial1, changed
  state to down
```

```
00:00:42: %LINEPROTO-5-UPDOWN: Line protocol on Interface
   Ethernet0, changed state to up
00:00:42: %LINEPROTO-5-UPDOWN: Line protocol on Interface
   Serial0, changed state to down
00:00:42: %LINEPROTO-5-UPDOWN: Line protocol on Interface
   Serial1, changed state to down
00:01:30: %LINEPROTO-5-UPDOWN: Line protocol on Interface
   Ethernet0, changed state to down
00:01:31: %LINK-5-CHANGED: Interface Serial0, changed
   state to administratively down
00:01:31: %LINK-5-CHANGED: Interface Ethernet0, changed
   state to administratively down
00:01:31: %LINK-5-CHANGED: Interface Serial1, changed
   state to administratively down
00:01:32: %IP-5-WEBINST_KILL: Terminating DNS process
00:01:38: %SYS-5-RESTART: System restarted --
Cisco Internetwork Operating System Software
IOS (tm) 2500 Software (C2500-DS-L), Version 11.3(9),
   RELEASE SOFTWARE (fc1)
Copyright (c) 1986-1999 by cisco Systems, Inc.
Compiled Tue 06-Apr-99 19:23 by dschwart
```

Logging into the Router

After the interface status messages appear and you press Enter, the Router> prompt will appear. This is called *user mode* and is mostly used to view statistics, though it is also a stepping-stone to logging into privileged mode. You can only view and change the configuration of a Cisco router in privileged mode, which you get into with the enable command.

```
Router>
Router>enable
Router#
```

You now end up with a Router# prompt, which indicates you're now in *privileged mode*, where you can both view and change the router's configuration. You can go back from privileged mode into user mode by using the disable command.

```
Router#disable
Router>
```

At this point, you can type **logout** to exit the console:

```
Router>logout
```

```
Router con0 is now available
Press RETURN to get started.
```

Or you could just type **logout** or **exit** from the privileged-mode prompt to log out:

```
Router>en
Router#logout
```

```
Router con0 is now available
Press RETURN to get started.
```

Overview of Router Modes

To configure from a CLI, you can make global changes to the router by typing **configure terminal** (or **config t** for short), which puts you in global configuration mode and changes what's known as the running-config. You can type **config** from the privileged-mode prompt and then just press Enter to take the default of terminal.

```
Router#config
Configuring from terminal, memory, or network
  [terminal]? [Enter]
Enter configuration commands, one per line. End with
  CNTL/Z.
Router(config)#
```

At this point, you make changes that affect the router as a whole, hence the term *global* configuration mode.

To change the running-config—the current configuration running in dynamic RAM (DRAM)—you use the **configure terminal** command, or just **config t**. To change the startup-config—the configuration stored in NVRAM—you use the **configure memory** command, or **config mem** for short. If you want to change a router configuration stored on a TFTP host (which is covered in Chapter 7), you use the `configure network` command, or just `config net`.

However, you need to understand that for a router to actually make a change to a configuration, it needs to put that configuration in RAM. So, if you actually type `config mem` or `config net`, you'll replace the current running-config with the config stored in NVRAM or a configuration stored on a TFTP host. I'll be going over this in much greater detail in Chapter 7.

Configure terminal, configure memory, and configure network are all considered commands that are used to configure information into RAM on a router; however, typically only the configure terminal command is used.

CLI Prompts

It's really important that you understand the different prompts you can find when configuring a router. Knowing these well will help you navigate and recognize where you are at any time within configuration mode. In this section, I'm going to demonstrate the prompts that are used on a Cisco router. (Always check your prompts before making any changes to a router's configuration!)

I'm not going into every different command offered. Doing that would be reaching beyond the scope of this exam. Instead, I'm going to describe all the different prompts you'll see throughout this chapter and the rest of the book. These commands are the ones you'll use most in your real life—and the ones you'll need to know for the exam.

Interfaces

To make changes to an interface, you use the `interface` command from global configuration mode:

```
Router(config)#interface ?
  Async              Async interface
  BVI                Bridge-Group Virtual Interface
  Dialer             Dialer interface
  FastEthernet       FastEthernet IEEE 802.3
  Group-Async        Async Group interface
  Lex                Lex interface
```

```
Loopback          Loopback interface
Multilink         Multilink-group interface
Null              Null interface
Port-channel      Ethernet Channel of interfaces
Tunnel            Tunnel interface
Virtual-Template  Virtual Template interface
Virtual-TokenRing Virtual TokenRing
Router(config)#interface fastethernet 0/0
Router(config-if)#
```

Did you notice the prompt changed to `Router(config-if)#`? This tells you that you're in *interface configuration mode*. And wouldn't it would be nice if it also gave you an indication of what interface you were configuring? Well, at least for now we'll have to live without it because it doesn't. (Could this be one of the reasons Cisco administrators make more money than Windows administrators? Or is it just that we're smarter?) One thing is for sure: You really have to pay attention when configuring a router!

Subinterfaces

Subinterfaces allow you to create logical interfaces within the router. The prompt then changes to `Router(config-subif)#`. (You can read more about subinterfaces in Chapters 8 and 10, but don't skip ahead just yet!)

```
Router(config)#int f0/0.?
<0-4294967295> FastEthernet interface number
Router(config)#int f0/0.1
Router(config-subif)#
```

Line Commands

To configure user-mode passwords, use the `line` command. The prompt then becomes `Router(config-line)#`.

```
Router#config t
Enter configuration commands, one per line. End with
  CNTL/Z.
Router(config)#line ?
<0-4>    First Line number
aux      Auxiliary line
```

```
    console Primary terminal line
    vty     Virtual terminal
```

```
Router(config)#line console 0
Router(config-line)#
```

The line console 0 command is known as a major command (also called a *global command*), and any command typed from the (config-line) prompt is known as a subcommand.

Routing Protocol Configurations

To configure routing protocols like RIP and IGRP, use the prompt (config-router)#:

```
Router#config t
Enter configuration commands, one per line. End with
    CNTL/Z.
Router(config)#router rip
Router(config-router)#
```

It's not important that you understand what each of these commands does at this time, because all of them will be explained later in great detail. At this point, you really need to concentrate on becoming familiar with the different prompts available.

Editing and Help Features

You can use the Cisco advanced editing features to help you configure your router. If you type in a question mark (**?**) at any prompt, you'll be given the list of all the commands available from that prompt:

```
Router#?
Exec commands:
 access-enable    Create a temporary Access-List entry
 access-profile   Apply user-profile to interface
 access-template  Create a temporary Access-List entry
 bfe              For manual emergency modes setting
```

```
clear          Reset functions
clock          Manage the system clock
configure      Enter configuration mode
connect        Open a terminal connection
copy           Copy configuration or image data
debug          Debugging functions (see also 'undebug')
disable        Turn off privileged commands
disconnect     Disconnect an existing network connection
enable         Turn on privileged commands
erase          Erase flash or configuration memory
exit           Exit from the EXEC
help           Description of the interactive help system
lock           Lock the terminal
login          Log in as a particular user
logout         Exit from the EXEC
mrinfo         Request neighbor and version information
               from a multicast router
--More-
```

Plus, at this point, you can press the spacebar to get another page of information, or you can press Enter to go one command at a time. You can also press Q or any other key to quit and return to the prompt.

And here's a shortcut… To find commands that start with a certain letter, use the letter and the question mark (?) with no space between them:

```
Router#c?
clear clock configure connect copy


Router#c
```

See that? By typing **c?**, we received a response listing all the commands that start with *c*. Also notice that the Router# prompt that appeared with our command is still present. This can be helpful when you have long commands and need the next possible command. It would be pretty lame if you had to retype the entire command every time you used a question mark!

To find the next command in a string, type the first command and then a question mark:

```
Router#clock ?
 set Set the time and date
```

```
Router#clock set ?
 hh:mm:ss Current Time
Router#clock set 10:30:10 ?
 <1-31> Day of the month
 MONTH  Month of the year
Router#clock set 10:30:10 28 ?
 MONTH  Month of the year
Router#clock set 10:30:10 28 may ?
 <1993-2035> Year
Router#clock set 10:30:10 28 may 2002 ?
 <cr>
Router#
```

By typing the clock command, followed with a space and a question mark, you'll get a list of the next possible commands and what they do. Notice that you should just keep typing a command, a space, and then a question mark until <cr> (carriage return) is your only option.

If you are typing commands and receive this:

```
Router#clock set 10:30:10
% Incomplete command.
```

you'll know that the command string isn't yet done. Just press the Up arrow key to receive the last command entered, then continue with the command by using your question mark.

And if you receive this error:

```
Router(config)#access-list 110 permit host 1.1.1.1
                                           ^
% Invalid input detected at '^' marker.
```

you've entered a command incorrectly. See that little caret—the ^? It's a very helpful tool that marks the point where you have entered the command wrong.

Now if you receive this error:

```
Router#sh te
% Ambiguous command: "sh te"
```

it means you didn't enter all the keywords or values required by this command. Use the question mark to find the command you need:

```
Router#sh te?
WORD tech-support terminal
```

Table 4.1 shows the list of the enhanced editing commands available on a Cisco router.

TABLE 4.1 Enhanced Editing Commands

Command	Meaning
Ctrl+A	Moves your cursor to the beginning of the line
Ctrl+E	Moves your cursor to the end of the line
Esc+B	Moves back one word
Ctrl+F	Moves forward one character
Esc+F	Moves forward one word
Ctrl+D	Deletes a single character
Backspace	Deletes a single character
Ctrl+R	Redisplays a line
Ctrl+U	Erases a line
Ctrl+W	Erases a word
Ctrl+Z	Ends configuration mode and returns to EXEC
Tab	Finishes typing a command for you

Another cool editing feature I need to show you is the automatic scrolling of long lines. In the following example, the command typed had reached the right margin and automatically moved eleven spaces to the left. The dollar sign ($) indicates that the line has been scrolled to the left.

```
Router#config t
Enter configuration commands, one per line. End with CNTL/Z.
Router(config)#$110 permit host 171.10.10.10 0.0.0.0 host
```

You can review the router-command history with the commands shown in Table 4.2.

The following example demonstrates the show history command and how to change the history size, as well as how to verify it with the show terminal command.

TABLE 4.2 Router-Command History

Command	Meaning
Ctrl+P or Up arrow	Shows last command entered
Ctrl+N or Down arrow	Shows previous commands entered
show history	Shows last 10 commands entered by default
show terminal	Shows terminal configurations and history buffer size
terminal history size	Changes buffer size (max 256)

First, use the show history command to see the last 10 commands that were entered on the router:

```
Router#sh history
  en
  sh history
  show terminal
  sh cdp neig
  sh ver
  sh flash
  sh int e0
  sh history
  sh int s0
  sh int s1
```

Now you use the show terminal command to verify the terminal history size:

```
Router#sh terminal
Line 0, Location: "", Type: ""
[output cut]
History is enabled, history size is 10.
Full user help is disabled
```

```
Allowed transports are lat pad v120 telnet mop rlogin
  nasi. Preferred is lat.
No output characters are padded
No special data dispatching characters
Group codes:  0
```

The terminal history size command, used from privileged mode, can change the size of the history buffer:

```
Router#terminal history size ?
 <0-256> Size of history buffer
Router#terminal history size 25
```

Verify the change with the show terminal command.

```
Router#sh terminal
Line 0, Location: "", Type: ""
[output cut]
Editing is enabled.
History is enabled, history size is 25.
Full user help is disabled
Allowed transports are lat pad v120 telnet mop rlogin
  nasi. Preferred is lat.
No output characters are padded
No special data dispatching characters
Group codes:  0
```

 Real World Scenario

When do you use the Cisco editing features?

There are a couple of editing features that are used quite often; some are not used as much, if at all. Understand that Cisco didn't make these up; these are just old Unix commands. However, Ctrl+A is really helpful to negate a command.

For example, if you were to put in a long command and then decide you didn't want to use that command in your configuration or that it didn't work, then you can press your Up arrow key to show the last command entered, press Ctrl+A, type **no** then a space, and press Enter, and poof, the command is negated. This doesn't work on every command, but it works on a lot of them.

Gathering Basic Routing Information

The show version command will provide basic configuration for the system hardware as well as the software version, the names and sources of configuration files, and the boot images:

```
Router#sh version
Cisco Internetwork Operating System Software
IOS (tm) 2500 Software (C2500-JS-L), Version 12.0(8),
  RELEASE SOFTWARE (fc1)
Copyright (c) 1986-1999 by cisco Systems, Inc.
Compiled Mon 29-Nov-99 14:52 by kpma
Image text-base: 0x03051C3C, data-base: 0x00001000
```

The preceding section of output describes the Cisco IOS running on the router. The following section describes the read-only memory (ROM) used, which is used to boot the router.

```
ROM: System Bootstrap, Version 11.0(10c), SOFTWARE
BOOTFLASH: 3000 Bootstrap Software (IGS-BOOT-R), Version
  11.0(10c), RELEASE SOFTWARE (fc1)
```

The next section shows how long the router has been running, how it was restarted (if you see a "system restarted by bus-error," that is a very bad thing) as well as where the Cisco IOS was loaded from, plus the IOS name. Flash is the default:

```
RouterA uptime is 5 minutes
System restarted by power-on
System image file is "flash:c2500-js-l_120-8.bin"
```

And this next section displays the processor (a whopping 68030!), the amount of DRAM and Flash memory, and the interfaces the POST test found on the router:

```
cisco 2522 (68030) processor (revision N) with 14336K
  /2048K bytes of memory.
Processor board ID 15662842, with hardware revision
  00000003
Bridging software.
X.25 software, Version 3.0.0.
SuperLAT software (copyright 1990 by Meridian Technology
  Corp).
```

```
TN3270 Emulation software.
Basic Rate ISDN software, Version 1.1.
1 Ethernet/IEEE 802.3 interface(s)
2 Serial network interface(s)
8 Low-speed serial(sync/async) network interface(s)
1 ISDN Basic Rate interface(s)
32K bytes of non-volatile configuration memory.
16384K bytes of processor board System flash (Read ONLY)
Configuration register is 0x2102
```

The configuration register value is listed last—it's something I'll cover in Chapter 7.

Setting Passwords

There are five passwords used to secure your Cisco routers. Just as you learned earlier in the chapter, the first two passwords are used to set your enable password, which is used to secure privileged mode. This will prompt a user for a password when the enable command is used. The other three are used to configure a password when user mode is accessed either through the console port, the auxiliary port, or via Telnet.

Enable Passwords

You set the enable passwords from global configuration mode like this:

```
Router(config)#enable ?
  last-resort Define enable action if no TACACS servers
              respond
  password    Assign the privileged level password
  secret      Assign the privileged level secret
  use-tacacs  Use TACACS to check enable passwords
```

Last-resort Allows you to still enter the router if you set up authentication through a TACACS server and it's not available. But it isn't used if the TACACS server is working.

Password Sets the enable password on older, pre-10.3 systems, and isn't ever used if an enable secret is set.

Secret Is the newer, encrypted password that overrides the enable password if it's set.

Use-tacacs   Tells the router to authenticate through a TACACS server. It's convenient if you have dozens or even hundreds of routers, because, well, would you like to change the password on 200 routers? If you go through the TACACS server, you only have to change the password once.

```
Router(config)#enable secret todd
Router(config)#enable password todd
The enable password you have chosen is the same as your
   enable secret. This is not recommended. Re-enter the
   enable password.
```

If you try and set the enable secret and enable passwords the same, the router will give you a nice, polite warning to change the second password. If you don't have older legacy routers, don't even bother to use the enable password.

User-mode passwords are assigned by using the `line` command:

```
Router(config)#line ?
 <0-4>   First Line number
 aux     Auxiliary line
 console Primary terminal line
 vty     Virtual terminal
```

Aux   Sets the user-mode password for the auxiliary port. It's usually used for configuring a modem on the router, but it can be used as a console as well.

Console   Sets a console user-mode password.

Vty   Sets a Telnet password on the router. If this password isn't set, then Telnet can't be used by default.

To configure the user-mode passwords, you configure the line you want and use either the `login` or `no login` command to tell the router to prompt for authentication. The next section will provide a line-by-line example of each line configuration.

Auxiliary Password

To configure the auxiliary password, go into global configuration mode and type `line aux ?`. You can see that you only get a choice of 0–0. That's because there's only one port:

```
Router#config t
Enter configuration commands, one per line. End with CNTL/Z.
```

```
Router(config)#line aux ?
 <0-0> First Line number
Router(config)#line aux 0
Router(config-line)#login
Router(config-line)#password todd
```

It's important to remember the login command, or the auxiliary port won't prompt for authentication.

Console Password

To set the console password, use the line console 0 command. But look… when I tried to type line console 0 ? from the aux line configuration, I received an error. You can still type line console 0 and it will accept it; but the help screens just don't work from that prompt. Type **exit** to get back one level and you'll find that your help screens now work. This is a "feature."

```
Router(config-line)#line console ?
% Unrecognized command
Router(config-line)#exit
Router(config)#line console ?
 <0-0> First Line number
Router(config)#line console 0
Router(config-line)#login
Router(config-line)#password todd1
```

Since there is only one console port, I can only choose line console 0. You can set all your line passwords to the same password, but for security reasons, I'd recommend that you make them different.

Other Console Port Commands

There are a few other important commands to know for the console port.

For one, the exec-timeout 0 0 command sets the timeout for the console EXEC session to zero, which means to never time out. The default timeout is 10 minutes. (If you're feeling mischievous, try this on your friends at work: Set it to 0 1. That will make the console time out in 1 second! And to fix it, you have to continually press the Down arrow key while changing the time-out time with your free hand!)

Logging synchronous is a very cool command, and it should be a default command, but it's not. What it does is stop annoying console messages from popping up and disrupting the input you're trying to type, making your input messages oh-so-much easier to read.

Here's an example of how to configure both commands:

```
Router(config)#line con 0
Router(config-line)#exec-timeout ?
 <0-35791> Timeout in minutes
Router(config-line)#exec-timeout 0 ?
 <0-2147483> Timeout in seconds
 <cr>
Router(config-line)#exec-timeout 0 0
Router(config-line)#logging synchronous
```

Telnet Password

To set the user-mode password for Telnet access into the router, use the line vty command. Routers that aren't running the Enterprise edition of the Cisco IOS default to five VTY lines; 0 through 4. But if you have the Enterprise edition, you'll have significantly more. The best way to find out how many lines you have is to use the question mark:

```
Router(config-line)#line vty 0 ?
 <1-4> Last Line Number
 <cr>
Router(config-line)#line vty 0 4
Router(config-line)#login
Router(config-line)#password todd2
```

What happens if you try to telnet into a router that doesn't have a VTY password set? You'll receive an error stating that the connection is refused because the password isn't set. But you can get around this and tell the router to allow Telnet connections without a password by using the no login command:

```
Router(config-line)#line vty 0 4
Router(config-line)#no login
```

After your routers are configured with an IP address, you can use the Telnet program to configure and check your routers instead of having to use a console cable. You can use the Telnet program by typing **telnet** from any command prompt (DOS or Cisco). Anything Telnet is covered more thoroughly in Chapter 7.

If you can ping a router but are unable to telnet into it, the likely problem is that you didn't set the password on the VTY lines.

Encrypting Your Passwords

Because only the enable secret password is encrypted by default, you'll need to manually configure the user-mode and enable passwords.

And notice that you can see all the passwords except the enable secret when performing a show running-config on a router:

```
Router#sh running-config
[output cut]
!
enable secret 5 $1$rFbM$8.aXocHg6yHrM/zzeNkAT.
enable password todd1
!
[output cut]
line con 0
 password todd1
 login
line aux 0
 password todd
 login
line vty 0 4
 password todd2
 login
line vty 5 197
 password todd2
 login
!
end

Router#
```

To manually encrypt your passwords, use the service password-encryption command. Here's an example of how to do it:

```
Router#config t
Enter configuration commands, one per line. End with CNTL/Z.
Router(config)#service password-encryption

Router(config)#no service password-encryption
Router(config)#^Z
```

There you have it! The passwords will now be encrypted. You just encrypt the passwords and then turn off the command. By typing the show running-config command, you can see the enable password and the line passwords are all encrypted:

```
Router#sh run
Building configuration...
[output cut]
!
enable secret 5 $1$rFbM$8.aXocHg6yHrM/zzeNkAT.
enable password 7 0835434A0D
!
[output cut]
!
line con 0
 password 7 111D160113
 login
line aux 0
 password 7 071B2E484A
 login
line vty 0 4
 password 7 0835434A0D
 login
line vty 5 197
 password 7 09463724B
 login
!
end

Router#
```

Banners

A good reason for having a banner is to add a security notice to users dialing into your internetwork. You can set a banner on a Cisco router so that when either a user logs into the router or an administrator telnets into the router, a banner will give them the information you want them to have. There are four different banners available:

```
Router(config)#banner ?
  LINE     c banner-text c, where 'c' is a delimiting
           character
  exec     Set EXEC process creation banner
  incoming Set incoming terminal line banner
  login    Set login banner
  motd     Set Message of the Day banner
```

Message of the day (MOTD) is the most extensively used banner. It gives a message to every person dialing into or connecting to the router via Telnet, auxiliary port, or through a console port.

```
Router(config)#banner motd ?
LINE c banner-text c, where 'c' is a delimiting character
Router(config)#banner motd #
Enter TEXT message. End with the character '#'.
$ Acme.com network, then you must disconnect immediately.
#
Router(config)#^Z
Router#
00:25:12: %SYS-5-CONFIG_I: Configured from console by
  console
Router#exit


Router con0 is now available


Press RETURN to get started.


If you are not authorized to be in Acme.com network, then
  you must disconnect immediately.


Router>
```

The preceding MOTD banner tells anyone connecting to the router that if they're not on the guest list, get lost! The part to understand is the delimiting character—the thing that's used to tell the router when the message is done. You can use any character you want for it, but you can't use the delimiting character in the message itself. Also, once the message is complete, press Enter, then the delimiting character, then Enter again. It'll still work if you don't do that, but if you have more than one banner, they'll be combined as one message and put on a single line.

These are the other banners:

Exec banner   You can configure a line-activation (exec) banner to be displayed when an EXEC process (such as a line-activation or incoming connection to a VTY line) is created.

Incoming banner   You can configure a banner to be displayed on terminals connected to reverse Telnet lines. This banner is useful for providing instructions to users who use reverse Telnet.

Login banner   You can configure a login banner to be displayed on all connected terminals. This banner is displayed after the MOTD banner but before the login prompts. The login banner can't be disabled on a per-line basis, so to globally disable the login banner, you must delete it with the no banner login command.

Router Interfaces

Interface configuration is one of the most important configurations of the router, because without interfaces, a router is totally useless. Plus, interface configurations must be exact to enable communication with other devices. Some of the configurations used to configure an interface are Network layer addresses, media type, bandwidth, and other administrator commands.

Different routers use different methods to choose the interfaces used on them. For instance, the following command shows a 2522 router with 10 serial interfaces, labeled 0 through 9:

```
Router(config)#int serial ?
  <0-9> Serial interface number
```

Now it's time to choose the interface you want to configure. Once you do that, you will be in interface configuration for that specific interface. The command to choose serial port 5, for example, would be:

```
Router(config)#int serial 5
Router(config)-if)#
```

The 2522 router has one Ethernet 10BaseT port, and typing **interface ethernet 0** can configure that interface:

```
Router(config)#int ethernet ?
 <0-0> Ethernet interface number
Router(config)#int ethernet 0
Router(config-if)#
```

The 2500 router, as previously demonstrated, is a fixed configuration router, which means that when you buy that model, you're stuck with that configuration.

To configure an interface, you always use the interface *type number* sequence, but the 2600, 3600, 4000, and 7000 series routers use a physical slot in the router, with a port number on the module plugged into that slot. For example, on a 2600 router, the configuration would be interface *type slot/port*:

```
Router(config)#int fastethernet ?
 <0-1> FastEthernet interface number
Router(config)#int fastethernet 0
% Incomplete command.
Router(config)#int fastethernet 0?
 /
Router(config)#int fastethernet 0/?
 <0-1> FastEthernet interface number
```

And make note of the fact that you can't just type **int fastethernet 0**. You must type the full command—*type slot/port*, or int fastethernet 0/0, or int fa 0/0.

To set the type of connector used, use the media-type command. This is usually auto-detected:

```
Router(config)#int fa 0/0
Router(config-if)#media-type ?
 100BaseX Use RJ45 for -TX; SC FO for -FX
 MII      Use MII connector
```

Bringing Up an Interface

You can turn an interface off with the interface command shutdown, and turn it on with the no shutdown command. If an interface is shut down, it'll display administratively down when using the show interface command.

Another way to check an interface's status is via the show running-config command. All interfaces are shut down by default.

```
Router#sh int ethernet0
Ethernet0 is administratively down, line protocol is down
[output cut]
```

Bring up the interface with the no shutdown command.

```
Router#config t
Enter configuration commands, one per line. End with
    CNTL/Z.
Router(config)#int ethernet0
Router(config-if)#no shutdown
Router(config-if)#^Z
00:57:08: %LINK-3-UPDOWN: Interface Ethernet0, changed
    state to up
00:57:09: %LINEPROTO-5-UPDOWN: Line protocol on Interface
    Ethernet0, changed state to up

Router#sh int ethernet0
Ethernet0 is up, line protocol is up
[output cut]
```

Configuring an IP Address on an Interface

Even though you don't have to use IP on your routers, it's most often what people use. To configure IP addresses on an interface, use the ip address command from interface configuration mode:

```
Router(config)#int e0
Router(config-if)#ip address 172.16.10.2 255.255.255.0
Router(config-if)#no shut
```

Don't forget to turn on an interface with the no shutdown command (no shut for short). Remember to look at the command show interface e0, for example, to see if it's administratively shut down or not. Show running-config will also give you this information.

The ip address *address mask* command starts the IP processing on the interface.

If you want to add a second subnet address to an interface, you have to use the secondary command. If you type another IP address and press Enter, it will replace the existing IP address and mask. This is definitely a most excellent feature of the Cisco IOS.

So, let's try it. To add a secondary IP address, just use the secondary command:

```
Router(config-if)#ip address 172.16.20.2 255.255.255.0
  secondary
Router(config-if)#^Z
```

You can verify both addresses are configured on the interface with the show running-config command (sh run for short):

```
Router#sh run
Building configuration...
Current configuration:
[output cut]
!
interface Ethernet0
 ip address 172.16.20.2 255.255.255.0 secondary
 ip address 172.16.10.2 255.255.255.0
!
```

I really wouldn't recommend having multiple IP addresses on an interface because it's inefficient, but I showed you anyway just in case you someday find yourself dealing with an MIS manager who loves a really lame network design and makes you administrate it!

Serial Interface Commands

Before you jump in and configure a serial interface, there are a couple of things you need to know. First, the interface will usually be attached to a CSU/DSU type of device that provides clocking for the line. But if you have a back-to-back configuration (for example, one that's used in a lab environment), one end—the data communication equipment (DCE) end of the cable—must provide clocking. By default, Cisco routers are all data terminal equipment (DTE) devices, so you must tell an interface to provide clocking if you need it to act like a DCE device. You configure a DCE serial interface with the clock rate command:

```
Router#config t
Enter configuration commands, one per line. End with CNTL/Z.
```

```
Router(config)#int s0
Router(config-if)#clock rate ?
    Speed (bits per second)
  1200
  2400
  4800
  9600
  19200
  38400
  56000
  64000
  72000
  125000
  148000
  250000
  500000
  800000
  1000000
  1300000
  2000000
  4000000

  <300-4000000>  Choose clockrate from list above

Router(config-if)#clock rate 64000
%Error: This command applies only to DCE interfaces
Router(config-if)#int s1
Router(config-if)#clock rate 64000
```

It doesn't hurt anything to try and put a clock rate on an interface. Notice that the clock rate command is in bits per second.

The next command you need to get acquainted with is the bandwidth command. Every Cisco router ships with a default serial link bandwidth of T-1 (1.544Mbps). But this has nothing to do with how data is transferred over a link. The bandwidth of a serial link is used by routing protocols such as IGRP, EIGRP, and OSPF to calculate the best cost (path) to a remote network. So if you're using RIP routing, then the bandwidth setting of a serial link is irrelevant, since RIP uses only hop count to determine that. (If you need to brush up on routing protocols and metrics, look for them in Chapter 5).

```
Router(config-if)#bandwidth ?
 <1-10000000> Bandwidth in kilobits

Router(config-if)#bandwidth 64
```

Did you notice that, unlike the clock rate command, the bandwidth command is configured in kilobits?

Hostnames

You can set the identity of the router with the hostname command. This is only locally significant, which means it has no bearing on how the router performs name lookups or how the router works on the internetwork.

```
Router#config t
Enter configuration commands, one per line. End with
  CNTL/Z.
Router(config)#hostname todd
todd(config)#hostname Atlanta
Atlanta(config)#
```

Even though it's pretty tempting to configure the hostname after your own name, it's a better idea to name the router something pertinent to the location.

Descriptions

Setting descriptions on an interface is helpful to the administrator and, like the hostname, only locally significant. This is a helpful command because you can use it to keep track of circuit numbers, for example.

```
Atlanta(config)#int e0
Atlanta(config-if)#description Sales Lan
Atlanta(config-if)#int s0
Atlanta(config-if)#desc Wan to Miami circuit:6fdda4321
```

You can view the description of an interface either with the show running-config command or the show interface command.

```
Atlanta#sh run
[cut]
interface Ethernet0
 description Sales Lan
 ip address 172.16.10.30 255.255.255.0
 no ip directed-broadcast
!
interface Serial0
 description Wan to Miami circuit:6fdda4321
 no ip address
 no ip directed-broadcast
 no ip mroute-cache
Atlanta#sh int e0
Ethernet0 is up, line protocol is up
 Hardware is Lance, address is 0010.7be8.25db (bia
  0010.7be8.25db)
 Description: Sales Lan
 [output cut]
Atlanta#sh int s0
Serial0 is up, line protocol is up
 Hardware is HD64570
 Description: Wan to Miami circuit:6fdda4321
 [output cut]
Atlanta#
```

 Real World Scenario

Description: The Helpful Command

The interface description command is very helpful if, for example, you have many administrators and no one can remember where any interface is connected. Also, if you have many WAN serial links, you can keep track of circuit numbers and the contact number for the responsible party. Spending just a few minutes describing where each interface goes will help tremendously when troubleshooting your network.

Viewing and Saving Configurations

If you run through setup mode, you'll be asked if you want to use the configuration you just created. If you say Yes, then it will copy the configuration running in DRAM, known as the running-config, into NVRAM, and name the file startup-config.

You can manually save the file from DRAM to NVRAM by using the copy running-config startup-config command. You can use the shortcut copy run start also:

```
Atlanta#copy run start
Destination filename [startup-config]?[Enter]
Warning: Attempting to overwrite an NVRAM configuration
    previously written by a different version of the system
    image.
Overwrite the previous NVRAM configuration?[confirm]
    [Enter]
Building configuration...
```

Notice that the message we got tells us we're trying to write over the older startup-config. The IOS had been just upgraded to version 12.2, and the last time the file was saved, 11.3 was running. When you see a question with an answer in [], it means that if you just press Enter, you're choosing the default answer.

Also, when the command asked for the destination filename, the default answer was startup-config. The "feature" aspect of this command output is that you can't even type anything else in or you will get an error!

```
Atlanta#copy run start
Destination filename [startup-config]?todd
%Error opening nvram:todd (No such file or directory)
Atlanta#
```

Okay, you're right—it's weird! Why on earth do they even ask if you can't change it at all? Well... since this "feature" was first introduced with the release of the 12.x IOS, we're pretty sure it will turn out to be relevant and important some time in the future.

Anyway, you can view the files by typing **show running-config** or **show startup-config** from privileged mode. The sh run command, which is the shortcut for show running-config, tells us that we are viewing the current configuration:

```
Router#sh run
Building configuration...
```

```
Current configuration:
!
version 12.0
service timestamps debug uptime
service timestamps log uptime
no service password-encryption
!
hostname Router
ip subnet-zero
frame-relay switching
!
```
[output cut]

The sh start command—the shortcut for the show startup-config command—shows us the configuration that will be used the next time the router is reloaded. It also tells us how much NVRAM is being used to store the startup-config file:

```
Router#sh start
Using 4850 out of 32762 bytes
!
version 12.0
service timestamps debug uptime
service timestamps log uptime
no service password-encryption
!
hostname Router
!
!
ip subnet-zero
frame-relay switching
!
```
[output cut]

You can delete the startup-config file by using the erase startup-config command, after which you'll receive an error if you ever try to view the startup-config file.

```
Router#erase startup-config
Erasing the nvram filesystem will remove all files!
  Continue? [confirm]
```

```
[OK]
Erase of nvram: complete
Router#sh start
%% Non-volatile configuration memory is not present
Router#
```

If you reload the router after using the erase startup-config command, you'll be put into setup mode. You can press Ctrl+C to exit setup mode at any time.

At this point, you shouldn't use setup mode to configure your router. Setup mode was designed to help people who do not know how to use the Cash Line Interface, and this no longer applies to you!

Verifying Your Configuration

Obviously, show running-config would be the best way to verify your configuration, and show startup-config would be the best way to verify the configuration that'll be used the next time the router is reloaded—right?

Well, once you take a look at the running-config, and if all appears well, you can verify your configuration with utilities like Ping and Telnet. Ping is Packet Internet Groper, a program that uses ICMP echo requests and replies. (ICMP is discussed in Chapter 3.) Ping sends a packet to a remote host, and if that host responds, you know that the host is alive. But you don't know if it's alive and also *well*—just because you can ping an NT server does not mean you can log in. Even so, Ping is an awesome starting point for troubleshooting an internetwork.

Did you know that you can ping with different protocols? You can, and you can test this by typing **ping ?** at either the router user-mode or privileged mode prompt:

```
Router#ping ?
  WORD      Ping destination address or hostname
  appletalk Appletalk echo
  decnet    DECnet echo
  ip        IP echo
  ipx       Novell/IPX echo
  srb       srb echo
  <cr>
```

To find a neighbor's Network layer address, you either need to go to the router or switch itself, or you can type **show cdp entry * protocol** to get the Network layer addresses you need for pinging. (Cisco Discovery Protocol [CDP] is covered in Chapter 7.)

Traceroute uses ICMP timeouts to track the path a packet takes through an internetwork, in contrast to Ping that just finds the host and responds. Traceroute can also be used with multiple protocols.

```
Router#traceroute ?
  WORD      Trace route to destination address or hostname
  appletalk AppleTalk Trace
  clns      ISO CLNS Trace
  ip        IP Trace
  oldvines  Vines Trace (Cisco)
  vines     Vines Trace (Banyan)
  <cr>
```

Telnet is the best tool, since it uses IP at the Network layer and TCP at the Transport layer to create a session with a remote host. If you can telnet into a device, your IP connectivity just has to be good. You can only telnet to IP addresses, and you can use Windows hosts or router prompts to telnet to a remote device.

```
Router#telnet ?
  WORD IP address or hostname of a remote system
  <cr>
```

From the router prompt, you just type a hostname or IP address and it will assume you want to telnet—you don't need to type the actual command, telnet.

Verifying with the *Show Interface* Command

Another way to verify your configuration is by typing show interface commands, the first of which is show interface ?. That will reveal all the available interfaces to configure. The only interfaces that aren't logical are Ethernet and Serial.

```
Router#sh int ?
  Ethernet  IEEE 802.3
  Null      Null interface
  Serial    Serial
```

```
accounting Show interface accounting
crb       Show interface routing/bridging info
irb       Show interface routing/bridging info
<cr>
```

The next command is show interface ethernet 0; it reveals to us the hardware address, logical address, and encapsulation method, as well as statistics on collisions:

```
Router#sh int e0
Ethernet0 is up, line protocol is up
 Hardware is Lance, address is 0010.7b7f.c26c (bia
  0010.7b7f.c26c)
Internet address is 172.16.10.1/24
 MTU 1500 bytes, BW 10000 Kbit, DLY 1000 usec,
   reliability 255/255, txload 1/255, rxload 1/255
 Encapsulation ARPA, loopback not set, keepalive set
 (10 sec)
 ARP type: ARPA, ARP Timeout 04:00:00
 Last input 00:08:23, output 00:08:20, output hang never
 Last clearing of "show interface" counters never
 Queueing strategy: fifo
 Output queue 0/40, 0 drops; input queue 0/75, 0 drops
 5 minute input rate 0 bits/sec, 0 packets/sec
 5 minute output rate 0 bits/sec, 0 packets/sec
   25 packets input, 2459 bytes, 0 no buffer
   Received 25 broadcasts, 0 runts, 0 giants, 0 throttles
   0 input errors, 0 CRC, 0 frame, 0 overrun, 0 ignored,
   0 abort
   0 input packets with dribble condition detected
   33 packets output, 7056 bytes, 0 underruns
   0 output errors, 0 collisions, 1 interface resets
   0 babbles, 0 late collision, 0 deferred
   0 lost carrier, 0 no carrier
   0 output buffer failures, 0 output buffers swapped out
```

The most important statistic of the show interface command is the output of the line and data-link protocol status. If the output reveals that Ethernet 0 is up and the line protocol is up, then the interface is up and running.

```
RouterA#sh int e0
Ethernet0 is up, line protocol is up
```

The first parameter refers to the Physical layer, and it's up when it receives carrier detect. The second parameter refers to the Data Link layer, and it looks for keepalives from the connecting end. (Keepalives are used between devices to make sure connectivity has not dropped.)

```
RouterA#sh int s0
Serial0 is up, line protocol is down
```

If you see the line is up but the protocol is down, as shown above, you are experiencing a clocking (keepalive) or framing problem. Check the keepalives on both ends to make sure that they match, the clock rate is set, if needed, and the encapsulation type is the same on both ends. This would be considered a Data Link layer problem.

```
RouterA#sh int s0
Serial0 is down, line protocol is down
```

If you discover that both the line interface and the protocol are down, it's a cable or interface problem. This would be considered a Physical layer problem.

If one end is administratively shut down (as shown next), the remote end would present as down and down.

```
RouterB#sh int s0
Serial0 is administratively down, line protocol is down
```

To enable the interface, use the command no shutdown from interface configuration mode.

The next show interface serial 0 command demonstrates the serial line and the maximum transmission unit (MTU)—1500 bytes by default. It also shows the default bandwidth (BW) on all Cisco serial links: 1.544Kbs. This is used to determine the bandwidth of the line for routing protocols like IGRP, EIGRP, and OSPF.

Another important configuration to notice is the keepalive, which is 10 seconds by default. Each router sends a keepalive message to its neighbor every 10 seconds, and if both routers aren't configured for the same keepalive time, it won't work.

You can clear the counters on the interface by typing the command clear counters.

```
Router#sh int s0
Serial0 is up, line protocol is up
```

```
Hardware is HD64570
MTU 1500 bytes, BW 1544 Kbit, DLY 20000 usec,
  reliability 255/255, txload 1/255, rxload 1/255
Encapsulation HDLC, loopback not set, keepalive set
 (10 sec)
Last input never, output never, output hang never
Last clearing of "show interface" counters never
Queueing strategy: fifo
Output queue 0/40, 0 drops; input queue 0/75, 0 drops
5 minute input rate 0 bits/sec, 0 packets/sec
5 minute output rate 0 bits/sec, 0 packets/sec
  0 packets input, 0 bytes, 0 no buffer
  Received 0 broadcasts, 0 runts, 0 giants, 0 throttles
  0 input errors, 0 CRC, 0 frame, 0 overrun, 0 ignored,
  0 abort
  0 packets output, 0 bytes, 0 underruns
  0 output errors, 0 collisions, 16 interface resets
  0 output buffer failures, 0 output buffers swapped out
  0 carrier transitions
  DCD=down DSR=down DTR=down RTS=down CTS=down

Router#clear counters ?
 Ethernet IEEE 802.3
 Null   Null interface
 Serial  Serial
 <cr>

Router#clear counters s0
Clear "show interface" counters on this interface
  [confirm][Enter]
Router#
00:17:35: %CLEAR-5-COUNTERS: Clear counter on interface
  Serial0 by console
Router#
```

Verifying with the *Show IP Interface* Command

The show ip interface command will provide you with information
regarding the layer-3 configurations of a router's interfaces.

```
Router#sh ip interface
FastEthernet0/0 is up, line protocol is down
  Internet address is 1.1.1.1/24
  Broadcast address is 255.255.255.255
  Address determined by setup command
  MTU is 1500 bytes
  Helper address is not set
  Directed broadcast forwarding is disabled
  Outgoing access list is not set
  Inbound  access list is not set
  Proxy ARP is enabled
  Security level is default
  Split horizon is enabled
[output cut]
```

The status of the interface, the IP address and mask, and information on whether an access list is set on the interface as well as basic IP information is included in this output.

Using the *Show Controllers* Command

The show controllers command displays information about the physical interface itself. It will also give you the type of serial cable plugged into a serial port. Usually, this will only be a DTE cable that plugs into a type of data service unit (DSU).

```
Router#sh controllers serial 0
HD unit 0, idb = 0x1229E4, driver structure at 0x127E70
buffer size 1524 HD unit 0, V.35 DTE cable
cpb = 0xE2, eda = 0x4140, cda = 0x4000

Router#sh controllers serial 1
HD unit 1, idb = 0x12C174, driver structure at 0x131600
buffer size 1524 HD unit 1, V.35 DCE cable
cpb = 0xE3, eda = 0x2940, cda = 0x2800
```

Notice that serial 0 has a DTE cable, whereas the serial 1 connection has a DCE cable. Serial 1 would have to provide clocking with the clock rate command. Serial 0 would get its clocking from the DSU.

Summary

Well, that concludes your introduction to the Cisco Internetwork Operating System (IOS)! And, as usual, it's super-important for you to have the basics that we went over in this chapter fully "dialed in" before you move on to subsequent chapters. So, here's a list of those important basics for you to go through point by point to make sure you're where you should be:

- Understanding the Cisco Internetwork Operating System (IOS) and how you can use the IOS to run and configure Cisco routers

- Connecting to a router with console connections and LAN connections

- Bringing up a router and entering setup mode

- Logging into a router and understanding the difference between user mode and privileged mode

- Understanding router prompts within router configuration mode

- Understanding editing and help features available from the router CLI

- Gathering basic routing information using the show commands

- Setting router passwords for both user-mode and privileged-mode access

- Setting router banners for identification

- Performing interface configurations to set the IP address on an interface

- Setting router hostnames for router identification

- Setting interface descriptions to identify each interface on a router

- Viewing and saving router configurations using the show commands and the copy run start command

- Verifying routing configurations using show commands

Exam Essentials

Understand the sequence of what happens when you power on a router. When you first bring up a Cisco router, it will run a power-on self-test (POST), and if that passes, it will then look for and load the Cisco IOS from Flash memory, if a file is present. The IOS then proceeds to load and look for a valid configuration in NVRAM called the startup-config. If no file is present in NVRAM, the router will go into setup mode.

Remember what setup mode provides. Setup mode is automatically started if a router boots and no startup-config is in NVRAM. You can also bring up setup mode by typing **setup** from the privileged mode. Setup provides a minimum amount of configuration in an easy format for someone who does not understand how to configure a Cisco router from the command line.

Understand the difference between user mode and privileged mode. User mode provides a command-line interface with very few available commands by default. User mode does not allow the configuration to be viewed or changed. Privileged mode allows a user to both view and change the configuration of a router. You can enter privileged mode by typing the command **enable** and entering the enable password or enable secret password, if set.

Remember what the command *show version* provides. The show version command will provide basic configuration for the system hardware as well as the software version, the names and sources of configuration files, and the boot images.

Remember how to set the hostname of a router. The command sequence to set the hostname of a router is:

```
enable
config t
hostname Todd
```

Remember the difference between the enable password and enable secret password. Both of these passwords are used to gain access into privilege mode. However, the enable secret is newer and encrypted by default. Also, if you set the enable password and then set the enable secret, only the enable secret will be used.

Remember how to set the enable secret on a router. To set the enable secret, you use the command enable secret. Do not use enable secret password *password*, or you will set your password to "password *password*". Here is an example:

```
enable
config t
enable secret todd
```

Remember how to set the console password on a router. To set the console password, the sequence is:

```
enable
config t
line console 0
login
password todd
```

Remember how to set the Telnet password on a router. To set the Telnet password, the sequence is:

```
enable
config t
line vty 0 4
login
password todd
```

Be able to understand how to troubleshoot a serial link problem. If you type show interface serial 0 and see that it is "down, line protocol is down", this will be considered a Physical layer problem. If you see it as "up, line protocol is down", then you have a Data Link layer problem.

Key Terms

Before taking the exam, be sure you're familiar with the following terms:

auxiliary port	global command
Basic Management Setup	interface configuration mode
Cisco Internetwork Operating System (IOS)	privileged mode
command-line interface (CLI)	setup mode
console port	Telnet
EXEC session	user mode
Extended Setup	

Commands Used in This Chapter

$\mathbf{T}$he following list contains a summary of all the commands used in this chapter:

Command	Description
?	Gives you a help screen
Backspace	Deletes a single character
bandwidth	Sets the bandwidth on a serial interface
banner	Creates a banner for users who log into the router
clear counters	Clears the statistics from an interface
clock rate	Provides clocking on a serial DCE interface
config memory	Copies the startup-config to running-config
config network	Copies a configuration stored on a TFTP host to running-config
config terminal	Puts you in global configuration mode and changes the running-config
copy run start	Short for copy running-config startup-config; places a configuration into NVRAM
Ctrl+A	Moves your cursor to the beginning of the line
Ctrl+D	Deletes a single character
Ctrl+E	Moves your cursor to the end of the line
Ctrl+F	Moves forward one character
Ctrl+R	Redisplays a line
Ctrl+U	Erases a line
Ctrl+W	Erases a word
Ctrl+Z	Ends configuration mode and returns to EXEC
description	Sets a description on an interface
disable	Takes you from privileged mode back to user mode
enable	Puts you into privileged mode
enable password	Sets the unencrypted enable password

Command	Description
enable secret	Sets the encrypted enable secret password; supersedes the enable password if set
erase startup	Deletes the startup-config
Esc+B	Moves back one word
Esc+F	Moves forward one word
exec-timeout	Sets the timeout in seconds and minutes for the console connection
hostname	Sets the name of a router
interface	Puts you in interface configuration mode; also used with show commands
interface fastethernet 0/0	Puts you in interface configuration mode for a FastEthernet port; also used with show commands
interface fastethernet 0/0.1	Creates a subinterface
interface serial 5	Puts you in configuration mode for interface serial 5 and can be used for show commands
ip address	Sets an IP address on an interface
line	Puts you in configuration mode to change or set your user mode passwords
line aux	Puts you in the auxiliary interface configuration mode
line console 0	Puts you in console configuration mode
line vty	Puts you in VTY (Telnet) interface configuration mode
logging synchronous	Stops console messages from overwriting your command-line input
logout	Logs you out of your console session
media-type	Sets the hardware media type on an interface
no shutdown	Turns on an interface
ping	Tests IP connectivity
router rip	Puts you in router rip configuration mode
service password-encryption	Encrypts the user mode and enable password
show controllers s 0	Shows the DTE or DCE status of an interface

Command	Description
show history	Shows you the last 10 commands entered by default
show interface s0	Shows the statistics of interface serial 0
show run	Short for show running-config; shows the configuration currently running on the router
show start	Short for show startup-config; shows the backup configuration stored in NVRAM
show terminal	Shows you your configured history size
show version	Shows you statistics of the router
shutdown	Puts an interface in administratively-down mode
Tab	Finishes typing a command for you
telnet	Tests IP connectivity and configures a router
terminal history size	Changes your history size from the default of 10 up to 256
trace	Tests IP connectivity

Written Lab 4

Write out the command or commands for the following questions:

1. What command is used to set a serial interface to provide clocking to another router at 64k?

2. If you telnet into a router and get the response "connection refused, password not set," what would you do to stop receiving this message and not be prompted for a password?

3. If you type **show inter et 0** and notice the port is administratively down, what would you do?

4. If you wanted to delete the configuration stored in NVRAM, what would you type?

5. If you wanted to set a user-mode password for the console port, what would you type?

6. If you wanted to set the enable secret password to *cisco*, what would you type?

7. If you wanted to see if a serial interface needed to provide clocking, what command would you use?

8. What command would you use to see the terminal history size?

9. What old Cisco command will change a configuration stored on a TFTP host?

10. How would you set the name of a router to *Chicago*?

(The answers to Written Lab 4 can be found following the answers to the Review Questions for this chapter.)

Hands-on Labs

In this section, you will perform commands on a Cisco router that will help you understand what you learned in this chapter.

You'll need at least one Cisco router—two would be better, three would be outstanding. The hands-on labs in this section are included for use with real Cisco routers. If you are using the Sybex Router Fundamentals Simulator provided on this book's companion CD, please use the hands-on labs found within that software program.

The labs in this chapter include the following:

Lab 4.1: Logging into a Router

Lab 4.2: Using the Help and Editing Features

Lab 4.3: Saving a Router Configuration

Lab 4.4: Setting Your Passwords

Lab 4.5: Setting the Hostname, Descriptions, IP Address, and Clock Rate

Hands-on Lab 4.1: Logging into a Router

1. Press Enter to connect to your router. This will put you into user mode.

2. At the Router> prompt, type a question mark (**?**).

3. Notice the –more– at the bottom of the screen.

4. Press the Enter key to view the commands line by line.

5. Press the spacebar to view the commands a full screen at a time.

6. You can type **q** at any time to quit.

7. Type **enable** or **en** and press Enter. This will put you into privileged where you can change and view the router configuration.

8. At the Router# prompt, type a question mark (**?**). Notice how many options are available to you in privileged mode.

9. Type **q** to quit.

10. Type **config** and press Enter.

11. Press Enter to configure your router using your terminal.

12. At the Router(config)# prompt, type a question mark (**?**), then **q** to quit, or hit the spacebar to view the commands.

13. Type **interface e0** or **int e0**, and press Enter. This will allow you to configure interface Ethernet 0.

14. At the Router(config-if)# prompt, type a question mark (**?**).

15. Type **int s0** or **interface s0** (same as the interface serial 0 command) and press Enter. This will allow you to configure interface serial 0. Notice that you can go from interface to interface easily.

16. Type **encapsulation ?**.

17. Type **exit**. Notice how this brings you back one level.

18. Press Ctrl+Z. Notice how this brings you out of configuration mode and places you back into privileged mode.

19. Type **disable**. This will put you into user mode.

20. Type **exit**, which will log you out of the router.

Hands-on Lab 4.2: Using the Help and Editing Features

1. Log into the router and go to privileged mode by typing **en** or **enable**.

2. Type a question mark (**?**).

3. Type **cl?** and then press Enter. Notice that you can see all the commands that start with *cl*.

4. Type **clock ?** and press Enter.

Notice the difference between Steps 3 and 4. Step 3 has you type letters with no space and a question mark, which will give you all the commands that start with *cl*. Step 4 has you type a command, space, and question mark. By doing this, you will see the next available commands.

5. Set the router's clock by typing **clock ?** and following the help screens; set the router's time and date.

6. Type **clock ?**.

7. Type **clock set ?**.

8. Type **clock set 10:30:30 ?**.

9. Type **clock set 10:30:30 14 March ?**.

10. Type **clock set 10:30:30 14 March 2002**.

11. Press Enter.

12. Type **show clock** to see the time and date.

13. From privileged mode, type **show access-list 10**. Don't press Enter.

14. Press Ctrl+A. This takes you to the beginning of the line.

15. Press Ctrl+E. This should take you back to the end of the line.

16. Press Ctrl+A, then Ctrl+F. This should move you forward one character.

17. Press Ctrl+B, which will move you back one character.

18. Press Enter, then press Ctrl+P. This will repeat the last command.

19. Press the Up arrow on your keyboard. This will also repeat the last command.

20. Type **sh history**. This shows you the last 10 commands entered.

21. Type **terminal history size ?**. This changes the history entry size.

22. Type **show terminal** to gather terminal statistics and history size.

23. Type **terminal no editing**. This turns off advanced editing. Repeat Steps 14–18 to see that the shortcut editing keys have no effect until you type **terminal editing**.

24. Type **terminal editing** and press Enter to re-enable advanced editing.

25. Type **sh run**, then press your Tab key. This will finish typing the command for you.

26. Type **sh star**, then press your Tab key. This will finish typing the command for you.

Hands-on Lab 4.3: Saving a Router Configuration

1. Log into the router and go into privileged mode by typing **en** or **enable**, then press Enter.

2. To see the configuration stored in NVRAM, type **sh start** and press Tab and Enter, or type **show startup-config** and press Enter. However, if no configuration has been saved, you will get an error message.

3. To save a configuration to NVRAM, which is known as startup-config, you can do one of the following:

   - Type **copy run start** and press Enter.

   - Type **copy running**, press Tab, type **start**, press Tab, and press Enter.

   - Type **copy running-config startup-config** and press Enter.

4. Type **sh start**, press tab, then press Enter.

5. Type **sh run**, press tab, then press Enter.

6. Type **erase start**, press Tab, then press Enter.

7. Type **sh start**, press Tab, then press Enter. You should get an error message.

8. Type **reload**, then press Enter. Acknowledge the reload by pressing Enter. Wait for the router to reload.

9. Say no to entering setup mode, or just press Ctrl+C.

Hands-on Lab 4.4: Setting Your Passwords

1. Log into the router and go into privileged mode by typing **en** or **enable**.

2. Type **config t** and press Enter.

3. Type **enable ?**.

4. Set your enable secret password by typing **enable secret** *password* (the third word should be your own personalized password) and pressing Enter. Do not add the command `password` after the command `secret` (this would make your password the word *password*). An example would be `enable secret todd`.

5. Now let's see what happens when you log all the way out of the router and then log in. Log out by pressing Ctrl+Z, then type **exit** and press Enter. Go to privileged mode. Before you are allowed to enter privileged mode, you will be asked for a password. If you successfully enter the secret password, you can proceed.

6. Remove the secret password. Go to privileged mode, type **config t**, and press Enter. Type **no enable secret** and press Enter. Log out and then log back in again, and now you should not be asked for a password.

7. One more password used to enter privileged mode is called the enable password. It is an older, less secure password and is not used if an enable secret password is set. Here is an example of how to set it:

```
config t
enable password todd1
```

8. Notice that the enable secret and enable passwords are different. They cannot be the same.

9. Type **config t** to be at the right level to set your console and auxiliary passwords, then type **line ?**.

10. Notice the output for the line commands is `auxiliary`, `vty`, and `console`. You will set all three.

11. To set the Telnet or VTY password, type **line vty 0 4** and then press Enter. The 0 4 is the five available virtual lines used to connect with Telnet. If you have an enterprise IOS, the number of lines may vary. Use the question mark to determine the last line number available on your router.

12. The next command is used to set the authentication on or off. Type **login** and press Enter to prompt for a user-mode password when telnetting into the router. You will not be able to telnet into a router if the password is not set.

You can use the `no login` command to disable the user-mode password prompt when using Telnet.

13. One more command you need to set for your VTY password is password. Type **password *password*** to set the password. (*password* is your password.)

14. Here is an example of how to set the VTY passwords:

```
config t
line vty 0 4
login
password todd
```

15. Set your auxiliary password by first typing **line auxiliary 0** or **line aux 0**.

16. Type **login**.

17. Type **password *password***.

18. Set your console password by first typing **line console 0** or **line con 0**.

19. Type **login**.

20. Type **password *password***. Here is an example of the last two commands:

```
config t
line con 0
login
password todd1
line aux 0
login
password todd
```

21. You can add the Exec-timeout 0 0 command to the console 0 line. This will stop the console from timing out and logging you out. The command will now look like this:

```
config t
line con 0
login
password todd2
exec-timeout 0 0
```

22. Set the console prompt to not overwrite the command you're typing with console messages by using the command logging synchronous.

```
config t
line con 0
logging synchronous
```

Hands-on Lab 4.5: Setting the Hostname, Descriptions, IP Address, and Clock Rate

1. Log into the router and go into privileged mode by typing **en** or **enable**.

2. Set your hostname on your router by using the hostname command. Notice that it is one word. Here is an example of setting your hostname:

```
Router#config t
Router(config)#hostname RouterA
RouterA(config)#
```

Notice that the hostname of the router changed as soon as you pressed Enter.

3. Set a banner that the network administrators will see by using the banner command.

4. Type **config t**, then **banner ?**.

5. Notice that you can set four different banners. For this exam we are only interested in the login and message of the day (MOTD) banners.

6. Set your MOTD banner, which will be displayed when a console, auxiliary, or Telnet connection is made to the router by typing

```
config t
banner motd #
This is an motd banner
#
```

7. The preceding example used a # sign as a delimiting character. This tells the router when the message is done. You cannot use the delimiting character in the message.

8. You can remove the MOTD banner by typing

```
config t
no banner motd
```

9. Set the login banner by typing

```
config t
banner login #
This is a login banner
#
```

10. The login banner will display immediately after the MOTD but before the user-mode password prompt. Remember that you set your user-mode passwords by setting the console, auxiliary, and VTY line passwords.

11. You can remove the login banner by typing:

```
config t
no banner login
```

12. You can add an IP address to an interface with the ip address command. You need to get into interface configuration mode first; here is an example of how you do that:

```
config t
int e0 (you can use int Ethernet 0 too)
ip address 1.1.1.1 255.255.0.0
no shutdown
```

Notice the IP address (1.1.1.1) and subnet mask (255.255.0.0) are configured on one line. The no shutdown (or no shut for short) command is used to enable the interface. All interfaces are shut down by default.

13. You can add identification to an interface by using the description command. This is useful for adding information about the connection. Only administrators see this, not users. Here is an example:

```
config t
int s0
ip address 1.1.1.2 255.255.0.0
no shut
description Wan link to Miami
```

14. You can add the bandwidth of a serial link as well as the clock rate when simulating a DCE WAN link. Here is an example:

```
config t
int s0
bandwidth 64
clock rate 64000
```

Review Questions

1. Which of the following messages displays the code image running in router memory?

A. System Bootstrap, Version 12.1(3r)T2, RELEASE SOFTWARE (fc1)Copyright (c) 2000 by cisco Systems, Inc.C2600 platform with 32768 Kbytes of main memory

B. program load complete, entry point: 0x80008000, size: 0x43b7fc. Self decompressing the image : ### ### #############################[OK]

C. Cisco Internetwork Operating System Software IOS (tm) C2600 Software (C2600-I-M), Version 12.1(8), RELEASE SOFTWARE (fc1)Copyright (c) 1986-2001 by cisco Systems, Inc.Compiled Tue 17-Apr-01 04:55 by kellythw Image text-base: 0x80008088, data-base: 0x8080853C

D. cisco 2621 (MPC860) processor (revision 0x101) with 26624K/6144K bytes of memory.Processor board ID JAD050697JB (146699779)M860 processor: part number 0, mask 49 Bridging software. X.25 software, Version 3.0.0.2 FastEthernet/IEEE 802.3 interface(s)1 Serial network interface(s)32K bytes of non-volatile configuration memory.8192K bytes of processor board System flash (Read/Write)

2. Which of the following prompts indicates that you are in privileged mode?

A. >

B. (config)#

C. #

D. !

3. If you type a command and receive the error "% incomplete command" from a switch CLI, what would you do to get help?

    A. Type **history** to review the error

    B. Re-enter the command followed by a question mark to view the keywords

    C. Type **help**

    D. Enter a question mark to see all the console commands

4. Which command will show you whether a DTE or DCE cable is plugged into serial 0?

    A. sh int s0

    B. sh int serial 0

    C. sho controllers s 0

    D. sho controllers s0

5. What keystroke will terminate setup mode?

    A. Ctrl+Z

    B. Ctrl+^

    C. Ctrl+C

    D. Ctrl+Shift+^

6. Which of the following commands will display a backup configuration?

    A. sh running-config

    B. show startup-config

    C. show version

    D. show backup-config

7. Which of the following commands will configure all the default VTY ports on a router?

    A. Router#line vty 0 4

    B. Router(config)#line vty 0 4

    C. Router(config-if)#line vty 0 4

    D. Router(config)#line vty all

8. Which of the following commands sets the secret password to "Cisco"?

   A. `enable secret password Cisco`

   B. `enable secret cisco`

   C. `enable secret Cisco`

   D. `enable password Cisco`

9. If you wanted administrators to see a message when logging into the router, which command would you use?

   A. `message banner motd`

   B. `banner message motd`

   C. `banner motd`

   D. `message motd`

10. Which of the following commands will reload the router?

   A. `Router>`**`reload`**

   B. `Router#`**`reset`**

   C. `Router#`**`reload`**

   D. `Router(config)#`**`reload`**

11. What command do you type to save the configuration stored in RAM to NVRAM?

   A. `Router(config)#`**`copy current to starting`**

   B. `Router#`**`copy starting to running`**

   C. `Router(config)#`**`copy running-config startup-config`**

   D. `Router#`**`copy run startup`**

12. What command will display all the valid commands at the given mode?

   A. `help`

   B. `help all`

   C. `?`

   D. `list`

13. Which command will delete the contents of NVRAM on a router?

   A. delete NVRAM

   B. delete startup-config

   C. erase NVRAM

   D. erase start

14. What is the problem with an interface if you type show interface serial 0 and receive the following message?

   Serial0 is administratively down, line protocol is down

   A. The keepalives are different times.

   B. The administrator has the interface shut down.

   C. The administrator is pinging from the interface.

   D. No cable is attached.

15. What do the square brackets indicate when in setup mode?

   A. That the router needs to be reloaded

   B. Values entered are not saved

   C. Current or default settings

   D. Hard-coded values that cannot be changed

16. If you delete the contents of NVRAM and reboot the router, what mode will you be in?

   A. Privileged mode

   B. Global mode

   C. Setup mode

   D. NVRAM loaded mode

17. Which of the following is stored in RAM? (Choose all that apply.)

A. Packet buffers

B. Startup-config

C. Cisco IOS

D. ARP cache

E. Routing table

F. Running-config

G. Configuration register

18. If you want to display all the commands in the history buffer, which command will you use?

A. Ctrl+Shift+6 then X

B. Ctrl+Z

C. `show history`

D. `show history buffer`

19. Which of the following commands starts the IP processing on a router interface?

A. `enable ip`

B. `network` *ip_address*

C. `ip address` *ip_address netmask*

D. `reload` and `restart`

20. Which command will provide you with information regarding the layer-3 configuration of a router's interfaces?

A. `show cdp neighbors`

B. `show cdp neighbors detail`

C. `show ip route`

D. `show ip interface`

E. `telnet`

21. If you type **line console 0**, what likely operation will follow?

    A. Setting of the telnet password

    B. Setting of the console password

    C. Configuration of a terminal type

    D. Change from privileged to user mode

22. Which of the following is a correct command for setting the console terminal line password to "todd"?

    A. line vty 0
       login
       password todd

    B. line vty 0 4
       login
       password todd

    C. line console 0
       login
       password todd

    D. line console0
       login
       password todd

23. When in setup mode, which of the following are true? (Choose two.)

    A. The enable password is encrypted.

    B. The enable secret is encrypted.

    C. The enable password is not encrypted.

    D. The enable secret is not encrypted.

24. If you type **erase startup-config** and reboot your router, what router mode will you be in?

    A. Global config

    B. Interface config

    C. Setup

    D. User mode

25. What layer of the OSI model would you assume the problem is in if you type **show interface serial 1** and receive the following message?

`Serial1 is a down, line protocol is down`

    A. Physical layer

    B. Data Link layer

    C. Network layer

    D. None; it is a router problem.

Answers to Review Questions

1. C. The only message that states the type of Cisco IOS running in memory is the third option.

2. C. The pound sign (#) indicates that you are in privileged mode.

3. B. If you receive the "% incomplete command" error, just press your Up arrow key then a question mark to see what the next available command is in the command string.

4. C. The `show controllers serial 0` command will show you whether either a DTE or DCE cable is connected to the interface.

5. C. You can exit setup mode at any time by using the keystroke Ctrl+C.

6. B. The `show startup-config` command will display the configuration that will be loaded the next time the router is booted.

7. B. From global configuration mode, use the `line vty 0 4` command to set all five default VTY lines.

8. C. The enable secret password is case sensitive, so the second option is wrong. To set the enable secret password, use the `enable secret password` command from global configuration mode.

9. C. The typically banner is a message of the day (MOTD) and is set by using the global configuration mode command `banner motd`.

10. C. To reload the router, use the command `reload` from privileged mode.

11. D. To copy the current config to NVRAM so that it will be used if the router is restarted, use the `copy run start` command.

12. C. You can get a list of commands from any prompt by using the question mark (?).

13. D. The `erase startup-config` command erases the contents of NVRAM and will put you in setup mode if the router is restarted.

14. B. If an interface is shut down, the `show interface` command will show the interface as administratively shut down. (It is possible no cable is attached, but you can't tell that from this message.)

15. C. If you are using setup mode, which you really shouldn't be doing, the square brackets indicate the current or default commands.

16. C. If you delete the startup-config and reload the router, the router will automatically enter setup mode. You can also type **setup** from privileged mode at any time.

17. A, D, E, F. RAM is used to store the packet buffers, ARP cache, and routing tables as well as the running-config.

18. C. The show history command will display the last 10 commands entered by default. You can change the amount of commands displayed with the terminal history size command.

19. C. By typing an IP address on an interface and then typing no shutdown on the interface, the router's interface will be enabled with IP.

20. D. Both the show cdp neighbors detail command (discussed in Chapter 7) and the command show ip interface will show you an interface's layer-3 information. However, the show cdp neighbors command only displays information about one interface, and show ip interface displays information about all interfaces on a router. The question stated "interfaces," not interface.

21. B. From the line console 0 command, you can then set the user-mode console password.

22. C. The line console 0 command will allow you to set the user-mode console password. You cannot type line console0; you must have a space between console and 0.

23. B, C. The enable password is not encrypted by default; however, the enable secret is encrypted by default.

24. C. You can enter setup mode by erasing the configuration and rebooting the router or by typing **setup** from privileged mode.

25. A. If you see that a serial interface and the protocol are both down, then you have a Physical layer problem.

Answers to Written Lab 4

1. clock rate 64000
2. config t, line vty 0 4, no login
3. config t, int e0, no shut
4. erase startup-config
5. config t, line console 0, login, password todd
6. config t, enable secret cisco
7. show controllers s 0
8. show terminal
9. config net
10. config t, hostname Chicago

Chapter

5

IP Routing

THE CCNA EXAM TOPICS COVERED IN THIS CHAPTER INCLUDE THE FOLLOWING:

✓ **Network Protocols**

- Configure IP addresses.

✓ **Routing**

- Add the RIP routing protocol to your configuration.
- Add the IGRP routing protocol to your configuration.

✓ **Cisco Basics, IOS & Network Basics**

- List problems that each routing type encounters when dealing with topology changes, and describe techniques to reduce the number of these problems.

his chapter will discuss the IP routing process. This is an important subject to understand, as it pertains to all routers and configurations that use IP. IP routing is the process of moving packets from one network to another network using routers.

Before you read this chapter, you must understand the difference between a routing protocol and a routed protocol. A *routing protocol* is used by routers to dynamically find all the networks in the internetwork and to make sure that all routers have the same routing table. Basically, a routing protocol determines the path of a packet through an internetwork. Examples of routing protocols are RIP and IGRP.

Once all routers know about all networks, a *routed protocol* can be used to send user data (packets) through the internetwork. Routed protocols are assigned to an interface and determine the method of packet delivery. Examples of routed protocols are IP and IPX.

It is imperative to understand that this is a very, very important chapter to comprehend. IP routing is what Cisco routers basically do, and they do this very well.

In this chapter, I'll tell you how to configure and verify IP routing with Cisco routers. I'll cover the following:

- Static routing

- Default routing

- Dynamic routing

Routing Basics

Once you create an internetwork by connecting your WANs and LANs to a router, you then need to configure logical network addresses, such as IP addresses, to all hosts on the internetwork so that they can communicate across the internetwork.

The term *routing* is used for taking a packet from one device and sending it through the network to another device on a different network. Routers don't care about hosts—they only care about networks and the best path to each network. The logical network address of the destination host is used to get packets to a network through a routed network, then the hardware address of the host is used to deliver the packet from a router to the destination host.

If your network has no routers, then you are not routing. (Makes sense, huh?) Routers route traffic to all the networks in your internetwork. To be able to route packets, a router must know, at a minimum, the following:

- Destination address

- Neighbor routers from which it can learn about remote networks

- Possible routes to all remote networks

- The best route to each remote network

- How to maintain and verify routing information

The router learns about remote networks from neighbor routers or from an administrator. The router then builds a routing table that describes how to find the remote networks. If a network is directly connected, then the router already knows how to get to it. If a network is not connected, the router must learn how to get to the remote network using either static routing, which means that the administrator must hand-type all network locations into the routing table, or dynamic routing.

In *dynamic routing*, a protocol on one router communicates with the same protocol running on neighbor routers. The routers then update each other about all the networks they know about and place this information in the routing table. If a change occurs in the network, the dynamic routing protocols automatically inform all routers about the change. If *static routing* is used, the administrator is responsible for updating all changes by hand into all routers. Typically, in a large network, a combination of both dynamic and static routing is used.

The IP Routing Process

The IP routing process is fairly simple and doesn't change, regardless of the size of network you have. For an example, we'll use Figure 5.1 to describe step by step what happens when Host A wants to communicate with Host B on a different network.

FIGURE 5.1 IP routing example using two hosts and one router

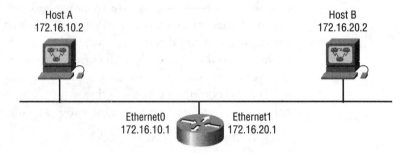

In our example, a user on Host A pings Host B's IP address. Routing will not get simpler than this, but it still involves a lot of steps. Let's work through them:

1. Internet Control Message Protocol (ICMP) creates an echo request payload (which is just the alphabet in the data field).

2. ICMP hands that payload to Internet Protocol (IP), which then creates a packet. At a minimum, this packet contains an IP source address, IP destination address, and a protocol field with 01h. All that tells the receiving host to whom it should hand the payload when the destination is reached—in this example, ICMP.

3. Once the packet is created, IP works with Address Resolution Protocol (ARP) to determine whether the destination IP address is on the local network or a remote one.

4. Since ARP and IP determine this is a remote request, the packet needs to be sent to the default gateway so the packet can be routed to the remote network. The Registry in Windows is parsed to find the configured default gateway.

5. The default gateway of host 172.16.10.2 is configured to 172.16.10.1. To be able to send this packet to the default gateway, the hardware

address of the router's interface Ethernet 0 (configured with the IP address of 172.16.10.1) must be known. Why? So the packet can be handed down to the Data Link layer, framed, and sent to the router's interface connected to the 172.16.10.0 network. Hosts communicate only via hardware addresses on the local LAN.

6. First, the ARP cache is checked to see if the IP address of the default gateway has been already resolved to a hardware address:

   - If it has, the packet is then free to be handed to the Data Link layer for framing. (The hardware destination address is also handed down with that packet.)

   - If the hardware address isn't already in the ARP cache of the host, an ARP broadcast is sent out onto the local network to search for the hardware address of 172.16.10.1. The router responds to the request and provides the hardware address of Ethernet 0, and the host caches this address. The router also caches the hardware address of Host A in the ARP cache.

7. Once the packet and destination hardware address are handed to the Data Link layer, the LAN driver is used to provide media access via the type of LAN being used (in this example, Ethernet). A frame is then generated, encapsulating the packet with control information. Within that frame are the hardware destination and source addresses, plus an Ether-Type field that describes the Network layer protocol that handed the packet to the Data Link layer—in this case, IP. At the end of the frame is something called a Frame Check Sequence field (FCS) that houses the answer to the cyclic redundancy check (CRC).

8. Once the frame is completed, the frame is handed down to the Physical layer to be put on the physical medium (in this example, twisted-pair wire) one bit at a time.

9. Every device in the collision domain receives these bits and builds the frame. They each run a CRC and check the answer in the FCS field. If the answers don't match, the frame is discarded. If the CRC matches (which, in this example, is the router's interface Ethernet 0), then the hardware destination address is checked to see if it matches too. If it's a match, then the Ether-Type field is checked to find the protocol used at the Network layer.

10. The packet is pulled from the frame, and the frame is discarded. The packet is handed to the protocol listed in the Ether-Type field—it's given to IP.

11. IP receives the packet and checks the IP destination address. Since the packet's destination address doesn't match any of the addresses configured on the receiving router itself, the router will look up the destination IP network address in its routing table.

12. The routing table must have an entry for the network 172.16.20.0, or the packet will be discarded immediately and an ICMP message will be sent back to the originating device with a "destination network unavailable" message.

13. If the router does find an entry for the destination network in its table, the packet is switched to the exit interface—in this example, interface Ethernet 1.

14. The router packet-switches the packet to the Ethernet 1 buffer.

15. The Ethernet 1 buffer needs to know the hardware address of the destination host and first checks the ARP cache. If the hardware address of Host B has already been resolved, then the packet and the hardware address are handed down to the Data Link layer to be resolved.

16. If the hardware address has not already been resolved, the router sends an ARP request looking for the hardware address of 172.16.20.2.

17. Host B responds with its hardware address, and the packet and destination hardware address are both sent to the Data Link layer for framing.

18. The Data Link layer creates a frame with the destination and source hardware address, Ether-Type field, and FCS field at the end of the frame. The frame is handed to the Physical layer to be sent out on the physical medium one bit at a time.

19. Host B receives the frame and immediately runs a CRC. If the answer matches what's in the FCS field, the hardware destination address is then checked. If the host finds a match, the Ether-Type field is then checked to determine protocol where the packet should be handed to at the Network layer—IP, in this example.

20. At the Network layer, IP receives the packet and checks the IP destination address. Since there's finally a match made, the protocol field is checked to find out whom the payload should be given to.

21. The payload is handed to ICMP, which understands that this is an echo request. ICMP responds to this by immediately discarding the packet and generating a new payload as an echo reply.

22. A packet is then created including the source and destination address, protocol field, and payload. The destination device is now Host A.

23. ARP then checks to see whether the destination IP address is a device on the local LAN or on a remote network. Since the destination device is on a remote network, the packet needs to be sent to the default gateway.

24. The default gateway address is found in the Registry of the Windows device, and the ARP cache is checked to see if the hardware address has already been resolved from an IP address.

25. Once the hardware address of the default gateway is found, the packet and destination hardware address are handed down to the Data Link layer for framing.

26. The Data Link layer frames the packet of information and includes the following in the header:

    - The destination and source hardware address

    - Ether-Type field with IP in it

    - FCS field with the CRC answer in tow

27. The frame is now handed down to the Physical layer to be sent out over the network medium one bit at a time.

28. The router's Ethernet 1 interface receives the bits and build a frame. The CRC is run, and the FCS field is checked to make sure the answers match.

29. One the CRC is found to be OK, the hardware destination address is checked. Since the router's interface is a match, the packet is pulled from the frame and the Ether-Type field is checked to see what protocol at the Network layer the packet should be delivered to.

30. The protocol is determined to be IP, so it gets the packet. IP runs a CRC check on the IP header first, and then checks the destination IP address. (Note: IP does not run a complete CRC like the Data Link layer—it only checks the header for errors.) Since the IP destination address doesn't match any of the router's interfaces, the routing table is checked to see whether it has a route to 172.16.10.0. If it doesn't

have a route over to the destination network, the packet will be discarded immediately. (This is the source point of confusion for a lot of administrators—when a ping fails, most people think the packet never reached the destination host. But as we see here, that's not *always* the case! All it takes is for just one of the remote routers to be lacking a route back to the originating host's network and POOF! The packet is dropped on the *return trip*, not on its way to the host.)

31. But the router does know how to get to network 172.16.10.0—the exit interface is Ethernet 0—so the packet is switched to interface Ethernet 0.

32. The router checks the ARP cache to determine if the hardware address for 172.16.10.2 has already been resolved.

33. Since the hardware address to 172.16.10.2 is already cached from the originating trip to Host B, the hardware address and packet are handed to the Data Link layer.

34. The Data Link layer builds a frame with the destination hardware address and source hardware address, then puts IP in the Ether-Type field. A CRC is run on the frame, and the answer is placed in the FCS field.

35. The frame is then handed to the Physical layer to be sent out onto the local network one bit at a time.

36. The destination host receives the frame, runs a CRC, checks the destination hardware address, and looks in the Ether-Type field to find who to hand the packet to.

37. IP is the designated receiver, and after the packet is handed to IP at the Network layer, it checks the protocol field for further direction. IP finds instructions to give the payload to ICMP, and ICMP determines the packet to be an ICMP echo reply.

38. ICMP acknowledges it has received the reply by sending an exclamation point (!) to the user interface. ICMP then attempts to send four more echo requests to the destination host.

You just experienced 38 easy steps to understanding IP routing. The key point to understand here is that if you had a much larger network, the process would be the same, with the packet simply going through more hops before it finds the destination host.

A very important subject to remember is that when you check the ARP table on Host A, it will show the MAC address for Host B as the MAC address of the local router's Ethernet port (default gateway). This is because frames cannot be placed on remote networks, only local networks, and packets destined for remote networks must go to the default gateway.

IP Routing in a Larger Network

In the example given in the previous section, the router already has both IP networks in its routing table because the networks are directly connected to the router. But what if we add three more routers? Figure 5.2 shows four routers: 2500A, 2500B, 2500C, and 2621A. These routers, by default, only know about their directly connected networks.

FIGURE 5.2   IP routing example with more routers

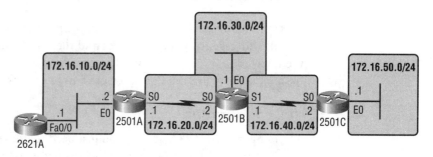

Figure 5.2 shows the three 2501 routers connected via a WAN and the 2621 router connected via the Ethernet network off 2501A. Each router also has an Ethernet network connected. I circled each logical network so you can see them easily on the figure. The idea is that each router must know about all five networks. The networks I'll use to configure the network are listed on the figure as well.

The first step is to configure each router with the correct configuration. Table 5.1 shows the IP address scheme I'll use to configure the network. After we go over how the network is configured, I'll discuss how to configure IP routing. Each network in the following table has a 24-bit subnet mask (255.255.255.0).

TABLE 5.1 Network Addressing for the IP Network

Router	Network Address	Interface	Address
2621A	172.16.10.0	f0/0	172.16.10.1
2501A	172.16.10.0	e0	172.16.10.2
2501A	172.16.20.0	s0	172.16.20.1
2501B	172.16.20.0	s0	172.16.20.2
2501B	172.16.40.0	s1	172.16.40.1
2501B	172.16.30.0	e0	172.16.30.1
2501C	172.16.40.0	s0	172.16.40.2
2501C	172.16.50.0	e0	172.16.50.1

Router configuration is a fairly simple process, since you just need to add IP addresses to your interfaces and then perform a no shutdown on the interfaces. It will get a tad bit more complex in the next section, but first, let's configure the IP addresses in the network.

2621A Configuration

To configure the 2621A router, you just need to add an IP address to interface FastEthernet 0/0. Configuring the hostnames of each router will make identification easier. Here is how I did that:

```
Router>en
Router#config t
Router(config)#hostname 2621A
2621A(config)#interface fa0/0
2621A(config-if)#ip address 172.16.10.1 255.255.255.0
2621A(config-if)#no shut
```

The configuration is only a few lines. If you have a hard time understanding this process, refer to Chapter 4.

To view the IP routing tables created on a Cisco router, use the privileged mode command show ip route. The command output is shown as follows.

Notice that only the configured network is shown in the routing table. This means the router only knows how to get to network 172.16.10.0.

```
2621A#sh ip route
Codes: C - connected, S - static, I - IGRP, R - RIP,
  M - mobile, B - BGP D - EIGRP, EX - EIGRP external, O -
  OSPF, IA - OSPF inter area N1 - OSPF NSSA external type
  1, N2 - OSPF NSSA external type 2 E1 - OSPF external
  type 1, E2 - OSPF external type 2, E - EGP i - IS-IS,
  L1 - IS-IS level-1, L2 - IS-IS level-2, * - candidate
  default, U - per-user static route, o - ODR, P -
  periodic downloaded static route, T - traffic
  engineered route
Gateway of last resort is not set
    172.16.0.0/24 is subnetted, 1 subnets
C       172.16.10.0 is directly connected, FastEthernet0/0
2621A#
```

The preceding routing table shows the directly connected network 172.16.10.0. Notice the C; this means that the network is directly connected. The codes for each type of connection are listed at the top of the show ip route command with their abbreviations.

In the interest of brevity, the codes will be cut in the rest of this chapter.

2501A Configuration

It is now time to configure the next router. To configure 2501A, two interfaces need to be configured: Ethernet 0 and serial 0.

```
Router>en
Router#config t
Router(config)#hostname 2501A
2501A(config)#int e0
2501A(config-if)#ip address 172.16.10.2 255.255.255.0
2501A(config-if)#no shut
2501A(config-if)#int s0
2501A(config-if)#ip address 172.16.20.1 255.255.255.0
2501A(config-if)#no shut
```

These commands configured serial 0 into network 172.16.20.0 and Ethernet 0 into network 172.16.10.0. The show ip route command displays the following:

```
2501A#sh ip route
[output cut]
Gateway of last resort is not set
      172.16.0.0/24 is subnetted, 2 subnets
C       172.16.20.0 is directly connected, Serial0
C       172.16.10.0 is directly connected, Ethernet0
2501A#
```

Notice that router 2501A knows how to get to networks 172.16.10.0 and 172.16.20.0. Router 2621A and Router 2501A can now communicate because they are connected on the same LAN.

2501B Configuration

The configuration of 2501B is more of the same, except that you also need to add the clock rate command to the data communication equipment (DCE) interfaces connected to both serial interfaces. For more information on the DCE interfaces and the clock rate command, please see Chapter 4.

```
Router>en
Router#config t
Router(config)#hostname 2501B
2501B(config)#int e0
2501B(config-if)#ip address 172.16.30.1 255.255.255.0
2501B(config-if)#no shut
2501B(config-if)#int s0
2501B(config-if)#ip address 172.16.20.2 255.255.255.0
2501B(config-if)#clock rate 64000
2501B(config-if)#no shut
2501B(config-if)#int s1
2501B(config-if)#ip address 172.16.40.1 255.255.255.0
2501B(config-if)#clock rate 64000
2501B(config-if)#no shut
```

These commands configured the hostname and IP addresses as well as the clock rate on the serial interfaces. The output of the following show ip route command displays the directly connected networks of 172.16.20.0, 172.16.30.0, and 172.16.40.0.

```
2501B#sh ip route
[output cut]
Gateway of last resort is not set
     172.16.0.0/24 is subnetted, 3 subnets
C       172.16.40.0 is directly connected, Serial1
C       172.16.30.0 is directly connected, Ethernet0
C       172.16.20.0 is directly connected, Serial0
2501B#
```

Routers 2501A and 2501B can communicate because they are on the same WAN network. However, Router 2501B cannot communicate with the 2621A router because it does not know about network 172.16.10.0. Router 2501A can ping both the 2621A router and 2501B, but 2501B and 2621A cannot see each other—yet.

2501C Configuration

The configuration of 2501C is the same as 2501A except that it has different network IDs.

```
Router>en
Router#config t
Router(config)#hostname 2501C
2501C(config)#int e0
2501C(config-if)#ip address 172.16.50.1 255.255.255.0
2501C(config-if)#no shut
2501C(config-if)#int s0
2501C(config-if)#ip address 172.16.40.2 255.255.255.0
2501C(config-if)#no shut
```

Interface Ethernet 0 is configured to participate in the 172.16.50.0 network, and serial 0 is configured into the 172.16.40.0 WAN network. The output of the show ip route command, displayed below, shows the directly connected networks on Router 2501C.

```
2501C#sh ip route
[output cut]
Gateway of last resort is not set
     172.16.0.0/24 is subnetted, 2 subnets
```

```
C       172.16.50.0 is directly connected, Ethernet0
C       172.16.40.0 is directly connected, Serial0
2501C#
```

Router 2501C can communicate with 2501B since they are on the same WAN network. However, by default, 2501C cannot see any other router or remote network.

Configuring IP Routing in Our Network

The network in the previous section has now been configured correctly with IP addressing. However, how does a router send packets to remote networks? The routers can only send packets by looking at the routing table and discovering how to get to the remote networks. But our configured routers only have information containing directly connected networks in each routing table. What happens when a router receives a packet with a network that is not listed in the routing table? It doesn't send a broadcast looking for the remote network—the router just discards it. Period.

There are a few different ways to configure the routing tables to include all the networks in our little internetwork so that packets will be forwarded. However, the best way for one network is not necessarily best for another. If you understand the different routing types, you'll be able to decide what fits best in your business requirements.

The different types of routing you will learn about in this chapter are:

- Static routing

- Default routing

- Dynamic routing

We will start off by describing and implementing static routing on our network. Why? Because if you can implement static routing and make it work, it means you have a good understanding of the internetwork.

Static Routing

Static routing occurs when an administrator manually adds routes in each router's routing table. There are both benefits and disadvantages to static routing, as there are for all routing processes.

Static routing has the following benefits:

- No overhead on the router CPU

- No bandwidth usage between routers

- Security (because the administrator only allows routing to certain networks)

Static routing has the following disadvantages:

- The administrator must really understand the internetwork and how each router is connected to configure the routes correctly.

- If one network is added to the internetwork, the administrator must add a route to it on all routers.

- It's not feasible in large networks because it would be a full-time job.

The command used to add a static route to a routing table is

```
ip route [destination_network] [mask] [next-hop_address
    or exitinterface] [administrative_distance] [permanent]
```

The following list describes each command in the string:

Ip route   The command used to create the static route.

Destination network   The network you are placing in the routing table.

Mask   The subnet mask being used on the network.

Next-hop address   The address of the next-hop router that will receive the packet and forward it to the remote network. This is a router interface that is on a directly connected network. You must be able to ping the router interface before you add the route. If you type in the wrong next-hop address, or the interface to that router is down, the static route will show up in the configuration of the router, but not in the routing table.

Exit interface   Used in place of the next-hop address if desired. Must be on a point-to-point link, such as a WAN. This command does not work on a LAN, such as Ethernet.

Administrative distance   By default, static routes have an administrative distance of 1. You can change the default value by adding an administrative weight at the end of the command. Administrative distance will be discussed further in the dynamic routing section later in this chapter.

Permanent   If the interface is shut down or the router cannot communicate to the next-hop router, the route is automatically discarded from the routing table. Choosing the `permanent` option keeps the entry in the routing table no matter what happens.

To be able to understand how static routes work, I'll demonstrate the configuration on my sample internetwork, as shown previously in Figure 5.2.

2621A

Each routing table automatically includes directly connected networks. To be able to route to all networks in the internetwork, the routing table must include information that defines where these other networks are located and how to get there.

The 2621A router is connected only to network 172.16.10.0. For the 2621A router to be able to route to all networks, the following networks must be configured in the routing table:

- 172.16.20.0
- 172.16.30.0
- 172.16.40.0
- 172.16.50.0

The following router output shows the configuration of static routes on the 2621A router and the routing table after the configuration. For the 2621A router to find the remote networks, an entry is placed in the routing table describing the network, the mask, and where to send the packets. Notice that each static route sends the packets to 172.16.10.2, which is the 2621A router's next hop.

```
2621A(config)#ip route 172.16.20.0 255.255.255.0
    172.16.10.2
2621A(config)#ip route 172.16.30.0 255.255.255.0
    172.16.10.2
2621A(config)#ip route 172.16.40.0 255.255.255.0
    172.16.10.2
2621A(config)#ip route 172.16.50.0 255.255.255.0
    172.16.10.2
```

After the router is configured, you can type `show running-config` and `show ip route` to see the static routes. Remember that if the routes don't appear in the routing table, it is because the router cannot communicate with the next-hop address you configured. You can use the permanent parameter to keep the route in the routing table even if the next-hop device cannot be contacted.

```
2621A#sh ip route
[output cut]
      172.16.0.0/24 is subnetted, 5 subnets
S       172.16.50.0 [1/0] via 172.16.10.2
S       172.16.40.0 [1/0] via 172.16.10.2
S       172.16.30.0 [1/0] via 172.16.10.2
S       172.16.20.0 [1/0] via 172.16.10.2
C       172.16.10.0 is directly connected, FastEthernet0/0
2621A#
```

The S in the routing table entries means that the network is a static entry. The [1/0] is the administrative distance and number of hops to the remote network, which is 0.

The 2621A router now has all the information it needs to communicate with the other remote networks. However, if the 2501A router is not configured with all the same information, the packets will be discarded at 2501A.

2501A

The 2501A router is connected to the networks 172.16.10.0 and 172.16.20.0. The following static routes must be configured on the 2501A router:

- 172.16.30.0

- 172.16.40.0

- 172.16.50.0

Here is the configuration for the 2501A router.

```
2501A(config)#ip route 172.16.30.0 255.255.255.0
   172.16.20.2
2501A(config)#ip route 172.16.40.0 255.255.255.0
   172.16.20.2
2501A(config)#ip route 172.16.50.0 255.255.255.0
   172.16.20.2
```

By looking at the routing table, you can see that the 2501A router now understands how to find each network.

```
2501A#sh ip route
[output cut]
       172.16.0.0/24 is subnetted, 5 subnets
S         172.16.50.0 [1/0] via 172.16.20.2
S         172.16.40.0 [1/0] via 172.16.20.2
S         172.16.30.0 [1/0] via 172.16.20.2
C         172.16.20.0 is directly connected, Serial0
C         172.16.10.0 is directly connected, Ethernet0
2501A#
```

The 2501A router now has a complete routing table. As soon as the other routers in the internetwork have the same routing table, 2501A can communicate to all remote networks.

2501B

The 2501B router is directly connected to networks 172.16.20.0, 172.16.30.0, and 172.16.40.0. Only two routes need to be added: 172.16.10.0 and 172.16.50.0.

```
2501B(config)#ip route 172.16.10.0 255.255.255.0
    172.16.20.1
2501B(config)#ip route 172.16.50.0 255.255.255.0
    172.16.40.2
```

The following output shows the routing table on the 2501B router.

```
2501B#sh ip route
[output cut]
       172.16.0.0/24 is subnetted, 5 subnets
S         172.16.50.0 [1/0] via 172.16.40.2
C         172.16.40.0 is directly connected, Serial1
C         172.16.30.0 is directly connected, Ethernet0
C         172.16.20.0 is directly connected, Serial0
S         172.16.10.0 [1/0] via 172.16.20.1
2501B#
```

2501B now shows all the networks in the internetwork and can communicate with all routers and networks, with the exception of the hosts on network 172.16.50.0; this is because 2501C is not configured yet.

2501C

Router 2501C is directly connected to networks 172.16.40.0 and 172.16.50.0. The routing table needs to know about networks 172.16.10.0, 172.16.20.0, and 172.16.30.0. Here is the configuration:

```
2501C(config)#ip route 172.16.10.0 255.255.255.0
  172.16.40.1
2501C(config)#ip route 172.16.20.0 255.255.255.0
  172.16.40.1
2501C(config)#ip route 172.16.30.0 255.255.255.0
  172.16.40.1
```

Below is the output of the show ip route command as run on the 2501C router.

```
2501C#sh ip route
[output cut]
      172.16.0.0/24 is subnetted, 5 subnets
C        172.16.50.0 is directly connected, Ethernet0
C        172.16.40.0 is directly connected, Serial0
S        172.16.30.0 [1/0] via 172.16.40.1
S        172.16.20.0 [1/0] via 172.16.40.1
S        172.16.10.0 [1/0] via 172.16.40.1
2501C#
```

Now all the routers have the correct routing table, and all the routers and hosts should be able to communicate without a problem. However, if you add even one more network or another router to the internetwork, you will have to update all routers' routing tables by hand. This is fine for a small network, but it is too time-consuming a task for a large internetwork.

Verifying Your Configuration

Once all the routers' routing tables are configured, they need to be verified. The best way to do this is with the Ping program. By pinging from routers 2621A and 2501C, the whole internetwork will be tested end-to-end.

Here is the output of a ping to network 172.16.50.0 from the 2621A router:

```
2621A#ping 172.16.50.1
Type escape sequence to abort.
```

```
Sending 5, 100-byte ICMP Echos to 172.16.50.1, timeout is
  2 seconds:
.!!!!
Success rate is 80 percent (4/5), round-trip min/avg/max
  = 64/66/68 ms
2621A#
```

Notice that the first response is a period. This is because the first ping times out waiting for the ARP request and response. Once the ARP has found the hardware address of the default gateway, the IP-to-Ethernet mapping will be in the ARP cache and will stay in the router's cache for four hours. Any other IP connectivity to the next-hop router will not time out, as no ARP broadcasts have to be performed.

From Router 2501C, a ping to 172.16.10.0 will test for good IP connectivity. Here is the router output:

```
2501C#ping 172.16.10.1
Type escape sequence to abort.
Sending 5, 100-byte ICMP Echos to 172.16.10.1, timeout
  is 2 seconds:
!!!!!
Success rate is 100 percent (5/5), round-trip min/avg/max
  = 64/67/72 ms
```

Notice that the first ping was not a time-out, since the ARP broadcasts are sent only on a LAN, not a WAN. And, since we can ping from end-to-end without a problem, our static route configuration was a success!

Default Routing

We use *default routing* to send packets with a remote destination network not in the routing table to the next-hop router. You can only use default routing on stub networks—those with only one exit port out of the network.

In the internetworking example used in the previous section, the only routers that are considered to be in a stub network are 2621A and 2501C. If you tried to put a default route on Routers 2501A and 2501B, packets would not be forwarded to the correct networks because they have more than one interface routing to other routers. However, even though Router 2501C has two connections, it does not have a router on the 172.16.50.0 network that needs packets sent to it. 2501C will only send packets to

172.16.40.1, which is the interface of 2501B. Router 2621A will only send packets to the 172.16.10.2 interface of 2501A.

To configure a default route, you use wildcards in the network address and mask locations of a static route. (In fact, you can just think of a default route as a static route that uses wildcards instead of network and mask information.) In this section, you'll create a default route on the 2501C router.

Router 2501C is directly connected to networks 172.16.40.0 and 172.16.50.0. The routing table needs to know about networks 172.16.10.0, 172.16.20.0, and 172.16.30.0. To configure the router to route to the other three networks, I placed three static routes in the routing table. By using a default route, you can just create one static route entry instead. First, you must delete the existing static routes from the router, then add the default route.

```
2501C(config)#no ip route 172.16.10.0 255.255.255.0
    172.16.40.1
2501C(config)#no ip route 172.16.20.0 255.255.255.0
    172.16.40.1
2501C(config)#no ip route 172.16.30.0 255.255.255.0
    172.16.40.1
2501C(config)#ip route 0.0.0.0 0.0.0.0 172.16.40.1
```

If you look at the routing table now, you'll see only the two directly connected networks, plus an S*, which indicates that this entry is a candidate for a default route.

```
2501C#sh ip route
[output cut]
Gateway of last resort is 172.16.40.1 to network 0.0.0.0
    172.16.0.0/24 is subnetted, 5 subnets
C       172.16.50.0 is directly connected, Ethernet0
C       172.16.40.0 is directly connected, Serial0
S*      0.0.0.0/0 [1/0] via 172.16.40.1
2501C#
```

Notice also in the routing table that the gateway of last resort is now set. However, there is one more command you must be aware of when using default routes: the ip classless command.

All Cisco routers are classful routers, which means they expect a default subnet mask on each interface of the router. When a router receives a packet for a destination subnet not in the routing table, it will drop the packet by default. If you are using default routing, you must use the ip classless command because no remote subnets will be in the routing table.

Since I have version 12.*x* of the IOS on my routers, the ip classless command is on by default. If you are using default routing and this command is not in your configuration, you need to add it. The command is shown here:

2501C(config)#**ip classless**

Notice that it is a global configuration mode command. The interesting part of the ip classless command is that default routing sometimes works without it, but sometimes it doesn't. Just to be on the safe side, you should always turn on the ip classless command when you use default routing.

Dynamic Routing

Dynamic routing is when protocols are used to find and update routing tables on routers. (This is easier than static or default routing, but you use it at the expense of router CPU processes and bandwidth on the network links.) A routing protocol defines the set of rules used by a router when it communicates between neighbor routers.

The two routing protocols discussed in this book are Routing Information Protocol (RIP) and Interior Gateway Routing Protocol (IGRP).

Enhanced Interior Gateway Routing Protocol (EIGRP) is an advanced distance-vector routing protocol and is Cisco proprietary. Open Shortest Path First (OSPF) is a non-proprietary link-state routing protocol used in the TCP/IP stack. For information on other types of routing protocols such as these, read *CCNP: Routing Study Guide* (Sybex, 2001), which covers the CCNP: Routing exam from Cisco.

EIGRP utilizes the features of both distance-vector and link-state routing protocols.

There are two types of routing protocols used in internetworks: interior gateway protocols (IGPs) and exterior gateway protocols (EGPs).

IGPs are used to exchange routing information with routers in the same autonomous system (AS). An AS is a collection of networks under a common administrative domain, which basically means that all routers sharing the same routing table information are in the same AS.

EGPs are used to communicate between ASs. An example of an EGP is Border Gateway Protocol (BGP), which is also discussed in *CCNP: Routing Study Guide*.

Since routing protocols are so essential to dynamic routing, in the next section we'll look at some basic information you should know about these protocols. In the section after that, we'll get nitty-gritty with RIP in particular.

Routing Protocol Basics

There are some fundamentals you should know about routing protocols before we look deeper into RIP. Specifically, you should understand administrative distances, the three different kinds of routing protocols, and routing loops.

Administrative Distances

The *administrative distance (AD)* is used to rate the trustworthiness of routing information received on a router from a neighbor router. An administrative distance is an integer from 0 to 255, where 0 is the most trusted and 255 means no traffic will be passed via this route.

If a router receives two updates listing the same remote network, the first thing the router checks is the AD. If one of the advertised routes has a lower AD than the other, then the route with the lowest AD will be placed in the routing table.

If both advertised routes to the same network have the same AD, then routing protocol metrics (such as *hop count* or bandwidth of the lines) will be used to find the best path to the remote network. The advertised route with the lowest metric will be placed in the routing table. However, if both advertised routes have the same AD as well as the same metrics, then the routing protocol will load-balance to the remote network.

Table 5.2 shows the default administrative distances that a Cisco router will use to decide which route to use to a remote network.

TABLE 5.2 Default Administrative Distances

Route Source	Default AD
Connected interface	0
Static route	1
EIGRP	90
IGRP	100
OSPF	110
RIP	120
External EIGRP	170
Unknown	255 (this route will never be used)

If a network is directly connected, the router will always use the interface connected to the network. If an administrator configures a static route, the router will believe that route over any other learned routes. You can change the administrative distance of static routes, but, by default, they have an AD of 1.

If you have a static route, a RIP-advertised route, and an IGRP-advertised route listing the same network, then by default, the router will always use the static route unless you change the AD of the static route.

Routing Protocols

There are three classes of routing protocols:

Distance vector   The *distance-vector protocols* find the best path to a remote network by judging distance. Each time a packet goes through a router, that's called a *hop*. The route with the least number of hops to the network is determined to be the best route. The vector indicates the direction to the remote network. Both RIP and IGRP are distance-vector routing protocols.

Link state   In *link-state protocols*, also called *shortest-path-first proto-cols*, the routers each create three separate tables. One of these tables keeps track of directly attached neighbors, one determines the topology of the entire internetwork, and one is used as the routing table. Link-state routers know more about the internetwork than any distance-vector routing protocol. OSPF is an IP routing protocol that is completely link state. For more information on OSPF, please see the Sybex *CCNP: Routing Study Guide*.

Hybrid   The *hybrid protocols* use aspects of both distance vector and link state—for example, EIGRP. For more information on EIGRP, please see the Sybex *CCNP: Routing Study Guide*.

There is no set way of configuring routing protocols for use with every business. This is a task that is performed on a case-by-case basis. However, if you understand how the different routing protocols work, you can make good business decisions. This book and the equivalent exam only cover distance-vector routing protocols and theory.

Distance-Vector Routing Protocols

The distance-vector routing algorithm passes complete routing tables to neighbor routers. The neighbor routers then combine the received routing table with their own routing tables to complete the internetwork map. This is called routing by rumor, because a router receiving an update from a neighbor router believes the information about remote networks without actually finding out for itself.

It is possible to have a network that has multiple links to the same remote network. If that is the case, the administrative distance is checked first. If the AD is the same, the protocol will have to use other metrics to determine the best path to use to that remote network.

RIP uses only hop count to determine the best path to an internetwork. If RIP finds more than one link to the same remote network with the same hop count, it will automatically perform a round-robin load balancing. RIP can perform load balancing for up to six equal-cost links.

However, a problem with this type of routing metric arises when the two links to a remote network are different bandwidths but the same hop count. Figure 5.3, for example, shows two links to remote network 172.16.10.0.

FIGURE 5.3 Pinhole congestion

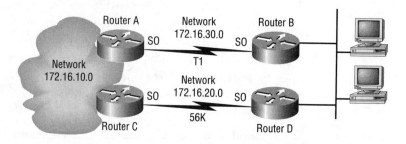

Since network 172.16.30.0 is a T1 link with a bandwidth of 1.544Mbps, and network 172.16.20.0 is a 56K link, you would want the router to choose the T1 over the 56K link. However, since hop count is the only metric used with RIP routing, they would both be seen as equal-cost links. This is called *pinhole congestion*.

It is important to understand what a distance-vector routing protocol does when it starts up. In Figure 5.4, the four routers start off with only their directly connected networks in the routing table. After a distance-vector routing protocol is started on each router, the routing tables are updated with all route information gathered from neighbor routers.

FIGURE 5.4 The internetwork with distance-vector routing

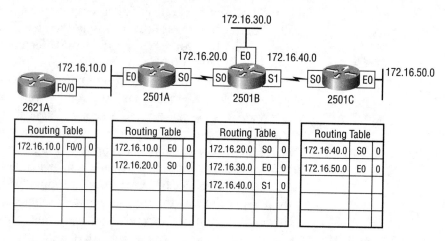

As shown in Figure 5.4, each router has only the directly connected networks in each routing table. Each router sends its complete routing table out

to each active interface on the router. The routing table of each router includes the network number, exit interface, and hop count to the network.

In Figure 5.5, the routing tables are complete because they include information about all the networks in the internetwork. They are considered *converged*. When the routers are converging, no data is passed. That's why fast convergence time is a plus. One of the problems with RIP, in fact, is its slow convergence time.

FIGURE 5.5 Converged routing tables

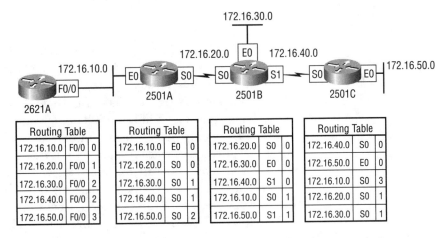

The routing table in each router keeps information regarding the remote network number, the interface to which the router will send packets to reach that network, and the hop count or metric to the network.

Routing Loops

Distance-vector routing protocols keep track of any changes to the internetwork by broadcasting periodic routing updates to all active interfaces. This broadcast includes the complete routing table. This works fine, although it takes up CPU process and link bandwidth. However, if a network outage happens, problems can occur. The slow convergence of distance-vector routing protocols can cause inconsistent routing tables and routing loops.

Routing loops can occur because every router is not updated close to the same time. Let's say that the interface to Network 5 in Figure 5.6 fails. All routers know about Network 5 from Router E. Router A, in its tables, has a path to Network 5 through Router B.

FIGURE 5.6 Routing loop example

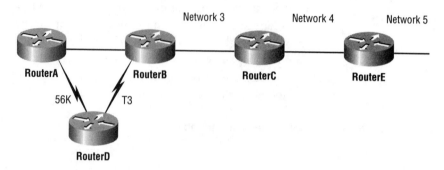

When Network 5 fails, Router E tells Router C. This causes Router C to stop routing to Network 5 through Router E. But Routers A, B, and D don't know about Network 5 yet, so they keep sending out update information. Router C will eventually send out its update and cause B to stop routing to Network 5, but Routers A and D are still not updated. To them, it appears that Network 5 is still available through Router B with a metric of 3.

The problem becomes when Router A sends out its regular 30-second "Hello, I'm still here—these are the links I know about" message, which includes reachability for Network 5. Routers B and D then receive the wonderful news that Network 5 can be reached from Router A, so they send out the information that Network 5 is available. Any packet destined for Network 5 will go to Router A, to Router B, and then back to Router A. This is a routing loop—how do you stop it?

Maximum Hop Count

The routing loop problem just described is called *counting to infinity*, and it's caused by gossip and wrong information being communicated and propagated throughout the internetwork. Without some form of intervention, the hop count increases indefinitely each time a packet passes through a router.

One way of solving this problem is to define a *maximum hop count*. Distance vector (RIP) permits a hop count of up to 15, so anything that requires 16 hops is deemed unreachable. In other words, after a loop of 15 hops, Network 5 will be considered down. Thus, the maximum hop count will keep packets from going around the loop forever. Though this is a workable solution, it won't remove the routing loop itself. Packets will still go into the loop, but instead of traveling on unchecked, they'll just whirl around for 16 bounces and die.

Split Horizon

Another solution to the routing loop problem is called *split horizon*. This reduces incorrect routing information and routing overhead in a distance-vector network by enforcing the rule that information cannot be sent back in the direction from which it was received.

In other words, the routing protocol differentiates which interface a network route was learned on and then will not advertise that route back out that same interface. This would have prevented Router A from sending the updated information it received from Router B back to Router B.

Route Poisoning

Another way to avoid problems caused by inconsistent updates and stop network loops is *route poisoning*. For example, when Network 5 goes down, Router E initiates route poisoning by entering a table entry for Network 5 as 16, or unreachable (sometimes referred to as *infinite*).

By this poisoning of the route to Network 5, Router C is not susceptible to incorrect updates about the route to Network 5. When Router C receives a route poisoning from Router E, it sends an update, called a *poison reverse*, back to Router E. This makes sure all routes on the segment have received the poisoned route information.

Route poisoning and split horizon create a much more resilient and dependable distance-vector network than we'd have otherwise and stop network loops. However, this isn't all you need to know about loop prevention in distance-vector networks; read on.

Holddowns

And then there are holddowns. A *holddown* prevents regular update messages from reinstating a route that is going up and down (called *flapping*). Typically this will happen on a serial link that is losing connectivity and then coming back up. If there was no way to stabilize this, the network would never converge and the flapping interface could bring the network down.

Holddowns prevent routes from changing too rapidly by allowing time for either the downed route to come back or the network to stabilize somewhat before changing to the next best route. These also tell routers to restrict, for a specific time period, any changes that might affect recently removed routes. This prevents inoperative routes from being prematurely restored to other routers' tables.

When a router receives an update from a neighbor indicating that a previously accessible network is not working and is inaccessible, the holddown timer will start. If a new update arrives from a neighbor with a better metric than the original network entry, the holddown is removed and data is passed. However, if an update is received from a neighbor router before the holddown timer expires and it has an equal or lower metric than the previous route, the update is ignored and the holddown timer keeps ticking. This allows more time for the network to stabilize before trying to converge.

Holddowns use triggered updates, which reset the holddown timer, to alert the neighbor routers of a change in the network. Unlike update messages from neighbor routers, triggered updates create a new routing table that is sent immediately to neighbor routers because a change was detected in the internetwork.

There are three instances when triggered updates will reset the holddown timer:

Memorize these!

- The holddown timer expires.

- Another update is received with a better metric.

- A flush timer, which is the time a route would be held before being removed, removes the route from the routing table.

Routing Information Protocol (RIP)

Routing Information Protocol (RIP) is a true distance-vector routing protocol. It sends the complete routing table out to all active interfaces every 30 seconds. RIP only uses hop count to determine the best way to a remote network, but it has a maximum allowable hop count of 15 by default, meaning that 16 is deemed unreachable. RIP works well in small networks, but it is inefficient on large networks with slow WAN links or on networks with a large number of routers installed.

RIP version 1 uses only *classful routing*, which means that all devices in the network must use the same subnet mask. This is because RIP version 1 does not send updates with subnet mask information in tow. RIP version 2 provides what is called *prefix routing* and does send subnet mask information with the route updates. This is called *classless routing*. Only RIP version 1 is discussed in this book because that is what the CCNA objectives cover.

RIP Timers

RIP uses three different kinds of timers to regulate its performance:

Route update timer   Sets the interval (typically 30 seconds) between periodic routing updates, in which the router sends a complete copy of its routing table out to all neighbors.

Route invalid timer   Determines the length of time that must elapse (90 seconds) before a router determines that a route has become invalid. It will come to this conclusion if it hasn't heard any updates about a particular route for that period. When that happens, the router will send out updates to all its neighbors letting them know that the route is invalid.

Route flush timer   Sets the time between a route becoming invalid and its removal from the routing table (240 seconds). Before it is removed from the table, the router notifies its neighbors of that route's impending doom. The value of the route invalid timer must be less than that of the route flush timer. This is to provide the router with enough time to tell its neighbors about the invalid route before the routing table is updated.

Configuring RIP Routing

To configure RIP routing, just turn on the protocol with the `router rip` command and tell the RIP routing protocol which networks to advertise.

That's it. As an example, let's configure our four-router internetwork (shown again in Figure 5.7) with RIP routing.

FIGURE 5.7 IP routing example with more routers

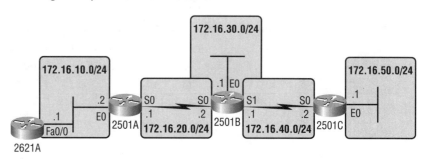

2621A

RIP has an administrative distance of 120. Static routes have an administrative distance of 1 by default and, since you currently have static routes configured, the routing tables won't be propagated with RIP information. The first thing you need to do is to delete the static routes off each router. This is done with the no ip route command. Notice that in the following 2621A router output, you must type the whole ip route command to delete the entry.

```
2621A#config t
Enter configuration commands, one per line. End with CNTL/Z.
2621A(config)#no ip route 172.16.20.0 255.255.255.0
    172.16.10.2
2621A(config)#no ip route 172.16.30.0 255.255.255.0
    172.16.10.2
2621A(config)#no ip route 172.16.40.0 255.255.255.0
    172.16.10.2
2621A(config)#no ip route 172.16.50.0 255.255.255.0
    172.16.10.2
```

Once the static routes are deleted from the configuration, you can add the RIP routing protocol by using the router rip command and the network command. The network command tells the routing protocol which network to advertise.

Notice that in the next router configuration, the routing protocol is not told which subnets to advertise; instead, it's told the classful boundary. RIP will find the subnets and advertise them.

```
2621A(config)#router rip
2621A(config-router)#network 172.16.0.0
2621A(config-router)#^Z
2621A#
```

That's it. Two commands, and you're done—sure makes your job a lot easier than when using static routes, doesn't it? However, keep in mind the extra router CPU process and bandwidth that you're consuming.

Remember that the network command just configured uses the network address of 172.16.0.0 even though the router is connected to many different subnets. RIP and IGRP use the classful address when configuring the network address. Because of this, all subnet masks must be the same on all devices in the network (this is called classful routing).

You must understand that RIP is configured with classful routing network addresses!

2501A

To configure RIP on the 2501A router, you need to remove the three static routes you added from the earlier example. Once you make sure no routes are in the routing table with a better administrative distance than 120, you can add RIP. Again, if you do not remove the static routes, RIP routes will never be found in the routing table, although RIP will be running in the background using CPU processing on the routers and bandwidth.

```
2501A#config t
Enter configuration commands, one per line. End with CNTL/Z.
2501A(config)#no ip route 172.16.30.0 255.255.255.0
    172.16.20.2
2501A(config)#no ip route 172.16.40.0 255.255.255.0
    172.16.20.2
2501A(config)#no ip route 172.16.50.0 255.255.255.0
    172.16.20.2
```

```
2501A(config)#router rip
2501A(config-router)#network 172.16.0.0
2501A(config-router)#^Z
2501A#
```

It doesn't get much easier than this.

2501B

The 2501B router had only two static routes. Once you remove those, you can turn on RIP routing.

```
2501B#config t
Enter configuration commands, one per line. End with CNTL/Z.
2501B(config)#no ip route 172.16.10.0 255.255.255.0
   172.16.20.1
2501B(config)#no ip route 172.16.50.0 255.255.255.0
   172.16.40.2
2501B(config)#router rip
2501B(config-router)#network 172.16.0.0
2501B(config-router)#^Z
2501B#
```

There is still one more router to configure RIP routing.

2501C

The 2501C has only a default route because our use of the `default route` command. Once you remove the default route, you can add RIP routing.

```
RouterC#config t
Enter configuration commands, one per line. End with CNTL/Z.
RouterC(config)#no ip route 0.0.0.0 0.0.0.0 172.16.40.1
RouterC(config)#router rip
RouterC(config-router)#network 172.16.0.0
RouterC(config-router)#^Z
RouterC#
05:10:31: %SYS-5-CONFIG_I: Configured from console by
   console
```

It is important to remember why we are doing this. Directly connected routes have an administrative distance of 0, static routes have an administrative distance of 1, and RIP has an administrative distance of 120. I call RIP the "gossip protocol" because it reminds me of junior high school, where if you hear a rumor (advertised route), it must be true. That's how RIP behaves on an internetwork—exactly like my 14-year-old son.

Verifying the RIP Routing Tables

Each routing table should now have the routers' directly connected routes as well as RIP-injected routes received from neighbor routers.

This router output shows the contents of the 2621A routing table:

```
2621A#sh ip route
[output cut]
        172.16.0.0/24 is subnetted, 5 subnets
R       172.16.50.0 [120/3] via 172.16.10.2, FastEthernet0/0
R       172.16.40.0 [120/2] via 172.16.10.2, FastEthernet0/0
R       172.16.30.0 [120/2] via 172.16.10.2, FastEthernet0/0
R       172.16.20.0 [120/1] via 172.16.10.2, FastEthernet0/0
C       172.16.10.0 is directly connected, FastEthernet0/0
2621A#
```

In this output, notice that the routing table has the same entries that the routing tables had when you were using static routes. However, the R means that the networks were added dynamically using the RIP routing protocol. The [120/3] is the administrative distance of the route (120) along with the number of hops to that remote network (3).

The next router output displays the routing table of the 2501A routers.

```
2501A#sh ip route
[output cut]
        172.16.0.0/24 is subnetted, 5 subnets
R   172.16.50.0 [120/2] via 172.16.20.2, 00:00:11, Serial0
R   172.16.40.0 [120/1] via 172.16.20.2, 00:00:11, Serial0
R   172.16.30.0 [120/1] via 172.16.20.2, 00:00:11, Serial0
C   172.16.20.0 is directly connected, Serial0
C   172.16.10.0 is directly connected, Ethernet0
2501A#
```

Notice that in this output, the same networks are again in the routing table, and you didn't have to add them there manually.

The following router output shows the routing tables for the 2501B and 2501C routers.

```
2501B#sh ip route
[output cut]
Gateway of last resort is not set
     172.16.0.0/24 is subnetted, 5 subnets
R   172.16.50.0 [120/1] via 172.16.40.2, 00:00:26, Serial1
C   172.16.40.0 is directly connected, Serial1
C   172.16.30.0 is directly connected, Ethernet0
C   172.16.20.0 is directly connected, Serial0
R   172.16.10.0 [120/1] via 172.16.20.1, 00:00:04, Serial0
2501B#
```

```
RouterC#sh ip route
[output cut]
Gateway of last resort is not set
     172.16.0.0/24 is subnetted, 5 subnets
C   172.16.50.0 is directly connected, Ethernet0
C   172.16.40.0 is directly connected, Serial0
R   172.16.30.0 [120/1] via 172.16.40.1, 00:00:06, Serial0
R   172.16.20.0 [120/1] via 172.16.40.1, 00:00:06, Serial0
R   172.16.10.0 [120/2] via 172.16.40.1, 00:00:06, Serial0
RouterC#
```

RIP has worked well in our little internetwork. However, since this technique has a maximum hop count of only 15 hops (where 16 is deemed unreachable) and performs full routing-table updates every 30 seconds, it can cause havoc on a larger internetwork.

One more thing I want to show you about RIP routing tables and the parameters used to advertise remote networks. Notice that the following routing table shows [120/15] in the 172.16.10.0 network metric. This means that the administrative distance is 120, the default for RIP, but that the hop count is 15. Remember that each time a router receives an update from another router, it increments the hop count by one for each route.

```
RouterC#sh ip route
[output cut]
Gateway of last resort is not set
     172.16.0.0/24 is subnetted, 5 subnets
```

```
C  172.16.50.0 is directly connected, Ethernet0
C  172.16.40.0 is directly connected, Serial0
R  172.16.30.0 [120/1] via 172.16.40.1, 00:00:06, Serial0
R  172.16.20.0 [120/1] via 172.16.40.1, 00:00:06, Serial0
R  172.16.10.0 [120/15] via 172.16.40.1, 00:00:06, Serial0
RouterC#
```

The [120/15] is bad, because the next router that receives the table from router 2501B will discard the route to network 172.16.10.0, since the hop count would then be 16, which is invalid.

Holding Down RIP Propagations

You may not want your RIP network advertised everywhere on your LAN and WAN. For instance, there is no advantage to advertising your RIP network to the Internet.

There are a few different ways to stop unwanted RIP updates from propagating across your LANs and WANs. The easiest way to do this is through the `passive-interface` command. This command prevents RIP update broadcasts from being sent out a defined interface, but that same interface can still receive RIP updates.

The following is an example of how to configure a `passive-interface` on a router:

RouterA#**config t**

RouterA(config)#**router rip**

RouterA(config-router)#**network 172.16.0.0**

RouterA(config-router)#**passive-interface serial 0**

This command will stop RIP updates from being propagated out serial interface 0, but serial interface 0 can still receive RIP updates.

 Real World Scenario

Should we really use RIP in an internetwork?

No, probably not. However, what happens if you just have old routers that don't support anything but RIP? Well, then you have to use RIP, at least in some fashion. If you have an old network and need to support it, then you can run RIP on a router connecting that old network, but you do not need to run RIP throughout your entire internetwork.

> You can do what is called *redistribution,* which is basically translating from one type of routing protocol to another. This means that you can support that old network using RIP but use Enhanced IGRP, for example, on the rest of your network. This will stop RIP routes from being sent all through the network and using up precious bandwidth.
>
> Redistribution is covered in the Sybex *CCNP: Routing Study Guide.*

Interior Gateway Routing Protocol (IGRP)

Interior Gateway Routing Protocol (IGRP) is a Cisco-proprietary distance-vector routing protocol. This means that all your routers must be Cisco routers to use IGRP in your network. Cisco created this routing protocol to overcome the problems associated with RIP.

IGRP has a maximum hop count of 255 with a default of 100. This is helpful in larger networks and solves the problem of 15 hops being the maximum possible in a RIP network.

IGRP also uses a different metric from RIP. IGRP uses bandwidth and delay of the line by default as a metric for determining the best route to an internetwork. This is called a *composite metric*. Reliability, load, and maximum transmission unit (MTU) can also be used, although they are not used by default.

 The main difference between RIP and IGRP configuration is that when you configure IGRP, you supply the autonomous system number. All routers must use the same number in order to share routing table information.

IGRP Timers

To control performance, IGRP includes the following timers with default settings:

Update timers   These specify how frequently routing-update messages should be sent. The default is 90 seconds.

Invalid timers These specify how long a router should wait before declaring a route invalid if it doesn't receive a specific update about it. The default is three times the update period.

Holddown timers These specify the holddown period. The default is three times the update timer period plus 10 seconds.

Flush timers These indicate how much time should pass before a route should be flushed from the routing table. The default is seven times the routing update period. If the update timer is 90 seconds by default, then $7 \times 90 = 630$ seconds elapse before a route will be flushed from the route table.

Configuring IGRP Routing

The command used to configure IGRP is the same as the one used to configure RIP routing with one important difference: you use an autonomous system (AS) number. All routers within an autonomous system must use the same AS number, or they will not communicate with routing information. Here is an example of how to turn on IGRP routing:

```
RouterA#config t
RouterA(config)#router igrp 10
RouterA(config-router)#network 172.16.0.0
```

Notice that the configuration in the above router commands is as simple as in RIP routing except that IGRP uses an AS number. This number advertises only to routers you want to share routing information with.

You absolutely *must* remember that you type a classful network number in when configuring IGRP!

IGRP can load-balance up to six unequal links. RIP networks must have the same hop count to load-balance, whereas IGRP uses bandwidth to determine how to load-balance. To load-balance over unequal-cost links, the variance command controls the load balancing between the best metric and the worst acceptable metric.

Load balancing and traffic sharing are covered more in depth in Sybex's *CCNP: Routing Study Guide*.

Configuring IGRP is pretty straightforward and not much different from configuring RIP. You do need to decide on an AS number before you configure your routers. Remember that all routers in your internetwork must use the same AS number if you want them to share routing information. In the sample internetwork we've been using throughout this chapter, we'll use AS 10 to configure the routers.

Okay, let's configure our internetwork with IGRP routing.

2621A

The AS number, as shown in the router output below, can be any number from 1 to 65535. A router can be a member of as many ASs as you need it to be.

```
2621A#config t
Enter configuration commands, one per line. End with CNTL/Z.
2621A(config)#router igrp ?
  <1-65535>  Autonomous system number

2621A(config)#router igrp 10
2621A(config-router)#netw 172.16.0.0
2621A(config-router)#^Z
2621A#
```

The `router igrp` command turns IGRP routing on in the router. As with RIP, you still need to add the network number you want to advertise. IGRP uses classful routing, which means that subnet mask information is not sent with the routing protocol updates.

Understand that if you did type in network 172.16.10.0, the router would accept it and then change the configuration to a classful entry of 172.16.0.0. However, the exam will not be so forgiving and will mark your answer wrong if you type the wrong network number. I cannot stress this enough: think classful!

2501A

To configure the 2501A router, all you need to do is turn on IGRP routing using AS 10 and then add the network number, as shown next.

```
2501A#config t
Enter configuration commands, one per line. End with CNTL/Z.
2501A(config)#router igrp 10
```

```
2501A(config-router)#netw 172.16.0.0
2501A(config-router)#^Z
2501A#
```

2501B

To configure 2501B, you need, once again, to turn on IGRP using AS 10.

```
2501B#config t
Enter configuration commands, one per line. End with CNTL/Z.
2501B(config)#router igrp 10
2501B(config-router)#netw 172.16.0.0
2501B(config-router)#^Z
2501B#
```

2501C

The last router is 2501C; you need to use AS 10 here as well.

```
2501C#config t
Enter configuration commands, one per line. End with CNTL/Z.
2501C(config)#router igrp 10
2501C(config-router)#netw 172.16.0.0
2501C(config-router)#^Z
RouterC#
```

Verifying the IGRP Routing Tables

Once the routers are configured, you need to verify the configuration with the show ip route command.

In all of the following router outputs, notice that the only routes to networks are either directly connected or IGRP-injected routes. Since we did not turn off RIP, it is still running in the background and taking up both router CPU cycles and bandwidth. However, the routing tables will never use a RIP-found route because IGRP has a better administrative distance than RIP does.

The router output below is from the 2621A router. Notice that all routes are in the routing table.

```
2621A#sh ip route
[output cut]
     172.16.0.0/24 is subnetted, 5 subnets
I       172.16.50.0 [100/160360] via 172.16.10.2,
   FastEthernet0/0
```

```
I       172.16.40.0 [100/160260] via 172.16.10.2,
   FastEthernet0/0
I       172.16.30.0 [100/158360] via 172.16.10.2,
   FastEthernet0/0
I       172.16.20.0 [100/158260] via 172.16.10.2,
   FastEthernet0/0
C       172.16.10.0 is directly connected,
   FastEthernet0/0
```

The I means IGRP-injected routes. The 100 in [100/160360] is the administrative distance of IGRP. The 160360 is the composite metric. The lower the composite metric, the better the route.

Remember that the composite metric is calculated by using the bandwidth and delay of the line by default. The delay of the line can also be referred to as the *cumulative interface delay*.

The following output shows the routing table for the 2501A router.

```
2501A#sh ip route
[output cut]
       172.16.0.0/24 is subnetted, 5 subnets
I       172.16.50.0 [100/160350] via 172.16.20.2,
   00:00:49, Serial0
I       172.16.40.0 [100/160250] via 172.16.20.2,
   00:00:49, Serial0
I       172.16.30.0 [100/158350] via 172.16.20.2,
   00:00:49, Serial0
C       172.16.20.0 is directly connected, Serial0
C       172.16.10.0 is directly connected, Ethernet0
2501A#
```

The following router output shows the 2501B routing table.

```
2501B#sh ip route
[output cut]
       172.16.0.0/24 is subnetted, 5 subnets
I       172.16.50.0 [100/8576] via 172.16.40.2,
   00:01:11, Serial1
C       172.16.40.0 is directly connected, Serial1
```

```
C        172.16.30.0 is directly connected, Ethernet0
C        172.16.20.0 is directly connected, Serial0
I        172.16.10.0 [100/158350] via 172.16.20.1,
   00:00:36, Serial0
2501B#
```

The following router output shows the 2501C routing table.

```
2501C#sh ip route
[output cut]
     172.16.0.0/24 is subnetted, 5 subnets
C        172.16.50.0 is directly connected, Ethernet0
C        172.16.40.0 is directly connected, Serial0
I        172.16.30.0 [100/8576] via 172.16.40.1,
   00:00:28, Serial0
I        172.16.20.0 [100/160250] via 172.16.40.1,
   00:00:28, Serial0
I        172.16.10.0 [100/160350] via 172.16.40.1,
   00:00:28, Serial0
2501C#
```

Verifying Your Configurations

It is important to verify your configurations once you have completed them, or at least, once you *think* you have completed them. The following list includes the commands you can use to verify the routed and routing protocols configured on your Cisco routers. The first command was covered in the previous section; the others are covered in upcoming sections.

- show ip route
- show protocols
- show ip protocol
- debug ip rip
- debug ip igrp events
- debug ip igrp transactions

The *Show Protocols* Command

The show protocols command is useful because it displays all the routed protocols and the interfaces on which the protocol is enabled.

```
2501B#sh protocol
Global values:
  Internet Protocol routing is enabled
Ethernet0 is up, line protocol is up
  Internet address is 172.16.30.1/24
Serial0 is up, line protocol is up
  Internet address is 172.16.20.2/24
Serial1 is up, line protocol is up
  Internet address is 172.16.40.1/24
2501B#
```

The output above shows the IP address of the Ethernet 0, serial 0, and serial 1 interfaces of the 2501B router. If IPX or AppleTalk were configured on the router, those network addresses would have appeared as well.

The *Show IP Protocol* Command

The show ip protocol command shows you the routing protocols that are configured on your router. Notice in the output below that both RIP and IGRP are running on the router, but only IGRP appears in the routing table because of its lower administrative distance (AD).

The show ip protocols command also displays the timers used in the routing protocol. Notice in the next output that RIP is sending updates every 30 seconds, which is the default. Notice further down that RIP is routing for network 172.16.0.0, and the two neighbors it found are 172.16.40.2 and 172.16.20.1.

```
2501B#sh ip protocols
Routing Protocol is "rip"
  Sending updates every 30 seconds, next due in 6 seconds
  Invalid after 180 seconds, hold down 180, flushed after
  240
  Outgoing update filter list for all interfaces is
  Incoming update filter list for all interfaces is
  Redistributing: rip
```

```
Default version control: send version 1, receive any
version
   Interface        Send  Recv   Key-chain
   Ethernet0         1     1 2
   Serial0           1     1 2
   Serial1           1     1 2
Routing for Networks:
   172.16.0.0
Routing Information Sources:
   Gateway          Distance       Last Update
   172.16.40.2           120       00:00:21
   172.16.20.1           120       00:00:23
Distance: (default is 120)
```

In the preceding router output, the last entry is the default AD for RIP (120).

The next router output shows the IGRP routing information. The default update timer is 90 seconds by default, and the administrative distance is 100.

```
Routing Protocol is "igrp 10"
   Sending updates every 90 seconds, next due in 42 seconds
   Invalid after 270 seconds, hold down 280, flushed after
   630
   Outgoing update filter list for all interfaces is
   Incoming update filter list for all interfaces is
   Default networks flagged in outgoing updates
   Default networks accepted from incoming updates
   IGRP metric weight K1=1, K2=0, K3=1, K4=0, K5=0
   IGRP maximum hopcount 100
   IGRP maximum metric variance 1
   Redistributing: eigrp 10, igrp 10
   Routing for Networks:
      172.16.0.0
   Routing Information Sources:
      Gateway          Distance      Last Update
      172.16.40.2           100      00:00:47
      172.16.20.1           100      00:01:18
   Distance: (default is 100)
```

The information included in the show ip protocols command includes the AS, routing timers, networks being advertised, gateways, and AD (100).

The invalid timer is set at 270 seconds (three times the update timer). If a router update is not received in three update periods, the route is considered invalid. The holddown timer is 280, which is around three times the update timer. This is the number of seconds a route is suppressed while waiting for a new update to be received. If a new update is not received before the hold-down timer expires, the flush timer will start. When the flush timer expires, the route is removed from the routing table.

The *Debug IP RIP* Command

The debug ip rip command sends routing updates as they are sent and received on the router to the console session. If you are telnetted into the router, you'll need to use the terminal monitor command to be able to receive the output from the debug commands.

Notice in the following router output that RIP is both sent and received on serial 1, serial 0, and Ethernet 0 interfaces. This is a great troubleshooting tool. The metric is the hop count.

```
2501B#debug ip rip
RIP protocol debugging is on
2501B#
07:12:56: RIP: received v1 update from 172.16.40.2 on
   Serial1
07:12:56:        172.16.50.0 in 1 hops
07:12:56: RIP: received v1 update from 172.16.20.1 on
   Serial0
07:12:56:        172.16.10.0 in 1 hops
```

In the above debug output, notice the route updates received on the 2501B serial 0 and serial 1 interfaces. These are from Routers 2501A and 2501C, respectively. What you want to notice is that spit horizon rules stop the 2501A and C routers from advertising back routes that they learned from 2501B, which means only network 172.16.50.0 is being advertised from 2501C and 172.16.10.0 is being advertised to 2501B from 2501A.

```
07:12:58: RIP: sending v1 update to 255.255.255.255 via
   Ethernet0 (172.16.30.1)
07:12:58:        subnet  172.16.40.0, metric 1
07:12:58:        subnet  172.16.20.0, metric 1
```

```
07:12:58: RIP: sending v1 update to 255.255.255.255 via
   Serial0 (172.16.20.2)
07:12:58:       subnet  172.16.40.0, metric 1
07:12:58:       subnet  172.16.30.0, metric 1
07:12:58: RIP: sending v1 update to 255.255.255.255 via
   Serial1 (172.16.40.1)
07:12:58:       subnet  172.16.30.0, metric 1
07:12:58:       subnet  172.16.20.0, metric 1
```

In the above output, split horizon rules only allow networks 172.16.20, 30, and 40 to be advertised to 2501A and 2501C. Router 2501B will not advertise the 172.16.10.0 and 172.16.50.0 networks back to the 2501A and 2501C routers.

If the metric of a route shows 16, this is a route poison, and the route being advertised is unreachable.

```
2501B#undebug all
All possible debugging has been turned off
2501B#
```

To turn off debugging, use the undebug all or the no debug all command. You can also use the un all shortcut command.

The *Debug IP IGRP* Command

With the debug ip igrp command, there are two options, events and transactions, as shown in the following router output:

```
2501B#debug ip igrp ?
  events        IGRP protocol events
  transactions  IGRP protocol transactions
```

The difference between these commands is explained in the following sections.

The *Debug IP IGRP Events* Command

The debug ip igrp events command is a summary of the IGRP routing information that is running on the network. The following router output shows the source and destination of each update as well as the number of routers in each update. Information about individual routes is not generated with this command.

```
2501B#debug ip igrp events
IGRP event debugging is on
07:13:50: IGRP: received request from 172.16.40.2 on
   Serial1
07:13:50: IGRP: sending update to 172.16.40.2 via Serial1
   (172.16.40.1)
07:13:51: IGRP: Update contains 3 interior, 0 system, and
   0 exterior routes.
07:13:51: IGRP: Total routes in update: 3
07:13:51: IGRP: received update from 172.16.40.2 on
   Serial1
07:13:51: IGRP: Update contains 1 interior, 0 system, and
   0 exterior routes.
07:13:51: IGRP: Total routes in update: 1
```

You can turn the command off with the undebug or undebug all command.

```
2501B#un
07:13:52: IGRP: received update from 172.16.40.2 on
   Serial1
07:13:52: IGRP: Update contains 1 interior, 0 system, and
   0 exterior routes.
07:13:52: IGRP: Total routes in update: 1
2501B#un all
All possible debugging has been turned off
```

The *Debug IP IGRP Transactions* Command

The debug ip igrp transactions command shows message requests from neighbor routers asking for an update and the broadcasts sent from your router towards that neighbor router.

In the following output, a request was received from a neighbor router on network 172.16.40.2 to serial 1 of Router 2501B, which responded with an update packet.

```
2501B#debug ip igrp transactions
IGRP protocol debugging is on
07:14:05: IGRP: received request from 172.16.40.2 on
   Serial1
07:14:05: IGRP: sending update to 172.16.40.2 via Serial1
   (172.16.40.1)
07:14:05:          subnet 172.16.30.0, metric=1100
07:14:05:          subnet 172.16.20.0, metric=158250
07:14:05:          subnet 172.16.10.0, metric=158350
07:14:06: IGRP: received update from 172.16.40.2 on
   Serial1
07:14:06:          subnet 172.16.50.0, metric 8576 (neighbor
   1100)
```

You can turn off the command with the undebug all command (un all for short).

```
2501B#un all
All possible debugging has been turned off
```

Summary

This chapter covered IP routing in detail. It is important that you understand the basics covered in this chapter, because everything that is done on a Cisco router must have some type of IP routing configured and running.

This chapter covered the following topics:

- IP routing and how frames are used to transport packets between routers and to the destination host

- Static routing and how an administrator can use it in a Cisco internetwork

- Default routing and how default routing can be used in stub networks

- Dynamic routing and how to solve loops in distance-vector routing protocols

- Configuring and verifying RIP routing

- Configuring and verifying IGRP routing

Exam Essentials

Understand that basic IP routing process.   You need to remember that the frame changes at each hop, but that the packet is never changed or manipulated in any way until it reaches the destination device.

You must understand how to configure RIP routing.   To configure RIP routing, you must first be in global configuration mode:

```
enable config t
```

Then you type the command:

```
router rip
```

Then you add all directly connected networks, but make sure to use the classful address. For example, if you have network 10.1.1.0 directly connected to your network, the command would be:

```
network 10.0.0.0
```

Remember how to verify RIP routing.   Show ip route will provide you with the contents of the routing table. An R on the left side of the table indicates a RIP-found route. The debug ip rip command will show you RIP updates being sent and received on your router. If you see a route with a metric of 16, that route is considered down.

You must understand how to configure IGRP routing.   IGRP is configured mostly like RIP, but with just one major difference: you must configure the autonomous system (AS). Here is an example:

```
Router igrp 10
```

This put your router into AS 10. The router will not accept any routes except from AS 10. Like RIP, you configure only classful networks with IGRP.

```
Network 10.0.0.0
```

Remember how to verify IGRP routing.   Show ip route will show you the routing table, and an I on the left side of the table indicates an IGRP-found route. The [100/123456] indicates the administrative distance, 100 for IGRP, the composite metric. The composite metric is determined by bandwidth and delay of the line, by default.

Key Terms

Before you take the exam, be sure you're familiar with the following terms:

administrative distance (AD)	hybrid protocols
classful routing	link-state protocols
classless routing	maximum hop count
composite metric	pinhole congestion
counting to infinity	poison reverse
default routing	prefix routing
distance-vector protocols	route poisoning
dynamic routing	routing
flapping	routing protocol
holddown	shortest-path-first protocols
hop	split horizon
hop count	static routing

Commands Used in This Chapter

The following list contains a summary of all the commands used in this chapter:

Command	Description
show ip route	Displays the IP routing table
ip route	Creates static and default routes on a router
ip classless	Is a global configuration command used to tell a router to forward packets to a default route when the destination network is not in the routing table
router rip	Turns on IP RIP routing on a router

Command	Description
`network`	Tells the routing protocol what network to advertise
`no ip route`	Removes a static or default route
`router igrp as`	Turns on IP IGRP routing on a router
`variance`	Controls the load balancing between the best metric and the worst acceptable metric
`show protocols`	Shows the routed protocols and network addresses configured on each interface
`show ip protocols`	Shows the routing protocols and timers associated with each routing protocol configured on a router
`debug ip rip`	Sends console messages displaying information about RIP packets being sent and received on a router interface
`debug ip igrp events`	Provides a summary of the IGRP routing information running on the network
`debug ip igrp transactions`	Shows message requests from neighbor routers asking for an update and the broadcasts sent from your router to that neighbor router

Written Lab 5

Write the answers to the following questions:

1. Create a static route to network 172.16.10.0/24 with a next-hop gateway of 172.16.20.1 and an administrative distance of 150.

2. Write the commands used to turn RIP routing on in a router and advertise network 10.0.0.0.

3. Write the commands to stop a router from propagating RIP information out serial 1.

4. Write the commands to create an AS 10 with IGRP in your 172.16.0.0 network.

5. Write the commands to configure a default route on a router to go to 172.16.50.3.

6. What works with triggered updates to help stop routing loops in distance-vector networks?

7. What stops routing loops in distance-vector networks by sending out a maximum hop count as soon as a link fails?

8. What stops routing loops in distance-vector networks by not resending information learned on an interface out that same interface?

9. What network number do you type to configure IGRP when a router is directly connected to subnets 172.16.10.0 and 172.16.35.0?

10. What command is used to send routing updates as they are sent and received on the router to the console session?

(The answers to Written Lab 5 can be found following the answers to the Review Questions for this chapter.)

Hands-on Labs

In the following hands-on labs, you will configure a network with three 2501 routers and one 2621 router.

The hands-on labs printed here are for use with real Cisco routers. If you are using the Sybex Router Fundamentals Simulator provided on this book's companion CD, please use the hands-on labs found within that software program.

The following labs will be covered:

Lab 5.1: Creating Static Routes

Lab 5.2: Dynamic Routing with RIP

Lab 5.3: Dynamic Routing with IGRP

Figure 5.8 will be used to configure all routers.

FIGURE 5.8 Hands-on lab internetwork

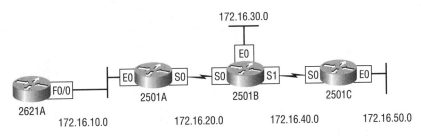

Hands-on Lab 5.1: Creating Static Routes

In this first lab, you will create a static route in all four routers so that the routers see all networks. Verify with the Ping program when complete.

1. The 2621A router is connected to network 172.16.10.0/24. It does not know about networks 172.16.20.0/24, 172.16.30.0/24, 172.16.40.0/24, and 172.16.50.0/24. The 2621A router fa0/1 interface has an IP address of 172.16.10.2/24, and the 2501A Ethernet 0 interface is 172.16.10.1/24. Create static routes so that the 2621A Router can see all networks, as shown here.

   ```
   2621A#config t
   2621A(config)#ip route 172.16.20.0 255.255.255.0
      172.16.10.1
   2621A(config)#ip route 172.16.30.0 255.255.255.0
      172.16.10.1
   2621A(config)#ip route 172.16.40.0 255.255.255.0
      172.16.10.1
   2621A(config)#ip route 172.16.50.0 255.255.255.0
      172.16.10.1
   ```

2. Save the current configuration for the 2621A router by going to the enabled mode, typing **copy run start**, and pressing Enter.

3. On Router 2501A, which is already directly connected to networks 172.16.10.0/24 and 172.16.20.0/24, create a static route to see networks 172.16.30.0/24, 172.16.40.0/24, and 172.16.50.0/24, as shown here. The 2501B serial 0 interface IP address is 172.16.20.2/24, which we will use as our next hop address.

   ```
   2501A#config t
   2501A(config)#ip route 172.16.30.0 255.255.255.0
      172.16.20.2
   2501A(config)#ip route 172.16.40.0 255.255.255.0
      172.16.20.2
   2501A(config)#ip route 172.16.50.0 255.255.255.0
      172.16.20.2
   ```

   These commands told Router 2501A to get to network 172.16.30.0/24 and use either IP address 172.16.20.2, which is the closet neighbor interface connected to network 172.16.30.0/24, or Router 2501B.

This is the same interface you will use to get to networks 172.16.40.0/24 and 172.16.50.0/24.

4. Save the current configuration for Router 2501A by going to the enabled mode, typing **copy run start**, and pressing Enter.

5. On Router 2501B, create a static route to see networks 172.16.10.0/24 and 172.16.50.0/24, which are not directly connected. Create static routes so that Router 2501B can see all networks, as shown here.

```
2501B#config t
2501B(config)#ip route 172.16.10.0 255.255.255.0
  172.16.20.1
2501B(config)#ip route 172.16.50.0 255.255.255.0
  172.16.40.2
```

The first command told Router 2501B that to get to network 172.16.10.0/24, it needs to use 172.16.20.1. The next command told Router 2501B to get to network 172.16.50.0/24 through 172.16.40.2, which is the 2501C serial 0 interface IP address.

Save the current configuration for Router 2501B by going to the enable mode, typing **copy run start**, and pressing Enter.

6. Router 2501C is connected to networks 172.16.50.0/24 and 172.16.40.0/24. It does not know about networks 172.16.30.0/24, 172.16.20.0/24, and 172.16.10.0/24. Create static routes so that Router 2501C can see all networks, as shown here. Use the 2501B serial 1 interface address of 172.16.40.1.

```
2501C#config t
2501C(config)#ip route 172.16.30.0 255.255.255.0
  172.16.40.1
2501C(config)#ip route 172.16.20.0 255.255.255.0
  172.16.40.1
2501C(config)#ip route 172.16.10.0 255.255.255.0
  172.16.40.1
```

Save the current configuration for Router 2501C by going to the enable mode, typing **copy run start**, and pressing Enter.

Now ping from each router to your hosts and from each router to each router. If it is set up correctly, it will work.

Hands-on Lab 5.2: Dynamic Routing with RIP

In this lab, we will use the dynamic routing protocol RIP instead of static and default routing.

1. Remove any static routes or default routes configured on your routers by using the `no ip route` command. For example, here is how you would remove the static routes on the 2501A router:

```
2501A#config t
2501A(config)#no ip route 172.16.30.0 255.255.255.0
    172.16.20.2
2501A(config)#no ip route 172.16.40.0 255.255.255.0
    172.16.20.2
2501A(config)#no ip route 172.16.50.0 255.255.255.0
    172.16.20.2
```

   Do the same thing for Routers 2501B and 2501C as well as the 2621A router. Type **sh run** and press Enter on each router to verify that all static and default routes are cleared.

2. After your static and default routers are clear, go into configuration mode on Router 2501A by typing **config t**.

3. Tell your router to use RIP routing by typing **router rip** and pressing Enter, as shown here:

```
config t
router rip
```

4. Add the network number you want to advertise by typing **network 172.16.0.0** and pressing Enter.

5. Press Ctrl+Z to get out of configuration mode.

6. Go to Routers 2501B and 2501C as well as the 2621A router and type the same commands, as shown here:

```
Config t
Router rip
Network 172.16.0.0
```

7. Verify that RIP is running at each router by typing the following commands at each router:

```
show ip protocol
```

```
show ip route
show running-config or show run
```

8. Save your configurations by typing **copy run start** or **copy running-config startup-config** and pressing Enter at each router.

9. Verify the network by pinging all remote networks and hosts.

Hands-on Lab 5.3: Dynamic Routing with IGRP

In this lab, you will run the IGRP routing protocol simultaneously with RIP routing.

1. Log into your routers and go into privileged mode by typing **en** or **enable**.

2. Keep RIP running on your routers and verify that it is running on each router. If you want to remove RIP, you can use the `no router rip` global configuration command to remove it from each router. For example,

   ```
   config t
   no router rip
   ```

3. From the configuration mode on Router 2501A, type **router igrp ?**.

4. Notice that it asks for an autonomous system number. This is used to allow only routers with the same AS number to communicate. Type 10 and press Enter. Your router can be configured to be part of as many different ASs as necessary.

5. At the config-router prompt, type **network 172.16.0.0**. Notice that we add the classful network boundary to advertise, rather than the subnet numbers.

6. Press Ctrl+Z to get out of configuration mode.

7. Go to Routers 2501B and 2501C as well as the 2621A router and type the commands shown here:

   ```
   2501B(config)#router igrp 10
   2501B(config-router)#network 172.16.0.0
   ```

8. Verify that IGRP is running by typing the following command at each router:

   ```
   show ip protocol
   ```

Notice that this shows you your RIP and IGRP routing protocols and the update timers.

`sh ip route`

This should let you see all five subnets: 10, 20, 30, 40, and 50. Some will be directly connected, and some will be I routes, which are IGRP-injected routes. RIP is still running, but if you look at the routing table, you'll notice the network entry has a network number (100/23456). The first number (100) is the trustworthiness rating. Since RIP's default trustworthiness rating is 120, the IGRP route is used before a RIP route is used. The second number is the metric, or weight, of the route that is used to determine the best path to a network.

`show running-config`

This lets you see that RIP and IGRP are configured.

9. To save your configurations, type **copy running-config startup-config** or **copy run start** and press Enter at each router.

10. Verify the network by pinging all routers, switches, and hosts.

Review Questions

1. Which routing protocol uses the properties of both distance-vector and link-state?

   A. RIP

   B. IGRP

   C. EIGRP

   D. OSPF

2. What command is used to stop routing updates from exiting out an interface?

   A. Router(config-if)#**no routing**

   B. Router(config-if)#**passive-interface**

   C. Router(config-router)#**passive-interface s0**

   D. Router(config-router)#**no routing updates**

3. Which of the following are solutions for reducing distance vector routing loops?

   A. Split horizon

   B. Hierarchical networking

   C. Holddown timers

   D. Link-state routing

   E. Count to infinity

4. Which command displays all the routed protocols and the interfaces on which each protocol is enabled?

   A. show protocols

   B. show protocols brief

   C. show interfaces protocol

   D. show interfaces

   E. show ip protocols

5. What are holddowns used for?

   A. To hold down the protocol from going to the next hop

   B. To prevent regular update messages from reinstating a route that has gone down

   C. To prevent regular update messages from reinstating a route that has just come up

   D. To prevent irregular update messages from reinstating a route that has gone down

6. What is split horizon?

   A. It causes a router to differentiate which interface a route advertisement is received on and not advertise that information back out the same interface.

   B. It splits the traffic when you have a large bus (horizon) physical network.

   C. It holds the regular updates from broadcasting to a downed link.

   D. It prevents regular update messages from reinstating a route that has gone down.

7. What is poison reverse?

   A. It sends back the protocol received from a router as a poison pill, which stops the regular updates.

   B. It is information received from a router that can't be sent back to the originating router.

   C. It prevents regular update messages from reinstating a route that has just come up.

   D. It describes when a router sets the metric for a downed link to infinity.

8. What is the default administrative distance for IGRP?

   A. 90

   B. 100

   C. 120

   D. 220

9. Which of the following is a correct default route?

   A. route ip 172.0.0.0 255.0.0.0 s0

   B. ip route 0.0.0.0 0.0.0.0 172.16.20.1

   C. ip route 0.0.0.0 255.255.255.255 172.16.20.1

   D. route ip 0.0.0.0 0.0.0.0 172.16.10.115 0

10. Which of the following is an Internet Protocol (IP) link-state protocol used in the TCP/IP stack?

   A. RIP V2

   B. EIGRP

   C. OSPF

   D. IGRP

11. Which of the following tasks need to be completed to start RIP routing? (Choose all that apply.)

   A. Specify the routing protocol

   B. Configure static routes

   C. Specify directly connected subnets

   D. Specify directly connected networks

12. What is the next command that must be entered after you type router rip?

   A. network 172.16.30.0

   B. network 172.16.0.0

   C. passive-interface ethernet 0

   D. No command is needed.

13. Which Cisco IOS command can you use to see the IP routing table?

   A. sh ip config

   B. sh ip arp

   C. sh ip route

   D. sh ip table

14. What is the administrative distance used for in routing?

  A. Determining the network administrator for entering that route

  B. Creating a database

  C. Rating the source's trustworthiness, expressed as a numeric value from 0 to 255

  D. Rating the source's trustworthiness, expressed as a numeric value from 0 to 1023

15. Which of the following commands will start RIP version 1 on a router?

  A. `rip routing`

  B. `routing rip`

  C. `router rip`

  D. `rip router`

16. Which command displays RIP routing updates?

  A. `show ip route`

  B. `debug ip rip`

  C. `show protocols`

  D. `debug ip route`

17. Which of the following shows the correct parameters for configuring IGRP?

  A. `router igrp 10`
     `network 10.1.2.0`

  B. `router igrp`
     `network 10.0.0.0`

  C. `router igrp 100`
     `network 10.0.0.0`
     `network 192.168.19.0`

  D. `router igrp 100`
     `network 10.0.0.0`
     `network 192.168.10.32`

18. What is the difference between routed and routing protocols? (Choose all that apply.)

    A. Routed protocols update the routing tables of a router.

    B. Routing protocols determine the path of a packet through a network.

    C. Routed protocols are assigned to a router interface and determine the method of packet delivery.

    D. Routing protocols are assigned to a router interface and determine the method of packet delivery.

19. How is the 16300 calculated in the following? (Choose two.)

    ```
    I   192.168.10.0 [100/16300] via 192.168.20.1
    ```

    A. Maximum transmission unit

    B. Bandwidth

    C. Hop count

    D. Delay

    E. Administrative distance

20. If an IGRP advertised route has been determined to be invalid, when will the entry be removed from the routing table?

    A. 30 seconds

    B. 90 seconds

    C. 180 seconds

    D. 360 seconds

    E. 630 seconds

21. You type **debug ip rip** on your router console and see that 172.16.10.0 is being advertised with a metric of 16. What does this mean?

    A. The route is 16 hops away.

    B. The route has a delay of 16 microseconds.

    C. The route is inaccessible.

    D. The route is queued at 16 messages a second.

22. IGRP uses which of the following as default parameters for finding the best path to a remote network? Select all that apply.

A. Hop count

B. MTU

C. Cumulative interface delay

D. STP

E. Path bandwidth value

23. If you have a routing table listing both I's, S's, and R's on the left side of the table, what does this mean?

A. That your table needs to be flushed

B. That static, RIP, and OSPF routes are in the routing table

C. That static, RIP, and IGRP routes are in the routing table

D. That a Reliable port was used to find Serial WAN information by using an Internal routing protocol

24. If your routing table has a static, a RIP, and an IGRP route to the same network, which route will be used to route packets?

A. Any available route

B. RIP route

C. Static route

D. IGRP route

E. They will all load-balance

25. You have the following IGRP configuration:

```
Corporate(config)#router igrp 10
Corporate(config-router)#network 172.16.10.0
Corporate(config-router)#network 172.16.20.0
Corporate(config-router)#network 172.16.30.0
Corporate(config-router)#network 10.0.0.0
```

```
Branch(config)#router igrp 11
Branch(config-router)#network 172.16.1.0
Branch(config-router)#network 172.16.2.0
Branch(config-router)#network 172.16.3.0
```

Which networks will be in the Branch router's IP routing table?

A. 172.16.10.0, 172.16.20.0, 172.16.30.0, 10.0.0.0, 172.16.1.0, 172.16.2.0, 172.16.3.0

B. 172.16.10.0, 172.16.20.0, 172.16.30.0, 10.0.0.0

C. 172.16.1.0, 172.16.2.0, 172.16.3.0

D. None, it won't work with this configuration.

Answers to Review Questions

1. C.   Enhanced Interior Gateway Routing Protocol (EIGRP) uses the properties of both distance-vector and link-state.

2. C.   The config-router `passive-interface` command stops updates from being sent out an interface.

3. A, C.   Distance-vector routing loops are solved by using split horizon and route holddown timers.

4. A.   The `show protocols` command provides routed protocols information. The `show ip protocols` command provides routing protocol information.

5. C.   Holddowns prevent regular update messages from reinstating a route that has just come up.

6. A.   A split horizon will not advertise a route back to the same router it learned the route from.

7. D.   A poison reverse is used to communicate to a router that the link is down and that the hop count to that network is set to infinity or unreachable.

8. B.   Interior Gateway Routing Protocol (IGRP)'s default administrative distance is 100; Routing Information Protocol (RIP)'s default administrative distance is 120.

9. B.   An IP route with a wildcard of all zeros for the destination network and subnet mask is used to create a default route.

10. C.   OSPF (Open Shortest Path First) is a true link-state IP routing protocol. It uses only bandwidth as a way to determine the best path to a remote network.

11. A, D.   To turn on Routing Information Protocol (RIP) routing, use the `router rip` command followed by the `network` command using a classful network address.

12. B.   After you type in `router rip`, you must type in the network you want to advertise. Also, it must be the classful address, which is why the first option is wrong.

13. C.   The `show ip route` command shows the Internet Protocol (IP) routing table, the metric used, and the interface used to find a remote network.

14. C.   The administrative distance is used in routing to decide the trustworthiness of a route. 0 is the highest rating.

15. C.   To start Routing Information Protocol (RIP) version 1 on a router, type the global configuration mode command `router rip`.

16. B.   `Debug ip rip` is used to show the Internet Protocol (IP) Routing Information Protocol (RIP) updates being sent and received on the router.

17. C.   You configure Interior Gateway Routing Protocol (IGRP) with an autonomous system number and then use the `network` command to tell the routing protocol which networks you want to advertise. The entry must be a classful entry, which is why the first and last answers are wrong.

18. B, C.   Routing protocols are used to update routing tables on routers, and routed protocols send user data through the internetwork. IP is an example of a routed protocol.

19. B, D.   Interior Gateway Routing Protocol (IGRP) uses bandwidth and delay of the line, by default, to determine the best path to a remote network.

20. E.   IGRP update timers are set by default at 90 seconds. After a route has been determined to be invalid, the routing table flushes the entry after seven update periods, or 630 seconds.

21. C.   You cannot have 16 hops on a RIP network by default. If you receive a route advertised with a metric of 16, this means it is inaccessible.

22. C, E.   IGRP uses bandwidth and delay of the line, by default, to determine the best path to a remote network. Delay of the line can sometimes be called the cumulative interface delay.

23. C.   An I in a routing table means it is an IGRP-found route. An S means it is a static entry to a remote network, and R means it is a RIP route.

24. C.   Static routes have an administrative distance of zero (0) by default. Unless you change this, a static route will always be used over any other found route. IGRP has an administrative distance of 100, and RIP has an administrative distance of 120, by default.

25. C.   The Branch router will only accept routes from other routers with the same autonomous system (AS) configured. The Corporate router has an AS of 10 and the Branch router was configured with an AS of 11, so Branch will never accept any routes from Corporate.

Answers to Written Lab 5

1. `ip route 172.16.10.0 255.255.255.0 172.16.20.1 150`
2. `config t, router rip, network 10.0.0.0`
3. `config t, router rip, passive-interface serial 1`
4. `config t, router igrp 10, network 172.16.0.0`
5. `config t, ip route 0.0.0.0 0.0.0.0 172.16.50.3`
6. Holddown timers
7. Poison reverse
8. Split horizon
9. `172.16.0.0`
10. `debug ip rip`

Chapter

6

Virtual LANs (VLANs)

THE CCNA EXAM TOPICS COVERED IN THIS CHAPTER INCLUDE THE FOLLOWING:

✓ **Bridging/Switching**

- Describe the benefits of virtual LANs.

know I keep telling you this, but I've just got to be sure you never forget it, so here I go one last time: By default, switches break up collision domains and routers break up broadcast domains. Okay, I feel better! Now let's move on.

In contrast to the networks of yesterday, which were based on collapsed backbones, today's network design is characterized by a flatter architecture—thanks to switches. So now what? How do we break up broadcast domains in a pure switched internetwork? By creating a virtual local area network (VLAN), that's how! A VLAN is a logical grouping of network users and resources connected to administratively defined ports on a switch. When you create VLANs, you are given the ability to create smaller broadcast domains within a layer-2 switched internetwork by assigning different ports on the switch to different subnetworks. A VLAN is treated like its own subnet or broadcast domain, which means that frames broadcasted onto the network are only switched between the ports logically grouped within the same VLAN—very nice!

So, does this mean we no longer need routers? Maybe yes; maybe no. It really depends on what you want to do. By default, all hosts in a VLAN cannot communicate with hosts that are members of another VLAN, so if you want inter-VLAN communication, the answer is yes—you still need a router.

In this chapter, you're going to learn exactly what a VLAN is and how VLAN memberships are used in a switched internetwork. Also, I'm going to tell you all about how VLAN Trunk Protocol (VTP) is used to update switch databases with VLAN information, and how trunking is used to send information about all VLANs across one link. And then I'll wrap things up by discussing how you can make inter-VLAN communication happen by introducing a router into your switched internetwork.

Introduction to VLANs

As shown in Figure 6.1, layer-2 switched networks are typically designed as a flat network. Every broadcast packet transmitted is seen by every device on the network, regardless of whether the device needs to receive that data or not.

FIGURE 6.1   Flat network structure

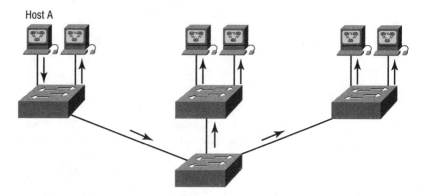

By default, routers allow broadcasts only within the originating network, but switches forward broadcasts to all segments. The reason it's called a *flat network* is because it's one *broadcast domain*, not because its design is physically flat.

In Figure 6.1 we see Host A sending a broadcast and all ports on all switches forwarding this broadcast, except the port that originally received it. Now look at Figure 6.2, which pictures a switched network. It shows Host A sending a frame with Host D as its destination, and as you can see, that frame is only forwarded out the port where Host D is located. This is a huge improvement over the old hub networks, unless having one *collision domain* by default is what you really want.

Now you already know that the largest benefit gained by having a layer-2 switched network is that it creates individual collision domain segments for each device plugged into the switch. This scenario frees us from the Ethernet distance constraints, so now larger networks can be built. But with each new advance, we often encounter new issues—the larger the number of users and devices, the more broadcasts and packets each switch must handle!

FIGURE 6.2 The benefit of a switched network

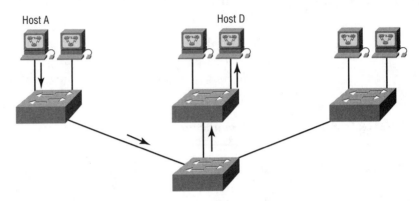

And here's another one—security! This one's a real problem because within the typical layer-2 switched internetwork, all users can see all devices by default. And you can't stop devices from broadcasting, nor users trying to respond to broadcasts. Your security options are dismally limited to placing passwords on the servers and other devices.

But not if you create a *virtual LAN (VLAN)*, my friend! Yes, indeed, you can solve many of the problems associated with layer-2 switching with VLANs—as you'll soon see!

There are several ways that VLANs simplify network management:

- The VLAN can group several broadcast domains into multiple logical subnets.

- Network adds, moves, and changes are achieved by configuring a port into the appropriate VLAN.

- A group of users needing high security can be put into a VLAN so that no users outside of the VLAN can communicate with them.

- As a logical grouping of users by function, VLANs can be considered independent from their physical or geographic locations.

- VLANs can enhance network security.

- VLANs increase the number of broadcast domains while decreasing their size.

Broadcast Control

Broadcasts occur in every protocol, but how often they occur depends upon three things:

- Type of protocol
- The application(s) running on the internetwork
- How these services are used

Some older applications have been rewritten to reduce their bandwidth needs, but there's a new generation of applications that are incredibly bandwidth-greedy, consuming all they can find. These bandwidth abusers are multimedia applications that use broadcasts and multicasts extensively. Faulty equipment, inadequate segmentation, and poorly designed firewalls only serve to compound the problems that these broadcast-intensive applications create. All of this has truly added a new dimension to network design, as well as generating new challenges for an administrator. Making sure the network is properly segmented in order to isolate one segment's problems and keep those problems from propagating throughout the internetwork is imperative. The most effective way of doing this is through strategic switching and routing.

Since switches have become more cost-effective lately, many companies are replacing their flat hub networks with a pure switched network and VLANs environment. All devices in a VLAN are members of the same broadcast domain and receive all broadcasts. The broadcasts, by default, are filtered from all ports on a switch that are not members of the same VLAN. This is great because it offers all the benefits you gain with a switched design without the serious anguish you would experience if all your users were in the same broadcast domain!

Security

But it seems there's always a catch, so let's get back to those security issues. A flat internetwork's security used to be tackled by connecting hubs and switches together with routers. So it was basically the router's job to maintain security. This arrangement was pretty ineffective for several reasons: First, anyone connecting to the physical network could access the network resources located on that physical LAN. Secondly, all anyone had to do to observe any and all traffic happening in that network was to simply plug a network analyzer into the hub. And in that same vein, users could join a workgroup by just plugging their workstations into the existing hub. So basically, this was non-security!

This is why VLANs are so cool. By building them and creating multiple broadcast groups, administrators can now have control over each port and user! The days where users could just plug their workstations into any switch port and gain access to network resources are history, because the administrator is now awarded control over each port and whatever resources that port could access.

Also, because VLANs can be created in accordance with the network resources a user requires, switches can be configured to inform a network management station of any unauthorized access to network resources. And if you need inter-VLAN communication, you can implement restrictions on a router to achieve it. You can also place restrictions on hardware addresses, protocols, and applications—now we're talking security!

Flexibility and Scalability

If you were paying attention to what you've read so far, you know that layer-2 switches only read frames for filtering—they don't look at the Network layer protocol. And by default, switches forward all broadcasts. But if you create and implement VLANs, you're essentially creating smaller broadcast domains at layer-2.

This means that broadcasts sent out from a node in one VLAN won't be forwarded to ports configured to be in a different VLAN. So by assigning switch ports or users to VLAN groups on a switch or group of connected switches (called a *switch fabric*), you gain the flexibility to add only the users you want into that broadcast domain regardless of their physical location! This setup can also work to block broadcast storms caused by a faulty network interface card (NIC), as well as prevent an application from propagating the storms throughout the entire internetwork. Those evils can still happen on the VLAN where the problem originated, but the disease will just be quarantined to that one ailing VLAN.

Another advantage is when a VLAN gets too big, you can create more VLANs to keep the broadcasts from consuming too much bandwidth—the fewer users in a VLAN, the fewer users affected by broadcasts. This is well and good, but you absolutely need to keep network services in mind and understand how the users connect to these services when you create your VLAN. It's a good move to try and keep all services, except for the e-mail and Internet access that everyone needs, local to all users when possible.

To understand how a VLAN looks to a switch, it's helpful to begin by first looking at a traditional network. Figure 6.3 shows how a network was created by connecting physical LANs using hubs to a router.

FIGURE 6.3   Physical LANs connected to a router

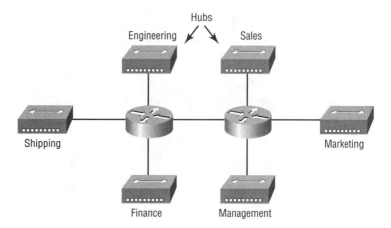

Here you can see that each network was attached with a hub port to the router (each segment also had its own logical network number, though this is not obvious from the figure). Each node attached to a particular physical network had to match that network number in order to be able to communicate on the internetwork. Notice that each department had its own LAN, so if you needed to add new users to Sales, for example, you would just plug them into the Sales LAN and they would automatically be part of the Sales collision and broadcast domain. This design really did work well for many years.

But there was one major flaw: what happens if the hub for Sales is full and you need to add another user to the Sales LAN? Or, what do we do if there's no more physical space in the location where the Sales team is located for this new employee? Well, let's say there just happens to be plenty of room in the Finance section of the building. That new Sales team member will just have to sit on the same side of the building as the Finance people, and we'll just plug the poor soul into the hub for Finance.

Doing this obviously makes that the new user part of the Finance LAN, which is bad for many reasons. First and foremost, we now have a security issue, because this new user is a member of the Finance broadcast domain and can therefore see all the same servers and network services that all of the Finance folks can. Secondly, for this user to access the Sales network services they need to get the job done, they would need to go through the router to login to the Sales server—not exactly efficient!

Now let's look at what a switch accomplishes. Figure 6.4 demonstrates how switches remove the physical boundary to solve our problem.

FIGURE 6.4 Switches removing the physical boundary

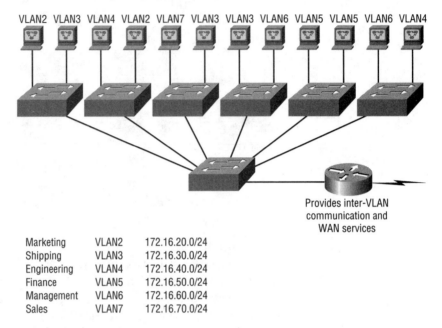

Marketing	VLAN2	172.16.20.0/24
Shipping	VLAN3	172.16.30.0/24
Engineering	VLAN4	172.16.40.0/24
Finance	VLAN5	172.16.50.0/24
Management	VLAN6	172.16.60.0/24
Sales	VLAN7	172.16.70.0/24

Figure 6.4 shows how six VLANs (numbered two through seven) were used to create a broadcast domain for each department. Each switch port is then administratively assigned a VLAN membership, depending on the host and which broadcast domain it must be in.

So now, if I needed to add another user to the Sales VLAN (VLAN 7), I could just assign the port needed to VLAN 7, regardless of where the new Sales team member is physically located—nice! This illustrates one of the sweetest advantages to designing your network with VLANs over the old collapsed backbone design. Now, cleanly and simply, each host that needs to be in the Sales VLAN is merely assigned to VLAN 7.

Notice that I started assigning VLANs with VLAN number 2. The number is irrelevant, but you might be wondering: What happened to VLAN 1? That VLAN is an administrative VLAN, and even though it can be used for a workgroup, Cisco recommends that you use this for administrative purposes only. You can't delete or change the name of VLAN 1, and by default, all ports on a switch are members of VLAN 1 until you change them.

Each VLAN is considered a broadcast domain, so it must also have its own subnet number, as shown in Figure 6.4. And if you're also using IPX, then each VLAN must also be assigned its own IPX network number.

Now let's get back to that "because of switches, we don't need routers anymore" misconception. In Figure 6.4, notice that there are seven VLANs or broadcast domains, counting VLAN 1. The nodes within each VLAN can communicate with each other, but not with anything in a different VLAN, because the nodes in any given VLAN "think" that they're actually in a collapsed backbone as in Figure 6.3.

And what handy little tool do we need to enable the hosts in Figure 6.3 to communicate to a node or host on a different network? You guessed it—a router! Those nodes positively need to go through a router, or some other layer-3 device, just like when they're configured for VLAN communication (as shown in Figure 6.4). It's the same as if we were trying to connect different physical networks. Communication between VLANs must go through a layer-3 device. So don't expect routers to disappear anytime soon!

VLAN Memberships

VLANs are usually created by an administrator, who then assigns switch ports to each VLAN. Such a VLAN is called a *static VLAN*. If the administrator wants to do a little more work up front and assign all the host devices' hardware addresses into a database, the switches can be configured to assign VLANs dynamically whenever a host is plugged into a switch.

Static VLANs

Static VLANs are the usual way of creating VLANs, and they're also the most secure. The switch port that you assign a VLAN association to always maintains that association until an administrator manually changes that port assignment.

This type of VLAN configuration is comparatively easy to set up and monitor, and it works well in a network where the movement of users within the network is controlled. And, although it can be helpful to use network management software to configure the ports, it's not mandatory.

In Figure 6.4, each switch port was configured with a VLAN membership by an administrator based on which VLAN the host needed to be a member of—the device's actual physical location doesn't matter. The broadcast domain the hosts will become a member of is an administrative choice.

Remember that each host must also have the correct IP address information. For example, each host in VLAN 2 must be configured into the 172.16.20.0/24 network. It is also important to remember that, if you plug a host into a switch, you must verify the VLAN membership of that port. If the membership is different than what is needed for that host, the host will not be able to reach the needed network services, such as a workgroup server.

Dynamic VLANs

A *dynamic VLAN* determines a node's VLAN assignment automatically. Using intelligent management software, you can enable hardware (MAC) addresses, protocols, or even applications to create dynamic VLANs. It's up to you! For example, suppose MAC addresses have been entered into a centralized VLAN management application. If a node is then attached to an unassigned switch port, the VLAN management database can look up the hardware address and assign and configure the switch port to the correct VLAN. This is very cool—it makes management and configuration easier because if a user moves, the switch will assign them to the correct VLAN automatically. But you have to do a lot more work initially setting up the database.

Cisco administrators can use the VLAN Management Policy Server (VMPS) service to set up a database of MAC addresses that can be used for dynamic addressing of VLANs. A VMPS database maps MAC addresses to VLANs.

Identifying VLANs

As frames are switched throughout the internetwork, switches must be able to keep track of all the different types, plus understand what to do with them depending on the hardware address. And remember, frames are handled differently according to the type of link they are traversing.

There are two different types of links in a switched environment:

Access links   This type of link is only part of one VLAN, and it's referred to as the *native VLAN* of the port. Any device attached to an *access link* is unaware of a VLAN membership—the device just assumes it's part of a broadcast domain, but it has no understanding of the physical network.

Switches remove any VLAN information from the frame before it's sent to an access-link device. Access-link devices cannot communicate with devices outside their VLAN unless the packet is routed through a router.

Trunk links Trunks can carry multiple VLANs and originally gained their name after the telephone system trunks that carry multiple telephone conversations.

A *trunk link* is a 100- or 1000Mbps point-to-point link between two switches, between a switch and router, or between a switch and server. These carry the traffic of multiple VLANs—from 1 to 1005 at a time. You can't run them on 10Mbps links.

Trunking allows you to make a single port part of multiple VLANs at the same time. This can be a real advantage. For instance, you can actually set things up to have a server in two broadcast domains simultaneously, so that your users won't have to cross a layer-3 device (router) to log in and access it. Another benefit to trunking is when you're connecting switches. Trunk links can carry some or all VLAN information across the link, but if the links between your switches aren't trunked, only VLAN 1 information will be switched across the link by default. This is why all VLANs are configured on a trunked link unless cleared by an administrator by hand.

Figure 6.5 shows how the different links are used in a switched network. Both switches can communicate to all VLANs because of the trunk link between them. And remember, using an access link only allows one VLAN to be used between switches. As you can see, these hosts are using access links to connect to the switch, so that means they're communicating in one VLAN only.

FIGURE 6.5 Access and trunk links in a switched network

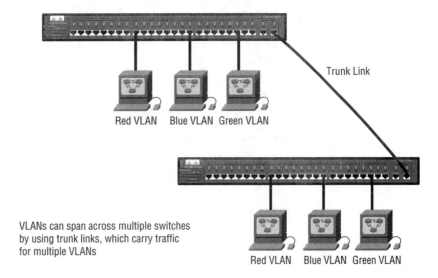

Trunk Link

Red VLAN Blue VLAN Green VLAN

VLANs can span across multiple switches
by using trunk links, which carry traffic
for multiple VLANs

Red VLAN Blue VLAN Green VLAN

Frame Tagging

You can also create your VLANs to span more than one connected switch. In Figure 6.4, hosts from various VLANs are spread across many switches. This flexible, power-packed capability is probably the main advantage to implementing VLANs!

But this can get kind of complicated—even for a switch—so there needs to be a way for each one to keep track of all the users and frames as they travel the switch fabric and VLANs. (Remember, a switch fabric is a group of switches sharing the same VLAN information.) This is where *frame tagging* comes in. This frame identification method uniquely assigns a user-defined ID to each frame. Sometimes people refer to it as a "VLAN ID" or "color."

Here's how it works: Each switch that the frame reaches must first identify the VLAN ID from the frame tag, then it finds out what to do with the frame by looking at the information in the filter table. If the frame reaches a switch that has another trunked link, the frame will be forwarded out the trunk-link port.

Once the frame reaches an exit to an access link, the switch removes the VLAN identifier. This is so the destination device can receive the frames without having to understand their VLAN identification.

VLAN Identification Methods

So VLAN identification is what switches use to keep track of all those frames as they're traversing a switch fabric. It's how switches identify which frames belong to which VLANs, and there's more than one trunking method:

Inter-Switch Link (ISL)   This is proprietary to Cisco switches, and it's used for Fast Ethernet and Gigabit Ethernet links only. *ISL routing* can be used on a switch port, router interfaces, and server interface cards to trunk a server. This is a very good approach if you're creating functional VLANs and you don't want to break the 80/20 rule.

Wait a minute—what's the 80/20 rule? Well, it's a formula that says 80 percent of the data traffic should stay on the local segment while 20 percent or less crosses a segmentation device. A trunked server is part of all VLANs (broadcast domains) simultaneously, so users don't have to cross a layer-3 device to access it.

IEEE 802.1Q   Created by the IEEE as a standard method of frame tagging, it actually inserts a field into the frame to identify the VLAN. If you're trunking between a Cisco switched link and a different brand of switch, you have to use 802.1Q for the trunk to work.

The basic purpose of ISL and 802.1Q frame-tagging methods is to provide interswitch VLAN communication.

LAN emulation (LANE)   This is used to communicate multiple VLANs over ATM.

802.10 (FDDI)   Employed for sending VLAN information over FDDI, it uses a SAID field in the frame header to identify the VLAN. This is also proprietary to Cisco devices.

The CCNA exam covers only the ISL method of VLAN identification, but it's good to know about the others too.

Inter-Switch Link (ISL) Protocol

Inter-Switch Link (ISL) is a way of explicitly tagging VLAN information onto an Ethernet frame. This tagging information allows VLANs to be multiplexed over a trunk link through an external encapsulation method, which allows the switch to identify the VLAN membership of a frame over the trunked link.

By running ISL, you can interconnect multiple switches and still maintain VLAN information as traffic travels between switches on trunk links. ISL provides a low-latency, full wire-speed performance, in contrast to Fast Ethernet, which uses either half- or full-duplex mode.

Cisco created the ISL protocol, and it's proprietary to Cisco devices only. If you need a non-proprietary VLAN protocol, use the 802.1Q that's covered in the Sybex *CCNP: Switching Study Guide*.

Anyway, ISL is an external tagging process, which means the original frame isn't altered—it's only encapsulated with a new 26-byte ISL header. It also adds a second 4-byte frame check sequence (FCS) field at the end of the frame. Because the frame has been encapsulated by ISL with information, only ISL-aware devices can read it. These frames can be up to a whopping 1522 bytes long, and devices that receive them may record them as a giant frame because it's over the maximum of 1518 bytes allowed on an Ethernet segment.

On multi-VLAN (trunk) ports, each frame is tagged as it enters the switch. ISL network interface cards (NICs) allow servers to send and receive frames tagged with multiple VLANs so they can traverse multiple VLANs without going through a router. This is good because it reduces latency. ISL makes it easy for users to access servers quickly and efficiently without having to go through a router every time they need to communicate with a resource. This technology can also be used with probes and certain network analyzers, and administrators can use it to include file servers in multiple VLANs simultaneously.

ISL VLAN information is added to a frame only if the frame is forwarded out a port configured as a trunk link The ISL encapsulation is removed from the frame if the frame is forwarded out an access link—this is an important ISL fact, so make a mental note, and don't forget it!

VLAN Trunk Protocol (VTP)

Cisco created this one too, but this time it isn't proprietary. The goal of *VLAN Trunk Protocol (VTP)* is to manage all configured VLANs across a switched internetwork and to maintain consistency throughout that network. VTP allows an administrator to add, delete, and rename VLANs—information that is then propagated to all switches in the network.

Here's a list of some of the benefits VTP has to offer:

- Consistent VLAN configuration across all switches in the network

- Allowing VLANs to be trunked over mixed networks, like Ethernet to ATM LANE or FDDI

- Accurate tracking and monitoring of VLANs

- Dynamic reporting of added VLANs to all switches

- Plug-and-Play VLAN adding

Very cool, but before you can get VTP to manage your VLANs across the network, you have to create a VTP server. All servers that need to share VLAN information must use the same domain name, and a switch can only be in one domain at a time. So, this means that a switch can only share VTP domain information with other switches if they're configured into the same VTP domain. You can use a VTP domain if you have more than one switch connected in a network, but if you've got all your switches in only one VLAN, you don't need to use VTP. VTP information is sent between switches via a trunk port.

Switches advertise VTP-management domain information, as well as a configuration revision number and all known VLANs with any specific parameters. And there's also something called *VTP transparent mode*. In it, you can configure switches to forward VTP information through trunk ports, but not to accept information updates or update their VTP databases.

If you find yourself having problems with users adding switches to your VTP domain, you can include passwords, but don't forget—every switch must be set up with the same password, and this can be difficult.

Switches detect the additional VLANs within a VTP advertisement and then prepare to receive information on their trunk ports with the newly defined VLAN in tow. This information would be either VLAN ID, 802.10 SAID fields, or LANE information. Updates are sent out as revision numbers that are the notification plus 1. Any time a switch sees a higher revision number, it knows the information that it's receiving is more current, and it will overwrite the current database with that new information.

VTP Modes of Operation

There are three different modes of operation within a VTP domain. Figure 6.6 shows you all three:

FIGURE 6.6   VTP modes

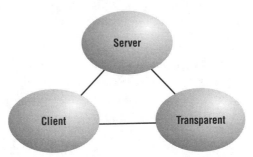

Server The default for all Catalyst switches. You need at least one server in your VTP domain to propagate VLAN information throughout the domain. The switch must be in server mode to be able to create, add, or delete VLANs in a VTP domain. Changing VTP information must also be done in server mode, and any change made to a switch in server mode will be advertised to the entire VTP domain.

Client In client mode, switches receives information from VTP servers, and they also send and receives updates. But they can't make any changes. Plus, none of the ports on a client switch can be added to a new VLAN before the VTP server notifies the client switch of the new VLAN. Here's a hint: If you want a switch to become a server, first make it a client so it receives all the correct VLAN information, then change it to a server—much easier!

Transparent Switches in transparent mode don't participate in the VTP domain, but they will still forward VTP advertisements through any configured trunk links. These switches can add and delete VLANs because they keep their own database—one they do not share with other switches. Transparent mode is really considered locally significant only.

 Real World Scenario

When do I need to worry about VTP?

Whenever you have more than one switch and you have multiple VLANs. If you have only one switch, then VTP is irrelevant. It also isn't important if you are not configuring VLANs in your network. However, if you do have multiple switches and use multiple VLANs, then you better configure your VTP server and clients correctly!

When you first bring up your switched network, all switches are VTP servers by default. Physically connect your switches, then configure the main switch to be the VTP server and all others to be VTP clients. When you create VLANs on the main VTP server, all switches will receive the VLAN database.

If you have an existing switched network and you want to add a new switch, make sure to configure it as a VTP client before you install it. If not, it's possible that this switch could send out a new VTP database to all other switches, effectively wiping out all your VLANs!

VTP Pruning

VTP provides a way for you to preserve bandwidth by configuring it to reduce the amount of broadcasts, multicasts, and other unicast packets. This is called *pruning*. VTP pruning only sends broadcasts to trunk links that truly must have the information. Here's an example: If Switch A doesn't have any ports configured for VLAN 5, and a broadcast is sent throughout VLAN 5, that broadcast would not traverse the trunk link to this Switch A. By default, VTP pruning is disabled on all switches.

When you enable pruning on a VTP server, you enable it for the entire domain. By default, VLANs 2 through 1005 are pruning-eligible, but VLAN 1 can never prune because it's an administrative VLAN.

Routing between VLANs

Hosts in a VLAN live in their own broadcast domain and can communicate freely. VLANs create network partitioning and traffic separation at layer 2 of the OSI, and like I said when I told you why we still need routers, if you want hosts or any other device to communicate between VLANs, a layer-3 device is absolutely necessary.

For this, you can use a router that has an interface for each VLAN or a router that supports ISL routing. The least expensive router that supports ISL routing is the 2600 series router. The 1600, 1700, and 2500 series don't support ISL routing.

As shown in Figure 6.7, if you only had a few VLANs (two or three), you could get a router with two or three 10BaseT or Fast Ethernet connections. And 10BaseT is okay, but I'd recommend Fast Ethernet—that will work really well.

What we see in Figure 6.7 is that each router interface is plugged into an access link. This means that each of the routers' interface IP addresses would then become the default gateway address for each host in each VLAN.

If you have more VLANs available than router interfaces, you can either run ISL routing on one Fast Ethernet interface, or buy a route switch module (RSM) for a 5000 series switch. The RSM can support up to 1005 VLANs and run on the backplane of the switch.

FIGURE 6.7 Router with individual VLAN associations

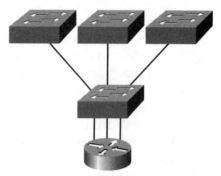

Router connecting three VLANs
together for inter-VLAN communication,
one interface for each VLAN.

Instead of using a router interface for each VLAN, you use one Fast Ethernet interface and run ISL routing. Figure 6.8 shows how a Fast Ethernet interface on a router will look when configured with ISL routing. This allows all VLANs to communicate through one interface. Cisco calls this "a router-on-a-stick."

FIGURE 6.8 Router-on-a-stick

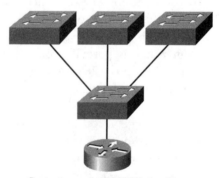

Router connecting all VLANs together
allowing for inter-VLAN communication,
using only one router interface
(Router on a stick).

Summary

This chapter introduced you to the world of virtual LANs and described how Cisco switches can use them. We talked about how VLANs break up broadcast domains in a switched internetwork, which is important because layer-2 switches only break up collision domains and, by default, all switches make up one large broadcast domain. I also described trunked VLANs across a Fast Ethernet link.

Trunking is a crucial technology to understand well when you're dealing with a network with multiple switches running several VLANs. I also talked at length about VLAN Trunk Protocol (VTP), which really has nothing to do with trunking. You learned that it does send VLAN information down a trunked link, but that the trunk configuration in itself is not part of VTP.

Exam Essentials

Understand the term "frame tagging."   Frame tagging refers to VLAN identification; this is what switches use to keep track of all those frames as they're traversing a switch fabric. It's how switches identify which frames belong to which VLANs.

Understand the ISL VLAN identification method.   Inter-Switch Link (ISL) is a way of explicitly tagging VLAN information onto an Ethernet frame. This tagging information allows VLANs to be multiplexed over a trunk link through an external encapsulation method, which allows the switch to identify the VLAN membership of a frame over the link. ISL is a Cisco-proprietary frame-tagging method that can only be used with Cisco switches.

Understand the 802.1Q VLAN identification method.   A nonpropri-etary IEEE method of frame tagging. If you're trunking between a Cisco switched link and a different brand of switch, you have to use 802.1Q for the trunk to work.

Remember the benefits of VLANs.   There are several benefits of VLANs:

- The VLAN can group several broadcast domains into multiple logical subnets.

- Network adds, moves, and changes are achieved by configuring a port into the appropriate VLAN.

- A group of users needing high security can be put into a VLAN so that no users outside of the VLAN can communicate with them.

- As a logical grouping of users by function, VLANs can be considered independent from their physical or geographic locations.

- VLANs can enhance network security.

- VLANs increase the number of broadcast domains while decreasing their size.

Remember to check a switch port's VLAN assignment when plugging in a new host. If you plug a new host into a switch, then you must verify the VLAN membership of that port. If the membership is different than what is needed for that host, the host will not be able to reach the needed network services, such as a workgroup server.

Key Terms

Be sure you're familiar with the following terms before taking the exam:

access link	pruning
broadcast domain	static VLAN
collision domain	switch fabric
dynamic VLAN	trunk link
flat network	virtual LAN (VLAN)
frame tagging	VLAN Trunk Protocol (VTP)
ISL routing	VTP transparent mode
native VLAN	

There are no hands-on labs associated with this chapter. Please see the companion CD or www.routersim.com for programs that provides practice in configuring switches and VLANs.

Written Lab 6

In this section, write the answers to the following questions:

1. What VTP mode can only accept VLAN information and not change VLAN information?

2. What VLAN identification method is proprietary to Cisco routers?

3. VLANs break up _____ domains.

4. Switches, by default, only break up _____ domains.

5. What is the default VTP mode?

6. What does trunking provide?

7. What is frame tagging?

8. True/False: The ISL encapsulation is removed from the frame if the frame is forwarded out an access link.

9. What type of link is only part of one VLAN and is referred to as the "native VLAN" of the port?

10. What type of Cisco tagging information allows VLANs to be multiplexed over a trunk link through an external encapsulation method?

(The answers to Written Lab 6 can be found following the answers to the Review Questions for this chapter.)

Review Questions

1. Which of the following are true regarding VLANs? (Choose all that apply.)

   A. You must have at least two VLANs defined in every Cisco switched network.

   B. All VLANs are configured at the fastest switch and, by default, propagate this information to all other switches.

   C. You should not have more than 10 switches in the same VTP domain.

   D. VTP is used to send VLAN information to switches in a configured VTP domain.

2. How does inter-VLAN communication take place?

   A. Using a layer-2 switch

   B. Using a router

   C. Using a hub

   D. Using a repeater

3. Which two statements about frame tagging are true?

   A. A filtering table is loaded into each switch.

   B. Frame tagging assigns a user-defined ID to each frame.

   C. A unique identifier is placed in the header of each frame as it is forwarded between switches.

   D. It is used by switches to control broadcasts.

4. How are dynamic VLANs configured?

   A. Statically

   B. By an administrator

   C. Via a DHCP server

   D. Via a VLAN Management Policy Server

5. Which of the following protocols are used to configure trunking on a switch? (Choose all that apply.)

   A. VLAN Trunk Protocol

   B. VLAN

   C. Trunk

   D. ISL

6. What is Cisco's proprietary frame-tagging method?

   A. 802.1Q

   B. 802.3

   C. ISL

   D. VTP

7. Which switching technology reduces the size of a broadcast domain?

   A. ISL

   B. 802.1Q

   C. VLANs

   D. STP

8. What does setting the VTP mode to transparent accomplish?

   A. Transparent mode will only forward messages and advertisements, not add them to their own database.

   B. Transparent mode will both forward messages and advertisements and add them to their own database.

   C. Transparent mode will not forward messages and advertisements.

   D. Transparent mode makes a switch dynamically secure.

9. What is the main purpose of creating VLANs?

   A. Break up collision domains at layer 2

   B. Break up collision domains at layer 3

   C. Break up broadcast domains at layer 2

   D. Break up broadcast domains at layer 3

10. Which of the following is true regarding VTP?

    A. All switches are VTP servers by default.

    B. All switches are VTP transparent by default.

    C. VTP is on by default with a domain name of Cisco on all Cisco switches.

    D. All switches are VTP clients by default.

11. Which of the following is true regarding trunked links?

    A. They are configured by default on all switch ports.

    B. They only work with a type of Ethernet network—not with Token Ring, FDDI, or ATM.

    C. You can set trunk links on any 10-, 100-, and 1000Mbps ports.

    D. You must clear the unwanted VLANs by hand.

12. Which of the following are benefits of VLANs? (Select all that apply.)

    A. The VLAN can group several broadcast domains into multiple logical subnets.

    B. Network adds, moves, and changes are achieved by configuring a port into the appropriate VLAN.

    C. A group of users needing high security can be put into a VLAN so that no users outside of that VLAN can communicate with them.

    D. VLANs allow logical grouping of users by function

    E. VLANs make it unnecessary to install cables to move a user from one network to another.

    F. VLANs can enhance network security.

    G. VLANs increase the number of broadcast domains, while decreasing their size.

13. Which of the following is an IEEE standard for frame tagging?

    A. ISL

    B. 802.3Z

    C. 802.1Q

    D. 802.3U

14. Which of the following statements describe a trunked link? (Select all that apply.)

   A. A trunked link can carry multiple VLANs.

   B. Switches remove any VLAN information from the frame before it is sent to an access link device.

   C. Access-link devices cannot communicate with devices outside their VLAN unless the packet is routed through a router.

   D. Trunked links are used to transport VLANs between devices and can be configured to transport all VLANs or just a few.

15. Which of the following are true regarding an access link? (Choose all that apply.)

   A. They can carry multiple VLANs.

   B. Switches remove any VLAN information from the frame before it is sent to an access-link device.

   C. Access-link devices cannot communicate with devices outside their VLAN unless the packet is routed through a router.

   D. Access links are used to transport VLANs between devices and can be configured to transport all VLANs or just a few.

16. Which of the following statements is true regarding access links?

   A. They can carry multiple VLANs.

   B. They are used to transport VLANs between devices and can be configured to transport all VLANs or just a few.

   C. They can only be used with Fast Ethernet or Gigabit Ethernet.

   D. They are only part of one VLAN and are referred to as the native VLAN of the port.

17. Which of the following is a nonproprietary method of frame tagging?

   A. ISL

   B. STP

   C. VLAN

   D. 802.1Q

18. You connect a host to a switch port, but the new host cannot log into the server that is plugged into the same switch. What could the problem be? (Choose the most likely answer.)

    A. The router is not configured for the new host.

    B. The VTP configuration on the switch is not updated for the new host.

    C. The host has an invalid MAC address.

    D. The switch port the host is connected to is not configured to the correct VLAN membership.

19. What advantage is offered by LAN segmentation? (Choose the best answer.)

    A. More broadcasts can be sent onto the network.

    B. More bandwidth is provided to each user.

    C. Fewer administrators are needed to run the network.

    D. More collision domains always means faster network services.

20. When is frame tagging used?

    A. When VLANs are traversing an access link

    B. When VLANs are traversing a trunked link

    C. When ISL is used on an access link

    D. When 802.1Q is used on an access link

21. When talking about frame tagging with VLAN ID, which of the following would be used to describe this?

    A. VTP with multiple switches and VLANs

    B. VLAN color and placement

    C. Identifying VLAN memberships over trunked links

    D. Creating an access port to on a switch a router with ISL

22. Which of the following provide interswitch VLAN communication? (Choose two.)

A. ISL

B. VTP

C. 802.1Q

D. 802.3Z

23. You have two switches connected with a trunked link running two VLANs. VLAN1 is assigned to ports 1 through 3 of each switch and VLAN2 has been assigned port 8 through 12 of each switch. HostA and HostB are in VLAN1. HostG and HostH are in VLAN2. There is *no* inter-VLAN routing. What should you do to verify proper VLAN and trunk operations? (Choose three.)

A. Verify that HostA can ping HostB.

B. Verify that HostA can ping HostG.

C. Verify that HostG can ping HostH.

D. Verify that HostG cannot ping HostA.

E. Verify that HostA cannot ping HostB.

24. You need to add a new VLAN named ROUTERSIM to your switched network. Which of the following are true regarding configuration of this VLAN? (Select all that apply.)

A. You must name the VLAN.

B. You must assign ports on a switch for this VLAN.

C. You must add this VLAN to the VTP domain.

D. The VLAN must be created.

E. You must add an IP address for the ROUTERSIM VLAN.

25. Which of the following protocols is used to exchange VLAN configuration information between switches?

A. 802.10

B. VLAN Trunking Protocol (VTP)

C. Inter-Switch Link (ISL)

D. 802.1Q

Answers to Review Questions

1. D.   Switches do not propagate VLAN information by default; you must configure the VTP domain. VLAN Trunk Protocol (VTP) is used to propagate VLAN information across a trunked link.

2. B.   Inter-VLAN communication must take place with a router or layer-3 switch.

3. B, C.   Frame tagging is used to keep track of frames as they traverse a switched fabric.

4. D.   A VMPS server must be configured with the hardware addresses of all hosts on the internetworks.

5. C, D.   VTP is not right because it has nothing to do with trunking, except that it sends VLAN information across a trunked link. Trunk protocol and ISL are used to configure trunking on a port.

6. C.   The Cisco proprietary frame-tagging method is Inter-Switch Link (ISL) routing.

7. C.   Virtual LANs break up broadcast domains in layer-2 switched internetworks.

8. A.   The transparent switch is a stand-alone switch that can be connected to your network for management. It does not add VLAN information to its VLAN database, nor does it share its configured VLAN information. It will pass VLAN-received trunked ports out a different trunked port if configured.

9. C.   Virtual LANs were created so that broadcast domains can be broken up in a layer-2 switched internetwork.

10. A.   All Cisco switches are VTP servers by default. No other VTP information is configured on a Cisco switch by default.

11. D.   By default, if you create a trunked link, all VLANs are allowed on that trunked link. You must delete any unwanted VLANs by hand.

12. A, B, C, D, F, G.   Virtual LANs create security, flexibility, and ease of management as well as create smaller broadcast domains. You still need to run cables to connect users to the network.

13. C. 802.1Q was created to allow trunked links between disparate switches.

14. A, D. Trunks are used to carry VLAN information between switches.

15. B, C. When a frame traverses a trunked link, it is encapsulated in ISL information. The ISL information is removed before the frame is sent down an access link.

16. D. Access links only carry information about one VLAN.

17. D. 802.1Q is the IEEE standard for identifying VLANs as they cross a trunked link.

18. D. This question is a little vague, but the best answer is that the VLAN membership for the port is not configured.

19. B. The typical reason for creating network segmentation is to provide more bandwidth to each user.

20. B. Cisco created frame tagging to be used when an Ethernet frame traverses a trunked link.

21. C. Frame tagging is the process of identifying frames as they traverse a trunked link. Cisco uses the propriety ISL version, where 802.1Q is a nonproprietary version.

22. A, C. ISL is a Cisco proprietary frame-tagging method. IEEE 802.1Q is the nonproprietary version of frame tagging.

23. A, C, D. If you are not providing a type of inter-VLAN routing, then hosts not in the same VLAN will not be able to communicate. HostA and HostB can communicate, and HostG and HostH can communicate, but HostA and B cannot communicate to HostG and HostH.

24. A, B, D. To establish a VLAN, you must first create the VLAN, name it, and then add the VLAN to the desired ports of a switch. Since the Network layer protocol is irrelevant to the VLAN, the IP address answer is not correct.

25. B. VLAN Trunking Protocol is responsible for distributing and synchronizing information about configured VLANs between switches throughout the network. VTP manages additions, deletions, and name changes for network VLANs.

Answers to Written Lab 6

1. Client

2. Inter-Switch Link (ISL)

3. Broadcast

4. Collision

5. Server

6. Trunking allows you to make a single port part of multiple VLANs at the same time.

7. Frame identification (frame tagging) uniquely assigns a user-defined ID to each frame. This is sometimes referred to as a VLAN ID or color.

8. True

9. Access link

10. Inter-Switch Link (ISL)

Managing a Cisco Internetwork

THE CCNA EXAM TOPICS COVERED IN THIS CHAPTER INCLUDE THE FOLLOWING:

✓ **Network Protocols**

  ▪ Verify IP addresses.

✓ **Cisco Basics, IOS & Network Basics**

  ▪ Examine router elements.

  ▪ Manage configuration files from the privilege EXEC mode.

  ▪ List the commands to load Cisco IOS software from: Flash memory, a TFTP server, or ROM.

  ▪ Prepare to backup, upgrade, and load a backup Cisco IOS software image.

In this chapter, you will learn how to manage Cisco routers on an internetwork. The Internetwork Operating System (IOS) and configuration files reside in different locations in a Cisco device, and it's important to understand where these files are located and how they work.

You will learn about the main components of a router, the router boot sequence, and the configuration register, including how to use the configuration register for password recovery. Then you will learn how to manage routers by performing the following tasks:

- Backing up and restoring the Cisco IOS

- Backing up and restoring the Cisco configuration

- Gathering information about neighbor devices through CDP and Telnet

- Resolving hostnames

- Using the `ping` and `trace` commands to test network connectivity

The Internal Components of a Cisco Router

In order to configure and troubleshoot a Cisco internetwork, you need to know the major components of Cisco routers and understand what these components do. Table 7.1 describes the major Cisco router components.

TABLE 7.1   Cisco Router Components

Component	Description
Bootstrap	Stored in the microcode of the ROM, the bootstrap is used to bring a router up during initialization. It will boot the router and then load the IOS.
POST (power-on self-test)	Stored in the microcode of the ROM, the POST is used to check the basic functionality of the router hardware and determines which interfaces are present.
ROM monitor	Stored in the microcode of the ROM, the ROM monitor is used for manufacturing testing and troubleshooting.
Mini-IOS	Called the RXBOOT or bootloader by Cisco, the mini-IOS is a small IOS in ROM that can be used to bring up an interface and load a Cisco IOS into flash memory. The mini-IOS can also perform a few other maintenance operations.
RAM (random-access memory)	Used to hold packet buffers, ARP cache, routing tables, and also the software and data structures that allow the router to function. Running-config is stored in RAM, and the IOS can also be run from RAM in some routers.
ROM (read-only memory)	Used to start and maintain the router.
Flash memory	Used on the router to hold the Cisco IOS. Flash memory is not erased when the router is reloaded. It is an EEPROM created by Intel.
NVRAM (non-volatile RAM)	Used to hold the router and switch configuration. NVRAM is not erased when the router or switch is reloaded.
Configuration register	Used to control how the router boots up. This value can be seen with the show version command and typically is 0x2102, which tells the router to load the IOS from flash memory.

The Router Boot Sequence

When a router boots up, it performs a series of steps, called the *boot sequence*, to test the hardware and load the necessary software. The boot sequence consists of the following steps:

1. The router performs a POST. The POST tests the hardware to verify that all components of the device are operational and present. For example, the POST checks for the different interfaces on the router. The POST is stored in and run from *ROM (read-only memory)*.

2. The bootstrap looks for and loads the Cisco IOS software. The bootstrap is a program in ROM that is used to execute programs. The bootstrap program is responsible for finding where each IOS program is located and then loading the file. By default, the IOS software is loaded from flash memory in all Cisco routers.

3. The IOS software looks for a valid configuration file stored in NVRAM. This file is called startup-config and is only there if an administrator copies the running-config file into NVRAM.

4. If a startup-config file is in NVRAM, the router will load and run this file. The router is now operational. If a startup-config file is not in NVRAM, the router will start the setup mode configuration upon bootup.

Managing Configuration Registers

All Cisco routers have a 16-bit software register, which is written into NVRAM. By default, the *configuration register* is set to load the Cisco IOS from *flash memory* and to look for and load the startup-config file from NVRAM.

Understanding the Configuration Register Bits

The 16 bits of the configuration register are read from 15 to 0, from left to right. The default configuration setting on Cisco routers is 0x2102. This means that bits 13, 8, and 1 are on, as shown in Table 7.2. Notice that each set of four bits is read in binary with a value of 1, 2, 4, and 8, from right to left.

TABLE 7.2 The Configuration Register Bit Numbers

Configuration Register	2				1				0				2			
Bit number	15	14	13	12	11	10	9	8	7	6	5	4	3	2	1	0
Binary	0	0	1	0	0	0	0	1	0	0	0	0	0	0	1	0

Add the prefix 0x to the configuration register address. The 0x means that the digits that follow are in hexadecimal.

Table 7.3 lists the software configuration bit meanings. Notice that bit 6 can be used to ignore the NVRAM contents. This bit is used for password recovery, as described in the "Recovering Passwords" section later in this chapter.

TABLE 7.3 Software Configuration Meanings

Bit	Hex	Description
0–3	0x0000–0x000F	Boot field (see Table 7.4)
6	0x0040	Ignore NVRAM contents
7	0x0080	OEM bit enabled
8	0x101	Break disabled
10	0x0400	IP broadcast with all zeros
11–12	0x0800–0x1000	Console line speed
13	0x2000	Boot default ROM software if network boot fails
14	0x4000	IP broadcasts do not have net numbers
15	0x8000	Enable diagnostic messages and ignore NVM contents

The boot field, which consists of bits 0–3 in the configuration register, controls the router boot sequence. Table 7.4 describes the boot field bits.

TABLE 7.4 The Boot Field (Configuration Register Bits 00–03)

Boot Field	Meaning	Use
00	ROM monitor mode	To boot to ROM monitor mode, set the configuration register to 2100. You must manually boot the router with the b command. The router will show the rommon> prompt.
01	Boot image from ROM	To boot an IOS image stored in ROM, set the configuration register to 2101. The router will show the router(boot)> prompt.
02–F	Specifies a default boot filename	Any value from 2102 through 210F tells the router to use the boot commands specified in NVRAM.

Remember that in hex, the scheme is 0–9 and A–F (A = 10, B = 11, C = 12, D = 13, E = 14, and F = 15). This means that a 210F setting for the configuration register is actually 210(15), or 1111 in binary.

Checking the Current Configuration Register Value

You can see the current value of the configuration register by using the show version command (sh version or show ver for short), as in the following example:

```
Router#sh version
Cisco Internetwork Operating System Software
IOS (tm) C2600 Software (C2600-I-M), Version 12.0(3)T3,
   RELEASE SOFTWARE (fc1)
[output cut]
Configuration register is 0x2102
```

The last information given from this command is the value of the configuration register. In this example, the value is 0x2102, which is the default setting. The configuration register setting of 0x2102 tells the router to look in NVRAM for the boot sequence.

Notice the show version command also provides the IOS version, and in the example above, it shows the IOS version as 12.0(3)T3.

The show version command will display system hardware configuration information, software version, and the names and sources of configuration files and boot images on a router.

Changing the Configuration Register

You can change the configuration register value to modify how the router boots and runs, as follows:

- Force the system into the ROM monitor mode
- Select a boot source and default boot filename
- Enable or disable the Break function
- Control broadcast addresses
- Set the console terminal baud rate
- Load operating software from ROM
- Enable booting from a TFTP (Trivial File Transfer Protocol) server

Before you change the configuration register, make sure you know the current configuration register value. Use the show version command to get this information.

You can change the configuration register by using the config-register command. For example, the following commands tell the router to boot a small IOS from ROM monitor mode and then show the current configuration register value:

```
Router(config)#config-register 0x101
Router(config)#^Z
```

```
Router#sh ver
[output cut]
Configuration register is 0x2102 (will be 0x0101 at next
   reload)
```

Notice that the show version command shows the current configuration register value, as well as what it will be when the router reboots. Any change to the configuration register will not take effect until the router is reloaded. The 0x0101 will load the IOS from ROM the next time the router is rebooted. You may see it listed as 0x101, which is the same thing and can be written either way.

Recovering Passwords

If you are locked out of a router because you forgot the password, you can change the configuration register to help you recover. As noted earlier, bit 6 in the configuration register is used to tell the router whether to use the contents of NVRAM to load a router configuration.

The default configuration register value is 0x2102, which means that bit 6 is off. With the default setting, the router will look for and load a router configuration stored in NVRAM (startup-config). To recover a password, you need to turn on bit 6, which will tell the router to ignore the NVRAM contents. The configuration register value to turn on bit 6 is 0x2142.

Here are the main steps to password recovery:

1. Boot the router and interrupt the boot sequence by performing a break.

2. Change the configuration register to turn on bit 6 (with the value 0x2142).

3. Reload the router.

4. Enter privileged mode.

5. Copy the startup-config file to running-config.

6. Change the password.

7. Reset the configuration register to the default value.

8. Save the router configuration.

9. Reload the router.

These steps are discussed in more detail in the following sections, showing the commands to restore access to 2600 and 2500 series routers.

Interrupting the Router Boot Sequence

Your first step is to boot the router and perform a break. Typically, you perform a break by pressing the Ctrl+Break key combination when using HyperTerminal.

The Windows NT or 2000 default HyperTerminal program will not perform the break. You must upgrade the HyperTerminal program or use Windows 95/98.

You should see something like this:

```
System Bootstrap, Version 11.3(2)XA4, RELEASE SOFTWARE (fc1)
Copyright (c) 1999 by cisco Systems, Inc.
TAC:Home:SW:IOS:Specials for info
PC = 0xfff0a530, Vector = 0x500, SP = 0x680127b0
C2600 platform with 32768 Kbytes of main memory
PC = 0xfff0a530, Vector = 0x500, SP = 0x80004374
monitor: command "boot" aborted due to user interrupt
rommon 1 >
```

Notice the line "boot" aborted due to user interrupt. At this point, you will be at the rommon 1> prompt on some routers.

Changing the Configuration Register

As explained earlier, you can change the configuration register by using the config-register command. To turn on bit 6, use the configuration register value 0x2142.

Remember that if you change the configuration register to 0x2142, then the startup-config will be bypassed and the router will load into setup mode.

Cisco 2600 Series Commands

To change the bit value on a Cisco 2600 series router, simply enter the command at the rommon 1> prompt:

```
rommon 1 > confreg 0x2142
You must reset or power cycle for new config to take effect
```

Cisco 2500 Series Commands

To change the configuration register on a 2500 series router, type **o** after creating a break sequence on the router. This brings up a menu of configuration register option settings. To change the configuration register, enter the command **o/r**, followed by the new register value. Here is an example of turning on bit 6 on a 2501 router:

```
System Bootstrap, Version 11.0(10c), SOFTWARE
Copyright (c) 1986-1996 by cisco Systems
2500 processor with 14336 Kbytes of main memory
Abort at 0x1098FEC (PC)
>o
Configuration register = 0x2102 at last boot
Bit#    Configuration register option settings:
15      Diagnostic mode disabled
14      IP broadcasts do not have network numbers
13      Boot default ROM software if network boot fails
12-11   Console speed is 9600 baud
10      IP broadcasts with ones
08      Break disabled
07      OEM disabled
06      Ignore configuration disabled
03-00   Boot file is cisco2-2500 (or 'boot system' command)
>o/r 0x2142
```

Notice the last entry in the router output is 03-00, which tells the router what the IOS boot file is. By default, the router will use the first file found in the flash memory. If you want to boot a different file name you can either change the configuration register or use the boot system *ios_name* command. You can also load an IOS image from a TFTP host by using the command boot system *tftp ios_name ip_address*.

Reloading the Router and Entering Privileged Mode

At this point, you need to reset the router, as follows:

- From the 2600 series router, type **reset**.

- From the 2500 series router, type **I** (for initialize).

The router will reload and ask if you want to use setup mode (because no startup-config is used). Answer No to entering setup mode, press Enter to go into user mode, and then type **enable** to go into privileged mode.

Viewing and Changing the Configuration

Now you are past where you would need to enter the user mode and privileged mode passwords in a router. Copy the startup-config file to the running-config file:

```
copy startup-config running-config
```

or use the shortcut:

```
copy start run
```

The configuration is now running in *RAM (random access memory)*, and you are in privileged mode, which means that you can view and change the configuration. Although you cannot view the enable secret setting for the password, you can change the password, as follows:

```
config t
enable secret todd
```

Resetting the Configuration Register and Reloading the Router

After you are finished changing passwords, set the configuration register back to the default value with the config-register command:

```
config t
config-register 0x2102
```

Finally, save the new configuration with a copy running-config startup-config and reload the router.

Backing Up and Restoring the Cisco IOS

Before you upgrade or restore a Cisco IOS, you should copy the existing file to a *TFTP host* as a backup in case the new image does not work.

You can use any TFTP host to perform this function. By default, the flash memory in a router is used to store the Cisco IOS. The following sections describe how to check the amount of flash memory, copy the Cisco IOS from flash memory to a TFTP host, and then copy the IOS from a TFTP host to flash memory.

Before you backup an IOS image to a network server, complete the following:

- Make sure you can access the network server.

- Ensure the network server has adequate space for the code image.

- Verify the file naming and path requirement.

Verifying Flash Memory

Before you attempt to upgrade the Cisco IOS on your router with a new IOS file, you should verify that your flash memory has enough room to hold the new image. You can verify the amount of flash memory and the file or files being stored in flash memory by using the show flash command (sh flash for short):

```
Router#sh flash
System flash directory:
File  Length    Name/status
  1   8121000   c2500-js-1.112-18.bin
[8121064 bytes used, 8656152 available, 16777216 total]
16384K bytes of processor board System flash (Read ONLY)
Router#
```

Notice that the filename in this example is c2500-js-1.112-18.bin. The name of the file is platform-specific and is derived as follows:

- c2500 is the platform.

- j indicates that the file is an enterprise image.

- s indicates the file contains extended capabilities.

- 1 indicates that the file can be moved from flash memory if needed and is not compressed.

- 11.2-18 is the revision number.

- .bin indicates that the Cisco IOS is a binary executable file.

The last line in the router output shows that the flash is 16,384KB (or 16MB). So if the new file that you want to use is, say, 10MB in size, you know that there is plenty of room for it. Once you verify that flash memory can hold the IOS you want to copy, you can continue with your backup operation.

Backing Up the Cisco IOS

To back up the Cisco IOS to a TFTP host, you use the copy flash tftp command. This is a straightforward command that requires only the source filename and the IP address of the TFTP host.

The key to success in this backup routine is to make sure that you have good connectivity to the TFTP host. You can check this by pinging the device from the router console prompt, as in the following example:

```
Router#ping 192.168.0.120
Type escape sequence to abort.
Sending 5, 100-byte ICMP Echos to 192.168.0.120, timeout
  is 2 seconds:
!!!!!
Success rate is 100 percent (5/5), round-trip min/avg/max
  = 4/4/8 ms
```

The *Ping (Packet Internet Groper)* utility is used to test network connectivity. It is used in some examples in this chapter and discussed in more detail in the "Checking Network Connectivity" section later in this chapter.

After you ping the TFTP host to make sure that IP is working, you can use the copy flash tftp command to copy the IOS to the TFTP host, as shown next. Notice that after you enter the command, the name of the file in flash memory is displayed. This makes it easy for you. You can copy the filename and then paste it when prompted for the source filename.

```
Router#copy flash tftp
System flash directory:
File   Length    Name/status
  1    8121000   c2500-js-1.112-18.bin
[8121064 bytes used, 8656152 available, 16777216 total]
Address or name of remote host [255.255.255.255]?
  192.168.0.120
Source file name?c2500-js-1.112-18.bin
Destination file name [c2500-js-1.112-18.bin]?[Enter]
Verifying checksum for 'c2500-js-1.112-18.bin')file #1)
...OK
```

```
Copy '/c2500-js-1.112-18' from Flash to server
   as '/c2500-js-1.112-18'? [yes/no]y
!!!!!!!!!!!!!!!!!!!!!!!!!!!!!!!!!!!!!!!!!!!!!!!!!!!!!!!!!!!!!
   !!!!!!!!!!!!!!!!!!!! [output cut]
Upload to server done
Flash copy took 00:02:30 [hh:mm:ss]
Router#
```

In this example, the content of flash memory was copied successfully to the TFTP host. The address of the remote host is the IP address of the TFTP host. The source filename is the file in flash memory.

The copy flash tftp command does not prompt you for the location of any file or ask you where to put the file. TFTP is the "grab it and place it" program in this situation. The TFTP host must have a default directory specified, or it won't work.

Restoring or Upgrading the Cisco Router IOS

You may need to restore the Cisco IOS to flash memory to replace an original file that has been damaged or to upgrade the IOS. You can download the file from a TFTP host to flash memory by using the copy tftp flash command. This command requires the IP address of the TFTP host and the name of the file you want to download to flash memory.

Before you begin, make sure that the file you want to place in flash memory is in the default TFTP directory on your host. When you issue the command, TFTP will not ask you where the file is. If the file you want to restore is not in the default directory of the TFTP host, this procedure won't work.

Copying the IOS from the TFTP host to flash memory requires a router reboot. So, instead of upgrading or restoring the IOS at 9 a.m. on Monday morning, you should probably wait until lunchtime.

After you enter the copy tftp flash command, you will see a message informing you that the router must reboot and run a ROM-based IOS image to perform this operation:

```
Router#copy tftp flash
```

```
                    ****  NOTICE  ****
Flash load helper v1.0
This process will accept the copy options and then
terminate the current system image to use the ROM based
image for the copy. Routing functionality will not be
available during that time. If you are logged in via
telnet, this connection will terminate. Users with
console access can see the results of the copy operation.
                  ____ ******** ____
Proceed? [confirm][Enter]
```

After you press Enter to confirm you understand that the router needs to reboot, the following router output is displayed. Once the router has used the TFTP host, it will remember the address and just prompt you to press Enter.

```
System flash directory:
File  Length   Name/status
  1  8121000  /c2500-js-1.112-18
[8121064 bytes used, 8656152 available, 16777216 total]
Address or name of remote host [192.168.0.120]?[Enter]
```

The next prompt is for the name of the file you want to copy to flash memory. As noted earlier, this file must be in your TFTP host's default directory.

```
Source file name?c2500-js56i-1.120-9.bin
Destination file name [c2500-js56i-1.120-9.bin]?[Enter]
Accessing file 'c2500-js56i-1.120-9.bin' on 192.168.0.120
...
Loading c2500-js56i-1.120-9.bin from 192.168.0.120
  (via Ethernet0): ! [OK]
```

After you tell the router the filename and where the file is, it asks you to confirm that you understand the contents of flash memory will be erased.

If you do not have enough room in flash memory to store both copies, or if the flash memory is new and no file has been written to flash memory before, the router will ask to erase the contents of flash memory before writing the new file into flash memory.

You are prompted three times, just to make sure that you really want to proceed with erasing flash memory. If you have not issued a copy run start command, you will be prompted to do so, since the router needs to reboot.

```
Erase flash device before writing? [confirm][Enter]
Flash contains files. Are you sure you want to erase?
  [confirm][Enter]

System configuration has been modified. Save? [yes/no]: y
Building configuration...
[OK]
Copy 'c2500-js56i-1.120-9.bin' from server
  as 'c2500-js56i-1.120-9.bin' into Flash WITH erase?
  [yes/no] y
```

After you say Yes to erasing flash memory, the router must reboot to load a small IOS from ROM memory. You cannot delete the flash file if it is in use.

Then the contents of flash memory are erased, and the file from the TFTP host is accessed and copied to flash memory.

```
%SYS-5-RELOAD: Reload requested
%FLH: c2500-js56i-1.120-9.bin from 192.168.0.120 to flash
...
System flash directory:
File  Length    Name/status
  1   8121000   /c2500-js-1.112-18
[8121064 bytes used, 8656152 available, 16777216 total]
Accessing file 'c2500-js56i-1.120-9.bin' on 192.168.0.120
...
Loading c2500-js56i-1.120-9.bin .from 192.168.0.120
  (via Ethernet0): ! [OK]

Erasing device... eeeeeeeeeeeeeeeeeeeeeeeeeeeeeeeeeeeeeeeee
  eeeeeeeeeeeeeeeeeeeeee
Loading c2500-js56i-1.120-9.bin from 192.168.0.120
  (via Ethernet0):
  !!!!!!!!!!!!!!!!!!!!!!!!!!!!!!!!!!!!!!!!!!!!!!!!!!!!!!!!!!!!
  !!!!!!!!!!!!!!!!!!!!!!!!!!!!!!!!!!! [output cut]
```

The row of **e** characters shows the contents of flash memory being erased. Each exclamation point (!) means that one UDP segment has been successfully transferred.

Once the copy is complete, you should receive this message:

```
[OK - 10935532/16777216 bytes]

Verifying checksum...  OK (0x2E3A)
Flash copy took 0:06:14 [hh:mm:ss]
%FLH: Re-booting system after download
```

After the file is loaded into flash memory and a checksum is performed, the router is rebooted to run the new IOS file.

Cisco routers can become a TFTP-server host for a router system image that is run in flash. The global configuration command is `tftp-server tftp:`.

Backing Up and Restoring the Cisco Configuration

Any changes that you make to the router configuration are stored in the running-config file. If you do not perform a `copy run start` command after you make a change to running-config, that change will be gone if the router reboots or gets powered down. You may want to make another backup of the configuration information as an extra precaution, in case the router or switch completely dies, or for documentation. The following sections describe how to copy the configuration of a router and switch to a TFTP host and how to restore that configuration.

Backing Up the Cisco Router Configuration

To copy the router's configuration from a router to a TFTP host, you can use either the `copy running-config tftp` or `copy startup-config tftp` command. Either command will back up the router configuration that is currently running in DRAM or that is stored in NVRAM.

Verifying the Current Configuration

To verify the configuration in DRAM, use the `show running-config` command (`sh run` for short), as follows:

```
Router#sh run
Building configuration...

Current configuration:
!
version 12.0
```

The current configuration information indicates that the router is now running version 12.0 of the IOS.

Verifying the Stored Configuration

Next, you should check the configuration stored in NVRAM. To see this, use the `show startup-config` command (`sh start` for short), as follows:

```
Router#sh start
Using 366 out of 32762 bytes
!
version 11.2
```

The second line shows how much room your backup configuration is using. In this example, NVRAM is 32KB and only 366 bytes of it are used. Notice that the version of configuration in NVRAM is 11.2 (because I have not copied running-config to startup-config since upgrading the router).

If you are not sure that the files are the same, and the running-config file is what you want to use, then use the `copy running-config startup-config` to make sure both files are the same, as described in the next section.

Copying the Current Configuration to NVRAM

By copying running-config to NVRAM as a backup, as shown in the following output, you are assured that your running-config will always be reloaded if the router gets rebooted. In the new IOS version 12.0, you are prompted for the filename you want to use. Also, in this example, since the version of IOS was 11.2 the last time a `copy run start` was performed, the router will let you know that it is going to replace that file with the new 12.0 version.

```
Router#copy run start
Destination filename [startup-config]?[Enter]
```

```
Warning: Attempting to overwrite an NVRAM configuration
  previously written by a different version of the system
  image.
Overwrite the previous NVRAM configuration?
  [confirm][Enter]
Building configuration...
[OK]
```

Now when you run show startup-config, the version shows 12.0:

```
Router#sh start
Using 487 out of 32762 bytes
!
version 12.0
```

Copying the Configuration to a TFTP Host

Once the file is copied to NVRAM, you can make a second backup to a TFTP host by using the copy running-config tftp command (copy run tftp for short), as follows:

```
Router#copy run tftp
Address or name of remote host []?192.168.0.120
Destination filename [router-confg]?todd1-confg
!!
487 bytes copied in 12.236 secs (40 bytes/sec)
Router#
```

Notice that this took only two exclamation points (!!), which are two UDP acknowledgments. In this example, I named the file todd1-confg because I had not set a hostname for the router. If you have a hostname configured, the command will automatically use the hostname plus the extension -confg as the name of the file.

Restoring the Cisco Router Configuration

If you have changed your router's running-config and want to restore the configuration to the version in startup-config, the easiest way to do this is to use the copy startup-config running-config command (copy start run for short). You can also use the older Cisco command, config mem, to restore a configuration. Of course, this will work only if you first copied running-config into NVRAM before making any changes.

If you copied the router's configuration to a TFTP host as a second backup, you can restore the configuration using the copy tftp running-config command (copy tftp run for short) or the copy tftp startup-config command (copy tftp start for short), as shown below. Remember that the old command that provides this function is config net.

```
Router#copy tftp run
Address or name of remote host []?192.168.0.120
Source filename []?todd1-confg
Destination filename [running-config]?[Enter]
Accessing tftp://192.168.0.120/todd1-confg...
Loading todd1-confg from 192.168.0.120 (via Ethernet0):
!!
[OK - 487/4096 bytes]
487 bytes copied in 5.400 secs (97 bytes/sec)
Router#
00:38:31: %SYS-5-CONFIG: Configured from
   tftp://192.168.0.120/todd1-confg
Router#
```

The configuration file is an ASCII text file. This means that before you copy the configuration stored on a TFTP host back to a router, you can make changes to the file with any text editor.

Erasing the Configuration

To delete the startup-config file on a Cisco router, use the command erase startup-config, as follows:

```
Router#erase startup-config
Erasing the nvram filesystem will remove all files!
   Continue? [confirm][Enter]
[OK]
Erase of nvram: complete
Router#
```

The preceding command deletes the contents of NVRAM on the router. The next time the router boots, it will run the setup mode.

Using Cisco Discovery Protocol

Cisco Discovery Protocol (CDP) is a proprietary protocol designed by Cisco to help administrators collect information about both locally attached and remote devices. By using CDP, you can gather hardware and protocol information about neighbor devices. This information is useful for trouble-shooting and documenting the network.

Getting CDP Timers and Holdtime Information

The show cdp command (sh cdp for short) shows information about two CDP global parameters that can be configured on Cisco devices:

- *CDP timer* is how often CDP packets are transmitted to all active interfaces.

- *CDP holdtime* is the amount of time that the device will hold packets received from neighbor devices.

Both the Cisco routers and the Cisco switches use the same parameters. The output on a router looks like this:

```
Router#sh cdp
Global CDP information:
        Sending CDP packets every 60 seconds
        Sending a holdtime value of 180 seconds
Router#
```

Use the global commands cdp holdtime and cdp timer to configure the CDP holdtime and timer on a router.

```
Router#config t
Enter configuration commands, one per line.  End with
  CNTL/Z.
Router(config)#cdp ?
  holdtime   Specify the holdtime (in sec) to be sent in
             packets
  timer      Specify the rate at which CDP packets are
             sent (in sec)
  run

Router(config)#cdp timer 90
```

```
Router(config)#cdp holdtime 240
Router(config)#^Z
```

You can turn off CDP completely with the no cdp run command from global configuration mode of a router. To turn CDP off or on in a router interface, use the no cdp enable and cdp enable commands, which are discussed in more detail in the "Gathering Port and Interface Information" section a bit later in this chapter.

Gathering Neighbor Information

The show cdp neighbor command (sh cdp nei for short) shows information about directly connected devices. It is important to remember that CDP packets are not passed through a Cisco switch, and you only see what is directly attached. On a router connected to a switch, you will not see the other devices connected to the switch.

The following output shows the show cdp neighbor command used on a 2509 router.

```
Todd2509#sh cdp nei
Capability Codes: R - Router, T - Trans Bridge,
  B - Source Route Bridge, S - Switch, H - Host,
  I - IGMP, r - Repeater
Device ID  Local Intrfce Holdtme Capability Platform Port ID
1900Switch    Eth 0       238        T S        1900      2
2500B         Ser 0       138        R          2500     Ser 0
Todd2509#
```

Connected directly to the 2509 router are a switch with a hostname of 1900Switch and a 2500 router with a hostname of 2500B. Notice that no devices connected to the 1900Switch and the 2500B router show in the CDP table on the 2509 router. You can only see directly connected devices.

Table 7.5 summarizes the information displayed by the show cdp neighbor command for each device.

TABLE 7.5 Output of the *Show CDP Neighbor* Command

Field	Description
Device ID	The hostname of the device directly connected.
Local Interface	The port or interface on which you are receiving the CDP packet.

TABLE 7.5 Output of the *Show CDP Neighbor* Command *(continued)*

Field	Description
Holdtime	The amount of time the router will hold the information before discarding it if no more CDP packets are received.
Capability	The neighbor's capability, such as router, switch, or repeater. The capability codes are listed at the top of the command output.
Platform	The type of Cisco device. In the above output, a Cisco 2509, Cisco 2511, and Catalyst 5000 are attached to the switch. The 2509 only sees the switch and the 2501 router connected through its serial 0 interface.
Port ID	The neighbor device's port or interface on which the CDP packets are broadcast.

Another command that provides neighbor information is the show cdp neighbor detail command (show cdp nei de for short), which also can be run on the router or switch. This command shows detailed information about each device connected to the device, as in the router output below.

```
Todd2509#sh cdp neighbor detail
-----------------------
Device ID: 1900Switch
Entry address(es):
   IP address: 0.0.0.0
Platform: cisco 1900,  Capabilities: Trans-Bridge Switch
Interface: Ethernet0,  Port ID (outgoing port): 2
Holdtime : 166 sec
Version :
V9.00
-----------------------
Device ID: 2501B
Entry address(es):
   IP address: 172.16.10.2
Platform: cisco 2500,  Capabilities: Router
```

```
Interface: Serial0,  Port ID (outgoing port): Serial0
Holdtime : 154 sec
Version :
Cisco Internetwork Operating System Software
IOS (tm) 3000 Software (IGS-J-L), Version 11.1(5),
   RELEASE SOFTWARE (fc1)Copyright (c) 1986-1996 by cisco
   Systems, Inc.Compiled Mon 05-Aug-96 11:48 by mkamson
Todd2509#
```

The output above shows the hostname and IP address of the directly connected devices. In addition to the same information displayed by the show cdp neighbor command (see Table 7.5), the show cdp neighbor detail command shows the IOS version of the neighbor device.

The show cdp entry * command displays the same information as the show cdp neighbor details command. The following is an example of the router output of the show cdp entry * command.

```
Todd2509#sh cdp entry *
-------------------------
Device ID: 1900Switch
Entry address(es):
   IP address: 0.0.0.0
Platform: cisco 1900,  Capabilities: Trans-Bridge Switch
Interface: Ethernet0,  Port ID (outgoing port): 2
Holdtime : 223 sec
Version :
V9.00

-------------------------
Device ID: 2501B
Entry address(es):
   IP address: 172.16.10.2
Platform: cisco 2500,  Capabilities: Router
Interface: Serial0,  Port ID (outgoing port): Serial0
Holdtime : 151 sec
Version :
Cisco Internetwork Operating System Software
IOS (tm) 3000 Software (IGS-J-L), Version 11.1(5),
   RELEASE SOFTWARE (fc1)Copyright (c) 1986-1996 by cisco
   Systems, Inc.Compiled Mon 05-Aug-96 11:48 by mkamson
Todd2509#
```

Gathering Interface Traffic Information

The show cdp traffic command displays information about interface traffic, including the number of CDP packets sent and received and the errors with CDP.

The following output shows the show cdp traffic command used on a router.

```
Router#sh cdp traffic
CDP counters:
        Packets output: 13, Input: 8
        Hdr syntax: 0, Chksum error: 0, Encaps failed: 0
        No memory: 0, Invalid packet: 0, Fragmented: 0
Router#
```

This is not really the most important information you can gather from a router, but it does show how many CDP packets are sent and received on a device.

Gathering Port and Interface Information

The show cdp interface command (sh cdp inter for short) shows the CDP status on router interfaces or switch ports.

As explained earlier, you can turn off CDP completely on a router by using the no cdp run command. However, CDP can also be turned off per interface with the no cdp enable command. You can enable a port with the cdp enable command. All ports and interfaces default to cdp enable.

On a router, the show cdp interface command shows information about each interface using CDP, including the encapsulation on the line, the timer, and the holdtime for each interface. Here is an example of this command's output on a router:

```
Router#sh cdp interface
Ethernet0 is up, line protocol is up
  Encapsulation ARPA
  Sending CDP packets every 60 seconds
  Holdtime is 180 seconds
Serial0 is administratively down, line protocol is down
  Encapsulation HDLC
  Sending CDP packets every 60 seconds
  Holdtime is 180 seconds
```

```
Serial1 is administratively down, line protocol is down
  Encapsulation HDLC
  Sending CDP packets every 60 seconds
  Holdtime is 180 seconds
```

To turn off CDP on one interface on a router, use the no cdp enable command from interface configuration mode:

```
Router#config t
Enter configuration commands, one per line.  End with
  CNTL/Z.
Router(config)#int s0
Router(config-if)#no cdp enable
Router(config-if)#^Z
```

Verify the change with the show cdp interface command:

```
Router#sh cdp int
Ethernet0 is up, line protocol is up
  Encapsulation ARPA
  Sending CDP packets every 60 seconds
  Holdtime is 180 seconds
Serial1 is administratively down, line protocol is down
  Encapsulation HDLC
  Sending CDP packets every 60 seconds
  Holdtime is 180 seconds
Router#
```

Notice in the output above that serial 0 is not listed in the router output. When you perform a cdp enable on serial 0, it would then display in the output.

 Real World Scenario

CDP is your friend!

You can use CDP to help you draw out your network. It is easy and just takes some of your time. However, all the routers must be Cisco routers, or this won't work!

If you have all Cisco routers and switches, then CDP can be really helpful. Telnet or console into a router or switch and type **show cdp neighbor**. You will see directly connected neighbors. Write these down. Then type **show cdp neighbors detail** and write down the IP addresses for each of these devices.

Now go to each of these devices and do that same thing. Just keep writing down what you find until you have drawn out the entire network.

If you don't know the passwords of these devices, this will be a show-stopper unless you can find out the access passwords or perform password recovery.

Using Telnet

Telnet is a virtual terminal protocol that is part of the TCP/IP protocol suite. Telnet allows you to make connections to remote devices, gather information, and run programs.

After your routers and switches are configured, you can use the Telnet program to configure and check your routers and switches so that you don't need to use a console cable. You run the Telnet program by typing **telnet** from any command prompt (DOS or Cisco). VTY passwords must be set on the routers for this to work.

You cannot use CDP to gather information about routers and switches that are not directly connected to your device. However, you can use the Telnet application to connect to your neighbor devices and then run CDP on those remote devices to gather CDP information about remote devices.

You can issue the **telnet** command from any router prompt, as in the following example:

```
Todd2509#telnet 172.16.10.2
Trying 172.16.10.2 ... Open

Password required, but none set

[Connection to 172.16.10.2 closed by foreign host]
Todd2509#
```

As you can see, I didn't set my passwords—how embarrassing! Remember that the VTY ports on a router are configured as login, which means you must either set the VTY passwords or use the no login command. (See Chapter 4 for details on setting passwords.)

On a Cisco router, you do not need to use the telnet command. If you just type in an IP address from a command prompt, the router will assume that you want to telnet to the device, as shown below:

```
Todd2509#172.16.10.2
Trying 172.16.10.2 ... Open


Password required, but none set


[Connection to 172.16.10.2 closed by foreign host]
Todd2509#
```

It's time to set VTY passwords on the router I want to telnet into. Here is an example of what I did:

```
2501B#config t
Enter configuration commands, one per line.  End with
  CNTL/Z.
2501B(config)#line vty 0 4
2501B(config-line)#login
2501B(config-line)#password todd
2501B(config-line)#^Z
2501B#
%SYS-5-CONFIG_I: Configured from console by console
```

Now, let's try connecting to the router again (from the 2509 router console).

```
Todd2509#172.16.10.2
Trying 172.16.10.2 ... Open


User Access Verification


Password:
2501B>
```

Remember that the VTY password is the user-mode password, not the enable-mode password. Watch what happens when I try to go into privileged mode after telnetting into router 2501B:

```
2501B>en
% No password set
2501B>
```

This is a good security feature. You don't want anyone telnetting onto your device and then being able to just type the `enable` command to get into privileged mode. You must set your enable-mode password or enable-secret password to use Telnet to configure remote devices.

Telnetting into Multiple Devices Simultaneously

If you telnet to a router or switch, you can end the connection by typing **exit** at any time. However, what if you want to keep your connection to a remote device but still come back to your original router console? To keep the connection, you can press the Ctrl+Shift+6 key combination, release it, and then press X.

Here's an example of connecting to multiple devices from my Todd2509 router console:

```
Todd2509#telnet 172.16.10.2
Trying 172.16.10.2 ... Open

User Access Verification

Password:
2501B>[Cntl+Shift+6, then x]
Todd2509#
```

In the example above, I telnetted to the 2501B router then typed the password to enter user mode. I then pressed Ctrl+Shift+6, then X (this doesn't show on the screen output). Notice my command prompt is now back at the Todd2509 router.

You can also telnet into a 1900 switch. However, you must set the enable mode password level 15 on the switch before you can gain access via the Telnet application.

In the following example, I telnet to a 1900 switch, which then gives me the console output of the switch.

```
Todd2509#telnet 192.168.0.148
Trying 192.168.0.148 ... Open
```

```
Catalyst 1900 Management Console
Copyright (c) Cisco Systems, Inc.  1993-1999
All rights reserved.
Enterprise Edition Software
Ethernet Address:        00-B0-64-75-6B-C0

PCA Number:              73-3122-04
PCA Serial Number:       FAB040131E2
Model Number:            WS-C1912-A
System Serial Number:    FAB0401U0JQ
Power Supply S/N:        PHI033108SD
PCB Serial Number:       FAB040131E2,73-3122-04
-------------------------------------------------


1 user(s) now active on Management Console.


        User Interface Menu


    [M] Menus
    [K] Command Line


Enter Selection:
```

At this point, I pressed Ctrl+Shift+6, then X, which took me back to my Todd2509 router console.

Checking Telnet Connections

To see the connections made from your router to a remote device, use the show sessions command.

```
Todd2509#sh sessions
Conn Host             Address         Byte Idle Conn Name
   1 172.16.10.2      172.16.10.2       0    0  172.16.10.2
*  2 192.168.0.148    192.168.0.148     0    0  192.168.0.148
Todd2509#
```

Notice the asterisk (*) next to connection 2? This means that session 2 was the last session you were at. You can return to your last session by pressing Enter twice. You can also return to any session by typing the number of the connection and pressing Enter twice.

Checking Telnet Users

You can list all active consoles and VTY ports in use on your router with the show users command:

```
Todd2509#sh users
     Line     User     Host(s)          Idle Location
*   0 con 0            172.16.10.2      00:07:52
                       192.168.0.148    00:07:18
```

In the command's output, the con represents the local console. In this example, the console is connected to two remote IP addresses, or devices.

In the next example, I typed show users on the 2501B router, which the Todd2509 router had telnetted into.

```
2501B>sh users
     Line     User     Host(s)          Idle Location
    0 con 0            idle             9
*   2 vty 0
```

This output shows that the console is active and that VTY port 2 is being used. The asterisk represents the current terminal session user.

Closing Telnet Sessions

You can end Telnet sessions a few different ways. Typing exit or disconnect is probably the easiest and quickest.

To end a session from a remote device, use the exit command.

```
Todd2509#[Enter] and again [Enter]
[Resuming connection 2 to 192.168.0.148 ... ]

1900Switch>exit

[Connection to 192.168.0.148 closed by foreign host]
Todd2509#
```

Since the 1900Switch was my last session, I just pressed Enter twice to return to that session.

To end a session from a local device, use the disconnect command.

```
Todd2509#disconnect ?
  <1-2>  The number of an active network connection
  WORD   The name of an active network connection
  <cr>
```

Todd2509#**disconnect 1**
Closing connection to 172.16.10.2 [confirm]
Todd2509#

In this example, I used the session number 1 because that was the connection to the 2501B router that I wanted to end. As explained earlier, you can use the show sessions command to see the connection number.

If you want to end a session of a device attached to your router through Telnet, you might want to first check if any devices are attached to your router. Use the show users command to get that information.

2501B#**sh users**
```
      Line      User      Host(s)        Idle Location
*   0 con 0               idle           0
    1 aux 0               idle           0
    2 vty 0               idle           0 172.16.10.1
```

This output shows that VTY 2 has IP address 172.16.10.1 connected. That is the Todd2509 router.

To clear the connection, use the clear line # command.

2501B#**clear line 2**
[confirm]
 [OK]

Verify that the user has been disconnected with the show users command.

2501B#**sh users**
```
      Line      User      Host(s)        Idle Location
*   0 con 0               idle           0
    1 aux 0               idle           1
```

2501B#

This output shows that the line has been cleared.

Resolving Hostnames

In order to use a hostname rather than an IP address to connect to a remote device, the device that you are using to make the connection must be able to translate the hostname to an IP address.

There are two ways to resolve hostnames to IP addresses: building a host table on each router or building a Domain Name System (DNS) server, which is like a dynamic host table.

Building a Host Table

A host table provides name resolution only on the router on which it was built. The command to build a host table on a router is

```
ip host name tcp_port_number ip_address
```

The default is TCP port number 23. You can create a session using Telnet with a different TCP port number, if needed, and you can assign up to eight IP addresses to a hostname.

Here is an example of configuring a host table with two entries to resolve the names for the 2501B router and the switch:

```
Todd2509#config t
Enter configuration commands, one per line.  End with
  CNTL/Z.
Todd2509(config)#ip host ?
  WORD  Name of host

Todd2509(config)#ip host 2501B ?
  <0-65535>  Default telnet port number
  A.B.C.D    Host IP address (maximum of 8)

Todd2509(config)#ip host 2501B 172.16.10.2 ?
  A.B.C.D  Host IP address (maximum of 8)
  <cr>
Todd2509(config)#ip host 2501B 172.16.10.2
Todd2509(config)#ip host 1900Switch 192.168.0.148
Todd2509(config)#^Z
```

To see the host table, use the show hosts command.

```
Todd2509#sh hosts
Default domain is not set
Name/address lookup uses domain service
Name servers are 255.255.255.255
```

```
Host              Flags      Age Type  Address(es)
2501B             (perm, OK)  0  IP    172.16.10.2
1900Switch        (perm, OK)  0  IP    192.168.0.148
Todd2509#
```

In the preceding router output, you can see the two hostnames and their associated IP addresses. The perm in the Flags column means that the entry is manually configured. If it said temp, it would be an entry resolved by DNS.

To verify that the host table resolves names, try typing the hostnames at a router prompt. Remember that if you don't specify the command, the router assumes you want to telnet. In the following example, I used the hostnames to telnet into the remote devices and then pressed Ctrl+Shift+6, then X to return to the main console of the Todd2509 router.

```
Todd2509#2501b
Trying 2501B (172.16.10.2)... Open


User Access Verification


Password:
2501B>
Todd2509#[Ctrl+Shift+6, then x]
Todd2509#1900switch
Trying 1900switch (192.168.0.148)... Open


Catalyst 1900 Management Console
Copyright (c) Cisco Systems, Inc.  1993-1999
All rights reserved.
Enterprise Edition Software
Ethernet Address:       00-B0-64-75-6B-C0


PCA Number:             73-3122-04
PCA Serial Number:      FAB040131E2
Model Number:           WS-C1912-A
System Serial Number:   FAB0401U0JQ
Power Supply S/N:       PHI033108SD
PCB Serial Number:      FAB040131E2,73-3122-04
------------------------------------------------
```

```
1 user(s) now active on Management Console.

      User Interface Menu

   [M] Menus
   [K] Command Line

Enter Selection:[Ctrl+Shift+6, then x]
Todd2509#
```

I successfully used the host table to create a session to two devices and used the names to telnet into both devices. Notice in the entries in the show sessions output below that the hostname now shows up instead of the IP address.

```
Todd2509#sh sess
Conn Host              Address        Byte  Idle Conn Name
   1 1900switch        192.168.0.148     0     0 switch
*  2 2501b             172.16.10.2       0     0 2501b
Todd2509#
```

You can remove a hostname from the table by using the no ip host command, as in the following example:

```
RouterA(config)#no ip host routerb
```

The problem with the host table method is that you would need to create a host table on each router to be able to resolve names. If you have many routers and want to resolve names, using DNS is a better choice.

Using DNS to Resolve Names

If you have many devices and don't want to create a host table in each device, you can use a DNS server to resolve hostnames.

Any time a Cisco device receives a command it doesn't understand, it tries to resolve this through DNS by default. Watch what happens when I type the special command todd at a Cisco router prompt.

```
Todd2509#todd
Translating "todd"...domain server (255.255.255.255)
% Unknown command or computer name, or unable to find
  computer address
Todd2509#
```

It doesn't know my name, or what command I am trying to type, so it tries to resolve this through DNS. This is annoying for two reasons: first, because it doesn't know my name, and second, because I need to wait for the name lookup to time out. You can prevent the default DNS lookup by using the no ip domain-lookup command on your router from global configuration mode.

If you have a DNS server on your network, you need to add a few commands to make DNS name resolution work:

- The first command is ip domain-lookup, which is turned on by default. It only needs to be entered if you previously turned it off (with the no ip domain-lookup command).

- The second command is ip name-server. This sets the IP address of the DNS server. You can enter the IP addresses of up to six servers.

- The last command is ip domain-name. Although this command is optional, it should be set. It appends the domain name to the hostname you type in. Since DNS uses a fully qualified domain name (FQDN) system, you must have a full DNS name, in the form domain.com.

Here is an example of using these three commands:

```
Todd2509#config t
Enter configuration commands, one per line.  End with
  CNTL/Z.
Todd2509(config)#ip domain-lookup
Todd2509(config)#ip name-server ?
  A.B.C.D  Domain server IP address (maximum of 6)
Todd2509(config)#ip name-server 192.168.0.70
Todd2509(config)#ip domain-name lammle.com
Todd2509(config)#^Z
Todd2509#
```

After the DNS configurations are set, you can test the DNS server by using a hostname to ping or telnet a device, as shown below.

```
Todd2509#ping 2501b
Translating "2501b"...domain server (192.168.0.70) [OK]
Type escape sequence to abort.
Sending 5, 100-byte ICMP Echos to 172.16.10.2, timeout is
  2 seconds:
!!!!!
```

```
Success rate is 100 percent (5/5), round-trip min/avg/max
  = 28/31/32 ms
```

Notice that the DNS server is used by the router to resolve the name.

After a name is resolved using DNS, use the show hosts command to see that the device cached this information in the host table, as shown below.

```
Todd2509#sh hosts
Default domain is lammle.com
Name/address lookup uses domain service
Name servers are 192.168.0.70


Host                   Flags       Age Type   Address(es)
2501b.lammle.com       (temp, OK)  0   IP     172.16.10.2
1900switch             (perm, OK)  0   IP     192.168.0.148
Todd2509#
```

The entry that was resolved is shown as temp, but the 1900 switch device is still perm, which means that it is a static entry. Notice that the hostname is a full domain name. If I hadn't used the ip domain-name lammle.com command, I would have needed to type in ping 2501b.lammle.com, which is a pain.

 Real World Scenario

Should you use a host table or DNS server?

Depends. How many routers do you have? If you have dozens of routers, then you don't want to build a static host table on each router. You can build one table on a DNS server.

Most networks should have a DNS server now, so adding a dozen or so hostnames into a DNS server would be pretty easy. Just add the three commands on your router and your resolving names.

Using a DNS sever makes it easy to update one entry as well. If you have static host tables, then you must go to each router to update the entry if anything changed.

Checking Network Connectivity

You can use the ping and traceroute commands to test connectivity to remote devices. Both commands can be used with many protocols, not just IP.

Using the *Ping* Command

In this chapter, you've seen many examples of pinging devices to test IP connectivity and name resolution using the DNS server. To see all the different protocols that you can use with ping, use the ping ? command, as shown below.

```
Todd2509#ping ?
  WORD      Ping destination address or hostname
  apollo    Apollo echo
  appletalk Appletalk echo
  clns      CLNS echo
  decnet    DECnet echo
  ip        IP echo
  ipx       Novell/IPX echo
  srb       srb echo
  tag       Tag encapsulated IP echo
  vines     Vines echo
  xns       XNS echo
  <cr>
```

The ping output displays the minimum, average, and maximum times it takes for a Ping packet to find a specified system and return. Here is another example of its use:

```
Todd2509#ping todd2509
Translating "todd2509"...domain server (192.168.0.70)[OK]
Type escape sequence to abort.
Sending 5, 100-byte ICMP Echos to 192.168.0.121, timeout
  is 2 seconds:
!!!!!
Success rate is 100 percent (5/5), round-trip min/avg/max
  = 32/32/32 ms
Todd2509#
```

You can see that the DNS server was used to resolve the name and the device was pinged in 32ms (milliseconds).

Using the *Traceroute* Command

Traceroute (the `traceroute` command, or `trace` for short) shows the path a packet takes to get to a remote device. To see the protocols that you can use with `traceroute`, use the `traceroute ?` command, as shown below:

```
Todd2509#traceroute ?
  WORD        Trace route to destination address or
              hostname
  appletalk   AppleTalk Trace
  clns        ISO CLNS Trace
  ip          IP Trace
  ipx         IPX Trace
  oldvines    Vines Trace (Cisco)
  vines       Vines Trace (Banyan)
  <cr>
```

The `trace` command shows the hop or hops that a packet traverses on its way to a remote device. Here is an example of its use:

```
Todd2509#trace 2501b
Type escape sequence to abort.
Tracing the route to 2501b.lammle.com (172.16.10.2)

  1 2501b.lammle.com (172.16.10.2) 16 msec *  16 msec
Todd2509#
```

You can see that the packet went through only one hop to find the destination.

Do not get confused on the exam. You cannot use the `tracert` command, which is a Windows command. For a router, use the `traceroute` command!

Summary

In this chapter, you learned how Cisco routers are configured and how to manage the configuration. The following router internal information was covered in this chapter:

- The internal components of a Cisco router

- The router boot sequence

- The configuration register and how to change it

- Password recovery

Next, you learned how to back up and restore a Cisco IOS, as well as how to back up and restore the configuration of a Cisco router. Then you learned how to use CDP and Telnet to gather information about neighbor devices. Finally, the chapter covered how to resolve hostnames and use the `ping` and `trace` commands to test network connectivity.

Exam Essentials

Remember the various configuration register commands and settings. The 2102 setting is the default on all Cisco routers and tells the router to look in NVRAM for the boot sequence. 2101 tells the router to boot from ROM, and 2142 tells the router to not load the startup-config in NVRAM to provide password recovery.

Remember how to back up an IOS image.   By using the privileged-mode command `copy flash tftp`, you can backup a file from flash memory to a TFTP (network) host.

Remember how to restore or upgrade an IOS image.   By using the privileged-mode command `copy tftp flash`, you can restore or upgrade a file from a TFTP (network) server to flash memory.

Remember what you must complete before you back up an IOS image to a network server.   Make sure you can access the network server, ensure the network server has adequate space for the code image, and verify the file naming and path requirement.

Remember how to save the configuration of a router.   There are a couple ways to do this, but the most common, as well as most tested, method is `copy running-config startup-config`.

Remember how to erase the configuration of a router.   Type the privileged-mode command `erase startup-config` and reload the router.

Understand when you would use CDP.   Cisco Discovery Protocol can be used to help you document your network as well as troubleshoot your network.

Remember the output from the show cdp neighbors command.   The `show cdp neighbors` command provides the following information: device ID, local interface, holdtime, capability, platform, and port ID.

Understand how to telnet into a router, keep your connection, but return to your originating console.   If you telnet to a router or switch, you can end the connection by typing **exit** at any time. However, if you want to keep your connection to a remote device but still come back to your original router console, you can press the Ctrl+Shift+6 key combination, release it, and then press X.

Remember the command to verify your Telnet sessions.   The command `show sessions` will provide you with all the sessions your router has to other routers.

Remember how to build a static host table on a router.   By using the global configuration mode command `ip host *host_name ip_address*`, you can build a static host table on your router.

Remember how to verify your host table on a router.   You can verify the host table with the `show hosts` command.

Understand when you would use the *ping* command.   Packet Internet Groper (Ping) uses ICMP echo request and ICMP echo replies to verify an active IP address on a network.

Remember how to ping a valid host ID.   You can ping an IP address from a router's user mode or privileged mode, but not from configuration mode. You must ping a valid address, like 1.1.1.1. Examples of invalid addresses are 192.168.10.0, 192.168.10.255, and 192.168.10.256. (See Chapter 3 for information on IP addressing if you do not understand this.)

Key Terms

Before taking the exam, be sure you're familiar with the following terms:

boot sequence	random access memory (RAM)
CDP holdtime	read-only memory (ROM)
CDP timer	Telnet
configuration register	TFTP host
flash memory	Traceroute
Packet Internet Groper (Ping)	

Commands Used in This Chapter

The following list contains a summary of all the commands used in this chapter:

Command	Description
cdp enable	Turns on CDP on an individual interface
cdp holdtime	Changes the holdtime of CDP packets
cdp run	Turns on CDP on a router
cdp timer	Changes the CDP update timer
clear line	Clears a connection connected via Telnet to your router
config-register	Tells the router how to boot and to change the configuration register setting
copy flash tftp	Copies a file from flash memory to a TFTP host

Command	Description
copy run start	Copies the running-config file to the startup-config file
copy run tftp	Copies the running-config file to a TFTP host
copy tftp flash	Copies a file from a TFTP host to flash memory
copy tftp run	Copies a configuration from a TFTP host to the running-config file
Ctrl+Shift+6, then X (keyboard combination)	Returns you to the originating router when you telnet to numerous routers
delete nvram	Deletes the contents of NVRAM on a 1900 switch
disconnect	Disconnects a connection to a remote router from the originating router
erase startup-config	Deletes the contents of NVRAM on a router
exit	Disconnects a connection to a remote router via Telnet
ip domain-lookup	Turns on DNS lookup (which is on by default)
ip domain-name	Appends a domain name to a DNS lookup
ip host	Creates a host table on a router
ip name-server	Sets the IP address of up to six DNS servers
no cdp enable	Turns off CDP on an individual interface
no cdp run	Turns off CDP completely on a router
no ip domain-lookup	Turns off DNS lookup
no ip host	Removes a hostname from a host table
o/r 0x2142	Changes a 2501 to boot without using the contents of NVRAM
ping	Tests IP connectivity to a remote device
show cdp	Displays the CDP timer and holdtime frequencies
show cdp entry *	Same as show cdp neighbor detail, but does not work on a 1900 switch
show cdp interface	Shows the individual interfaces enabled with CDP

Command	Description
show cdp neighbor	Shows the directly connected neighbors and the details about them
show cdp neighbor detail	Shows the IP address and IOS version and type, and includes all of the information from the show cdp neighbor command
show cdp traffic	Shows the CDP packets sent and received on a device and any errors
show flash	Shows the files in flash memory
show hosts	Shows the contents of the host table
show run	Displays the running-config file
show sessions	Shows your connections via Telnet to remote devices
show start	Displays the startup-config file
show version	Displays the IOS type and version as well as the configuration register
telnet	Connects, views, and runs programs on a remote device
tftp-server system ios-name	Creates a TFTP-server host for a router system image that is run in flash.
trace	Tests a connection to a remote device and shows the path it took through the internetwork to find the remote device

Written Lab 7

Write in the answers to the following questions.

1. What is the command to copy a Cisco IOS to a TFTP host?

2. What is the command to copy a Cisco startup-config file to a TFTP host?

3. What is the command to copy the startup-config file to DRAM?

4. What is an older command that you can use to copy the `startup-config` file to DRAM?

5. What command can you use to see the neighbor router's IP address from your router prompt?

6. What command can you use to see the hostname, local interface, platform, and remote port of a neighbor router?

7. What keystrokes can you use to telnet into multiple devices simultaneously?

8. What command will show you your active Telnet connections to neighbor and remote devices?

9. What command can you use to upgrade a Cisco IOS?

10. What command can you use to create a host table entry for Bob, using IP addresses 172.16.10.1 and 172.16.20.2?

(The answers to Written Lab 7 can be found following the answers to the Review Questions for this chapter.)

Hands-on Labs

To complete the labs in this section, you need at least one router (more is better) and at least one PC running as a TFTP host. Remember that the labs listed here were created for use with real routers; if you are using the Sybex Router Fundamentals Simulator provided on this book's companion CD, please use the hands-on labs found within that software program.

Here is a list of the labs in this chapter:

Lab 7.1: Backing Up Your Router IOS

Lab 7.2: Upgrading or Restoring Your Router IOS

Lab 7.3: Backing Up the Router Configuration

Lab 7.4: Using the Cisco Discovery Protocol (CDP)

Lab 7.5: Using Telnet

Lab 7.6: Resolving Hostnames

Hands-on Lab 7.1: Backing Up Your Router IOS

1. Log into your router and go into privileged mode by typing **en** or **enable**.

2. Make sure you can connect to the TFTP host that is on your network by pinging the IP address from the router console.

3. Type **show flash** to see the contents of flash memory.

4. Type **show version** at the router privileged mode prompt to get the name of the IOS currently running on the router. If there is only one file in flash memory, the show flash and show version commands show the same file. Remember that the show version command shows you the file that is currently running, and the show flash command shows you all of the files in flash memory.

5. Once you know you have good Ethernet connectivity to the TFTP host, and you also know the IOS filename, back up your IOS by typing **copy flash tftp**. This command tells the router to copy the contents of flash memory (this is where the IOS is stored by default) to a TFTP host.

6. Enter the IP address of the TFTP host and the source IOS filename. The file is now copied and stored in the TFTP host's default directory.

Hands-on Lab 7.2: Upgrading or Restoring Your Router IOS

1. Log into your router and go into privileged mode by typing **en** or **enable**.

2. Make sure you can connect to the TFTP host by pinging the IP address of the host from the router console.

3. Once you know you have good Ethernet connectivity to the TFTP host, issue the copy tftp flash command.

4. Confirm that the router is not functioning during the restore or upgrade by following the prompts provided on the router console.

5. Enter the IP address of the TFTP host.

6. Enter the IOS filename you want to restore or upgrade.

7. Confirm that you understand that the contents of flash memory will be erased.

8. Watch in amazement as your IOS is deleted out of flash memory, and your new IOS is copied to flash memory.

If the file that was in flash memory is deleted, but the new version wasn't copied to flash memory, the router will boot from ROM monitor mode. You'll need to figure out why the copy operation did not take place.

Hands-on Lab 7.3: Backing Up the Router Configuration

1. Log into your router and go into privileged mode by typing **en** or **enable**.

2. Ping the TFTP host to make sure you have IP connectivity.

3. From Router B, type **copy run tftp**.

4. Type the IP address of the TFTP host (for example, 172.16.30.2) and press Enter.

5. The router will prompt you for a filename. The hostname of the router is followed by the suffix -confg (yes, I spelled that correctly). You can use any name you want.

   ```
   Name of configuration file to write [RouterB-confg]?
   ```
   Press Enter to accept the default name.

   ```
   Write file RouterB-confg on host 172.16.30.2? [confirm]
   ```
   Press Enter.

   The !! are UDP acknowledgments that the file was transferred successfully.

Hands-on Lab 7.4: Using the Cisco Discovery Protocol (CDP)

1. Log into your router and go into privileged mode by typing **en** or **enable**.

2. From the router, type **sh cdp** and press Enter. You should see that CDP packets are being sent out to all active interfaces every 60 seconds and the holdtime is 180 seconds (these are the defaults).

3. To change the CDP update frequency to 90 seconds, type **cdp timer 90** in global configuration mode.

   ```
   RouterC#config t
   Enter configuration commands, one per line.  End with
     CNTL/Z.
   ```

```
RouterC(config)#cdp timer ?
  <5-900>  Rate at which CDP packets are sent (in sec)
RouterC(config)#cdp timer 90
```

4. Verify your CDP timer frequency has changed by using the command show cdp in privileged mode.

```
RouteC#sh cdp
Global CDP information:
Sending CDP packets every 90 seconds
Sending a holdtime value of 180 seconds
```

5. Now, use CDP to gather information about neighbor routers. You can get the list of available commands by typing **sh cdp ?**.

```
RouterC#sh cdp ?
  entry     Information for specific neighbor entry
  interface CDP interface status and configuration
  neighbors CDP neighbor entries
  traffic   CDP statistics
  <cr>
```

6. Type **sh cdp int** to see the interface information plus the default encapsulation used by the interface. It also shows the CDP timer information.

7. Type **sh cdp entry** * to see the CDP information received from all routers.

8. Type **show cdp** neighbor to gather information about all connected neighbors. (You should know the specific information output by this command.)

9. Type **show cdp neighbor detail**. Notice that it produces the same output as show cdp entry *.

Hands-on Lab 7.5: Using Telnet

1. Log into your router and go into privileged mode by typing **en** or **enable**.

2. From Router A, telnet into your remote router by typing **telnet** *ip_address* from the command prompt.

3. Type in Router B's IP address from Router A's command prompt. Notice that the router automatically tries to telnet to the IP address you specified. You can use the `telnet` command or just type in the IP address.

4. From Router B, press Ctrl+Shift+6, then X to return to Router A's command prompt. Now telnet into your third router, Router C. Press Ctrl+Shift+6, then X to return to Router A.

5. From Router A, type **show sessions**. Notice your two sessions. You can press the number displayed to the left of the session and press Enter twice to return to that session. The asterisk shows this default session. You can press Enter twice to return to that session.

6. Go to the session for your Router B. Type **show user**. This shows the console connection and the remote connection. You can use the `disconnect` command to clear the session, or just type **exit** from the prompt to close your session with Router B.

7. Go to the Router C's console port by typing **show sessions** on the first router and using the connection number to return to Router C. Type **show user** and notice the connection to your first router, Router A.

8. Type **clear line** to disconnect the Telnet session.

Hands-on Lab 7.6: Resolving Hostnames

1. Log into your router and go into privileged mode by typing **en** or **enable**.

2. From Router A, type **todd** and press Enter at the command prompt. Notice the error you receive and the delay. The router is trying to resolve the hostname to an IP address by looking for a DNS server. You can turn this feature off by using the `no ip domain-lookup` command from global configuration mode.

3. To build a host table, you use the `ip host` command. From Router A, add a host table entry for Router B and Router C by entering the following commands:

```
ip host routerb ip_address
ip host routerc ip_address
```

Here is an example:

```
ip host routerb 172.16.20.2
ip host routerc 172.16.40.2
```

4. Test your host table by typing **ping routerb** from the command prompt (not the `config` prompt).

```
RouterA#ping routerb
Type escape sequence to abort.
Sending 5, 100-byte ICMP Echos to 172.16.20.2, timeout
  is 2 seconds:
!!!!!
Success rate is 100 percent (5/5), round-trip
  min/avg/max = 4/4/4 ms
```

5. Test your host table by typing **ping routerc**.

```
RouterA#ping routerc
Type escape sequence to abort.
Sending 5, 100-byte ICMP Echos to 172.16.40.2, timeout
  is 2 seconds:
!!!!!
Success rate is 100 percent (5/5), round-trip
  min/avg/max = 4/6/8 ms
```

6. Keep your session to Router B open, and then return to Router A by pressing Ctrl+Shift+6, then X.

7. Telnet to Router C by typing **routerc** at the command prompt.

8. Return to Router A and keep the session to Router C open by pressing Ctrl+Shift+6, then X.

9. View the host table by typing **show hosts** and pressing Enter.

```
Default domain is not set
Name/address lookup uses domain service
Name servers are 255.255.255.255
Host                Flags        Age Type   Address(es)
routerb             (perm, OK)   0   IP     172.16.20.2
routerc             (perm, OK)   0   IP     172.16.40.2
```

Review Questions

1. Which command will show you the hostname resolved to the IP address on a router?

   A. `sh router`

   B. `sho hosts`

   C. `sh ip hosts`

   D. `sho name resolution`

2. Which command will copy the IOS to a backup host on your network?

   A. `transfer IOS to 172.16.10.1`

   B. `copy run start`

   C. `copy tftp flash`

   D. `copy start tftp`

   E. `copy flash tftp`

3. Which command will copy a router configuration stored on a TFTP host to the router's NVRAM?

   A. `transfer IOS to 172.16.10.1`

   B. `copy run start`

   C. `copy tftp startup`

   D. `copy tftp run`

   E. `copy flash tftp`

4. To copy a configuration from a TFTP host to a Cisco router's DRAM on your network, what two commands can you use?

   A. `config netw`

   B. `config mem`

   C. `config term`

   D. `copy tftp run`

   E. `copy tftp start`

5. Which memory in a Cisco router stores packet buffers, ARP cache, and routing tables?

A. Flash

B. RAM

C. ROM

D. NVRAM

6. Which of the following is the correct command to create a host table on a Cisco router?

A. `bob ip host 172.16.10.1`

B. `host 172.16.10.1 bob`

C. `ip host bob 172.16.10.1 172.16.10.2`

D. `host bob 172.16.10.1`

7. Which command loads a new version of the Cisco IOS into a router?

A. `copy flash ftp`

B. `copy ftp flash`

C. `copy flash tftp`

D. `copy tftp flash`

8. Which command will show you the IOS version running on your router?

A. `sh IOS`

B. `sh flash`

C. `sh version`

D. `sh running-config`

9. Which of the following saves the configuration stored in RAM to NVRAM?

A. `copy running-config startup-config`

B. `copy tftp running-config`

C. `copy startup-config running-config`

D. `copy active backup`

10. To copy a configuration from the Cisco router's DRAM to a TFTP host on your network, what command can you use?

   A. config netw

   B. config mem

   C. config term

   D. copy run tftp

   E. copy start tftp

11. If you want to have more than one Telnet session open at the same time, what keystroke combination would you use?

   A. Tab+spacebar

   B. Ctrl+X, then 6

   C. Ctrl+Shift+X, then 6

   D. Ctrl+Shift+6, then X

12. Which of the following commands will load an image named "beta" from a network server at 1.1.1.1 during the next router reload?

   A. load system tftp beta 1.1.1.1

   B. load system tftp 1.1.1. beta

   C. boot system tftp beta 1.1.1.1

   D. load system tftp 1.1.1.1 beta

13. Which exec command displays system hardware config information, software version, and the names and sources of config files and boot images on a router?

   A. show flash

   B. show running-config

   C. show version

   D. show config

14. Which three commands can be used to check LAN connectivity problem on a router?

    A. `show interfaces`

    B. `show ip route`

    C. `tracert`

    D. `ping`

    E. `dns lookups`

15. Which command is used to find the path a packet takes through an internetwork?

    A. `ping`

    B. `trace`

    C. `rip`

    D. `sap`

16. Which two commands can be used to test IP through your network and verify address configuration?

    A. `ping`

    B. `trace`

    C. `rip`

    D. `sap`

17. Which of the following will copy the active configuration to a backup configuration?

    A. `copy active backup`

    B. `copy starting-config running-config`

    C. `copy running-config startup-config`

    D. `copy tftp running-config`

18. Which command displays Cisco Discovery Protocol adjacencies?

    A. `show cdp neighbor`

    B. `show cdp neighbor adjacencies`

    C. `show cdp adjacencies`

    D. `show adjacencies cdp`

19. Which command displays the configuration register setting?

   A. show ip route

   B. show boot version

   C. show version

   D. show flash

20. In what two modes can the ICMP ping command be used?

   A. User

   B. Privileged

   C. Global config

   D. Interface configuration

21. Which of the following should be done before you back up an IOS on a router? (Choose three.)

   A. Make sure you are logged in as root.

   B. Make sure the TFTP server has enough space for the image.

   C. Make sure you can access the server.

   D. Verify the IOS name and path requirements.

   E. Make sure the server can run the IOS code.

22. The configuration register setting of 0x2102 provides what function to a router?

   A. Tells the router to boot into ROM monitor mode

   B. Provides password recovery

   C. Tells the router to look in NVRAM for the boot sequence

   D. Boots the IOS from a TFTP host

   E. Boots an IOS image stored in ROM

23. If your router is working fine with the running-config and you do a copy run start, but you reboot the router and it goes into setup mode, which of the following could the problem be?

A. Faulty startup-config file

B. Configuration register setting

C. Hardware failure

D. Flash is corrupt

24. The configuration register setting of 0x2100 provides what function to a router?

   A. Tells the router to boot into ROM monitor mode

   B. Provides password recovery

   C. Tells the router to look in NVRAM for the boot sequence

   D. Boots the IOS from a TFTP host

   E. Boots an IOS image stored in ROM

25. The configuration register setting of 0x101 provides what function to a router?

   A. Tells the router to boot into ROM monitor mode

   B. Provides password recovery

   C. Tells the router to look in NVRAM for the boot sequence

   D. Boots the IOS from a TFTP host

   E. Boots an IOS image stored in ROM

Answers to Review Questions

1. B.   The command to see the host table, which resolves hostnames to IP addresses, is `show host` or `show hosts`.

2. E.   To copy the IOS to a backup host, which is stored in flash memory by default, use the `copy flash tftp` command.

3. C.   To copy a configuration of a router stored on a TFTP host to a router's NVRAM, use the `copy tftp startup-config` command.

4. A, D.   To copy a configuration of a router stored on a TFTP host to a router's RAM, you can use `copy tftp running-config` or `config net`.

5. B.   RAM is used to store packet buffers and routing tables, among other things.

6. C.   The command `ip host hostname ip_addresses` is used to create a host table on a Cisco router. The second IP address will only be tried if the first one does not work.

7. D.   The command `copy tftp flash` will allow you to copy a new IOS into flash memory on your router.

8. C.   The best answer is `show version`, which shows you the IOS file running currently on your router. The `show flash` shows you the contents of flash and not which file is running.

9. A.   The `copy running-config startup-config` command copies the configuration stored in RAM to NVRAM.

10. D.   To copy a configuration of a router from DRAM to a TFTP host, use the `copy running-config tftp` command.

11. D.   To keep open multiple Telnet sessions, use the Ctrl+Shift+6, then X keystroke combination.

12. C.   The command `boot system tftp IOS-name TFTP_server_address` will load an IOS image file from a TFTP server when the router is reloaded.

13. C.   The `show version` command will show you the IOS names and the source from which it was loaded, the configuration register setting, and the software version.

14. A, B, D. The `tracert` command is a Windows command and will not work on a router! A router uses the `traceroute` command.

15. B. The `trace` command displays the path a packet takes to find a remote destination by using ICMP timeouts.

16. A, B. The `ping` and `trace` commands can both be used to test IP connectivity in an internetwork.

17. C. The command `copy running-config startup-config` will copy the active router configuration and make it a backup configuration stored in NVRAM.

18. A. The command `show cdp neighbor` displays all the directly connected devices that CDP knows about.

19. C. The `show version` command provides you with the current configuration register setting.

20. A, B. `ping` and `traceroute` can be used from either user mode or privileged mode only.

21. B, C, D. Before you back up an IOS image to a network server (TFTP), make sure you can ping the server, that the server has enough space to hold the file, and that you know the IOS name.

22. C. The default configuration setting of 0x2102 tells the router to look in NVRAM for the boot sequence.

23. B. If your configuration setting is set to 0x2142, then the router will bypass the startup-config upon boot.

24. A. To boot to ROM monitor mode, set the configuration register to 0x2100. You must manually boot the router with the b command.

25. E. To boot an IOS image stored in ROM, set the configuration register to 0x2101 or 0x101. The router will show the `router(boot)>` prompt.

Answers to Written Lab 7

1. `copy flash tftp`

2. `copy start tftp`

3. `copy start run`

4. `config mem`

5. `show cdp neighbor detail` or `show cdp entry *`

6. `show cdp neighbor`

7. Ctrl+Shift+6, then X

8. `show sessions`

9. `copy tftp flash`

10. `ip host bob 172.16.10.1 172.16.20.2`

Configuring Novell IPX

THE CCNA EXAM TOPICS COVERED IN THIS CHAPTER INCLUDE THE FOLLOWING:

✓ **OSI Reference Model & Layered Communications**

- Describe the two parts of network addressing; then identify the parts in specific protocol address examples.

- Identify the parts in specific protocol address examples.

✓ **Network Protocols**

- List the required IPX address and encapsulation type.

ost network administrators have, at some point, encountered IPX for two reasons: first, Novell NetWare uses IPX as its default protocol; second, it was the most popular network operating system during the late 1980s and early 1990s. As a result, millions of IPX networks have been installed. But Novell changed things with the release of NetWare 5. TCP/IP is now the default communications protocol instead of IPX, although Novell still supports IPX. Why do they still bother? Well, considering the multitude of installed IPX clients and servers, it would be pretty impractical to yank the support for it.

There's little doubt that IPX will be around for a while, so it's no surprise that the Cisco IOS provides full support for large IPX internetworks. But to really take advantage of Novell IPX's functions and features, we need to review the way it operates and handles addressing because it varies significantly from the TCP/IP method we covered earlier. Armed with a solid grasp of things IPX, we'll then explore the configuration of IPX in the Cisco IOS and, from there, cover the monitoring of IPX traffic.

Introduction to Novell IPX

ovell Internetwork Packet Exchange (IPX) has been in use since its release in the early 1980s. It's quite similar to Xerox Network Systems (XNS), which was developed by Xerox at its Palo Alto Research Center in the 1960s; it even shares a likeness with TCP/IP. IPX is really a family of protocols that coexist and interact to empower sound network communications.

Novell IPX Protocol Stack

IPX doesn't map directly to the OSI model, but its protocols do function in layers. Back when they designed IPX, engineers were more concerned with performance than they were with strict compliance to existing standards or models. Even so, comparisons can be made.

Figure 8.1 illustrates the IPX protocols, layers, and functions relative to those of the OSI model.

FIGURE 8.1   IPX protocol stack and the OSI model

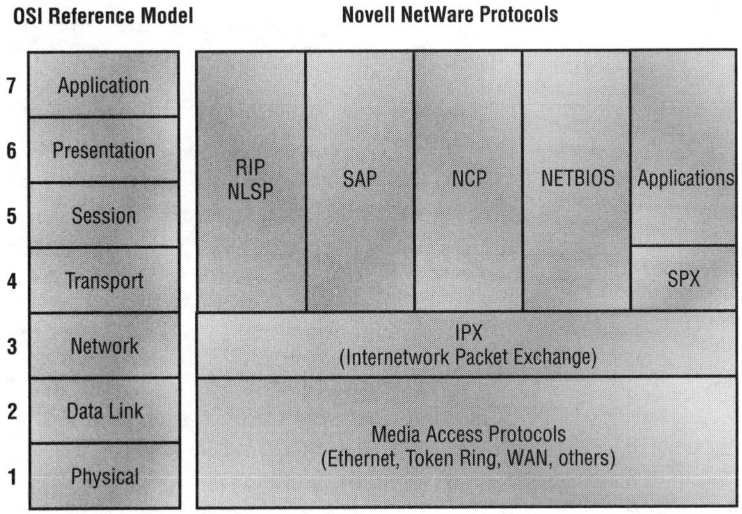

OSI Reference Model		Novell NetWare Protocols				
7	Application	RIP NLSP	SAP	NCP	NETBIOS	Applications
6	Presentation					
5	Session					
4	Transport					SPX
3	Network	IPX (Internetwork Packet Exchange)				
2	Data Link	Media Access Protocols (Ethernet, Token Ring, WAN, others)				
1	Physical					

IPX   Internetwork Packet Exchange performs functions at layers 3 and 4 of the OSI model. It controls the assignment of IPX addresses (software addressing) on individual nodes, governs packet delivery across internetworks, and makes routing decisions based on information provided by the routing protocols, RIP, Cisco EIGRP, or Novell NLSP. IPX is a connectionless protocol (similar to TCP/IP's IP), so it doesn't require any acknowledgment that packets were received from the destination node. To communicate with the upper-layer protocols, IPX uses sockets. A *socket* is similar to TCP/IP ports in that it's used to address multiple, independent applications running on the same machine.

SPX   Sequenced Packet Exchange adds connection-oriented communications to the otherwise connectionless IPX. Through it, upper-layer protocols can ensure data delivery between source and destination nodes. SPX works by creating a *virtual circuit* or connection between machines, with each connection having a specific connection ID included in the SPX header.

RIP Routing Information Protocol is a distance-vector routing protocol used to discover IPX routes through internetworks. It employs ticks (1/18 of a second) and *hop counts* (number of routers between nodes) as metrics for determining preferred routes.

SAP Service Advertising Protocol is used to advertise and request services. Servers use it to advertise the services they offer, and clients use it to locate network services.

NLSP NetWare Link Services Protocol is an advanced link-state routing protocol developed by Novell. It's intended to replace both RIP and SAP.

Cisco EIGRP Cisco Enhanced Interior Gateway Routing Protocol is a proprietary routing protocol that can be used instead of IPX RIP. It is considered an advanced distance-vector routing protocol, but it uses some link-state properties and some distance-vector properties to make routing decisions and keep bandwidth usage at a minimum.

NCP NetWare Core Protocol provides clients with access to server resources; functions such as file access, printing, synchronization, and security are all handled by NCP.

What does the presence of routing protocols, connection and connectionless transport protocols, and application protocols indicate to you? All of these factors add up to the fact that IPX is capable of supporting large internetworks running many applications. Understanding how Novell uses these protocols clears the way for you to include third-party devices (such as Cisco routers) into an IPX network.

Client-Server Communication

Novell NetWare follows a strict client-server model (there's no overlap): a NetWare node is either a client or a server, and that is that. You won't find peer machines that both provide and consume network resources here. Clients can be workstations running MacOS, DOS, Microsoft Windows, Windows NT, OS/2, Unix, or VMS. Servers generally run Novell NetWare. NetWare servers provide the following services to clients:

- File

- Print

- Message

- Application

- Database

As you would think, NetWare clients need servers to locate all network resources. Every NetWare server builds a SAP table comprising all the network resources that it's aware of. (We'll explain how they do this a bit later in the chapter.) When clients require access to a certain resource, they issue an IPX broadcast called a *Get Nearest Server (GNS)* request so they can locate a NetWare server that provides the particular resource the client needs. In turn, the servers receiving the GNS check their SAP tables to locate a NetWare server that matches the specific request; they respond to the client with a GNS reply. The GNS reply points the client to a specific server to contact for the resource it requested. If none of the servers receiving the client's GNS request have or know of another server that has the requested service, they simply don't respond, which leaves the requesting client without the ability to access the requested resource.

Why do we care? Because Cisco routers build SAP tables, too, and because they can respond to client GNS requests just as if they were NetWare servers. This doesn't mean they *offer* the services that NetWare servers do, just that their replies are identical when it comes to locating services. The GNS reply to a client can come from a local NetWare server or a Cisco router, and generally, if there are local NetWare servers present, they should respond to the client's request.

If there are no local NetWare servers, however, the local Cisco router that connects the client's segment to the IPX internetwork can respond to the client's GNS. This saves the client from having to wait for remote NetWare servers to respond. A second advantage of this arrangement is that precious WAN bandwidth isn't occupied with GNS conversations between clients on a segment with no local NetWare server and remote NetWare servers, as shown in Figure 8.2.

In this figure, you can see client workstations at the remote office site: they require access to server resources at the main office. In this situation, Router B would answer client GNS requests from its SAP table rather than forwarding the request across the WAN to the main office servers. The clients never realize or care that there isn't a NetWare server present on their LAN.

FIGURE 8.2 Remote IPX clients on a serverless network

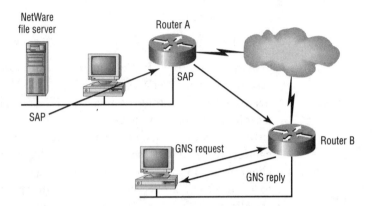

This communication insulates the client from the task of locating and tracking available network resources; it places that burden on the server instead. The client simply broadcasts a GNS and waits for a reply. From the client's perspective, all network resources respond as though they were local, regardless of their physical location in the internetwork.

Server-Server Communication

Communication between two NetWare servers is a bit more complicated than client-server communication. As mentioned earlier, servers are responsible for maintaining tables of all available network resources, regardless of whether those resources are local to the server. Also, keep in mind that each server must be able to locate *any* resource on the internetwork.

Servers exchange two types of information using two separate protocols: SAP (Service Advertising Protocol) and RIP (Routing Information Protocol). As their names suggest, SAP communicates service information, and RIP communicates routing information.

Please don't confuse RIP in IPX with RIP in TCP/IP. They're both routing protocols, but they're not the same routing protocol.

Service Advertising Protocol

NetWare servers use SAP to advertise the services they offer by sending out an SAP broadcast every 60 seconds. The broadcast includes all services that the server has learned about from other servers—not just the ones they furnish. All servers receiving the SAP broadcast incorporate the information into their own SAP tables; they then rebroadcast the SAP entries in their own SAP updates. Because SAP information is shared among all servers, all servers eventually become aware of all available services and are thereby equipped to respond to client GNS requests. As new services are introduced, they're added to SAP tables on local servers and are rebroadcast until every server knows they exist and knows where to get them.

So how does a Cisco router fit in here? Well, as far as SAP is concerned, the Cisco router acts just like another NetWare server. By default, an SAP broadcast won't cross a Cisco router. A Cisco router catalogs all SAPs heard on any of its IPX-enabled interfaces into its SAP table; unless you change the settings, the router then broadcasts the whole table from each of those interfaces at 60-second intervals (just as a NetWare server does). This is an important point, especially with WAN links. The router isolates SAP broadcasts to individual segments and passes along only the summarized information to each segment. Let's take a look at an SAP broadcast with the Etherpeek analyzer.

```
Flags:          0x00
   Status:        0x00
   Packet Length:306
   Timestamp:     23:48:36.362000 06/28/1998
Ethernet Header
   Destination:  ff:ff:ff:ff:ff:ff Ethernet Brdcast
   Source:       00:80:5f:ad:14:e4
   Protocol Type:81-37  NetWare
IPX - NetWare Protocol
   Checksum:              0xffff
   Length:                288
   Transport Control:
      Reserved:           %0000
      Hop Count:          %0000
   Packet Type:           4  PEP
   Destination Network:   0xcc715b00
   Destination Node:      ff:ff:ff:ff:ff:ff Ethernet
      Brdcast
   Destination Socket:    0x0452   Service Advertising
      Protocol
```

```
Source Network:      0xcc715b00
Source Node:         00:80:5f:ad:14:e4
Source Socket:       0x0452  Service Advertising
   Protocol
SAP - Service Advertising Protocol
Operation:           2  NetWare General Service Response
Service Advertising Set #1
Service Type:        263  NetWare 386
Service Name:
   BORDER3..................................
Network Number:      0x12db8494
Node Number:         00:00:00:00:00:01
Socket Number:       0x8104
Hops to Server:      1
Service Advertising Set #2
Service Type:        4  File Server
Service Name:
   BORDER3..................................
Network Number:      0x12db8494
Node Number:         00:00:00:00:00:01
Socket Number:       0x0451
Hops to Server:      1
Service Advertising Set #3
Service Type:        632
Service Name:
   BORDER_____R.S.I@@@@@D.PJ..
Network Number:      0x12db8494
Node Number:         00:00:00:00:00:01
Socket Number:       0x4006
Hops to Server:      1
```

This SAP is from a NetWare server named BORDER3. Notice that it is advertising three separate services that it offers. These services—their address and socket information—will be included in the SAP table of all IPX-enabled devices attached to this network (including the routers) and rebroadcast throughout the internetwork.

Routing Information Protocol

RIP information is exchanged between servers much the same way that SAP information is. Servers build routing tables that contain entries for the networks they're directly connected to, they then broadcast this information to all IPX-enabled interfaces.

Other servers on those segments receive those updates and broadcast their RIP tables on their IPX interfaces. Just as SAP information travels from server to server until all servers are enlightened, RIP information is spread until all servers and routers know of the internetwork's routes. Like SAP information, RIP information is broadcast at 60-second intervals. Let's take a look at an IPX RIP packet with the Etherpeek analyzer.

```
Flags:          0x80  802.3
   Status:        0x00
   Packet Length:94
   Timestamp:     15:23:05.642000 06/28/1998
802.3 Header
   Destination:   ff:ff:ff:ff:ff:ff Ethernet Brdcast
   Source:        00:00:0c:8d:5c:9d
   LLC Length:    76
802.2 Logical Link Control (LLC) Header
   Dest. SAP:     0xe0  NetWare
   Source SAP:    0xe0  NetWare  Null LSAP
   Command:       0x03  Unnumbered Information
IPX - NetWare Protocol
   Checksum:               0xffff
   Length:                 72
   Transport Control:
      Reserved:            %0000
      Hop Count:           %0000
   Packet Type:            1  RIP
   Destination Network:  0x00002300
   Destination Node:       ff:ff:ff:ff:ff:ff Ethernet
      Brdcast
   Destination Socket:   0x0453   Routing Information
      Protocol
   Source Network:         0x00002300
```

Source Node: 00:00:0c:8d:5c:9d

Source Socket: 0x0453 Routing Information
   Protocol

RIP - Routing Information Protocol

Operation: 2 *Response*

Network Number Set # 1

  Network Number: 0x00005200

  Number of Hops: 3

  Number of Ticks: 14

Network Number Set # 2

  Network Number: 0x00004100

  Number of Hops: 2

  Number of Ticks: 8

Network Number Set # 3

  Network Number: 0x00003200

  Number of Hops: 1

  Number of Ticks: 2

Network Number Set # 4

  Network Number: 0x00002200

  Number of Hops: 1

  Number of Ticks: 2

Network Number Set # 5

  Network Number: 0x00002100

  Number of Hops: 1

  Number of Ticks: 2

Extra bytes (Padding):

  r   72

See that? It looks a lot like an IP RIP packet, but it's missing the IP addresses. In their place are IPX addresses and network numbers. Also, notice that it has both ticks and hops in the updates. Ticks are how many 1/18 of a second it takes to get to a remote network. This is IPX's way of using link delay to find the best way to a remote network.

There are only three routers in this example, and this packet is sent out every 60 seconds—imagine this happening on a large network with hundreds of routers!

IPX Addressing

After sweating through IP addressing, IPX addressing should seem like a day at the beach. The IPX addressing scheme has several features that make it a lot easier to understand and administer than the TCP/IP scheme.

IPX addresses use 80 bits, or 10 bytes, of data. As with TCP/IP addresses, they are hierarchical and divided into a network and node portion. The first four bytes always represent the network address, and the last six bytes always represent the node address. There's none of that Class A, Class B, or Class C TCP/IP stuff in IPX addressing—the network and node portions of the address are always the same lengths. After subnet masking, this is sweet indeed!

Just as with IP network addresses, the network portion of the address is assigned by administrators and must be unique on the entire IPX internetwork. Node addresses are automatically assigned to every node. In most cases, the MAC address of the machine is used as the node portion of the address. This offers several notable advantages over TCP/IP addressing. Since client addressing is dynamic (automatic), you don't have to run DHCP or manually configure each individual workstation with an IPX address. Also, since the hardware address (layer 2) is included as part of the software address (layer 3), there's no need for a TCP/IP ARP equivalent in IPX.

As with TCP/IP addresses, IPX addresses can be written in several formats. Most often, though, they're written in hex, such as 0000.7C80.0000.8609.33E9.

The first eight hex digits (0000.7C80) represent the network portion of the address. It's a common IPX custom when referring to the IPX network to drop leading zeros. Thus, the above network address would be referred to as IPX network 7C80.

The remaining 12 hex digits (0000.8609.33E9) represent the node portion and are commonly divided into three sections of four hex digits divided by periods. They are the MAC address of the workstation.

You must understand IPX addressing and be able to differentiate between the network number and node number when looking at an IPX address.

Encapsulation

The process of *encapsulation*, or framing, is taking packets from upper-layer protocols and building frames to transmit them across the network. As you probably recall, frames live at layer 2 of the OSI model. When you're dealing with IPX, encapsulation is the specific process of taking IPX datagrams (layer 3) and building frames (layer 2) for one of the supported media. We'll cover IPX encapsulation on the following physical networks:

- Ethernet
- Token Ring
- FDDI

Why is encapsulation significant? Well, for the very good reason that NetWare supports multiple, incompatible framing methods, and it does so on the same media. For instance, take Ethernet. NetWare has four different *frame types* to choose from, depending on your needs (see Table 8.1), and each one of those frame types is incompatible with the other ones. It's like this: Say your servers are using Ethernet_802.2 and your clients are configured for Ethernet_II. Does this mean you don't have to worry about anything? Not necessarily. If they're communicating with each other via a router that supports both frame types, you're set. If not, you're cooked—they just won't talk! When configuring any IPX device (including a router) on a network, the frame type has to be consistent for things to work.

TABLE 8.1 Novell Ethernet Encapsulations

NetWare Frame Type	Features
Ethernet_802.3	Default up to NetWare 3.11
Ethernet_802.2	Default since NetWare 3.12
Ethernet_II	Supports both TCP/IP and IPX
Ethernet_SNAP	AppleTalk, IPX, and TCP/IP

Sometimes—and only sometimes—you can intentionally have multiple frame types present on the same network. Typically, you'll start working in an environment that already has all frame types configured—usually because the administrator didn't know what to do and just configured all available frame types on all routers and servers, as shown in Figure 8.3.

FIGURE 8.3 Multiple frame types on a single Ethernet segment

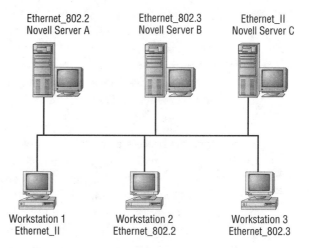

Each frame type in Figure 8.3 has a unique IPX network address. Even though there's a single Ethernet segment, there are three *virtual* IPX networks and, therefore, three unique IPX network addresses. Each network will be broadcast across the internetwork every 60 seconds.

In Figure 8.3, Workstation 1 can communicate only with Server C because they're both running Ethernet_II. Workstation 2 can communicate only with Server A, and Workstation 3 can communicate only with Server B. But what if you wanted all the workstations to communicate with all the servers—what would you do? You can add a router that supports all frame types, or you can add more frame types to each server. Adding a router would allow any workstation to communicate with any of the servers, but that router would have to route all packets among all the servers and clients with dissimilar frame types. Adding multiple frame types to servers and routers is not a good solution. It's best to have one frame type, probably 802.2, in your internetwork. However, NetWare 5 introduced a native IP, so all this is irrelevant unless you have to support older servers.

When configuring a router, you'll need to know both the frame type and the IPX network address information for each segment that you plan to attach that router to. To find this information, ask the network administrator or go to one of the NetWare servers and type **config** at the server console.

> ### 🌐 Real World Scenario
>
> ### Should I support multiple Ethernet frame types?
>
> No, not if you can help it. The reason this was even developed was to support older hosts that couldn't run the newer 802.2 frame type when it was released. It was never intended to support the network indefinitely—only long enough so you can keep the network running while you are updating the hosts. Of course, this never happens, so you have to keep supporting multiple frame types forever.
>
> Why is this bad? Because for every frame type you have configured on your network, the packets sent out are doubled. For example, if you have an IPX Ethernet network with 802.3 configured, and you add a new server to your network that is running only 802.2, you have to configure all hosts to run both 802.3 and 802.2 frame types so they will talk to both servers. This means that every packet transmitted from every host is sent twice, once in an 802.3 frame and once in an 802.2 frame. If you have all four possible frame types configured, then you send every packet out four times. Yikes!

Enabling IPX on Cisco Routers

Cool—with the basics behind you, it's *finally* time to configure IPX on the router! This is easy compared to IP. The only confusing part can be the multiple frame types. But don't worry, I'll show you the configuration in detail.

There are two main tasks to activate IPX across Cisco routers:

- Enabling IPX routing
- Enabling IPX on each individual interface

Enabling IPX Routing

To configure IPX routing, use the `ipx routing` global configuration command. Here is an example:

```
RouterA#config t
RouterA(config)#ipx routing
```

Once you enable IPX routing on the router, RIP and SAP are automatically enabled as well. However, nothing happens until you configure the individual interfaces with IPX addresses.

Enabling IPX on Individual Interfaces

Once you have IPX routing enabled on the router, the next step is to enable IPX on individual interfaces. To enable IPX on an interface, first enter the interface configuration mode, and then issue the following command:

ipx network *number* [encapsulation *encapsulation-type*] [secondary]

The various parts are defined as follows:

number	The IPX network address.
encapsulation *encapsulation-type*	Optional. Table 8.2 shows the default encapsulation-type on different media.
[secondary]	Indicates a secondary encapsulation (frame type) and network address on the same interface.

Here is an example of configuring IPX on 2501A:

```
2501A#config t
2501A(config)#ipx routing
2501A(config)#int e0
2501A(config-if)#ipx network 10
```

That's all there is to it. Just add the network number, and the rest is done for you. IPX is a very resilient routed protocol because it broadcasts for everything. However, this is also why it causes problems in larger internetworks.

What frame type is now running on Ethernet 0 on 2501A? By default, the frame type is Novell-Ether (802.3). To change the frame type, or to add another frame type, add the encapsulation command to the interface configuration. Table 8.2 shows the different encapsulations (frame types) available with IPX.

TABLE 8.2 Novell IPX Frame Types

Interface Type	Novell Frame Type	Cisco Keyword
Ethernet	Ethernet_802.3	novell-ether (default)
	Ethernet_802.2	sap
	Ethernet_II	arpa
	Ethernet_snap	snap
Token Ring	Token-Ring	sap (default)
	Token-Ring_snap	snap
FDDI	Fddi_snap	snap (default)
	Fddi_802.2	sap
	Fddi_raw	novell-fddi

You absolutely must know your Novell Ethernet IPX frame types for the CCNA exam!

To change the IPX frame type on Ethernet 0 of 2501A to sap (802.2), use the encapsulation command, as shown below:

```
2501A#config t
2501A(config)#int e0
2501A(config-if)#ipx network 10 encapsulation sap
```

This replaced the existing network number and encapsulation with the 802.2 frame type. If you want to add multiple frame types, you need to either use the secondary command at the end of the network command line, or create subinterfaces. Both the secondary command and subinterfaces are discussed later in this chapter.

To configure a Cisco router into an existing IPX internetwork, you'll need the IPX network address and frame type information from the "config" screen of your NetWare servers for this step. When specifying the encapsulation type on the router, make sure to use the Cisco keyword, *not* the Novell frame type.

Configuring Our Internetwork with IPX

Before you start configuring IPX routing with Cisco routers, let's take another look at our internetwork. Figure 8.4 shows the four routers plus the IPX addressing you'll be using.

FIGURE 8.4   Our internetwork

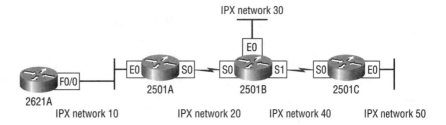

Notice that there are IPX network numbers for all network segments in this figure. The IPX network numbers are the same as the IP subnet numbers. Remember that IPX addressing has nothing to do with IP, and that I am using the IP subnet numbers as IPX network numbers only for ease of administration.

Let's start off by adding the Novell-Ether (802.3) frame type to the internetwork Ethernet networks. Since that is the default encapsulation, the configuration is really simple. The default encapsulation on the serial links is HDLC, and you'll use that as well. (HDLC is discussed in Chapter 10.)

Configuring IPX on the 2621A Router

To configure IPX on the 2621A router, you just need to start IPX routing on the router with the global configuration command ipx routing. Then tell interface FastEthernet 0/0 that it is on IPX network 10.

Here is the configuration for 2621A:

```
2621A(config)#ipx routing
2621A(config)#int f0/0
2621A(config-if)#ipx network 10
```

That's it. The 2621A router will now route IPX traffic through interface FastEthernet 0/0 using IPX network 10.

Configuring IPX on the 2501A Router

The same commands are used on the 2501A router as on the 2621A router. However, the 2501A router has two connections into the internetwork: interface Ethernet 0 is on IPX network 10 and interface serial 0 is on IPX network 20.

Here is the configuration for the 2501A router:

```
2501A(config)#ipx routing
2501A(config)#int e0
2501A(config-if)#ipx network 10
2501A(config-if)#int s0
2501A(config-if)#ipx network 20
```

That's all you need to do to configure IPX on the 2501A router. Much easier than IP, isn't it?

Configuring IPX on the 2501B Router

To configure IPX routing on the 2501B router, you need to configure three interfaces: interface Ethernet 0 is on network 30, interface serial 0 is on IPX network 20, and interface serial 1 is on network 40.

Here is the configuration for the 2501B router:

```
2501B(config)#ipx routing
2501B(config)#int e0
2501B(config-if)#ipx network 30
2501B(config-if)#int s0
2501B(config-if)#ipx network 20
2501B(config-if)#int s1
2501B(config-if)#ipx network 40
```

That is all you need to do to configure IPX on the 2501B router.

Configuring IPX on the 2501C Router

To configure IPX routing on the 2501C router, you need to configure interface Ethernet 0 into IPX network 50 and interface serial 0 into IPX network 40.

Here is the configuration for the 2501C router:

```
2501C(config)#ipx routing
2501C(config)#int e0
```

```
2501C(config-if)#ipx network 50
2501C(config-if)#int s0
2501C(config-if)#ipx network 40
```

All four of the routers are now configured and should be up and working. The best way to verify the configuration is with the show ipx route command.

Verifying the IPX Routing Tables

To view the IPX routing tables, use the show ipx route command. Like IP, IPX routers only know about directly connected networks by default. However, when I turned on IPX routing in the configuration examples above, IPX RIP was automatically started on all routers.

IPX RIP will find all IPX networks in the internetwork and update all routers' routing tables. Let's take a look at all routers in our internetwork and see the IPX routing table.

2621A

The 2621A router is only connected to IPX network 10, so IPX RIP would have to update the routing table of the other four IPX networks in the internetwork.

Here is the routing table on the 2621A router:

```
2621A#sh ipx route
[output cut]
5 Total IPX routes. Up to 1 parallel paths and 16 hops
  allowed.
No default route known.
C    10 (NOVELL-ETHER),  Fa0/0
R    20 [07/01] via      10.0000.0c8d.3a7b,   16s, Fa0/0
R    30 [07/02] via      10.0000.0c8d.3a7c,   17s, Fa0/0
R    40 [07/02] via      10.0000.0c8d.3a7c,   17s, Fa0/0
R    50 [13/03] via      10.0000.0c8d.3a7c,   17s, Fa0/0
2621A#
```

The C means a directly connected IPX network, and the Rs are IPX RIP-found networks. The [07/01] is the tick and hops needed to get to the remote network.

2501A

The 2501A router knows only about IPX networks 10 and 20 since that is what is directly connected. IPX RIP will tell router 2501A about networks 30, 40, and 50. Here is the routing table from the 2501A router:

```
2501A#sh ipx route
[output cut]
5 Total IPX routes. Up to 1 parallel paths and 16 hops
  allowed.
No default route known.
C      20 (HDLC),         Se0
C      10 (NOVELL-ETHER),  Et0
R      30 [13/02] via       20.0000.0c8d.2b8c,    16s, Se0
R      40 [07/02] via       20.0000.0c8d.2b8c,    17s, Se0
R      50 [07/03] via       20.0000.0c8d.2b8c,    17s, Se0
2501A#
```

In the routing table above, notice the two directly connected networks and the three RIP-found networks. The IPX address of the neighbor's interface is included in the routing table as well as the interface the router will use to get to the remote network.

2501B

The routes found from IPX RIP in the 2501B router are 10 and 20. Here is the output from the 2501B router:

```
2501B#sh ipx route
[output cut]
5 Total IPX routes. Up to 1 parallel paths and 16 hops
  allowed.
No default route known.
C      20 (HDLC),         Se0
C      40 (HDLC),         Se1
C      30 (NOVELL-ETHER),  Et0
R      10 [07/01] via       20.0000.0c8d.3d8e,    16s, Se0
R      50 [07/01] via       40.0000.0c8d.5c9d,    17s, Se1
2501B#
```

2501C

In the 2501C router, the routes that are found by IPX RIP are networks 10, 20, and 30. Here is the output from the 2501C router:

```
2501C#sh ipx route
[output cut]
5 Total IPX routes. Up to 1 parallel paths and 16 hops
   allowed.
No default route known.
C      40 (HDLC),          Se0
C      50 (NOVELL-ETHER),  Et0
R      10 [13/02] via        40.0000.0c8d.5c9d,    16s, Se0
R      20 [07/01] via        40.0000.0c8d.5c9d,    17s, Se0
R      30 [07/01] via        40.0000.0c8d.5c9d,    17s, Se0
2501C#
```

Adding Secondary Addresses

What is the Ethernet frame type we are running on our sample inter-network? Novell-Ether (802.3). Since we didn't use the `encapsulation` command, the default frame type was used.

In this section, I will show you how to configure the other three available frame types on our Ethernet networks. This is not so you can go and do this in production—that would be a bad thing. Rather, this is so that when you see this type of configuration, you know what it is and how to fix it.

To configure multiple frame types on the same LAN network, you can either use the `secondary` command or create a subinterface. There is absolutely no functional difference on how the `secondary` command or how a subinterface runs on the internetwork. The difference is for administration purposes only.

Configuring Secondary Addresses

To configure a secondary address on an Ethernet LAN to support multiple frame types, use the `ipx network` command with the `secondary` parameter at the end of the command.

Here is an example of adding a secondary network to 2501A's Ethernet connection:

```
2501A#config t
Enter configuration commands, one per line.  End with CNTL/Z.
2501A(config)#int e0
2501A(config-if)#ipx network 10a encap sap sec
```

If you don't use the `secondary` command at the end of the line, the `ipx network` command will replace the existing entry. (The shortcut commands `encap` and `sec` were used here instead of the whole command `encapsulation` and `secondary`.)

The important thing to understand is that each frame type must have a different IPX network number. Notice the 10a in the above example. The 802.3 frame type is using 10 so that you cannot configure the 802.2 frame type with that number.

Subinterfaces

To define IPX network numbers to router interfaces that support multiple networks, you can use a subinterface instead of the `secondary` command. This allows one physical interface to support multiple logical IPX networks. Each subinterface, like a secondary, must have a unique IPX network number and a unique encapsulation type.

To define subinterfaces, use the `interface ethernet port.number` command. You can use numbers between e0.0 and e0.4292967295—that's a lot of subinterfaces! An example of adding the 802.2 frame type is shown below:

```
2621A(config)#int e0.10
2621A(config-subif)#ipx network 10a encap sap
2621A(config-subif)#^Z
2621A#
```

As I have mentioned before, there is no functional difference between subinterfaces and the `secondary` command on the IPX internetwork; it is merely an administrative difference. You create subinterfaces instead of a secondary for administrative control because you can place commands under the subinterface that allow more granular control over the subinterface and associated networks. If you use the `secondary` command instead, the network is placed under the physical interface and any change you make to the physical interface affects that network.

Configuring Our Internetwork with Multiple Ethernet Frame Types

You never really want to do this in a real product network. The only time you would is if you were trying to support clients that just couldn't run the 802.2 frame type and you needed to support 802.3. Remember, the best IPX network is one that uses only one frame type.

However, you should be aware of the different frame types and how they are configured. This section will teach you just that. Let's configure our internetwork to run all possible frame types on the Ethernet LANs. This way, when you see this configuration in a production network, you'll know what is wrong with it and why everyone is complaining that the network is a *not*work.

It is important to understand that this is performed only on the LAN interfaces and that you do not run LAN frames on a WAN interface.

Configuring Multiple Frame Types on the 2621A Router

To configure multiple frame types on the 2621A router, you'll need to add three new IPX network numbers, one for each frame type you want to add. When configuring multiple frame types, I like to use the primary number plus a letter. In this configuration, use 10a for 802.2, 10b for Ethernet_II, and 10c for SNAP.

For the following configuration, you will create one secondary address on each router and two subinterfaces. You can do this any way you want, but this is just the way I chose do it.

Here is the configuration for 2621A. Notice that when you use the ipx network 10a encap command and a question mark, you can see all the supported encapsulation types and the Cisco keywords.

```
2621A(config)#int f0/0
2621A(config-if)#ipx network 10a encap ?
  arpa          Novell Ethernet_II
  hdlc          HDLC on serial links
  novell-ether  Novell Ethernet_802.3
  novell-fddi   Novell FDDI RAW
```

```
sap           IEEE 802.2 on Ethernet, FDDI, Token Ring
snap          IEEE 802.2 SNAP on Ethernet, Token Ring,
              and FDDI
RouterA(config-if)#ipx network 10a encap sap sec
```

After you configure the secondary address, you need to add two sub-interfaces. If you were configuring this network for a real production network and needed to support multiple frame types, you would use only subinterfaces and no secondary networks because Cisco will not support secondary commands in the future (so they say). The secondary command is only included here so you understand what it is if you see it in a configuration.

The subinterface numbers can be any number, as the help screen (int f0/0.?) shows below. The subinterface numbers are only locally significant and have no bearing on how IPX runs on the internetwork.

```
2621A(config)#int f0/0.?
  <0-4294967295>  Ethernet interface number
2621A(config)#int f0/0.10
2621A(config-subif)#ipx network 10b encap arpa
2621A(config)#int f0/0.100
2621A(config-subif)#ipx network 10c encap snap
```

All four frame types are now configured on the FastEthernet 0/0 interface of the 2621 router. For any device to communicate with the 2621A router with IPX, they must support the same network numbers configured with each frame type.

Configuring Multiple Frame Types on the 2501A Router

For the 2501A router to communicate to the 2621A router with IPX, it must be configured with the same IPX network numbers for each frame type configured.

Here is the configuration for the 2501A router:

```
2501A(config)#int e0
2501A(config-if)#ipx network 10a encap sap sec
2501A(config-if)#int e0.10
2501A(config-subif)#ipx network 10b encap arpa
2501A(config-subif)#int e0.100
2501A(config-subif)#ipx network 10c encap snap
```

In the above example, the same subinterface numbers were used, but they can be any numbers you want to use. Here is a copy of the `running-config` after the router is configured with all four IPX Ethernet frame types:

```
hostname RouterA
!
ipx routing 0060.7015.63d6
!
interface Ethernet0
ip address 172.16.10.1 255.255.255.0
ipx network 10
ipx network 10A encapsulation SAP secondary
!
interface Ethernet0.10
ipx network 10B encapsulation ARPA
!
interface Ethernet0.100
ipx network 10C encapsulation SNAP
!
interface Serial0
ip address 172.16.20.1 255.255.255.0
ipx network 20
```

Notice that under the main Ethernet interface there are two IPX network numbers, one for the Novell-Ether (802.3) frame type and one for the SAP (802.2) frame type. The Ethernet_II (ARPA) frame type and the SNAP frame type have their own subinterfaces, and the `secondary` command does not need to be used.

Configuring Multiple Frame Types on the 2501B Router

To configure the 2501B router, you need to be concerned with only the Ethernet 0 interface. IPX network 30 is running the 802.3 frame type on the primary interface. I will add the other three possible frame types to Ethernet 0. Here is the configuration for the 2501B router:

```
2501B(config)#int e0
2501B(config-if)#ipx network 30a encap sap sec
2501B(config-if)#int e0.30
```

```
2501B(config-subif)#ipx network 30b encap arpa
2501B(config-subif)#int e0.300
2501B(config-subif)#ipx network 30c encap snap
```

The 2501B router now has all four IPX Ethernet frame types configured on the Ethernet 0 interface. Plenty of bandwidth on the Ethernet network is now being wasted.

Configuring Multiple Frame Types on the 2501C Router

The 2501C has only one LAN connection, and that is to IPX network 50. IPX network 50 is running the 802.3 frame type. Let's configure the other three supported IPX network numbers on Ethernet 0.

Here is the configuration for the 2501C router:

```
2501C(config)#int e0
2501C(config-if)#ipx network 50a encap sap sec
2501C(config-if)#int e0.50
2501C(config-subif)#ipx network 50b encap arpa
2501C(config-subif)#int e0.500
2501C(config-subif)#ipx network 50c encap snap
```

All four of the routers are now configured and should be up and working with all four possible IPX Ethernet frame types.

Are you ready to find out why using multiple frame types is so bad for your internetwork? Let's use the show ipx route command and find out.

Verifying the IPX Routing Tables

Remember, when we verified the IPX routing tables earlier, there was one connection for each IPX network in the routing tables of each router. Let's run the command again and see what it shows now. (This is the IPX routing table for the 2621A router only. The other routers will have the same routing table.)

```
2621A#sh ipx route
[output cut]
14 Total IPX routes. Up to 1 parallel paths and 16 hops
    allowed.
No default route known.
C      10 (NOVELL-ETHER),  Fa0/0
C      10A(SAP),           Fa0/0
```

```
C       10B(ARPA),          Fa0/0.10
C       10C(SNAP),          Fa0/0.100
R       20 [07/01] via      10.0000.0c8d.3a7b,    16s, Fa0/0
R       30A[07/02] via      10.0000.0c8d.3a7c,    17s, Fa0/0
R       30B[07/02] via      10.0000.0c8d.3a7c,    17s, Fa0/0
R       30C[07/02] via      10.0000.0c8d.3a7c,    17s, Fa0/0
R       30D[07/02] via      10.0000.0c8d.3a7c,    17s, Fa0/0
R       40 [07/02] via      10.0000.0c8d.3a7c,    17s, Fa0/0
R       50A[13/03] via      10.0000.0c8d.3a7c,    17s, Fa0/0
R       50B[13/03] via      10.0000.0c8d.3a7c,    17s, Fa0/0
R       50C[13/03] via      10.0000.0c8d.3a7c,    17s, Fa0/0
R       50D[13/03] via      10.0000.0c8d.3a7c,    17s, Fa0/0
2621A#
```

Notice that the routing table has 14 IPX routes now instead of the five we had earlier. I did not add any new physical networks, but the new networks are the new encapsulations you added for each network. The three LANs each advertise four IPX networks every 60 seconds out of each active interface. Imagine if you had 20 routers and you added all the frame types!

There is one more consideration when adding multiple frame types on a LAN: the SAP activity. Service Advertisement Protocol (SAP) is broadcast over every active interface every 60 seconds. If you have multiple frame types configured on a LAN, the broadcast is sent out in every frame type possible. If you only send one SAP packet, which is unlikely, you would send that same packet out four times. If you have multiple SAP packets, you send each packet out four times every 60 seconds.

Monitoring IPX on Cisco Routers

Once you have IPX configured and running, there are several ways to verify and track that your router is communicating correctly. The following commands will be covered:

- show ipx servers
- show ipx route
- show ipx traffic

- show ipx interface

- show protocol

- debug ipx

- IPX ping

The *Show IPX Servers* Command

The show ipx servers command is a lot like the display servers command in NetWare—it displays the contents of the SAP table in the Cisco router, so you should see the names of all SAP services here. Remember that if the router doesn't have entries for remote servers in its own SAP table, local clients will never see those servers. If there are servers missing from this table that shouldn't be, double check your IPX network addresses and encapsulation settings.

```
2501A#sho ipx servers
Codes: S - Static, P - Periodic, E - EIGRP, N - NLSP,
       H - Holddown, + = detail
9 Total IPX Servers
Table ordering is based on routing and server info
Type Name          Net       Address              Port Route Hops  Itf
P    4 BORDER1     350ED6D2.0000.0000.0001:0451   2/01   1   Et0
P    4 BORDER3     12DB8494.0000.0000.0001:0451   2/01   1   Et0
P    107 BORDER1   350ED6D2.0000.0000.0001:8104   2/01   1   Et0
P    107 BORDER3   12DB8494.0000.0000.0001:8104   2/01   1   Et0
P    26B BORDER    350ED6D2.0000.0000.0001:0005   2/01   1   Et0
P    278 BORDER    12DB8494.0000.0000.0001:4006   2/01   1   Et0
P    278 BORDER    350ED6D2.0000.0000.0001:4006   2/01   1   Et0
P    3E1 BORDER1   350ED6D2.0000.0000.0001:9056   2/01   1   Et0
P    3E1 BORDER3   12DB8494.0000.0000.0001:9056   2/01   1   Et0
```

The output from the router allows you to see all the IPX servers discovered through the SAP advertisements.

The Type field is the type of SAP service being advertised, with 4 being a file service and 7 a print service. The other service numbers listed are specific for that type of application running on the NetWare server. The **Net** and **Address** fields are the IPX Internal network numbers configured on each server. The Port field identifies the upper layer application. The socket number for the NetWare Core Protocol (NCP) is 451.

The *Show IPX Route* Command

The show ipx route command displays the IPX routing table entries that the router knows about. The router reports networks to which it is directly connected, then it reports networks that it has learned of since the router came online.

```
2501A#sh ipx route
Codes: C - Connected primary network, c - Connected
    secondary network, S - Static, F - Floating static,
    L - Local (internal), W - IPXWAN, R - RIP, E - EIGRP,
    N - NLSP, X - External, A - Aggregate, s - seconds,
    u - uses
6 Total IPX routes. Up to 1 parallel paths and 16 hops
    allowed.
No default route known.
C       10 (NOVELL-ETHER),   Et0
C       20 (HDLC),           Se0
c       10a (sap),           Et0
C       10b (ARPA),          Et0.10
R       40 [07/01] via    20.00e0.1ea9.c418,    13s, Se0
R       50 [13/02] via    20.00e0.1ea9.c418,    13s, Se0
```

The small c in the routing table tells you that it is a secondary configured IPX network.

Load Balancing with IPX

If you set up parallel IPX paths between routers, the Cisco IOS will not learn about these paths by default. The router will learn a single path to a destination and discard information about alternative, parallel, equal-cost paths.

Notice in the show ipx route output above the phrase Up to 1 parallel paths and 16 hops allowed. To be able to perform a round-robin load balance over multiple equal-cost paths, you need to add the command ipx maximum-paths # (with # being any number up to 64); this will allow the router to accept the possibility that there might be more than one path to the same destination.

The Cisco IOS will perform per-packet load sharing by default over these parallel lines. Packets will be sent on a round-robin basis between all equal-cost lines, without regard to the destination. However, if you want to ensure that all packets sent to a destination or host will always go over the same line, use the ipx per-host-load-share command.

The ipx maximum-paths command is shown below. It tells the IPX RIP protocol to perform round-robin load balancing across two equal-cost paths.

```
Router#config t
Router(config)#ipx maximum-paths 2
Router(config)#^Z
Router#sh ipx route
Codes: C - Connected primary network, c - Connected
[output cut]
5 Total IPX routes. Up to 2 parallel paths and 16 hops
    allowed. [output cut]
```

The show ipx route command shows that two parallel paths are now supported.

The *Show IPX Traffic* Command

The show ipx traffic command gives you a summary of the number and type of IPX packets received and transmitted by the router. Notice that this command will show you both the IPX RIP and SAP update packets.

```
2501A#sh ipx traffic
System Traffic for 0.0000.0000.0001 System-Name: RouterA
Rcvd:   15 total, 0 format errors, 0 checksum errors,
   0 bad hop count, 0 packets pitched, 15 local
   destination, 0 multicast
Bcast:  10 received, 249 sent
Sent:   255 generated, 0 forwarded
        0 encapsulation failed, 0 no route
SAP:    1 SAP requests, 0 SAP replies, 0 servers
        0 SAP Nearest Name requests, 0 replies
        0 SAP General Name requests, 0 replies
        0 SAP advertisements received, 0 sent
        0 SAP flash updates sent, 0 SAP format errors
```

```
RIP:    1 RIP requests, 0 RIP replies, 6 routes
        8 RIP advertisements received, 230 sent
        12 RIP flash updates sent, 0 RIP format errors
Echo:   Rcvd 0 requests, 5 replies
        Sent 5 requests, 0 replies
        0 unknown: 0 no socket, 0 filtered, 0 no helper
        0 SAPs throttled, freed NDB len 0
Watchdog:
        0 packets received, 0 replies spoofed
Queue lengths:
        IPX input: 0, SAP 0, RIP 0, GNS 0
        SAP throttling length: 0/(no limit), 0 nets
  pending lost route reply
  --More-
```

Remember that the show ipx traffic command shows you the statistics for IPX RIP and SAP information received on the router. If you wanted to view the statistics of RIP and SAP information received only on a specific interface, use the next command we discuss: show ipx interface.

The *Show IPX Interface* Command

The show ipx interface command gives you the interface status of IPX and the IPX parameters configured on each interface.

The show ipx interface e0 command shows you the IPX address and encapsulation type of the interface. If you use the show interface e0 command, remember that it does not provide the IPX address of the interface, only the IP address.

Notice the IPX address is 10.0000.0c8d.5c9d and the frame type is Novell-Ether (802.3).

```
2501A#sh ipx int e0
Ethernet0 is up, line protocol is up
  IPX address is 10.0000.0c8d.5c9d, NOVELL-ETHER [up]
  Delay of this IPX network, in ticks is 1 throughput 0
  link delay 0
  IPXWAN processing not enabled on this interface.
  IPX SAP update interval is 1 minute(s)
  IPX type 20 propagation packet forwarding is disabled
```

```
  Incoming access list is not set
  Outgoing access list is not set
  IPX helper access list is not set
  SAP GNS processing enabled, delay 0 ms, output filter
  list is not set
  SAP Input filter list is not set
  SAP Output filter list is not set
  SAP Router filter list is not set
  Input filter list is not set
  Output filter list is not set
  Router filter list is not set
  Netbios Input host access list is not set
  Netbios Input bytes access list is not set
  Netbios Output host access list is not set
  Netbios Output bytes access list is not set
  Updates each 60 seconds, aging multiples RIP: 3 SAP: 3
  SAP interpacket delay is 55 ms, maximum size is 480
  bytes
  RIP interpacket delay is 55 ms, maximum size is 432
  bytes
 --More-
```

This command shows you the RIP and SAP information received on a certain interface. The show ipx traffic command shows the RIP and SAP information received on the router in whole.

The *Show Protocols* Command

There is one more command that shows the IPX address and encapsulation type of an interface: the show protocols command. This command shows the routed protocols configured on your router and the interface addresses.

Here is the show protocol command run on the 2501A router:

```
2501A#sh protocols
Global values:
  Internet Protocol routing is enabled
  IPX routing is enabled
Ethernet0 is up, line protocol is up
```

```
    Internet address is 172.16.10.1/24
    IPX address is 10.0060.7015.63d6 (NOVELL-ETHER)
    IPX address is 10A.0060.7015.63d6 (SAP)
  Ethernet0.10 is up, line protocol is up
    IPX address is 10B.0060.7015.63d6
  Ethernet0.100 is up, line protocol is up
    IPX address is 10C.0060.7015.63d6
  Serial0 is up, line protocol is up
    Internet address is 172.16.20.1/24
    IPX address is 20.0060.7015.63d6
```

Notice that you can see all configured interfaces' addresses, even for the subinterfaces. However, although the primary, secondary, and subinterfaces show the interface addresses, the subinterfaces do not show the encapsulation types.

Remember, there are only two commands that show you the IPX address of an interface: show ipx interface and show protocols.

The *Debug IPX* Command

The debug ipx commands show you IPX as it's running through your internetwork. It's noteworthy that you can see the IPX RIP and SAP updates with this command, but be careful—it can consume your precious CPU if you don't use it wisely.

The two commands that are the most useful with IPX are debug ipx routing activity and debug ipx sap activity, as shown in the router output below:

```
RouterA#debug ipx routing ?
  activity  IPX RIP routing activity
  events    IPX RIP routing events
```

Let's take a look at each command.

The *Debug IPX Routing Activity* Command

The debug ipx routing activity command shows information about IPX routing updates that are transmitted or received on the router.

```
RouterA#debug ipx routing act
IPX routing debugging is on
RouterA#
```

```
IPXRIP: update from 20.00e0.1ea9.c418
    50 in 2 hops, delay 13
    40 in 1 hops, delay 7
IPXRIP: positing full update to 10.ffff.ffff.ffff via
  Ethernet0 (broadcast)
IPXRIP: src=10.0000.0c8d.5c9d, dst=20.ffff.ffff.ffff,
  packet sent
    network 50, hops 3,  delay 14
    network 40, hops 2,  delay 8
    network 30, hops 1,  delay 2
    network 20, hops 1,  delay 2
    network 10, hops 1,  delay 2
```

You can turn this command off by using undebug all (un al, for short),
or you can type the whole command as demonstrated below:

```
RouterA#undebug ipx routing act
IPX routing debugging is off
RouterA#
```

The debug ipx routing activity command is an important one—be sure to
remember it!

The *Debug IPX SAP Activity* Command

The debug ipx sap activity command shows you the IPX SAP packets
that are transmitted and received on your router. SAPs are broadcast over
every active interface every 60 seconds, just as IPX RIP is. Each SAP packet
shows up as multiple lines in the debug output.

In the router output below, the first two lines are IPX SAPs; the other four
lines are a packet summary and service detail message.

```
RouterA#debug ipx sap activity
05:31:18: IPXSAP: positing update to 1111.ffff.ffff.ffff
  via Ethernet0 (broadcast) (full)
02:31:18: IPXSAP: Update type 0x2 len 288
  src:1111.00e0.2f5d.bf2e dest:1111.ffff.ffff.ffff(452)
02:31:18:  type 0x7, " MarketingPrint ",
  10.0000.0000.0001(451), 2 hops
```

```
02:31:18:  type 0x4, "SalesFS", 30.0000.0000.0001(451),
   2 hops
02:31:18:  type 0x4, "MarketingFS",
   30.0000.0000.0001(451), 2 hops
02:31:18:  type 0x7, "SalesFS", 50.0000.0000.0001(451),
   2 hops
```

You can turn the debug command off by using undebug all (un al, for short), or you can type the whole command as demonstrated below:

```
RouterA#undebug ipx sap activity
IPX routing debugging is off
```

The *Ping IPX* Command

By either telnetting into a remote router or using the show cdp neighbor detail or show cdp entry * commands, you can find the IPX address of a neighbor router. This will allow you to ping that address with IPX and test your internetwork.

You can ping an IPX address from a router through a regular ping or through an extended ping. The following command was run on Router C and was used to find the IPX network address for Router B.

```
RouterC#sh cdp entry *
-------------------------
Device ID: RouterB
Entry address(es):
   IP address: 172.16.40.1
   Novell address: 40.0000.0c8d.5c9d
Platform: cisco 2500,  Capabilities: Router
Interface: Serial0,  Port ID (outgoing port): Serial1
Holdtime : 155 sec
```

Now that you have the IPX address for Router B, you can ping the router. You can use the ping ipx *address* command from any router prompt, as shown below:

```
RouterC#ping ipx 40.0000.0c8d.5c9d
Sending 5, 100-byte IPX Novell Echoes to
   40.0000.0c8d.5c9d, timeout is 2 seconds:
!!!!!
```

You can also use an extended ping, which has more capabilities than a standard ping.

```
RouterC#ping
Protocol [ip]: ipx
Target IPX address: 40.0000.0c8d.5c9d
Repeat count [5]:
Datagram size [100]:
Timeout in seconds [2]:
Verbose [n]:
Novell Standard Echo [n]: y
Type escape sequence to abort.
Sending 5, 100-byte IPX Novell Echoes to
  40.0000.0c8d.5c9d, timeout is 2 seconds:
!!!!!
Success rate is 100 percent (5/5), round-trip min/avg/max
  = 4/7/12 ms
```

Summary

In this chapter, we covered the following points:

- The required IPX address and encapsulation types and the frame types that Cisco routers can use when running IPX.

- How to enable the Novell IPX protocol and configure router interfaces. We talked about and gave examples of how to configure IPX on Cisco routers and its interfaces.

- How to monitor the Novell IPX operation on the router. We covered some basic tools for monitoring IPX on your routers.

- The two parts of network addressing and these parts in specific protocol address examples.

- The IPX host address and the different parts of this address.

Exam Essentials

You must understand IPX addressing.   An Internetwork Packet Exchange (IPX) address is 10 bytes long. The network portion is 4 bytes, and the host part is 6 bytes. The network portion is made up by the network administrator. All network numbers must be the same on a network segment. An example of an IPX address is 10.*abcd.abcd.abcd*. The first number, 10, is the network number. This can be up to four bytes (eight characters hex). The last six bytes is the hardware address of the host.

Remember your Ethernet frame types.   There are four Ethernet frame types that can be configured on your router with IPX: 802.3, which is the default on an IPX interface, and is called Novell-Ether; 802.2, which is called SAP; Ethernet_II (also called ARPA); and SNAP.

Understand how to configure basic IPX.   From global configuration mode, type `ipx routing` to enable IPX. Then assign your network numbers on all your router's interfaces with the `ipx network` *number* command.

Understand how to create a secondary interface.   You can create a secondary interface to support multiple frame types on an Ethernet interface, in two ways. One is to use the `secondary` command:

```
ipx network 10a encapsulation sap secondary
```

This will add the 802.2 frame type support on the interface. You can also create a subinterface:

```
int e0.10
ipx network 10a encapsulation sap
```

This configuration accomplishes the same thing as the secondary command, but it is just done differently.

Key Terms

Be sure you're familiar with the following terms before taking the exam:

encapsulation	hop counts
frame types	socket
Get Nearest Server (GNS)	virtual circuit

Commands Used in This Chapter

The following list contains a summary of all the commands used in this chapter:

Command	Description
debug ipx	Shows the RIP and SAP information as it passes through the router.
encapsulation	Sets the frame type used on an interface.
int e0.10	Creates a subinterface.
ipx network	Assigns an IPX network number to an interface.
ipx ping	A Packet Internet Groper used to test IPX packet on an internetwork.
ipx routing	Turns on IPX routing.
secondary	Adds a second IPX network on the same physical interface.
show ipx interface	Shows the RIP and SAP information being sent and received on an individual interface. Also shows the IPX address of the interface.
show ipx route	Shows the IPX routing table.
show ipx servers	Shows the SAP table on a Cisco router.
show ipx traffic	Shows the RIP and SAP information sent and received on a Cisco router.
show protocols	Shows the routed protocols and the addresses on each interface.

Written Lab 8

Write out the answers to the following IPX-related questions.

1. Write the command that lets you view your configured routed protocols on your router.

2. Write the command to enable the IPX-routed protocol.

3. Write the command that enables IPX on individual interfaces. Configure an Ethernet 0 interface with IPX network 11, Token Ring with IPX network 15, and serial 0 with IPX network 20.

4. Write the command that lets you see the IPX routing table.

5. Write the two commands you can use to see the IPX address of an interface.

6. Write the two commands that will find your neighbor's IPX address.

7. Add the Ethernet_II frame type to an Ethernet 0 interface, but don't use a subinterface to accomplish this. Use IPX network number 11a.

8. Add the 802.2 and SNAP frame types to an Ethernet 0 interface using subinterfaces. Use 11b and 11c IPX network numbers.

9. Write the commands that you can use to verify your IPX configuration.

10. A host with a MAC address of 0c2c.3dgf.7211 is to be inserted into network 5be2. Write the complete IPX address of this host.

(The answers to Written Lab 8 can be found following the answers to the Review Questions for this chapter.)

Hands-on Labs

In this section, you will configure three 2501 routers with IPX routing. Remember, the hands-on labs printed here are included for use with real Cisco routers. If you are using the Sybex Router Fundamentals Simulator provided on this book's companion CD, please use the labs found within that software program.

There are two labs in this chapter. The first configures IPX routing with 802.3 frame types; the second lab configures multiple frame types on the same physical LAN.

Lab 8.1: Configuring Internetworking Packet Exchange (IPX)

Lab 8.2: Adding Secondary Network Addresses and Multiple Frame Types with IPX

Both labs will use Figure 8.5 to configure the network.

FIGURE 8.5 IPX lab figure

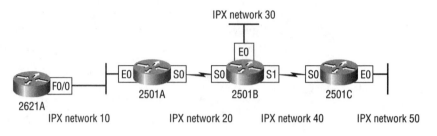

Hands-on Lab 8.1: Configuring Internetworking Packet Exchange (IPX)

1. Log in a router and go into privileged mode by typing **en** or **enable**.

2. Type **show protocol** or **sh prot** to see your routed protocols configured. Notice that this shows the routed protocol (IP) as well as the configured addresses for each interface.

3. Enable the IPX-routed protocol on your router by using the IPX `routing` command:

   ```
   2501A#config t
   2501A(config)#ipx routing
   2501A(config)#^Z
   ```

4. Check your routed protocols again to see if IPX routing is enabled by typing the commands **sh prot** or **show protocol**. Notice that IPX routing is enabled, but the interfaces don't have IPX addresses, only IP addresses.

5. Enable IPX on the individual interfaces by using the interface command `ipx network`. You can use any number, up to eight characters, hexadecimal (A through F and 0 through 9). Here is an example for Router 2501A:

   ```
   2501A#config t
   2501A(config)#int e0
   2501A(config-if)#ipx network 10
   2501A(config-if)#int s0
   2501A(config-if)#ipx network 20
   ```

6. Configure the other routers in the lab with IPX networking.

7. Test your configuration. One of the best ways to do this is with the `show ipx route` command.

8. Use the `show protocol` and `show ipx interface` commands to see the IPX addresses of an interface.

9. Once you find the IPX address of your neighbor routers, ping using the IPX protocol. (You can either go to the neighbor routers' console port, use the `show protocol` or `show ipx interface` command, or use the CDP protocol to gather the protocol information, as `sh cdp entry *`.)

10. Use the `ipx maximum-paths` command to tell a Cisco router that it is possible there is more than one link to a remote network. (The IPX protocol, by default, only looks for one route to a remote network. Once it finds a valid route, it will not consider looking for another route, even if a second route exists.)

11. Verify this command with the `show ipx route` command.

Hands-on Lab 8.2: Adding Secondary Network Addresses and Multiple Frame Types with IPX

In Lab 8.1, you added IPX routing to your routers and IPX network numbers to your interfaces. By default, Cisco routers run the 802.3 Ethernet frame type. To add a second frame type (Ethernet supports four) to your Ethernet, use the `encapsulation` command. However, you need to remember two things: You must use a different network number for each frame type and you cannot add Ethernet frame types to a serial link. Let's configure Router 2501A with a second frame type on the Ethernet LAN.

1. In Ethernet configuration mode, use the `IPX network` command with a different IPX network number and then use the `encapsulation` command. Here is an example on Router 2501A:

```
2501A#config t
2501A(config)#int e0
2501A(config-if)#ipx network 10a encapsulation ?
  arpa          Novell Ethernet_II
  hdlc          HDLC on serial links
  novell-ether  Novell Ethernet_802.3
  novell-fddi   Novell FDDI RAW
  sap           IEEE 802.2 on Ethernet, FDDI, Token Ring
  snap          IEEE 802.2 SNAP on Ethernet, Token
                  Ring, and FDDI
```

2. Notice the different options available. To use the Ethernet_II frame type, you need to use the **arpa** keyword. You can use **sec** instead of the full command **secondary**. Notice that you are adding the Ethernet_II frame type to your Ethernet LAN off of interface E0 on Router 2501A.

```
2501A(config-if)#ipx network 10a encapsulation arpa ?
secondary  Make this network a secondary network
  <cr>
2501A(config-if)#ipx network 10a encapsulation arpa
  secondary
```

3. You can also add a secondary network number and frame type by using subinterfaces. There is not a functional difference between using the **secondary** command and subinterfaces. However, using subinterfaces will possibly allow you more configuration control over using the **secondary** command. Use a subinterface command on an Ethernet network:

```
2501A#config t
2501A(config)#int e0.?
  <0-4294967295>  Ethernet interface number
2501A(config)#int e0.1500
2501A(config-subif)#ipx network 10b encap ?
  arpa          Novell Ethernet_II
  hdlc          HDLC on serial links
  novell-ether  Novell Ethernet_802.3
  novell-fddi   Novell FDDI RAW
  sap           IEEE 802.2 on Ethernet, FDDI, Token Ring
  snap          IEEE 802.2 SNAP on Ethernet, Token
                  Ring, and FDDI
2501A(config-subif)#ipx network 10b encap sap
```

4. Notice that you can create over four billion subinterfaces. In the commands above, I used a number (1500), with no particular significance. I also configured the frame type of 802.2 to run on the LAN. You do not have to use the **secondary** command when using subinterfaces.

5. There is one more frame type that can be used on Ethernet: SNAP. Create another subinterface on Ethernet 0.

```
2501A#config t
2501A(config)#int e0.?
  <0-4294967295>  Ethernet interface number
2501A(config)#int e0.1600
2501A(config-subif)#ipx network 10c encap ?
  arpa          Novell Ethernet_II
  hdlc          HDLC on serial links
  novell-ether  Novell Ethernet_802.3
  novell-fddi   Novell FDDI RAW
  sap           IEEE 802.2 on Ethernet, FDDI, Token Ring
  snap          IEEE 802.2 SNAP on Ethernet, Token
                  Ring, and FDDI
2501A(config-subif)#ipx network 10c encap snap
```

6. Verify your IPX configuration by using the show ipx route, show ipx interface, and show protocol commands.

7. For practice, configure secondary and subinterfaces on all other routers.

Review Questions

1. Which of the following provides connection-oriented transport to upper-layer protocols?

   A. RIP

   B. NLSP

   C. SPX

   D. NCP

2. You type show ipx interface fa0/0 on your router and receive the following output:

   ```
   FastEthernet0/0 is up, line protocol is up
   IPX address is 6FC2.00b0.6483.2120, NOVELL-ETHER [up]
   Delay of this IPX network, in ticks is 1 throughput 0
     link delay 0
   IPXWAN processing not enabled on this interface
   IPX SAP update interval is 60 seconds
   IPX type 20 propagation packet forwarding is disabled
   Incoming access list is not set
   Outgoing access list is not set
   ```

   What is the layer-2 address?

   A. 6FC2

   B. 6FC2.00b0

   C. 6FC2.00b0.6483

   D. 6FC2.00b0.6483.2120

   E. Novell-Ether [up]

3. How often do servers exchange RIP and SAP information unless set otherwise?

A. Every 15 seconds

B. Every 30 seconds

C. Every 60 seconds

D. Every 120 seconds

4. How can you configure a secondary subinterface on your Ethernet interface?

    A. `config t, int e0.24010`

    B. `config t, int e100.0`

    C. `config t, 24000 e0`

    D. `config t, 24000 e100`

5. Given the IPX address 71.00A0.2494.E939, which of the following is the associated IPX network and node address?

    A. Net 00a0, node 2494 E939

    B. Net 71, node 00a0.2494.e939

    C. Net 00A0.2494, node E939

    D. Net 71 00a0, node 2494.e939

6. If you bring up a new NetWare server and the Novell clients cannot see the server, what could the problem be?

    A. You need to upgrade the client software.

    B. You need to load the NetWare patches.

    C. You have a frame type mismatch.

    D. New NetWare servers do not support IPX.

7. Which of the following are valid methods of including multiple encapsulations on a single interface? (Choose all that apply.)

    A. Secondary networks

    B. Subinterfaces

    C. Additional physical interfaces

    D. There is no method for using multiple encapsulations on a single interface.

8. Which command would you use to see if you were receiving SAP and RIP information on an interface?

A. sho ipx route

B. sho ipx traffic

C. sho ipx interface

D. sho ipx servers

9. How do you see the SAP table?

A. sho ipx route

B. sho ipx traffic

C. sho ipx interface

D. sho ipx servers

10. Which commands allow you to display the IPX address assignments on a router (i.e., show the interface IPX addresses)? (Choose all that apply.)

A. sh ipx route

B. sh int

C. sh prot

D. debug ipx int

E. show ipx inter

11. You want to forward IPX packets over multiple paths. What command do you use?

A. ipx forward maximum-paths

B. ipx maximum-paths

C. ipx forward

D. ipx forward-paths

12. Which of the following are valid Cisco encapsulation names? (Choose all that apply.)

A. `arpa` = IPX Ethernet_II

B. `hdlc` = HDLC on serial links

C. `novell-ether` = IPX Ethernet_802.3

D. `novell-fddi` = IPX FDDI_Raw

E. `sap` = IEEE 802.2 on Ethernet, FDDI, and Token Ring

F. `snap` = IEEE 802.2 SNAP on Ethernet, FDDI, and Token Ring

13. Which commands, at a minimum, must be used to enable IPX networking?

   A. `ipx routing, ipx number, network 790`

   B. `ipx routing, int e0, ipx network number 980`

   C. `ipx routing, int e0, ipx network 77790 encapsulation arpa`

   D. `ipx routing, ipx encapsulation sap, int e0, network 789`

14. What is the default encapsulation on an Ethernet interface when enabling Novell?

   A. SAP

   B. 802.2

   C. SNAP

   D. Token_SNAP

   E. 802.3

   F. Ethernet_II

15. IPX addresses have two configurable parts. The network administrator specifies the IPX network number. How is the node number determined?

   A. It is set by the administrator.

   B. From a DHCP server.

   C. It is usually the MAC address of one interface.

   D. It is downloaded by the NCP protocol.

16. If you want to run the 802.2 frame type on your Ethernet interface, which encapsulation type should you choose?

A. SNAP

B. 802.2

C. Ethernet_II

D. SAP

E. Novell-Ether

17. If you want to enable the Ethernet_II frame type on your Ethernet interface, which encapsulation should you use?

A. arpa

B. rarpa

C. sap

D. rip

E. snap

F. novell-ether

18. Which of the following commands will show you the routed protocols running on your Cisco router?

A. show ipx traffic

B. show ip route

C. show protocols

D. show ipx protocols

19. Which command will show the network servers advertising on your network?

A. sh novell

B. sh ipx sap

C. sh ipx servers

D. sh servers

20. Which command will show you the IPX RIP packets being sent and received on your router?

    A. `show ip rip`

    B. `sh ipx int`

    C. `debug ipx routing activity`

    D. `debug ipx interface`

21. Which of the following is/are part of the Novell IPX Protocol suite? (Select all that apply.)

    A. NetBIOS

    B. Traceroute

    C. NCP

    D. RTMP

22. An IPX address is _____ bits in length. It consists of a _____-bit network component and a _____-bit node component.

    A. 10, 4, 6

    B. 80, 32, 48

    C. 10, 6, 4

    D. 80, 48, 32

23. Which of the following are valid IPX addresses? (Select all that apply.)

    A. `b126.00c0.3c93`

    B. `a5.00c0.3ca5.g553`

    C. `abcd88022.00d0.034c.3914`

    D. `c0ffee.0000.0000.0001`

24. Which of the following statements are *true* concerning the operation of IPX? (Select all that apply.)

    A. The use of a MAC address as part of the network layer address eliminates the need for an administrator to configure Layer-3 node addressing on end-devices.

    B. IPX cannot be used over serial links, because serial interfaces do not have MAC addresses.

    C. IPX does not require the use of an address resolution protocol.

    D. Multiple encapsulation types can be specified for an IPX network.

25. Which of the following protocols is used by an IPX client to locate servers available for user authentication?

    A. GNS

    B. SAP

    C. NCP

    D. NetBIOS

Answers to Review Questions

1. C. Sequenced Packet Exchange (SPX) works with Internetwork Packet Exchange (IPX) to make a connection-oriented service at the Transport layer.

2. D. The layer-2 address includes the Internetwork Packet Exchange (IPX) network number of 6FC2, plus the MAC address of the interface.

3. C. By default, IPX RIP and SAP are broadcast every 60 seconds by every router and server on the internetwork.

4. A. The only correct answer is the first one. The command to create a sub-interface is `int type number.number` (`int e0.10`, for example).

5. B. The IPX address is four bytes for the network and six bytes for the node address, in hex.

6. C. It is possible that the frame types on a LAN interface are not the same between the server and the clients. This would cause the clients to not see the server.

7. A, B. You can either use the `secondary` command or create subinterfaces on a LAN interface to create multiple virtual IPX networks.

8. C. The `show ipx traffic` command shows all the RIP and SAP information received on the router, but the `show ipx interface` command shows the RIP and SAP information received only on a certain interface.

9. D. `show ipx servers` lets you see if the router is hearing the server SAPs. Although `show ipx traffic` and `show ipx interface` show Service Advertising Protocol (SAP) information sent and received, they don't show from whom it is received.

10. C, E. The `show interface` command does not show you the IPX address of an interface, it only shows you the IP address. Only the `show ipx interface` and `show protocols` commands show the IPX address of the routers' interfaces.

11. B. The `ipx maximum-paths` command provides round-robin load-balancing between multiple equal-cost links.

12. A, B, C, D, E, F. Each of the answers matches to its respective Cisco keyword.

13. C. At a minimum, you must turn on IPX routing and enable one interface with an IPX network address.

14. E. The Cisco default encapsulation on an Ethernet interface is Novell-Ether (802.3).

15. C. The IPX node number is typically the MAC address of the host or router interface.

16. D. The Cisco keyword `sap` is used to enable the 802.2 frame type on Ethernet.

17. A. The Cisco keyword `arpa` is used to enable the Ethernet_II frame type on Ethernet.

18. C. The `show protocols` command shows the routed protocols and the configured interfaces and addresses of each routed protocol.

19. C. The `show ipx servers` command shows you all the IPX servers advertising SAPs on your network.

20. C. The `debug ipx routing activity` command will show you the IPX RIP packets being sent and received on your router.

21. A, C. Novell's IPX implementation includes NetBIOS and the NetWare Core Protocol (NCP). Traceroute is from the TCP/IP protocol suite. RTMP is a routing protocol used by AppleTalk and is part of the AppleTalk protocol suite.

22. B. A Novell IPX address is 80 bits (10 bytes) in length. It is built with a 32-bit (4-byte) network component and a 48-bit (6-byte) node component, expressed in hexadecimal format. The node component is generally the MAC address of the local interface.

23. D. An IPX network number can be up to 8 hexadecimal digits in length. An IPX node number (MAC address) is 12 hexadecimal digits in length. The IPX address is written in the form *nnnnnnnn.hhhh.hhhh.hhhh*.

24. A, C. The node portion of an IPX address uses the MAC address of the host's interface. Since IPX includes the MAC address within the IPX address, there's no need for an address resolution protocol's mapping of the Network layer address to the Data Link layer address. When IPX is run over a WAN serial interface, the serial interface borrows a MAC address from one of its LAN interfaces.

25. A. The Get Nearest Server (GNS) protocol is used by an IPX client to request the nearest server for end-user authentication purposes. A router or NetWare server uses information contained in SAP packets to provide the information requested in a GNS reply packet.

Answers to Written Lab 8

1. show protocol

2. config t ipx routing

3. RouterA#**config t**
   Enter configuration commands, one per line
   End with CNTL/Z
   RouterA(config)#**int e0**
   RouterA(config-if)#**ipx network 11**
   RouterA(config-if)#**int to0**
   RouterA(config-if)#**ipx network 15**
   RouterA(config-if)#**int s0**
   RouterA(config-if)#**ipx network 20**

4. show ipx route

5. show proto and show ipx int

6. sh cdp nei detail and show cdp entry *

7. RouterA#**config t**
   RouterA(config)#**int e0**
   RouterA(config-if)#**ipx network 11a encap arpa sec**

8. RouterA#**config t**
   RouterA(config)#**int e0.10**
   RouterA(config-subif)#**ipx network 11b encap sap**
   RouterA(config-subif)#**int e0.11**
   RouterA(config-subif)#**ipx network 11c encap snap**

9. sh ipx route
   sh protocol
   sh ipx int

10. 5be2.0c2c.3dgf.7211

Chapter

9

Managing Traffic with Access Lists

THE CCNA EXAM TOPICS COVERED IN THIS CHAPTER INCLUDE THE FOLLOWING:

✓ **Network Management**

- Configure standard access lists to figure IP traffic.

- Configure extended access lists to filter IP traffic.

- Monitor and verify selected access list operations on the router.

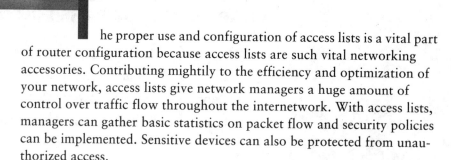

The proper use and configuration of access lists is a vital part of router configuration because access lists are such vital networking accessories. Contributing mightily to the efficiency and optimization of your network, access lists give network managers a huge amount of control over traffic flow throughout the internetwork. With access lists, managers can gather basic statistics on packet flow and security policies can be implemented. Sensitive devices can also be protected from unauthorized access.

Access lists can be used to permit or deny packets moving through the router, permit or deny Telnet (VTY) access to or from a router, and create dial-on-demand interesting traffic that triggers dialing to a remote location.

In this chapter, we'll discuss access lists for both TCP/IP and IPX, and we'll cover some of the tools available to test and monitor the functionality of applied access lists.

Access Lists

An *access list* is essentially a list of conditions that control access both to and from a network segment. Access lists can filter unwanted packets and be used to implement security policies. With the right combination of access lists, network managers arm themselves with the power to enforce nearly any access policy they can invent.

The IP and IPX access lists work similarly—they're both packet filters that packets are compared with, categorized by, and acted upon. Once the lists are built, they can be applied to either inbound or outbound traffic on any interface. Applying an access list will then cause the router to analyze every packet crossing that interface in the specified direction and take action accordingly.

There are a few important rules a packet follows when it's being compared with an access list:

- It's always compared with each line of the access list in sequential order, i.e., it'll always start with line 1, then go to line 2, then line 3, and so on.

- It's compared with lines of the access list only until a match is made. Once the packet matches a line of the access list, it's acted upon, and no further comparisons take place.

- There is an implicit "deny" at the end of each access list—this means that if a packet doesn't match up to any lines in the access list, it'll be discarded.

Each of these rules has some powerful implications when filtering IP and IPX packets with access lists.

There are two types of access lists used with IP and IPX:

Standard access lists   These use only the source IP address in an IP packet to filter the network. This basically permits or denies an entire suite of protocols. IPX standards can filter on both source and destination IPX address.

Extended access lists   These check for both source and destination IP address, protocol field in the Network layer header, and port number at the Transport layer header. IPX extended access lists use source and destination IPX addresses, Network layer protocol fields, and socket numbers in the Transport layer header.

Once you create an access list, you apply it to an interface with either an inbound or outbound list:

Inbound access lists   Packets are processed through the access list before being routed to the outbound interface.

Outbound access lists   Packets are routed to the outbound interface and then processed through the access list.

There are also some access list guidelines that should be followed when creating and implementing access lists on a router:

- You can only assign one access list per interface, per protocol, or per direction. This means that if you are creating IP access lists, you can only have one inbound access list and one outbound access list per interface.

- Organize your access lists so that the more specific tests are at the top of the access list.

- Any time a new entry is added to the access list, it will be placed at the bottom of the list.

- You cannot remove one line from an access list. If you try to do this, you will remove the entire list. It is best to copy the access list to a text editor before trying to edit the list. The only exception is when using named access lists.

- Unless your access list ends with a `permit any` command, all packets will be discarded if they do not meet any of the lists' tests. Every list should have at least one permit statement, or you might as well shut the interface down.

- Create access lists and then apply them to an interface. Any access list applied to an interface without an access list present will not filter traffic.

- Access lists are designed to filter traffic going through the router. They will not filter traffic that has originated from the router.

- Place IP standard access lists as close to the destination as possible.

- Place IP extended access lists as close to the source as possible.

Standard IP Access Lists

Standard IP access lists filter the network by using the source IP address in an IP packet. You create a *standard IP access list* by using the access-list numbers 1–99.

Below is an example of the access-list numbers that you can use to filter your network. The different protocols that you can use with access lists depend on your IOS version.

```
RouterA(config)#access-list ?
  <1-99>       IP standard access list
  <100-199>    IP extended access list
  <1000-1099>  IPX SAP access list
  <1100-1199>  Extended 48-bit MAC address access list
  <1200-1299>  IPX summary address access list
  <200-299>    Protocol type-code access list
  <300-399>    DECnet access list
```

```
<400-499>    XNS standard access list
<500-599>    XNS extended access list
<600-699>    Appletalk access list
<700-799>    48-bit MAC address access list
<800-899>    IPX standard access list
<900-999>    IPX extended access list
```

By using the access-list numbers between 1 and 99, you tell the router that you want to create a standard IP access list.

```
RouterA(config)#access-list 10 ?
  deny    Specify packets to reject
  permit  Specify packets to forward
```

After you choose the access-list number, you need to decide if you are creating a permit or deny list. For this example, you will create a deny statement:

```
RouterA(config)#access-list 10 deny ?
  Hostname or A.B.C.D  Address to match
  any                  Any source host
  host                 A single host address
```

The next step requires a more detailed explanation. There are three options available. You can use the any command to permit or deny any host or network, you can use an IP address to specify or match a specific network or IP host, or you can use the host command to specify a specific host only.

Here is an example of using the host command:

```
RouterA(config)#access-list 10 deny host 172.16.30.2
```

This tells the list to deny any packets from host 172.16.30.2. The default command is host. In other words, if you type **access-list 10 deny 172.16.30.2**, the router assumes you mean host 172.16.30.2.

However, there is another way to specify a specific host: you can use wildcards. In fact, to specify a network or a subnet, you have no option but to use wildcards in the access list.

Wildcards

Wildcards are used with access lists to specify a host, network, or part of a network. To understand a *wildcard*, you need to understand what a *block size* is; these are used to specify a range of addresses. Some of the different block sizes available are 64, 32, 16, 8, and 4.

When you need to specify a range of addresses, you choose the next-largest block size for your needs. For example, if you need to specify 34 networks, you need a block size of 64. If you want to specify 18 hosts, you need a block size of 32. If you only specify two networks, then a block size of 4 would work.

Wildcards are used with the host or network address to tell the router a range of available addresses to filter. To specify a host, the address would look like this:

172.16.30.5 0.0.0.0

The four zeros represent each octet of the address. Whenever a zero is present, it means that octet in the address must match exactly. To specify that an octet can be any value, the value of 255 is used. As an example, here is how a full subnet is specified with a wildcard:

172.16.30.0 0.0.0.255

This tells the router to match up the first three octets exactly, but the fourth octet can be any value.

Now, that was the easy part. What if you want to specify only a small range of subnets? This is where the block sizes come in. You have to specify the range of values in a block size. In other words, you can't choose to specify 20 networks. You can only specify the exact amount as the block size value. For example, the range would either have to be 16 or 32, but not 20.

Let's say that you want to block access to part of network that is in the range from 172.16.8.0 through 172.16.15.0. That is a block size of 8. Your network number would be 172.16.8.0, and the wildcard would be 0.0.7.255. Whoa! What is that? The 7.255 is what the router uses to determine the block size. The network and wildcard tell the router to start at 172.16.8.0 and go up a block size of eight addresses to network 172.16.15.0.

It is actually easier than it looks. I could certainly go through the binary math for you, but actually all you have to do is remember that the wildcard is always one number less than the block size. So, in our example, the wildcard would be 7 since our block size is 8. If you used a block size of 16, the wildcard would be 15. Easy, huh?

We'll go through some examples to help you really understand it. The following example tells the router to match the first three octets exactly but that the fourth octet can be anything.

RouterA(config)#**access-list 10 deny 172.16.10.0 0.0.0.255**

The next example tells the router to match the first two octets and that the last two octets can be any value.

```
RouterA(config)#access-list 10 deny 172.16.0.0
   0.0.255.255
```

Try to figure out this next line:

```
RouterA(config)#access-list 10 deny 172.16.16.0 0.0.3.255
```

The above configuration tells the router to start at network 172.16.16.0 and use a block size of 4. The range would then be 172.16.16.0 through 172.16.19.0.

The example below shows an access list starting at 172.16.16.0 and going up a block size of 8 to 172.16.23.0.

```
RouterA(config)#access-list 10 deny 172.16.16.0 0.0.7.255
```

The next example starts at network 172.16.32.0 and goes up a block size of 32 to 172.16.63.0.

```
RouterA(config)#access-list 10 deny 172.16.32.0
   0.0.31.255
```

The last example starts at network 172.16.64.0 and goes up a block size of 64 to 172.16.127.0.

```
RouterA(config)#access-list 10 deny 172.16.64.0
   0.0.63.255
```

Here are two more things to keep in mind when working with block sizes and wildcards:

- Each block size must start at 0. For example, you can't say that you want a block size of 8 and then start at 12. You must use 0–7, 8–15, 16–23, etc. For a block size of 32, the ranges are 0–31, 32–63, 64–95, etc.

- The command any is the same thing as writing out the wildcard 0.0.0.0 255.255.255.255.

Standard IP Access List Example

In this section, you'll learn how to use a standard IP access list to stop certain users from gaining access to the finance-department LAN.

In Figure 9.1, a router has three LAN connections and one WAN connection to the Internet. Users on the Sales LAN should not have access to the Finance LAN, but they should be able to access the Internet and the marketing department. The Marketing LAN needs to access the Finance LAN for application services.

FIGURE 9.1 IP access list example with three LANs and a WAN connection

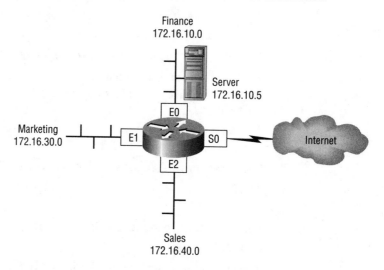

On the Acme router, the following standard IP access list is applied:

```
Acme#config t
Acme(config)#access-list 10 deny 172.16.40.0 0.0.0.255
Acme(config)#access-list 10 permit any
```

It is very important to understand that the any command is the same thing as saying this:

```
Acme(config)#access-list 10 permit 0.0.0.0
    255.255.255.255
```

At this point, the access list is denying the Sales LAN and allowing everyone else. But where should this access list be placed? If you place it as an incoming access list on E2, you might as well shut down the Ethernet interface because all of the Sales LAN devices are denied access to all networks attached to the router. The best place to put this router is the E0 interface as an outbound list.

```
Acme(config)#int e0
Acme(config-if)#ip access-group 10 out
```

This completely stops network 172.16.40.0 from getting out Ethernet 0, but it can still access the Marketing LAN and the Internet.

Real World Scenario

Should I use standard IP access lists?

Probably not.

Unless you are studying for the test and running through the labs, standard IP access lists have somewhat outlived their usefulness. In a small network or home network, they might be okay to use, but they are not flexible enough for a real-world, large production environment. Extended access lists provide many more options and flexibility when creating access lists for large networks.

Controlling VTY (Telnet) Access

You will have a difficult time trying to stop users from telnetting into a router because any active port on a router is fair game for VTY access. However, you can use a standard IP access list to control access by placing the access list on the VTY lines themselves.

To perform this function:

1. Create a standard IP access list that permits only the host or hosts you want to be able to telnet into the routers.

2. Apply the access list to the VTY line with the `access-class` command.

Here is an example of allowing only host 172.16.10.3 to telnet into a router:

```
RouterA(config)#access-list 50 permit 172.16.10.3
RouterA(config)#line vty 0 4
RouterA(config-line)#access-class 50 in
```

Because of the implied deny any at the end of the list, the access list stops any host from telnetting into the router except the host 172.16.10.3.

 Real World Scenario

Should you secure your Telnet lines on a router?

Yes, absolutely, and the `access-class` command is the best way to do this. Why? Because it doesn't use an access list that just sits on an interface looking at every packet that is coming and going. This can cause latency on the packets trying to be routed.

> By putting the `access-class` command on the VTY lines, only packets trying to telnet into the router will be looked at and compared. This provides a nice, easy-to-configure security for your router.

Extended IP Access Lists

In the standard IP access list example, notice how you had to block the whole subnet from getting to the finance department. What if you wanted them to gain access to only a certain server on the Finance LAN, but not to other network services, for obvious security reasons? With a standard IP access list, you can't allow users to get to one network service and not another. However, an *extended IP access list* allows you to do this. Extended IP access lists allow you to choose your IP source and destination address as well as the protocol and port number, which identify the upper-layer protocol or application. By using extended IP access lists, you can effectively allow users access to a physical LAN and stop them from using certain services.

Here is an example of an extended IP access list. The first command shows the access-list numbers available. You'll use the extended access list range from 100 to 199.

```
RouterA(config)#access-list ?
  <1-99>       IP standard access list
  <100-199>    IP extended access list
  <1000-1099>  IPX SAP access list
  <1100-1199>  Extended 48-bit MAC address access list
  <1200-1299>  IPX summary address access list
  <200-299>    Protocol type-code access list
  <300-399>    DECnet access list
  <400-499>    XNS standard access list
  <500-599>    XNS extended access list
  <600-699>    Appletalk access list
  <700-799>    48-bit MAC address access list
  <800-899>    IPX standard access list
  <900-999>    IPX extended access list
```

At this point, you need to decide what type of list entry you are making. For this example, you'll choose a deny list entry.

```
RouterA(config)#access-list 110 ?
  deny     Specify packet
```

```
dynamic   Specify a DYNAMIC list of PERMITs or DENYs
permit    Specify packets to forward
```

Once you choose the access list type, you must choose a Network layer protocol field entry. It is important to understand that if you want to filter the network by Application layer, you must choose an entry here that allows you to go up through the OSI model. For example, to filter by Telnet or FTP, you must choose TCP here. If you were to choose IP, you would never leave the Network layer, and you would not be allowed to filter by upper-layer applications.

```
RouterA(config)#access-list 110 deny ?
  <0-255>  An IP protocol number
  eigrp    Cisco's EIGRP routing protocol
  gre      Cisco's GRE tunneling
  icmp     Internet Control Message Protocol
  igmp     Internet Gateway Message Protocol
  igrp     Cisco's IGRP routing protocol
  ip       Any Internet Protocol
  ipinip   IP in IP tunneling
  nos      KA9Q NOS compatible IP over IP tunneling
  ospf     OSPF routing protocol
  tcp      Transmission Control Protocol
  udp      User Datagram Protocol
```

Once you choose to go up to the Application layer through TCP, you will be prompted for the source IP address of the host or network. You can choose the any command to allow any source address.

```
RouterA(config)#access-list 110 deny tcp ?
  A.B.C.D  Source address
  any      Any source host
  host     A single source host
```

After the source address is selected, the destination address is chosen.

```
RouterA(config)#access-list 110 deny tcp any ?
  A.B.C.D  Destination address
  any      Any destination host
  eq       Match only packets on a given port number
  gt       Match only packets with a greater port number
  host     A single destination host
```

```
lt       Match only packets with a lower port number
neq      Match only packets not on a given port number
range    Match only packets in the range of port numbers
```

In the example below, any source IP address that has a destination IP address of 172.16.30.2 has been denied.

```
RouterA(config)#access-list 110 deny tcp any host
    172.16.30.2 ?
    eq          Match only packets on a given port number
    established Match established connections
    fragments   Check fragments
    gt          Match only packets with a greater port
                number
    log         Log matches against this entry
    log-input   Log matches against this entry,including
                inputinterface
    lt          Match only packets with a lower port
                number
    neq         Match only packets not on a given port
                number
    precedence  Match packets with given precedence value
    range       Match only packets in the range of port
                numbers
    tos         Match packets with given TOS value
    <cr>
```

Now, you can press Enter here and leave the access list as is. However, you can be even more specific: once you have the host addresses in place, you can specify the type of service you are denying. The following help screen gives you the options. You can choose a port number or use the application or even the program name.

```
RouterA(config)#access-list 110 deny tcp any host
    172.16.30.2 eq ?
    <0-65535>   Port number
    bgp         Border Gateway Protocol (179)
    chargen     Character generator (19)
    cmd         Remote commands (rcmd, 514)
    daytime     Daytime (13)
```

discard	Discard (9)
domain	Domain Name Service (53)
echo	Echo (7)
exec	Exec (rsh, 512)
finger	Finger (79)
ftp	File Transfer Protocol (21)
ftp-data	FTP data connections (20, 21)
gopher	Gopher (70)
hostname	NIC hostname server (101)
ident	Ident Protocol (113)
irc	Internet Relay Chat (194)
klogin	Kerberos login (543)
kshell	Kerberos shell (544)
login	Login (rlogin, 513)
lpd	Printer service (515)
nntp	Network News Transport Protocol (119)
pim-auto-RP	PIM Auto-RP
pop2	Post Office Protocol v2 (109)
pop3	Post Office Protocol v3 (110)
smtp	Simple Mail Transport Protocol (25)
sunrpc	Sun Remote Procedure Call (111)
syslog	Syslog (514)
tacacs	TAC Access Control System (49)
talk	Talk (517)
telnet	Telnet (23)
time	Time (37)
uucp	Unix-to-Unix Copy Program (540)
whois	Nicname (43)
www	World Wide Web (HTTP, 80)

At this point, let's block Telnet (port 23) to host 172.16.30.2 only. If the users want to FTP, that is allowed. The log command is used to send messages to the console every time the access list is hit. This would not be a good thing to do in a busy environment, but it is great when used in a class or in a home network.

```
RouterA(config)#access-list 110 deny tcp any host
    172.16.30.2 eq 23 log
```

You need to keep in mind that the next line is an implicit deny any by default. If you apply this access list to an interface, you might as well just shut the interface down, since by default there is an implicit deny all at the end of every access list. You must follow up the access list with the following command:

```
RouterA(config)#access-list 110 permit ip any any
```

Remember, the 0.0.0.0 255.255.255.255 is the same command as any, so the command could look like this:

```
RouterA(config)#access-list 110 permit ip 0.0.0.0
    255.255.255.255 0.0.0.0 255.255.255.255
```

Once the access list is created, you need to apply it to an interface. It is the same command as the IP standard list:

```
RouterA(config-if)#ip access-group 110 in
```

or

```
RouterA(config-if)#ip access-group 110 out
```

Extended IP Access List Example

Using Figure 9.1 from the IP standard access list example again, let's use the same network and deny access to a server on the finance-department LAN for both Telnet and FTP services on server 172.16.10.5. All other services on the LAN are acceptable for the sales and marketing departments to access.

The following access list should be created:

```
Acme#config t
Acme(config)#access-list 110 deny tcp any host
    172.16.10.5 eq 21
Acme(config)#access-list 110 deny tcp any host
    172.16.10.5 eq 23
Acme(config)#access-list 110 permit ip any any
```

The access-list 110 tells the router you are creating an extended IP Access list. The tcp is the protocol field in the Network layer header. If the list doesn't say tcp here, you cannot filter by port numbers 21 and 23 as shown in the example. (These are FTP and Telnet, and they both use TCP for connection-oriented services.) The any command is the source, which means any IP address, and the host is the destination IP address.

It is important to understand why the deny commands were placed first in the list. If you had configured the permits first and the deny commands second, the Finance LAN would have not been able to go to any other LAN or to the Internet because of the implicit deny at the end of the list. It would be difficult to configure the list any other way than the preceding example.

After the lists are created, they need to be applied to the Ethernet 0 port. This is because the other three interfaces on the router need access to the LAN. However, if this list were created to only block Sales, then we would have wanted to put this list closest to the source, or on Ethernet interface 2.

```
Acme(config-if)#ip access-group 110 out
```

Monitoring IP Access Lists

It is important to be able to verify the configuration on a router. The following commands can be used to verify the configuration:

Command	Effect
show access-list	Displays all access lists and their parameters configured on the router. This command does not show you which interface the list is set on.
show access-list 110	Shows only the parameters for the access list 110. This command does not show you the interface the list is set on.
show ip access-list	Shows only the IP access lists configured on the router.
show ip interface	Shows which interfaces have access lists set.
show running-config	Shows the access lists and which interfaces have access lists set.

IPX Access Lists

IPX access lists are configured the same way as any other list. You use the access-list command to create your access list of packet tests and then apply the list to an interface with the access-group command.

I will discuss the following IPX access lists:

IPX standard   These access lists filter on IPX source and destination host or network number. They use the access-list numbers 800–899. IPX standard access lists are similar to IP standard access lists, except that IP standards only filter on source IP addresses, whereas IPX standards filter on both source and destination IPX addresses.

IPX extended   These access lists filter on IPX source and destination host or network number, IPX protocol field in the Network layer header, and socket number in the Transport layer header. They use the access-list numbers 900–999.

IPX SAP filter   These filters are used to control SAP traffic on LANs and WANs. IPX SAP filters use the access-list numbers 1000–1099. Network administrators can set up IPX access lists to control the amount of IPX traffic, including IPX SAPs across slow WAN links.

Standard IPX Access Lists

Standard IPX access lists use the source or destination IPX host or network address to filter the network. This is configured much the same way IP standard access lists are. The parameter to configure a *standard IPX access list* is

access-list {*number*} {permit|deny} {*source_address*}
    {*destination_address*}

Wildcards can be used for the source and destination IPX addresses; however, the wildcard is –1, which means it is equal to any host and network.

Figure 9.2 shows an example of an IPX network and how IPX standard access lists can be configured.

FIGURE 9.2   IPX access list example

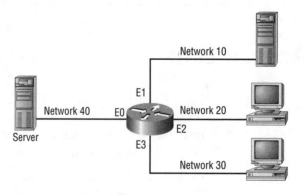

The following configuration is used with Figure 9.2. Interface Ethernet 0 is on Network 40; interface Ethernet 1 is on Network 10; interface Ethernet 2 is on Network 20; interface Ethernet 3 is on Network 30.

The access list is configured and applied as shown. This IPX access list permits packets generated from IPX Network 20 out interface Ethernet 0 to Network 40.

```
Router(config)#access-list 810 permit 20 40
Router(config)#int e0
Router(config-if)#ipx access-group 810 out
```

Think about what this configuration accomplishes. First and most obvious, any IPX devices on IPX Network 20 off interface Ethernet 2 can communicate to the server on Network 40, which is connected to interface Ethernet 0. However, notice what else this configuration accomplishes with only one line (remember that there is an implicit deny all at the end of the list):

- Hosts on Network 10 cannot communicate to the server on Network 40.

- Hosts on Network 40 can get to Network 10, but the packets cannot get back.

- Hosts on Network 30 can communicate to Network 10, and Network 10 can communicate to Network 30.

- Hosts on Network 30 cannot communicate to the server on Network 40.

- Hosts on Network 40 can get to hosts on Network 30, but the packets can't come back from Network 30 in response.

- Hosts on Network 20 can communicate to all devices in the internetwork.

Extended IPX Access Lists

An *extended IPX access list* can filter based on any of the following:

- Source network/node

- Destination network/node

- IPX protocol (SAP, SPX, etc.)

- IPX socket

These are access lists in the range of 900–999 and are configured just like standard access lists, with the addition of protocol and socket information. Let's take a look at a template for building lines in an IPX extended access list.

```
access-list {number} {permit|deny} {protocol} {source}
  {socket} {destination} {socket}
```

Again, when you move from standard to extended access lists, you're simply adding the ability to filter based on protocol and socket (port for IP).

IPX SAP Filters

IPX SAP filters are implemented using the same tools we've been discussing all along in this chapter. They have an important place in controlling IPX SAP traffic. Why is this important? Because if you can control the SAPs, you can control the access to IPX devices. IPX SAP filters use access lists in the 1000–1099 range. IPX SAP filters should be placed as close as possible to the source of the SAP broadcasts; this is to stop unwanted SAP traffic from crossing a network because it will only be discarded.

Two types of access list filters control SAP traffic:

IPX input SAP filter This is used to stop certain SAP entries from entering a router and updating the SAP table.

IPX output SAP filter This stops certain SAP updates from being sent in the regular 60-second SAP updates.

Here's the template for each line of an IPX SAP filter:

```
access-list {number} {permit|deny} {source}
  {service type}
```

Here is an example of an IPX SAP filter that allows service type 4 (file services) from a NetWare service named Sales.

```
Router(config)#access-list 1010 permit ?
  -1          Any IPX net
  <0-FFFFFFFF>  Source net
  N.H.H.H        Source net.host address
Router(config)#access-list 1010 permit -1 ?
  <0-FFFF>  Service type-code (0 matches all services)
  N.H.H.H    Source net.host mask
  <cr>
```

```
Router(config)#access-list 1010 permit -1 4 ?
  WORD  A SAP server name
  <cr>
Router(config)#access-list 1010 permit -1 4 Sales
```

The −1 in the access list is a wildcard that says any node, any network. After the list is created, apply it to an interface with either of the two following commands:

```
RouterA(config-if)#ipx input-sap-filter 1010
```

or

```
RouterA(config-if)#ipx output-sap-filter 1010
```

The `input-sap-filter` is used to stop SAP entries from being added to the SAP table on the router, and `output-sap-filter` is used to stop SAP entries from being propagated out of the router.

Verifying IPX Access Lists

To verify the IPX access lists and their placement on a router, use the commands `show ipx interface` and `show ipx access-list`.

Notice in the output of the `show ipx interface` command that the IPX address is shown, the outgoing access list is set with list 810, and the SAP input filter is 1010.

```
Router#sh ipx int
Ethernet0 is up, line protocol is up
  IPX address is 10.0060.7015.63d6, NOVELL-ETHER [up]
  Delay of this IPX network, in ticks is 1 throughput 0
  link delay 0
  IPXWAN processing not enabled on this interface.
  IPX SAP update interval is 1 minute(s)
  IPX type 20 propagation packet forwarding is disabled
  Incoming access list is not set
  Outgoing access list is 810
  IPX helper access list is not set
  SAP GNS processing enabled, delay 0 ms, output filter
  list is not set
  SAP Input filter list is 1010
```

```
SAP Output filter list is not set
SAP Router filter list is not set
Input filter list is not set
Output filter list is not set
Router filter list is not set
Netbios Input host access list is not set
Netbios Input bytes access list is not set
Netbios Output host access list is not set
Netbios Output bytes access list is not set
Updates each 60 seconds, aging multiples RIP: 3 SAP: 3
SAP interpacket delay is 55 ms, maximum size is 480 bytes
RIP interpacket delay is 55 ms, maximum size is 432 bytes
--More-
```

The show ipx access-list shows the two IPX lists set on the router.

```
Router#sh ipx access-list
IPX access list 810
    permit FFFFFFFF 30
IPX SAP access list 1010
    permit FFFFFFFF 4 Sales
Router#
```

The Fs are hexadecimal and are the same as all 1s or permit any. Since you used the –1 in the IPX commands, the running-config shows them as all Fs.

Summary

In this chapter, we covered the following points:

- How to configure standard access lists to filter IP traffic. You learned what a standard access list is and how to apply it to a Cisco router to add security to your network.

- How to configure extended access lists to filter IP traffic. You learned the difference between a standard and an extended access list and how to apply these lists to Cisco routers.

- How to configure IPX access lists and SAP filters to control basic Novell traffic. You learned the difference between a standard and extended IPX access list and how to apply the lists to a Cisco router.

- How to monitor and verify selected access list operations on the router. We went over some basic monitoring commands to verify and test IP and IPX access lists.

Exam Essentials

Remember the standard and extended IP access-list number ranges. The numbered range you can use to configure a standard IP access list is 1–99. The numbered range for an extended IP access list is 100–199.

Understand the term "implicit deny."   At the end of every access list is an implicit deny. What this means is that if a packet does not match any of the lines in the access list, then it will be discarded. Also, if you have nothing but denys in your list, then the list will pass no packets.

Understand the standard IP access list configuration command.   To configure a standard IP access list, use the access-list numbers 1–99 in global configuration mode. Choose permit or deny, then choose the source IP address you want to filter on.

Understand the extended IP access list configuration command.   To configure an extended IP access list, use the access-list numbers 100–199 in global configuration mode. Choose permit or deny, the Network layer protocol, the source IP address you want to filter on, the destination address you want to filer on, and finally the Transport layer protocol.

Remember the command to verify an access list on an interface.   To see whether an access list is set on an interface and in which direction it is filtering, use the show ip interface command.

Remember the command to verify the access lists configuration.   To see the *configured* access lists on your router, use the show access-list command. This command will not show you which interfaces have an access list set.

Key Terms

Before you take the exam, be sure you're familiar with the following terms:

access list	standard IP access list
block size	standard IPX access list
extended IP access list	wildcard
extended IPX access list	

Commands Used in This Chapter

The following list contains a summary of all the commands used in this chapter:

Command	Description
`0.0.0.0 255.255.255.255`	A wildcard command; same as the **any** command
`access-class`	Applies a standard IP access list to a VTY line
`access-list`	Creates a list of tests to filter the networks
`any`	Specifies any host or any network; same as the `0.0.0.0 255.255.255.255` command
`host`	Specifies a single host address
`ip access-group`	Applies an IP access list to an interface
`ipx access-group`	Applies an IPX access list to an interface
`ipx input-sap-filter`	Applies an inbound IPX SAP filter to an interface
`ipx output-sap-filter`	Applies an outbound IPX SAP filter to an interface
`show access-list`	Shows all the access lists configured on the router

Command	Description
`show access-list 110`	Shows only access list 110
`show ip access-list`	Shows only the IP access lists
`show ip interface`	Shows which interfaces have IP access lists applied
`show ipx access-list`	Shows the IPX access lists configured on a router
`show ipx interface`	Shows which interfaces have IPX access lists applied

Written Lab 9

In this section, write the answers to the following questions:

1. Configure a standard IP access list to prevent all machines on network 172.16.0.0 from accessing your Ethernet network.

2. Apply the access list to your Ethernet interface.

3. Create an access list that denies host 196.22.15.5 access to your Ethernet network.

4. Write the command to verify that you've entered the access list correctly.

5. Write the two commands that verify the access list was properly applied to the Ethernet interface.

6. Create an extended access list that stops host 172.16.10.1 on Ethernet 0 from telnetting to host 172.16.30.5 on Ethernet 1.

7. Apply the access list to the correct interface.

8. Configure an IPX SAP access list that prevents any file service SAP messages other than those from IPX address 45.0000.0000.0001 from leaving the Ethernet 0 network.

9. Apply the IPX SAP access list to the Ethernet interface.

(The answers to Written Lab 9 can be found following the answers to the Review Questions for this chapter.)

Hands-on Labs

In this section, you will complete three labs. To complete these labs, you will need at least three 2500 series routers. If you are using the Sybex Router Fundamentals Simulator provided on this book's companion CD, please use the hands-on labs found within that software program.

Lab 9.1: Standard IP Access Lists

Lab 9.2: Extended IP Access Lists

Lab 9.3: Standard IPX Access Lists

All of the labs will use Figure 9.3 for configuring the routers.

FIGURE 9.3 Access list lab figure

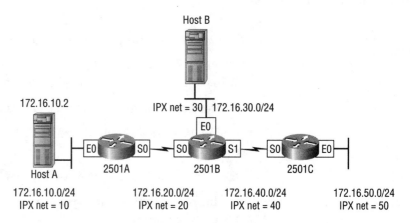

Hands-on Lab 9.1: Standard IP Access Lists

In this lab, you will allow only Host B from network 172.16.30.0 to enter network 172.16.10.0.

1. Go to 2501A and enter global configuration mode by typing **config t**.

2. From global configuration mode, type **access-list ?** to get a list of all the different access lists available.

3. Choose an access-list number that will allow you to create an IP standard access list. This is a number between 1 and 99.

4. Choose to permit host 172.16.30.2 which is Host B's address:

```
2501A(config)#access-list 10 permit 172.16.30.2 ?
  A.B.C.D  Wildcard bits
  <cr>
```

To specify only host 172.16.30.2, use the wildcards 0.0.0.0:

```
RouterA(config)#access-list 10 permit 172.16.30.2
  0.0.0.0
```

5. Now that the access list is created, you must apply it to an interface to make it work:

```
2501A(config)#int e0
2501A(config-if)#ip access-group 10 out
```

6. Verify your access lists with the following commands:

```
RouterA#sh access-list
Standard IP access list 10
    permit 172.16.30.2
RouterA#sh run
[output cut]
interface Ethernet0
 ip address 172.16.10.1 255.255.255.0
 ip access-group 10 out
 ipx network 10A
```

7. Test your access list by pinging from Host B (172.16.30.2) to Host A (172.16.10.2).

8. Ping from 2501B and 2501C to Host A (172.16.10.2); this should fail if your access list is correct.

Hands-on Lab 9.2: Extended IP Access Lists

In this lab, you will use an extended IP access list to stop host 172.16.10.2 from creating a Telnet session to router 2501B (172.16.20.2). However, the host still should be able to ping the 2501B router. IP extended lists should be placed closest to the source, so add the extended list on router 2501A.

1. Remove any access lists on 2501A and add an extended list to 2501A.

2. Choose a number to create an extended IP list. The IP extended lists use 100–199.

3. Use a deny statement (you'll add a permit statement in step 7 to allow other traffic to still work).

```
2501A(config)#access-list 110 deny ?
  <0-255>  An IP protocol number
  ahp      Authentication Header Protocol
  eigrp    Cisco's EIGRP routing protocol
  esp      Encapsulation Security Payload
  gre      Cisco's GRE tunneling
  icmp     Internet Control Message Protocol
  igmp     Internet Gateway Message Protocol
  igrp     Cisco's IGRP routing protocol
  ip       Any Internet Protocol
  ipinip   IP in IP tunneling
  nos      KA9Q NOS compatible IP over IP tunneling
  ospf     OSPF routing protocol
  pcp      Payload Compression Protocol
  tcp      Transmission Control Protocol
  udp      User Datagram Protocol
```

4. Since you are going to deny Telnet, you must choose TCP as a Transport layer protocol:

```
2501A(config)#access-list 110 deny tcp ?
  A.B.C.D  Source address
  any      Any source host
  host     A single source host
```

5. Add the source IP address you want to filter on, then add the destination host IP address. Use the host command instead of wildcard bits.

```
2501A(config)#access-list 110 deny tcp host
172.16.10.2 host 172.16.20.2 ?
  ack          Match on the ACK bit
  eq           Match only packets on a given port
               number
  established  Match established connections
  fin          Match on the FIN bit
  fragments    Check fragments
```

gt	Match only packets with a greater port number
log	Log matches against this entry
log-input	Log matches against this entry, including input interface
lt	Match only packets with a lower port number
neq	Match only packets not on a given port number
precedence	Match packets with given precedence value
psh	Match on the PSH bit
range	Match only packets in the range of port numbers
rst	Match on the RST bit
syn	Match on the SYN bit
tos	Match packets with given TOS value
urg	Match on the URG bit
<cr>	

6. At this point, you can add the eq telnet command. The log command can also be used at the end of the command so that whenever the access-list line is hit, a log will be generated on the console.

```
2501A(config)#access-list 110 deny tcp host
   172.16.10.2 host 172.16.20.2 eq telnet log
```

7. It is important to add this line next to create a permit statement.

```
2501A(config)#access-list 110 permit ip any 0.0.0.0
   255.255.255.255
```

8. You must create a permit statement; if you just add a deny statement, nothing will be permitted at all. Please see the sections earlier in this chapter for more detailed information on the permit command.

9. Apply the access list to the Ethernet 0 on 2501A to stop the Telnet traffic as soon as it hits the first router interface.

```
2501A(config)#int e0
2501A(config-if)#ip access-group 110 in
2501A(config-if)#^Z
```

10. Try telnetting from host 172.16.10.2 to 2501A using the destination IP address of 172.16.20.2. The following messages should be generated on 2501A's console. However, the ping command should work.

```
From host 172.16.10.2: >telnet 172.16.20.2
```

On 2501A's console, this should appear as follows:

```
01:11:48: %SEC-6-IPACCESSLOGP: list 110 denied tcp
    172.16.10.2(1030) -> 172.16.20.2(23), 1 packet
01:13:04: %SEC-6-IPACCESSLOGP: list 110 denied tcp
    172.16.10.2(1030) -> 172.16.20.2(23), 3 packets
```

Hands-on Lab 9.3: Standard IPX Access Lists

In this lab, you will configure IPX to allow only IPX traffic from IPX Network 30 and not from IPX Network 50.

1. Remove any existing access lists on the 2501A router. Because this is an IPX standard access list, the filtering can be placed anywhere on the network since it can filter based on IPX source and destination IP addresses.

2. Verify that you have the IPX network working as shown in Figure 9.3. Use the show ipx route command to see all networks on your routers.

3. Configure an access list on 2501A to allow only IPX traffic from Network 30 and to deny IPX Network 50. IPX standard lists use the access-list numbers 800–899.

```
2501A#config t
RouterC(config)#access-list 810 ?
  deny     Specify packets to reject
  permit   Specify packets to permit
```

4. First, deny IPX Network 50, then permit everything else. The −1 is a wildcard in IPX.

```
2501A(config)#access-list 810 deny ?
  -1           Any IPX net
  <0-FFFFFFFF> Source net
  N.H.H.H      Source net.host address
```

5. Choose Network 50 as a source address:

```
2501A(config)#access-list 810 deny 50
  -1              Any IPX net
  <0-FFFFFFFF>    Destination net
  N.H.H.H         Destination net.host address
  <cr>
```

6. Choose Network 10 as the destination network:

```
2501A(config)#access-list 810 deny 50 10
```

7. Permit everything else with an IPX wildcard:

```
2501A(config)#access-list 810 permit -1 -1
```

8. Apply the list to the serial interface of 2501A to stop the packets as they reach the router:

```
2501A(config)#int s0
2501A(config-if)#ipx access-group 810 in
2501A(config-if)#^Z
```

9. Verify the list by looking at the IPX routing table. Network 50 should not be in the 2501A IPX routing table. Also, use the show access-list and show ipx access-list commands to vary the list.

Review Questions

1. Which of the following is an example of a standard IP access list?

   A. `access-list 110 permit host 1.1.1.1`

   B. `access-list 1 deny 172.16.10.1 0.0.0.0`

   C. `access-list 1 permit 172.16.10.1 255.255.0.0`

   D. `access-list standard 1.1.1.1`

2. Extended IP access lists use which of the following as a basis for permitting or denying packets?

   A. Source address

   B. Destination address

   C. Protocol

   D. Port

   E. All of the above

3. To specify all hosts in the Class B IP network 172.16.0.0, which wild-card access-list mask would you use?

   A. 255.255.0.0

   B. 255.255.255.0

   C. 0.0.255.255

   D. 0.255.255.255

   E. 0.0.0.255

4. Which of the following are valid ways to refer only to host 172.16.30.55 in an IP access list? Select all that apply.

   A. `172.16.30.55 0.0.0.255`

   B. `172.16.30.55 0.0.0.0`

   C. `any 172.16.30.55`

   D. `host 172.16.30.55`

   E. `0.0.0.0 172.16.30.55`

   F. `ip any 172.16.30.55`

5. Which of the following access lists will allow only WWW traffic into network 196.15.7.0? Select all that apply.

A. `access-list 100 permit tcp any 196.15.7.0 0.0.0.255 eq www`

B. `access-list 10 deny tcp any 196.15.7.0 eq www`

C. `access-list 100 permit 196.15.7.0 0.0.0.255 eq www`

D. `access-list 110 permit ip any 196.15.7.0 0.0.0.255`

E. `access-list 110 permit www 196.15.7.0 0.0.0.255`

6. What router command allows you to determine whether an IP access list is enabled on a particular interface?

A. `show ip port`

B. `show access-list`

C. `show ip interface`

D. `show access-list interface`

7. Which router command allows you to view the entire contents of all access lists?

A. `Router#show interface`

B. `Router>show ip interface`

C. `Router#show access-lists`

D. `Router>show all access-lists`

8. If you wanted to deny all Telnet connections to network 192.168.10.0, which command could you use?

A. `access-list 100 deny tcp 192.168.10.0 255.255.255.0 eq telnet`

B. `access-list 100 deny tcp 192.168.10.0 255.255.255.0 eq telnet`

C. `access-list 100 deny tcp any 192.168.10.0 0.0.0.255 eq 23`

D. `access-list 100 deny 192.168.10.0 0.0.0.255 any eq 23`

9. If you wanted to deny FTP access from network 200.200.10.0 to network 200.199.11.0, but allow everything else, which of the following command strings is valid?

   A. `access-list 110 deny 200.200.10.0 to network`
   `200.199.11.0 eq ftp`
   `access-list 111 permit ip any 0.0.0.0 255.255.255.255`

   B. `access-list 1 deny ftp 200.200.10.0 200.199.11.0 any any`

   C. `access-list 100 deny tcp 200.200.10.0 0.0.0.255`
   `200.199.11.0 0.0.0.255 eq ftp`

   D. `access-list 198 deny tcp 200.200.10.0 0.0.0.255`
   `200.199.11.0 0.0.0.255 eq ftp`
   `access-list 198 permit ip any 0.0.0.0 255.255.255.255`

10. Which of the following commands will apply IPX SAP access list 1050 for incoming traffic, assuming you're already at interface configuration?

   A. `ipx access-group 1050 in`

   B. `ipx input-sap-filter 1050`

   C. `ipx access-list 1050 in`

   D. `ipx input-sap-filter 1050 in`

   E. `ipx access-group 1050`

11. Which of the following commands will show extended access list 187? Select all that apply.

   A. `sh ip int`

   B. `sh ip access-list`

   C. `sh access-list 187`

   D. `sh access-list 187 extended`

12. What is the extended IP access list range?

   A. 1–99

   B. 200–299

   C. 1000–1999

   D. 100–199

13. Which of the following commands is valid for creating an extended IP access list?

    A. `access-list 101 permit ip host 172.16.30.0 any eq 21`

    B. `access-list 101 permit tcp host 172.16.30.0 any eq 21 log`

    C. `access-list 101 permit icmp  host 172.16.30.0 any ftp log`

    D. `access-list 101 permit ip any eq 172.16.30.0 21 log`

14. What is the extended IPX access-list range?

    A. 100–199

    B. 900–999

    C. 1000–1999

    D. 700–799

15. Which command would you use to apply an access list to a router interface?

    A. `ip access-list 101 out`

    B. `access-list ip 101 in`

    C. `ip access-group 101 in`

    D. `access-group ip 101 in`

16. Which command is used to display the placement and direction of an IP access control list on a router?

    A. `sh int`

    B. `sh ip interface`

    C. `sh run`

    D. `sh access-list`

17. Which of the following commands should follow this command: `access-list 110 deny tcp any any eq ftp`?

A. access-list 110 deny ip any any

B. access-list 110 permit tcp any any

C. access-list 110 permit ip any

D. access-list 110 permit ip any 0.0.0.0 255.255.255.255

18. Which access configuration allows only traffic from network 172.16.0.0 to enter interface s0?

A. access-list 10 permit 172.16.0.0 0.0.255.255
int s0
ip access-list 10 in

B. access-group 10 permit 172.16.0.0 0.0.255.255
int s0
ip access-list 10 out

C. access-list 10 permit 172.16.0.0 0.0.255.255
int s0
ip access-group 10 in

D. access-list 10 permit 172.16.0.0 0.0.255.255
int s0
ip access-group 10 out

19. Which of the following commands connect access list 110 inbound to interface ethernet0?

A. Router(config)#**ip access-group 110 in**

B. Router(config)#**ip access-list 110 in**

C. Router(config-if)#**ip access-group 110 in**

D. Router(config-if)#**ip access-list 110 in**

20. What command will permit SMTP mail to only host 1.1.1.1?

A. access-list 10 permit smtp host 1.1.1.1

B. access-list 110 permit ip smtp host 1.1.1.1

C. access-list 10 permit tcp any host 1.1.1.1 eq smtp

D. access-list 110 permit tcp any host 1.1.1.1. eq smtp

21. If you configure the following access list:

```
access-list 110 deny 10.1.1.128 0.0.0.63 eq smtp
access-list 110 deny any any eq 23
int ethernet 0
ip access-group 110 out
```

What will the result of this access list be?

A. E-mail and Telnet will be allowed out E0.

B. E-mail and Telnet will be allowed in E0.

C. Everything but e-mail and Telnet will be allowed out E0.

D. No IP traffic will be allowed out E0.

22. Which of the following series of commands will restrict Telnet access to the router?

A. RouterA(config)#**access-list 10 permit 172.16.1.1**
RouterA(config)#**line con 0**
RouterA(config-line)#**ip access-group 10 in**

B. RouterA(config)#**access-list 10 permit 172.16.1.1**
RouterA(config)#**line vty 0 4**
RouterA(config-line)#**access-class 10 out**

C. RouterA(config)#**access-list 10 permit 172.16.1.1**
RouterA(config)#**line vty 0 4**
RouterA(config-line)#**access-class 10 in**

D. RouterA(config)#**access-list 10 permit 172.16.1.1**
RouterA(config)#**line vty 0 4**
RouterA(config-line)#**ip access-group 10 in**

23. While reviewing your running configuration, you notice an access-list line that reads access-list 10 deny 192.168.5.19. The wildcard mask field is notably absent. How is this access-list line interpreted by the router?

A. A wildcard mask of 0.0.0.0 is assumed.

B. A wildcard mask of 255.255.255.0 is assumed.

C. A wildcard mask of 0.0.0.255 is used as the default for a Class C address.

D. A wildcard mask of 255.255.255.255 is assumed.

24. You are working on a router that has established privilege levels that restrict access to certain functions. You discover that you are not able to execute the command show running-configuration. How can you view and confirm the access lists that have been applied to the Ethernet 0 interface on your router?

A. show access-lists

B. show interface Ethernet 0

C. show ip access-lists

D. show ip interface Ethernet 0

25. What happens when an access list is applied to an interface when the keywords in or out have *not* been included in the command syntax?

A. The access list will not be applied to the interface.

B. The access list will be applied inbound by default.

C. The access list will be applied outbound by default.

D. The access list will be applied inbound and outbound.

Answers to Review Questions

1. B.   Standard IP access lists use the numbers 1–99 and filter based on source IP address only.

2. E.   IP extended lists use source and destination IP addresses, Network layer protocol files, and port fields in the Transport layer header.

3. C.   The mask 0.0.255.255 tells the router to match the first two octets and that the last two octets can be any value.

4. B, D.   The wildcard 0.0.0.0 tells the router to match all four octets. The wildcard command can be replaced with the host command.

5. A.   The first thing to check in a question like this is the access-list number. Right away, you can see that the second option is wrong because it is using a standard IP access-list number. The second thing to check is the protocol. If you are filtering by upper-layer protocol, then you must be using either UDP or TCP; this eliminates the fourth option. The second and last answers have the wrong syntax.

6. C.   Only the `show ip interface` command will tell you which ports have access lists applied. `show access-lists` will not show you which interfaces have an access list applied.

7. C.   The `show access-lists` command will allow you to view the entire contents of all access lists, but will not show you to which interfaces the access lists are applied.

8. C.   The extended access list range is 100–199, so the access-list number of 100 is valid. Telnet uses TCP, so the protocol TCP is valid. Now, you just need to look for the source and destination address. Only the third option has the correct sequence of commands.

9. D.   Extended IP access lists use numbers from 100–199 and filter based on source and destination IP address, protocol number, and port number. The command 0.0.0.0 255.255.255.255 is the same as the any command. The reason the last option is correct is because of the second line that "permits IP any any;" the third answer does not.

10. B.   You don't add the `in` or `out` parameters at the end of the list with SAP access lists.

11. B, C. You can see the access lists with the `show ip access-list` command or the `show access-list #` command.

12. D. Extended IP access lists use the range from 100 to 199.

13. B. Remember to first look for the access-list numbers. Since all of the access lists are using 101, they are all set for IP extended access lists. The second thing to look for is the protocol. Only one list is using TCP, which is needed to access the FTP protocol.

14. B. Standard IPX uses the range 800–899, and extended IPX lists use the range 900–999.

15. C. To apply an access list, the proper command is: `ip access-group 101 in`.

16. B. The command `show ip interface` will show you whether an access list is set on an interface and in which direction it is filtering.

17. D. The `access-list 110 permit ip any any` command is used to specify and permit all traffic. The `0.0.0.0 255.255.255.255` command is the same as the `any` command.

18. C. This is a standard IP access list that only filters on source IP addresses. The number range for IP access list is 1–99. The command to place an IP access list on an interface is `ip access-group`. Since the question specified incoming traffic, only the third option works.

19. C. To place an access list on an interface use the `ip access-group` command.

20. D. When trying to find the best answer to an access-list question, always check the access-list number and then the protocol. When filtering to an upper-layer protocol, you must use an extended list, numbers 100–199. Also, when you filter to an upper-layer protocol, you must use either `tcp` or `udp` in the protocol field. If it says `ip` in the protocol field, you cannot filter to an upper-layer protocol.

21. D. If you add an access list to an interface and you do not have at least one permit statement, then you will effectively shut down the interface because of the implicit `deny any` at the end of every list.

22. C. Telnet access to the router is restricted by using either a standard or extended IP access list to the VTY lines on the router. The command `access-class` is used to apply the access list to the VTY lines.

23. A. The wildcard mask is optional when configuring a standard access list. If a wildcard mask is not specified, the router interprets the statement to be that the list is to match all bits of the source address.

24. D. The only command that shows which access lists have been applied to an interface is `show ip interface Ethernet 0`. The command `show access-lists` displays all configured access lists, and `show ip access-lists` displays all configured IP access lists, but neither command indicates whether the displayed access lists have been applied to an interface.

25. C. If neither the keyword `in` nor `out` is used when applying an access list to an interface, the access list will be applied outbound by default. If you have planned to implement security inbound to the interface, ensure that you have used the `in` keyword.

Answers to Written Lab 9

1. access-list 10 deny 172.16.0.0 0.0.255.255
   access-list 10 permit any

2. ip access-group 10 out

3. access-list 10 deny host 196.22.15.5
   access-list 10 permit any

4. show access-list

5. show running-config
   sh ip interface

6. access-list 110 deny tcp host 172.16.10.1 host
   172.16.30.5 eq 23
   access-list 110 permit ip any any

7. int e0
   ip access-group 110 in

8. access-list 1010 permit 45.0000.0000.0001 4

9. int e0
   ipx input-sap-filter 1010

Wide Area Networking Protocols

THE CCNA EXAM TOPICS COVERED IN THIS CHAPTER INCLUDE THE FOLLOWING:

✓ **WAN Protocols**

- Recognize key Frame Relay terms and features.
- List commands to configure Frame Relay LMIs, maps, and subinterfaces.
- List commands to monitor Frame Relay operation in the router.
- State a relevant use and context for ISDN networking.
- Identify ISDN protocols, function groups, reference points, and channels.
- Identify PPP operations to encapsulate WAN data on Cisco routers.

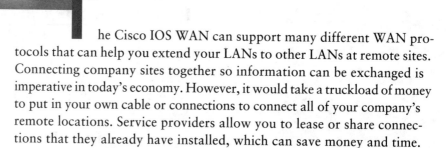

The Cisco IOS WAN can support many different WAN protocols that can help you extend your LANs to other LANs at remote sites. Connecting company sites together so information can be exchanged is imperative in today's economy. However, it would take a truckload of money to put in your own cable or connections to connect all of your company's remote locations. Service providers allow you to lease or share connections that they already have installed, which can save money and time.

It is important to understand the different types of WAN support provided by Cisco. Although this chapter does not cover every type of Cisco WAN support, it does cover the HDLC, PPP, Frame Relay, and ISDN protocols.

Wide Area Networks

To understand WAN technologies, you first need to understand the different WAN terms and connection types that can be used to connect your networks together. This section will discuss the different WAN terms and connection types typically used by service providers.

Defining WAN Terms

Before you order a WAN service type, it is important to understand the terms that the service providers use.

CPE   Equipment that is owned by the subscriber and located at the subscriber's premises is called *customer premises equipment (CPE)*.

Demarcation   The *demarc* is the last responsibility of the service provider, usually an RJ-45 jack located close to the CPE. The CPE at this point would be a CSU/DSU or ISDN interface that plugs into the demarc.

Local loop   The *local loop* connects the demarc to the closest switching office, called a central office.

Central office (CO)   This point connects the customers to the provider's switching network. A *central office (CO)* is sometimes referred to as a *point of presence (POP)*.

Toll network   These are trunk lines inside a WAN provider's network. The toll network is a collection of switches and facilities.

It is important to familiarize yourself with these terms, as they are crucial to understanding WAN technologies.

WAN Connection Types

Figure 10.1 shows the different WAN connection types that can be used to connect your LANs together over a DCE network.

FIGURE 10.1   WAN connection types

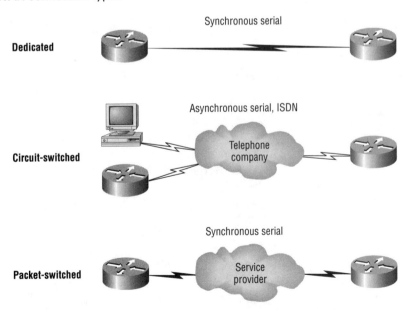

The following list explains the WAN connection types:

Leased lines   Typically referred to as a *point-to-point connection* or dedicated connection; a *leased line* is a pre-established WAN communications path from the CPE, through the DCE switch, to the CPE of the remote site, allowing DTE networks to communicate at any time with no setup procedures before transmitting data. It uses synchronous serial lines up to 45Mbps.

Circuit switching   Sets up a line like a phone call. No data can transfer before the end-to-end connection is established; *circuit switching* uses dial-up modems and ISDN. It is used for low-bandwidth data transfers.

Packet switching   WAN switching method that allows you to share bandwidth with other companies to save money. Think of packet switching networks as a party line. As long as you are not constantly transmitting data and are instead using bursty data transfers, packet switching can save you a lot of money. However, if you have constant data transfers, you will need to get a leased line. Frame Relay and X.25 are packet-switching technologies. Speeds can range from 56Kbps to 2.048Mbps.

WAN Support

In this section, we will define the most prominent WAN protocols used today. These are Frame Relay, ISDN, LAPB, HDLC, and PPP. The rest of the chapter will be dedicated to explaining in depth how WAN protocols work and how to configure them with Cisco routers.

Frame Relay   A packet-switched technology that emerged in the early 1990s, *Frame Relay* is a Data Link and Physical layer specification that provides high performance. Frame Relay assumes that the facilities used are less error prone than when X.25 was used and that they transmit data with less overhead. Frame Relay is more cost-effective than point-to-point links and can typically run at speeds of 64Kbps to 1.544Mbps. Frame Relay provides features for dynamic bandwidth allocation and congestion control.

ISDN   *Integrated Services Digital Network (ISDN)* is a set of digital services that transmit voice and data over existing phone lines. ISDN can offer a cost-effective solution for remote users who need a higher-speed connection than analog dial-up links offer. ISDN is also a good choice as a backup link for other types of links such as Frame Relay or a T-1 connection.

LAPB *Link Access Procedure, Balanced (LAPB)* was created to be used as a connection-oriented protocol at the Data Link layer for use with X.25. It can also be used as a simple Data Link transport. LAPB has a tremendous amount of overhead because of its strict timeout and windowing techniques. You can use LAPB instead of the lower-overhead HDLC if your link is very error prone. However, that typically is not a problem any longer.

HDLC *High-Level Data Link Control (HDLC)* was derived from Synchronous Data Link Control (SDLC), which was created by IBM as a Data Link connection protocol. HDLC is a connection-oriented protocol at the Data Link layer, but it has very little overhead compared to LAPB. HDLC was not intended to encapsulate multiple Network layer protocols across the same link. The HDLC header carries no identification of the type of protocol being carried inside the HDLC encapsulation. Because of this, each vendor that uses HDLC has their own way of identifying the Network layer protocol, which means that each vendor's HDLC is proprietary for their equipment.

PPP *Point-to-Point Protocol (PPP)* is an industry-standard protocol. Because many versions of HDLC are proprietary, PPP can be used to create point-to-point links between different vendors' equipment. It uses a Network Control Protocol field in the Data Link header to identify the Network layer protocol. It allows authentication and multilink connections and can be run over asynchronous and synchronous links.

ATM Asynchronous Transfer Mode (ATM) was created for time-sensitive traffic, providing simultaneous transmission of voice, video, and data. ATM uses cells instead of packets that are a fixed 53-bytes long. It also uses isochronous clocking (external clocking) to help the data move faster. Local area network emulation (LANE) is used to allow ATM to run on Ethernet and Token Ring LANs.

 Real World Scenario

Which of the listed WAN services is the best?

Well, none, really. The best WAN service is the one service that you can get in your neighborhood or at your company. Since you don't have the option of just choosing whatever you want, you must first call your local service provider and ask what they can provide to you. Then you can choose from that list. Hopefully, they won't just say dial-up modem!

One of the newer WAN services that Cisco doesn't list as a WAN service in the CCNA objectives is a wireless connection. You can get from 1Mbps to over 50Mbps, depending on the service, and it works too! For the speed, it is relatively inexpensive. If you want to connect two buildings together, then you should consider a wireless solution. Of course, Cisco sells everything you need to do this, at a decent price (compared to an wired solution).

You can even use a wireless solution for connecting your business to the Internet. The problem with wireless ISPs (WISPs) is that they come and go—they are in business one day and then gone the next. Make sure you have a backup solution if you decide on a WISP, in case they don't answer the phone one day. Eventually, things will mellow out and we'll find carriers that stay in business.

If you cannot get wireless for your business, then Frame Relay is a fast, cost-effective WAN service. ATM is nice and fast, but expensive.

High-Level Data-Link Control Protocol (HDLC)

The High-Level Data-Link Control protocol (HDLC) is a popular ISO-standard, bit-oriented Data Link layer protocol. It specifies an encapsulation method for data on synchronous serial data links using frame characters and checksums. HDLC is a point-to-point protocol used on leased lines. No authentication can be used with HDLC.

In byte-oriented protocols, control information is encoded using entire bytes. Bit-oriented protocols, on the other hand, may use single bits to represent control information. Bit-oriented protocols include SDLC, LLC, HDLC, TCP, IP, etc.

HDLC is the default encapsulation used by Cisco routers over synchronous serial links. Cisco's HDLC is proprietary—it won't communicate with any other vendor's HDLC implementation—but don't give Cisco grief for it; *everyone's* HDLC implementation is proprietary. Figure 10.2 shows the Cisco HDLC format.

FIGURE 10.2   Cisco HDLC frame format

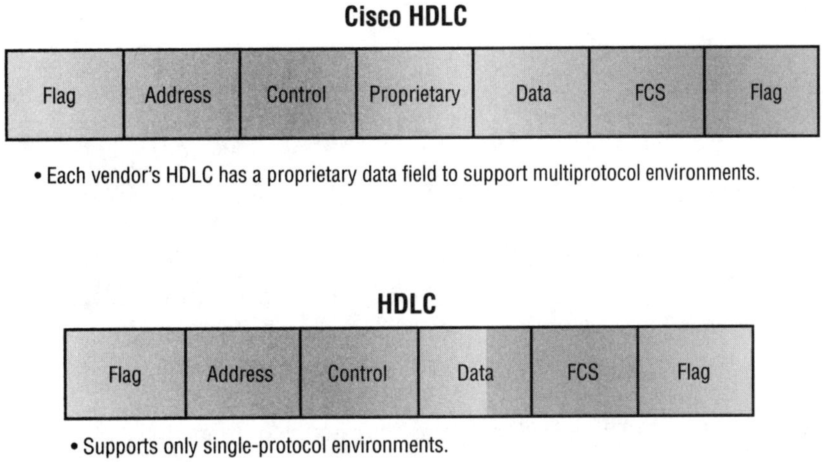

Cisco HDLC

| Flag | Address | Control | Proprietary | Data | FCS | Flag |

• Each vendor's HDLC has a proprietary data field to support multiprotocol environments.

HDLC

| Flag | Address | Control | Data | FCS | Flag |

• Supports only single-protocol environments.

As shown in the figure, the reason that every vendor has a proprietary HDLC encapsulation method is that each vendor has a different way for the HDLC protocol to communicate with the Network layer protocols. If the vendors didn't have a way for HDLC to communicate with the different layer-3 protocols, then HDLC would only be able to carry one protocol. This proprietary header is placed in the data field of the HDLC encapsulation.

If you had only one Cisco router and you needed to connect to, say, a Bay router because you had your other Cisco router on order, then you couldn't use the default HDLC serial encapsulation. You would use something like PPP, which is an ISO-standard way of identifying the upper-layer protocols.

Point-to-Point Protocol (PPP)

PPP (Point-to-Point Protocol) is a data-link protocol that can be used over either asynchronous serial (dial-up) or synchronous serial (ISDN) media and that uses the LCP (Link Control Protocol) to build and maintain data-link connections.

The basic purpose of PPP is to transport layer-3 packets across a Data Link layer point-to-point link. Figure 10.3 shows the protocol stack compared to the OSI reference model.

FIGURE 10.3 Point-to-point protocol stack

OSI layer

3	Upper-layer Protocols (such as IP, IPX, AppleTalk)
	Network Control Protocol (NCP) (specific to each Network-layer protocol)
2	Link Control Protocol (LCP)
	High-Level Data Link Control Protocol (HDLC)
1	Physical layer (such as EIA/TIA-232, V.24, V.35, ISDN)

PPP contains four main components:

EIA/TIA-232-C   A Physical layer international standard for serial communication.

HDLC   A method for encapsulating datagrams over serial links.

LCP   A method of establishing, configuring, maintaining, and terminating the point-to-point connection.

NCP   A method of establishing and configuring different Network layer protocols. PPP is designed to allow the simultaneous use of multiple Network layer protocols. Some examples of protocols here are IPCP (Internet Protocol Control Protocol) and IPXCP (Internetwork Packet Exchange Control Protocol).

It is important to understand that the PPP protocol stack is specified at the Physical and Data Link layers only. NCP is used to allow communication of multiple Network layer protocols by encapsulating the protocols across a PPP data link.

Remember that if you have a Cisco router and a non-Cisco router connected with a serial connection, you must configure PPP or another encapsulation method, like Frame Relay, because the default of HDLC will not work!

Link Control Protocol (LCP) Configuration Options

Link Control Protocol offers different PPP encapsulation options, including the following:

Authentication   This option tells the calling side of the link to send information that can identify the user. The two methods relevant to the CCNA exam are PAP and CHAP.

Compression   This is used to increase the throughput of PPP connections. PPP decompresses the data frame on the receiving end. Cisco uses the Stacker and Predictor compression methods, discussed in *CCNP: Routing Study Guide* (Sybex, 2000).

Error detection   PPP uses Quality and Magic Number options to ensure a reliable, loop-free data link.

Multilink   Starting in IOS version 11.1, multilink is supported on PPP links with Cisco routers. This splits the load for PPP over two or more parallel circuits and is called a bundle.

PPP Session Establishment

PPP can be used with authentication. This means that communicating routers must provide information to identify the link as a valid communication link. When PPP connections are started, the links go through three phases of session establishment:

Link-establishment phase   LCP packets are sent by each PPP device to configure and test the link. The LCP packets contain a field called the Configuration Option that allows each device to see the size of the data, compression, and authentication. If no Configuration Option field is present, then the default configurations are used.

Authentication phase   If configured, either CHAP or PAP can be used to authenticate a link. Authentication takes place before Network layer protocol information is read.

Network layer protocol phase   PPP uses the Network Control Protocol to allow multiple Network layer protocols to be encapsulated and sent over a PPP data link.

PPP Authentication Methods

There are two methods of authentication that can be used with PPP links, either Password Authentication Protocol (PAP) or Challenge Authentication Protocol (CHAP).

Password Authentication Protocol (PAP)

The *Password Authentication Protocol (PAP)* is the less secure of the two methods. Passwords are sent in clear text, and PAP is only performed upon the initial link establishment. When the PPP link is first established, the remote node sends back to the sending router the username and password until authentication is acknowledged. That's it.

Challenge Authentication Protocol (CHAP)

The *Challenge Authentication Protocol (CHAP)* is used at the initial startup of a link and at periodic checkups on the link to make sure the router is still communicating with the same host.

After PPP finishes its initial phase, the local router sends a challenge request to the remote device. The remote device sends a value calculated using a one-way hash function called MD5. The local router checks this hash value to make sure it matches. If the values don't match, the link is immediately terminated.

Configuring PPP on Cisco Routers

Configuring PPP encapsulation on an interface is a fairly straightforward process. To configure it, follow these router commands:

```
Router#config t
Enter configuration commands, one per line. End with CNTL/Z.
Router(config)#int s0
Router(config-if)#encapsulation ppp
Router(config-if)#^Z
Router#
```

Of course, PPP encapsulation must be enabled on both interfaces connected to a serial line to work, and there are several additional configuration options available by using the `help` command.

Configuring PPP Authentication

After you configure your serial interface to support PPP encapsulation, you can then configure authentication using PPP between routers. First set the hostname of the router if it is not already set. Then set the username and password for the remote router connecting to your router.

```
Router#config t
Enter configuration commands, one per line. End with CNTL/Z.
Router(config)#hostname RouterA
RouterA(config)#username todd password cisco
```

When using the hostname command, remember that the username is the hostname of the remote router connecting to your router. It is case sensitive. Also, the password on both routers must be the same. It is a plain-text password and can be seen with a show run command. You can configure the password to be encrypted by using the command service password-encryption. You must have a username and password configured for each remote system you are going to connect to. The remote routers must also be configured with usernames and passwords.

After you set the hostname, usernames, and passwords, choose the authentication type, either CHAP or PAP.

```
RouterA#config t
Enter configuration commands, one per line. End with CNTL/Z.
RouterA(config)#int s0
RouterA(config-if)#ppp authentication chap
RouterA(config-if)#ppp authentication pap
RouterA(config-if)#^Z
RouterA#
```

If both methods are configured, as shown in the preceding configuration example, then only the first method is used during link negotiation. If the first method fails, then the second method will be used.

Verifying PPP Encapsulation

Now that we have PPP encapsulation enabled, let's take a look to verify that it's up and running. You can verify the configuration with the show interface command:

```
RouterA#show int s0
Serial0 is up, line protocol is up
 Hardware is HD64570
 Internet address is 172.16.20.1/24
```

```
MTU 1500 bytes, BW 1544 Kbit, DLY 20000 usec, rely
 255/255, load 1/255
Encapsulation PPP, loopback not set, keepalive set (10 sec)
LCP Open
Listen: IPXCP
Open: IPCP, CDPCP, ATCP
Last input 00:00:05, output 00:00:05, output hang never
Last clearing of "show interface" counters never
Input queue: 0/75/0 (size/max/drops); Total output drops: 0
Queueing strategy: weighted fair
Output queue: 0/1000/64/0 (size/max total/threshold/drops)
  Conversations 0/2/256 (active/max active/max total)
  Reserved Conversations 0/0 (allocated/max allocated)
5 minute input rate 0 bits/sec, 0 packets/sec
5 minute output rate 0 bits/sec, 0 packets/sec
  670 packets input, 31845 bytes, 0 no buffer
  Received 596 broadcasts, 0 runts, 0 giants,
    0 throttles
  0 input errors, 0 CRC, 0 frame, 0 overrun, 0 ignored,
    0 abort
  707 packets output, 31553 bytes, 0 underruns
  0 output errors, 0 collisions, 18 interface resets
  0 output buffer failures, 0 output buffers swapped out
21 carrier transitions
  DCD=up DSR=up DTR=up RTS=up CTS=up
RouterA#
```

Notice that the sixth line lists encapsulation as PPP, and the seventh line tells us that LCP is open. Remember that LCP's job is to build and maintain connections. The ninth line tells us that IPCP, CDPCP, and ATCP are open. This shows the IP, CDP, and AppleTalk support from NCP. The eighth line reports that we are listening for IPXCP.

You can verify the PPP authentication configuration by using the debug ppp authentication command.

Frame Relay

Recently, the high-performance WAN encapsulation method known as Frame Relay has become one of the most popular technologies in use. It operates at the Physical and Data Link layers of the OSI reference model and was originally designed for use across Integrated Services Digital Network (ISDN) interfaces. But today, Frame Relay is used over a variety of other network interfaces.

Cisco Frame Relay supports the following protocols:

- IP
- DECnet
- AppleTalk
- Xerox Network Service (XNS)
- Novell IPX
- Connectionless Network Service (CLNS)
- International Organization for Standardization (ISO)
- Banyan Vines
- Transparent bridging

Frame Relay provides a communications interface between DTE (data terminal equipment) and DCE (data communication equipment, such as packet switches) devices. DTE consists of terminals, PCs, routers, and bridges—customer-owned end-node and internetworking devices. DCE consists of carrier-owned internetworking devices.

Popular opinion maintains that Frame Relay is more efficient and faster than X.25 because it assumes error checking will be done through higher-layer protocols and application services.

Frame Relay provides connection-oriented, Data Link layer communication via virtual circuits just as X.25 does. These virtual circuits are logical connections created between two DTEs across a packet-switched network, which is identified by a *Data Link Connection Identifier (DLCI)*. (We'll get to DLCIs in a bit.) Also, like X.25, Frame Relay uses both permanent virtual circuits (PVCs) and switched virtual circuits (SVCs), although most Frame Relay networks use only PVCs. This virtual circuit provides the complete path to the destination network prior to the sending of the first frame.

Frame Relay Terminology

To understand the terminology used in Frame Relay networks, first you need to know how the technology works. Figure 10.4 is labeled with the various terms used to describe different parts of a Frame Relay network.

FIGURE 10.4 Frame Relay technology and terms

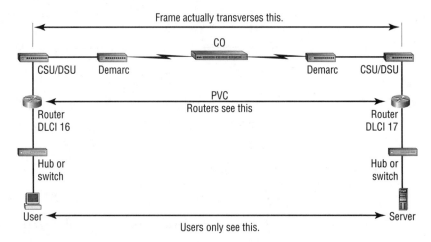

The basic idea behind Frame Relay networks is to allow users to communicate between two DTE devices through DCE devices. The users should not see the difference between connecting to and gathering resources from a local server and a server at a remote site connected with Frame Relay. Chances are this connection will be slower than a 10Mbps Ethernet LAN, but the physical difference in the connection should be transparent to the user.

Figure 10.4 illustrates everything that must happen in order for two DTE devices to communicate. Here is how the process works:

1. The user's network device sends a frame out on the local network. The hardware address of the router (default gateway) will be in the header of the frame.

2. The router picks up the frame, extracts the packet, and discards the frame. It then looks at the destination IP address within the packet and checks to see whether it knows how to get to the destination network by looking in the routing table.

3. The router then forwards the data out the interface that it thinks can find the remote network. (If it can't find the network in its routing table, it will discard the packet.) Because this will be a serial interface

encapsulated with Frame Relay, the router puts the packet onto the Frame Relay network encapsulated within a Frame Relay frame. It will add the DLCI number associated with the serial interface. DLCIs identify the virtual circuit (PVC or SVC) to the routers and provider's switches participating in the Frame Relay network.

4. The channel service unit/data service unit (CSU/DSU) receives the digital signal and encodes it into the type of digital signaling that the switch at the packet switching exchange (PSE) can understand. The PSE receives the digital signal and extracts the ones and zeros from the line.

5. The CSU/DSU is connected to a demarcation (demarc) installed by the service provider, and its location is the service provider's first point of responsibility (last point on the receiving end). The demarc is typically just an RJ-45 jack installed close to the router and CSU/DSU.

6. The demarc is typically a twisted-pair cable that connects to the local loop. The local loop connects to the closest central office (CO), sometimes called a point of presence (POP). The local loop can connect using various physical mediums, but twisted-pair or fiber is very common.

7. The CO receives the frame and sends it through the Frame Relay "cloud" to its destination. This cloud can be dozens of switching offices—or more! It looks for the destination DLCI address based on the local DLCI number the frame was transmitted from. It typically can find the DLCI number of the remote device or router by looking up a DLCI mapping created by the service provider. Frame Relay mappings are usually created statically by the service provider, but they can be created dynamically using the Inverse ARP (IARP) protocol. Remember that before data is sent through the cloud, the virtual circuit is created from end to end.

It is important to remember that the Frame Relay PVC identifies the DLCI of 100 from the first router and the DLCI number of 200 from the second router by the configuration of what are called "local significant DLCI numbers." We'll discuss this more in a minute.

8. Once the frame reaches the switching office closest to the destination office, it is sent through the local loop. The frame is received at the demarc and then is sent to the CSU/DSU. Finally, the router extracts the packet, or datagram, from the frame and puts the packet in a

new LAN frame to be delivered to the destination host. The frame on the LAN will have the final destination hardware address in the header. This was found in the router's ARP cache, or an ARP broadcast was performed. Whew!

The user and server do not need to know, nor should they know, everything that happens as the frame makes its way across the Frame Relay network. The remote server should be as easy to use as a locally connected resource.

Frame Relay Encapsulation

When configuring Frame Relay on Cisco routers, you need to specify it as an encapsulation on serial interfaces. There are only two encapsulation types: Cisco and IETF (Internet Engineering Task Force). The following router output shows the two different encapsulation methods when choosing Frame Relay on your Cisco router:

```
RouterA(config)#int s0
RouterA(config-if)#encapsulation frame-relay ?
  ietf  Use RFC1490 encapsulation
  <cr>
```

The default encapsulation is Cisco unless you manually type in IETF, and Cisco is the type used when connecting two Cisco devices. You'd opt for the IETF-type encapsulation if you needed to connect a Cisco device to a non-Cisco device with Frame Relay. So before choosing an encapsulation type, check with your ISP and find out which one they use. (If they don't know, hook up with a different ISP!)

Data Link Connection Identifiers (DLCIs)

Frame Relay virtual circuits (PVCs) are identified by DLCIs. A Frame Relay service provider, such as the telephone company, typically assigns DLCI values, which are used by Frame Relay to distinguish between different virtual circuits on the network. Because many virtual circuits can be terminated on one multipoint Frame Relay interface, many DLCIs are often affiliated with it.

For the IP devices at each end of a virtual circuit to communicate, their IP addresses need to be mapped to DLCIs. This mapping can function as a multipoint device—one that can identify to the Frame Relay network the appropriate destination virtual circuit for each packet that is sent over the single physical interface. The mappings can be done dynamically through IARP or manually through the Frame Relay map command.

Frame Relay uses DLCIs the same way that X.25 uses X.121 addresses, and every DLCI number can be given either global or local meaning everywhere within the Frame Relay network.

Sometimes a provider can give a site a DLCI that is advertised to all remote sites as the same PVC. This PVC is said to have a global significance. For example, a corporate office might have a DLCI of 20. All remote sites would know that the corporate office is DLCI 20 and use this PVC to communicate to the corporate office. However, the customary implementation is to give each DLCI local meaning. What does this mean? It means that DLCI numbers do not necessarily need to be unique. Two DLCI numbers can be the same on different sides of a link because Frame Relay maps a local DLCI number to a virtual circuit on each interface of the switch. Basically, this means that a DLCI is only locally significant to the physical serial interface. Each remote office can have its own DLCI number and communicate with the corporate office using unique DLCI numbers, which is called the *local significant DLCI number*.

DLCI numbers, used to identify a PVC, are typically assigned by the provider and start at 16. Configuring a DLCI number to be applied to an interface is shown below:

```
RouterA(config-if)#frame-relay interface-dlci ?
  <16-1007> Define a DLCI as part of the current
            subinterface
RouterA(config-if)#frame-relay interface-dlci 16
```

Local Management Interface (LMI)

The *Local Management Interface (LMI)* was developed in 1990 by Cisco Systems, StrataCom, Northern Telecom, and Digital Equipment Corporation and became known as the Gang-of-Four LMI or Cisco LMI. This gang took the basic Frame Relay protocol from the CCITT and added extensions onto the protocol features that allow internetworking devices to communicate easily with a Frame Relay network.

The LMI is a signaling standard between a CPE device (router) and a frame switch. The LMI is responsible for managing and maintaining status between these devices. LMI messages provide information about the following:

Keepalives   Verify data is flowing.

Multicasting   Provides a local DLCI PVC.

Multicast addressing   Provides global significance.

Status of virtual circuits   Provides DLCI status.

Beginning with IOS version 11.2, the LMI type is auto-sensed. This enables the interface to determine the LMI type supported by the switch.

If you're not going to use the auto-sense feature, you'll need to check with your Frame Relay provider to find out which type to use instead. The default type is Cisco, but you may need to change to ANSI or Q.933A. The three different LMI types are depicted in the following router output:

```
RouterA(config-if)#frame-relay lmi-type ?
  cisco
  ansi
  q933a
```

As seen in the output, all three standard LMI signaling formats are supported:

Cisco   LMI defined by the Gang of Four (default).

ANSI   Annex D defined by ANSI standard T1.617.

ITU-T (q933a)   Annex A defined by Q.933.

Routers receive LMI information on a frame-encapsulated interface and update the virtual circuit status to one of three different states:

Active state   Everything is up, and routers can exchange information.

Inactive state   The router's interface is up and working with a connection to the switching office, but the remote router is not working.

Deleted state   No LMI information is being received on the interface from the switch. It could be a mapping problem or a line failure.

Subinterfaces

You can have multiple virtual circuits on a single serial interface and yet treat each as a separate interface. These are known as *subinterfaces*. Think of a subinterface as a hardware interface defined by the IOS software. An advantage gained through using subinterfaces is the ability to assign different Network layer characteristics to each subinterface and virtual circuit, such as IP routing on one virtual circuit and IPX on another.

Partial Meshed Networks

You can use subinterfaces to mitigate partial meshed Frame Relay networks and split horizon protocols. For example, say you were running the IP protocol on a LAN network. If, on the same physical network, Router A can talk to Router B, and Router B to Router C, you can usually assume that Router A can talk to Router C. Though this is true with a LAN, it's not true with a Frame Relay network, unless Router A has a PVC to Router C.

In Figure 10.5, Network 1 is configured with five locations. To be able to make this network function, you would have to create a meshed network as shown in Network 2. However, even though Network 2's example works, it's an expensive solution—configuring subinterfaces as shown in the Network 3 solution is much more cost-effective.

FIGURE 10.5   Partial meshed network examples

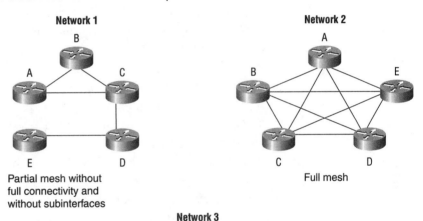

Network 1

Partial mesh without
full connectivity and
without subinterfaces

Network 2

Full mesh

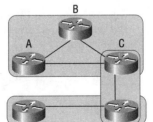

Network 3

Partial mesh with full
connectivity using
subinterfaces

In Network 3, configuring subinterfaces actually works to subdivide the Frame Relay network into smaller subnetworks—each with its own network number. So locations A, B, and C connect to a fully meshed network, while locations C and D, and D and E, are connected via point-to-point connections. Locations C and D connect to two subinterfaces and forward packets.

Subinterfaces also solve the problem with routing protocols that use split horizon. As you may recall, split horizon protocols do not advertise routes out the same interface they received the route update on. This can cause a problem on a meshed Frame Relay network. However, by using subinterfaces, routing protocols that receive route updates on one subinterface can send out the same route update on another subinterface.

Creating Subinterfaces

You define subinterfaces with the int s0.subinterface number command as shown below. You first set the encapsulation on the serial interface, then you can define the subinterfaces.

```
RouterA(config)#int s0
RouterA(config)#encapsulation frame-relay
RouterA(config)#int s0.?
  <0-4294967295>  Serial interface number
RouterA(config)#int s0.16 ?
  multipoint      Treat as a multipoint link
  point-to-point  Treat as a point-to-point link
RouterA(config)#int s0.16 point-to-point
```

You can define an almost limitless number of subinterfaces on a given physical interface (keeping router memory in mind). In the above example, we chose to use subinterface 16 because that represents the DLCI number assigned to that interface. However, you can choose any number between 0 and 4,292,967,295.

There are two types of subinterfaces:

Point-to-point Used when a single virtual circuit connects one router to another. Each point-to-point subinterface requires its own subnet.

Multipoint Used when the router is the center of a star of virtual circuits. Uses a single subnet for all routers' serial interfaces connected to the frame switch.

An example of a production router running multiple subinterfaces is shown next. Notice that the subinterface number matches the DLCI number. This is not a requirement but helps in the administration of the interfaces. Also notice that there is no LMI type defined, which means they are running either the default of Cisco or using autodetect if running Cisco IOS version 11.2 or newer. This configuration was taken from one of my customers' production routers (used by permission). Notice that each interface is defined as a separate subnet, separate IPX network, and separate AppleTalk cable range (Apple-Talk is beyond the scope of this exam):

```
interface Serial0
 no ip address
 no ip directed-broadcast
 encapsulation frame-relay
!
interface Serial0.102 point-to-point
 ip address 10.1.12.1 255.255.255.0
 no ip directed-broadcast
 appletalk cable-range 12-12 12.65
 appletalk zone wan2
 appletalk protocol eigrp
 no appletalk protocol rtmp
 ipx network 12
 frame-relay interface-dlci 102
!
interface Serial0.103 point-to-point
 ip address 10.1.13.1 255.255.255.0
 no ip directed-broadcast
 appletalk cable-range 13-13 13.174
 appletalk zone wan3
 appletalk protocol eigrp
 no appletalk protocol rtmp
 ipx network 13
 frame-relay interface-dlci 103
!
interface Serial0.104 point-to-point
 ip address 10.1.14.1 255.255.255.0
```

```
   no ip directed-broadcast
   appletalk cable-range 14-14 14.131
   appletalk zone wan4
   appletalk protocol eigrp
   no appletalk protocol rtmp
   ipx network 14
   frame-relay interface-dlci 104
 !
interface Serial0.105 point-to-point
  ip address 10.1.15.1 255.255.255.0
  no ip directed-broadcast
  appletalk cable-range 15-15 15.184
  appletalk zone wan5
  appletalk protocol eigrp
  no appletalk protocol rtmp
  ipx network 15
  frame-relay interface-dlci 105
 !
interface Serial0.106 point-to-point
  ip address 10.1.16.1 255.255.255.0
  no ip directed-broadcast
  appletalk cable-range 16-16 16.28
  appletalk zone wan6
  appletalk protocol eigrp
  no appletalk protocol rtmp
  ipx network 16
  frame-relay interface-dlci 106
 !
interface Serial0.107 point-to-point
  ip address 10.1.17.1 255.255.255.0
  no ip directed-broadcast
  appletalk cable-range 17-17 17.223
  appletalk zone wan7
  appletalk protocol eigrp
  no appletalk protocol rtmp
  ipx network 17
```

```
frame-relay interface-dlci 107
!
interface Serial0.108 point-to-point
 ip address 10.1.18.1 255.255.255.0
 no ip directed-broadcast
 appletalk cable-range 18-18 18.43
 appletalk zone wan8
 appletalk protocol eigrp
 no appletalk protocol rtmp
 ipx network 18
 frame-relay interface-dlci 108
```

Mapping Frame Relay

As we explained earlier, in order for IP devices at the ends of virtual circuits to communicate, their addresses must be mapped to the DLCIs. There are two ways to make this mapping happen:

- Use the frame-relay map command.

- Use the inverse-arp function.

Here's an example using the frame-relay map command on a multipoint Frame Relay network:

```
RouterA(config)#int s0
RouterA(config-if)#encap frame
RouterA(config-if)#int s0.16 multipoint
RouterA(config-subif)#no inverse-arp
RouterA(config-subif)#ip address 172.16.30.1
  255.255.255.0
RouterA(config-subif)#frame-relay map ip 172.16.30.17 16
  ietf broadcast
RouterA(config-subif)#frame-relay map ip 172.16.30.18 17
  broadcast
RouterA(config-subif)#frame-relay map ip 172.16.30.19 18
```

Here's what we did: First, we configured interface serial 0 to use the encapsulation type of Cisco (default), then we created our subinterface. We then turned off inverse arp and mapped three virtual circuits and their corresponding DLCI numbers.

Notice that we changed the encapsulation type for the first mapping. The frame map command is the only way to configure multiple frame encapsulation types on an interface.

The broadcast keyword at the end of the map command tells the router to forward broadcasts for this interface to this specific virtual circuit. Remember that Frame Relay is a nonbroadcast multiaccess (NBMA) encapsulation method, which will not broadcast routing protocols. You can either use the map command with the broadcast keyword or the neighbor command within the routing process.

Instead of putting in map commands for each virtual circuit, you can use the inverse-arp function to perform dynamic mapping of the IP address to the DLCI number. This makes our configuration look like this:

```
RouterA(config)#int s0.16 multipoint
RouterA(config-subif)#encap frame-relay ietf
RouterA(config-subif)#ip address 172.16.30.1
   255.255.255.0
```

Yes, this configuration is a whole lot easier to do, but it's not as stable as using the map command. Why? Sometimes, when using the inverse-arp function, configuration errors occur because virtual circuits can be insidiously and dynamically mapped to unknown devices.

Frame Relay Congestion Control

In this section, we will define how the Frame Relay switch handles congestion problems.

DE   When a Frame Relay router detects congestion on the Frame Relay network, it will turn the *Discard Eligibility (DE)* bit on in a Frame Relay packet header. If the switch is congested, the Frame Relay switch will discard the packets with the DE bit set first. If your bandwidth is configured with a committed information rate (CIR) of zero, the DE will always be on.

FECN   When the Frame Relay network recognizes congestion in the cloud, the switch will set the *Forward-Explicit Congestion Notification (FECN)* bit to 1 in a Frame Relay packet header. This will indicate to the destination DCE that the path just traversed is congested.

BECN   When the switch detects congestion in the Frame Relay network, it will set the *Backward-Explicit Congestion Notification (BECN)* bit in a Frame Relay packet and send it to the source router, telling it to slow down the rate at which it is transmitting packets.

Committed Information Rate (CIR)

Frame Relay provides a packet-switched network to many different customers at the same time. This is a great idea because it spreads the cost of the switches among many customers. However, Frame Relay is based on the assumption that not all customers need to transmit constant data all at the same time. Frame Relay works best with bursty traffic.

Think of Frame Relay as a party line. Remember party lines? That's when many people on your block had to share the same phone number. Okay, I'm showing my age here, but understand that party lines were created on the assumption that few people needed to use the phone each day. If you needed to talk excessively, you had to pay for the more expensive dedicated circuit. Frame Relay works somewhat on the same principle, except many devices can transmit at the same time. However, if you need a constant data-stream connection, then Frame Relay is not for you. Buy a dedicated, point-to-point T-1 instead.

Frame Relay works by providing a dedicated bandwidth to each user, who is committed to that bandwidth at any given time. Frame Relay providers allow customers to buy a lower amount of bandwidth than what they really might need. This is called the *committed information rate (CIR)*. What this means is that the customer can buy bandwidth of, for example, 256K, but it is possible to burst up to T-1 speeds. The CIR specifies that as long as the data input by a device to the Frame Relay network is below or equal to the CIR, then the network will continue to forward data for the PVC. However, if data rates exceed the CIR, it is not guaranteed.

The CIR is the rate, in bits per second, at which the Frame Relay switch agrees to transfer data.

It is sometimes possible to also purchase an excess burst (Be), which allows customers to exceed their CIR for a specified amount of time. In this situation, the DE bit will always be set.

Choose a CIR based on realistic, anticipated traffic rates. Some Frame Relay providers allow you to purchase a CIR of zero. You can use a zero CIR to save money if retransmission of packets is acceptable. However, understand that the DE bit will always be turned on in every frame.

Monitoring Frame Relay

There are several ways to check the status of your interfaces and PVCs once you have Frame Relay encapsulation set up and running:

```
RouterA>sho frame ?
  ip      show frame relay IP statistics
  lmi     show frame relay lmi statistics
  map     Frame-Relay map table
  pvc     show frame relay pvc statistics
  route   show frame relay route
  traffic Frame-Relay protocol statistics
```

The Show Frame Relay LMI Command

The show frame relay lmi command will give you the LMI traffic statistics exchanged between the local router and the Frame Relay switch.

```
Router#sh frame lmi

LMI Statistics for interface Serial0 (Frame Relay DTE)
LMI TYPE = CISCO
  Invalid Unnumbered info 0      Invalid Prot Disc 0
  Invalid dummy Call Ref 0       Invalid Msg Type 0
  Invalid Status Message 0       Invalid Lock Shift 0
  Invalid Information ID 0        Invalid Report IE Len 0
  Invalid Report Request 0       Invalid Keep IE Len 0
  Num Status Enq. Sent 0         Num Status msgs Rcvd 0
  Num Update Status Rcvd 0       Num Status Timeouts 0
Router#
```

The router output from the show frame relay lmi command shows you LMI errors as well as the LMI type.

The Show Frame Relay PVC Command

The show frame pvc command will list all configured PVCs and DLCI numbers. It provides the status of each PVC connection and traffic statistics. It will also give you the number of BECN and FECN packets received on the router.

```
RouterA#sho frame pvc

PVC Statistics for interface Serial0 (Frame Relay DTE)
```

```
DLCI = 16,DLCI USAGE = LOCAL,PVC STATUS =ACTIVE,
INTERFACE = Serial0.1
  input pkts 50977876     output pkts 41822892
   in bytes 3137403144
  out bytes 3408047602    dropped pkts 5
   in FECN pkts 0
  in BECN pkts 0       out FECN pkts 0      out BECN pkts 0
  in DE pkts 9393      out DE pkts 0
  pvc create time 7w3d, last time pvc status changed 7w3d

DLCI = 18,DLCI USAGE =LOCAL,PVC STATUS =ACTIVE,
INTERFACE = Serial0.3
  input pkts 30572401     output pkts 31139837
   in bytes 1797291100
  out bytes 3227181474    dropped pkts 5
   in FECN pkts 0
  in BECN pkts 0       out FECN pkts 0      out BECN pkts 0
  in DE pkts 28        out DE pkts 0
  pvc create time 7w3d, last time pvc status changed 7w3d
```

To see information about only PVC 16, you can type the command show frame relay pvc 16.

The Show Interface Command

We can also use the show interface command to check for LMI traffic. The show interface command displays information about the encapsulation as well as layer-2 and layer-3 information.

The LMI DLCI, as highlighted in the following, is used to define the type of LMI being used. If it is 1023, it is the default LMI type of Cisco. If the LMI DLCI is zero, then it is the ANSI LMI type. If the LMI DLCI is anything other then 0 or 1023, then call your provider because they have a problem.

```
RouterA#sho int s0
Serial0 is up, line protocol is up
  Hardware is HD64570
  MTU 1500 bytes, BW 1544 Kbit, DLY 20000 usec, rely
   255/255, load 2/255
  Encapsulation FRAME-RELAY, loopback not set, keepalive
   set (10 sec)
```

```
    LMI enq sent 451751,LMI stat recvd 451750,LMI upd recvd
      164,DTE LMI up
    LMI enq recvd 0, LMI stat sent 0, LMI upd sent 0
    LMI DLCI 1023 LMI type is CISCO frame relay DTE
    Broadcast queue 0/64, broadcasts sent/dropped 0/0,
      interface broadcasts 839294
```

The show interface command displays line, protocol, DLCI, and LMI information.

The Show Frame Map Command

The show frame map command will show you the Network layer–to–DLCI mappings.

```
RouterB#show frame map
Serial0 (up): ipx 20.0007.7842.3575 dlci 16(0x10,0x400),
                dynamic, broadcast,, status defined, active
Serial0 (up): ip 172.16.20.1 dlci 16(0x10,0x400),
                dynamic, broadcast,, status defined, active
Serial1 (up): ipx 40.0007.7842.153a dlci 17(0x11,0x410),
                dynamic, broadcast,, status defined, active
Serial1 (up): ip 172.16.40.2 dlci 17(0x11,0x410),
                dynamic, broadcast,, status defined, active
```

Notice that the serial interface has two mappings, one for IP and one for IPX. Also, notice that the Network layer addresses were resolved with the dynamic protocol Inverse ARP (IARP). If an administrator mapped the addresses, the output would say "static."

After the DLCI number is listed, you can see some numbers in parentheses. Notice the first number is 0x10, which is the hex equivalent for the DLCI number 16 used on serial 0, and the 0x11 is the hex for DLCI 17 used on serial 1. The second numbers, 0x400 and 0x410, are the DLCI numbers configured in the Frame Relay frame. They are different because of the way the bits are spread out in the frame.

NOTE To clear the dynamic mappings, you can use the clear frame-relay-inarp command.

The Debug Frame LMI Command

The debug frame lmi command will show output on the router consoles by default. The information from this command will allow you to verify and troubleshoot the Frame Relay connection by helping you to determine whether the router and switch are exchanging the correct LMI information.

```
Router#debug frame-relay lmi
Serial3/1(in): Status, myseq 214
RT IE 1, length 1, type 0
KA IE 3, length 2, yourseq 214, myseq 214
PVC IE 0x7 , length 0x6 , dlci 130, status 0x2 , bw 0
Serial3/1(out): StEnq, myseq 215, yourseen 214, DTE up
datagramstart = 0x1959DF4, datagramsize = 13
FR encap = 0xFCF10309
00 75 01 01 01 03 02 D7 D6

Serial3/1(in): Status, myseq 215
RT IE 1, length 1, type 1
KA IE 3, length 2, yourseq 215, myseq 215
Serial3/1(out): StEnq, myseq 216, yourseen 215, DTE up
datagramstart = 0x1959DF4, datagramsize = 13
FR encap = 0xFCF10309
00 75 01 01 01 03 02 D8 D7
```

Integrated Services Digital Network (ISDN)

Integrated Services Digital Network (ISDN) is a digital service designed to run over existing telephone networks. ISDN can support both data and voice—a telecommuter's dream. But ISDN applications require bandwidth. Typical ISDN applications and implementations include high-speed image applications (such as Group IV facsimile), high-speed file transfer, videoconferencing, and multiple links into homes of telecommuters.

ISDN is actually a set of communication protocols proposed by telephone companies that allows them to carry a group of digital services that simultaneously convey data, text, voice, music, graphics, and video to end users, and it was designed to achieve this over the telephone systems already in place. ISDN is referenced by a suite of ITU-T standards that encompass the OSI model's Physical, Data Link, and Network layers.

The ISDN standards define the hardware and call-setup schemes for end-to-end digital connectivity.

PPP is typically used with ISDN to provide data encapsulation, link integrity, and authentication.

These are the benefits of ISDN:

- It can carry voice, video, and data simultaneously.

- Call setup is faster than with a modem.

- Data rates are faster than on a modem connection.

- Full-time connectivity across the ISDN is spoofed by the Cisco IOS routers using dial-on-demand (DDR) routing.

- Small office and home office sites can be economically supported with ISDN BRI services.

- ISDN can be used as a backup service for a leased line connection between the remote and central offices.

- Modem racking and cabling can be eliminated by integration of digital modem cards on Cisco IOS Network Access Server (NAS).

ISDN Components

The components used with ISDN include functions and reference points. Figure 10.6 shows how the different types of terminal and reference points can be used in an ISDN network.

In North America, ISDN uses a two-wire connection, called a U reference point, into a home or office. The NT1 device is used to convert the typical four-wire connection to a two-wire connection that is used by ISDN phones and terminal adapters (TAs). Most routers can now be purchased with a built-in NT1 (U) interface.

Figure 10.7 shows the different reference points and terminal equipment that can be used with Cisco ISDN BRI interfaces.

FIGURE 10.6   ISDN functions and reference points

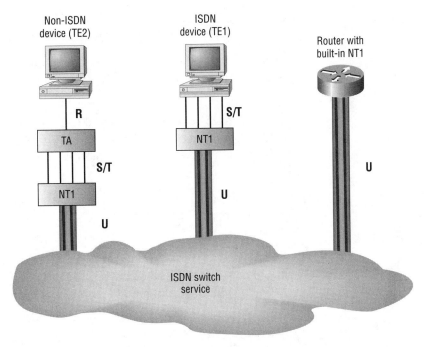

FIGURE 10.7   ISDN BRI reference points and terminal equipment

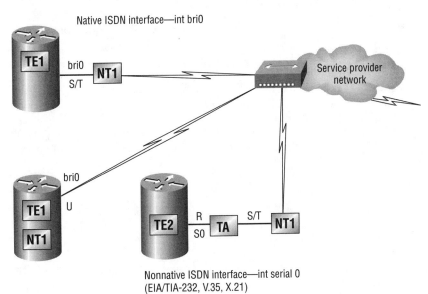

ISDN Terminals

Devices connecting to the ISDN network are known as terminal equipment (TE) and *network termination (NT)* equipment. There are two types of each:

TE1   A *terminal equipment type 1 (TE1)* device refers to those terminals that understand ISDN standards and can plug right into an ISDN network.

TE2   A *terminal equipment type 2 (TE2)* device refers to those that predate ISDN standards. To use a TE2, you have to use a terminal adapter (TA) to be able to plug into an ISDN network.

NT1   The *network termination 1 (NT1)* device implements the ISDN Physical layer specifications and connects the user devices to the ISDN network by converting the network from a four-wire to the two-wire network used by ISDN.

NT2   The *network termination 2 (NT2)* device is typically a provider's equipment, such as a switch or PBX. It also provides Data Link and Network layer implementation. It's very rare at customer premises.

TA   A *terminal adapter (TA)* converts TE2 non-ISDN signaling to signaling used by the ISDN switch and then connects into an NT1 device for conversion into a two-wire ISDN network.

ISDN Reference Points

Reference points are a series of specifications that define the connection between the various equipment used in an ISDN network. ISDN has four reference points that define logical interfaces:

R   The *R reference point* defines the point between non-ISDN equipment (TE2) and a TA.

S   The *S reference point* defines the point between the customer router and an NT2. Enables calls between the different customer equipment.

T   The *T reference point* defines the point between NT1 and NT2 devices. S and T reference points are electrically the same and can perform the same function. Therefore, they are sometimes referred to as an S/T reference point.

U   The *U reference point* defines the point between NT1 devices and line-termination equipment in a carrier network. (This is only in

North America, where the NT1 function isn't provided by the carrier network.)

ISDN Protocols

ISDN protocols are defined by the ITU, and there are several series of protocols dealing with diverse issues:

- Protocols beginning with the letter *E* deal with using ISDN on the existing telephone network.

- Protocols beginning with the letter *I* deal with concepts, aspects, and services.

- Protocols beginning with the letter *Q* cover switching and signaling. These are the protocols that we used to connect to an ISDN network as well as troubleshoot.

ISDN Switch Types

We can credit AT&T and Nortel for the majority of the ISDN switches in place today, but additional companies also make them.

In Table 10.1 under "Keyword," you'll find the right keyword to use along with the isdn switch-type command to configure a router for the variety of switches it's going to connect to. If you don't know which switch your provider is using at their central office, simply call them to find out.

TABLE 10.1 ISDN Switch Types

Switch Type	Keyword
AT&T basic rate switch	basic-5ess
Nortel DMS-100 basic rate switch	basic-dms100
National ISDN-1 switch	basic-ni
AT&T 4ESS (ISDN PRI only)	primary-4ess
AT&T 5ESS (ISDN PRI only)	primary-5ess
Nortel DMS-100 (ISDN PRI only)	primary-dms100

Basic Rate Interface (BRI)

ISDN *Basic Rate Interface (BRI)* service, also known as 2B+1D, provides two B channels and one D channel. The BRI B-channel service operates at 64Kbps and carries data, while the BRI D-channel service operates at 16Kbps and usually carries control and signaling information. The total bandwidth for ISDN BRI is then 144K (64 + 64 + 16 = 144).

The D-channel signaling protocol spans the OSI reference model's Physical, Data Link, and Network layers. The D channel carries signaling information to set up and control calls. The D channel can also be used for other functions like an alarm system for a building, or anything that doesn't need much bandwidth, since it is only a whopping 16K. D channels work with LAPD at the Data Link layer for reliable connections.

When configuring ISDN BRI, you will need to obtain service profile identifiers (SPIDs), and you should have one SPID for each B channel. SPIDs can be thought of as the telephone number of each B channel. The ISDN device gives the SPID to the ISDN switch, which then allows the device to access the network for BRI or PRI service. Without a SPID, many ISDN switches don't allow an ISDN device to place a call on the network.

To set up a BRI call, four events must take place:

1. The D channel between the router and the local ISDN switch comes up.

2. The ISDN switch uses the SS7 signaling technique to set up a path to a remote switch.

3. The remote switch sets up the D-channel link to the remote router.

4. The B channels are then connected end-to-end.

Primary Rate Interface (PRI)

In North America and Japan, the ISDN *Primary Rate Interface* (PRI, also known as 23B+D1) service delivers 23 64Kbps B channels and one 64Kbps D channel, for a total bit rate of up to 1.544Mbps.

In Europe, Australia, and other parts of the world, ISDN provides 30 64Kbps B channels and one 64Kbps D channel, for a total bit rate of up to 2.048Mbps.

ISDN with Cisco Routers

Accessing ISDN with a Cisco router means that you will need to purchase either a router with a built-in NT1 (U reference point) or an ISDN modem (called a terminal adapter or TA). If your router has a BRI interface, you're ready to rock. Otherwise, you can use one of your router's serial interfaces if you can get a hold of a TA. A router with a BRI interface is called a TE1 (terminal equipment type 1), and one that requires a TA is called a TE2 (terminal equipment type 2).

ISDN supports virtually every upper-layer network protocol (IP, IPX, AppleTalk, you name it), and you can choose PPP, HDLC, or LAPD as your encapsulation protocol.

When configuring ISDN, you'll need to know the type of switch that your service provider is using. To see which switches your router will support, use the isdn switch-type ? command in global configuration mode or interface configuration mode. You need to do this because each manufacturer has a proprietary protocol for signaling.

For each ISDN BRI interface, you need to specify the SPIDs that are using the isdn spid1 and isdn spid2 interface subcommands. These are provided by the ISDN provider and identify you on the switch, sort of like a telephone number. However, some providers no longer require SPIDs to be configured on the router. Check with your provider to be sure.

The second part of the SPID configuration is the local dial number for that SPID. It is optional, but some switches need to have those set on the router in order to use both B channels simultaneously.

An example is shown below:

```
RouterA#config t
Enter configuration commands, one per line. End with CNTL/Z.
RouterA(config)#isdn switch-type basic-ni
RouterA(config)#int bri0
RouterA(config-if)#encap ppp (optional)
RouterA(config-if)#isdn spid1 086506610100 8650661
RouterA(config-if)#isdn spid2 086506620100 8650662
```

The isdn switch-type command can be configured in either global configuration or interface configuration mode. Configuring the switch type global will set the switch type for all BRI interfaces in the router. If you only have one interface, it doesn't matter where you use the isdn switch-type command.

Real World Scenario

Should we really still use ISDN?

Only if you cannot get anything else. If your only option is a 56Kbps dial-up modem, then yes, ISDN will be better. Since it is a true 128Kbps data service, it will provide much better performance then any modem.

However, if you can get DSL, a cable modem, Frame Relay, or even a wireless connection, you will be much better off.

Dial-on-Demand Routing (DDR)

*D*ial-on-demand routing (DDR) is used to allow two or more Cisco routers to dial an ISDN dial-up connection on an as-needed basis. DDR is only used for low-volume, periodic network connections using either a public switched telephone network (PSTN) or ISDN. This was designed to reduce WAN costs if you have to pay on a per-minute or per-packet basis.

DDR works when a packet received on an interface meets the requirements of an access list defined by an administrator, which defines interesting traffic. The following five steps give a basic description of how DDR works when an interesting packet is received in a router interface:

1. Route to the destination network is determined.

2. Interesting packets dictate a DDR call.

3. Dialer information is looked up.

4. Traffic is transmitted.

5. Call is terminated when no more traffic is being transmitted over a link and the idle-timeout period ends.

Configuring DDR

To configure legacy DDR, you need to perform three tasks:

1. Define static routes, which define how to get to the remote networks and what interface to use to get there.

2. Specify the traffic that is considered interesting to the router.

3. Configure the dialer information that will be used to dial the interface to get to the remote network.

Configuring Static Routes

To forward traffic across the ISDN link, you configure static routes in each of the routers. You certainly can configure dynamic routing protocols to run on your ISDN link, but then the link will never drop. The suggested routing method is static routes. Keep the following in mind when creating static routes:

- All participating routers must have static routes defining all routes of known networks.

- Default routing can be used if the network is a stub network.

An example of static routing with ISDN is shown below:

```
RouterA(config)#ip route 172.16.50.0 255.255.255.0
    172.16.60.2
RouterA(config)#ip route 172.16.60.2 255.255.255.255 bri0
```

What this does is tell the router how to get to network 172.16.50.0, which is through 172.16.60.2. The second line tells the router how to get to 172.16.60.2.

Specifying Interesting Traffic

After setting the route tables in each router, you need to configure the router to determine what brings up the ISDN line. An administrator using the `dialer-list` global configuration command defines interesting packets. The command to turn on all IP traffic is shown as follows:

```
804A(config)#dialer-list 1 protocol ip permit
804A(config)#int bri0
804A(config-if)#dialer-group 1
```

The `dialer-group` command sets the access list on the BRI interface. Extended access lists can be used with the `dialer-list` command to define interesting traffic to just certain applications. We'll cover that in a minute.

If you use the `dialer-list` command, you must enter the `dialer-group` command on an interface before this will work!

Configuring the Dialer Information

There are five steps in the configuration of the dialer information.

1. Choose the interface.

2. Set the IP address.

3. Configure the encapsulation type.

4. Link interesting traffic to the interface.

5. Configure the number or numbers to dial.

Here is an example of how to configure the five steps:

```
804A#config t
804A(config)#int bri0
804A(config-if)#ip address 172.16.60.1 255.255.255.0
804A(config-if)#no shut
804A(config-if)#encapsulation ppp
804A(config-if)#dialer-group 1
804A(config-if)#dialer string 8350661
```

Instead of the dialer string command, you can use a dialer map, which provides more security.

```
804A(config-if)#dialer map ip 172.16.60.2 name 804B
   8350661
```

The dialer map command can be used with the dialer-group command and its associated access list to initiate dialing. The dialer map command uses the IP address of the next hop router, the hostname of the remote router for authentication, and then the number to dial to get there.

Remember, the dialer map command is used to associate an ISDN phone number with the next hop router address.

Take a look at the following configuration of an 804 router:

```
804B#sh run
Building configuration...
Current configuration:
!
version 12.0
no service pad
```

```
service timestamps debug uptime
service timestamps log uptime
no service password-encryption
!
hostname 804B
!
ip subnet-zero
!
isdn switch-type basic-ni
!
interface Ethernet0
 ip address 172.16.50.10 255.255.255.0
 no ip directed-broadcast
!
interface BRI0
 ip address 172.16.60.2 255.255.255.0
 no ip directed-broadcast
 encapsulation ppp
 dialer idle-timeout 300
 dialer string 8358661
 dialer load-threshold 2 either
 dialer-group 1
 isdn switch-type basic-ni
 isdn spid1 0835866201 8358662
 isdn spid2 0835866401 8358664
 hold-queue 75 in
!
ip classless
ip route 172.16.30.0 255.255.255.0 172.16.60.1
ip route 172.16.60.1 255.255.255.255 BRI0
!
dialer-list 1 protocol ip permit
!
```

The BRI interface is running the PPP encapsulation and has a timeout value of 300 seconds. The load-threshold command makes both BRI interfaces come up immediately (okay, I feel that if I am paying for both, I want them both up all the time). The one thing you really want to notice is the `dialer-group 1` command. That number must match the dialer-list number. The `hold-queue 75 in` command tells the router that when it receives an interesting packet, it should queue up to 75 packets while it is waiting for the BRI to come up. If there are more than 75 packets queued before the link comes up, the packets will be dropped.

Optional Commands

There are two other commands that you should configure on your BRI interface: the `dialer load-threshold` command and the `dialer idle-timeout` command.

The `dialer load-threshold` command tells the BRI interface when to bring up the second B channel. The option is from 1 to 255, where 255 tells the BRI to bring up the second B channel only when the first channel is 100 percent loaded. The second option for that command is in, out, or either. This calculates the actual load on the interface either on outbound traffic, inbound traffic, or combined. The default is outbound.

The `dialer idle-timeout` command specifies the number of seconds before a call is disconnected after the last interesting traffic is sent. The default is 120 seconds.

```
RouterA(config-if)#dialer load-threshold 125 either
RouterA(config-if)#dialer idle-timeout 180
```

The `dialer load-threshold` 125 tells the BRI interface to bring up the second B channel if either the inbound or outbound traffic load is 50 percent. The `dialer idle-timeout` 180 changes the default disconnect time from 120 to 180 seconds.

DDR with Access Lists

You can use access lists to be more specific about what is interesting traffic. In the preceding example we just set the dialer list to allow any IP traffic to bring up the line. That is great if you are testing, but it can defeat the purpose of why you use a DDR line in the first place. You can use extended access lists to set the restriction, for example, to only e-mail or Telnet.

Here is an example of how you define the dialer list to use an access list:

```
804A(config)#dialer-list 1 list 110
804A(config)#access-list 110 permit tcp any any eq smtp
```

```
804A(config)#access-list 110 permit tcp any any eq telnet
804A(config)#int bri0
804A(config-if)#dialer-group 1
```

In the preceding example, you configure the `dialer-list` command to look at an access list. This doesn't have to be IP; it can be used with any protocol. Create your list, then apply it to the BRI interface with the `dialer-group` command.

Verifying the ISDN Operation

The following commands can be used to verify legacy DDR and ISDN:

Command	Description
`ping` and `telnet`	Great IP tools for any network. However, your interesting traffic must dictate that Ping and Telnet are acceptable as interesting traffic to bring up a link. Once a link is up, you can ping or telnet to your remote router regardless of your interesting traffic lists.
`show dialer`	Gives good information about your dialer diagnostic information and shows the number of times the dialer string has been reached, the idle-timeout values of each B channel, the length of the call, and the name of the router to which the interface is connected.
`show isdn active`	Shows the number called and whether a call is in progress.
`show isdn status`	A good command to use before trying to dial. Shows if your SPIDs are valid and if you are connected and communicating with layers 1 through 3 information to the provider's switch.
`sho ip route`	Shows all routes the router knows about.
`debug isdn q921`	Used to see layer-2 information only.
`debug isdn q931`	Used to see layer-3 information, including call setup and teardown.
`debug dialer`	Gives you call-setup and teardown activity.
`isdn disconnect int bri0`	Clears the interface and drops the connection. Performing a shutdown on the interface can give you the same results.

Summary

In this chapter, we covered the following key points:

- The difference between the following WAN services: X.25/LAPB, Frame Relay, ISDN/LAPD, SDLC, HDLC, and PPP

- Important Frame Relay and X.25 terms and features

- The commands to configure Frame Relay LMIs, maps, and sub-interfaces

- The commands to monitor Frame Relay operation in the router

- How to identify PPP operations to encapsulate WAN data on Cisco routers

- How to state a relevant use and context for ISDN networking

- How to identify ISDN protocols, function groups, reference points, and channels

- How to describe Cisco's implementation of ISDN BRI

Exam Essentials

Remember the default serial encapsulation on Cisco routers. Cisco routers use a proprietary High-Level Data Link Control (HDLC) encapsulation on all their serial links by default.

Understand what the LMI is in Frame Relay. The LMI is a signaling standard between a CPE device (router) and a frame switch. The LMI is responsible for managing and maintaining status between these devices. This also provides transmission keepalives to ensure that the PVC does not shut down because of inactivity.

Understand the different Frame Relay encapsulations. Cisco uses two different Frame Relay encapsulation methods on their routers. Cisco is the default, and means that the router is connected to a Cisco Frame Relay switch; Internet Engineering Task Force (IETF) means your router is connecting to anything but a Cisco Frame Relay switch.

Remember what the CIR is in Frame Relay. The CIR is the rate, in bits per second, at which the Frame Relay switch agrees to transfer data.

Remember the commands for verifying Frame Relay. The `show frame relay lmi` command will give you the LMI traffic statistics exchanged between the local router and the Frame Relay switch. The `show frame pvc` command will list all configured PVCs and DLCI numbers.

Remember the PPP Data Link layer protocols. The three Data Link layer protocols are: Network Control Protocol (NCP), which defines the Network layer protocols; Link Control Protocol (LCP), a method of establishing, configuring, maintaining, and terminating the point-to-point connection; and High-Level Data Link Control (HDLC), the MAC layer protocol that encapsulates the packets.

Understand what the basic standards of ISDN provide. The ISDN standards define the hardware and call-setup schemes for end-to-end digital connectivity.

Remember what the total bandwidth of BRI provides. Basic Rate Interface provides two 64Kbps bearer (B) channels and one data (D) channel of 16K, for a total of 144Kbps.

Remember what the command show isdn status provides. Shows if your SPIDs are valid and if you are connected and communicating with layers 1 through 3 information to the provider's switch.

Key Terms

Be sure you are familiar with these terms before you take the exam:

Backward-Explicit Congestion Notification (BECN)	circuit switching
Basic Rate Interface (BRI)	committed information rate (CIR)
central office (CO)	customer premises equipment (CPE)
Challenge Authentication Protocol (CHAP)	Data Link Connection Identifier (DLCI)

demarc	network termination 2 (NT2)
Dial-on-demand routing (DDR)	Password Authentication Protocol (PAP)
Discard Eligibility (DE)	point of presence (POP)
Forward-Explicit Congestion Notification (FECN)	point-to-point
Frame Relay	Point-to-Point Protocol (PPP)
High-Level Data Link Control (HDLC)	R reference point
Integrated Services Digital Network (ISDN)	S reference point
leased line	subinterfaces
Link Access Procedure, Balanced (LAPB)	T reference point
local loop	terminal adapter (TA)
Local Management Interface (LMI)	terminal equipment type 1 (TE1)
network termination (NT)	terminal equipment type 2 (TE2)
network termination 1 (NT1)	U reference point

Commands Used in This Chapter

The following list contains a summary of all the commands used in this chapter:

Command	Description
debug dialer	Shows you the call setup and teardown procedures.
debug frame-relay lmi	Shows the LMI exchanges between the router and the Frame Relay switch.

Command	Description
`debug isdn q921`	Shows layer-2 processes.
`debug isdn q931`	Shows layer-3 processes.
`dialer idle-timeout number`	Tells the BRI line when to drop if no interesting traffic is found.
`dialer list number protocol protocol permit/deny`	Specifies interesting traffic for a DDR link.
`dialer load-threshold number inbound/outbound/ either`	Sets the parameters that describe when the second BRI comes up on a ISDN link.
`dialer map protocol address name hostname number`	Used instead of a dialer string to provide more security in an ISDN network.
`dialer string`	Sets the phone number to dial for a BRI interface.
`encapsulation frame-relay`	Changes the encapsulation to Frame Relay on a serial link.
`encapsulation frame-relay ietf`	Sets the encapsulation type to the Internet Engineering Task Force (IETF). Connects Cisco routers to off-brand routers.
`encapsulation hdlc`	Restores the default encapsulation of HDLC on a serial link.
`encapsulation ppp`	Changes the encapsulation on a serial link to PPP.
`frame-relay interface-dlci`	Configures the PVC address on a serial interface or subinterface.
`frame-relay lmi-type`	Configures the LMI type on a serial link.
`frame-relay map protocol address`	Creates a static mapping for use with a Frame Relay network.
`interface s0.16 multipoint`	Creates a multipoint subinterface on a serial link that can be used with Frame Relay networks.

Command	Description
`interface s0.16 point-to-point`	Creates a point-to-point subinterface on a serial link that can be used with Frame Relay.
`isdn spid1`	Sets the number that identifies the first DS0 to the ISDN switch.
`isdn spid2`	Sets the number that identifies the second DS0 to the ISDN switch.
`isdn switch-type`	Sets the type of ISDN switch that the router will communicate with. Can be set at interface level or global configuration mode.
`no inverse-arp`	Turns off the dynamic IARP used with Frame Relay. Static mappings must be configured.
`ppp authentication chap`	Tells PPP to use CHAP authentication.
`ppp authentication pap`	Tells PPP to use PAP authentication.
`show dialer`	Shows the number of times the dialer string has been reached, the idle-timeout values of each B channel, the length of call, and the name of the router to which the interface is connected.
`show frame-relay lmi`	Sets the LMI type on a serial interface.
`show frame-relay map`	Shows the static and dynamic Network layer–to–PVC mappings.
`show frame-relay pvc`	Shows the configured PVCs and DLCI numbers configured on a router.
`show ip route`	Shows the IP routing table.
`show isdn active`	Shows the number called and whether a call is in progress.
`show isdn status`	Shows if your SPIDs are valid and if you are connected and communicating with the provider's switch.
`username name password password`	Creates usernames and passwords for authentication on a Cisco router.

Written Lab 10

1. Write the command to see the encapsulation method on serial 0 of a Cisco router.

2. Write the commands to configure s0 to PPP encapsulation.

3. Write the commands to configure a username of *todd* and password of *cisco* that is used on a Cisco router.

4. Write the commands to enable CHAP authentication on a Cisco BRI interface.

5. Write the commands to configure the DLCI numbers for two serial interfaces, 0 and 1. Use 16 for s0 and 17 for s1.

6. Write the commands to configure a remote office using a point-to-point subinterface. Use DLCI 16 and IP address 172.16.60.1/24. The IPX network is 16.

7. Write the commands to set the switch type of basic-ni on a Cisco router BRI interface.

8. Set the switch type on a Cisco router at the interface level.

9. Write the command that will specify interesting traffic to bring up the ISDN link. Choose all IP traffic.

10. Write the commands necessary to apply the command that you specified in Question 9 to a Cisco router.

11. Write the commands to configure the dialer information on a Cisco router.

12. Write the commands to set the dialer load-threshold and the idle-time percentage.

13. Write the commands that will set the queue for packets at 75 when they are found interesting and need a place to wait for the ISDN link to come up.

14. Write out the five steps in the configuration of the dialer information.

15. Write out the five steps that give a basic description of how DDR works when an interesting packet is received in a router interface.

(The answers to Written Lab 10 can be found following the answers to the Review Questions for this chapter.)

Hands-on Labs

In this section, you will configure Cisco routers in four different WAN labs using the figure supplied in each lab. These labs are included for use with real Cisco routers. If you are using the Sybex Router Fundamentals Simulator provided on this book's companion CD, please use the hands-on labs found within that software program.

Lab 10.1: Configuring PPP Encapsulation and Authentication

Lab 10.2: Configuring and Monitoring HDLC

Lab 10.3: Configuring Frame Relay and Subinterfaces

Lab 10.4: Configuring ISDN and BRI Interfaces

Hands-on Lab 10.1: Configuring PPP Encapsulation and Authentication

By default, Cisco routers use High-Level Data Link Control (HDLC) as a point-to-point encapsulation method on serial links. If you are connecting to non-Cisco equipment, then you can use the PPP encapsulation method to communicate.

The lab you will configure is shown in Figure 10.8.

FIGURE 10.8 PPP lab

EO　SO　　　　　　　　SO　EO

RouterA　　　　　　　　RouterB

1. Type **sh int s0** on Routers A and B to see the encapsulation method.

2. Make sure that each router has the hostname assigned:

   RouterA#**config t**
   RouterA(config)#**hostname RouterA**

   RouterB#**config t**
   RouterB(config)#**hostname RouterB**

3. To change the default HDLC encapsulation method to PPP on both routers, use the `encapsulation` command at interface configuration. Both ends of the link must run the same encapsulation method.

```
RouterA#Config t
RouterA(config)#Int s0
RouterA(config)#Encap ppp
```

4. Now go to Router B and set serial 0 to PPP encapsulation.

```
RouterB#config t
RouterB(config)#int s0
RouterB(config)#encap ppp
```

5. Verify the configuration by typing **sh int s0** on both routers.

6. Notice the IPCP, IPXCP, and CDPCP. This is the information used to transmit the upper-layer (Network layer) information across the ISO HDLC at the MAC sublayer.

7. Define a username and password on each router. Notice that the username is the name of the remote router. Also, the password must be the same.

```
RouterA#config t
RouterA(config)#username RouterB password todd

RouterB#config t
RouterB(config)#username RouterA password todd
```

8. Enable CHAP or PAP authentication on each interface.

```
RouterA(config)#int s0
RouterA(config-if)#ppp authentication chap

RouterB(config)#int s0
RouterB(config-if)#ppp authentication chap
```

9. Verify the PPP configuration on each router by using these two commands:

```
sh int s0
debug PPP authentication
```

Hands-on Lab 10.2: Configuring and Monitoring HDLC

There is no configuration for HDLC, but if you completed Lab 10.1, then the PPP encapsulation would be set on both routers. This is why I put the PPP lab first. This allows you to actually configure HDLC encapsulation on a router.

This second lab will use the same Figure 10.8 as Lab 10.1 used.

1. Set the encapsulation for each serial interface by using the encapsulation hdlc command.

   RouterA#**config t**
   RouterA(config)#**int s0**
   RouterA(config-if)#**encapsulation hdlc**

   RouterB#**config t**
   RouterB(config)#**int s0**
   RouterB(config-if)#**encapsulation hdlc**

2. Verify the HDLC encapsulation by using the show interface s0 command on each router.

Hands-on Lab 10.3: Configuring Frame Relay and Subinterfaces

This lab will use Figure 10.9 to describe and configure Frame Relay configurations.

FIGURE 10.9 Frame Relay lab

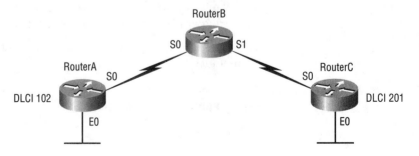

In my seminars I usually use a 2522 router as a frame switch, which provides 10 serial connections. But, since it is possible you may only have some 2501s, I have written this lab to work with three 2501 routers.

1. Set the hostname, `frame-relay switching` command, and the encapsulation of each serial interface on the Frame Relay switch.

```
Router#config t
Router(config)#hostname RouterB
RouterB(config)#frame-relay switching
RouterB(config)#int s0
RouterB(config-if)#encapsulation frame-relay
RouterB(config-if)#int s1
RouterB(config-if)#encapsulation frame-relay
```

2. Configure the Frame Relay mappings on each interface. You do not have to have IP addresses on these interfaces, as they are only switching one interface to another with Frame Relay frames.

```
RouterB(config-if)#int s0
RouterB(config-if)#frame-relay route 102 interface
   Serial1 201
RouterB(config-if)#frame intf-type dce
RouterB(config-if)#clock rate 64000 [if you have this
   as DCE]

RouterB(config-if)#int s1
RouterB(config-if)#frame-relay route 201 interface
   Serial0 102
RouterB(config-if)#frame intf-type dce
RouterB(config-if)#clock rate 64000 [if you have this
   as DCE]
```

This is not as hard as it looks. The `route` command just says that if you receive frames from PVC 102, send them out `int s1` using PVC 201. The second mapping on serial 1 is just the opposite. Anything that comes in `int s1` is routed out serial 0 using PVC 102.

3. Configure your Router A with a point-to-point subinterface.

```
Router#config t
Router(config)#hostname RouterA
```

```
RouterA(config)#int s0
RouterA(config-if)#encapsulation frame-relay
RouterA(config-if)#int s0.102 point-to-point
RouterA(config-if)#ip address 172.16.10.1
  255.255.255.0
RouterC(config-if)#ipx network 10
RouterA(config-if)#frame-relay interface-dlci 102
```

4. Configure Router C with a point-to-point subinterface.

```
Router#config t
Router(config)#hostname RouterC
RouterC(config)#int s0
RouterC(config-if)#encapsulation frame-relay
RouterC(config-if)#int s0.102 point-to-point
RouterC(config-if)#ip address 172.16.10.2
  255.255.255.0
RouterC(config-if)#ipx network 10
RouterC(config-if)#frame-relay interface-dlci 201
```

5. Verify your configurations with the following commands:

```
RouterA>sho frame ?
 ip       show frame relay IP statistics
 lmi      show frame relay lmi statistics
 map      Frame-Relay map table
 pvc      show frame relay pvc statistics
 route    show frame relay route
 traffic  Frame-Relay protocol statistics
```

6. Also, use Ping and Telnet to verify connectivity.

Hands-on Lab 10.4: Configuring ISDN and BRI Interfaces

This lab will use Figure 10.10 as a reference for configuring and monitoring ISDN on Cisco routers. In this lab, you will configure routers 804A and 804B to dial ISDN between the networks 172.16.30.0 and 172.16.50.0, using network 172.16.60.0 on the ISDN BRI interfaces.

FIGURE 10.10 ISDN lab

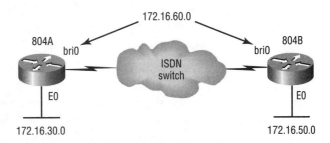

1. Go to 804B and set the hostname and ISDN switch type.

   Router#**config t**
   Router(config)#**hostname 804B**
   804B(config)#**isdn switch-type basic-ni**

2. Set the hostname and switch type on 804A at the interface level. The point of steps 1 and 2 is to show you that you can configure the switch type either through global configuration mode or interface level.

   Router#**config t**
   Router(config)#**hostname 804A**
   804A(config)#**int bri0**
   804B(config-if)#**isdn switch-type basic-ni**

3. On 804A, set the SPID numbers on BRI 0 and make the IP address 171.16.60.1/24. If you have either a real connection into an ISDN network or an ISDN simulator, put your SPID numbers in.

   804a#**config t**
   804A(config)#**int bri0**
   804A(config-if)#**isdn spid 1 0835866101 8358661**
   804A(config-if)#**isdn spid 2 0835866301 8358663**
   804A(config-if)#**ip address 172.16.60.1 255.255.255.0**
   804A(config-if)#**no shut**

4. Set the SPIDs on 804B and make the IP address of the interface 172.16.60.2/24.

   804A#**config t**
   804A(config)#**int bri0**

```
804A(config-if)#isdn spid 1 0835866201 8358662
804A(config-if)#isdn spid 2 0835866401 8358664
804A(config-if)#ip address 172.16.60.2 255.255.255.0
804A(config-if)#no shut
```

5. Create static routes on the routers to use the remote ISDN interface. Dynamic routing will create two problems: (1) the ISDN line will always stay up, and (2) a network loop will occur because of multiple links between the same location. The CCNA exam only discusses distant vector routing protocols (RIP and IGRP). Static routes are recommended with ISDN.

```
804A(config)#ip route 172.16.50.0 255.255.255.0
  172.16.60.2
804A(config)#ip route 172.16.60.2 255.255.255.255 bri0


804B(config)#ip route 172.16.30.0 255.255.255.0
  172.16.60.1
804B(config)#ip route 172.16.60.1 255.255.255.255 bri0
```

6. Specify interesting traffic to bring up the ISDN link. Let's choose all IP traffic. This is a global configuration mode command.

```
804A(config)#dialer-list 1 protocol ip permit


804B(config)#dialer-list 1 protocol ip permit
```

7. Under the BRI interface of both routers, add the command dialer-group 1, which matches the dialer-list number.

```
804B(config)#config t
804B(config)#int bri0
804B(config)#dialer-group 1
```

8. Configure the dialer information on both routers.

```
804A#config t
804A(config)#int bri0
804A(config-if)#dialer string 8358662


804B#config t
804B(config)#int bri0
804B(config-if)#dialer string 8358661
```

9. Set the `dialer load-threshold` and `multilink` commands, as well as the idle-time percentage on both 804 routers.

```
804A#config t
804A(config)#int bri0
804B(config-if)#dialer load-threshold 125 either
804B(config-if)#dialer idle-timeout 180

804B#config t
804B(config)#int bri0
804B(config-if)#dialer load-threshold 125 either
804B(config-if)#dialer idle-timeout 180
```

10. Set the hold queue for packets when they are found interesting and need a place to wait for the ISDN link to come up.

```
804A#config t
804A(config)#int bri0
804B(config-if)#hold-queue 75 in

804B#config t
804B(config)#int bri0
804B(config-if)#hold-queue 75 in
```

11. Verify the ISDN connection.

```
ping
telnet
show dialer
show isdn status
sh ip route
```

Review Questions

1. Regarding Frame Relay, which of the following statements is true?

   A. You must use Cisco encapsulation if connecting to non-Cisco equipment.

   B. You must use ANSI encapsulation if connecting to non-Cisco equipment.

   C. You must use IETF encapsulation if connecting to non-Cisco equipment.

   D. You must use Q.933A encapsulation if connecting to non-Cisco equipment.

2. Which of the following WAN protocols was initially intended to replace standard telephone service?

   A. Frame Relay

   B. ISDN BRI

   C. T1

   D. X.25

3. Which of the following uses a PVC at layer 2?

   A. X.25

   B. ISDN

   C. Frame Relay

   D. HDLC

4. Which ISDN protocol prefix specifies signaling and switching?

   A. I

   B. E

   C. S

   D. Q

5. If you wanted to view the DLCI numbers configured for your Frame Relay network, which command or commands would you use? (Choose all that apply.)

A. `sh frame-relay`

B. `show running`

C. `sh int s0`

D. `sh frame-relay dlci`

E. `sh frame-relay pvc`

6. Which of the following commands would you use to view the Frame Relay Local Management Interface (LMI) traffic statistics?

A. `show lmi`

B. `show ip route`

C. `show frame-relay lmi`

D. `show frame-relay pvc`

7. What does the ISDN Basic Rate Interface (BRI) provide?

A. 23 B channels and one 64Kbps D channel

B. Total bit rate of up to 1.544Mbps

C. Two 56Kbps B channels and one 64Kbps D channel

D. Two 64Kbps B channels and one 16Kbps D channel

8. What is true about Frame Relay DLCI? Select all that apply.

A. DLCI is optional in a Frame Relay network.

B. DLCI represents a single physical circuit.

C. DLCI identifies a logical connection between DTE devices.

D. DLCI is used to tag the beginning of a frame when using LAN switching.

9. Which command will list all configured PVCs and DLCIs?

   A. `sh frame pvc`

   B. `sh frame`

   C. `sh frame lmi`

   D. `sh pvc`

10. What is the default encapsulation on point-to-point links between two Cisco routers?

   A. SDLC

   B. HDLC

   C. Cisco

   D. ANSI

11. What information is provided by the Local Management Interface? (Choose all that apply.)

   A. The status of virtual circuits

   B. The current DLCI values

   C. The global or local significance of the DLCI values

   D. LMI encapsulation type

12. Which protocol used in PPP allows multiple Network layer protocols to be used during a connection?

   A. LCP

   B. NCP

   C. HDLC

   D. X.25

13. Which protocol is used with PPP to establish, configure, and authenticate a data-link connection?

A. LCP

B. NCP

C. HDLC

D. X.25

14. In Frame Relay, what identifies the PVC?

A. NCP

B. LMI

C. IARP

D. DLCI

15. What WAN protocol would you use to create a WAN that provides simultaneous transmission of voice, video, and data?

A. X.25

B. Frame Relay

C. ATM

D. 56K dedicated line

16. Which of the following protocols provide connections between computers via dial-up telephone lines? Select all that apply.

A. SLIP

B. X.25

C. LABP

D. PPP

17. Which of the following is a valid second subinterface on serial interface 0?

A. `interface s0 sub 2 point-to-point sub 2`

B. `interface s0.2 point-to-point`

C. `interface 2 s0 point-to-point`

D. `subinterface serial0.2 point-to-point`

18. Which of the following is true regarding CIR?

   A. It is used in ISDN to allow separate B and D channels.

   B. It is a signaling standard between the CPE device and Frame Relay switch.

   C. It is responsible for managing the connection and maintaining status between devices.

   D. It is the rate, in bits per second, at which the Frame Relay switch agrees to transfer data.

19. What is the bandwidth of one ISDN B channel?

   A. 64Kbps

   B. 128Kbps

   C. 144Kbps

   D. 1.544Mbps

20. Which of the following are benefits of ISDN networking? Select all that apply.

   A. Full-time connectivity across the ISDN is spoofed by the Cisco IOS routers using dial-on-demand routing (DDR).

   B. Small office and home office sites can be economically supported with ISDN BRI services.

   C. ISDN can be used as a backup service for a leased-line connection between the remote and central offices.

   D. Modem racking and cabling can be eliminated by integration of digital modem cards on Cisco IOS Network Access Server (NSA).

   E. ISDN replaces the SS7 signaling in the PSTN backbone.

21. If you have a remote router with a hostname of "Bob" and you want to set up a PPP authentication link using the password "Cisco" to a local router with a hostname "Todd", which of the following commands is correct?

A. username bob password cisco

B. username Bob password Cisco

C. username todd password cisco

D. username Todd password Cisco

22. Which of the following technologies use high-quality digital lines and is packet switched? (Select all that apply.)

    A. ATM

    B. Frame Relay

    C. ISDN

    D. HDLC

    E. PPP

23. The following ISDN command verifies which of the following?

show isdn status

    A. Shows that a router has established layer-1 and layer-2 connectivity to the telephone company ISDN switch

    B. Shows the number called and whether a call is in progress

    C. Shows the idle-timeout values of each B channel, the length of the call, and the name of the router to which the interface is connected

    D. Shows the dialer diagnostic information and the number of times the dialer string has been reached, the idle-timeout values of each B channel, the length of the call, and the name of the router to which the interface is connected

24. What is the default encapsulation type for Frame Relay in a Cisco router?

    A. HDLC

    B. IEFT

    C. Cisco

    D. PPP

    E. Ansi

    F. Q933i

25. The Local Management Interface (LMI) is responsible for which of the following?

A. For keeping routers up and running with less memory overhead

B. For telling the switch what type of router is running on each end

C. For broadcasting IP routing protocol information

D. For transmission keepalives to ensure that the PVC does not shut down because of inactivity

Answers to Review Questions

1. C. Internet Engineering Task Force (IETF) is the encapsulation method used when connecting Frame Relay to non-Cisco routers.

2. B. ISDN BRI was intended to replace standard dial-up modems.

3. C. Frame Relay uses a PVC at the Data Link layer.

4. D. The ISDN specification that is used for switching and signaling is the Q specification.

5. B, E. You can use the `show running-config` and `show frame-relay pvc` commands to see the DLCI numbers configured on your router.

6. C. The `show frame-relay lmi` command will allow you to view the LMI traffic statistics.

7. D. BRI is two DS0s, which are 64Kbps each. It also has one data channel of 16Kbps to provide clocking.

8. C. DLCI is required to be used on each circuit with Frame Relay. The DLCI number identifies the PVC of each circuit. PVCs are logical links between two DTE devices.

9. A. The `show frame-relay pvc` command will show the PVCs configured and the associated DLCI numbers.

10. B. Cisco uses a proprietary HDLC as the default encapsulation on all their serial interfaces.

11. A, B, C. The LMI provides PVC status messaging, the DLCI values associated with a PV, and global or local significance of the DLCI values.

12. B. Network Control Protocol works at the LLC sublayer of the Data Link layer and is responsible for allowing multiple Network layer protocols to be used with Point-to-Point Protocol.

13. A. Link Control Protocol works at the MAC sublayer of the Data Link layer to establish, maintain, and authenticate a data-link connection.

14. D. Data Link Connection Identifiers (DLCIs) are used to identify a permanent virtual circuit.

15. C. Asynchronous Transfer Mode (ATM) provide simultaneous transmission of voice, video, and data.

16. A, D. Serial Line Internet Protocol (SLIP) and Point-to-Point Protocol (PPP) are the protocols typically used for communications on dial-up connections.

17. B. Subinterfaces are created with the `interface serial0.#` command. This is followed by the type of subinterface used, either point-to-point or multipoint.

18. D. The committed information rate is used in Frame Relay to set the transfer rate between the router and the Frame Relay switch.

19. A. The ISDN B channel used in BRI is 64Kbps. Each Basic Rate Interface used two Bearer (B channels) and one Data (D Channel).

20. A, B, C, D. ISDN uses SS7 signaling.

21. B. To set up authentication, you must use the `username` command with the hostname of the remote router. This is case sensitive.

22. B. Frame Relay is a packet-switching technology that uses high-quality digital lines to get speeds up to T3.

23. A. The command `show isdn status` shows that a router has established layer-1 and layer-2 connectivity to the telephone company ISDN switch.

24. C. If you just type from interface configuration mode, `encapsulation frame-relay`, the encapsulation type will be Cisco.

25. D. The LMI provides keepalives between the router and the frame switch to verify that the link and connection are still active.

Answers to Written Lab 10

1. sh int s0

2. config t
   int s0
   encap ppp

3. config t
   username todd password cisco

4. config t
   int bri0
   ppp authentication chap

5. config t
   int s0
   frame interface-dlci 16
   int s1
   frame interface-dlci 17

6. config t
   int s0
   encap frame
   int s0.16 point-to-point
   ip address 172.16.60.1 255.255.255.0
   ipx netw 16
   frame interface-dlci 16

7. config t
   isdn switch-type basic-ni

8. config t
   interface bri 0
   isdn switch-type basic-ni

9. Router(config)#**dialer-list 1 protocol ip permit**

10. config t
    int bri0
    dialer-group 1

11. config t
    int bri0
    dialer string 8358662

12. config t
    int bri0
    dialer load-threshold 125 either
    dialer idle-timeout 180

13. config t
    int bri0
    hold-queue 75 in

14. These are the steps you should take to configure the dialer information:

    1. Choose the interface.

    2. Set the IP address.

    3. Configure the encapsulation type.

    4. Link interesting traffic to the interface.

    5. Configure the number or numbers to dial.

15. These are the steps that DDR follows when an interesting packet is received in a router interface:

    1. Route to the destination network is determined.

    2. Interesting packets dictate a DDR call.

    3. Dialer information is looked up.

    4. Traffic is transmitted.

    5. Call is terminated when no more traffic is being transmitted over a link and the idle-timeout period ends.

Appendix

A

Introduction to the Cisco IOS: Hands-on Labs

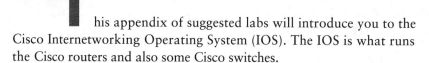

his appendix of suggested labs will introduce you to the Cisco Internetworking Operating System (IOS). The IOS is what runs the Cisco routers and also some Cisco switches.

In this appendix, you'll learn how to configure Cisco routers using a command-line interface (CLI). The CLI is really the best way to configure a router because it gives you the most flexibility.

These labs were designed and written to work with the Router Fundamentals Simulator that is found on the CD bundled with this book. You can find other products that have more labs and more routers and switches at www.routersim.com.

The following suggested labs will be covered in this chapter:

- Lab A.1: Logging into a Cisco Router

- Lab A.2: Editing and Help Features

- Lab A.3: Gathering Basic Router Information

- Lab A.4: Setting the Passwords

- Lab A.5: Setting Router Banners

- Lab A.6: Configuring Router Interfaces

- Lab A.7: Bringing up an Interface

- Lab A.8: Configuring an IP Address on an Interface

- Lab A.9: Serial Interface Commands

Lab A.1: Logging into a Cisco Router

This first lab will have you connect to a router and teach you how to log in using the `enable` and `disable` commands.

1. Connect to a router through the Network Visualizer and press Return. The `Router>` prompt will appear. This is called *user mode* and is mostly used to view statistics, though it is also a stepping-stone to logging into *privileged mode*. You can only view and change the configuration of a Cisco router in privileged mode, which you enter with the `enable` command.

```
Router>
Router>enable
Router#
```

2. You now end up with a `Router#` prompt, which indicates you are in privileged mode. You can both view and change the configuration in this mode. You can go back from privileged mode to user mode by using the `disable` command.

```
Router#disable
Router>
```

3. At this point, you can type **logout** to exit the console.

```
Router>logout
Router con0 is now available
Press RETURN to get started.
```

Lab A.2: Editing and Help Features

You can use the Cisco advanced editing features to help you configure your router. This lab will teach you how and where to use a question mark (?) from the CLI as well as how to use keystrokes to help you edit your command strings.

1. By using a question mark (?) at any prompt, you can see the list of commands available from that prompt.

```
Router#?
Exec commands:
  access-enable    Create a temporary Access-List entry
  access-profile   Apply user-profile to interface
  access-template  Create a temporary Access-List entry
  bfe              For manual emergency modes setting
  clear            Reset functions
  clock            Manage the system clock
  configure        Enter configuration mode
  connect          Open a terminal connection
  copy             Copy configuration or image data
  debug            Debugging functions (see also
                     'undebug')
  disable          Turn off privileged commands
  disconnect       Disconnect an existing network
                     connection
  enable           Turn on privileged commands
  erase            Erase flash or configuration memory
  exit             Exit from the EXEC
  help             Description of the interactive help
                     system
  lock             Lock the terminal
  login            Log in as a particular user
  logout           Exit from the EXEC
  mrinfo           Request neighbor and version
     information from a multicast router
--More-
```

At this point, you can press the spacebar to get another page of information, or you can press Return to go one command at a time. You can also press any other key to quit and return to the prompt.

2. To find commands that start with a certain letter, use the letter and the question mark (?) with no space between them.

```
Router#c?
clear  clock  configure  connect  copy

Router#c
```

Notice that by typing c?, we received a response of all the commands that start with *c*. Also notice that the `Router#` prompt returned with our command still present. This is helpful when you have long commands and need the next possible command.

3. To find the next command in a string, type the first command and then a question mark. Set the router's clock by typing **clock ?** and following the help screens; set the router's time and date.

```
Router#clock ?
  set  Set the time and date
Router#clock set ?
  hh:mm:ss  Current Time
Router#clock set 10:30:10 ?
  <1-31>  Day of the month
  MONTH   Month of the year
Router#clock set 10:30:10 28 ?
  MONTH  Month of the year
Router#clock set 10:30:10 28 jun ?
  <1993-2035>  Year
Router#clock set 10:30:10 28 jun 2002 ?
  <cr>
Router#
```

By using the `clock` command, then a space and a question mark, you will get a list of the next possible commands and what they do. Notice that we just kept typing a command, a space, and then a question mark until `<cr>` (carriage return) was our only option.

4. Type **show clock** to see the time and date you have set.

5. If you are typing commands and receive this:

    ```
    Router#clock set 10:30:10
    % Incomplete command.
    ```

    then you know that the command string is not done. Just press the Up arrow key to receive the last command entered, then continue with the command by using your question mark.

6. Also, if you receive this error:

    ```
    Router#clock set 10:30:10 28 8
                              ^
    % Invalid input detected at '^' marker.
    ```

    you should notice that the ^ marks the point where you have entered the command incorrectly. This is very helpful.

7. If you receive this error:

    ```
    Router#sh te
    % Ambiguous command:  "sh te"
    ```

    it means you did not enter all the keywords or values required by this command. Use the question mark to find the command you need.

    ```
    Router#sh te?
    WORD  tech-support  terminal
    ```

8. From privileged mode, type **show access-list 10**. *Don't* press Enter.

9. Notice the cursor is at the end of the line. Press Ctrl+A. This takes you to the beginning of the line.

10. Press Ctrl+E. This should take you back to the end of the line.

11. Press Ctrl+A, then press Ctrl+F. This should move you forward one character.

12. Press Ctrl+B, which will move you back one character.

13. Press Return, then press Ctrl+P. This will repeat the last command.

14. Press the Up arrow on your keyboard. This will also repeat the last command.

Lab A.3: Gathering Basic Router Information

This lab will provide the commands used to gather basic information about a Cisco router.

1. The show version command provides basic configuration for the system hardware as well as the software version, the names and sources of configuration files, and the boot images.

```
Router#sh version
Cisco Internetwork Operating System Software
IOS (tm) 2500 Software (C2500-JS-L), Version 12.0(8),
  RELEASE SOFTWARE (fc1)
Copyright (c) 1986-1999 by cisco Systems, Inc.
Compiled Mon 29-Nov-99 14:52 by kpma
Image text-base: 0x03051C3C, data-base: 0x00001000

ROM: System Bootstrap, Version 11.0(10c), SOFTWARE
BOOTFLASH: 3000 Bootstrap Software (IGS-BOOT-R),
  Version 11.0(10c), RELEASE SOFTWARE (fc1)

RouterA uptime is 5 minutes
System restarted by power-on
System image file is "flash:c2500-js-l_120-8.bin"

cisco 2522 (68030) processor (revision N) with 14336K/
  2048K bytes of memory.
Processor board ID 15662842, with hardware revision
  00000003
Bridging software.
X.25 software, Version 3.0.0.
SuperLAT software (copyright 1990 by Meridian
  Technology Corp).
TN3270 Emulation software.
Basic Rate ISDN software, Version 1.1.
```

```
1 Ethernet/IEEE 802.3 interface(s)
2 Serial network interface(s)
8 Low-speed serial(sync/async) network interface(s)
1 ISDN Basic Rate interface(s)
32K bytes of non-volatile configuration memory.
16384K bytes of processor board System flash (Read ONLY)
Configuration register is 0x2102
```

The show version command tells you how long the router has been running, how it was restarted, the IOS filename running, the model hardware and processor versions, and the amount of DRAM. Also, the configuration register value is listed last.

2. You can view the router files by typing **show running-config** or **show startup-config** from privileged mode. The sh run command, which is the shortcut for show running-config, tells us that we are viewing the current configuration.

```
Router#sh run
Building configuration...

Current configuration:
!
version 12.0
service timestamps debug uptime
service timestamps log uptime
no service password-encryption
!
hostname Router
ip subnet-zero
!
[output cut]
```

3. The sh start command, which is the shortcut for the show startup-config command, shows us the configuration that will be used the next time the router is reloaded and also shows us the amount of NVRAM used to store the startup-config file.

```
Router#sh start
Using 4850 out of 32762 bytes
!
```

```
version 12.0
service timestamps debug uptime
service timestamps log uptime
no service password-encryption
!
hostname Router
!
!
ip subnet-zero
[output cut]
```

4. You can delete the startup-config file by using the `erase startup-config` command. Once you perform this command, you will receive an error if you try to view the startup-config file.

```
Router#erase startup-config
Erasing the nvram filesystem will remove all files!
  Continue? [confirm]
[OK]
Erase of nvram: complete
Router#sh start
%% Non-volatile configuration memory is not present
Router#
```

Lab A.4: Setting the Passwords

There are five passwords used to secure your Cisco routers. The first two passwords discussed are used to set your enable password, which is used to secure privileged mode. This will prompt a user for a password when the `enable` command is used. The other three are used to configure a password when user mode is accessed either through the console port, the auxiliary port, or Telnet.

1. Set the two enable passwords on your router. You set the enable passwords from global configuration mode.

```
Router(config)#enable secret todd
Router(config)#enable password cisco
```

2. The enable secret, if set, supersedes the enable password.

3. Set your user-mode passwords by using the `line` command.

```
Router(config)#line ?
  <0-4>    First Line number
  aux      Auxiliary line
  console  Primary terminal line
  vty      Virtual terminal
```

- Aux is used to set the user-mode password for the auxiliary port. This is typically used for configuring a modem on the router but can be used as a console as well.

- Console is used to set a console user-mode password.

- Vty is used to set a Telnet password on the router. If this password is not set, then Telnet cannot be used by default.

To configure the user-mode passwords, you configure the line you want and use the `login` command to tell the router to prompt for authentication.

4. Set the auxiliary password on your router. To configure the auxiliary password, go to global configuration mode and type **line aux ?**. Notice that you only get a choice of 0–0 because there is only one port.

```
Router#config t
Enter configuration commands, one per line. End with
  CNTL/Z.
Router(config)#line aux ?
  <0-0>  First Line number
Router(config)#line aux 0
Router(config-line)#login
Router(config-line)#password todd
```

It is important to remember the `login` command, or the auxiliary port won't prompt for authentication.

5. Set your console password on your router. To set the console password, use the `line console 0` command.

```
Router(config)#line console 0
Router(config-line)#login
Router(config-line)#password todd1
```

6. Set your Telnet password on your router. To set the user-mode password for Telnet access into the router, use the line vty command.

```
Router(config-line)#line vty 0 ?
<1-4>Last Line Number
<cr>
Router(config-line)#line vty 0 4
Router(config-line)#login
Router(config-line)#password todd2
```

After your routers are configured with an IP address, you can use the Telnet program to configure and check your routers instead of having to use a console cable.

Lab A.5: Setting Router Banners

You can set a banner on a Cisco router so that, for example, when either a user logs into the router or an administrator telnets into the router, a banner will give them information you want them to have.

1. The command to use is from global configuration mode and shown below:

```
Router(config)#banner ?
  LINE      c banner-text c, where 'c' is a delimiting
              character
  exec      Set EXEC process creation banner
  incoming  Set incoming terminal line banner
  login     Set login banner
  motd      Set Message of the Day banner
```

2. The message of the day is the most used and gives a message to every person dialing in or connecting to the router, via Telnet, auxiliary port, or console port.

```
Router(config)#banner motd ?
  LINE  c banner-text c, where 'c' is a delimiting
      character
Router(config)#banner motd #
Enter TEXT message.  End with the character '#'.
```

```
Authorized personnel only.
#
Router(config)#^Z
Router#
00:25:12: %SYS-5-CONFIG_I: Configured from console by
  console
Router#exit

Router con0 is now available
Press RETURN to get started.

Authorized personnel only.

Router>
```

3. The above MOTD banner tells anyone connecting to the router that they must be authorized.

For information on the other available banners, please see Chapter 4.

Lab A.6: Configuring Router Interfaces

Interface configuration is one of the most important configurations of the router. Without interfaces, the router is useless. Interface configurations must be exact to be able to communicate with other devices.

1. Connect to a router and enter global configuration mode. Type **interface ?** to see all the interfaces available on the router.

```
Router(config)#interface ?
```

The output will vary depending on the device you are connected to.

2. Type **interface serial ?**. This output shows a 2501 router with two serial interfaces, which are labeled 0 and 1:

```
Router(config)#interface serial ?
  <0-1>  Serial interface number
```

3. At this point you must choose the interface you want to configure. Once you do that, you will be in interface configuration for that interface. The command to choose serial port 1, for example, would be

```
Router(config)#interface serial 1
Router(config-if)#
```

4. The 2501 router has one Ethernet 10BaseT port. Typing **interface ethernet 0** can configure the interface.

```
Router(config)#int ethernet ?
  <0-0>  Ethernet interface number
Router(config)#int ethernet 0
Router(config-if)#
```

Lab A.7: Bringing up an Interface

You can turn an interface off with the shutdown interface command or enable it with the no shutdown command. If an interface is shut down, it will display administratively down when using the show interface command, and the show running-config command will show the interface as shut down. All interfaces are shut down by default.

1. Type **show interface Ethernet 0** and see that it is administratively down.

```
Router#sh int e0
Ethernet0 is administratively down, line protocol is down
[output cut]
```

2. Bring up interface serial 0 with the no shutdown command.

```
Router#config t
Enter configuration commands, one per line. End with
  CNTL/Z.
Router(config)#int e0
Router(config-if)#no shutdown
Router(config-if)#^Z
```

```
00:57:08: %LINK-3-UPDOWN: Interface Ethernet0, changed
   state to up
00:57:09: %LINEPROTO-5-UPDOWN: Line protocol on
   Interface Ethernet0, changed state to up
```

Router#**sh int e0**
Ethernet0 is up, line protocol is up

3. Configure the router to enable all interfaces by issuing the no shutdown command on all interfaces.

Lab A.8: Configuring an IP Address on an Interface

You don't *have* to use Internet Protocol (IP) on your routers; however, IP is typically used on all routers. To configure IP addresses on an interface, use the ip address command from interface configuration mode.

1. Configure the Ethernet 0 interface with the IP address of 172.16.10.2/24.

Router(config)#**int e0**
Router(config-if)#**ip address 172.16.10.2 255.255.255.0**
Router(config-if)#**no shut**

Notice that you turn on an interface with the no shut command. Remember to look at the command show interface e0, for example, which will show you if it is administratively shut down or not. show running-config will also show you if the interface is shut down.

2. If you want to add a second subnet address to an interface, then you must use the secondary command. If you type another IP address and press Enter, it will replace the existing IP address and mask. To add a secondary IP address, use the secondary command.

Router(config-if)#**ip address 172.16.20.2 255.255.255.0 secondary**
Router(config-if)#**^Z**

You can verify that both addresses are configured on the interface with the show running-config command (sh run for short).

```
Router#sh run
Building configuration...
Current configuration:
[output cut]
!
interface Ethernet0
 ip address 172.16.20.2 255.255.255.0 secondary
 ip address 172.16.10.2 255.255.255.0
!
```

Lab A.9: Serial Interface Commands

To configure a serial interface, a couple of specifics need to be discussed. Typically, the interface will be attached to a CSU/DSU type of device that provides clocking for the line. However, if you have a back-to-back configuration—for example, in a lab environment—one end must provide clocking. This would be the data communication equipment (DCE) end of the cable. Cisco routers, by default, are all data terminal equipment (DTE) devices, and you must tell an interface to provide clocking if it is to act as a DCE device.

1. You configure a DCE serial interface with the clock rate command.

```
Router#config t
Enter configuration commands, one per line. End with
   CNTL/Z.
Router(config)#int s0
Router(config-if)#clock rate ?
      Speed (bits per second)
  1200
  2400
  4800
  9600
  19200
```

```
        38400
        56000
        64000
        72000
        125000
        148000
        250000
        500000
        800000
        1000000
        1300000
        2000000
        4000000

  <300-4000000>    Choose clockrate from list above
Router(config-if)#clock rate 64000
%Error: This command applies only to DCE interfaces
Router(config-if)#int s1
Router(config-if)#clock rate 64000
```

It does not hurt anything to try and put a clock rate on an interface. Notice that the clock rate command is in bits per second.

2. The next command you need to understand is the bandwidth command. Every Cisco router ships with a default serial link bandwidth of T-1, or 1.544Mbps. However, understand that this has nothing to do with how data is transferred over a link. The bandwidth of a serial link is used by routing protocols such as IGRP, EIGRP, and OSPF to calculate the best cost to a remote network. If you are using RIP routing, for example, the bandwidth setting of a serial link is irrelevant.

```
Router(config-if)#bandwidth ?
  <1-10000000>  Bandwidth in kilobits

Router(config-if)#bandwidth 64
```

Notice that unlike the clock rate command, the bandwidth command is configured in kilobits.

Lab A.10: Setting the Router Hostnames

You can set the hostname of the router with the hostname command. This is only locally significant, which means it has no bearing on how the router performs name lookups on the internetwork.

1. Set the hostname of your router.

```
Router#config t
Enter configuration commands, one per line. End with
   CNTL/Z.
Router(config)#hostname Todd
Todd(config)#
```

Notice that when you pressed Return, the command took effect immediately.

Lab A.11: Setting Interface Descriptions

Setting descriptions on an interface is helpful to the administrator and, like the hostname, only locally significant. This is a helpful command because it can be used to keep track of circuit numbers, among other things.

1. Set the description of the interface Ethernet 0 to Sales LAN and the serial 0 interface to WAN to Miami with a circuit number of 6fdda4321.

```
Todd(config)#int e0
Todd(config-if)#description Sales Lan
Todd(config-if)#int s0
Todd(config-if)#description Wan to Miami
   circuit:6fdda4321
```

2. You can view the description of an interface either with the show running-config or the show interface command.

```
Todd#sh run
[output cut]
interface Ethernet0
```

```
                    description Sales Lan
                    ip address 172.16.10.30 255.255.255.0
                    no ip directed-broadcast
                    !
                    interface Serial0
                    description Wan to Miami circuit:6fdda4321
                    no ip address
                    no ip directed-broadcast
                    no ip mroute-cache

               Todd#sh int e0
               Ethernet0 is up, line protocol is up
                  Hardware is Lance, address is 0010.7be8.25db (bia
                  0010.7be8.25db)
                  Description: Sales Lan
               [output cut]

               Todd#sh int s0
               Serial0 is up, line protocol is up
                  Hardware is HD64570
                  Description: Wan to Miami circuit:6fdda4321
               [output cut]
               Atlanta#
```

Lab A.12: Saving Your Configurations

You can manually save the file from DRAM to NVRAM by using the copy running-config startup-config command. You can use the shortcut copy run start also.

1. Save the configuration on your router.

```
Router#copy run start
Destination filename [startup-config]?return
Building configuration...
```

This will now place the file you created into NVRAM, which will be used the next time the router is booted up.

2. You can view this file with the show startup-config command.

Router#**show start**

Lab A.13: Verifying Your Configuration

Once you take a look at the running-config, and it appears that everything is in order, you can verify your configuration with utilities such as Ping and Telnet.

1. You can ping with different protocols, and you can see this by typing **ping ?** at the router user-mode or privileged-mode prompt.

```
Router#ping ?
  WORD      Ping destination address or hostname
  appletalk Appletalk echo
  decnet    DECnet echo
  ip        IP echo
  ipx       Novell/IPX echo
  srb       srb echo
  <cr>
```

2. Telnet can be used to test IP connectivity and to gain access into remote routers. From the router prompt, you do not need to use the telnet command. If you just type a hostname or IP address, it will assume you want to telnet. The following example shows how to use Telnet from a router prompt. However, you need to have a configured and working network for Telnet to be successful.

```
Router#telnet ?
  WORD  IP address or hostname of a remote system
  <cr>
```

3. Another way to verify your configuration is by using the show interface commands. The first command is show interface ?, which shows us all the available interfaces to configure. The only interfaces that are not logical are Ethernet and Serial.

```
Router#sh int ?
  Ethernet    IEEE 802.3
  Null        Null interface
  Serial      Serial
  accounting  Show interface accounting
  crb         Show interface routing/bridging info
  irb         Show interface routing/bridging info
  <cr>
```

4. You can be specific with the command and use **show interface ethernet** 0 or **serial** 0.

```
Router#sh int e0
Ethernet0 is up, line protocol is up
  Hardware is Lance, address is 0010.7b7f.c26c (bia
     0010.7b7f.c26c)
Internet address is 172.16.10.1/24
  MTU 1500 bytes, BW 10000 Kbit, DLY 1000 usec,
     reliability 255/255, txload 1/255, rxload 1/255
  Encapsulation ARPA, loopback not set, keepalive set
     (10 sec)
  ARP type: ARPA, ARP Timeout 04:00:00
  Last input 00:08:23, output 00:08:20, output hang
     never
  Last clearing of "show interface" counters never
  Queueing strategy: fifo
  Output queue 0/40, 0 drops; input queue 0/75, 0 drops
  5 minute input rate 0 bits/sec, 0 packets/sec
  5 minute output rate 0 bits/sec, 0 packets/sec
     25 packets input, 2459 bytes, 0 no buffer
     Received 25 broadcasts, 0 runts, 0 giants, 0
        throttles
     0 input errors, 0 CRC, 0 frame, 0 overrun, 0
        ignored, 0 abort
     0 input packets with dribble condition detected
     33 packets output, 7056 bytes, 0 underruns
     0 output errors, 0 collisions, 1 interface resets
     0 babbles, 0 late collision, 0 deferred
```

```
0 lost carrier, 0 no carrier
0 output buffer failures, 0 output buffers swapped
  out
```

Lab A.14: Final Lab

This final lab will have you log into both routers and configure the routers using all the commands discussed in this chapter.

1. Connect to the 2501A router and log in. Set the hostname and passwords.

```
Router#config t
Router(config)#hostname 2501A
2501A(config)#enable secret todd
2501A(config)#enable password bill
2501A(config)#line console 0
2501A(config-line)#login
2501A(config-line)#password todd
2501A(config-line)#line aux 0
2501A(config-line)#login
2501A(config-line)#password todd
2501A(config-line)#line vty 0 4
2501A(config-line)#login
2501A(config-line)#password todd
2501A(config-line)#
```

2. On the 2501A router, set the IP address of 172.16.10.1/24 on the Ethernet 0 interface and 172.16.20.1/24 on the serial 0 interface. Set the clock rate to 64000 on serial 0.

```
2501A(config-line)#interface serial 0
2501A(config-if)#ip address 172.16.20.1 255.255.255.0
2501A(config-if)#clock rate 64000
2501A(config-if)#no shut
2501A(config-if)#interface ethernet 0
2501A(config-if)#ip address 172.16.10.1 255.255.255.0
2501A(config-if)#no shut
2501A(config-if)#
```

3. Set the interface descriptions and router banner.

```
2501A(config-if)#description Ethernet LAN on 2501A
2501A(config-if)#interface serial 0
2501A(config-if)#description WAN to 2501B
2501A(config-if)#banner motd #
This is the 2501A router
#
2501A(config-if)#
```

4. Save the configuration.

```
2501A(config-if)#^z
2501A#copy running-config startup-config
2501A#
```

5. Connect to the 2501B router and log in. Set the hostname and passwords.

```
Router#config t
Router(config)#hostname 2501B
2501B(config)#enable secret todd
2501B(config)#enable password bill
2501B(config)#line console 0
2501B(config-line)#login
2501B(config-line)#password todd
2501B(config-line)#line aux 0
2501B(config-line)#login
2501B(config-line)#password todd
2501B(config-line)#line vty 0 4
2501B(config-line)#login
2501B(config-line)#password todd
2501B(config-line)#
```

6. On the 2501B router, set the IP address of 172.16.30.1/24 on the Ethernet 0 interface and 172.16.20.2/24 on the serial 0 interface.

```
2501B(config-line)#interface serial 0
2501B(config-if)#ip address 172.16.20.2 255.255.255.0
2501B(config-if)#no shut
2501B(config-if)#interface ethernet 0
```

```
2501B(config-if)#ip address 172.16.30.1 255.255.255.0
2501B(config-if)#no shut
2501B(config-if)#
```

7. Set the interface descriptions and router banner.

```
2501B(config-if)#description Ethernet LAN on 2501B
2501B(config-if)#interface serial 0
2501B(config-if)#description WAN to 2501A
2501B(config-if)#banner motd #
This is the 2501B router
#
2501B(config-if)#
```

8. Save the configuration.

```
2501B(config-if)#^z
2501B#copy running-config startup-config
2501B#
```

9. Turn on RIP routing with the following commands on each router:

```
2501A#config t
2501A(config)#router rip
2501A(config-router)#network 172.16.0.0
2501A(config-router)#^z
2501A#

2501B#config t
2501B(config)#router rip
2501B(config-router)#network 172.16.0.0
2501B(config-router)#^z
2501B#
```

10. From the 2501A router, type **show ip route** to view the routing table. All three networks should be in the routing table.

11. Ping from the console of the 2501A router to 172.16.30.1, which will verify that the routers are communicating.

Appendix B

Commands in This Study Guide

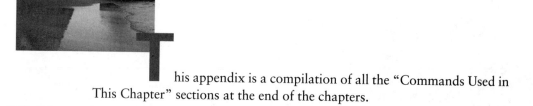

T his appendix is a compilation of all the "Commands Used in This Chapter" sections at the end of the chapters.

Command	Description	Chapter
?	Gives you a help screen	4
0.0.0.0 255.255.255.255	A wildcard command; same as the **any** command	9
access-class	Applies a standard IP access list to a VTY line	9
access-list	Creates a list of tests to filter the networks	9
any	Specifies any host or any network; same as the 0.0.0.0 255.255.255.255 command	9
Backspace	Deletes a single character	4
bandwidth	Sets the bandwidth on a serial interface	4
banner	Creates a banner for users who log into the router	4
cdp enable	Turns on CDP on an individual interface	7
cdp holdtime	Changes the holdtime of CDP packets	7
cdp run	Turns on CDP on a router	7
cdp timer	Changes the CDP update timer	7
clear counters	Clears the statistics from an interface	4
clear line	Clears a connection connected via Telnet to your router	7

Command	Description	Chapter
`clock rate`	Provides clocking on a serial DCE interface	4
`config memory`	Copies the `startup-config` to `running-config`	4
`config network`	Copies a configuration stored on a TFTP host to `running-config`	4
`config terminal`	Puts you in global configuration mode and changes the running-config	4
`config-register`	Tells the router how to boot and to change the configuration register setting	7
`copy flash tftp`	Copies a file from flash memory to a TFTP host	7
`copy run start`	Short for `copy running-config startup-config`; places a configuration into NVRAM	4, 7
`copy run tftp`	Copies the `running-config` file to a TFTP host	7
`copy tftp flash`	Copies a file from a TFTP host to flash memory	7
`copy tftp run`	Copies a configuration from a TFTP host to the `running-config` file	7
Ctrl+A	Moves your cursor to the beginning of the line	4
Ctrl+D	Deletes a single character	4
Ctrl+E	Moves your cursor to the end of the line	4
Ctrl+F	Moves forward one character	4
Ctrl+R	Redisplays a line	4
Ctrl+Shift+6, then X (keyboard combination)	Returns you to the originating router when you telnet to numerous routers	7
Ctrl+U	Erases a line	4
Ctrl+W	Erases a word	4

Command	Description	Chapter
Ctrl+Z	Ends configuration mode and returns to EXEC	4
debug dialer	Shows you the call setup and teardown procedures	10
debug frame-relay lmi	Shows the lmi exchanges between the router and the Frame Relay switch	10
debug ip igrp events	Provides a summary of the IGRP routing information running on the network	5
debug ip igrp transactions	Shows message requests from neighbor routers asking for an update and the broadcasts sent from your router to that neighbor router	5
debug ip rip	Sends console messages displaying information about RIP packets being sent and received on a router interface	5
debug ipx	Shows the RIP and SAP information as it passes through the router	8
debug isdn q921	Shows layer-2 processes	10
debug isdn q931	Shows layer-3 processes	10
delete nvram	Deletes the contents of NVRAM on a 1900 switch	7
description	Sets a description on an interface	4
dialer idle-timeout number	Tells the BRI line when to drop if no interesting traffic is found	10
dialer list number protocol protocol permit/deny	Specifies interesting traffic for a DDR link	10
dialer load-threshold number inbound/outbound/either	Sets the parameters that describe when the second BRI comes up on an ISDN link	10
dialer map protocol address name hostname number	Used instead of a dialer string to provide more security in an ISDN network	10

Command	Description	Chapter
`dialer string`	Sets the phone number to dial for a BRI interface	10
`disable`	Takes you from privileged mode back to user mode	4
`disconnect`	Disconnects a connection to a remote router from the originating router	7
`enable`	Puts you into privileged mode	4
`enable password`	Sets the unencrypted enable password	4
`enable secret`	Sets the encrypted enable secret password. Supersedes the enable password if set	4
`encapsulation`	Sets the frame type used on an interface	8
`encapsulation frame-relay`	Changes the encapsulation to Frame Relay on a serial link	10
`encapsulation frame-relay ietf`	Sets the encapsulation type to the Internet Engineering Task Force (IETF); connects Cisco routers to off-brand routers	10
`encapsulation hdlc`	Restores the default encapsulation of HDLC on a serial link	10
`encapsulation ppp`	Changes the encapsulation on a serial link to PPP	10
`erase startup`	Deletes the `startup-config`	4
`erase startup-config`	Deletes the contents of NVRAM on a router	7
`Esc+B`	Moves back one word	4
`Esc+F`	Moves forward one word	4
`exec-timeout`	Sets the timeout in seconds and minutes for the console connection	4
`exit`	Disconnects a connection to a remote router via Telnet	7
`frame-relay interface-dlci`	Configures the PVC address on a serial interface or subinterface	10

Command	Description	Chapter
`frame-relay lmi-type`	Configures the LMI type on a serial link	10
`frame-relay map protocol address`	Creates a static mapping for use with a Frame Relay network	10
`Host`	Specifies a single host address	9
`hostname`	Sets the name of a router or a switch	4
`int e0.10`	Creates a subinterface	8
`interface`	Puts you in interface configuration mode; also used with `show` commands	4
`interface fastethernet 0/0`	Puts you in interface configuration mode for a Fast Ethernet port; also used with show commands	4
`interface fastethernet 0/0.1`	Creates a subinterface	4
`interface s0.16 multipoint`	Creates a multipoint subinterface on a serial link that can be used with Frame Relay networks	10
`interface s0.16 point-to-point`	Creates a point-to-point subinterface on a serial link that can be used with Frame Relay	10
`interface serial 5`	Puts you in configuration mode for interface serial 5 and can be used for `show` commands	4
`ip access-group`	Applies an IP access list to an interface	9
`ip address`	Sets an IP address on an interface or a switch	4
`ip classless`	A global configuration command used to tell a router to forward packets to a default route when the destination network is not in the routing table	5
`ip domain-lookup`	Turns on DNS lookup (which is on by default)	7
`ip domain-name`	Appends a domain name to a DNS lookup	7
`ip host`	Creates a host table on a router	7

Command	Description	Chapter
`ip name-server`	Sets the IP address of up to six DNS servers	7
`IP route`	Creates static and default routes on a router	5
`ipx access-group`	Applies an IPX access list to an interface	9
`ipx input-sap-filter`	Applies an inbound IPX SAP filter to an interface	9
`ipx network`	Assigns an IPX network number to an interface	8
`ipx output-sap-filter`	Applies an outbound IPX SAP filter to an interface	9
`ipx ping`	A Packet Internet Groper used to test IPX packet on an internetwork	8
`ipx routing`	Turns on IPX routing	8
`isdn spid1`	Sets the number that identifies the first DS0 to the ISDN switch	10
`isdn spid2`	Sets the number that identifies the second DS0 to the ISDN switch	10
`isdn switch-type`	Sets the type of ISDN switch that the router will communicate with; can be set at interface level or global configuration mode	10
`line`	Puts you in configuration mode to change or set your user mode passwords	4
`line aux`	Puts you in the auxiliary interface configuration mode	4
`line console 0`	Puts you in console configuration mode	4
`line vty`	Puts you in VTY (Telnet) interface configuration mode	4
`logging synchronous`	Stops console messages from overwriting your command-line input	4
`logout`	Logs you out of your console session	4
`media-type`	Sets the hardware media type on an interface	4

Command	Description	Chapter
network	Tells the routing protocol what network to advertise	5
no cdp enable	Turns off CDP on an individual interface	7
no cdp run	Turns off CDP completely on a router	7
no inverse-arp	Turns off the dynamic IARP used with Frame Relay; static mappings must be configured	10
no ip domain-lookup	Turns off DNS lookup	7
no ip host	Removes a hostname from a host table	7
No IP route	Removes a static or default route	5
no shutdown	Turns on an interface	4
o/r 0x2142	Changes a 2501 to boot without using the contents of NVRAM	7
ping	Tests IP connectivity to a remote device	4, 7
ppp authentication chap	Tells PPP to use CHAP authentication	10
ppp authentication pap	Tells PPP to use PAP authentication	10
router igrp as	Turns on IP IGRP routing on a router	5
router rip	Puts you in router rip configuration mode	4, 5
secondary	Adds a second IPX network on the same physical interface	8
Service password-encryption	Encrypts the user mode and enable password	4
show access-list	Shows all the access lists configured on the router	9
show access-list 110	Shows only access list 110	9
show cdp	Displays the CDP timer and holdtime frequencies	7
show cdp entry *	Same as show cdp neighbor detail, but does not work on a 1900 switch	7

Command	Description	Chapter
show cdp interface	Shows the individual interfaces enabled with CDP	7
show cdp neighbor	Shows the directly connected neighbors and the details about them	7
show cdp neighbor detail	Shows the IP address and IOS version and type, and includes all of the information from the show cdp neighbor command	7
show cdp traffic	Shows the CDP packets sent and received on a device and any errors	7
Show controllers s 0	Shows the DTE or DCE status of an interface	4
show dialer	Shows the number of times the dialer string has been reached, the idle-timeout values of each B channel, the length of call, and the name of the router to which the interface is connected	10
show flash	Shows the files in flash memory	7
show frame-relay lmi	Shows the LMI type on a serial interface	10
show frame-relay map	Shows the static and dynamic Network layer–to–PVC mappings	10
show frame-relay pvc	Shows the configured PVCs and DLCI numbers configured on a router	10
show history	Shows you the last 10 commands entered by default	4
show hosts	Shows the contents of the host table	7
show interface s0	Shows the statistics of interface serial 0	4
show ip access-list	Shows only the IP access lists	9
show ip interface	Shows which interfaces have IP access lists applied	9
show ip protocols	Shows the routing protocols and timers associated with each routing protocol configured on a router	5

Command	Description	Chapter
show ip route	Displays the IP routing table	5, 10
show ipx access-list	Shows the IPX access lists configured on a router	9
show ipx interface	Shows the RIP and SAP information being sent and received on an individual interface; also shows the IPX address of the interface	8, 9
show ipx route	Shows the IPX routing table	8
show ipx servers	Shows the SAP table on a Cisco router	8
show ipx traffic	Shows the RIP and SAP information sent and received on a Cisco router	8
show isdn active	Shows the number called and whether a call is in progress	10
show isdn status	Shows if your SPIDs are valid and if you are connected and communicating with the provider's switch	10
show protocols	Shows the routed protocols and network addresses configured on each interface	5, 8
show run	Short for show running-config; shows the configuration currently running on the router	4, 7
show sessions	Shows your connections via Telnet to remote devices	7
show start	Short for show startup-config; shows the backup configuration stored in NVRAM	4, 7
show terminal	Shows you your configured history size	4
show version	Gives the IOS information of the switch, as well as the uptime and base Ethernet address	4, 7
shutdown	Puts an interface in administratively down mode	4
Tab	Finishes typing a command for you	4

Command	Description	Chapter
telnet	Connects, views, and runs programs on a remote device	4, 7
terminal history size	Changes your history size from the default of 10 up to 256	4
trace	Tests a connection to a remote device and shows the path it took through the internetwork to find the remote device	4, 7
traffic-share balanced	Tells the IGRP routing protocol to share links inversely proportional to the metrics	5
traffic-share min	Tells the IGRP routing process to use routes that have only minimum costs	5
username name password password	Creates usernames and passwords for authentication on a Cisco router	10
variance	Controls the load balancing between the best metric and the worst acceptable metric	5

Glossary

10BaseT Part of the original IEEE 802.3 standard, 10BaseT is the Ethernet specification of 10Mbps baseband that uses two pairs of twisted-pair, Category 3, 4, or 5 cabling—using one pair to send data and the other to receive. 10BaseT has a distance limit of about 100 meters per segment. *See also: Ethernet* and *IEEE 802.3.*

100BaseT Based on the IEEE 802.3U standard, 100BaseT is the Fast Ethernet specification of 100Mbps baseband that uses UTP wiring. 100BaseT sends link pulses (containing more information than those used in 10BaseT) over the network when no traffic is present. *See also: 10BaseT, Fast Ethernet,* and *IEEE 802.3.*

100BaseTX Based on the IEEE 802.3U standard, 100BaseTX is the 100Mbps baseband Fast Ethernet specification that uses two pairs of UTP or STP wiring. The first pair of wires receives data; the second pair sends data. To ensure correct signal timing, a 100BaseTX segment cannot be longer than 100 meters.

A&B bit signaling Used in T-1 transmission facilities and sometimes called "24th channel signaling." Each of the 24 T-1 subchannels in this procedure uses one bit of every sixth frame to send supervisory signaling information.

AAA Authentication, Authorization, and Accounting: A system developed by Cisco to provide network security. *See also: authentication, authorization,* and *accounting.*

AAL ATM Adaptation Layer: A service-dependent sublayer of the Data Link layer, which accepts data from other applications and brings it to the ATM layer in 48-byte ATM payload segments. CS and SAR are the two sublayers that form AALs. Currently, the four types of AAL recommended by the ITU-T are AAL1, AAL2, AAL3/4, and AAL5. AALs are differentiated by the source-destination timing they use, whether they are CBR or VBR, and whether they are used for connection-oriented or connectionless mode data transmission. *See also: AAL1, AAL2, AAL3/4, AAL5, ATM,* and *ATM layer.*

AAL1 ATM Adaptation Layer 1: One of four AALs recommended by the ITU-T, it is used for connection-oriented, time-sensitive services that need constant bit rates, such as isochronous traffic and uncompressed video. *See also: AAL.*

AAL2   ATM Adaptation Layer 2: One of four AALs recommended by the ITU-T, it is used for connection-oriented services that support a variable bit rate, such as voice traffic. *See also: AAL.*

AAL3/4   ATM Adaptation Layer 3/4: One of four AALs (a product of two initially distinct layers) recommended by the ITU-T, supporting both connectionless and connection-oriented links. Its primary use is in sending SMDS packets over ATM networks. *See also: AAL.*

AAL5   ATM Adaptation Layer 5: One of four AALs recommended by the ITU-T, it is used to support connection-oriented VBR services primarily to transfer classical IP over ATM and LANE traffic. This least complex of the AAL recommendations uses SEAL, offering lower bandwidth costs and simpler processing requirements but also providing reduced bandwidth and error-recovery capacities. *See also: AAL.*

AARP   AppleTalk Address Resolution Protocol: The protocol in an AppleTalk stack that maps data-link addresses to network addresses.

AARP probe packets   Packets sent by the AARP to determine whether a given node ID is being used by another node in a nonextended AppleTalk network. If the node ID is not in use, the sending node appropriates that node's ID. If the node ID is in use, the sending node will select a different ID and then send out more AARP probe packets. *See also: AARP.*

ABM   Asynchronous Balanced Mode: When two stations can initiate a transmission, ABM is an HDLC (or one of its derived protocols) communication technology that supports peer-oriented, point-to-point communications between both stations.

ABR   Area Border Router: An OSPF router that is located on the border of one or more OSPF areas. ABRs are used to connect OSPF areas to the OSPF backbone area.

access layer   One of the layers in Cisco's three-layer hierarchical model. The access layer provides users with access to the internetwork.

access link   A link used with switches that is part of only one virtual LAN (VLAN). Trunk links carry information from multiple VLANs.

access list   A set of test conditions kept by routers that determines "interesting traffic" to and from the router for various services on the network.

access method   The manner in which network devices approach gaining access to the network itself.

access rate   Defines the bandwidth rate of the circuit. For example, the access rate of a T-1 circuit is 1.544Mbps. In Frame Relay and other technologies, there may be a fractional T-1 connection—256Kbps, for example—however, the access rate and clock rate is still 1.544Mbps.

access server   Also known as a "network access server," it is a communications process connecting asynchronous devices to a LAN or WAN through network and terminal emulation software, providing synchronous or asynchronous routing of supported protocols.

accounting   One of the three components in AAA. Accounting provides auditing and logging functionalities to the security model.

acknowledgment   Verification sent from one network device to another signifying that an event has occurred. May be abbreviated as ACK. *Contrast with: NAK.*

ACR   allowed cell rate: A designation defined by the ATM Forum for managing ATM traffic. Dynamically controlled using congestion control measures, the ACR varies between the minimum cell rate (MCR) and the peak cell rate (PCR). *See also: MCR and PCR.*

active monitor   The mechanism used to manage a Token Ring. The network node with the highest MAC address on the ring becomes the active monitor and is responsible for management tasks such as preventing loops and ensuring tokens are not lost.

address learning   Used with transparent bridges to learn the hardware addresses of all devices on an internetwork. The switch then filters the network with the known hardware (MAC) addresses.

address mapping   By translating network addresses from one format to another, this methodology permits different protocols to operate interchangeably.

address mask   A bit combination descriptor identifying which portion of an address refers to the network or subnet and which part refers to the host. Sometimes simply called the mask. *See also: subnet mask.*

address resolution   The process used for resolving differences between computer addressing schemes. Address resolution typically defines a method for tracing network layer (layer-3) addresses to Data Link layer (layer-2) addresses. *See also: address mapping.*

adjacency   The relationship made between defined neighboring routers and end nodes, using a common media segment, to exchange routing information.

administrative distance   A number between 0 and 255 that expresses the value of trustworthiness of a routing information source. The lower the number, the higher the integrity rating.

administrative weight   A value designated by a network administrator to rate the preference given to a network link. It is one of four link metrics exchanged by PTSPs to test ATM network resource availability.

ADSU   ATM Data Service Unit: The terminal adapter used to connect to an ATM network through an HSSI-compatible mechanism. *See also: DSU.*

advertising   The process whereby routing or service updates are transmitted at given intervals, allowing other routers on the network to maintain a record of viable routes.

AEP   AppleTalk Echo Protocol: A test for connectivity between two AppleTalk nodes where one node sends a packet to another and receives an echo, or copy, in response.

AFI   Authority and Format Identifier: The part of an NSAP ATM address that delineates the type and format of the IDI section of an ATM address.

AFP   AppleTalk Filing Protocol: A presentation-layer protocol, supporting AppleShare and Mac OS File Sharing, that permits users to share files and applications on a server.

AIP   ATM Interface Processor: Supporting AAL3/4 and AAL5, this interface for Cisco 7000 series routers minimizes performance bottlenecks at the UNI. *See also: AAL3/4 and AAL5.*

algorithm   A set of rules or processes used to solve a problem. In networking, algorithms are typically used for finding the best route for traffic from a source to its destination.

alignment error   An error occurring in Ethernet networks, in which a received frame has extra bits; that is, a number not divisible by eight. Alignment errors are generally the result of frame damage caused by collisions.

all-routes explorer packet   An explorer packet that can move across an entire SRB network, tracing all possible paths to a given destination. Also known as an all-rings explorer packet. *See also: explorer packet, local explorer packet,* and *spanning explorer packet.*

AM   Amplitude modulation: A modulation method that represents information by varying the amplitude of the carrier signal. *See also: modulation.*

AMI   Alternate Mark Inversion: A line-code type on T-1 and E-1 circuits that shows zeros as "01" during each bit cell, and ones as "11" or "00," alternately, during each bit cell. The sending device must maintain ones density in AMI but not independently of the data stream. Also known as binary-coded, alternate mark inversion. *Contrast with: B8ZS. See also: ones density.*

amplitude   An analog or digital waveform's highest value.

analog transmission   Signal messaging whereby information is represented by various combinations of signal amplitude, frequency, and phase.

ANSI   American National Standards Institute: The organization of corporate, government, and other volunteer members that coordinates standards-related activities, approves U.S. national standards, and develops U.S. positions in international standards organizations. ANSI assists in the creation of international and U.S. standards in disciplines such as communications, networking, and a variety of technical fields. It publishes over 13,000 standards, for engineered products and technologies ranging from screw threads to networking protocols. ANSI is a member of the IEC and ISO.

anycast   An ATM address that can be shared by more than one end system, allowing requests to be routed to a node that provides a particular service.

AppleTalk   Currently in two versions, the group of communication protocols designed by Apple Computer for use in Macintosh environments. The earlier Phase 1 protocols support one physical network with only one network number that resides in one zone. The later Phase 2 protocols support more than one logical network on a single physical network, allowing networks to exist in more than one zone. *See also: zone.*

Application layer   Layer 7 of the OSI reference network model, supplying services to application procedures (such as electronic mail or file transfer) that are outside the OSI model. This layer chooses and determines the availability of communicating partners along with the resources necessary to make the connection, coordinates partnering applications, and forms a consensus on procedures for controlling data integrity and error recovery. *See also: Data Link layer, Network layer, Physical layer, Presentation layer, Session layer,* and *Transport layer.*

ARA   AppleTalk Remote Access: A protocol for Macintosh users establishing their access to resources and data from a remote AppleTalk location.

area   A logical, rather than physical, set of segments (based on either CLNS, DECnet, or OSPF) along with their attached devices. Areas are commonly connected to others using routers to create a single autonomous system. *See also: autonomous system.*

ARM   Asynchronous Response Mode: An HDLC communication mode using one primary station and at least one additional station, in which transmission can be initiated from either the primary or one of the secondary units.

ARP   Address Resolution Protocol: Defined in RFC 826, the protocol that traces IP addresses to MAC addresses. *See also: RARP.*

AS   autonomous system: A group of networks under mutual administration that share the same routing methodology. Autonomous systems are subdivided by areas and must be assigned an individual 16-bit number by the IANA. *See also: area.*

AS path prepending   The use of route maps to lengthen the autonomous system path by adding false ASNs.

ASBR   Autonomous System Boundary Router: An area border router placed between an OSPF autonomous system and a non-OSPF network that operates both OSPF and an additional routing protocol, such as RIP. ASBRs must be located in a non-stub OSPF area. *See also: ABR, non-stub area,* and *OSPF.*

ASCII   American Standard Code for Information Interchange: An 8-bit code for representing characters, consisting of seven data bits plus one parity bit.

ASICs application-specific integrated circuits: Used in layer-2 switches to make filtering decisions. The ASIC looks in the filter table of MAC addresses and determines which port the destination hardware address of a received hardware address is destined for. The frame will be allowed to traverse only that one segment. If the hardware address is unknown, the frame is forwarded out all ports.

ASN.1 Abstract Syntax Notation One: An OSI language used to describe types of data that is independent of computer structures and depicting methods. Described by ISO International Standard 8824.

ASP AppleTalk Session Protocol: A protocol employing ATP to establish, maintain, and tear down sessions, as well as sequence requests. *See also: ATP.*

AST Automatic Spanning Tree: A function that supplies one path for spanning explorer frames traveling from one node in the network to another, supporting the automatic resolution of spanning trees in SRB networks. AST is based on the IEEE 802.1 standard. *See also: IEEE 802.1 and SRB.*

asynchronous transmission Digital signals sent without precise timing, usually with different frequencies and phase relationships. Asynchronous transmissions generally enclose individual characters in control bits (called start and stop bits) that show the beginning and end of each character. *Contrast with: isochronous transmission and synchronous transmission.*

ATCP AppleTalk Control Program: The protocol for establishing and configuring AppleTalk over PPP, defined in RFC 1378. *See also: PPP.*

ATDM Asynchronous Time-Division Multiplexing: A technique for sending information, it differs from normal TDM in that the time slots are assigned when necessary rather than preassigned to certain transmitters. *Contrast with: FDM, statistical multiplexing, and TDM.*

ATG Address Translation Gateway: The mechanism within Cisco DECnet routing software that enables routers to route multiple, independent DECnet networks and to establish a user-designated address translation for chosen nodes between networks.

ATM Asynchronous Transfer Mode: The international standard, identified by fixed-length 53-byte cells, for transmitting cells in multiple service systems, such as voice, video, or data. Transit delays are reduced because the fixed-length cells permit processing to occur in the hardware. ATM is designed to maximize the benefits of high-speed transmission media, such as SONET, E3, and T3.

ATM ARP server   A device that supplies logical subnets running classical IP over ATM with address-resolution services.

ATM endpoint   The initiating or terminating connection in an ATM network. ATM endpoints include servers, workstations, ATM-to-LAN switches, and ATM routers.

ATM Forum   The international organization founded jointly by Northern Telecom, Sprint, Cisco Systems, and NET/ADAPTIVE in 1991 to develop and promote standards-based implementation agreements for ATM technology. The ATM Forum broadens official standards developed by ANSI and ITU-T and creates implementation agreements before official standards are published.

ATM layer   A sublayer of the Data Link layer in an ATM network that is service-independent. To create standard 53-byte ATM cells, the ATM layer receives 48-byte segments from the AAL and attaches a 5-byte header to each. These cells are then sent to the physical layer for transmission across the physical medium. *See also: AAL.*

ATMM   ATM Management: A procedure that runs on ATM switches, managing rate enforcement and VCI translation. *See also: ATM.*

ATM user-user connection   A connection made by the ATM layer to supply communication between at least two ATM service users, such as ATMM processes. These communications can be uni- or bidirectional, using one or two VCCs, respectively. *See also: ATM layer and ATMM.*

ATP   AppleTalk Transaction Protocol: A transport-level protocol that enables reliable transactions between two sockets, where one requests the other to perform a given task and to report the results. ATP fastens the request and response together, assuring a loss-free exchange of request-response pairs.

attenuation   In communication, weakening or loss of signal energy, typically caused by distance.

AURP   AppleTalk Update-based Routing Protocol: A technique for encapsulating AppleTalk traffic in the header of a foreign protocol that allows the connection of at least two noncontiguous AppleTalk internetworks through a foreign network (such as TCP/IP) to create an AppleTalk WAN. The connection made is called an AURP tunnel. By exchanging routing information between exterior routers, the AURP maintains routing tables for the complete AppleTalk WAN. *See also: AURP tunnel.*

AURP tunnel   A connection made in an AURP WAN that acts as a single, virtual link between AppleTalk internetworks separated physically by a foreign network such as a TCP/IP network. *See also: AURP.*

authentication   The first component in the AAA model. Users are typically authenticated via a username and password, which are used to uniquely identify them.

authority zone   A portion of the domain-name tree associated with DNS for which one name server is the authority. *See also: DNS.*

authorization   The act of permitting access to a resource based on authentication information in the AAA model.

auto-detect mechanism   Used in Ethernet switch, hub, and interface cards to determine the duplex and speed that can be used.

auto duplex   A setting on layer-1 and -2 devices that sets the duplex of a switch or hub port automatically.

automatic call reconnect   A function that enables automatic call rerouting away from a failed trunk line.

autonomous confederation   A collection of self-governed systems that depend more on their own network accessibility and routing information than on information received from other systems or groups.

autonomous switching   The ability of Cisco routers to process packets more quickly by using the ciscoBus to switch packets independently of the system processor.

autonomous system   *See: AS.*

autoreconfiguration   A procedure executed by nodes within the failure domain of a Token Ring, wherein nodes automatically perform diagnostics, trying to reconfigure the network around failed areas.

auxiliary port   The console port on the back of Cisco routers that allows you to dial the router and make console configuration settings.

B8ZS   Binary 8-Zero Substitution: A line-code type, interpreted at the remote end of the connection, that uses a special code substitution whenever eight consecutive zeros are transmitted over the link on T-1 and E-1 circuits. This technique assures ones density independent of the data stream. Also known as bipolar 8-zero substitution. *Contrast with: AMI. See also: ones density.*

backbone   The basic portion of the network that provides the primary path for traffic sent to and initiated from other networks.

back end   A node or software program supplying services to a front end. *See also: server.*

bandwidth   The gap between the highest and lowest frequencies employed by network signals. More commonly, it refers to the rated throughput capacity of a network protocol or medium.

bandwidth on demand (BoD)   This function allows an additional B channel to be used to increase the amount of bandwidth available for a particular connection.

baseband   A feature of a network technology that uses only one carrier frequency. Ethernet is an example. Also named "narrowband." *Compare with: broadband.*

baseline   Baseline information includes historical data about the network and routine utilization information. This information can be used to determine whether there were recent changes made to the network that may contribute to the problem at hand.

Basic Management Setup   Used with Cisco routers when in setup mode. Only provides enough management and configuration to get the router working so someone can telnet into the router and configure it.

baud   Synonymous with bits per second (bps), if each signal element represents one bit. It is a unit of signaling speed equivalent to the number of separate signal elements transmitted per second.

B channel   Bearer channel: A full-duplex, 64Kbps channel in ISDN that transmits user data. *Compare with: D channel, E channel, and H channel.*

BDR   Backup Designated Router: This is used in an OSPF network to backup the designated router in case of failure.

beacon   An FDDI device or Token Ring frame that points to a serious problem with the ring, such as a broken cable. The beacon frame carries the address of the station thought to be down. *See also: failure domain.*

BECN   Backward Explicit Congestion Notification: BECN is the bit set by a Frame Relay network in frames moving away from frames headed into a congested path. A DTE that receives frames with the BECN may ask higher-level protocols to take necessary flow control measures. *Compare with: FECN.*

BGP4   BGP version 4: Version 4 of the interdomain routing protocol most commonly used on the Internet. BGP4 supports CIDR and uses route-counting mechanisms to decrease the size of routing tables. *See also: CIDR.*

BGP Identifier   This field contains a value that identifies the BGP speaker. This is a random value chosen by the BGP router when sending an OPEN message.

BGP neighbors   Two routers running BGP that begin a communication process to exchange dynamic routing information; they use a TCP port at Layer 4 of the OSI reference model. Specifically, TCP port 179 is used. Also known as "BGP peers."

BGP peers   *See: BGP neighbors.*

BGP speaker   A router that advertises its prefixes or routes.

bidirectional shared tree   A method of shared tree multicast forwarding. This method allows group members to receive data from the source or the RP, whichever is closer. *See also: RP (rendezvous point).*

binary   A two-character numbering method that uses ones and zeros. The binary numbering system underlies all digital representation of information.

binding   Configuring a Network layer protocol to use a certain frame type on a LAN.

BIP   Bit Interleaved Parity: A method used in ATM to monitor errors on a link, sending a check bit or word in the link overhead for the previous block or frame. This allows bit errors in transmissions to be found and delivered as maintenance information.

BISDN   Broadband ISDN: ITU-T standards created to manage high-bandwidth technologies such as video. BISDN presently employs ATM technology along SONET-based transmission circuits, supplying data rates between 155Mbps and 622Mbps and beyond. *See also: BRI, ISDN, and PRI.*

bit   One digit; either a one or a zero. Eight bits make a byte.

bit-oriented protocol   Regardless of frame content, the class of Data Link layer communication protocols that transmits frames. Bit-oriented protocols, as compared with byte-oriented, supply more efficient and trustworthy full-duplex operation. *Compare with: byte-oriented protocol.*

block size   Number of hosts that can be used in a subnet. Block sizes typically can be used in increments of 4, 8, 16, 32, 64, and 128.

Boot ROM   Used in routers to put the router into bootstrap mode. Bootstrap mode then boots the device with an operating system. The ROM can also hold a small Cisco IOS.

boot sequence   Defines how a router boots. The configuration register tells the router where to boot the IOS from as well as the configuration.

bootstrap protocol   A protocol used to dynamically assign IP addresses and gateways to requesting clients.

border gateway   A router that facilitates communication with routers in different autonomous systems.

border peer   The device in charge of a peer group; it exists at the edge of a hierarchical design. When any member of the peer group wants to locate a resource, it sends a single explorer to the border peer. The border peer then forwards this request on behalf of the requesting router, thus eliminating duplicate traffic.

border router   Typically defined within Open Shortest Path First (OSPF) as a router that connected an area to the backbone area. However, a border router can be a router that connects a company to the Internet as well. *See also: OSPF.*

BPDU   Bridge Protocol Data Unit: A Spanning Tree Protocol initializing packet that is sent at definable intervals for the purpose of exchanging information among bridges in networks.

BRI Basic Rate Interface: The ISDN interface that facilitates circuit-switched communication between video, data, and voice; it is made up of two B channels (64Kbps each) and one D channel (16Kbps). *Compare with: PRI. See also: BISDN.*

bridge A device for connecting two segments of a network and transmitting packets between them. Both segments must use identical protocols to communicate. Bridges function at the Data Link layer, layer 2 of the OSI reference model. The purpose of a bridge is to filter, send, or flood any incoming frame, based on the MAC address of that particular frame.

bridge group Used in the router configuration of bridging, bridge groups are defined by a unique number. Network traffic is bridged between all interfaces that are a member of the same bridge group.

bridge identifier Used to find and elect the root bridge in a layer-2 switched internetwork. The bridge ID is a combination of the bridge priority and base MAC address.

bridge priority Sets the STP priority of the bridge. All bridge priorities are set to 32768 by default.

bridging loop Loops occur in a bridged network if more then one link to a network exists and the STP protocol is not turned on.

broadband A transmission methodology for multiplexing several independent signals onto one cable. In telecommunications, broadband is classified as any channel with bandwidth greater than 4kHz (typical voice grade). In LAN terminology, it is classified as a coaxial cable on which analog signaling is employed. Also known as "wideband." *Contrast with: baseband.*

broadcast A data frame or packet that is transmitted to every node on the local network segment (as defined by the broadcast domain). Broadcasts are known by their broadcast address, which is a destination network and host address with all the bits turned on. Also called "local broadcast." *Compare with: directed broadcast.*

broadcast address Used in both logical addressing and hardware addressing. In logical addressing, the host addresses will be all ones. With hardware addressing, the hardware address will be all ones in hex (all Fs).

broadcast domain   A group of devices receiving broadcast frames initiating from any device within the group. Because they do not forward broadcast frames, broadcast domains are generally surrounded by routers.

broadcast storm   An undesired event on the network caused by the simultaneous transmission of any number of broadcasts across the network segment. Such an occurrence can overwhelm network bandwidth, resulting in time-outs.

buffer   A storage area dedicated to handling data while in transit. Buffers are used to receive/store sporadic deliveries of data bursts, usually received from faster devices, compensating for the variations in processing speed. Incoming information is stored until everything is received prior to sending data on. Also known as an "information buffer."

bursting   Some technologies, including ATM and Frame Relay, are considered burstable. This means that user data can exceed the bandwidth normally reserved for the connection; however, this cannot exceed the port speed. An example of this would be a 128Kbps Frame Relay CIR on a T-1—depending on the vendor, it may be possible to send more than 128Kbps for a short time.

bus topology   A linear LAN architecture in which transmissions from various stations on the network are reproduced over the length of the medium and are accepted by all other stations. *Compare with: ring* and *star.*

bus   Any physical path, typically wires or copper, through which a digital signal can be used to send data from one part of a computer to another.

BUS   broadcast and unknown servers: In LAN emulation, the hardware or software responsible for resolving all broadcasts and packets with unknown (unregistered) addresses into the point-to-point virtual circuits required by ATM. *See also: LANE, LEC, LECS,* and *LES.*

BX.25   AT&T's use of X.25. *See also: X.25.*

bypass mode   An FDDI and Token Ring network operation that deletes an interface.

bypass relay   A device that enables a particular interface in the Token Ring to be closed down and effectively taken off the ring.

byte   Eight bits. *See also: octet.*

byte-oriented protocol   Any type of data-link communication protocol that, in order to mark the boundaries of frames, uses a specific character from the user character set. These protocols have generally been superseded by bit-oriented protocols. *Compare with: bit-oriented protocol.*

cable range   In an extended AppleTalk network, the range of numbers allotted for use by existing nodes on the network. The value of the cable range can be anywhere from a single to a sequence of several touching network numbers. Node addresses are determined by their cable range value.

CAC   Connection Admission Control: The sequence of actions executed by every ATM switch while connection setup is performed in order to determine if a request for connection is violating the guarantees of QoS for established connections. Also, CAC is used to route a connection request through an ATM network.

call admission control   A device for managing of traffic in ATM networks, determining the possibility of a path containing adequate bandwidth for a requested VCC.

call establishment   Used to reference an ISDN call setup scheme when the call is working.

call priority   In circuit-switched systems, the defining priority given to each originating port; it specifies in which order calls will be reconnected. Additionally, call priority identifies which calls are allowed during a bandwidth reservation.

call setup   Handshaking scheme that defines how a source and destination device will transmit data to each other.

call setup time   The length of time necessary to effect a switched call between DTE devices.

CBR   constant bit rate: An ATM Forum QoS class created for use in ATM networks. CBR is used for connections that rely on precision clocking to guarantee trustworthy delivery. *Compare with: ABR and VBR.*

CD   carrier detect: A signal indicating that an interface is active or that a connection generated by a modem has been established.

CDP   Cisco Discovery Protocol: Cisco's proprietary protocol that is used to tell a neighbor Cisco device about the type of hardware, software version, and active interfaces that the Cisco device is using. It uses a SNAP frame between devices and is not routable.

CDP holdtime   The amount of time a router will hold Cisco Discovery Protocol information received from a neighbor router before discarding it if the information is not updated by the neighbor. This timer is set to 180 seconds by default.

CDP timer   The amount of time Cisco Discovery Protocol is transmitted out of all router interfaces, by default. The cdp timer is 90 seconds, by default.

CDVT   Cell Delay Variation Tolerance: A QoS parameter for traffic management in ATM networks specified when a connection is established. The allowable fluctuation levels for data samples taken by the PCR in CBR transmissions are determined by the CDVT. *See also: CBR and PCR.*

cell   In ATM networking, the basic unit of data for switching and multiplexing. Cells have a defined length of 53 bytes, including a 5-byte header that identifies the cell's data stream and 48 bytes of payload. *See also: cell relay.*

cell payload scrambling   The method by which an ATM switch maintains framing on some medium-speed edge and trunk interfaces (T-3 or E-3 circuits). Cell payload scrambling rearranges the data portion of a cell to maintain the line synchronization with certain common bit patterns.

cell relay   A technology that uses small packets of fixed size, known as cells. Their fixed length enables cells to be processed and switched in hardware at high speeds, making this technology the foundation for ATM and other high-speed network protocols. *See also: cell.*

Centrex   A local exchange carrier service, providing local switching that resembles that of an on-site PBX. Centrex has no on-site switching capability. Therefore, all customer connections return to the CO. *See also: CO.*

CER   cell error ratio: The ratio in ATM of transmitted cells having errors to the total number of cells sent in a transmission within a certain span of time.

CGMP Cisco Group Management Protocol: A proprietary protocol developed by Cisco. The router uses CGMP to send multicast membership commands to Catalyst switches.

channelized E-1 Operating at 2.048Mpbs, an access link that is sectioned into 29 B-channels and one D-channel, supporting DDR, Frame Relay, and X.25. *Compare with: channelized T-1.*

channelized T-1 Operating at 1.544Mbps, an access link that is sectioned into 23 B-channels and one D-channel of 64Kbps each, where individual channels or groups of channels connect to various destinations, supporting DDR, Frame Relay, and X.25. *Compare with: channelized E-1.*

CHAP Challenge Handshake Authentication Protocol: Supported on lines using PPP encapsulation, it is a security feature that identifies the remote end, helping keep out unauthorized users. After CHAP is performed, the router or access server determines whether a given user is permitted access. It is a newer, more secure protocol than PAP. *Compare with: PAP.*

checksum A test for ensuring the integrity of sent data. It is a number calculated from a series of values taken through a sequence of mathematical functions, typically placed at the end of the data from which it is calculated, and then recalculated at the receiving end for verification. *Compare with: CRC.*

choke packet When congestion exists, it is a packet sent to inform a transmitter that it should decrease its sending rate.

CIDR Classless Interdomain Routing: A method supported by classless routing protocols, such as OSPF and BGP4, based on the concept of ignoring the IP class of address, permitting route aggregation and VLSM that enable routers to combine routes in order to minimize the routing information that needs to be conveyed by the primary routers. It allows a group of IP networks to appear to other networks as a unified, larger entity. In CIDR, IP addresses and their subnet masks are written as four dotted octets, followed by a forward slash and the numbering of masking bits (a form of subnet notation shorthand). *See also: BGP4.*

CIP Channel Interface Processor: A channel attachment interface for use in Cisco 7000 series routers that connects a host mainframe to a control unit. This device eliminates the need for an FBP to attach channels.

CIR committed information rate: Averaged over a minimum span of time and measured in bps, a Frame Relay network's agreed-upon minimum rate of transferring information.

circuit switching Used with dial-up networks such as PPP and ISDN. Passes data, but needs to set up the connection first—just like making a phone call.

Cisco FRAD Cisco Frame Relay Access Device: A Cisco product that supports Cisco IPS Frame Relay SNA services, connecting SDLC devices to Frame Relay without requiring an existing LAN. May be upgraded to a fully functioning multiprotocol router. Can activate conversion from SDLC to Ethernet and Token Ring, but does not support attached LANs. *See also: FRAD.*

CiscoFusion Cisco's name for the internetworking architecture under which its Cisco IOS operates. It is designed to "fuse" together the capabilities of its disparate collection of acquired routers and switches.

Cisco IOS Cisco Internet Operating System software. The kernel of the Cisco line of routers and switches that supplies shared functionality, scalability, and security for all products under its CiscoFusion architecture. *See also: CiscoFusion.*

CiscoView GUI-based management software for Cisco networking devices, enabling dynamic status, statistics, and comprehensive configuration information. Displays a physical view of the Cisco device chassis and provides device-monitoring functions and fundamental troubleshooting capabilities. May be integrated with a number of SNMP-based network management platforms.

Class A network Part of the Internet Protocol hierarchical addressing scheme. Class A networks have only 8 bits for defining networks and 24 bits for defining hosts on each network.

Class B network Part of the Internet Protocol hierarchical addressing scheme. Class B networks have 16 bits for defining networks and 16 bits for defining hosts on each network.

Class C network Part of the Internet Protocol hierarchical addressing scheme. Class C networks have 24 bits for defining networks and only 8 bits for defining hosts on each network.

classful routing   Routing protocols that do not send subnet mask information when a route update is sent out.

classical IP over ATM   Defined in RFC 1577, the specification for running IP over ATM that maximizes ATM features. Also known as "CIA."

classless routing   Routing that sends subnet mask information in the routing updates. Classless routing allows Variable-Length Subnet Mask (VLSM) and supernetting. Routing protocols that support classless routing are RIP version 2, EIGRP, and OSPF.

CLI   command-line interface: Allows you to configure Cisco routers and switches with maximum flexibility.

CLP   Cell Loss Priority: The area in the ATM cell header that determines the likelihood of a cell being dropped during network congestion. Cells with CLP = 0 are considered insured traffic and are not apt to be dropped. Cells with CLP = 1 are considered best-effort traffic that may be dropped during congested episodes, delivering more resources to handle insured traffic.

CLR   Cell Loss Ratio: The ratio of discarded cells to successfully delivered cells in ATM. CLR can be designated a QoS parameter when establishing a connection.

CO   central office: The local telephone company office where all loops in a certain area connect and where circuit switching of subscriber lines occurs.

collapsed backbone   A nondistributed backbone where all network segments are connected to each other through an internetworking device. A collapsed backbone can be a virtual network segment at work in a device such as a router, hub, or switch.

collision   The effect of two nodes sending transmissions simultaneously in Ethernet. When they meet on the physical media, the frames from each node collide and are damaged. *See also: collision domain.*

collision domain   The network area in Ethernet over which frames that have collided will spread. Collisions are propagated by hubs and repeaters, but not by LAN switches, routers, or bridges. *See also: collision.*

composite metric   Used with routing protocols, such as IGRP and EIGRP, that use more than one metric to find the best path to a remote network.

IGRP and EIGRP both use bandwidth and delay of the line by default. However, maximum transmission unit (MTU), load, and reliability of a link can be used as well.

compression   A technique to send more data across a link than would be normally permitted by representing repetitious strings of data with a single marker.

configuration register   A 16-bit configurable value stored in hardware or software that determines how Cisco routers function during initialization. In hardware, the bit position is set using a jumper. In software, it is set by specifying specific bit patterns used to set startup options, configured using a hexadecimal value with configuration commands.

congestion   Traffic that exceeds the network's ability to handle it.

congestion avoidance   To minimize delays, the method an ATM network uses to control traffic entering the system. Lower-priority traffic is discarded at the edge of the network when indicators signal it cannot be delivered, thus using resources efficiently.

congestion collapse   The situation that results from the retransmission of packets in ATM networks where little or no traffic successfully arrives at destination points. It usually happens in networks made of switches with ineffective or inadequate buffering capabilities combined with poor packet discard or ABR congestion feedback mechanisms.

connection ID   Identifications given to each Telnet session into a router. The show sessions command will give you the connections a local router will have to a remote router. The show users command will show the connection IDs of users telnetted into your local router.

connectionless   Data transfer that occurs without the creating of a virtual circuit. It has no overhead, best-effort delivery, and is not reliable. *Contrast with: connection-oriented. See also: virtual circuit.*

connection-oriented   Data transfer method that sets up a virtual circuit before any data is transferred. Uses acknowledgments and flow control for reliable data transfer. *Contrast with: connectionless. See also: virtual circuit.*

console port   Typically an RJ-45 port on a Cisco router and switch that allows Command-Line Interface capability.

control direct VCC   One of three control connections defined by Phase I LAN emulation; a bidirectional virtual control connection (VCC) established in ATM by an LEC to an LES. *See also: control distribute VCC.*

control distribute VCC   One of three control connections defined by Phase 1 LAN emulation; a unidirectional virtual control connection (VCC) set up in ATM from an LES to an LEC. Usually, the VCC is a point-to-multipoint connection. *See also: control direct VCC.*

convergence   The process required for all routers in an internetwork to update their routing tables and create a consistent view of the network, using the best possible paths. No user data is passed during a convergence time.

core layer   Top layer in the Cisco three-layer hierarchical model, which helps you design, build, and maintain Cisco hierarchical networks. The core layer passes packets quickly to distribution-layer devices only. No packet filtering should take place at this layer.

cost   Also known as path cost, an arbitrary value, based on hop count, bandwidth, or other calculation, that is typically assigned by a network administrator and used by the routing protocol to compare different routes through an internetwork. Routing protocols use cost values to select the best path to a certain destination: the lowest cost identifies the best path. Also known as "path cost." *See also: routing metric.*

count to infinity   A problem occurring in routing algorithms that are slow to converge where routers keep increasing the hop count to particular networks. To avoid this problem, various solutions have been implemented into each of the different routing protocols. Some of those solutions include defining a maximum hop count (defining infinity), route poising, poison reverse, and split horizon.

CPCS   Common Part Convergence Sublayer: One of two AAL sublayers that is service-dependent, it is further segmented into the CS and SAR sublayers. The CPCS prepares data for transmission across the ATM network; it creates the 48-byte payload cells that are sent to the ATM layer. *See also: AAL* and *ATM layer.*

CPE   customer premises equipment: Items such as telephones, modems, and terminals installed at customer locations and connected to the telephone company network.

crankback   In ATM, a correction technique used when a node somewhere on a chosen path cannot accept a connection setup request, blocking the request. The path is rolled back to an intermediate node, which then uses GCAC to attempt to find an alternate path to the final destination.

CRC   cyclical redundancy check: A methodology that detects errors, whereby the frame recipient makes a calculation by dividing frame contents with a prime binary divisor and compares the remainder to a value stored in the frame by the sending node. *Contrast with: checksum.*

crossover cable   Type of Ethernet cable that connects a switch to switch, host to host, hub to hub, or switch to hub.

CSMA/CD   Carrier Sense Multiple Access/Collision Detect: A technology defined by the Ethernet IEEE 802.3 committee. Each device senses the cable for a digital signal before transmitting. Also, CSMA/CD allows all devices on the network to share the same cable, but one at a time. If two devices transmit at the same time, a frame collision will occur and a jamming pattern will be sent; the devices will stop transmitting, wait a predetermined amount of time, and then try to transmit again.

CSU   channel service unit: A digital mechanism that connects end-user equipment to the local digital telephone loop. Frequently referred to along with the data service unit as CSU/DSU. *See also: DSU.*

CSU/DSU   channel service unit/data service unit: Physical layer device used in wide area networks to convert the digital signals to what is understood by the provider's switch. A CSU/DSU is typically one device that plugs into a RJ-45 jack, known as the demarcation location.

CTD   Cell Transfer Delay: For a given connection in ATM, the time period between a cell exit event at the source user-network interface (UNI) and the corresponding cell entry event at the destination. The CTD between these points is the sum of the total inter-ATM transmission delay and the total ATM processing delay.

cut-through frame switching   A frame-switching technique that flows data through a switch so that the leading edge exits the switch at the output port before the packet finishes entering the input port. Frames will be read, processed, and forwarded by devices that use cut-through switching as soon as the destination address of the frame is confirmed and the outgoing port is identified.

data circuit-terminating equipment   DCE is used to provide clocking to DTE equipment.

data compression   *See: compression*

data direct VCC   A bidirectional point-to-point virtual control connection (VCC) set up between two LECs in ATM and one of three data connections defined by Phase 1 LAN emulation. Because data direct VCCs do not guarantee QoS, they are generally reserved for UBR and ABR connections. *Compare with: control distribute VCC and control direct VCC.*

data encapsulation   The process in which the information in a protocol is wrapped, or contained, in the data section of another protocol. In the OSI reference model, each layer encapsulates the layer immediately above it as the data flows down the protocol stack.

data frame   Protocol Data Unit encapsulation at the Data Link layer of the OSI reference model. Encapsulates packets from the network layer and prepares the data for transmission on a network medium.

datagram   A logical collection of information transmitted as a network-layer unit over a medium without a previously established virtual circuit. IP datagrams have become the primary information unit of the Internet. At various layers of the OSI reference model, the terms *cell, frame, message, packet,* and *segment* also define these logical information groupings.

Data Link Control layer   Layer 2 of the SNA architectural model, it is responsible for the transmission of data over a given physical link and compares somewhat to the Data Link layer of the OSI model.

Data Link layer   Layer 2 of the OSI reference model, it ensures the trustworthy transmission of data across a physical link and is primarily concerned with physical addressing, line discipline, network topology, error notification, ordered delivery of frames, and flow control. The IEEE has further segmented this layer into the MAC sublayer and the LLC sublayer. Also known as the link layer. Can be compared somewhat to the data link control layer of the SNA model. *See also: Application layer, LLC, MAC, Network layer, Physical layer, Presentation layer, Session layer,* and *Transport layer.*

data terminal equipment   *See: DTE.*

DCC   Data Country Code: Developed by the ATM Forum, one of two ATM address formats designed for use by private networks. *Compare with: ICD.*

DCE data communications equipment (as defined by the EIA) or data circuit-terminating equipment (as defined by the ITU-T): The mechanisms and links of a communications network that make up the network portion of the user-to-network interface, such as modems. The DCE supplies the physical connection to the network, forwards traffic, and provides a clocking signal to synchronize data transmission between DTE and DCE devices. *Compare with: DTE.*

D channel 1) data channel: A full-duplex, 16Kbps (BRI) or 64Kbps (PRI) ISDN channel. *Compare with: B channel, E channel,* and *H channel.* 2) In SNA, anything that provides a connection between the processor and main storage with any peripherals.

DDP Datagram Delivery Protocol: Used in the AppleTalk suite of protocols as a connectionless protocol that is responsible for sending datagrams through an internetwork.

DDR dial-on-demand routing: A technique that allows a router to automatically initiate and end a circuit-switched session per the requirements of the sending station. By mimicking keepalives, the router fools the end station into treating the session as active. DDR permits routing over ISDN or telephone lines via a modem or external ISDN terminal adapter.

DE Discard Eligibility: Used in Frame Relay networks to tell a switch that a frame can be discarded if the switch is too busy. The DE is a field in the frame that is turned on by transmitting routers if the committed information rate (CIR) is oversubscribed or set to 0.

dedicated line Point-to-point connection that does not share any bandwidth.

de-encapsulation The technique used by layered protocols in which a layer removes header information from the Protocol Data Unit (PDU) from the layer below. *See: encapsulation.*

default route The static routing table entry used to direct frames whose next hop is not spelled out in the dynamic routing table.

delay The time elapsed between a sender's initiation of a transaction and the first response they receive. Also, the time needed to move a packet from its source to its destination over a path. *See also: latency.*

demarc The demarcation point between the customer premises equipment (CPE) and the telco's carrier equipment.

demodulation A series of steps that return a modulated signal to its original form. When receiving, a modem demodulates an analog signal to its original digital form (and, conversely, modulates the digital data it sends into an analog signal). *See also: modulation.*

demultiplexing The process of converting a single multiplex signal, comprising more than one input stream, back into separate output streams. *See also: multiplexing.*

designated bridge In the process of forwarding a frame from a segment to the route bridge, the bridge with the lowest path cost.

designated port Used with the Spanning Tree Protocol (STP) to designate forwarding ports. If there are multiple links to the same network, STP will shut a port down to stop network loops.

designated router (DR) An OSPF router that creates LSAs for a multiaccess network and is required to perform other special tasks in OSPF operations. Multiaccess OSPF networks that maintain a minimum of two attached routers identify one router that is chosen by the OSPF Hello protocol, which makes possible a decrease in the number of adjacencies necessary on a multiaccess network. This in turn reduces the quantity of routing protocol traffic and the physical size of the database.

destination address The address for the network devices that will receive a packet.

DHCP Dynamic Host Configuration Protocol: DHCP is a superset of the BootP protocol. This means that it uses the same protocol structure as BootP, but it has enhancements added. Both of these protocols use servers that dynamically configure clients when requested. The two major enhancements are address pools and lease times.

dial backup Dial backup connections are typically used to provide redundancy to Frame Relay connections. The backup link is activated over an analog modem.

directed broadcast A data frame or packet that is transmitted to a specific group of nodes on a remote network segment. Directed broadcasts are known by their broadcast address, which is a destination subnet address with all the bits turned on.

discovery mode   Also known as dynamic configuration, this technique is used by an AppleTalk interface to gain information from a working node about an attached network. The information is subsequently used by the interface for self-configuration.

distance-vector routing algorithm   In order to find the shortest path, this group of routing algorithms repeats on the number of hops in a given route, requiring each router to send its complete routing table with each update, but only to its neighbors. Routing algorithms of this type tend to generate loops, but they are fundamentally simpler than their link-state counterparts. *See also: link-state routing algorithm* and *SPF.*

distribution layer   Middle layer of the Cisco three-layer hierarchical model, which helps you design, install, and maintain Cisco hierarchical networks. The distribution layer is the point where access-layer devices connect. Routing is performed at this layer.

DLCI   Data-Link Connection Identifier: Used to identify virtual circuits in a Frame Relay network.

DLSw   Data Link Switching: IBM developed Data Link Switching (DLSw) in 1992 to provide support for SNA (Systems Network Architecture) and NetBIOS protocols in router-based networks. SNA and NetBIOS are non-routable protocols that do not contain any logical layer 3 network information. DLSw encapsulates these protocols into TCP/IP messages that can be routed and is an alternative to Remote Source-Route Bridging (RSRB).

DLSw+   Cisco's implementation of DLSw. In addition to support for the RFC standards, Cisco added enhancements intended to increase scalability and to improve performance and availability.

DNS   Domain Name System: Used to resolve host names to IP addresses.

DSAP   Destination Service Access Point: The service access point of a network node, specified in the destination field of a packet. *See also: SSAP* and *SAP.*

DSR   Data Set Ready: When a DCE is powered up and ready to run, this EIA/TIA-232 interface circuit is also engaged.

DSU   data service unit: This device is used to adapt the physical interface on a data terminal equipment (DTE) mechanism to a transmission facility such as T-1 or E-1 and is also responsible for signal timing. It is commonly grouped with the channel service unit and referred to as the CSU/DSU. *See also: CSU.*

DTE data terminal equipment: Any device located at the user end of a user-network interface serving as a destination, a source, or both. DTE includes devices such as multiplexers, protocol translators, and computers. The connection to a data network is made through data communication equipment (DCE) such as a modem, using the clocking signals generated by that device. *See also: DCE.*

DTR Data Terminal Ready: An activated EIA/TIA-232 circuit communicating to the DCE the state of preparedness of the DTE to transmit or receive data.

DUAL Diffusing Update Algorithm: Used in Enhanced IGRP, this convergence algorithm provides loop-free operation throughout an entire route's computation. DUAL grants routers involved in a topology revision the ability to synchronize simultaneously, while routers unaffected by this change are not involved. *See also: Enhanced IGRP.*

DVMRP Distance Vector Multicast Routing Protocol: Based primarily on the Routing Information Protocol (RIP), this Internet gateway protocol implements a common, condensed-mode IP multicast scheme, using IGMP to transfer routing datagrams between its neighbors. *See also: IGMP.*

DXI Data Exchange Interface: Described in RFC 1482, DXI defines the effectiveness of a network device such as a router, bridge, or hub to act as an FEP to an ATM network by using a special DSU that accomplishes packet encapsulation.

dynamic entries Used in layer-2 and -3 devices to dynamically create a table of either hardware addresses or logical addresses dynamically.

dynamic routing Also known as "adaptive routing," this technique automatically adapts to traffic or physical network revisions.

dynamic VLAN An administrator will create an entry in a special server with the hardware addresses of all devices on the internetwork. The server will then dynamically assign used VLANs.

E-1 Generally used in Europe, a wide-area digital transmission scheme carrying data at 2.048Mbps. E-1 transmission lines are available for lease from common carriers for private use.

E.164 1) Evolved from standard telephone numbering system, the standard recommended by ITU-T for international telecommunication numbering, particularly in ISDN, SMDS, and BISDN. 2) Label of field in an ATM address containing numbers in E.164 format.

eBGP   External Border Gateway Protocol: Used to exchange route information between different autonomous systems.

E channel   Echo channel: A 64Kbps ISDN control channel used for circuit switching. Specific description of this channel can be found in the 1984 ITU-T ISDN specification, but was dropped from the 1988 version. *See also: B channel, D channel,* and *H channel.*

edge device   A device that enables packets to be forwarded between legacy interfaces (such as Ethernet and Token Ring) and ATM interfaces based on information in the data-link and network layers. An edge device does not take part in the running of any network layer routing protocol; it merely uses the route description protocol in order to get the forwarding information required.

EEPROM   electronically erasable programmable read-only memory: Programmed after their manufacture, these nonvolatile memory chips can be erased if necessary using electric power and reprogrammed. *See also: EPROM* and *PROM.*

EFCI   Explicit Forward Congestion Indication: A congestion feedback mode permitted by ABR service in an ATM network. The EFCI may be set by any network element that is in a state of immediate or certain congestion. The destination end-system is able to carry out a protocol that adjusts and lowers the cell rate of the connection based on value of the EFCI. *See also: ABR.*

EIGRP   *See: Enhanced IGRP.*

EIP   Ethernet Interface Processor: A Cisco 7000 series router interface processor card, supplying 10Mbps AUI ports to support Ethernet Version 1 and Ethernet Version 2 or IEEE 802.3 interfaces with a high-speed data path to other interface processors.

ELAN   emulated LAN: An ATM network configured using a client/server model in order to emulate either an Ethernet or Token Ring LAN. Multiple ELANs can exist at the same time on a single ATM network and are made up of a LAN emulation client (LEC), a LAN emulation server (LES), a broadcast and unknown server (BUS), and a LAN emulation configuration server (LECS). ELANs are defined by the LANE specification. *See also: LANE, LEC, LECS,* and *LES.*

ELAP EtherTalk Link Access Protocol: In an EtherTalk network, the link-access protocol constructed above the standard Ethernet Data Link layer.

encapsulation The technique used by layered protocols in which a layer adds header information to the Protocol Data Unit (PDU) from the layer above. As an example, in Internet terminology, a packet would contain a header from the Physical layer, followed by a header from the Network layer (IP), followed by a header from the Transport layer (TCP), followed by the application protocol data.

encryption The conversion of information into a scrambled form that effectively disguises it to prevent unauthorized access. Every encryption scheme uses some well-defined algorithm, which is reversed at the receiving end by an opposite algorithm in a process known as decryption.

Endpoints *See: BGP neighbors.*

end-to-end VLANs VLANs that span the switch-fabric from end to end; all switches in end-to-end VLANs understand about all configured VLANs. End-to-end VLANs are configured to allow membership based on function, project, department, and so on.

Enhanced IGRP Enhanced Interior Gateway Routing Protocol: An advanced routing protocol created by Cisco, combining the advantages of link-state and distance-vector protocols. Enhanced IGRP has superior convergence attributes, including high operating efficiency. *See also: IGP, OSPF,* and *RIP.*

enterprise network A privately owned and operated network that joins most major locations in a large company or organization.

EPROM erasable programmable read-only memory: Programmed after their manufacture, these nonvolatile memory chips can be erased if necessary using high-power light and reprogrammed. *See also: EEPROM* and *PROM.*

ESF Extended Superframe: Made up of 24 frames with 192 bits each, with the 193rd bit providing other functions including timing. This is an enhanced version of SF. *See also: SF.*

Ethernet A baseband LAN specification created by the Xerox Corporation and then improved through joint efforts of Xerox, Digital Equipment Corporation, and Intel. Ethernet is similar to the IEEE 802.3 series standard and, using CSMA/CD, operates over various types of cables at 10Mbps. Also called: DIX (Digital/Intel/Xerox) Ethernet. *See also: 10BaseT, Fast Ethernet, and IEEE.*

EtherTalk   A data-link product from Apple Computer that permits AppleTalk networks to be connected by Ethernet.

excess burst size   The amount of traffic by which the user may exceed the committed burst size.

excess rate   In ATM networking, traffic exceeding a connection's insured rate. The excess rate is the maximum rate less the insured rate. Depending on the availability of network resources, excess traffic can be discarded during congestion episodes. *Compare with: maximum rate.*

EXEC session   Cisco term used to describe the command-line interface. The EXEC session exists in user mode and privileged mode.

expansion   The procedure of directing compressed data through an algorithm, restoring information to its original size.

expedited delivery   An option that can be specified by one protocol layer, communicating either with other layers or with the identical protocol layer in a different network device, requiring that identified data be processed faster.

explorer frame   Used with Source Route Bridging to find the route to the remote bridged network before a frame is transmitted.

explorer packet   An SNA packet transmitted by a source Token Ring device to find the path through a source-route-bridged network.

extended IP access list   IP access list that filters the network by logical address, protocol field in the Network layer header, and even the port field in the Transport layer header.

extended IPX access list   IPX access list that filters the network by logical IPX address, protocol field in the Network layer header, or even socket number in the Transport layer header.

Extended Setup   Used in setup mode to configure the router with more detail than Basic Setup mode. Allows multiple-protocol support and interface configuration.

failure domain The region in which a failure has occurred in a Token Ring. When a station gains information that a serious problem, such as a cable break, has occurred with the network, it sends a beacon frame that includes the station reporting the failure, its NAUN, and everything between. This defines the failure domain. Beaconing then initiates the procedure known as autoreconfiguration. *See also: autoreconfiguration* and *beacon.*

fallback In ATM networks, this mechanism is used for scouting a path if it isn't possible to locate one using customary methods. The device relaxes requirements for certain characteristics, such as delay, in an attempt to find a path that meets a certain set of the most important requirements.

Fast Ethernet Any Ethernet specification with a speed of 100Mbps. Fast Ethernet is ten times faster than 10BaseT, while retaining qualities like MAC mechanisms, MTU, and frame format. These similarities make it possible for existing 10BaseT applications and management tools to be used on Fast Ethernet networks. Fast Ethernet is based on an extension of IEEE 802.3 specification (IEEE 802.3U). *Compare with: Ethernet. See also: 100BaseT, 100BaseTX,* and *IEEE.*

fast switching A Cisco feature that uses a route cache to speed packet switching through a router. *Contrast with: process switching.*

fault tolerance The extent to which a network device or a communication link can fail without communication being interrupted. Fault tolerance can be provided by added secondary routes to a remote network.

FDM Frequency-Division Multiplexing: A technique that permits information from several channels to be assigned bandwidth on one wire based on frequency. *See also: TDM, ATDM,* and *statistical multiplexing.*

FDDI Fiber Distributed Data Interface: A LAN standard, defined by ANSI X3T9.5 that can run at speeds up to 200Mbps and uses token-passing media access on fiber-optic cable. For redundancy, FDDI can use a dual-ring architecture.

FECN Forward Explicit Congestion Notification: A bit set by a Frame Relay network that informs the DTE receptor that congestion was encountered along the path from source to destination. A device receiving frames with the FECN bit set can ask higher-priority protocols to take flow-control action as needed. *See also: BECN.*

FEIP   Fast Ethernet Interface Processor: An interface processor employed on Cisco 7000 series routers, supporting up to two 100Mbps 100BaseT ports.

filtering   Used to provide security on the network with access lists.

firewall   A barrier purposefully erected between any connected public networks and a private network, made up of a router or access server or several routers or access servers, that uses access lists and other methods to ensure the security of the private network.

fixed configuration router   A router that cannot be upgraded with any new interfaces.

flapping   Term used to describe a serial interface that is going up and down.

Flash   electronically erasable programmable read-only memory (EEPROM). Used to hold the Cisco IOS in a router by default.

flash memory   Developed by Intel and licensed to other semiconductor manufacturers, it is nonvolatile storage that can be erased electronically and reprogrammed, physically located on an EEPROM chip. Flash memory permits software images to be stored, booted, and rewritten as needed. Cisco routers and switches use flash memory to hold the IOS by default. *See also: EPROM,* and *EEPROM.*

flat network   Network that is one large collision domain and one large broadcast domain.

floating routes   Used with dynamic routing to provide backup routes in case of failure.

flooding   When traffic is received on an interface, it is then transmitted to every interface connected to that device with exception of the interface from which the traffic originated. This technique can be used for traffic transfer by bridges and switches throughout the network.

flow control   A methodology used to ensure that receiving units are not overwhelmed with data from sending devices. Pacing, as it is called in IBM networks, means that when buffers at a receiving unit are full, a message is transmitted to the sending unit to temporarily halt transmissions until all the data in the receiving buffer has been processed and the buffer is again ready for action.

FQDN fully qualified domain name: Used within the DNS domain structure to provide name to IP address resolution on the Internet. An example of an FQDN is bob.acme.com.

FRAD Frame Relay access device: Any device affording a connection between a LAN and a Frame Relay WAN. *See also: Cisco FRAD and FRAS.*

fragment Any portion of a larger packet that has been intentionally segmented into smaller pieces. A packet fragment does not necessarily indicate an error and can be intentional. *See also: fragmentation.*

fragmentation The process of intentionally segmenting a packet into smaller pieces when sending data over an intermediate network medium that cannot support the larger packet size.

FragmentFree LAN switch type that reads into the data section of a frame to make sure fragmentation did not occur. Sometimes called modified cut-through.

frame A logical unit of information sent by the Data Link layer over a transmission medium. The term often refers to the header and trailer, employed for synchronization and error control, that surround the data contained in the unit.

frame filtering Frame filtering is used on a layer-2 switch to provide more bandwidth. A switch reads the destination hardware address of a frame and then looks for this address in the filter table, built by the switch. It then only sends the frame out the port where the hardware address is located, and the other ports do not see the frame.

frame identification (frame tagging) VLANs can span multiple connected switches, which Cisco calls a switch-fabric. Switches within this switch-fabric must keep track of frames as they are received on the switch ports, and they must keep track of the VLAN they belong to as the frames traverse this switch-fabric. Frame tagging performs this function. Switches can then direct frames to the appropriate port.

Frame Relay A more efficient replacement of the X.25 protocol (an unrelated packet relay technology that guarantees data delivery). Frame Relay is an industry-standard, shared-access, best-effort, switched Data Link layer encapsulation that services multiple virtual circuits and protocols between connected mechanisms.

Frame Relay bridging   Defined in RFC 1490, this bridging method uses the identical spanning-tree algorithm as other bridging operations but permits packets to be encapsulated for transmission across a Frame Relay network.

Frame Relay switching   When a router at a service provider provides packet switching for Frame Relay packets. A process that activates an interface that has been deactivated by the pruning process. It is initiated by an IGMP membership report sent to the router.

frame tagging   *See: frame identification.*

frame types   Used in LANs to determine how a packet is put on the local network. Ethernet provides four different frame types. These are not compatible with each other, so for two hosts to communicate, they must use the same frame type.

framing   Encapsulation at the Data Link layer of the OSI model. It is called framing because the packet is encapsulated with both a header and a trailer.

FRAS   Frame Relay Access Support: A feature of Cisco IOS software that enables SDLC, Ethernet, Token Ring, and Frame Relay-attached IBM devices to be linked with other IBM mechanisms on a Frame Relay network. *See also: FRAD.*

frequency   The number of cycles of an alternating current signal per time unit, measured in hertz (cycles per second).

FSIP   Fast Serial Interface Processor: The Cisco 7000 routers' default serial interface processor, it provides four or eight high-speed serial ports.

FTP   File Transfer Protocol: The TCP/IP protocol used for transmitting files between network nodes, it supports a broad range of file types and is defined in RFC 959. *See also: TFTP.*

full duplex   The capacity to transmit information between a sending station and a receiving unit at the same time. *See also: half duplex.*

full mesh   A type of network topology where every node has either a physical or a virtual circuit linking it to every other network node. A full mesh supplies a great deal of redundancy but is typically reserved for network backbones because of its expense. *See also: partial mesh.*

global command   Cisco term used to define commands that are used to change the router configuration that affect the whole router. In contrast, an interface command only affects that interface.

GMII   Gigabit MII: Media Independent Interface that provides 8 bits at a time of data transfer.

GNS   Get Nearest Server: On an IPX network, a request packet sent by a customer for determining the location of the nearest active server of a given type. An IPX network client launches a GNS request to get either a direct answer from a connected server or a response from a router disclosing the location of the service on the internetwork to the GNS. GNS is part of IPX and SAP. *See also: IPX and SAP.*

grafting   A process that activates an interface that has been deactivated by the pruning process. It is initiated by an IGMP membership report sent to the router.

GRE   Generic Routing Encapsulation: A tunneling protocol created by Cisco with the capacity for encapsulating a wide variety of protocol packet types inside IP tunnels, thereby generating a virtual point-to-point connection to Cisco routers across an IP network at remote points. IP tunneling using GRE permits network expansion across a single-protocol backbone environment by linking multiprotocol subnetworks in a single-protocol backbone environment.

guard band   The unused frequency area found between two communications channels, furnishing the space necessary to avoid interference between the two.

half duplex   The capacity to transfer data in only one direction at a time between a sending unit and receiving unit. *See also: full duplex.*

handshake   Any series of transmissions exchanged between two or more devices on a network to ensure synchronized operations.

H channel   high-speed channel: A full-duplex, ISDN primary rate channel operating at a speed of 384Kbps. *See also: B channel, D channel,* and *E channel.*

HDLC   High-Level Data Link Control: Using frame characters, including checksums, HDLC designates a method for data encapsulation on synchronous serial links and is the default encapsulation for Cisco routers. HDLC is a bit-oriented synchronous Data Link layer protocol created by ISO and derived from SDLC. However, most HDLC vendor implementations (including Cisco's) are proprietary. *See also: SDLC.*

helper address   The unicast address specified, which instructs the Cisco router to change the client's local broadcast request for a service into a directed unicast to the server.

hierarchical addressing   Any addressing plan employing a logical chain of commands to determine location. IP addresses are made up of a hierarchy of network numbers, subnet numbers, and host numbers to direct packets to the appropriate destination.

hierarchy   Term used in defining IP addressing; in heirarchical addressing, some bits are used for networking and some bits for host addressing.

HIP   HSSI Interface Processor: An interface processor used on Cisco 7000 series routers, providing one HSSI port that supports connections to ATM, SMDS, Frame Relay, or private lines at speeds up to T3 or E3.

holddown   The state a route is placed in so that routers can neither advertise the route nor accept advertisements about it for a defined time period. Holddown is used to discover bad information about a route from all routers in the network. A route is generally placed in holddown when one of its links fails.

hop   The movement of a packet between any two network nodes. *See also: hop count.*

hop count   A routing metric that calculates the distance between a source and a destination. RIP employs hop count as its sole metric. *See also: hop and RIP.*

host address   Logical address configured by an administrator or server on a device. Logically identifies this device on an internetwork.

Host-to-Host layer   Layer in the Internet Protocol suite that is equal to the Transport layer of the OSI model.

HSCI   High-Speed Communication Interface: Developed by Cisco, a single-port interface that provides full-duplex synchronous serial communications capability at speeds up to 52Mbps.

HSRP   Hot Standby Router Protocol: A protocol that provides high network availability and provides nearly instantaneous hardware fail-over without administrator intervention. It generates a Hot Standby router group, including a lead router that lends its services to any packet being transferred to the Hot Standby address. If the lead router fails, it will be replaced by any of the other routers—the standby routers—that monitor it.

HSSI   High-Speed Serial Interface: A network standard physical connector for high-speed serial linking over a WAN at speeds of up to 52Mbps.

hubs   Physical layer devices that are really just multiple port repeaters. When an electronic digital signal is received on a port, the signal is reamplified or regenerated and forwarded out all segments except the segment from which the signal was received.

hybrid protocol   Routing protocol that uses the attributes of both distance-vector and link-state. Enhanced Interior Gateway Routing Protocol (Enhanced IGRP) is a hybrid routing protocol.

ICD   International Code Designator: Adapted from the subnetwork model of addressing, this assigns the mapping of network layer addresses to ATM addresses. HSSI is one of two ATM formats for addressing created by the ATM Forum to be utilized with private networks. *See also: DCC.*

ICMP   Internet Control Message Protocol: Documented in RFC 792, it is a Network layer Internet protocol for the purpose of reporting errors and providing information pertinent to IP packet procedures.

IEEE   Institute of Electrical and Electronics Engineers: A professional organization that, among other activities, defines standards in a number of fields within computing and electronics, including networking and communications. IEEE standards are the predominant LAN standards used today throughout the industry. Many protocols are commonly known by the reference number of the corresponding IEEE standard.

IEEE 802.1   The IEEE committee specification that defines the bridging group. The specification for STP (Spanning Tree Protocol) is IEEE 802.1D. The STP uses SPA (spanning-tree algorithm) to find and prevent network loops in bridged networks. The specification for VLAN trunking is IEEE 802.1Q.

IEEE 802.3   The IEEE committee specification that defines the Ethernet group, specifically the original 10Mbps standard. Ethernet is a LAN protocol that specifies physical layer and MAC sublayer media access. IEEE 802.3 uses CSMA/CD to provide access for many devices on the same network. Fast Ethernet is defined as 802.3U, and Gigabit Ethernet is defined as 802.3Q. *See also: CSMA/CD.*

IEEE 802.5   IEEE committee that defines Token Ring media access.

IGMP   Internet Group Management Protocol: Employed by IP hosts, the protocol that reports their multicast group memberships to an adjacent multicast router.

IGP   interior gateway protocol: Any protocol used by the Internet to exchange routing data within an independent system. Examples include RIP, IGRP, and OSPF.

IGRP   Interior Gateway Routing Protocol: Cisco proprietary distance vector routing algorithm. Upgrade from the RIP protocol.

ILMI   Integrated (or Interim) Local Management Interface. A specification created by the ATM Forum, designated for the incorporation of network-management capability into the ATM UNI. Integrated Local Management Interface cells provide for automatic configuration between ATM systems. In LAN emulation, ILMI can provide sufficient information for the ATM end station to find an LECS. In addition, ILMI provides the ATM NSAP (Network Service Access Point) prefix information to the end station.

in-band management   In-band management is the management of a network device "through" the network. Examples include using Simple Network Management Protocol (SNMP) or Telnet directly via the local LAN. *Compare with: out-of-band management.*

in-band signaling   Configuration of a router from within the network. Examples are Telnet, Simple Network Management Protocol (SNMP), or a Network Management Station (NMS).

insured burst   In an ATM network, it is the largest, temporarily permitted data burst exceeding the insured rate on a PVC and not tagged by the traffic policing function for being dropped if network congestion occurs. This insured burst is designated in bytes or cells.

interarea routing Routing between two or more logical areas. *Contrast with: intra-area routing. See also: area.*

interface configuration mode Mode that allows you to configure a Cisco router or switch port with specific information, such as an IP address and mask.

interface processor Any of several processor modules used with Cisco 7000 series routers. *See also: AIP, CIP, EIP, FEIP, HIP, MIP, and TRIP.*

Internet The global "network of networks," whose popularity has exploded in the last few years. Originally a tool for collaborative academic research, it has become a medium for exchanging and distributing information of all kinds. The Internet's need to link disparate computer platforms and technologies has led to the development of uniform protocols and standards that have also found widespread use within corporate LANs. *See also: TCP/IP and MBONE.*

internet Before the rise of the Internet, this lowercase form was shorthand for "internetwork" in the generic sense. Now rarely used. *See also: internetwork.*

internet layer Layer in the Internet Protocol suite of protocols that provide network addressing and routing through and internetwork.

Internet protocol Any protocol belonging to the TCP/IP protocol stack. *See also: TCP/IP.*

internetwork Any group of private networks interconnected by routers and other mechanisms, typically operating as a single entity.

internetworking Broadly, anything associated with the general task of linking networks to each other. The term encompasses technologies, procedures, and products. When you connect networks to a router, you are creating an internetwork.

intra-area routing Routing that occurs within a logical area. *Contrast with: interarea routing.*

Inverse ARP Inverse Address Resolution Protocol: A technique by which dynamic mappings are constructed in a network, allowing a device such as a router to locate the logical network address and associate it with a permanent virtual circuit (PVC). Commonly used in Frame Relay to determine the far-end node's TCP/IP address by sending the Inverse ARP request to the local DLCI.

IP   Internet Protocol: Defined in RFC 791, it is a network layer protocol that is part of the TCP/IP stack and allows connectionless service. IP furnishes an array of features for addressing, type-of-service specification, fragmentation and reassembly, and security.

IP address   Often called an Internet address, this is an address uniquely identifying any device (host) on the Internet (or any TCP/IP network). Each address consists of four octets (32 bits), represented as decimal numbers separated by periods (a format known as "dotted-decimal"). Every address is made up of a network number, an optional subnetwork number, and a host number. The network and subnetwork numbers together are used for routing, while the host number addresses an individual host within the network or subnetwork. The network and subnetwork information is extracted from the IP address using the subnet mask. There are five classes of IP addresses (A–E), which allocate different numbers of bits to the network, subnetwork, and host portions of the address. *See also: CIDR, IP,* and *subnet mask.*

IPCP   IP Control Program: The protocol used to establish and configure IP over PPP. *See also: IP* and *PPP.*

IP multicast   A technique for routing that enables IP traffic to be reproduced from one source to several endpoints or from multiple sources to many destinations. Instead of transmitting only one packet to each individual point of destination, one packet is sent to a multicast group specified by only one IP endpoint address for the group.

IPX   Internetwork Packet eXchange: Network layer protocol (layer 3) used in Novell NetWare networks for transferring information from servers to workstations. Similar to IP and XNS.

IPXCP   IPX Control Program: The protocol used to establish and configure IPX over PPP. *See also: IPX* and *PPP.*

IPXWAN   Protocol used for new WAN links to provide and negotiate line options on the link using IPX. After the link is up and the options have been agreed upon by the two end-to-end links, normal IPX transmission begins.

ISDN Integrated Services Digital Network: Offered as a service by telephone companies, a communication protocol that allows telephone networks to carry data, voice, and other digital traffic. *See also: BISDN, BRI, and PRI.*

IS-IS Intermediate System-to-Intermediate System: An OSI link-state hierarchical routing protocol.

ISL routing Inter-Switch Link routing: A Cisco proprietary method of frame tagging in a switched internetwork. Frame tagging is a way to identify the VLAN membership of a frame as it traverses a switched internetwork.

isochronous transmission Asynchronous data transfer over a synchronous data-link, requiring a constant bit rate for reliable transport. *Compare with: asynchronous transmission and synchronous transmission.*

ITU-T International Telecommunication Union-Telecommunication Standardization Sector: This is a group of engineers that develops worldwide standards for telecommunications technologies.

Kerberos An authentication and encryption method that can be used by Cisco routers to ensure that data cannot be "sniffed" off of the network. Kerberos was developed at MIT and was designed to provide strong security using the Data Encryption Standard (DES) cryptographic algorithm.

LAN local area network: Broadly, any network linking two or more computers and related devices within a limited geographical area (up to a few kilometers). LANs are typically high-speed, low-error networks within a company. Cabling and signaling at the Physical and Data Link layers of the OSI are dictated by LAN standards. Ethernet, FDDI, and Token Ring are among the most popular LAN technologies. *Compare with: MAN.*

LANE LAN emulation: The technology that allows an ATM network to operate as a LAN backbone. To do so, the ATM network is required to provide multicast and broadcast support, address mapping (MAC-to-ATM), SVC management, in addition to an operable packet format. Additionally, LANE defines Ethernet and Token Ring ELANs. *See also: ELAN.*

LAN switch A high-speed, multiple-interface transparent bridging mechanism, transmitting packets between segments of data links, usually referred to specifically as an Ethernet switch. LAN switches transfer traffic based on

MAC addresses. Multilayer switches are a type of high-speed, special purpose, hardware-based router. *See also: multilayer switch* and *store-and-forward packet switching.*

LAPB Link Accessed Procedure, Balanced: A bit-oriented Data Link layer protocol that is part of the X.25 stack and has its origin in SDLC. *See also: SDLC* and *X.25.*

LAPD Link Access Procedure on the D channel: The ISDN Data Link layer protocol used specifically for the D channel and defined by ITU-T Recommendations Q.920 and Q.921. LAPD evolved from LAPB and is created to comply with the signaling requirements of ISDN basic access.

latency Broadly, the time it takes a data packet to get from one location to another. In specific networking contexts, it can mean either 1) the time elapsed (delay) between the execution of a request for access to a network by a device and the time the mechanism actually is permitted transmission, or 2) the time elapsed between when a mechanism receives a frame and the time that frame is forwarded out of the destination port.

layer Term used in networking to define how the OSI model works to encapsulate data for transmission on the network.

layer-3 switch *See: multilayer switch.*

layered architecture Industry standard way of creating applications to work on a network. Layered architecture allows the application developer to make changes in only one layer instead of the whole program.

LCP Link Control Protocol: The protocol designed to establish, configure, and test data-link connections for use by PPP. *See also: PPP.*

leaky bucket An analogy for the basic cell rate algorithm (GCRA) used in ATM networks for checking the conformance of cell flows from a user or network. The bucket's "hole" is understood to be the prolonged rate at which cells can be accommodated, and the "depth" is the tolerance for cell bursts over a certain time period.

learning bridge A bridge that transparently builds a dynamic database of MAC addresses and the interfaces associated with each address. Transparent bridges help to reduce traffic congestion on the network.

LE ARP LAN Emulation Address Resolution Protocol: The protocol providing the ATM address that corresponds to a MAC address.

leased line Permanent connection between two points leased from the telephone companies.

LEC LAN emulation client: Software providing the emulation of the link layer interface that allows the operation and communication of all higher-level protocols and applications to continue. The LEC runs in all ATM devices, which include hosts, servers, bridges, and routers. *See also: ELAN* and *LES.*

LECS LAN emulation configuration server: An important part of emulated LAN services, providing the configuration data that is furnished upon request from the LES. These services include address registration for Integrated Local Management Interface (ILMI) support, configuration support for the LES addresses and their corresponding emulated LAN identifiers, and an interface to the emulated LAN. *See also: LES* and *ELAN.*

LES LAN emulation server: The central LANE component that provides the initial configuration data for each connecting LEC. The LES typically is located on either an ATM-integrated router or a switch. Responsibilities of the LES include configuration and support for the LEC, address registration for the LEC, database storage and response concerning ATM addresses, and interfacing to the emulated LAN. *See also: ELAN, LEC,* and *LECS.*

link-state routing algorithm A routing algorithm that allows each router to broadcast or multicast information regarding the cost of reaching all its neighbors to every node in the internetwork. Link-state algorithms provide a consistent view of the network and are therefore not vulnerable to routing loops. However, this is achieved at the cost of somewhat greater difficulty in computation and more widespread traffic (compared with distance-vector routing algorithms). *See also: distance-vector routing algorithm.*

LLAP LocalTalk Link Access Protocol: In a LocalTalk environment, the data link-level protocol that manages node-to-node delivery of data. This protocol provides node addressing and management of bus access, and it also controls data sending and receiving to assure packet length and integrity.

LLC Logical Link Control: Defined by the IEEE, the higher of two Data Link layer sublayers. LLC is responsible for error detection (but not correction), flow control, framing, and software-sublayer addressing. The predominant LLC protocol, IEEE 802.2, defines both connectionless and connection-oriented operations. *See also: Data Link layer* and *MAC.*

LMI   Local Management Interface: An enhancement to the original Frame Relay specification. Among the features it provides are a keepalive mechanism, a multicast mechanism, global addressing, and a status mechanism.

LNNI   LAN Emulation Network-to-Network Interface: In the Phase 2 LANE specification, an interface that supports communication between the server components within one ELAN.

load balancing   The act of balancing packet load over multiple links to the same remote network.

local explorer packet   In a Token Ring SRB network, a packet generated by an end system to find a host linked to the local ring. If no local host can be found, the end system will produce one of two solutions: a spanning explorer packet or an all-routes explorer packet.

local loop   Connection from a demarcation point to the closest switching office.

LocalTalk   Utilizing CSMA/CD, in addition to supporting data transmission at speeds of 230.4Kbps, LocalTalk is Apple Computer's proprietary baseband protocol, operating at the Data Link and Physical layers of the OSI reference model.

logical address   Network layer address that defines how data is sent from one network to another. Examples of logical addresses are IP and IPX.

LPD   Line Printer Daemon: Used in Unix world to allow printing to an IP address.

LSA   Link-State Advertisement: Contained inside of link-state packets (LSPs), these advertisements are usually multicast packets, containing information about neighbors and path costs, that are employed by link-state protocols. Receiving routers use LSAs to maintain their link-state databases and, ultimately, routing tables.

LUNI   LAN Emulation User-to-Network Interface: Defining the interface between the LAN emulation client (LEC) and the LAN emulation server

(LES), LUNI is the ATM Forum's standard for LAN emulation on ATM networks. *See also: LES* and *LECS.*

MAC   Media Access Control: The lower sublayer in the Data Link layer, it is responsible for hardware addressing, media access, and error detection of frames. *See also: Data Link layer* and *LLC.*

MAC address   A Data Link layer hardware address that every port or device needs in order to connect to a LAN segment. These addresses are used by various devices in the network for accurate location of logical addresses. MAC addresses are defined by the IEEE standard and their length is six characters, typically using the burned-in address (BIA) of the local LAN interface. Variously called hardware address, physical address, burned-in address, or MAC-layer address.

MacIP   In AppleTalk, the network layer protocol encapsulating IP packets in Datagram Delivery Protocol (DDP) packets. MacIP also supplies substitute ARP services.

MAN   metropolitan area network: Any network that encompasses a metropolitan area; that is, an area typically larger than a LAN but smaller than a WAN. *See also: LAN.*

Manchester encoding   A method for digital coding in which a mid-bit–time transition is employed for clocking, and a 1 (one) is denoted by a high voltage level during the first half of the bit time. This scheme is used by Ethernet and IEEE 802.3.

maximum burst   Specified in bytes or cells, the largest burst of information exceeding the insured rate that will be permitted on an ATM permanent virtual connection for a short time and will not be dropped even if it goes over the specified maximum rate. *Compare with: insured burst. See also: maximum rate.*

maximum hop count   Number of routers a packet is allowed to pass before it is terminated. This is created to prevent a packet from circling a network forever.

maximum rate   The maximum permitted data throughput on a particular virtual circuit, equal to the total of insured and uninsured traffic from the traffic source. Should traffic congestion occur, uninsured information may be deleted from the path. Measured in bits or cells per second, the maximum rate represents the highest throughput of data the virtual circuit is ever able to deliver and cannot exceed the media rate. *Compare with: excess rate. See also: maximum burst.*

MBS   Maximum Burst Size: In an ATM signaling message, this metric, coded as a number of cells, is used to convey the burst tolerance.

MBONE   The multicast backbone of the Internet, it is a virtual multicast network made up of multicast LANs, including point-to-point tunnels interconnecting them.

MCDV   Maximum Cell Delay Variation: The maximum two-point CDV objective across a link or node for the identified service category in an ATM network. The MCDV is one of four link metrics that are exchanged using PTSPs to verify the available resources of an ATM network. Only one MCDV value is assigned to each traffic class.

MCLR   Maximum Cell Loss Ratio: The maximum ratio of cells in an ATM network that fail to transit a link or node compared with the total number of cells that arrive at the link or node. MCDV is one of four link metrics that are exchanged using PTSPs to verify the available resources of an ATM network. The MCLR applies to cells in VBR and CBR traffic classes whose CLP bit is set to zero. *See also: CBR, CLP, and VBR.*

MCR   Minimum cell rate: A parameter determined by the ATM Forum for traffic management of the ATM networks. MCR is specifically defined for ABR transmissions and specifies the minimum value for the allowed cell rate (ACR). *See also: ACR and PCR.*

MCTD   Maximum Cell Transfer Delay: In an ATM network, the total of the maximum cell delay variation and the fixed delay across the link or node. MCTD is one of four link metrics that are exchanged using PNNI topology state packets to verify the available resources of an ATM network. There is one MCTD value assigned to each traffic class. *See also: MCDV.*

media translation   A router property that allows two different types of LAN to communicate—for example, Ethernet to Token Ring.

MIB   Management Information Base: Used with SNMP management software to gather information from remote devices. The management station can poll the remote device for information, or the MIB running on the remote station can be programmed to send information on a regular basis.

MII Media Independent Interface: Used in Fast Ethernet and Gigabit Ethernet to provide faster bit transfer rates of four and eight bits at a time. Contrast to AUI interface that is one bit at a time.

MIP Multichannel Interface Processor: The resident interface processor on Cisco 7000 series routers, providing up to two channelized T-1 or E-1 connections by serial cables connected to a CSU. The two controllers are capable of providing 24 T-1 or 30 E-1 channel groups, with each group being introduced to the system as a serial interface that can be configured individually.

mips millions of instructions per second: A measure of processor speed.

MLP Multilink PPP: A technique used to split, recombine, and sequence datagrams across numerous logical data links.

MMP Multichassis Multilink PPP: A protocol that supplies MLP support across multiple routers and access servers. MMP enables several routers and access servers to work as a single, large dial-up pool with one network address and ISDN access number. MMP successfully supports packet fragmenting and reassembly when the user connection is split between two physical access devices.

modem modulator-demodulator: A device that converts digital signals to analog and vice-versa so that digital information can be transmitted over analog communication facilities, such as voice-grade telephone lines. This is achieved by converting digital signals at the source to analog for transmission and reconverting the analog signals back into digital form at the destination. *See also: modulation* and *demodulation.*

modem eliminator A mechanism that makes possible a connection between two DTE devices without modems by simulating the commands and physical signaling required.

modulation The process of modifying some characteristic of an electrical signal, such as amplitude (AM) or frequency (FM), in order to represent digital or analog information. *See also: AM.*

MOSPF Multicast OSPF: An extension of the OSPF unicast protocol that enables IP multicast routing within the domain. *See also: OSPF.*

MPOA Multiprotocol over ATM: An effort by the ATM Forum to standardize how existing and future network-layer protocols such as IP, IPv6, AppleTalk, and IPX run over an ATM network with directly attached hosts, routers, and multilayer LAN switches.

MTU maximum transmission unit: The largest packet size, measured in bytes, that an interface can handle.

multicast Broadly, any communication between a single sender and multiple receivers. Unlike broadcast messages, which are sent to all addresses on a network, multicast messages are sent to a defined subset of the network addresses; this subset has a group multicast address, which is specified in the packet's destination address field. *See also: broadcast* and *directed broadcast.*

multicast address A single address that points to more than one device on the network by specifying a special non-existent MAC address specified in that particular multicast protocol. Identical to group address. *See also: multicast.*

multicast send VCC A two-directional point-to-point virtual control connection (VCC) arranged by an LEC to a BUS, it is one of the three types of informational links specified by phase 1 LANE. *See also: control distribute VCC* and *control direct VCC.*

multilayer switch A highly specialized, high-speed, hardware-based type of LAN router, the device filters and forwards packets based on their layer-2 MAC addresses and layer-3 network addresses. It's possible that even layer-4 can be read. Sometimes called a layer-3 switch. *See also: LAN switch.*

multilink Used to combine multiple Async or ISDN links to provide combined bandwidth.

multiplexing The process of converting several logical signals into a single physical signal for transmission across one physical channel. *Contrast with: demultiplexing.*

NAK negative acknowledgment: A response sent from a receiver, telling the sender that the information was not received or contained errors. *Compare with: acknowledgment.*

NAT network address translation: An algorithm instrumental in minimizing the requirement for globally unique IP addresses, permitting an organization whose addresses are not all globally unique to connect to the Internet nevertheless, by translating those addresses into globally routable address space.

native VLAN   Cisco switches all have a native VLAN called VLAN 1. This cannot be deleted or changed in any way. All switch ports are in VLAN 1 by default.

NBP   Name Binding Protocol: In AppleTalk, the transport-level protocol that interprets a socket client's name, entered as a character string, into the corresponding DDP address. NBP gives AppleTalk protocols the capacity to discern user-defined zones and names of mechanisms by showing and keeping translation tables that map names to their corresponding socket addresses.

neighboring routers   Two routers in OSPF that have interfaces to a common network. On networks with multiaccess, these neighboring routers are dynamically discovered using the Hello protocol of OSPF.

NetBEUI   NetBIOS Extended User Interface: An improved version of the NetBIOS protocol used in a number of network operating systems including LAN Manager, Windows NT, LAN Server, and Windows for Workgroups, implementing the OSI LLC2 protocol. NetBEUI formalizes the transport frame not standardized in NetBIOS and adds more functions. *See also: OSI.*

NetBIOS   Network Basic Input/Output System: The API employed by applications residing on an IBM LAN to ask for services, such as session termination or information transfer, from lower-level network processes.

NetView   A mainframe network product from IBM, used for monitoring SNA (Systems Network Architecture) networks. It runs as a VTAM (Virtual Telecommunications Access Method) application.

NetWare   A widely used NOS created by Novell, providing a number of distributed network services and remote file access.

network access layer   Bottom layer in the Internet Protocol suite that provides media access to packets.

network address   Used with the logical network addresses to identify the network segment in an internetwork. Logical addresses are hierarchical in nature and have at least two parts: network and host. An example of a hierarchical address is 172.16.10.5, where 172.16 is the network and 10.5 is the host address.

Network layer   In the OSI reference model, it is layer 3—the layer in which routing is implemented, enabling connections and path selection between two end systems. *See also: Application layer, Data Link layer, Physical layer, Presentation layer, Session layer,* and *Transport layer.*

network segmentation   Breaking up a large network into smaller networks. Routers, switches, and bridges are used to create network segmentation.

NFS   Network File System: One of the protocols in Sun Microsystems' widely used file system protocol suite, allowing remote file access across a network. The name is loosely used to refer to the entire Sun protocol suite, which also includes RPC, XDR (External Data Representation), and other protocols.

NHRP   Next Hop Resolution Protocol: In a nonbroadcast multiaccess (NBMA) network, the protocol employed by routers in order to dynamically locate MAC addresses of various hosts and routers. It enables systems to communicate directly without requiring an intermediate hop, thus facilitating increased performance in ATM, Frame Relay, X.25, and SMDS systems.

NHS   Next Hop Server: Defined by the NHRP protocol, this server maintains the next-hop resolution cache tables, listing IP-to-ATM address maps of related nodes and nodes that can be reached through routers served by the NHS.

nibble   Four bits.

NIC   network interface card: An electronic circuit board placed in a computer. The NIC provides network communication to a LAN.

NLSP   NetWare Link Services Protocol: Novell's link-state routing protocol, based on the IS-IS model.

NMP   Network Management Processor: A Catalyst 5000 switch processor module used to control and monitor the switch.

node address   Used to identify a specific device in an internetwork. Can be a hardware address, which is burned into the network interface card or a logical network address, which an administrator or server assigns to the node.

nondesignated port   A switch port that will not forward frames in order to prevent a switching loop. Spanning Tree Protocol (STP) is responsible for deciding whether a port is designated (forwarding) or nondesignated (blocking).

non-stub area   In OSPF, a resource-consuming area carrying a default route, intra-area routes, interarea routes, static routes, and external routes. Non-stub areas are the only areas that can have virtual links configured across them and exclusively contain an anonymous system boundary router (ASBR). *Compare with: stub area. See also: ASBR* and *OSPF.*

NRZ   nonreturn to zero: One of several encoding schemes for transmitting digital data. NRZ signals sustain constant levels of voltage with no signal shifting (no return to zero-voltage level) during a bit interval. If there is a series of bits with the same value (1 or 0), there will be no state change. The signal is not self-clocking. *See also: NRZI.*

NRZI   nonreturn to zero inverted: One of several encoding schemes for transmitting digital data. A transition in voltage level (either from high to low or vice-versa) at the beginning of a bit interval is interpreted as a value of 1; the absence of a transition is interpreted as a 0. Thus, the voltage assigned to each value is continually inverted. NRZI signals are not self-clocking. *See also: NRZ.*

NT   network termination: A point in an ISDN network. *See: NT1* and *NT2.*

NT1   network termination 1: Is an ISDN designation to devices that understand ISDN standards.

NT2   network termination 2: Is an ISDN designation to devices that do not understand ISDN standards. To use a NT2, you must use a terminal adapter (TA).

NVRAM   nonvolatile RAM: Random-access memory that keeps its contents intact while power is turned off.

OC   Optical Carrier: A series of physical protocols, designated as OC-1, OC-2, OC-3, and so on, for SONET optical signal transmissions. OC signal levels place STS frames on a multimode fiber-optic line at various speeds, of which 51.84Mbps is the lowest (OC-1). Each subsequent protocol runs at a speed divisible by 51.84. *See also: SONET.*

octet   Base-8 numbering system used to identify a section of a dotted decimal IP address. Also referred to as a byte.

ones density   Also known as pulse density, this is a method of signal clocking. The CSU/DSU retrieves the clocking information from data that passes through it. For this scheme to work, the data needs to be encoded to contain at least one binary 1 for each eight bits transmitted. *See also: CSU and DSU.*

OSI   Open System Interconnection: International standardization program designed by ISO and ITU-T for the development of data networking standards that make multivendor equipment interoperability a reality.

OSI reference model   Open System Interconnection reference model: A conceptual model defined by the International Organization for Standardization (ISO), describing how any combination of devices can be connected for the purpose of communication. The OSI model divides the task into seven functional layers, forming a hierarchy with the applications at the top and the physical medium at the bottom, and it defines the functions each layer must provide. *See also: Application layer, Data Link layer, Network layer, Physical layer, Presentation layer, Session layer,* and *Transport layer.*

OSPF   Open Shortest Path First: A link-state, hierarchical IGP routing algorithm derived from an earlier version of the IS-IS protocol, whose features include multipath routing, load balancing, and least-cost routing. OSPF is the suggested successor to RIP in the Internet environment. *See also: Enhanced IGRP, IGP,* and *IP.*

OUI   organizationally unique identifier: Code assigned by the IEEE to an organization that makes network interface cards. The organization then puts this OUI on each and every card they manufacture. The OUI is 3 bytes (24 bits) long. The manufacturer then adds a 3-byte identifier to uniquely identify the host on an internetwork. The total length of the address is 48 bits (6 bytes) and is called a hardware address or MAC address.

out-of-band management   Management "outside" of the network's physical channels. For example, using a console connection not directly interfaced through the local LAN or WAN or a dial-in modem. *Compare to: in-band management.*

out-of-band signaling   Within a network, any transmission that uses physical channels or frequencies separate from those ordinarily used for data transfer. For example, the initial configuration of a Cisco Catalyst switch requires an out-of-band connection via a console port.

packet   In data communications, the basic logical unit of information transferred. A packet consists of a certain number of data bytes, wrapped or encapsulated in headers and/or trailers that contain information about where the packet came from, where it's going, and so on. The various protocols involved in sending a transmission add their own layers of header information, which the corresponding protocols in receiving devices then interpret.

packet switch   A physical device that makes it possible for a communication channel to share several connections, its functions include finding the most efficient transmission path for packets.

packet switching   A networking technology based on the transmission of data in packets. Dividing a continuous stream of data into small units—packets—enables data from multiple devices on a network to share the same communication channel simultaneously but also requires the use of precise routing information.

PAP   Password Authentication Protocol: In Point-to-Point Protocol (PPP) networks, a method of validating connection requests. The requesting (remote) device must send an authentication request, containing a password and ID, to the local router when attempting to connect. Unlike the more secure CHAP (Challenge Handshake Authentication Protocol), PAP sends the password unencrypted and does not attempt to verify whether the user is authorized to access the requested resource; it merely identifies the remote end. *See also: CHAP.*

parity checking   A method of error-checking in data transmissions. An extra bit (the parity bit) is added to each character or data word so that the sum of the bits will be either an odd number (in odd parity) or an even number (even parity).

partial mesh   A type of network topology in which some network nodes form a full mesh (where every node has either a physical or a virtual circuit linking it to every other network node), but others are attached to only one or two nodes in the network. A typical use of partial-mesh topology is in peripheral networks linked to a fully meshed backbone. *See also: full mesh.*

PAT port address translation: This process allows a single IP address to represent multiple resources by altering the source TCP or UDP port number.

PCM pulse code modulation: Process by which analog data is converted into digital information.

PCR peak cell rate: As defined by the ATM Forum, the parameter specifying, in cells per second, the maximum rate at which a source may transmit.

PDN public data network: Generally for a fee, a PDN offers the public access to a computer communication network operated by private concerns or government agencies. Small organizations can take advantage of PDNs, aiding them to create WANs without investing in long-distance equipment and circuitry.

PDU Protocol Data Unit: The processes at each layer of the OSI model. PDUs at the Transport layer are called segments; PDUs at the Network layer are called packets or datagrams; and PDUs at the Data Link layer are called frames. The Physical layer uses bits.

PGP Pretty Good Privacy: A popular public-key/private-key encryption application offering protected transfer of files and messages.

phantom router Used in a Hot Standby Routing Protocol (HSRP) network to provide an IP default gateway address to hosts.

Physical layer The lowest layer—layer 1—in the OSI reference model, it is responsible for converting data packets from the Data Link layer (layer 2) into electrical signals. Physical-layer protocols and standards define, for example, the type of cable and connectors to be used, including their pin assignments and the encoding scheme for signaling 0 and 1 values. *See also: Application layer, Data Link layer, Network layer, Presentation layer, Session layer,* and *Transport layer.*

PIM Protocol Independent Multicast: A multicast protocol that handles the IGMP requests as well as requests for multicast data forwarding.

PIM-DM Protocol Independent Multicast Dense Mode: PIM-DM utilizes the unicast route table and relies on the source root distribution architecture for multicast data forwarding.

PIM-SM Protocol Independent Multicast Sparse Mode: PIM-SM utilizes the unicast route table and relies on the shared root distribution architecture for multicast data forwarding.

Ping Packet Internet Groper: A Unix-based Internet diagnostic tool, consisting of a message sent to test the accessibility of a particular device on the IP network. The acronym (from which the "full name" was formed) reflects the underlying metaphor of submarine sonar. Just as the sonar operator sends out a signal and waits to hear it echo ("ping") back from a submerged object, the network user can ping another node on the network and wait to see if it responds.

pinhole congestion A problem associated with distance-vector routing protocols if more than one connection to a remote network is known, but they are different bandwidths.

pleisochronous Nearly synchronous, except that clocking comes from an outside source instead of being embedded within the signal as in synchronous transmissions.

PLP Packet Level Protocol: Occasionally called X.25 level 3 or X.25 Protocol, a network-layer protocol that is part of the X.25 stack.

PNNI Private Network-Network Interface: An ATM Forum specification for offering topology data used for the calculation of paths through the network, among switches and groups of switches. It is based on well-known link-state routing procedures and allows for automatic configuration in networks whose addressing scheme is determined by the topology.

point-to-multipoint connection In ATM, a communication path going only one way, connecting a single system at the starting point, called the "root node," to systems at multiple points of destination, called "leaves." *See also: point-to-point connection.*

point-to-point connection In ATM, a channel of communication that can be directed either one way or two ways between two ATM end systems. *See also: point-to-multipoint connection.*

poison reverse updates These update messages are transmitted by a router back to the originator (thus ignoring the split-horizon rule) after route poisoning has occurred. Typically used with DV routing protocols in order to overcome large routing loops and offer explicit information when a subnet or network is not accessible (instead of merely suggesting that the network is unreachable by not including it in updates). *See also: route poisoning.*

polling The procedure of orderly inquiry, used by a primary network mechanism, to determine if secondary devices have data to transmit. A message is sent to each secondary, granting the secondary the right to transmit.

POP 1) point of presence: The physical location where an interexchange carrier has placed equipment to interconnect with a local exchange carrier. 2) Post Office Protocol (currently at version 3) A protocol used by client e-mail applications for recovery of mail from a mail server.

port security Used with layer-2 switches to provide some security. Not typically used in production because it is difficult to manage. Allows only certain frames to traverse administrator-assigned segments.

port numbers Used at the transport layer with TCP to keep track of host-to-host virtual circuits.

positive acknowledgment with retransmission A connection-oriented session that provides acknowledgment and retransmission of the data if it is not acknowledged by the receiving host within a certain time frame.

POTS plain old telephone service: This refers to the traditional analog phone service that is found in most installations.

PPP Point-to-Point Protocol: The protocol most commonly used for dial-up Internet access, superseding the earlier SLIP. Its features include address notification, authentication via CHAP or PAP, support for multiple protocols, and link monitoring. PPP has two layers: the Link Control Protocol (LCP) establishes, configures, and tests a link; and then any of various Network Control Programs (NCPs) transport traffic for a specific protocol suite, such as IPX. *See also: CHAP, PAP,* and *SLIP.*

prefix routing Method of defining how many bits are used in a subnet and how this information is sent in a routing update. For example, RIP version 1 does not send subnet mask information in the route updates. However, RIP version 2 does. This means that RIP v2 updates will send /24, /25, /26, etc., with a route update, which RIP v1 will not.

Presentation layer Layer 6 of the OSI reference model, it defines how data is formatted, presented, encoded, and converted for use by software at the Application layer. *See also: Application layer, Data Link layer, Network layer, Physical layer, Session layer,* and *Transport layer.*

PRI Primary Rate Interface: A type of ISDN connection between a PBX and a long-distance carrier, which is made up of a single 64Kbps D channel in addition to 23 (T-1) or 30 (E-1) B channels. *See also: ISDN.*

priority queueing A routing function in which frames temporarily placed in an interface output queue are assigned priorities based on traits such as packet size or type of interface.

privileged mode Command-line EXEC mode used in Cisco routers and switches that provides both viewing and changing of configurations.

process/application layer Upper layer in the Internet Protocol stack. Responsible for network services.

process switching As a packet arrives on a router to be forwarded, it's copied to the router's process buffer, and the router performs a lookup on the layer-3 address. Using the route table, an exit interface is associated with the destination address. The processor forwards the packet with the added new information to the exit interface, while the router initializes the fast-switching cache. Subsequent packets bound for the same destination address follow the same path as the first packet.

PROM programmable read-only memory: ROM that is programmable only once, using special equipment. *Compare with: EPROM.*

propagation delay The time it takes data to traverse a network from its source to its destination.

protocol In networking, the specification of a set of rules for a particular type of communication. The term is also used to refer to the software that implements a protocol.

protocol stack A collection of related protocols.

pruning The act of trimming down the shortest-path tree. This deactivates interfaces that do not have group participants.

Proxy Address Resolution Protocol Proxy ARP: Used to allow redundancy in case of a failure with the configured default gateway on a host. Proxy ARP is a variation of the ARP protocol in which an intermediate device, such as a router, sends an ARP response on behalf of an end node to the requesting host.

PSE   packet switching exchange: The X.25 term for a switch.

PSN   packet-switched network: Any network that uses packet-switching technology. Also known as packet-switched data network (PSDN). *See also: packet switching.*

PSTN   public switched telephone network: Colloquially referred to as "plain old telephone service" (POTS). A term that describes the assortment of telephone networks and services available globally.

PVC   permanent virtual circuit: In a Frame Relay network, a logical connection, defined in software, that is maintained permanently. *Compare with: SVC. See also: virtual circuit.*

PVP   permanent virtual path: A virtual path made up of PVCs. *See also: PVC.*

PVP tunneling   permanent virtual path tunneling: A technique that links two private ATM networks across a public network using a virtual path, wherein the public network transparently trunks the complete collection of virtual channels in the virtual path between the two private networks.

QoS   quality of service: A set of metrics used to measure the quality of transmission and service availability of any given transmission system.

queue   Broadly, any list of elements arranged in an orderly fashion and ready for processing, such as a line of people waiting to enter a movie theater. In routing, it refers to a backlog of information packets waiting in line to be transmitted over a router interface.

R reference point   Used with ISDN networks to identify the connection between an NT1 and an S/T device. The S/T device converts the four-wire network to the two-wire ISDN standard network.

RADIUS   Reverse Address Resolution Protocol: A protocol that is used to communicate between the remote access device and an authentication server. Sometimes an authentication server running RADIUS will be called a RADIUS server.

RAM   random-access memory: Used by all computers to store information. Cisco routers use RAM to store packet buffers and routing tables, along with the hardware addresses cache.

RARP   Reverse Address Resolution Protocol: The protocol within the TCP/IP stack that maps MAC addresses to IP addresses. *See also: ARP.*

RARP server   A Reverse Address Resolution Protocol server is used to provide an IP address from a known MAC address.

rate queue   A value, assigned to one or more virtual circuits, that specifies the speed at which an individual virtual circuit will transmit data to the remote end. Every rate queue identifies a segment of the total bandwidth available on an ATM link. The sum of all rate queues should not exceed the total available bandwidth.

RCP   Remote Copy Protocol: A protocol for copying files to or from a file system that resides on a remote server on a network, using TCP to guarantee reliable data delivery.

redistribution   Command used in Cisco routers to inject the paths found from one type of routing protocol into another type of routing protocol. For example, networks found by RIP can be inserted into an IGRP network.

redundancy   In internetworking, the duplication of connections, devices, or services that can be used as a backup in the event that the primary connections, devices, or services fail.

reference model   Used by application developers to create applications that work on any type of network. The most popular reference model is the Open Systems Interconnection (OSI) model.

reload   An event or command that causes Cisco routers to reboot.

RIF   Routing Information Field: In source-route bridging, a header field that defines the path direction of the frame or token. If the Route Information Indicator (RII) bit is not set, the RIF is read from source to destination (left to right). If the RII bit is set, the RIF is read from the destination back to the source, so the RIF is read right to left. It is defined as part of the Token Ring frame header for source-routed frames, which contains path information.

ring   Two or more stations connected in a logical circular topology. In this topology, which is the basis for Token Ring, FDDI, and CDDI, information is transferred from station to station in sequence.

ring topology A network logical topology comprising a series of repeaters that form one closed loop by connecting unidirectional transmission links. Individual stations on the network are connected to the network at a repeater. Physically, ring topologies are generally organized in a closed-loop star. *Compare with: bus topology* and *star topology.*

RJ connector registered jack connector: Used with twisted-pair wiring to connect the copper wire to network interface cards, switches, and hubs.

RIP Routing Information Protocol: The most commonly used interior gateway protocol in the Internet. RIP employs hop count as a routing metric. *See also: Enhanced IGRP, IGP, OSPF, and hop count.*

robbed-bit signaling Used in Primary Rate Interface clocking mechanisms.

rolled cable Type of Ethernet cable that is used to connect a PC's COM port to a router or switch console port.

ROM read-only memory: Chip used in computers to help boot the device. Cisco routers use a ROM chip to load the bootstrap, which runs a power-on self test, and then find and load the IOS in flash memory by default.

root bridge Used with Spanning Tree Protocol to stop network loops from occurring. The root bridge is elected by having the lowest bridge ID. The bridge ID is determined by the priority (32,768 by default on all bridges and switches) and the main hardware address of the device. The root bridge determines which of the neighboring layer-2 devices' interfaces become the designated and nondesignated ports.

routed protocol Routed protocols (such as IP and IPX) are used to transmit user data through an internetwork. By contrast, routing protocols (such as RIP, IGRP, and OSPF) are used to update routing tables between routers.

route flap A route that is being announced in an up/down fashion.

route poisoning Used by various DV routing protocols in order to overcome large routing loops and offer explicit information about when a subnet or network is not accessible (instead of merely suggesting that the network is unreachable by not including it in updates). Typically, this is accomplished by setting the hop count to one more than maximum. *See also: poison reverse updates.*

route summarization   In various routing protocols, such as OSPF, EIGRP, and IS-IS, the consolidation of publicized subnetwork addresses so that a single summary route is advertised to other areas by an area border router.

router   A network-layer mechanism, either software or hardware, using one or more metrics to decide on the best path to use for transmission of network traffic. Sending packets between networks by routers is based on the information provided on network layers. Historically, this device has sometimes been called a gateway.

routing   The process of forwarding logically addressed packets from their local subnetwork toward their ultimate destination. In large networks, the numerous intermediary destinations a packet might travel before reaching its destination can make routing very complex.

routing domain   Any collection of end systems and intermediate systems that operate under an identical set of administrative rules. Every routing domain contains one or several areas, all individually given a certain area address.

routing metric   Any value that is used by routing algorithms to determine whether one route is superior to another. Metrics include such information as bandwidth, delay, hop count, path cost, load, MTU, reliability, and communication cost. Only the best possible routes are stored in the routing table, while all other information may be stored in link-state or topological databases. *See also: cost.*

routing protocol   Any protocol that defines algorithms to be used for updating routing tables between routers. Examples include IGRP, RIP, and OSPF.

routing table   A table kept in a router or other internetworking mechanism that maintains a record of only the best possible routes to certain network destinations and the metrics associated with those routes.

RP   Route Processor: Also known as a supervisory processor, a module on Cisco 7000 series routers that holds the CPU, system software, and most of the memory components used in the router.

RSP   Route/Switch Processor: A processor module combining the functions of RP and SP used in Cisco 7500 series routers. *See also: RP and SP.*

RTS Request To Send: An EIA/TIA-232 control signal requesting permission to transmit data on a communication line.

S reference point ISDN reference point that works with a T reference point to convert a four-wire ISDN network to the two-wire ISDN network needed to communicate with the ISDN switches at the network provider.

sampling rate The rate at which samples of a specific waveform amplitude are collected within a specified period of time.

SAP 1) Service Access Point: A field specified by IEEE 802.2 that is part of an address specification. 2) Service Advertising Protocol: The Novell NetWare protocol that supplies a way to inform network clients of resources and services availability on network, using routers and servers. *See also: IPX.*

SCR sustainable cell rate: An ATM Forum parameter used for traffic management, it is the long-term average cell rate for VBR connections that can be transmitted.

SDH Synchronous Digital Hierarchy: One of the standards developed for Fiberoptic Transmission Systems (FOTS).

SDLC Synchronous Data Link Control: A protocol used in SNA Data Link layer communications. SDLC is a bit-oriented, full-duplex serial protocol that is the basis for several similar protocols, including HDLC and LAPB. *See also: HDLC and LAPB.*

seed router In an AppleTalk network, the router that is equipped with the network number or cable range in its port descriptor. The seed router specifies the network number or cable range for other routers in that network section and answers to configuration requests from nonseed routers on its connected AppleTalk network, permitting those routers to affirm or modify their configurations accordingly. Every AppleTalk network needs at least one seed router physically connected to each network segment.

sequencing Used in virtual circuits and segmentation to number segments so they can be put back together again in the correct order.

server Hardware and software that provide network services to clients.

set-based Set-based routers and switches use the `set` command to configure devices. Cisco is moving away from set-based commands and is using the command-line interface (CLI) on all new devices.

session   1) Session layer of OSI model is responsible for keeping track of user data and keeping it separate on the network. 2) Reliable sessions can be set up between hosts.

Session layer   Layer 5 of the OSI reference model, responsible for creating, managing, and terminating sessions between applications and overseeing data exchange between presentation layer entities. *See also: Application layer, Data Link layer, Network layer, Physical layer, Presentation layer,* and *Transport layer.*

setup mode   Mode that a router will enter if no configuration is found in nonvolatile RAM when the router boots. Allows the administrator to configure a router step-by-step. Not as robust or flexible as the command-line interface.

SF   A super frame (also called a D4 frame) consists of 12 frames with 192 bits each, and the 193rd bit providing other functions including error checking. SF is frequently used on T-1 circuits. A newer version of the technology is Extended Super Frame (ESF), which uses 24 frames. *See also: ESF.*

shared tree   A method of multicast data forwarding. Shared trees use an architecture in which multiple sources share a common rendezvous point.

shortest-path-first   A type of routing protocol. The only true SPF protocol is Open Shortest Path First (OSPF).

signaling packet   An informational packet created by an ATM-connected mechanism that wants to establish connection with another such mechanism. The packet contains the QoS parameters needed for connection and the ATM NSAP address of the endpoint. The endpoint responds with a message of acceptance if it is able to support the desired QoS, and the connection is established. *See also: QoS.*

silicon switching   A type of high-speed switching used in Cisco 7000 series routers, based on the use of a separate processor (the Silicon Switch Processor, or SSP). *See also: SSE.*

simplex   The mode at which data or a digital signal is transmitted. Simplex is a way of transmitting in only one direction. Half duplex transmits in two directions but only one direction at a time. Full duplex transmits both directions simultaneously.

sliding window   The method of flow control used by TCP, as well as several Data Link layer protocols. This method places a buffer between the receiving application and the network data flow. The "window" available for accepting data is the size of the buffer minus the amount of data already there. This window increases in size as the application reads data from it and decreases as new data is sent. The receiver sends the transmitter announcements of the current window size, and it may stop accepting data until the window increases above a certain threshold.

SLIP   Serial Line Internet Protocol: An industry standard serial encapsulation for point-to-point connections that supports only a single routed protocol, TCP/IP. SLIP is the predecessor to PPP. *See also: PPP.*

SMDS   Switched Multimegabit Data Service: A packet-switched, datagram-based WAN networking technology offered by telephone companies that provides high speed.

SMTP   Simple Mail Transfer Protocol: A protocol used on the Internet to provide electronic mail services.

SNA   System Network Architecture: A complex, feature-rich, network architecture similar to the OSI reference model but with several variations; created by IBM in the 1970s and essentially composed of seven layers.

SNAP   Subnetwork Access Protocol: SNAP is a frame used in Ethernet, Token Ring, and FDDI LANs. Data transfer, connection management, and QoS selection are three primary functions executed by the SNAP frame.

snapshot routing   Snapshot routing takes a point-in-time capture of a dynamic routing table and maintains it even when the remote connection goes down. This allows the use of a dynamic routing protocol without requiring the link to remain active, which might incur per-minute usage charges.

SNMP   Simple Network Management Protocol: This protocol polls SNMP agents or devices for statistical and environmental data. This data can include device temperature, name, performance statistics and much more. SNMP works with MIB objects that are present on the SNMP agent. This information is queried then sent to the SNMP server.

socket   1) A software structure that operates within a network device as a destination point for communications. 2) In AppleTalk networks, an entity at a specific location within a node; AppleTalk sockets are conceptually similar to TCP/IP ports.

software address   Also called a logical address. This is typically an IP address, but can also be an IPX address.

SOHO   small office/home office: A contemporary term for remote users.

SONET   Synchronous Optical Network: The ANSI standard for synchronous transmission on fiber-optic media, developed at Bell Labs. It specifies a base signal rate of 51.84Mbps and a set of multiples of that rate, known as Optical Carrier levels, up to 2.5Gbps.

source tree   A method of multicast data forwarding. Source trees use the architecture of the source of the multicast traffic as the root of the tree.

SP   Switch Processor: Also known as a ciscoBus controller, it is a Cisco 7000 series processor module acting as governing agent for all CxBus activities.

span   A full-duplex digital transmission line connecting two facilities.

SPAN   Switched Port Analyzer: A feature of the Catalyst 5000 switch, offering freedom to manipulate within a switched Ethernet environment by extending the monitoring ability of the existing network analyzers into the environment. At one switched segment, the SPAN mirrors traffic onto a predetermined SPAN port, while a network analyzer connected to the SPAN port is able to monitor traffic from any other Catalyst switched port.

spanning explorer packet   Sometimes called limited-route or single-route explorer packet, it pursues a statically configured spanning tree when searching for paths in a source-route bridging network. *See also: all-routes explorer packet, explorer packet,* and *local explorer packet.*

spanning tree   A subset of a network topology, within which no loops exist. When bridges are interconnected into a loop, the bridge, or switch, cannot identify a frame that has been forwarded previously, so there is no mechanism for removing a frame as it passes the interface numerous times. Without a method of removing these frames, the bridges continuously forward them—consuming bandwidth and adding overhead to the network. Spanning trees prune the network to provide only one path for any packet. *See also: Spanning Tree Protocol* and *spanning-tree algorithm.*

spanning-tree algorithm (STA)   An algorithm that creates a spanning tree using the Spanning Tree Protocol (STP). *See also: spanning-tree* and *Spanning Tree Protocol.*

Spanning Tree Protocol (STP) The bridge protocol (IEEE 802.1D) that enables a learning bridge to dynamically avoid loops in the network topology by creating a spanning tree using the spanning-tree algorithm. Spanning-tree frames called Bridge Protocol Data Units (BPDUs) are sent and received by all switches in the network at regular intervals. The switches participating in the spanning tree don't forward the frames; instead, they're processed to determine the spanning-tree topology itself. Cisco Catalyst series switches use STP 802.1D to perform this function. *See also: BPDU, learning bridge, MAC address, spanning tree,* and *spanning-tree algorithm.*

SPF Shortest Path First algorithm: A routing algorithm used to decide on the shortest-path spanning tree. Sometimes called Dijkstra's algorithm and frequently used in link-state routing algorithms. *See also: link-state routing algorithm.*

SPID Service Profile Identifier: A number assigned by service providers or local telephone companies and assigned by administrators to a BRI port. SPIDs are used to determine subscription services of a device connected via ISDN. ISDN devices use SPID when accessing the telephone company switch that initializes the link to a service provider.

split horizon Useful for preventing routing loops, a type of distance-vector routing rule where information about routes is prevented from leaving the router interface through which that information was received.

spoofing 1) In dial-on-demand routing (DDR), where a circuit-switched link is taken down to save toll charges when there is no traffic to be sent, spoofing is a scheme used by routers that causes a host to treat an interface as if it were functioning and supporting a session. The router pretends to send "spoof" replies to keepalive messages from the host in an effort to convince the host that the session is up and running. *See also: DDR.* 2) The illegal act of sending a packet labeled with a false address, in order to deceive network security mechanisms such as filters and access lists.

spooler A management application that processes requests submitted to it for execution in a sequential fashion from a queue. A good example is a print spooler.

SPX Sequenced Packet Exchange: A Novell NetWare transport protocol that augments the datagram service provided by network layer (Layer 3) protocols, it was derived from the Switch-to-Switch Protocol of the XNS protocol suite.

SQE   Signal Quality Error: In an Ethernet network, a message sent from a transceiver to an attached machine that the collision-detection circuitry is working.

SRB   Source-Route Bridging: Created by IBM, the bridging method used in Token Ring networks. The source determines the entire route to a destination before sending the data and includes that information in route information fields (RIF) within each packet. *Contrast with: transparent bridging.*

SRT   Source-Route Transparent Bridging: A bridging scheme developed by IBM, merging source-route and transparent bridging. SRT takes advantage of both technologies in one device, fulfilling the needs of all end nodes. Translation between bridging protocols is not necessary. *Compare with: SR/TLB.*

SR/TLB   Source-Route Translational Bridging: A bridging method that allows source-route stations to communicate with transparent bridge stations aided by an intermediate bridge that translates between the two bridge protocols. Used for bridging between Token Ring and Ethernet. *Compare with: SRT.*

SSAP   Source Service Access Point: The SAP of the network node identified in the Source field of the packet. *See also: DSAP and SAP.*

SSE   Silicon Switching Engine: The software component of Cisco's silicon switching technology, hard-coded into the Silicon Switch Processor (SSP). Silicon switching is available only on the Cisco 7000 with an SSP. Silicon-switched packets are compared to the silicon-switching cache on the SSE. The SSP is a dedicated switch processor that offloads the switching process from the route processor, providing a fast-switching solution, but packets must still traverse the backplane of the router to get to the SSP and then back to the exit interface.

standard IP access list   IP access list that uses only the source IP addresses to filter a network.

standard IPX access list   IPX access list that uses only the source and destination IPX address to filter a network.

star topology   A LAN physical topology with endpoints on the network converging at a common central switch (known as a hub) using point-to-point links. A logical ring topology can be configured as a physical star topology using a unidirectional closed-loop star rather than point-to-point links. That is, connections within the hub are arranged in an internal ring. *See also: bus topology* and *ring topology.*

startup range   If an AppleTalk node does not have a number saved from the last time it was booted, then the node selects from the range of values from 65,280 to 65,534.

state transitions   Digital signaling scheme that reads the "state" of the digital signal in the middle of the bit cell. If it is five volts, the cell is read as a one. If the state of the digital signal is zero volts, the bit cell is read as a zero.

static route   A route whose information is purposefully entered into the routing table and takes priority over those chosen by dynamic routing protocols.

static VLAN   A VLAN that is manually configured port-by-port. This is the method typically used in production networks.

statistical multiplexing   Multiplexing in general is a technique that allows data from multiple logical channels to be sent across a single physical channel. Statistical multiplexing dynamically assigns bandwidth only to input channels that are active, optimizing available bandwidth so that more devices can be connected than with other multiplexing techniques. Also known as statistical time-division multiplexing or stat mux.

STM-1   Synchronous Transport Module Level 1. In the European SDH standard, one of many formats identifying the frame structure for the 155.52Mbps lines that are used to carry ATM cells.

store-and-forward packet switching   A technique in which the switch first copies each packet into its buffer and performs a cyclical redundancy check (CRC). If the packet is error-free, the switch then looks up the destination address in its filter table, determines the appropriate exit port, and sends the packet.

STP   1) shielded twisted-pair: A two-pair wiring scheme, used in many network implementations, that has a layer of shielded insulation to reduce EMI. 2) Spanning Tree Protocol.

straight-through cable   Type of Ethernet cable that connects a host to a switch, host to a hub, or router to a switch or hub.

stub area   An OSPF area carrying a default route, intra-area routes, and interarea routes, but no external routes. Configuration of virtual links cannot be achieved across a stub area, and stub areas are not allowed to contain an ASBR. *See also: non-stub area, ASBR, and OSPF.*

stub network   A network having only one connection to a router.

STUN   Serial Tunnel: A technology used to connect an HDLC link to an SDLC link over a serial link.

subarea   A portion of an SNA network made up of a subarea node and its attached links and peripheral nodes.

subarea node   An SNA communications host or controller that handles entire network addresses.

subchannel   A frequency-based subdivision that creates a separate broadband communications channel.

subinterface   One of many virtual interfaces available on a single physical interface.

subnet   *See: subnetwork.*

subnet address   The portion of an IP address that is specifically identified by the subnet mask as the subnetwork. *See also: IP address, subnetwork, and subnet mask.*

subnet mask   Also simply known as mask, a 32-bit address mask used in IP to identify the bits of an IP address that are used for the subnet address. Using a mask, the router does not need to examine all 32 bits, only those selected by the mask. *See also: address mask and IP address.*

subnetting   Used in IP networks to break up larger networks into smaller subnetworks.

subnetwork   1) Any network that is part of a larger IP network and is identified by a subnet address. A network administrator segments a network into subnetworks in order to provide a hierarchical, multilevel routing structure, and at the same time protect the subnetwork from the addressing complexity of networks that are attached. Also known as a subnet. *See also: IP address, subnet mask, and subnet address.* 2) In OSI networks, the term specifically refers to a collection of ESs and ISs controlled by only one administrative domain, using a solitary network connection protocol.

summarization   Term used to describe the process of summarizing multiple routing table entries into one entry.

supernetting   *See: summarization.*

SVC   switched virtual circuit: A dynamically established virtual circuit, created on demand and dissolved as soon as transmission is over and the circuit is no longer needed. In ATM terminology, it is referred to as a switched virtual connection. *See also: PVC.*

switch   1) In networking, a device responsible for multiple functions such as filtering, flooding, and sending frames. It works using the destination address of individual frames. Switches operate at the Data Link layer of the OSI model. 2) Broadly, any electronic/mechanical device allowing connections to be established as needed and terminated if no longer necessary.

switch block   A combination of layer-3 switches and layer-3 routers. The layer-2 switches connect users in the wiring closet into the access layer and provide 10 or 100Mbps dedicated connections. 1900/2820 and 2900 Catalyst switches can be used in the switch block.

switch fabric   Term used to identify a layer-2 switched internetwork with many switches.

switched LAN   Any LAN implemented using LAN switches. *See also: LAN switch.*

synchronous transmission   Signals transmitted digitally with precision clocking. These signals have identical frequencies and contain individual characters encapsulated in control bits (called start/stop bits) that designate the beginning and ending of each character. *See also: asynchronous transmission* and *isochronous transmission.*

syslog   A protocol used to monitor system log messages by a remote device.

T reference point   Used with an S reference point to change a 4-wire ISDN network to a two-wire ISDN network.

T-1   Digital WAN that uses 24 DS0s at 64K each to create a bandwidth of 1.536Mbps, minus clocking overhead, providing 1.544Mbps of usable bandwidth.

T3 Digital WAN that can provide bandwidth of 44.763Mbps.

TACACS+ Terminal Access Controller Access Control System: An enhanced version of TACACS, this protocol is similar to RADIUS. *See also: RADIUS.*

tag switching Based on the concept of label swapping, where packets or cells are designated to defined-length labels that control the manner in which data is to be sent, tag switching is a high-performance technology used for forwarding packets. It incorporates Data Link layer (Layer 2) switching and Network layer (Layer 3) routing and supplies scalable, high-speed switching in the network core.

tagged traffic ATM cells with their cell loss priority (CLP) bit set to 1. Also referred to as Discard Eligible (DE) traffic. Tagged traffic can be eliminated in order to ensure trouble-free delivery of higher priority traffic, if the network is congested. *See also: CLP.*

TCP Transmission Control Protocol: A connection-oriented protocol that is defined at the transport layer of the OSI reference model. Provides reliable delivery of data.

TCP/IP Transmission Control Protocol/Internet Protocol. The suite of protocols underlying the Internet. TCP and IP are the most widely known protocols in that suite. *See also: IP* and *TCP.*

TDM Time Division Multiplexing: A technique for assigning bandwidth on a single wire, based on preassigned time slots, to data from several channels. Bandwidth is allotted to each channel regardless of a station's ability to send data. *See also: ATDM, FDM,* and *multiplexing.*

TE terminal equipment: Any peripheral device that is ISDN-compatible and attached to a network, such as a telephone or computer. TE1s are devices that are ISDN-ready and understand ISDN signaling techniques. TE2s are devices that are not ISDN-ready and do not understand ISDN signaling techniques. A terminal adapter must be used with a TE2.

TE1 A device with a four-wire, twisted-pair digital interface is referred to as terminal equipment type 1. Most modern ISDN devices are of this type.

TE2 Devices known as terminal equipment type 2 do not understand ISDN signaling techniques, and a terminal adapter must be used to convert the signaling.

telco A common abbreviation for the telephone company.

Telnet The standard terminal emulation protocol within the TCP/IP protocol stack. Method of remote terminal connection, enabling users to log in on remote networks and use those resources as if they were locally connected. Telnet is defined in RFC 854.

terminal adapter (TA) A hardware interface between a computer without a native ISDN interface and an ISDN line. In effect, a device to connect a standard async interface to a non-native ISDN device, emulating a modem.

terminal emulation The use of software, installed on a PC or LAN server, that allows the PC to function as if it were a "dumb" terminal directly attached to a particular type of mainframe.

TFTP Conceptually, a stripped-down version of FTP, it's the protocol of choice if you know exactly what you want and where it's to be found. TFTP doesn't provide the abundance of functions that FTP does. In particular, it has no directory browsing abilities; it can do nothing but send and receive files.

TFTP host Trivial File Transfer Protocol is used to send files using IP at the Network layer and UDP at the Transport layer, which makes it unreliable.

thicknet Also called 10Base5. Bus network that uses a thick cable and runs Ethernet up to 500 meters.

thinnet Also called 10Base2. Bus network that uses a thin coax cable and runs Ethernet media access up to 185 meters.

three-way handshake Term used in a TCP session to define how a virtual circuit is set up. It is called a "three-way" handshake because it used three data packets.

token A frame containing only control information. Possessing this control information gives a network device permission to transmit data onto the network. *See also: token passing.*

token bus LAN architecture that is the basis for the IEEE 802.4 LAN specification and employs token passing access over a bus topology. *See also: IEEE.*

token passing   A method used by network devices to access the physical medium in a systematic way based on possession of a small frame called a token. *See also: token.*

Token Ring   IBM's token-passing LAN technology. It runs at 4Mbps or 16Mbps over a ring topology. Defined formally by IEEE 802.5. *See also: ring topology* and *token passing.*

toll network   WAN network that uses the public switched telephone network (PSTN) to send packets.

traceroute   also trace; IP command used to trace the path a packet takes through an internetwork.

transparent bridging   The bridging scheme used in Ethernet and IEEE 802.3 networks, it passes frames along one hop at a time, using bridging information stored in tables that associate end-node MAC addresses within bridge ports. This type of bridging is considered transparent because the source node does not know it has been bridged, because the destination frames are sent directly to the end node. *Contrast with: SRB.*

Transport layer   Layer 4 of the OSI reference model, used for reliable communication between end nodes over the network. The transport layer provides mechanisms used for establishing, maintaining, and terminating virtual circuits, transport fault detection and recovery, and controlling the flow of information. *See also: Application layer, Data Link layer, Network layer, Physical layer, Presentation layer,* and *Session layer.*

trap   Used to send SNMP messages to SNMP managers.

TRIP   Token Ring Interface Processor: A high-speed interface processor used on Cisco 7000 series routers. The TRIP provides two or four ports for interconnection with IEEE 802.5 and IBM media with ports set to speeds of either 4Mbps or 16Mbps set independently of each other.

trunk link   Link used between switches and from some servers to the switches. Trunk links carry information about many VLANs. Access links are used to connect host devices to a switch and carry only VLAN information that the device is a member of.

TTL   time to live: A field in an IP header, indicating the length of time a packet is valid.

TUD   Trunk Up-Down: A protocol used in ATM networks for the monitoring of trunks. Should a trunk miss a given number of test messages being sent by ATM switches to ensure trunk line quality, TUD declares the trunk down. When a trunk reverses direction and comes back up, TUD recognizes that the trunk is up and returns the trunk to service.

tunneling   A method of avoiding protocol restrictions by wrapping packets from one protocol in another protocol's packet and transmitting this encapsulated packet over a network that supports the wrapper protocol. *See also: encapsulation.*

U reference point   Reference point between a TE1 and an ISDN network. The U reference point understands ISDN signaling techniques and uses a 2-wire connection.

UDP   User Datagram Protocol: A connectionless transport layer protocol in the TCP/IP protocol stack that simply allows datagrams to be exchanged without acknowledgments or delivery guarantees, requiring other protocols to handle error processing and retransmission. UDP is defined in RFC 768.

unicast   Used for direct host-to-host communication. Communication is directed to only one destination and is originated only from one source.

unidirectional shared tree   A method of shared tree multicast forwarding. This method allows only multicast data to be forwarded from the RP.

unnumbered frames   HDLC frames used for control-management purposes, such as link startup and shutdown or mode specification.

user mode   Cisco IOS EXEC mode that allows an administrator to perform very few commands. You can only verify statistics in user mode; you cannot see or change the router or switch configuration.

UTP   unshielded twisted-pair: Copper wiring used in small-to-large networks to connect host devices to hubs and switches. Also used to connect switch to switch or hub to hub.

VBR   variable bit rate: A QoS class, as defined by the ATM Forum, for use in ATM networks that is subdivided into real time (RT) class and non-real time (NRT) class. RT is employed when connections have a fixed-time relationship between samples. Conversely, NRT is employed when connections do not have a fixed-time relationship between samples, but still need an assured QoS.

VCC   virtual channel connection: A logical circuit that is created by VCLs. VCCs carry data between two endpoints in an ATM network. Sometimes called a virtual circuit connection.

VIP   1) Versatile Interface Processor: An interface card for Cisco 7000 and 7500 series routers, providing multilayer switching and running the Cisco IOS software. The most recent version of VIP is VIP2. 2) Virtual IP: A function making it possible for logically separated switched IP workgroups to run Virtual Networking Services across the switch ports of a Catalyst 5000.

virtual circuit (VC)   A logical circuit devised to assure reliable communication between two devices on a network. Defined by a virtual path connection (VPC)/virtual path identifier (VCI) pair, a virtual circuit can be permanent (PVC) or switched (SVC). Virtual circuits are used in Frame Relay and X.25. Known as virtual channel in ATM. *See also: PVC and SVC.*

virtual ring   In an SRB network, a logical connection between physical rings, either local or remote.

VLAN   virtual LAN: A group of devices on one or more logically segmented LANs (configured by use of management software), enabling devices to communicate as if attached to the same physical medium, when they are actually located on numerous different LAN segments. VLANs are based on logical instead of physical connections and thus are tremendously flexible.

VLAN ID   Sometimes referred to as VLAN color, the VLAN ID is tagged onto a frame to tell a receiving switch which VLAN the frame is a member of.

VLSM   variable-length subnet mask: Helps optimize available address space and specify a different subnet mask for the same network number on various subnets. Also commonly referred to as "subnetting a subnet."

VMPS   VLAN Management Policy Server: Used to dynamically assign VLANs to a switch port.

VPN   virtual private network: A method of encrypting point-to-point logical connections across a public network, such as the Internet. This allows secure communications across a public network.

VTP   VLAN Trunk Protocol: Used to update switches in a switch fabric about VLANs configured on a VTP server. VTP devices can be a VTP server, client, or transparent device. Servers update clients. Transparent devices are only local devices and do not share information with VTP clients. VTPs send VLAN information down trunked links only.

VTP transparent mode   Switch mode that receives VLAN Trunk Protocol VLAN information and passes it on, but doesn't read the information.

WAN   wide area network: Is a designation used to connect LANs together across a DCE (data communications equipment) network. Typically, a WAN is a leased line or dial-up connection across a PSTN network. Examples of WAN protocols include Frame Relay, PPP, ISDN, and HDLC.

wildcard   Used with access-list, supernetting, and OSPF configurations. Wildcards are designations used to identify a range of subnets.

windowing   Flow-control method used with TCP at the Transport layer of the OSI model.

WINS   Windows Internet Name Service: Name resolution database for NetBIOS names to TCP/IP address.

WinSock   Windows Socket Interface: A software interface that makes it possible for an assortment of applications to use and share an Internet connection. The WinSock software consists of a dynamic link library (DLL) with supporting programs such as a dialer program that initiates the connection.

workgroup switching   A switching method that supplies high-speed (100Mbps) transparent bridging between Ethernet networks as well as high-speed translational bridging between Ethernet and CDDI or FDDI.

X Window   A distributed multitasking windowing and graphics system originally developed by MIT for communication between X terminals and Unix workstations.

X.25   An ITU-T packet-relay standard that defines communication between DTE and DCE network devices. X.25 uses a reliable Data Link layer protocol called LAPB. X.25 also uses PLP at the Network layer. X.25 has mostly been replaced by Frame Relay.

ZIP Zone Information Protocol: A session-layer protocol used by AppleTalk to map network numbers to zone names. NBP uses ZIP in the determination of networks containing nodes that belong to a zone. *See also: ZIP storm* and *zone.*

ZIP storm A broadcast storm occurring when a router running AppleTalk reproduces or transmits a route for which there is no corresponding zone name at the time of execution. The route is then forwarded by other routers downstream, thus causing a ZIP storm. *See also: broadcast storm* and *ZIP.*

zone A logical grouping of network devices in AppleTalk. *See also: ZIP.*

Index

Note to the Reader: Throughout this index **boldfaced** page numbers indicate primary discussions of a topic. *Italicized* page numbers indicate illustrations.

E

N

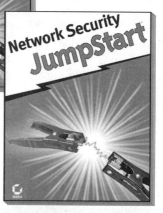

TELL US WHAT YOU THINK!

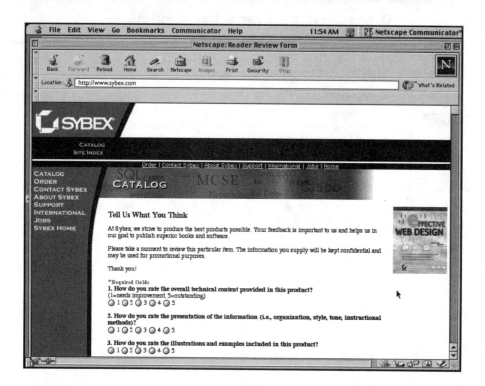

Your feedback is critical to our efforts to provide you with the best books and software on the market. Tell us what you think about the products you've purchased. It's simple:

1. Visit the Sybex website
2. Go to the product page
3. Click on **Submit a Review**
4. Fill out the questionnaire and comments
5. Click **Submit**

With your feedback, we can continue to publish the highest quality computer books and software products that today's busy IT professionals deserve.

www.sybex.com

SYBEX Inc. • 1151 Marina Village Parkway, Alameda, CA 94501 • 510-523-8233